**Applied
Structured
BASIC**

## WADSWORTH SERIES IN COMPUTER INFORMATION SYSTEMS

# Applied Structured BASIC

**ROY AGELOFF**
**University of Rhode Island**

**RICHARD MOJENA**
**University of Rhode Island**

Wadsworth Publishing Company
Belmont, California
A Division of Wadsworth, Inc.

To Wayne Corcoran, for helping me write my
first computer program, and much more   *RA*

To YARA, once again, all Love   *RM*

Data Processing Editor: Frank Ruggirello
Production Editor: Harold Humphrey
Design and Cover: Cynthia Bassett
Print Buyer: Karen Hunt
Copy Editor: Yvonne Howell
Compositor: Graphic Typesetting Service
Technical Illustrator: Blakeley Graphics
Cover Art: Jablonka

Printed in the United States of America
1 2 3 4 5 6 7 8 9 10——89 88 87 86 85

ISBN 0-534-04740-8

Library of Congress Cataloging in Publication Data

Ageloff, Roy, 1943–
    Applied structured BASIC.

    (Wadsworth series in computer information systems)
    Includes index.
    1. Basic (Computer program language)   2. Structured
programming.   I. Mojena, Richard.   II. Title.   III. Series.
QA76.73.B3A37   1985        001.64′24        84-25835
ISBN 0-534-04740-8

# Preface

This textbook is designed for a first course in BASIC programming. No prerequisite is required, other than a willingness to develop problem-solving skills coupled with patience and endurance. (Learning a computer language takes time, practice, and effort.)

The combination of features described below distinguishes this book from others in the field.

**Treatment of Dialects.** The nonstandardization of BASIC raises major presentation problems in any textbook that is not machine/dialect specific. Yet, there are now enough similarities across machines/dialects so that certain generic treatments make sense. For example, we can generically classify IF-type statements as traditional IF/THEN, enhanced IF/THEN, single-line IF/THEN/ELSE, and multi-line IF/THEN/ELSE. Whenever major differences appear (as in WHILE and multi-line IF/THEN/ELSE implementations) we use a table that shows the following four dialects: Minimal BASIC (the earlier ANS version), ANS BASIC (the currently proposed standard), VAX-11 BASIC, and Microsoft BASIC (on the IBM PC). For the most part, dialect-specific material is restricted to these clearly differentiated tables, so as to minimize student confusion. Moreover, each table has a section for the student's own dialect/machine, if different from those illustrated.

**Structured Programming.** Structured programming concepts are presented early in Chapter 3, elaborated upon in Chapters 4–6, and adhered to throughout the book. All programs strictly use defined control structures (sequence, selection, repetition). Both Minimal-BASIC and structured-statement versions are illustrated. GOTO-less programming is encouraged whenever it's possible in a given dialect.

**Top-Down Design.** Stepwise refinement is introduced and motivated at a point (Chapter 4) where programs start getting more elaborate. Other top-down design procedures like top-down execution, top-down structured programming, and top-down testing are discussed at strategic points.

**Modular Programming.**    Modular programs are discussed in Chapter 7 and used from that point forward when appropriate. This topic immediately follows advanced decision structures, to emphasize its place as a top-down/structured programming tool. The traditional placement of modular programs after arrays is discarded in favor of this current design emphasis. The implementation of modules is primarily illustrated through subroutines. The more modern external functions and subprograms are also illustrated.

**Design and Style.**    Program design and style is emphasized throughout in keeping with the current (and future) emphases on both reducing software development/maintenance costs and improving the user interface. Each chapter ends with a Pointers section that includes the following two subsections: Design and Style and Common Errors.

**Modular Chapters.**    The seven modules at the end of the text are meant to grant the instructor flexibility in choice and sequencing of topics like debugging, built-in functions, **PRINT USING** statements, external files, string processing, and **MAT** operations. The earliest assignments of modular chapters are:

| Module | | Can be assigned anytime after Chapter |
|---|---|---|
| A | Running BASIC Programs | 1 |
| B | Debugging Programs | 2 |
| C | Built-In and User-Defined Functions | 3 |
| D | PRINT USING Statement and Formatted Output | 2 |
| E | External Data Files and Transaction Processing | 5 |
| F | String Functions and Text Processing | 5 |
| G | Matrix Operations | 9 |

No one module depends on any other module, which adds even greater flexibility to topical selection and sequencing.

**Interactive Programming.**    Design issues regarding the user interface in interactive applications are discussed throughout the book. Menus, screen design, and input error trapping are treated where appropriate.

**Flowcharts and Pseudocode.**    Both flowcharts and pseudocode (program design language) are illustrated. Flowcharts are deemphasized, however, in keeping with their reduced use within commercial environments and their misuse from a structured point of view. We primarily use flowcharts to improve the pedagogy of control structures. We use pseudocode primarily as a program design and documentation tool.

**Applications Programs.**    The word "applied" in the title of this book suggests our emphasis throughout on meaningful applications of the computer. Applications include those relating to information processing and those relating to mathematical modeling. They are described in a wide variety of contexts, including areas in business, economics, mathematics, statistics, and the sciences, as well as public sector areas like health care delivery, governmental administration, and emergency response systems. The table inside the front cover of the book summarizes and references the applications described through examples and exercises. This table clearly illustrates our philosophy that problems should be presented in an *evolutionary* manner. As new material is learned, selected earlier applications are revisited. This approach is not only educationally sound but also is consistent with (but not identical to) the evolutionary nature of program design in the real world.

**Exercises.**    The book has a carefully designed set of over 440 exercises, many with multiple parts. The chapters on programming (Chapters 2–9) average better than 37 exercises per chapter. Exercises include both follow-up exercises (to reinforce, integrate, and extend preceding material) and additional exercises (for complete programming assignments at the end of chapters and modules). *Answers to most follow-up exercises (those without asterisks) are included at the end of the text.* The follow-up exercises with answers give the book a programmed learning flavor without the traditional regimentation of such an approach. Additionally, the follow-up exercises are an excellent basis for planning many classroom lectures.

**Software Development Cycle.**    A four-step software development cycle (Analysis, Design, Code, Test) is first described and illustrated in Chapter 1. Subsequently it's used in all major applications programs throughout the text. As in commercial environments, this stepwise organization facilitates the development of programs. Students are asked to structure each end-of-chapter assignment along these four steps.

**Evolutionary Treatment.**    The programming material and applications scenarios are developed patiently. This means, for example, that comprehensive topics like selection and repetition are not covered completely within the same chapters.

**FOR/NEXT Loops.**    Unlike traditional texts, FOR/NEXT loops are introduced early (Chapter 3) as the first of the loop structure implementations. We find that this loop implementation is the easiest for the students to master. Moreover, the early treatment of loops (before decision structure implementations) allows the very early illustration of realistic programs that show the power of repetitive processing (which, after all, is the *raison d'etre* for computing).

**String Processing.**    The processing of string data is emphasized throughout the text, which reflects the enormous extent of information processing applications in practice. The specialized and more difficult text processing and editing applications are covered in Module F.

**External Files.**    The use of external data files is a must in practice, but it's a difficult topic for beginning programmers. This topic is comprehensively covered in Module E, including both sequential and direct access files. This module also includes transaction processing applications, to add realism and explain fundamental procedures that use transaction, master, and sort files.

**Camera-Ready Programs.**    All complete programs and their input/output are reproduced by camera rather than typeset. This increases the realism of the programming material and ensures the reliability of programs. Moreover, many of the programs include color shading and margin notes to enhance student understanding. The camera-ready programs and runs feature either the **IBM PC**, the **VAX-11**, or both, depending on the topic.

**Other Aids.**    Additional learning aids include the following:

- Many short, complete programs presented as examples and exercises. These can be used more easily than long programs by instructors for classroom demonstrations, and by students as practice exercises on the computer.

- Use of color type (for user input in the computer runs, important terms, and notes), color screens (to highlight and draw attention to the topic of interest), and arrowed margin notes.
- Important concepts and explanations set off from the rest of the text by specially marked "Note" paragraphs.
- A table of names and page references on the front inside cover for all of the applications examples and exercises. The back inside cover includes a table of reserved words (keywords), applicable BASIC dialect, and page references.

**Text Supplements.**    The text is supplemented by an Instructor's Manual with lecture hints, answers not given in the text to follow-up exercises, and solutions to all end-of-chapter programming assignments; a set of Transparency Masters; a computerized Test Bank; and IBM PC diskettes with the textbook's sample programs and end-of-chapter programs.

## Acknowledgments

We wish to express our deep appreciation to many who have contributed to this project: to Frank Ruggirello, our editor, for unique humor, support, and expert advice; to Serina Beauparlant, the "Assistant Coach," for keeping us on track; to Hal Humphrey, our production editor, for production and time magic on a rather complex project; to Cynthia Bassett for outstanding design; to Joy Westberg for thoughtful advertising; to the rest of the Wadsworth team for all the help in getting the text "out the door"; to Richard R. Weeks, Dean, University of Rhode Island, for administrative support; to the Computer Laboratories at the University of Rhode Island, for obvious reasons; to our graduate assistants, Thodur Hemashree, Donna Rose, and Rohit Thukral; to Marco Urbano for generating the Test Bank; to our reviewers, who provided invaluable suggestions and corrections for manuscript revisions: John L. Callaghan, College of St. Thomas; Donald Davis, University of Mississippi; David Gustafson, Kansas State University; Larry Harvey, DeAnza College; Richard Lott, Bentley College; Lewis Miller, Cañada College; Tom Richard, Bemidji State University; and Clint Smullen, University of Tennessee; to our students, who always teach us something about teaching; and to our immediate families, who sometimes wonder what we look like.

Roy Ageloff
Richard Mojena
January, 1985
Kingston, Rhode Island

# Contents

C H A P T E R

# 4

## SIMPLE DECISIONS 107

C H A P T E R

# 5

## MORE LOOPS 146

C  H  A  P  T  E  R

TWO-DIMENSIONAL ARRAYS 314

M  O  D  U  L  E

A

RUNNING BASIC PROGRAMS 349

MODULE

# EXTERNAL DATA FILES AND TRANSACTION PROCESSING 399

MODULE

# STRING FUNCTIONS AND TEXT PROCESSING 461

**M  O  D  U  L  E**

# G

## MATRIX OPERATIONS  486

# Orientation

# 1

The electronic computer is one of our foremost technological inventions; for good or for bad, its presence affects each of us, and its future holds even more potential to affect our lives.

This chapter is an orientation to the course you are about to take. We first define the computer. Thereafter we provide a nontechnical overview of what makes up a computer system and how we communicate with the computer. Finally we outline how you might benefit from this course and include some advice that you might find helpful.

We see one major prerequisite to doing well in this course: A curiosity or better yet, a desire to learn more about computers. By the time this course is over, we hope that we (together with your instructor) shall have helped you translate that curiosity into a continuing, productive, and rewarding experience.

## 1.1 WHAT IS A COMPUTER?

An electronic **computer** is defined most generally as an electronic device that is capable of manipulating data to achieve some task. Given this definition, electronic cash registers, electronic gasoline pumps, and electronic calculators all qualify as simple computers. The machine we usually think of as a computer, however, has three significant characteristics.

1.  It's fast.
2.  It stores large amounts of data.
3.  It executes alterable, stored instructions.

### Characteristics of Electronic Computers

The great speed of today's electronic computers is a direct result of miniaturization in solid-state electronics. To get a rough idea of the speed capabilities of large electronic computers, consider the following estimates. One minute of computer time is equivalent to approximately 6700 hours of skilled labor by a person using a calculator. In other words, a person using a calculator would take one hour to accomplish what a computer can accomplish in less than one hundredth of a second. In fact, the electronic transfers within computers are so fast that computer designers use basic units of time equal to one billionth of a second (called a nanosecond) and one trillionth of a second (a picosecond)—quite a feat when you consider that the basic unit of time for us mortals is one second. Another measure of computer speed is how many million instructions per second (MIPS) are performed. Currently, large computers carry out around 25 MIPS. Expectations for the late 1980s include speeds of 100 MIPS.

Another significant characteristic of electronic computers is their capacity to store large amounts of data and instructions for recall. In other words, much like the human brain, the computer has "memory." For example, computers at most universities store several million characters of data in primary storage and hundreds of millions of characters in secondary storage.

An electronic computer also is differentiated from most other computing devices by its ability to store and obey instructions in memory. Moreover, these instructions are easily programmable (can be altered or changed). In other words, the computer executes instructions from different users without interference from human beings. This characteristic makes the computer flexible and efficient: it carries out multiple tasks automatically while we do something else. Of course, the computer cannot do without us completely, but more about that later.

### Computer Classifications

To distinguish among different types of electronic computers, we shall make the following comparisons: analog versus digital computers, special-purpose versus general-purpose computers, and mainframes versus minicomputers versus microcomputers.

The **analog computer** manipulates data representing continuous physical processes such as temperature, pressure, and voltage. The fuel injection system of an automobile, for example, deals with physical processes as it regulates the fuel/air ratio on the basis of engine speed, temperature, and pressure; the gasoline pump converts the flow of fuel into price (dollars and cents) and volume (gallons or liters to the nearest tenth).

You will be using the **digital computer,** which operates by counting digits. This type of computer manipulates data (numbers in our decimal system, letters in our alphabet, and special characters such as the comma and dollar sign) by counting binary (two-state or 0–1) digits. **Hybrid computers,** which combine the features of digital and analog computers, have been designed for various applications—for example, controlling the production of products such as steel and gasoline, providing on-board guidance for aircraft and spacecraft, regulating the peak energy demands of large office buildings and factories, and monitoring the vital life signs of patients in critical condition.

Computers are classified not only by how they process data, as in analog versus digital, but also by the functions they serve. **Special-purpose computers** are designed to accomplish a single task, whereas **general-purpose computers** are designed to accept programs of instruction for carrying out different tasks. For example, one special-purpose computer has been designed strictly to do navigational calculations for ships and aircraft. The instructions for carrying out this task are built into the electronic circuitry of the machine so that the navigator simply keys in data and receives the answer. Other special-purpose computers include word processors for preparing, storing, and printing letters, documents, reports, manuscripts, and anything else previously typed; computers used in color television sets to improve color reception; those used in PBX (Private Branch Exchange) telephones to perform various functions, such as automatic placement of a call at a preset time and simplified dialing of frequently used telephone numbers; and those used in automobiles to calculate such items as "miles of fuel left" and "time of destination" and to monitor and read out instantaneously the status of oil level, gasoline level, engine temperature, brake lining wear, and other operating conditions.

In contrast, a general-purpose computer used by a corporation might accomplish tasks relating to the preparation of payrolls and production schedules and the analyses of financial, marketing, and engineering data all in one day. Similarly, the academic computer you are about to use might run a management simulation one minute and analyze the results of a psychology experiment the next minute, or it might even accomplish both of these tasks (and more) concurrently.

Compared with the special-purpose computer, the general-purpose computer has the flexibility to satisfy the needs of a variety of users, but at the expense of speed and economy. In this textbook, we shall focus on the electronic, digital, general-purpose computer.

Another useful distinction among computers is size, which generally translates into storage capacity, speed, and cost. **Mainframe** computers are physically large, process huge amounts of data at incredible speeds, and strain data-processing budgets. Control Data Corporation (CDC), International Business Machines (IBM), and Burroughs are typical manufacturers. **Minicomputers** range in size from a filing cabinet to a closet. They contain less memory, work more slowly, and are cheaper than mainframe computers. Data General, Digital Equipment Corporation (DEC), Hewlett-Packard (HP), IBM, and Prime are popular suppliers. **Microcomputers** come in sizes that fit pockets to desktops, with correspondingly lower storage capacities, processing speeds, and prices. Apple Computer, Commodore, DEC, HP, IBM, Radio Shack, and Zenith are common suppliers.

In recent years microcomputer use has increased dramatically in homes, schools, and organizations, large and small. The reasons for this growth in popularity are improvements in storage capacity, speed, cost, ease of use, standardization, and task versatility, including word processing, data management, financial analysis, communications with other computers, and games.

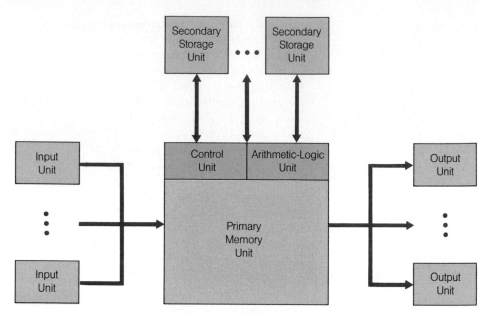

**Figure 1.1**   Functional organization of a digital general-purpose computer

## 1.2 ORGANIZATION OF A COMPUTER

Figure 1.1 should give you a feel for the makeup of a digital general-purpose computer. Six components are identified by the nature of their functions. Actual physical components for two popular computer systems are illustrated in Figure 1.2. But before describing each of these components, we define two terms that we use often.

An **instruction** is a specific task for the computer to accomplish. For example, the following represents three instructions.

1.  Read and store the name of a student and the grades received for the school term.
2.  Calculate and store the grade point average.
3.  Print the student's name and grade point average.

**Data** are facts or observations that the computer is to input, manipulate, and output. In the example, the student's name, grades, and grade point average are all data.

As you read through the remainder of this section, you might find it useful to look frequently at Figures 1.1 and 1.2. The first illustration relates components functionally, and the second shows specific components.

### Input Units

The input function of the computer brings data and instructions from the outside world to the computer's memory. To accomplish this transfer process, the data and instructions must be converted into a machine-readable input medium. The more commonly used **input media** are punched cards, magnetic tapes, hard magnetic disks, floppy magnetic diskettes, punched paper tape, optical characters, and magnetic ink characters.

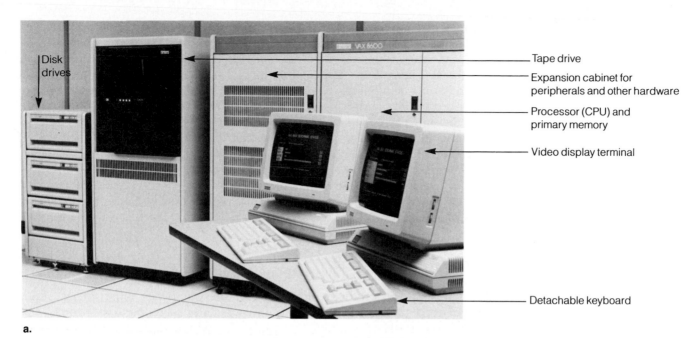

Disk drives

Tape drive

Expansion cabinet for peripherals and other hardware

Processor (CPU) and primary memory

Video display terminal

Detachable keyboard

**a.**

**Figure 1.2**  Two popular computer systems. *(a)* VAX-11 minicomputer system. Courtesy of DEC. *(b)* IBM personal computer system. Courtesy of IBM.

**b.**

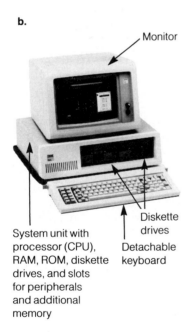

Monitor

System unit with processor (CPU), RAM, ROM, diskette drives, and slots for peripherals and additional memory

Diskette drives

Detachable keyboard

These media usually require **data preparation devices** to convert data from source documents (bills, invoices) to the desired medium. For example, the keypunch machine is a data preparation device for converting data on source documents to punched cards; a key-to-tape machine transfers data from source documents to magnetic tapes; and a microcomputer keyboard places data on a diskette.

Data, once in machine-readable form, are transferred to the computer through an **input unit.** This device reads the coded data on the input medium and converts them into electric impulses, which are transferred to the memory unit of the computer. For example, magnetically coded data on a magnetic disk are read by a disk drive and converted to appropriate electric signals, which are submitted to the computer's memory for storage. Table 1.1 lists some input units used with specific input media. (By the way, MICR units

**Table 1.1**  Input Units and Input Media

| Medium | Corresponding Input Unit |
|---|---|
| Punched card | Punched card reader |
| Punched paper tape | Paper tape reader |
| Optical characters | Optical character reader (OCR) |
| Magnetic ink characters | Magnetic ink character reader (MICR) |
| Magnetic tape | Tape drive (Figure 1.2b) |
| Magnetic disk | Disk drive (Figure 1.2) |
| Cassette tape | Cassette recorder |
| Keyboard | Online terminal (Figure 1.2b) or microcomputer keyboard and monitor (Figure 1.2a) |

are used by banks to process checks, and OCR units are widely used by universities for processing student records and grading exams.)

Data and instructions also can be entered into a computer through **online terminals** (Figure 1.2b). The terminals are connected directly to the computer (the meaning of *online*) by cable or telephone lines. Terminals have a keyboard for entering data and instructions and a visual (video) display or teleprinter for viewing. The Video Display Terminals (VDTs) are much more common than the teleprinter terminals. The keyboard and monitor (video display unit) of a microcomputer also serve as an input unit.

In general, a computer system will have more than one input unit. The mix of input units in any one computer system, however, will depend on factors such as cost, the amount of data to be processed, the method by which data originate, and the needs that must be satisfied by the computer.

## Primary Memory Unit

The **primary (internal) memory** unit of the computer temporarily stores instructions and data during input, output, and processing operations. Most computers use semiconductor memory, for which the basic memory component is the microelectronic (silicon) chip. In the early 1960s, engineers could place eight transistors on a chip; by 1982 they could manage nearly half a million transistors on a $\frac{1}{4}$-in. square chip. On microcomputers, primary memory is called random-access memory **(RAM),** to distinguish it from read-only memory **(ROM),** for which the data and instructions are "hard wired" at the factory.

Another type of primary memory is called bubble memory. This technology creates and manipulates tiny magnetic fields in a crystalline or semiconductor material. These fields appear under a microscope as little black specks or bubbles, hence the name bubble memory.

Regardless of the technology used to construct memory units, primary memory consists of storage locations that have numerical designations called addresses. Figure 1.3 represents a means of visualizing the storage locations of primary memory. Each storage location is assigned a number **(address)** that is used to reference the location whenever the item of data stored within that location **(contents)** is to be accessed. For example, in Figure 1.3 the character R is stored in location 1 and the character 8 is stored in location 2.

Figure 1.3 illustrates what is called a byte-addressable organization, a method of addressing storage that is common to many computers. It means that each address stores a single **character** (a letter, one of the digits 0 through 9, a comma, etc.), usually called a **byte.**

At the machine level, a byte is a packet or grouping of **binary digits.** A binary digit, or **bit** for short, takes on one of two possible values: 0 or 1 from a mathematical point of view; off or on from a mechanical perspective; and low voltage or high voltage from an electronic viewpoint.

A common coding scheme abbreviated as **ASCII** (American Standard Code for Information Interchange) uses seven bits to represent a byte or character. For example, in Figure 1.3 the letter R would be coded and stored as 1010010, and the digit 8 would be coded and stored as 0111000. It's common, as in the IBM Personal Computer, to enhance the ASCII code to eight bits, thereby expanding the character set with graphics, Greek, foreign language, and other characters. As a result, the usual assumption is that a byte is eight bits.

The storage capacity of computer memory usually is expressed as the number of characters (bytes) that can be stored. Because of the way memory units are constructed, storage capacity is often expressed as some multiple of 1024, where the number 1024 is represented by the letter K. For example,

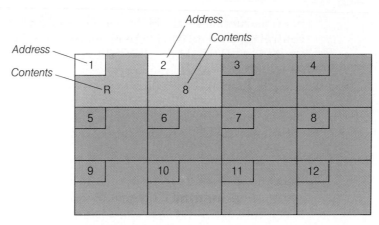

**Figure 1.3**  Visualization of storage in primary memory

many home computers have quoted memory capacities of 64KB (or 64 Kilo Bytes), which means that they store 65,536 (that is, 64 × 1024) bytes of data. Primary memory units usually range in storage capacity from 4KB for some pocket computers to 16 megabytes (or 16MB) for some mainframe computers, where a megabyte is one million bytes.

The primary memory itself consists of a series of microelectronic chips smaller than the tip of a finger. A common memory capacity for each chip is 64K bits.[1] Microcomputers are now being made with 256K-bit chips, and IBM has announced experimental 512K-bit chips.

## Central Processing Unit (CPU)

The arithmetic-logic unit and the control unit together make up what is called the **central processing unit (CPU),** or simply the **processor.** (See Figures 1.1 and 1.2.) The processor, together with primary memory, is what most professionals think of as *the* computer. Input and output units, secondary storage, and other components that attach to the CPU are called **peripherals.** These are not thought of as the "computer" since they are peripheral or external to the computer. The processor, primary memory, and peripherals together form a computer system.

Data stored in primary storage are transferred to the **arithmetic–logic unit (ALU)** whenever processing of data is required. Basic arithmetic operations such as addition, subtraction, multiplication, and division are performed within the ALU. Moreover, logical operations such as comparison of values can be made. This capability permits the testing of various conditions, such as whether an employee is entitled to receive overtime pay.

The **control unit** of a computer directs the operation of all other units associated with the computer, including peripheral devices (input/output units, external memory, and others). The control unit "fetches" or obtains an instruction from primary memory, interprets this instruction, and then executes the instruction by transmitting directions to the appropriate computer components. For example, suppose the instruction "read and store student's name and grades" is fetched from memory and interpreted by the control unit; the input unit would be directed to read these data into memory. The

---

[1]If 8 bits encode 1 byte, then each 64K-bit chip stores 8192 bytes (that is, 64 × 1024 or 65,536 bits divided by 8 bits per byte). In practice, 9 bits would encode 1 byte, with the 9th bit being used to check for storage errors. An even parity system, for example, places the proper 0 or 1 in the 9th bit-position to ensure that the sum of the 9 bits is an even number. Should a parity check reveal that the sum is not even, then the system has detected an electronic storage error.

next instruction might be "calculate and store the grade point average"; the control unit would direct the memory unit to provide the ALU with the data; then the ALU would be directed to perform the calculations and to transmit the result to primary memory.

The fundamental control-unit steps of fetch, interpret, and execute an instruction (which often includes fetch data from primary memory and store results back in primary memory) may seem cumbersome and slow. Yet, as mentioned earlier, modern processors perform millions of these steps in just one second.

Computers are often categorized by the number of bits they use to store data and instructions within the CPU. For example, many "super" minicomputers and mainframe computers are 32-bit machines, meaning that their processors use 32-bit *logic chips* to move data and instructions in 32-bit packets within the control and the arithmetic–logic units. Early microcomputers like the Apple II are 8-bit machines. The second generation of micros, typified by the IBM PC, are 16-bit machines. "Super" micros now include 32-bit logic chips, and "super" mainframe computers have 64-bit logic chips.

In general, the higher-bit machines are faster than the lower-bit machines, as the bigger packets of data and instructions require fewer steps. This speeds program execution and data transfers. Also, higher-bit machines are capable of addressing a greater number of storage locations than lower-bit machines; that is, they can support more primary memory.

Current technology can place an entire CPU on a single microelectronic chip that is less than one quarter of an inch square. These so-called **microprocessors** are as effective as earlier computers in terms of calculating and storage capabilities. In effect, a microprocessor that you can balance on the tip of your finger is equivalent to an early-1960s computer with a CPU as large as an office desk.

## Output Units

The function of an **output unit** is exactly opposite to that of an input unit: an output unit receives data from the computer in the form of electronic signals and converts these data into a form that can be used by either humans or computers. The list below summarizes output units; of these, you will most likely use line printers and online terminals.

**Line Printers.**    If output of data is meant for human consumption, then the line printer can be used. Some impact line printers output at the rate of 2000 lines per minute, each line having up to 132 characters. Picture yourself standing in front of such a printer. At 65 lines per page, you would see approximately 31 pages of printed output whiz by you in the time span of one minute. More recent nonimpact printers produce printed pages at stunning speeds. For example, laser printers operate at about 20,000 lines per minute and ink jet printers sprint at approximately 45,000 lines per minute!

**Online Terminals.**    If you are using either a VDT or teleprinter terminal as an input unit, then most likely you are also using the terminal as an output unit. This is convenient, but compared with a line printer the speed of output is slow. Many computer systems, however, allow input through terminals and output on line printers, a feature that is advantageous if a particular job requires a high volume of printed output on paper.

**Monitors.**    If you are using a microcomputer, then the monitor's screen shows both the keyboard input and the computer output. It's also possible either to dump output from the screen to an attached line printer or to route output to the line printer rather than to the screen.

**Other Output Units.**    Other output units include magnetic tape drives, which have both read (input) and write (output) capabilities using the magnetic tape medium (Figure 1.2b); paper tape units, some of which can be attached to remote, online terminals for the purpose of both input from and output to punched paper tape; magnetic disk drives, which allow both input from and output to magnetized disks that resemble a stack of LP phonograph records (Figure 1.2b); card punch units, which allow output onto punched cards; and voice response units, which process verbal output. Voice response units have been used by telephone companies for many years. Most likely you have listened to the computer give you someone's new telephone number.

## Secondary Storage Units

**Secondary storage (auxiliary** or **external storage)** is memory that is housed outside the CPU. Programs and data not currently in use are kept on secondary storage media and read into primary storage when needed. Magnetic tapes, disks, diskettes, drums, and data cells are commonly used media for secondary storage. Secondary storage units such as tape drives and disk drives (Figure 1.2b) are used to process specific media. Compared with primary storage, secondary storage has greater capacity (billions of bytes) at much less cost per byte, but the amount of time it takes to access data is greater.

## 1.3 COMMUNICATING WITH THE COMPUTER

If we wish to use a computer to solve a problem, we must communicate our instructions to the computer through a language. A language can be defined as patterns that have meaning. To a computer, these patterns are electronic; to a human being, they are symbolic (letters, numbers, punctuation). Unfortunately, no computer can understand any of the some 4000 languages used on Earth. It was necessary, therefore, to invent **computer languages** for person–machine communication. These are classified into the three categories shown in Figure 1.4. The designation **high-level** refers to a computer language that is far removed from the patterns "understood" directly by the computer, whereas a **low-level** language deals with patterns that are more nearly compatible with the electronic patterns of the machine.

### Procedure- and Problem-Oriented Languages

Any language can be distinguished from any other language by its syntax— that is, by the rules for arranging a specified set of symbols into recognizable patterns. We shall be communicating our instructions to the computer through a language called **BASIC.**[2] This is one of many **procedure-oriented languages.** In general, these computer languages are easily understood by us humans (after some education, of course) and are relatively machine-independent, which means that they can be used on a wide variety of computers. BASIC is the most widely used high-level language, especially on microcomputers.

The first standard for the BASIC language, approved in 1978 by the American National Standards Institute (ANSI), is called **Minimal BASIC.** This

---

[2]BASIC (Beginners All-purpose Symbolic Instruction Code) was developed at Dartmouth College in the mid-1960s to simplify the learning of computer programming using online terminals.

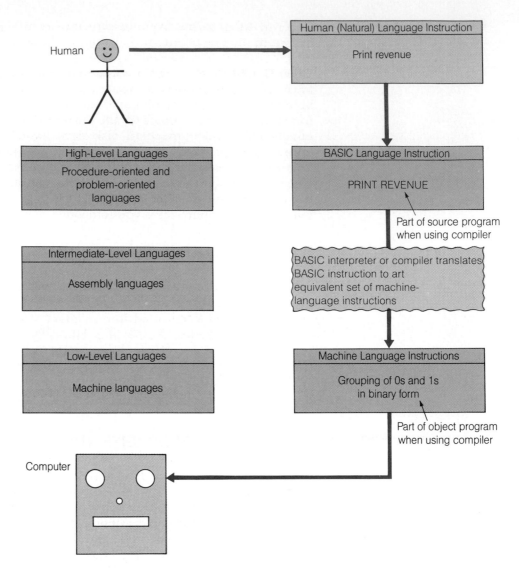

**Figure 1.4**　Language levels and compilation

version of **BASIC** covers a small portion of what is considered today to be the **BASIC** language. Computer manufacturers and software companies have developed full-feature versions of **BASIC** that include commands and enhancements beyond the original standard. Unfortunately, the enhanced instructions are not exactly the same for each version. Thus many different versions (dialects) of the **BASIC** language evolved and exist today.

In 1984 ANSI proposed a more comprehensive standard for the **BASIC** language and named it **ANS BASIC.** In time, if this new standard is accepted, **BASIC** should become a more consistent language. In this text we cover Minimal BASIC and the new ANS BASIC. We also illustrate two widely used dialects of BASIC: **Microsoft BASIC** on the IBM PC and **VAX-11 BASIC.**

Other popular procedure-oriented languages include FORTRAN, the first high-level language, widely used in mathematical, statistical, and scientific programming; COBOL, the traditional language of choice in commercial data-processing environments; and Pascal, a more recent language that incorporates many modern programming procedures, thereby especially gaining favor in many academic computer-science departments. Interestingly, the latest BASIC dialects also incorporate many of the modern programming procedures found in newer languages like Pascal. We introduce these procedures in Chapter 3.

**Problem-oriented languages** usually refer to a set of high-level languages that have been developed for solving certain special-purpose problems, such as the simulation of traffic flows in a city or the computer editing of newspaper articles.

More recently, **nonprocedual languages** or **fourth-generation languages** have gained popularity. These languages are higher level languages with a more user-friendly natural language syntax. The most popular of these are query languages that create, maintain, query, and generate reports from databases. *Focus* and *dBASE* are two popular commercial database management systems that offer nonprocedural languages.

## Assembly and Machine Languages

Each type of computer has associated with it an assembly language and a machine language. An **assembly language** is specifically designed for a particular type of computer; hence it can accomplish more detailed tasks and can execute faster for that computer than could a high-level language. Such a language, however, requires more specialized training for persons who would use it. In other words, it is more difficult for us to learn an assembly language than to learn a high-level language. To illustrate, consider the following assembly language instruction for the IBM 370 computer:

    S  2,COST

In plain English this instructs the computer to subtract the contents of the location named COST from the value currently in register 2 and store the result back in register 2. A *register* is a memory location within the ALU.

Another disadvantage of assembly languages is that they vary from one computer type to another. Thus, if we were restricted to programming only in assembly languages, we would need to learn a new assembly language for each computer type we might use—and worse yet, every computer program written for one computer would have to be rewritten for use on another computer.

After all this, you might be surprised to learn that computers do not directly "understand" either high-level or assembly languages! Computers understand only machine language. An instruction in **machine language** is written either in binary form as a series of 0s and 1s or in one of the shortcut notations for binary forms such as hexadecimal (base 16) or octal (base 8), because these schemes conform to the electronic circuitry in binary computers. For example, the hexadecimal instruction 5A20C01A says "Add the constant 14 to register 2 and store the result in register 2." Of course, this hexadecimal form would be stored in binary form within the computer itself. Needless to say, programming in machine language is tedious, which is one reason why high-level languages were developed.

## Interpreters and Compilers

How is it possible for the computer to understand the BASIC program that we write? Well, each computer manufacturer provides the means for that computer to translate our BASIC-language instruction into an equivalent instruction in machine language. This translation of a high-level language into its equivalent machine language is accomplished by a computer program called either an interpreter or a compiler. In other words, the interpreter or compiler acts as the language translator between you and the computer, much as a foreign language interpreter would translate from English into, say, Spanish.

The **interpreter** resides as a separate program in primary memory during the entire process of running the program. The interpreter first translates a single instruction into its machine language equivalent and then immediately executes, or carries out, this instruction. Then it processes the next instruction in the sequence in the same manner: first translation, then execution. If a particular instruction violates syntax, then the interpreter does not understand the instruction and prints an error message to that effect. (See Figure 1.4.)

A **compiler** is like an interpreter, except that all instructions are first translated line by line prior to execution. If there are no syntax errors, the result is a separate program in machine language called the **object program.** The object program is then executed by the computer. In this case, the program written in the high-level language is called the **source program.**

## 1.4 COMPUTER SYSTEMS

Your interactions with the computer involve much more than a simple communication between you and the CPU. In fact, you will be dealing with a comprehensive computer system.

### Hardware and Software

The **computer system** is a collection of related hardware and software. As the name implies, **hardware** refers to the physical equipment: input/output (I/O) units, CPU, primary memory, secondary storage, and other specialized machinery. The term **software** refers to computer programs. In general, software is classified as either systems software or applications software.

**Systems software** is a term for programs that are designed to facilitate the use of hardware. The **operating system** of a computer (supplied by the computer manufacturer) is the most important piece of systems software. This software, which is often called the **OS** (for Operating System) or **DOS** (for Disk Operating System), consists of a number of specialized programs for operating the computer efficiently. Among others, the following important functions are performed by the operating system.

1. Scheduling the sequence of jobs within the computer[3]
2. Supplying the appropriate compiler or interpreter
3. Allocating storage for programs and data
4. Controlling input and output operations
5. Performing housekeeping chores, such as accounting for the amount of CPU time used by each user

**Applications software** refers to programs written in either high-level or assembly languages to solve specific types of problems. These programs are often developed in-house (by the organizations's systems analysts and programmers) to process applications such as payroll, inventories, billing, and accounts receivable.

[3]Each computer program that is to be run (executed) is called a *job.*

Many computer manufacturers and independent software companies prepare generalized applications packages (off-the-shelf or canned software) for widely used applications. The cost of these packages ranges from less than $100 to more than $100,000. For example, the *Materials Requirement Planning (MRP)* packages provided by IBM are designed to assist a manufacturing company in managing its labor force, machines, materials, and money; Visicorp's *VisiCalc*, the original electronic spreadsheet program for microcomputers, has been widely used for an amazing variety of applications; *Student's Records System* from Information Associates, Inc. is used by many schools for generating class rosters, grade reports, and student transcripts; and *Statistical Analysis System (SAS)*, *Statistical Package for the Social Sciences (SPSS)*, and *BioMeDical (BMD)* are three statistical packages widely used by researchers. The types of programs that you will be writing in your computer class are examples of applications programs.

## Processing Environments

There are two major approaches to computing activity: batch processing and interactive processing. In this section we briefly describe these two processing environments and identify a related approach called distributed processing.

**Batch Processing.**     This method of processing accumulates programs (jobs) in groups, or batches, to await execution. Each program is then run, or executed, according to job priorities established by computing-center personnel. In some batch environments, each program is run serially, that is, one program at a time. In more sophisticated systems, with multiprogramming capabilities, several programs can be executed concurrently under the control of the operating system. In either case, it may take from a few minutes to several hours before the results of a program are available. Typical batch jobs include weekly payrolls, monthly billings, elaborate scientific analyses, and other jobs that require many computations and/or large amounts of input and output.

**Interactive Processing.**     In this method of processing, the user develops and/or executes programs while online (directly connected) to the computer; that is, the user directly interacts with the program while it executes. Interactive processing is usually implemented on either a microcomputer or a time-sharing system.

An example might include the following dialogue between a user and a program that resides within RAM in a microcomputer: The user types RUN; the computer interprets an instruction that prints a message on the screen (monitor) requesting entry of a data item; the user types a number at the keyboard; the computer performs a calculation and prints a result on the screen.

In a time-sharing system, many users working at online terminals have simultaneous use of the computer system. In this mode of processing jobs, we send data and instructions to the computer via terminals, and the computer responds within seconds. This dialogue between us and the computer continues until we complete our task. Thus we code, execute, and correct programs at a terminal that is connected directly to the computer via a cable or a telephone line.

If the connection is by cable, then the computer and terminal communicate directly by digital pulses. We typically activate a session by turning on the terminal and pressing the "Enter" or "Carriage Return" key. If the connection is by telephone line, then we dial the computer's phone number and communicate through modems at each end of the line. A modem is a peripheral that converts digital signals to audio signals at the transmission end and audio signals back to digital signals at the receiving end.

While sitting at a terminal it seems that we have the computer to ourselves. Actually, we and others who use terminals are sharing the computer's CPU in rotation under the control of the operating system (thus the term time sharing).

Time-sharing systems can also be accessed by microcomputers. In this case, transmission of data and instructions is typically via a telephone line through modems. In effect, the microcomputer emulates a terminal; that is, the microcomputer *is* a terminal from the point of view of the time-shared computer (it doesn't know any better).

Interactive processing is common in automated banking systems, in airline reservation and other inquiry systems, and in decision-oriented applications that implement "What if . . . ?" interactive analyses. This textbook emphasizes interactive programming.

**Distributed Processing.** Communications networks that link various computers and automated office equipment (such as word processors, copying machines, and electronic mail and teleconferencing equipment) at scattered locations are called distributed processing systems. A typical system at universities includes a central mainframe computer linked to satellite minicomputers and microcomputers at various locations on and off campus. Key advantages of this type of system include greater reliability (even if one computer "crashes," the others will continue to operate); greater convenience, custom-tailoring of jobs and software, and more timely information at the local level where each computer is located; and system-wide access to specialized software packages and databases.

Distributed processing systems usually include both batch and interactive processing. For example, jobs that transmit different sets of data from a computer in San Francisco to a computer in Boston might be batched for transmission during the graveyard shift; a student might interactively access the university's mainframe computer first and its minicomputer next to accomplish two different tasks, from home or campus, using either a terminal or a microcomputer.

## 1.5 SOFTWARE DEVELOPMENT CYCLE

A **computer program** is an organized set of instructions written in a computer language; its purpose is to solve a problem that has been defined. This problem is solved when the computer program is correctly executed by the computer.

Writing a computer program involves the following four-step procedure:

1. Problem analysis (understanding the problem and requirements)
2. Program design (flowchart or pseudocode version)
3. Program code (BASIC version)
4. Program test (getting out the "bugs")

These four steps are the basis of the **software development cycle.** Thus the act of writing a program includes a step-by-step process, beginning with an analysis of the problem and ending with a program that executes as intended. In actual environments, the software development cycle also includes steps for implementing the newly developed software on an ongoing basis, evaluating its usefulness, and maintaining or modifying it over time.

This four-step process is not a rigid, lock-step procedure. In practice, the development of software cycles through these four steps until the program executes correctly. This means, for example, that the test in Step 4 may indicate a change in design (which takes us back to Step 2) or even a change in the analysis (which takes us to Step 1). By the way, within commercial environments, the software development cycle never really ends throughout the life cycle of a program; new bugs, changes in the environment, and additional requirements are facts of computerized life that promote continued cycling through these steps.

### Step 1: Problem Analysis

First, it's essential to completely understand the structure of the problem and the requirements or needs of the user (or group of users) who will benefit from the program. A common approach is to specify:

**a.** The output we wish to receive as the solution to the problem

**b.** The data we shall provide the computer

**c.** The computations and/or logical processes by which the computer will convert the provided data to the output data.

As an illustration, suppose that the Board of Regents, which oversees the State College System, wants to have a program for assessing the effects of various policies on the tuition revenue collected by state institutions of higher education. For example, how much is revenue affected if there is a change in enrollment? What is the effect of increasing student tuition on tuition revenue?

In our problem analysis we need to specify clearly three aspects of this problem.

**a.** *Data output*
   Name of college
   Total tuition revenue received by the college

**b.** *Provided data*
   Name of college (Micro U)
   Tuition per student ($750)
   Number of students enrolled (1000)

**c.** *Computations*
   To determine tuition revenue, multiply the tuition per student by the enrollment.

**NOTE**   When describing the provided data, we need to ask ourselves: Does the provided data represent the information necessary to generate the required output?

In practice (the "real world"), the requirements for output include not only *what* is to be output but also *where* (VDT, line printer, etc.), *when* (daily, weekly, on demand, etc.), and *how* (design of the display, document, or report). Similar requirements apply to the provided data.

Other considerations in the problem analysis include how the proposed program fits into the organization's computer-based goals, the projected benefits and costs, the needs for additional hardware and software, and future expectations with respect to modifications, enhancements, and extensions.

For us, the analysis in Step 1 is fairly brief. In practice, however, this step is elaborate and can take many months to complete, especially for large applications programs that integrate within a complex system of programs and users.

## Step 2: Program Design

It's best to design a computer program before it is actually written, much as a building is designed before it is constructed. A program design identifies the necessary processing tasks and spells out the exact sequence or logic by which these tasks are to be carried out. The description of this design is often called an algorithm. The manner in which we specify the algorithm, however, is closer to the problem-solving logic of the computer than to the type of prose statement in our preceding step. Throughout this textbook we use flowcharts and/or pseudocode to specify the algorithm.

A **flowchart** is a drawing of the algorithm. It has two primary uses: to help us write the computer program by serving as a blueprint and to document the logic of the computer program for future review.

Flowcharts use specific symbols to represent different activities and a written message within each symbol to explain each activity. Table 1.2 shows the "traditional" flowcharting symbols we use in this textbook, and Figure 1.5 illustrates the flowchart for the tuition revenue problem.

The flowchart in Figure 1.5 breaks down the problem into several steps.

1. Store the name of the college in a memory location.
2. Store the tuition in a memory location.
3. Store the enrollment in a memory location.
4. Calculate tuition revenue.

**Table 1.2**   Flowcharting Symbols

| Symbol | Name | Meaning |
|---|---|---|
| | Terminal | Indicates the start or end of the program. |
| | Input/output | Indicates when an input or output operation is to be performed. |
| | Process | Indicates calculations or data manipulation. |
| | Flowline | Represents the flow of logic. |
| | Decision | Represents a decision point or question that requires a choice of which logical path to follow. |
| | Connector | Connects parts of the flowchart. |
| | Preparation | Indicates a preparation step as in describing a FOR/NEXT loop (Chapter 3). |
| | Predefined process | Indicates a predefined process or step where the details are not shown in this flowchart, as in calling a subprogram (Chapter 7). |

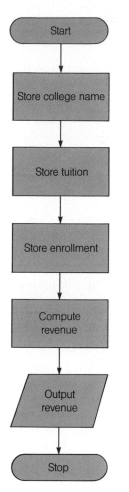

**Figure 1.5** Flowchart for the tuition revenue problem

5. Print the output.

6. Stop processing.

Note that this flowchart uses only the first four symbols of Table 1.2. The other symbols are introduced in later chapters, as our programming becomes more sophisticated.

In general, a flowchart must indicate a *Start* and must have at least one *Stop*. The flow generally runs from top to bottom and from left to right. As an option, you can use arrowheads to indicate the direction of flow, which is our preference.

A flowchart is one way of diagramming the logic of a program. Many professional programmers and systems analysts use them regularly; others do not. One reason for not using flowcharts is the difficulty in revising them once a program has been modified.

An increasingly popular alternative to flowcharts is called **pseudocode** or **program design language.** Pseudocode expresses the logic of the algorithm using English-like phrases. A key reason for the growing acceptance of pseudocode is its compatibility with the thinking processes of the programmer. The terms and expressions in this false (pseudo) code are often defined by the person doing the programming, and as a result there are many variations in writing pseudocode. The example that follows should give you some idea of the syntax and structure of pseudocode.

Before writing the tuition revenue program, we can map out its structure by using pseudocode as follows:

```
Store college name
Store tuition
Store enrollment
Revenue = tuition × enrollment
Output revenue
Stop
```

A program written in pseudocode is similar to a program written in a higher-level language such as BASIC. The major difference is the emphasis placed on content versus syntax. Pseudocode primarily concentrates on mapping out the algorithmic logic of a program, with little regard for the syntax of the actual programming language to be used. Thus we are free to concentrate on the design of the program by expressing its logic or structure in ordinary English, including abbreviations, symbols, and formulas.

Either flowcharts or pseudocode can be used to design and document programs, but the simplicity and compactness of pseudocode may tip the balance in its favor, particularly for documenting programs that are likely to undergo frequent modification.

A significant drop in the commercial sales of programs that generate flowcharts suggests the declining popularity of flowcharts as a design and documentation tool. Moreover, experimental research indicates that informal program design languages are more effective than flowcharts for program design and designer-programmer communication.[4]

We prefer pseudocode to flowcharts in designing and documenting programs but believe that flowcharts are useful tools for teaching certain programming concepts. Thus, in this textbook, we shall use either flowcharts or pseudocode, whichever is more appropriate.

Although the above example of a flowchart and pseudocode is rather simple, and you may be tempted not to use these aids for such an easy problem,

[4]H. R. Ramsey, M. E. Atwood, and J. R. Van Doren, "Flowcharts Versus Program Design Languages: An Experimental Comparison," *Communications of the acm,* June 1983, pp.445–49.

we strongly suggest that you get in the habit of using either pseudocode or flowcharts now. As programs become more complex, you will find these design tools increasingly helpful.

Later (in Module E), we shall show how the design of a program (and the program itself) fits into the design of a proposed or existing system of programs.

### Step 3: Program Code

**Coding** is the translation of our problem-solving logic from the design phase into a computer program. We use the flowchart or pseudocode as a guide for writing instructions to the computer.

The computer language that our instructions are to be written in must be decided by this step in the procedure. (Quite often the same flowchart or pseudocode can be used with any computer language.) Some languages are more suitable than others, depending on the application.

In this textbook we show several versions of the programming language called BASIC. The reasons for its widespread use, particularly among micro-computer users, include the following: The relative ease of learning BASIC; its excellent mathematical and character manipulation abilities; its capabilities with sound (music), color, and graphics; its simple syntax; and its interactive orientation (it was the first interactive language).

BASIC also has its faults, as do all programming languages. For example, it's been said that "BASIC is easy to learn, easy to write, and hard to follow." We shall clear up this seeming paradox (and show what to do about it) in the chapters that follow.

BASIC code for the tuition revenue program is shown below. Note the correspondence between the program and its flowchart and pseudocode predecessors.

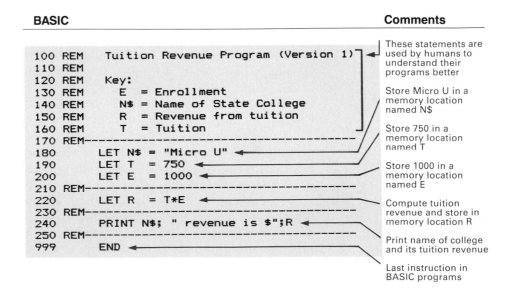

At this point you need not worry about the exact meaning of each instruction in the program, for we shall discuss them in (excruciating) detail in the next chapter. However, the program should make some sense to you.

Typically, we first design and then write our code on an ordinary sheet of paper. After we are reasonably sure that the program is correct, we enter the code through the appropriate input medium for our system, either an online terminal or a microcomputer. Details on these procedures are presented in Modules A and B at the end of the text, which you should study after reading this or the next chapter; in these modules, we briefly illustrate the IBM PC and the VAX-11. You will need to fill in the details for your particular system by consulting your instructor and your User Guide.

### Step 4: Program Test

The next step is to run, or execute, the program on the computer. By **run** or **execute** we mean that the instructions that make up the program code are processed (carried out) by the computer. Our purpose, in this case, is to test the program to ensure that it contains no errors. Testing involves running the program with test data to verify that the correct output is produced.

You will often write programs that fail to run or that run improperly. (It happens to all of us.) **Debugging** is the process of locating and correcting errors, or "getting out the bugs." Types of bugs and methods for correcting them are illustrated in Module B.

For the moment, let's assume that the program from Step 3 has been entered into primary memory and is currently awaiting execution. On most systems, we would execute the program by typing RUN, as the following test run indicates:

As you can see, the output of $750,000 for revenue at Micro U is correct, given a tuition of $750 per student and an enrollment of 1000 students.

## 1.6 BEFORE YOU LEAP

Before you leap into your course in BASIC, we offer some objectives for you to think about and some advice that we believe is sound.

### Objectives

You should be aware that the computer is used increasingly as an indispensable tool for clerical purposes, to satisfy information needs, and to make decisions. Increasingly, people have jobs that require either direct or indirect contact with a computer. Moreover, the job market in computer-related fields looks quite promising for years to come.

What does all of this mean to you? Well, we feel that if you don't accomplish the two objectives stated below, then you are shortchanging what will prove to be a very relevant part of your education.

**Objective 1.**   Achieving a modest level of programming and problem-solving skills

**Objective 2.**   Acquiring a basic knowledge of computer concepts, uses, and limitations

The first objective will develop your ability to access, utilize, and exploit the computer for the purpose of analyzing problems and making decisions more effectively, in subsequent academic courses and in your career. The second objective should dispel the mystique and misconceptions surrounding computers and thus help you to feel comfortable and operate effectively in a computerized environment.

## Advice

Some of you have a great aptitude for the material that follows. We hope you will get "turned on" to do fine things in this field. Others of you are less inclined to absorb this type of material readily. If you are in the latter category, then you should take the following advice seriously.

1. Pay close attention to *written detail*. The computer is not permissive. For example, if you spell PRENT instead of PRINT, the computer will not understand.

2. Pay close attention to *logical detail*. The computer is a machine. Therefore, you must tell it what to do in precise detail, which is broken down into logical steps.

3. Develop *good habits*. Work consistently (not constantly!). Try to rely on others as little as possible to sharpen your inherent problem-solving skills. Try to solve the Follow-up Exercises before looking up answers in the back of the book.

4. Take note of an interesting *paradox* in the act of programming. On one hand, good programming requires the type of "scientific method" outlined in items 1–3; on the other hand, art and creativity distinguish great programs from average programs. Look upon your programming as a written composition, and let your creative juices flow.

5. Be *patient*. Don't become frustrated by your mistakes. Don't get angry at the computer if it breaks down (after all, it also works hard). Finally, give yourself time. Our years of teaching this course have shown us that many students take about six to eight weeks before the material crystallizes.

## EXERCISES

1. Can you define the following terms?

| | | |
|---|---|---|
| computer | ASCII | compiler |
| analog computer | CPU | object program |
| digital computer | processor | source program |
| hybrid computer | peripherals | computer system |
| special-purpose computer | ALU | hardware |
| general-purpose computer | control unit | software |
| mainframe computer | microprocessor | systems software |
| minicomputer | output unit | applications software |
| microcomputer | line printer | operating system |
| instruction | monitor | OS |
| data | secondary storage units | DOS |
| input media | computer language | batch processing |
| data preparation devices | high-level language | interactive processing |
| input unit | low-level language | distributed processing |
| online terminal | procedure-oriented language | computer program |
| primary or internal memory | problem-oriented language | software development cycle |
| RAM | BASIC | algorithm |
| ROM | Minimal BASIC | flowchart |
| address | ANS BASIC | pseudocode |

contents

byte

character

binary digit

bit

nonprocedural language

fourth-generation language

assembly language

machine language

interpreter

program design language

coding

run

execute

debugging

2. Identify and briefly discuss the three outstanding characteristics of electronic computers.

3. Sketch the organization of a digital, general-purpose computer. Briefly describe the functions of each component.

4. Identify and briefly discuss types of computer languages.

5. Give some examples of hardware and software.

6. Briefly describe the functions of the operating system.

7. Briefly describe the functions of the compiler. How does an interpreter differ from a compiler?

8. Briefly describe and compare three processing environments.

9. How are you doing?

# Fundamentals of BASIC

C H A P T E R

# 2

This chapter introduces certain fundamental elements of BASIC. By the end of it, you will be writing and running complete, though simple, programs of the type presented in Example 2.1.

## 2.1 ELEMENTS OF BASIC

Nine elements describe the structure of the BASIC language. These are briefly described here for perspective and are elaborated upon in the remainder of this chapter and in other chapters. The tuition revenue program from Chapter 1 is reproduced here for easy reference.

**E X A M P L E   2 . 1**   **First Tuition Revenue Program**

```
100 REM    Tuition Revenue Program (Version 1)
110 REM
120 REM    Key:
130 REM      E  = Enrollment
140 REM      N$ = Name of State College
150 REM      R  = Revenue from tuition
160 REM      T  = Tuition
170 REM------------------------------------
180     LET N$ = "Micro U"
190     LET T  = 750
200     LET E  = 1000
210 REM------------------------------------
220     LET R  = T*E
230 REM------------------------------------
240     PRINT N$; " revenue is $";R
250 REM------------------------------------
999     END
```

**1. Character Set.**   The Minimal BASIC standard defines the following 60 characters.

**a.**  The 26 **alphabetic characters**, given by the letters A through Z

**b.**  The 10 **numeric characters**, or digits, given by 0 1 2 3 4 5 6 7 8 9

**c.**  The 24 **special characters**, given by a space or one of the following:
! " # $ % & ' ( ) * + − . / , : ; < = > ? ^ _

Most systems enhance the above character set with at least the full ASCII 128-character set, which includes lowercase letters and other special characters. The **character set** is the most fundamental element of the language, since it is used to construct the other eight elements.

**2. Strings.**   A string is a sequence of characters. For example, the string "Micro U" in Example 2.1 is a quoted string consisting of 7 characters, including the space but not the quotation marks.

**3. Numbers.**   A numeric value, or **number,** in BASIC includes whole numbers such as 750 and −80, numbers with decimal points such as 6.14, and numbers in scientific notation such as $5.1E-7$. These are discussed in the next section.

**4. Constants and Variables.**   **Constants** and **variables** are used to represent numeric and nonnumeric data within programs. For example, the tuition revenue program uses: the numeric variables T, E, and R; the string variable N$; the numeric constants 750 and 1000; and the string constants *Micro U* and *revenue is $*. We shall discuss these fully in the next section.

**5. Keywords.**   Certain words, called **reserved words** or **keywords,** are reserved to perform operations or communicate certain information to the computer. For example, REM, LET, PRINT, and END are keywords used in the tuition revenue program. Other keywords are introduced throughout this book, as summarized on the inside back cover.

**6. Functions.**   Certain operations are performed by using **functions.** For example, we can use the function SQR to take square roots and the function LOG to find natural logarithms. These and other functions are discussed in Module C.

**7. Expressions.**   An **expression** is a combination of one or more variables, constants, functions, and special characters. It is used to express arithmetic calculations, logical comparisons, or string manipulations. For example, T * E is a numeric expression in the tuition revenue program. Expressions are discussed in Section 2.5.

**8. Statements.**   A **statement,** or instruction, either directs the computer to perform a specific task or declares information. BASIC statements are combinations of characters, strings, numbers, variables, constants, keywords, functions, and expressions. Thus they use the first seven elements of BASIC. The tuition revenue program contains 17 statements. Note that each statement is identified by a unique keyword. This program illustrates REM, LET, PRINT, and END statements.

**9. Lines.**   A BASIC program is a sequence of **lines.** Minimal BASIC limits a line to 72 characters; however, many systems allow lines of 255 characters. Each line begins with a unique **line number,** usually one to four digits, which itself is part of the line.[1] For example, the tuition revenue program has 17 lines with line numbers 100, 110, 120, . . . , 250, 999. Leading zeros are usually ignored, and spaces before or within the line number are not permitted.

Line numbers order the lines in a program and attach unique labels to each line. The order or sequence established by the line numbers dictates the sequence of execution or action in the program. For example, lines in the tuition revenue program are executed in the sequence 180, 190, 200, 220, 240, and 999.[2] Moreover, these line numbers serve as labels that can be used to alter the sequence of execution, as discussed in Chapter 4.

It's good programming practice to number the lines in your program in increments (steps) of at least 5. For example, in the tuition revenue program we used an increment of 10. This practice allows us to insert new lines between old lines should we need to correct, expand, or otherwise modify the program.

Normally one statement is placed on each line, as in the tuition revenue program. On some systems, however, more than one statement can be typed on a line by separating the statements with a special character, such as a colon (:) on Microsoft systems or a backslash (\) on DEC systems. We shall return to this feature later.

## 2.2 CONSTANTS

A **constant** is a value that does not change during the execution of a program. BASIC requires a distinction between numeric and string constants.

### Numeric Constants

Numeric constants are positive or negative numbers; a constant is made up of the digits 0 to 9, an optional decimal point, and may be preceded by a plus or minus symbol. Numbers such as 175, −42, 3.14159, and +12 are examples of numeric constants. Commas and other special characters are *not* permitted within a numeric constant. For example, the numeric constants 6,000 and $54.50 would give syntax errors.

---

[1] All systems limit the size of a line number. For example, line numbers cannot exceed 65529 on Microsoft Systems. ANS BASIC does not require line numbers.

[2] Lines that contain a REM are ignored during program execution; hence, execution begins with line 180. We discuss this in Section 2.4.

**E-Notation.**    Very small or very large numeric constants can be represented by scientific notation, or **E-notation**, as follows:

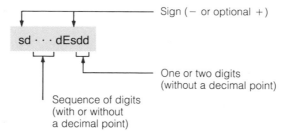

where

- *d* is a digit with or without a decimal point,
- *s* is an optional sign, and
- *E* means 10 raised to a power

For example, the constant 7,200,000,000 is written as 7.2E+09 in E-notation.

Table 2.1 shows several examples of conventional scientific notations and the equivalent E-notation used in the BASIC language. Thus E represents "times ten to the power given by the following digits." In other words, E+09 in the constant 7.2E+09 says to multiply 7.2 by 10 raised to the power 9, or multiply 7.2 by $10^9$, giving 7.2 × 1000000000 or 7200000000. In plain English, E+09 simply means move the decimal point nine places to the *right*, and E−10 says move the decimal point ten places to the *left*.

You will most likely see E-notation when reading computer output, since systems use this convention to store and print very large and very small values. Thus an understanding of E-notation facilitates the reading of computer output. For example, if in the tuition revenue program, enrollment (E) is 20000 instead of 1000, then revenue is $15 million. The output line appears as

```
Micro U revenue is $ 1.5E+07
```

**Precision and Range.**    You should be aware of the following issues when working with numeric values:

1.  The maximum number of significant digits, often called **precision**, differs from system to system. ANS BASIC specifies that numeric values can be rounded to a *minimum* of six digits. Six or seven digits is common on

**Table 2.1**    E-Notation Examples

| Standard Notation | Scientific Notation | E-Notation | Comment |
|---|---|---|---|
| 7,200,000,000 | $7.2 \times 10^9$ | 7.2E+09 | Move decimal point 9 places to the right (multiply by $10^9$) |
| −84,500,000 | $-8.45 \times 10^7$ | −8.45E+07 | Move decimal point 7 places to the right (multiply by $10^7$) |
| 0.0000000003 | $3 \times 10^{-10}$ | 3E−10 | Move decimal point 10 places to the left (divide by $10^{10}$) |

many systems. For example, the population of the U.S. in 1980 (223,324,111) would be represented on six-digit systems as 223324000 (actually 2.23324E + 08), on seven-digit systems as 2.233241E08, and on nine (or more)-digit systems exactly as is. Ask your instructor about precision on your system (and see Exercise 15).

2. The range of values allowed for a number also varies from system to system. According to the ANSI standard, all conforming systems must accommodate a range of at least 1E − 38 to 1E38 ($10^{-38}$ to $10^{38}$). Thus a value such as 2.5E82 may be too large for many systems. Values that exceed the maximum limit cause an **overflow** condition; values smaller than the lower limit cause an **underflow** condition. Systems normally print an error message whenever an overflow condition is encountered, as we illustrate in Module B. An underflow condition such as 8E − 5000 typically yields a value of zero for the constant. Ask your instructor about the range on your system (and see Exercise 15).

3. Many versions of BASIC allow the representation of distinct integer constants (whole number values), single-precision real constants (values with decimal points or E-notation with at least six-digit precision), and double-precision real constants (values with decimal points or E-notation with about double the usual precision). For example, the U.S. population of 223,324,111 could be precisely represented as a single-precision real constant on many systems; however, many other systems would have to express this number as a double-precision real constant, though the exact method of doing so varies from system to system. Ask your instructor about your system.

## String Constants

A **string constant** is a sequence of characters that may include letters, numbers, or special characters, usually enclosed between quotation marks. For example,

"Micro U"

identifies a string constant in line 180 of the tuition revenue program. Note that the length of the string constant is seven characters, including the space between the two words. Also note that the string constant does not include the quotes. Other examples of string constants are

"$2,324.25"    "327-23-3411"    "06/03/67"    "Clark Kent"

These examples are also called quoted strings, because they are enclosed by quotation marks. Later we shall show the use of unquoted strings as well.

String constants are commonly used to print labels, report headings, messages, and other text. Line 240 in the tuition revenue program uses the string constant

" revenue is $"

to label the output. Other examples and uses are shown in Section 2.6 and throughout the remainder of the text.

You should be aware of the following facts when using string constants:

1. Spaces within string constants are not ignored; that is, don't forget that a space counts as a valid character within the quoted string.

2. The maximum number of characters (length) allowed in a string constant varies from one version of BASIC to another. For example, Microsoft BASIC allows 255 characters, while other systems allow as many as 4095 characters. Ask your instructor or check your system's reference manual for the limit that applies to you.

---

### Follow-Up Exercises

1. Identify what, if anything, is wrong with each of the following constants.

   a. 1,000,000         j. 2.5E175
   b. 1000000           k. 2.5E1.5
   c. 1E6               l. "COST
   d. +7.3              m. "CO ST"
   e. 7.3               n. $500
   f. 614.25−           o. 65789024517
   g. −614.25           p. 154.612876
   h. 7 05              q. "$500"
   i. 7*5               r. "I'm OK; you're OK"

2. Express the following constants using E-notation.

   a. $-6.142 \times 10^{15}$       c. 0.00007
   b. $-6142 \times 10^{12}$        d. $7 \times 10^{-5}$

3. Express the following constants using standard notation.

   a. 123E9             c. 456E−4
   b. 0.123E12          d. 4.56E−2

---

## 2.3 VARIABLES

Programmers use symbolic names to reference unique memory locations that store data values. In BASIC this name is called a **variable**, since the value stored in that memory location can vary as the program executes; however, at any instant during the execution of a program, a variable is associated with a single value. Variables store either numeric or string values.

### Numeric Variables

A variable that stores numeric values is called a **numeric variable.** (We're not usually this straightforward!) For example, the numeric value 750 stored under the numeric variable $T$ might be represented as follows:

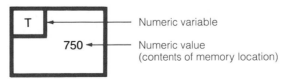

Numeric variables are classified as simple or subscripted. **Simple numeric variables** store a single numeric value, whereas **subscripted numeric variables** store multiple numeric values in related memory locations. The use of subscripted variables requires more advanced programming skills, so we shall delay this topic until Chapter 8.

The rules for forming variable names differ depending on the version of BASIC. Minimal BASIC allows 1- or 2-character variable names; however,

**Table 2.2**  Rules for Naming Numeric Variables for Selected Dialects

| Dialect | First Character | Other Characters |
|---|---|---|
| Minimal BASIC | Letter | 1 optional digit |
| ANS BASIC | Letter | 30 optional characters (letters, digits, and underscore) |
| Microsoft BASIC | Letter | 39 optional characters (letters, digits, and period) |
| VAX-11 BASIC | Letter | 30 optional characters (letters, digits, underscore, and period) |
| Your system (if different) | | |

Tables 2.3 and 2.4 illustrate some valid and invalid names for numeric variables.

**Table 2.3**  Sample Names for Numeric Variables

| Dialect | Variable Name | | | | |
| | T | T9 | TUITION | NET.PAY | NET_PAY |
|---|---|---|---|---|---|
| Minimal BASIC | Valid | Valid | Invalid | Invalid | Invalid |
| ANS BASIC | Valid | Valid | Valid | Invalid | Valid |
| Microsoft BASIC | Valid | Valid | Valid | Valid | Invalid |
| VAX-11 BASIC | Valid | Valid | Valid | Valid | Valid |
| Your system (if different) | | | | | |

many versions of BASIC allow longer multicharacter names. Table 2.2 provides different rules for naming numeric variables, depending on the BASIC dialect. Tables 2.3 and 2.4 illustrate some valid and invalid names for numeric variables.

When the size of a variable name is limited in length, as it is in Minimal BASIC, digits in a variable name are often used to distinguish among related variables. For example, if three different types of costs are to be represented by simple numeric variables in a program, then it makes sense to label these C1, C2, and C3. This practice of selecting a variable name that has meaning helps us to remember the attribute that is represented by this variable.

A good programming practice is to select variable names that have

**Table 2.4**  Invalid Names for Numeric Variables (All Dialects)

| Variable Name | Comment |
| --- | --- |
| A+ | + is an illegal character |
| 3A | Letter must be first character |
| NET PAY | No embedded blanks |
| NET-PAY | Hyphen is an illegal character |
| END | Reserved word in BASIC |

**Table 2.5**  Selection of Numeric Variable Names in Tuition Revenue Program

| Variable Description | Minimal BASIC | Multicharacter BASICs |
| --- | --- | --- |
| Tuition per student | T | TUITION |
| Enrollment at institution | E | ENROLLMENT |
| Revenue from tuition | R | REVENUE |

descriptive meaning within the context of the problem. For example, in the tuition revenue program, the variable names in Table 2.5 have contextual meaning.

**NOTE**  Issues regarding precision and range apply to numeric variables as well as to numeric constants. Items 1–3 on page 25–26 also apply to numeric variables.

## String Variables

**String variables** store string values and are indicated by placing a dollar sign ($) after the variable name. For example, N$, K$, and T$ are string variables. These variables are primarily used to store names, addresses, text, and other nonnumeric data. The tuition revenue illustration stores the name of the institution being processed. For example, the string value *Micro U* is stored in the string variable N$. The string variable N$ and its value can be pictured in memory as follows:

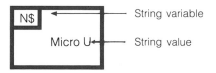

We might note the following facts and suggestions regarding string variables:

1. The rules for forming string variable names are essentially the same rules as those for naming numeric variable names, except for the trailing $ that identifies the variable as a string variable. (See Table 2.2.)
2. Select string variable names that have contextual meaning. For example, N$ is a good selection in Minimal BASIC to store the name of a college; COLLEGE$ conveys meaning in dialects that allow multicharacter names.

3. Dialects limit the maximum length of the string value that can be stored within the storage location defined by a string variable. For example, Microsoft BASIC allows up to 255 characters. Check on the limitation for your system.

4. As is true of numeric variables, string variables are classified as **simple string variables,** each of which stores a single string value, and **subscripted string variables,** each of which stores multiple strings within related memory locations. The variable N$ is a simple string variable. Subscripted string variables are discussed in Chapter 8.

**NOTE 1**    Don't use a variable name that's the same as a keyword (reserved word) in the BASIC dialect you're using. For example, END as a variable name is illegal for all dialects; NAME$ for storing names is illegal in Microsoft BASIC. In general, it's a good idea to have handy a list of reserved words for your dialect.

**NOTE 2**    Our illustrative programs will generally use multicharacter variable names for variables that store descriptive items. If your system limits variable names to one or two characters, then you should be aware that these programs will not run on your system as is.

---

### Follow-Up Exercise

4. Identify each of the following as numeric variable, string variable, or unacceptable variable.

| | | | | |
|---|---|---|---|---|
| **a.** | 1T | | **g.** | PROFIT |
| **b.** | T1 | | **h.** | $P |
| **c.** | ITEM NAME$ | | **i.** | P$ |
| **d.** | ITEM _ NAME$ | | **j.** | P |
| **e.** | ITEM.NAME$ | | **k.** | %K |
| **f.** | B+ | | **l.** | 7 |

## 2.4 END AND REM STATEMENTS

It's important to distinguish between two classes of statements called executable and nonexecutable statements, of which END and REM statements are examples.

### Executable and Nonexecutable Statements

Statements are classified as executable and nonexecutable. An **executable statement** causes activity in the CPU during execution of the program. The END, LET, PRINT, INPUT, READ, and RESTORE statements are all examples of executable statements; we introduce these statements in this chapter.

As illustrated in the tuition revenue program, programs end with the statement:

**END Statement**

```
END
```

This statement not only defines the physical end of a BASIC program but also causes execution of the program to terminate. Since the END statement is the last statement in the program, it follows that it must appear in the highest-numbered line. In our tuition revenue example, we placed it in line number 999. As a matter of programming style, we usually use the label 999 as the last line in a program with three-digit line numbers.

A **nonexecutable statement** is used to provide or declare certain information to the CPU during compilation or interpretation of the program. Nonexecutable statements are ignored during execution of the program. The REM and DATA statements introduced in this chapter are examples of nonexecutable statements.

### Documentation of Programs

The statement

**REM Statement**

```
REM unquoted string
```

is used to document programs for improved *human* readability. The next example illustrates a fully documented program.

## E X A M P L E   2 . 2   Revised Tuition Revenue Program

The following version of the tuition revenue program from Example 2.1 on page 23 includes multicharacter variable names and more extensive documentation.

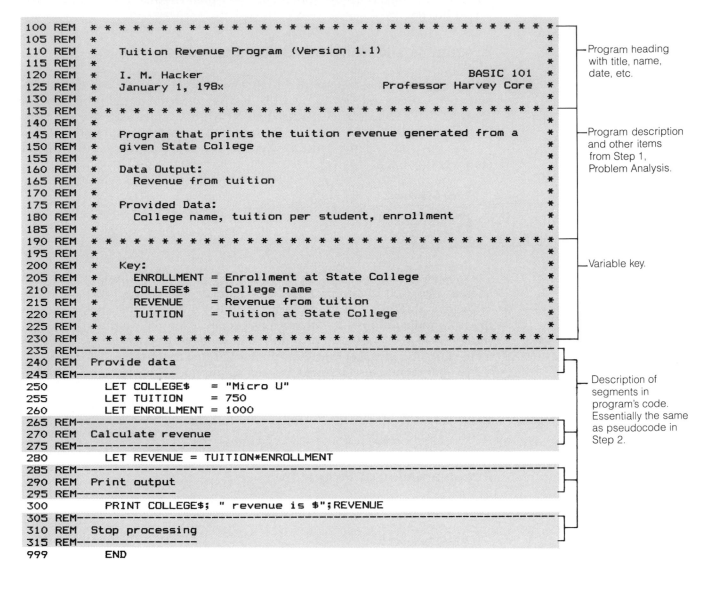

```
100 REM  * * * * * * * * * * * * * * * * * * * * * * * * * * * * * * * * * *
105 REM  *                                                               *          ─Program heading
110 REM  *    Tuition Revenue Program (Version 1.1)                      *            with title, name,
115 REM  *                                                               *            date, etc.
120 REM  *    I. M. Hacker                              BASIC 101        *
125 REM  *    January 1, 198x                 Professor Harvey Core      *
130 REM  *                                                               *
135 REM  * * * * * * * * * * * * * * * * * * * * * * * * * * * * * * * * * *
140 REM  *                                                               *
145 REM  *    Program that prints the tuition revenue generated from a   *          ─Program description
150 REM  *    given State College                                        *            and other items
155 REM  *                                                               *            from Step 1,
160 REM  *    Data Output:                                               *            Problem Analysis.
165 REM  *       Revenue from tuition                                    *
170 REM  *                                                               *
175 REM  *    Provided Data:                                             *
180 REM  *       College name, tuition per student, enrollment           *
185 REM  *                                                               *
190 REM  * * * * * * * * * * * * * * * * * * * * * * * * * * * * * * * * * *
195 REM  *                                                               *
200 REM  *    Key:                                                       *          ─Variable key.
205 REM  *       ENROLLMENT = Enrollment at State College                *
210 REM  *       COLLEGE$   = College name                               *
215 REM  *       REVENUE    = Revenue from tuition                       *
220 REM  *       TUITION    = Tuition at State College                   *
225 REM  *                                                               *
230 REM  * * * * * * * * * * * * * * * * * * * * * * * * * * * * * * * * * *
235 REM----------------------------------------------------------------
240 REM  Provide data
245 REM---------------
250          LET COLLEGE$    = "Micro U"                                            ─Description of
255          LET TUITION     = 750                                                    segments in
260          LET ENROLLMENT = 1000                                                    program's code.
265 REM----------------------------------------------------------------              Essentially the same
270 REM  Calculate revenue                                                           as pseudocode in
275 REM------------------                                                            Step 2.
280          LET REVENUE = TUITION*ENROLLMENT
285 REM----------------------------------------------------------------
290 REM  Print output
295 REM---------------
300          PRINT COLLEGE$; " revenue is $";REVENUE
305 REM----------------------------------------------------------------
310 REM  Stop processing
315 REM-----------------
999          END


RUN
Micro U revenue is $ 750000
```

Thus REM statements are used to document or describe programs as follows:

1. An introductory section that gives the title of the program, version, author, date, course/professor (in academic courses), and perhaps other items such as computer system and other system-dependent features. (See lines 110–125.)

2. A narrative section, which might include the purpose and scope of the program, a description of data input and output, and other information that relates to step 1 in our four-step procedure first described in Section 1.5. (See lines 145–180.)

**Table 2.6** Alternatives to the Keyword REM

| Dialect | | Sample Line | |
|---------|---|-------------|---|

Microsoft

Apostrophe ⎯┐ Placement of remark to right
└ of statement on same line ↓

255     LET T = 750     | Tuition is $750 per student |

VAX-11

255     LET T = 750   Exclamation ⎯→ | Tuition is $750 per student |

Your system
(if different)

3. An optional section might include abbreviated pseudocode (step 2 in our procedure) as an overall description of the program's design. This is useful in long and involved programs.

4. A section that defines each major variable in the program. (See lines 200–220.) This section may be unnecessary if multicharacter variable names are used.

5. Remarks that are interspersed within the code to identify major tasks, describe segments, explain logic, and otherwise improve the appearance and facilitate the readability of the program. (See lines 235–245, 265–275, 285–295, and 305–315.) As an option to item 3 above, these REMs can include abbreviated pseudocode. (See lines 240, 270, 290, and 310.)

**NOTE 1** *Good programming style dictates that programs be well documented,* since such programs are easier to follow, modify, or otherwise update at a later time. Our documentation may seem like overkill at this time, but you will come to appreciate this point as your programs (and others you might read) increase in length and complexity. In commercial environments, extensive documentation helps to reduce software maintenance costs.[3]

**NOTE 2** The REM statement is a *nonexecutable* statement. When the program in Example 2.1 is run, the first statement executed is the LET in line 250. Thus REM statements are ignored during execution. They simply serve to document a program for any user who views a listing of the program (such as your instructor).

Some versions of BASIC allow the placement of remarks to the right of a statement, as illustrated in Table 2.6.

These systems also allow the replacement of the keyword REM at the beginning of a line with the apostrophe or exclamation mark, which would give a cleaner look to the program in Example 2.2. Does your system allow the replacement of REM by a special character?

## 2.5 LET STATEMENT

A **LET statement** is used to perform and store calculations, to assign a constant to a storage location, or to copy the contents of one storage location into another. In the tuition revenue program, the statement

[3]This factor is rather important since software development and program changes account for more than 50% of computer budgets. One estimate is that the cost of changing the programs at financial institutions for the proposed dividend withholding in the early 1980s would have cost $1.5 billion!

190 LET T = 750

is an example of a LET statement. This statement stores the numeric value 750 in the storage location named T.

## Structure

In more general terms, the LET statement is structured as follows:

**LET Statement**

> **LET** *variable = expression*
>
> *LET L$ = "I love BASIC"*

On the left side of the equal sign, a single variable following the keyword LET identifies a storage location in internal computer memory.[4] The right side of the equal sign is either a string expression or a numeric expression.

**LET Statement and String Expressions.**   A **string expression** can be a string variable or a string constant.[5] We illustrate these next:

**E X A M P L E   2 . 3**   **LETs with String Expressions**

The shaded portion in the program below illustrates three string expressions.

**Program**
```
100 LET L$ = "I love BASIC"          String constants
110 LET P$ = L$                      String variable
120 LET L$ = "I'm not sure"
130 PRINT L$,P$
999 END
```
**Output**
```
I'm not sure  I love BASIC
```

After execution of line 100, L$ stores the following in memory:

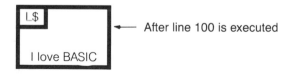

After line 100 is executed

In this case the string expression is the 12-character string constant I LOVE BASIC (including the two blank characters). The LET statement thus tells the computer to "replace the contents of L$ by the expression to the right of the equal sign."

---

[4]The keyword LET can be omitted on some systems.

[5]A string expression also may include string functions and string operators, which we discuss in Module F.

**Table 2.7** Numeric Operators

| Numeric Operation | Numeric Operator | Example |
|---|---|---|
| Addition | + | $x + 2$ |
| Subtraction | − | $x - 2$ |
| Division | / | $x / 2$ |
| Multiplication | * | $x * 2$ |
| Exponentiation (raise to a power)# | $\wedge$ | $x \wedge 2$ |

#Some systems allow the upward arrow ↑ or ** for exponentiation.

When the computer next executes line 110, memory for these two string variables would appear as follows:

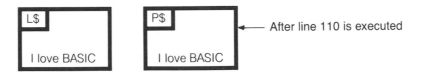

The string expression to the right of the equal sign in line 110 is the single string variable L\$. Note that the LET statement simply copies the contents of L\$ into P\$, leaving the contents of L\$ unaffected. When the computer next executes line 120, memory would appear as follows:

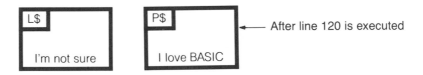

**LET Statement and Numeric Expressions.** A **numeric expression** may consist of a single numeric constant, a single numeric variable, or a combination of numeric constants and numeric variables separated by numeric operators and optional parentheses.[6] A **numeric operator** indicates the type of computation desired. Five symbols are used in the BASIC language to indicate the type of numeric operation, as described in Table 2.7.

**E X A M P L E   2 . 4**   **LETs with Numeric Expressions**

The shaded portion in the program below illustrates three numeric expressions.

**Program**
```
100 LET A = 5000
110 LET B = A
120 LET C = A + 3000
130 PRINT A,B,C
999 END
```

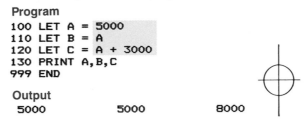

**Output**
```
 5000          5000          8000
```

[6]Module C includes numeric functions in this definition.

The relevant memory locations change as follows:

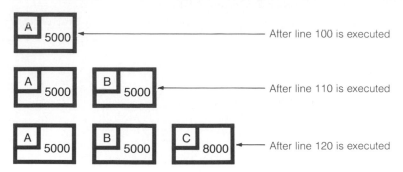

In line 100, the constant 5000 is placed in the storage location that is identified by A. In line 110, the contents of the storage location called A are copied by the storage location called B. Note, however, that this transfer is electronic; that is, whatever is in A remains there, but whatever was in B gets replaced by whatever is in A. Finally, line 120 places the computational result of the expression A + 3000 in the storage location called C. This means that the constant 3000 and the contents of A are added, and the result is stored in C.

## Follow-Up Exercises

5. Modify Example 2.3 as indicated and describe the output.
   a. 120 LET L$ = P$
   b. 120 LET L$ = L$

6. Modify Example 2.4 as indicated and describe the output.
   a. 120 LET C = A/2
   b. 120 LET C = A*2
   c. 120 LET C = A^2

7. Consider the following sequence
   10 LET A = 37/C
   15 LET B = A + 1.6
   20 LET D = B^2

   and the current contents given below.

   Indicate the new contents after the execution of the above statements.

8. Given the lines
   100 LET K = K + 1
   110 LET S = S + X
   and the current contents

   determine the new contents if these instructions are executed three times in sequence.

## Order of Evaluating Numeric Expressions

Computers do arithmetic on only one arithmetic operation at a time (pairwise arithmetic). Therefore, a numeric expression involving several computations must be computed in a certain sequence.

**Arithmetic Hierarchy.** In BASIC, the sequence for performing pairwise numeric operations is based on the following **arithmetic hierarchy:**

- First priority    All exponentiation is performed.
- Second priority  All multiplication and division is completed.
- Third priority   All addition and subtraction is performed.

**E X A M P L E   2 . 5**   Area Problem

An analyst for Prangles Potato Chips, a competitor of Pringles, wishes to determine the area of the top that would be required of a super-economy-size cylindrical container of radius 5 inches. As you might recall, the area of a circle is computed by using the formula *area* = $\pi r^2$, where *r* is the radius. This can be written in BASIC as

```
100 REM   Area Problem
110 REM
120       LET PI   = 3.141593
130       LET R    = 5
140       LET AREA = PI*R^2
150       PRINT AREA
999       END

run
 78.53983
```

The execution of the LET statement in line 140 is achieved as follows:

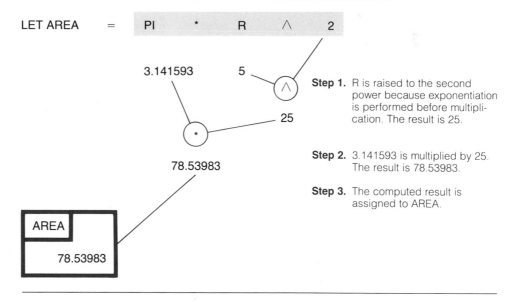

**Left-to-Right Rule.** The exact order of computation when two or more computations are at the same level of arithmetic hierarchy will be consistent with a *left-to-right scan* of the arithmetic expression, as the following example illustrates.

**E X A M P L E  2 . 6**  **Microeconomics Problem**

The daily cost in dollars (c) of operating a small manufacturing firm is described by the cost function

$$c = u^3 - 6u^2 + 250$$

where $u$ represents the number of units produced by the firm per day. The following program computes this daily cost.

```
100 REM   Microeconomics Problem
110 REM
120       LET U    = 20
130       LET COST = U^3 - 6*U^2 + 250
140       PRINT COST
999       END

run
 5850
```

The LET statement is executed as follows:

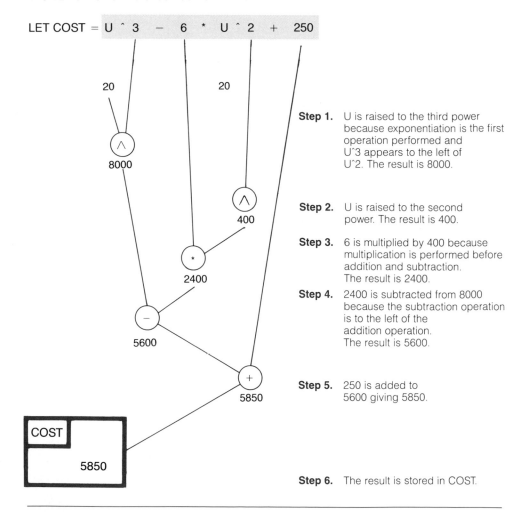

LET COST = U ˆ 3 − 6 * U ˆ 2 + 250

**Step 1.** U is raised to the third power because exponentiation is the first operation performed and U^3 appears to the left of U^2. The result is 8000.

**Step 2.** U is raised to the second power. The result is 400.

**Step 3.** 6 is multiplied by 400 because multiplication is performed before addition and subtraction. The result is 2400.

**Step 4.** 2400 is subtracted from 8000 because the subtraction operation is to the left of the addition operation. The result is 5600.

**Step 5.** 250 is added to 5600 giving 5850.

**Step 6.** The result is stored in COST.

**Use of Parentheses.**    The insertion of parentheses into arithmetic expressions changes the order of computation according to the following rules.

**1.** The operations inside parentheses are computed before operations that are not inside parentheses.

2. Parentheses can be embedded inside other parentheses in complicated expressions.

3. The innermost set of parentheses contains the computations done first. Note that within parentheses the hierarchy and left-to-right rules apply.

**E X A M P L E   2 . 7**   **Temperature Conversion**

Conversion of temperatures from Fahrenheit to Celsius is given by the formula

$$\text{Celsius} = \frac{5}{9}(\text{Fahrenheit} - 32)$$

The following program converts Fahrenheit to Celsius temperatures.

```
100 REM   Temperature Conversion
110 REM
120       LET F = 212
130       LET C = 5/9*(F - 32)
140       PRINT C
999       END

run
 100
```

The LET statement is executed as follows:

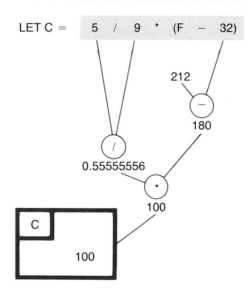

LET C =   5 / 9 * (F - 32)

**Step 1.** 32 is subtracted from F because this operation is enclosed in parentheses. The result is 180.

**Step 2.** 5 is divided by 9 because division is to the left of multiplication.

**Step 3.** 0.5555556 is multiplied by 180. The result is 100.

**Step 4.** The result is stored in C.

## Exceptions, Warnings, and Reminders

1. Avoid the following violations when forming numeric expressions.

   a. Don't place numeric operators adjacent to one another, because a syntax error will result. For example,

      2 * − 3        ⊘ Illegal

   is incorrect. Instead use

      2 * (−3)

or

$$-2 * 3$$

**b.** Don't raise negative quantities to a nonintegral power, because an error during execution will occur. Negative values can be raised only to integer powers. For example,

(−2) ^ **5.1**     ⊘ Illegal

is not allowed, but

(−2) ^ 5

is permitted.

**c.** Don't use implied multiplication such as 7V. This gives a syntax error. This error is made often, because it's a holdover from algebra days. Of course, we use 7*V.

**d.** Avoid division by zero, which gives an overflow execution error.

**2.** The keyword LET is optional on most systems. Thus the statement

220    **LET**  R = T*E

can be written as

```
                                        —— LET omitted
                     ↓
220                     R = T*E
```

Does your system allow this? We generally don't recommend this practice as a matter of style, since all BASIC statements have associated keywords.

**3.** Some versions of BASIC allow the assignment of the same value to two or more variables in a single LET statement. For example, we might use

10 LET A = B = C = 0

or

10 LET A, B, C = 0

instead of

10 LET A = 0
20 LET B = 0
30 LET C = 0

What about your system?

**4.** Carefully note the meaning of the equal sign (=) in BASIC; it means "place the *value* indicated by the expression to the right into the storage location indicated by the *variable* to the left." Because of this meaning, a LET statement such as

LET K = K + 1

makes sense in BASIC but not in algebra. Note that each time this statement is executed by the computer, the content (value) of K gets increased by 1. In other words, this statement instructs the computer to "add the content of K and 1, and place this result in K." This type of statement is used often in BASIC programs for the purpose of counting.

5. A simple variable can store only one value at a time. Storing another value in the same location erases the original value. For example, in the statements

190 LET T = 750

195 LET T = 800

the value 750 is stored in T after line 190 is executed. However, the execution of line 195 replaces the old value 750 with the new value 800 in memory location T.

6. We cannot assign a string value to a numeric variable or a numeric value to a string variable. Thus both these statements yield errors:

Can't pair numeric variable with string constant

100 LET A = "LOTUS"    ⊘ Illegal

110 LET B$ = 123    ⊘ Illegal

Can't pair string variable with numeric constant

7. Some BASIC dialects allow **multistatement lines,** that is, lines that include more than one statement per line. Table 2.8 illustrates two such dialects.

**Table 2.8**  Multistatement Line Examples

| Dialect | Multiple Lines | Multistatement Lines | Comment |
|---|---|---|---|
| Microsoft | 10 LET A = 1<br>20 LET B = 2<br>30 LET C = 3 | 10 LET A = 1 : LET B = 2 : LET C = 3<br>or<br>10 LET A = 1 : B = 2 : C = 3 | The colon separates each pair of statements on a line.<br>Deleting the last two LETs is visually appealing. |
| VAX-11 | 10 LET A = 1<br>20 LET B = 2<br>30 LET C = 3 | 10 LET A = 1 \ LET B = 2 \ LET C = 3<br>or<br>10 LET A = 1 \ B = 2 \ C = 3<br>or<br>10 LET A = 1<br>        B = 2<br>        C = 3 | The backslash separates each pair of statements on a line.<br><br>Here we have one *program* line, three statements, and three *visual* lines. Note that only the first visual line is numbered. Later in the text we illustrate the advantage of this approach for certain types of statements |

Your system
(if different)

**NOTE**    It's very important that you pay close attention to hierarchy, left-to-right, and parentheses rules when you're writing BASIC expressions. Inattention to these rules is a leading cause of logic errors. The following exercises emphasize this point.

---

## Follow-Up Exercises

**9.**  In Example 2.7, what would be stored under C if the LET statement were as follows:

20 LET C = 5/9*F − 32

**10.**  What values are stored in P and R after the following program segment is executed?

100 LET E = 1000
110 LET U = 5000
120 LET P = E/U*100
130 LET R = E/(U*100)

**11.**  Indicate what would be stored in A for each of the following, given that 3 is in B and 2 is in C.
  **a.**  80 LET A = (4 + B^3 − C)*C^2
  **b.**  82 LET A = (4 + B^(3 − C))*C^2
  **c.**  84 LET A = (4 + B^(3 − C))*(C^2)
  **d.**  86 LET A = 9/B*C + 5/C
  **e.**  88 LET A = 9/(B*C) + 5/C
  **f.**  90 LET A = 9/B/C + 5/C
  **g.**  92 LET A = 9/B*(C+5) /C

**12.**  Write numeric expressions for each of the following algebraic expressions.
  **a.**  $x^{i+1}$
  **b.**  $x^i + 1$
  **c.**  $\dfrac{s^2}{(p-1)}$
  **d.**  $\dfrac{(x-a)^2}{(p-1)}$
  **e.**  $(y - 3^{x-1} + 2)^5$
  **f.**  $(7 - x)^{1/2}$
  **g.**  $\sqrt{\dfrac{(x-a)^2}{(p-1)}}$
  **h.**  $[a/b]$, or integer portion of $a \div b$
  **i.**  $\ln(x + 3)$, or natural logarithm of $(x+3)$

**13.**  Identify what is wrong, if anything, with each of the following LET statements.
  **a.**  05 LET B + C = A
  **b.**  10 LET D = 4.1 * −X
  **c.**  15 LET 5 = A
  **d.**  20 LET X = Y = 5.3
  **e.**  25 LET K = J^3.2, where J stores a negative value.
  **f.**  30 LET K = J^3, where J stores a negative value.
  **g.**  35 L = 8^K + 4

## 2.6 PRINT STATEMENT

The PRINT statement is used to display output values at the terminal or monitor during the execution of a program. A general form of the PRINT statement is given by

**PRINT Statement**

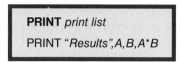

**PRINT** *print list*

PRINT *"Results",A,B,A*B*

where the print list contains one or more of the following items:

**1.** A constant (numeric or string)

**2.** A variable (numeric or string)

**3.** An expression (numeric or string)

Any combination of variables, constants, and expressions can be included in the PRINT statement. However, each item in the print list must be separated by either a comma or a semicolon.[7]

**E X A M P L E   2 . 8**  **Output from the Tuition Revenue Program**

In the program of Example 2.2 on page 32, lines 250 and 280 store the following:

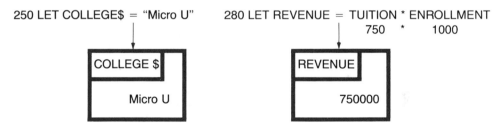

250 LET COLLEGE$ = "Micro U"    280 LET REVENUE = TUITION * ENROLLMENT
                                                750    *    1000

COLLEGE $

Micro U

REVENUE

750000

The PRINT statement in line 300 has three items in its print list.

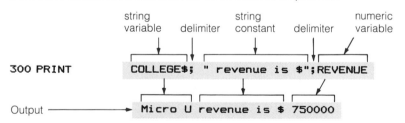

|  | string variable | delimiter | string constant | delimiter | numeric variable |

**300 PRINT**    `COLLEGE$;  " revenue is $";REVENUE`

Output ⟶    `Micro U revenue is $ 750000`

Execution of this print statement thus outputs three distinct values, one for each item in the print list, as shown. Note that each adjacent pair of items in the print list must be separated or *delimited,* in this case by a semicolon. More on this shortly.

---

[7]Some systems allow one or more blank spaces or other special characters to delimit items in the print list.

## Printing Numeric Values

Study the following points regarding the output of numeric values:

1. Output of a positive value is usually preceded by a space to account for the plus sign.

2. Output of a negative value is preceded by a minus sign.

3. Output of a numeric value is usually followed by a single space.

4. When an item in the print list is an expression, BASIC evaluates the expression before printing the value.

5. Numeric values are printed in different ways depending on the size of the value being output. Numeric values are normally printed in decimal form unless the value is too small or too large, in which case BASIC automatically outputs the value in E-notation rounded to at least six digits of precision.

6. Execution of a PRINT statement results in the output of a value for each item (constant, variable, and expression) in the print list.

7. When execution of a PRINT statement is completed, the printing element or cursor on the output unit automatically goes to the beginning (column 1) of the next print line. (As with most rules, there's an exception to this one, which we shall discuss shortly.)

8. Output on a print line is divided into print zones. The number of zones and the width of each zone vary from system to system. However, a typical setup for an 80-column display divides each print line into five print zones of 14 columns each, as seen in Figure 2.1. Is the output display screen different for your system?

9. When a comma in the print list precedes the item to be printed, the value is printed at the beginning of the next print zone; however, if a semicolon precedes the item, then the value is printed immediately after the last value.

10. Virtually all systems print values left-justified (at the extreme left) in a print zone.

**E X A M P L E  2 . 9**  Printing Numeric Values

The following example illustrates many of the points described above.

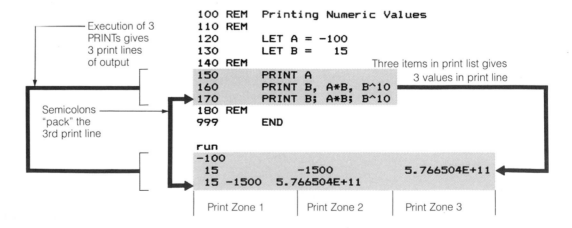

```
100 REM   Printing Numeric Values
110 REM
120       LET A = -100
130       LET B =    15
140 REM
150       PRINT A
160       PRINT B, A*B, B^10
170       PRINT B; A*B; B^10
180 REM
999       END

run
-100
    15              -1500         5.766504E+11
    15 -1500  5.766504E+11
```

Execution of 3 PRINTs gives 3 print lines of output

Three items in print list gives 3 values in print line

Semicolons "pack" the 3rd print line

Print Zone 1     Print Zone 2     Print Zone 3

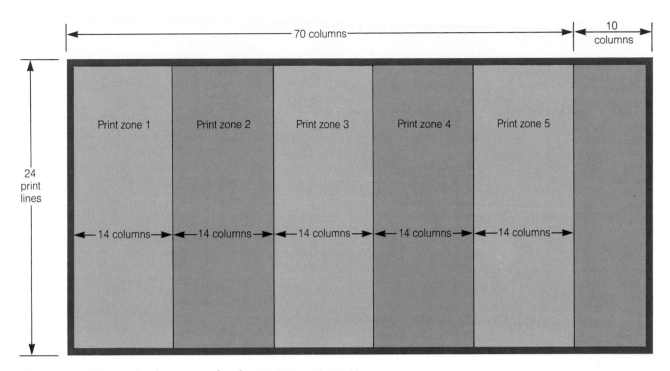

**Figure 2.1** Output display screen for the IBM PC or VAX-11

### Printing String Values

The print list can include not only string variables but also labels, report titles, column headings, and other textual matter. Note the following points:

1. A string constant must be enclosed by quotation marks.
2. In Minimal BASIC, the maximum length of a string constant is 72 characters; however, on many systems the length of a string constant can be longer. Check your system.
3. The string value is printed exactly as it appears within the quotation marks, without leading or trailing spaces.
4. Items 6–10 on page 44 also apply to the printing of string values.

**E X A M P L E   2 . 1 0**   **Tuition Revenue Problem with Revised Output**

The following revision of our tuition revenue problem shows a more elaborate output design.

Program

```
100 ,REM    Tuition Revenue Program (Version 1.2)
110 REM-------------------------------------------
250         LET COLLEGE$   = " Micro U"
255         LET TUITION    = 750
260         LET ENROLLMENT = 1000
265 REM-------------------------------------------
280         LET REVENUE = TUITION*ENROLLMENT
285 REM-------------------------------------------
290         PRINT "Tuition Revenue Report"
295         PRINT "----------------------"
300         PRINT "College .....", COLLEGE$
305         PRINT "Enrollment ..", ENROLLMENT
310         PRINT "Tuition ....$", TUITION
315         PRINT "Revenue ....$", REVENUE
320         PRINT "----------------------"
325 REM-------------------------------------------
999         END
```

Output

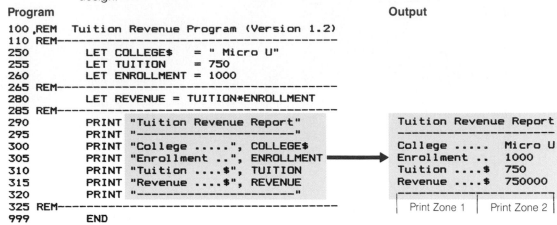

```
Tuition Revenue Report
----------------------
College .....   Micro U
Enrollment ..   1000
Tuition ....$   750
Revenue ....$   750000
----------------------
```
Print Zone 1 | Print Zone 2

Note that each print list in lines 300–315 has two elements, a string constant and a variable. The value of the string constant is printed left-justified in the first print zone of a print line, and the value of the variable is printed left-justified in the second print zone of the same print line. (Did you notice the cunning extra space we inserted just before M in Micro in line 250? This aligns the M over the numeric output in print zone 2.)

This output design shows how the use of titles, labels, and special characters like dashes and periods contributes to visually appealing and readable output.

## Output Spacing

Certain variations in the use of the PRINT statement allow us to better control horizontal and vertical spacing of printed output. Here are some points that will allow us to spread spacing, compact spacing, suppress printing on the next line, and achieve blank lines.

1. As you know, use of a semicolon to separate items in a print list "packs" the zones. Packed zones allow us to fit more output data on a print line. The semicolon causes the terminal to generate zero spaces, so that printing continues at the next column on the line, rather than moving to the next print zone.

2. A comma or semicolon at the end of the print list, called a trailing comma or trailing semicolon, instructs the system to print the next output on the same print line. Thus a trailing comma causes the cursor on a screen to stay on the same line and proceed to the beginning of the next print zone. On the other hand, the trailing semicolon causes the cursor to stay in its current location.

3. On many systems, commas can appear consecutively in the list of a PRINT statement. Each extra comma positions the cursor or printing element at

the beginning of the next zone, thus allowing us to print a blank zone. Does your system allow these blank-zone commas?[8]

4. If we omit the list of items in a PRINT statement, then a blank line is "printed." In effect, this allows us to control vertical spacing by moving the cursor down the video screen.

**EXAMPLE 2.11** Output Spacing

We now illustrate these points by example.

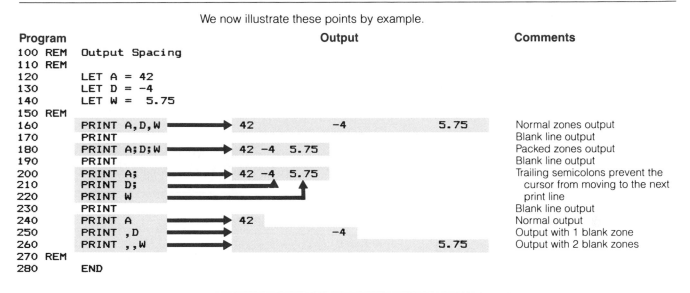

| Program | Output | Comments |
|---|---|---|
| 100 REM Output Spacing | | |
| 110 REM | | |
| 120      LET A = 42 | | |
| 130      LET D = -4 | | |
| 140      LET W =  5.75 | | |
| 150 REM | | |
| 160      PRINT A,D,W  →  42        -4        5.75 | | Normal zones output |
| 170      PRINT | | Blank line output |
| 180      PRINT A;D;W  →  42 -4 5.75 | | Packed zones output |
| 190      PRINT | | Blank line output |
| 200      PRINT A;  →  42 -4 5.75 | | Trailing semicolons prevent the |
| 210      PRINT D; | | cursor from moving to the next |
| 220      PRINT W | | print line |
| 230      PRINT | | Blank line output |
| 240      PRINT A  →  42 | | Normal output |
| 250      PRINT ,D  →           -4 | | Output with 1 blank zone |
| 260      PRINT ,,W  →                5.75 | | Output with 2 blank zones |
| 270 REM | | |
| 280      END | | |

## The TAB Function

Use of the comma (,) and the semicolon (;) to space output is sometimes inconvenient. The TAB function is a formatting feature that allows convenient spacing of output. This function is used only as an item within the print list of a PRINT statement. Its general form is

**TAB Function**

where the *argument* represents a numeric constant, numeric variable, or numeric expression that is evaluated and rounded to the nearest integer value. The value of the argument determines the column in which the next character is printed.

---

[8]Some systems don't allow the use of extra commas for blank zones. In these situations, a statement like
PRINT ,D ←——— Prints the value in D in the 2nd print zone
can be replaced by
PRINT " ", D ←——— Also prints the value in D in the 2nd print zone
Thus the output of a single blank within a zone ensures a blank zone.

**E X A M P L E   2 . 1 2**    **The TAB Function**

Study the following variations.

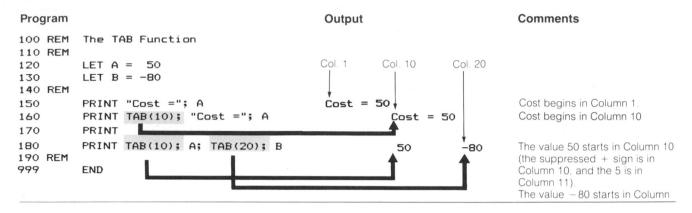

| Program | Output | Comments |
|---|---|---|
| 100 REM   The TAB Function | | |
| 110 REM | | Col. 1    Col. 10    Col. 20 |
| 120       LET A =  50 | | |
| 130       LET B = -80 | | |
| 140 REM | | |
| 150       PRINT "Cost ="; A | Cost = 50 | Cost begins in Column 1. |
| 160       PRINT TAB(10); "Cost ="; A | Cost = 50 | Cost begins in Column 10 |
| 170       PRINT | | |
| 180       PRINT TAB(10); A; TAB(20); B | 50        -80 | The value 50 starts in Column 10 (the suppressed + sign is in Column 10, and the 5 is in Column 11). |
| 190 REM | | The value -80 starts in Column |
| 999       END | | |

> **NOTE**  Use the semicolon delimiter following each TAB function and item in the print list; otherwise, output may revert back to standard print zones.

**E X A M P L E   2 . 13**    **Tuition Revenue Program with Report Headings**

In this program we use the TAB function to space headings and output conveniently for a report. Study the correspondence between the PRINT segment and the output.

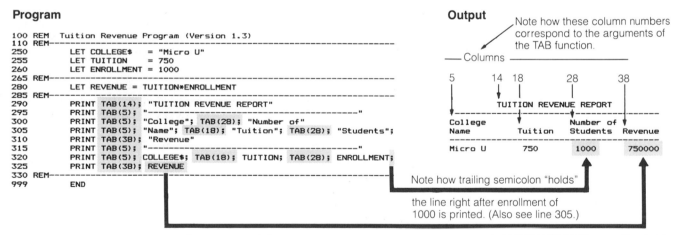

**Program**

```
100 REM  Tuition Revenue Program (Version 1.3)
110 REM-------------------------------------------
250        LET COLLEGE$   = "Micro U"
255        LET TUITION    = 750
260        LET ENROLLMENT = 1000
265 REM-------------------------------------------
280        LET REVENUE = TUITION*ENROLLMENT
285 REM-------------------------------------------
290        PRINT TAB(14); "TUITION REVENUE REPORT"
295        PRINT TAB(5); "------------------------------"
300        PRINT TAB(5); "College"; TAB(28); "Number of"
305        PRINT TAB(5); "Name"; TAB(18); "Tuition"; TAB(28); "Students";
310        PRINT TAB(38); "Revenue"
315        PRINT TAB(5); "------------------------------"
320        PRINT TAB(5); COLLEGE$; TAB(18); TUITION; TAB(28); ENROLLMENT;
325        PRINT TAB(38); REVENUE
330 REM-------------------------------------------
999        END
```

**Output**

Note how these column numbers correspond to the arguments of the TAB function.

```
—— Columns ——
5       14  18           28           38

            TUITION REVENUE REPORT
       ------------------------------
College
Name         Tuition     Number of
                         Students   Revenue
       ------------------------------
Micro U      750         1000       750000
```

Note how trailing semicolon "holds" the line right after enrollment of 1000 is printed. (Also see line 305.)

The 750000 in REVENUE gets printed on the same line as 1000 in ENROLLMENT. (Also see line 310.)

> **NOTE 1**  The print lists in lines 305 and 320 end with a semicolon, which effectively allows us to continue these print lists in lines 310 and 325, respectively. This is one way of continuing print lists that are too long to fit on one screen. Ask your instructor about other ways to continue long lines on your system.

> **NOTE 2**  The PRINT USING statement discussed in Module D is the ultimate tool for the precise control of output. Try reading this module after this or the *next* chapter.

## Follow-Up Exercises

**14.** Run the following program on your system:

```
10 PRINT "00000000011111111111222222222233333333334"
20 PRINT "12345678901234567890123456789012345678890"
30 LET A = −5.4
40 PRINT A,A,A,A,A,A,A
99 END
```

How long is each zone on your system? How many zones fit on a print line? What happens when you try to print too many items on one print line? Ask your instructor (or check your system's User Manual) if it's possible to increase or decrease the length of the print line.

**15.** Describe printed output for your system by running the following program.

```
10 LET A = 0.55
15 LET B = 0.00055
20 LET C = 1234.0
25 LET D = 1234567890123
30 LET E = 1234.56789
35 LET F = 2.5E82
40 LET G = 8E−5000
80 PRINT A,B,C,D,E,F,G
85 PRINT
90 PRINT A;B;C;D;E;F;G
99 END
```

How does your system's precision handle the values in D and E? Does your system have overflow for the value in F? How does it handle the underflow in G?

**16.** First describe the print lines for each case below. Then run these on your system. Assume −5 is stored in X, 10 is stored in Y, 15 is stored in Z, and AKA is stored in N$.

**a.** 15 PRINT X,Y;Z

**b.** 15 PRINT X;Y,Z

**c.** 15 PRINT X;Y,
    20 PRINT Z

**d.** 15 PRINT X;Y;
    20 PRINT Z

**e.** 15 PRINT X,Y,,,Z

**f.** 15 PRINT "X =";X
    20 PRINT
    25 PRINT "Y =",Y
    30 PRINT
    35 PRINT
    40 PRINT "Z =";Z;"%"
    45 LET L$ = "Z ="
    50 PRINT L$;Z;"%"

**g.** 15 PRINT "X","Y"
    20 PRINT X,Y

**h.** 15 PRINT "bXb";"bbY"
    20 PRINT "− − − − − −"
    25 PRINT X;Y

**i.** 15 PRINT N$,N$
    20 PRINT N$;N$
    25 PRINT N$;"b";N$

**17.** Describe the output, given the following storage in memory:

| | | |
|---|---|---|
| **a.** | 75 PRINT A,TAB(25);C | **f.** 75 PRINT TAB(15);D$ |
| **b.** | 75 PRINT A;TAB(25),C | **g.** 75 PRINT TAB(B);D$ |
| **c.** | 75 PRINT A;TAB(25);C | **h.** 75 PRINT TAB(2*B);D$ |
| **d.** | 75 PRINT TAB(15);B | **i.** 75 PRINT TAB(C);D$ |
| **e.** | 75 PRINT TAB(15);C | **j.** 75 PRINT INT(B),INT(B+0.5) |

Try running each of these on your system.

**18.**   The following PRINT statements contain some errors that are common for beginning programmers. Make necessary corrections.

**a.**   PRINT A = A          **c.**   PRINT QUANTITY PRICE REVENUE
**b.**   PRINT "B = "B        **d.**   PRINT A B C
                             **e.**   PRINT "MY NAME IS

**\*19.**   Replace the PRINT statement in

```
10 LET A = 15
20 LET B = 25
30 PRINT A,B
40 END
```

for each output case below:

**a.**   A = 15          **b.**   First value . . . . 15
         B = 25                  ← blank line
         ↑—— column 5            Second value . . . 25
                                 ↑———— column 10

**c.**   A = 15          B = 25
         ↑—— column 5    ↑—— column 15

**\*20.**   Modify the program in Example 2.10 to print the following output:

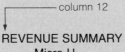

```
      ┌—— column 12
      ↓

REVENUE SUMMARY
    Micro U
      ←—— blank line
Revenues of $ 4500000 are expected
for a student body of 6000.
Tuition of $ 750 was assumed.
↑
└—— column 1
```

**\*21.**   Modify the program in Example 2.13 so that:
**a.**   The entire report is shifted 10 columns to the right.
**b.**   A dollar sign is placed in columns 17 and 37 on the last line of output.

**\*22.**   Supply PRINT statements that incorporate the TAB function for the following output:

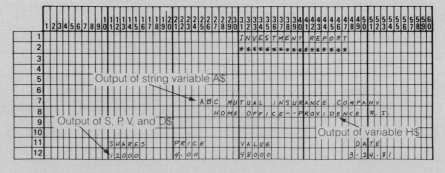

\*Answers to single-starred exercises are not given. Ask your instructor.

**\*23.** **LPRINT statement.** Those of us using microcomputers have a simple variation of the PRINT statement that prints output to an attached line printer:

**LPRINT statement**

> **LPRINT** *print list*
> LPRINT "Results",A,B,A\*B

This statement works pretty much like the PRINT statement, except for the printing unit. Additionally, new items called *control characters* can be included in the print list for special effects, such as bold-facing, condensed (small) print characters, expanded (large) print characters, and so on. Try the following parts if this statement is available to you:
**a.** Rework Exercise 19.
**b.** Rework Exercise 20.
**c.** Rework Exercise 21.
**d.** Rework Exercise 22.

Check the printer control characters for your system and try some special effects.

**\*24.** **Screen cursor location.** Microcomputer dialects allow us to position the cursor at any point on the active screen. For example, Microsoft BASIC on the IBM PC enables us to position the cursor at row 24 and column 10 as follows:

LOCATE 24, 10

This, of course, allows complete control of the screen for positioning output, including the placement of output in a bottom-to-top sequence on the screen (as opposed to the traditional top-to-bottom sequence). Additionally, optional parameters turn the cursor on and off and define its size. If your system has a LOCATE-type statement, then use it to locate output for:
**a.** Example 2.13.
**b.** Exercise 22.

Try running these programs on your system.

## 2.7 INPUT STATEMENT

In the previous sections, we provided data to programs by using LET statements. Normally, however, a program receives data in one or more of the following ways:

- We enter data interactively while the program is running by using INPUT statements.

- We enter data as we write the program by using READ and DATA statements.

- We enter data from data files outside the program.

We shall discuss the first two types of data entry in this chapter and wait until Module E to discuss data files.

The INPUT statement allows us to supply data to a program from the keyboard *while the program is running.* When the computer executes an INPUT statement, it prints a prompt on the screen, usually a question mark (?), and suspends execution of the program until we enter data. After the data are entered, the computer stores the data items within the variables indicated in the INPUT statement.

## Simple Form

A simple form of the INPUT statement is

**Simple INPUT Statement**

> **INPUT** *input list*
> INPUT A,B,C

where the input list contains variable names (separated by commas) in the exact sequence that data items are to be entered.

**E X A M P L E   2 . 1 4**    Simple INPUT Statement

Suppose we wish to enter interactively the values 5, 10, and 15 for storage in A, B, and C. The following program and run illustrate an approach that uses the simple INPUT statement.

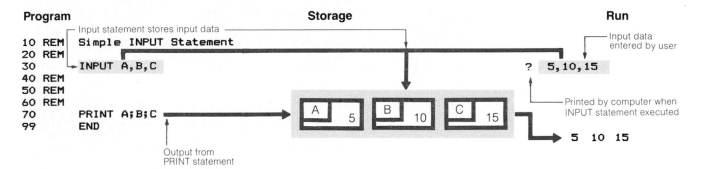

Note the following sequence:

**1.** The computer prints a question-mark prompt when it executes the INPUT statement and then awaits the input of three data items from the user.

**2.** The INPUT statement has three numeric variables in its input list; hence, the user must enter three numeric values following the question-mark prompt, each separated from the other by a comma.

**3.** The user then strikes the "Enter" or "Carriage Return" key, and the computer stores the three values 5, 10, and 15 in the respective memory locations A, B, and C. Note that the first value (5) is placed in the location corresponding to the first variable in the input list (A), the second value is matched with the second variable (10 with B), and so forth.

**NOTE 1**  The type of program shown in the preceding example is called an **interactive program,** because the user enters data in response to a prompt from the program. Thus the user and program (computer) interact with one another.

**NOTE 2**  In practice it's best to include a "message" or "conversation" just before the prompt, so as to alert the user to the required input.

### Conversational Input

A good programming practice is to print a prompting message that reminds the program user of which data are to be entered next. This is accomplished in various ways, depending on the BASIC dialect. The next example illustrates several approaches to **conversational input.**

**EXAMPLE 2.15** Conversational Input Approaches

Table 2.8 shows different approaches to conversational input, depending on the dialect.

**Table 2.8** Conversational Input Approaches (Example 2.15)

| BASIC Dialect | Code | Input/Output (I/0) |
|---|---|---|
| Minimal | 10  PRINT "Enter 3 values"; <br> 20  INPUT A,B,C <br> 30  PRINT A;B;C <br> 99  END | Enter 3 values?  5,10,15 <br><br> 5   10   15 |
| | Remarks: This approach works on any system. Each INPUT statement is immediately preceded by a PRINT statement that prints the message prompt. The trailing semicolon is used in line 10 so that the system places the ? prompt on the same line as the message, thereby allowing entry of the three data values to the right of the message. | |
| ANS | 20  INPUT PROMPT "Enter 3 values?":A,B,C <br> 30  PRINT A;B;C <br> 99  END | Enter 3 Values?  5,10,15 <br> 5   10   15 |
| | Remarks: This approach uses a new statement called the **INPUT PROMPT statement** to serve this purpose. Note that this statement suppresses the ? prompt, so we include it as part of the message. In practice we need not use the question mark. For example, we could leave it off altogether or substitute something more appropriate such as = or ---->. Also note that the colon (:) is used to separate the message prompt from the variable input list. | |
| Microsoft VAX-11 | 20  INPUT "Enter 3 values";A,B,C <br> 30  PRINT A;B;C <br> 99  END | Enter 3 values?  5,10,15 <br> 5   10   15 |
| | Remarks: This approach simply includes the message as a string constant within the input list. Note that the semicolon (;) is used to separate the message prompt from the input list of variables. | |

Your system
(if different)

**E X A M P L E   2 . 1 6**    **Tuition Revenue Problem with Data Input**

The program below replaces the three LET statements in lines 250–260 of Example 2.2 on page 32 with three INPUT statements. (We also redesigned the output.)

```
100 REM   Tuition Revenue Program (Version 1.4)
110 REM---------------------------------------------------
250         INPUT "Enter college name --->"; COLLEGE$
255         INPUT "Enter tuition --------->"; TUITION
260         INPUT "Enter enrollment ----->"; ENROLLMENT
265 REM---------------------------------------------------
280         LET REVENUE = TUITION*ENROLLMENT
285 REM---------------------------------------------------
290         PRINT
300         PRINT "Revenue ...............$"; REVENUE
325 REM---------------------------------------------------
999         END
```

```
RUN
Enter college name --->? Micro U
Enter tuition --------->? 750
Enter enrollment ----->? 1000

Revenue ...............$ 750000
```

Note the following:

1.  We used the Microsoft and VAX-11 approach to conversational input. Is your system different?

2.  The first input line illustrates how we can enter a string value. In this case we simply entered the unquoted string *Micro U* with no problem; however, suppose we were to enter as follows:

Enter college name ──► ? Micro U, Sunnyside Campus
                                      └──── Comma delimits input

This input would be interpreted as two separate values by most systems, since the comma acts as a delimiter. The typical system response is a request to reenter the data. For this situation we need to enter a quoted string:

                              ┌──── Quotes take care
                              │     of the problem
Enter college name ──►? "Micro U, Sunnyside Campus"

---

**NOTE**    Good input design dictates informative, pleasing, and uncluttered input areas. To view a poor input design, try replacing lines 250–260 in Example 2.16 with a single INPUT statement that inputs college name, tuition, and enrollment all in one line with no messages.

## Follow-Up Exercises

25.  Try the program in Table 2.8 on your system. Deliberately enter too few and then too many data values to familiarize yourself with the error response on your system. What would happen if you were to omit the trailing semicolon in the Minimal BASIC version?

**26.** Do the following for Example 2.16:
    **a.** Write pseudocode.
    **b.** Draw a flowchart. (Go back to Table 1.2 on page 6 for the proper input symbol.)

**27.** Write statements for the following conversational input:
    **a.** Enter name, SS Number, and age (separated by commas)?

                                                     └ Values for N\$,S,A

    **b.** Do you wish to print output (Y/N)?

                                    └ Value for R\$

    **\*c.** Enter principal ..........? ◄——— Value for P
           Enter number of years ...? ◄——— Value for N
           Enter interest rate ........? ◄——— Value for I

**28.** What do you expect will happen given the following?

```
10 PRINT "Enter name";
20 INPUT N$
30 PRINT N$
99 END
RUN


Enter name? Bogart, H.
```

Try it on your system and make any necessary correction.

**\*29.** Write the segment of code that prints the following on the screen:

```
SAMPLE PROGRAM
A – MUSIC
B – ART
C – MORTGAGE


Enter letter of program?
```
                           └——— Value for C\$

**\*30.** Write short programs and show I/O for the following cases:

    **a.** Input and print the month (M\$) of July, the 4th day (D), and the year (Y) 1776. Output should appear as follows:

       Date: 4 July, 1776

    **b.** Input and print faculty name (F\$) as Harvey Hacker, rank (R\$) as Instructor-1, and salary (S) as 25000 dollars. Output should appear as follows:

```
Name  ......  Harvey Hacker
Rank  .......  Instructor-1
Salary  ......  $ 25000
```

**\*31.** **LINPUT statement.** The LINPUT statement is similar to the INPUT statement, except that it inputs an entire line of data to a single string variable. For example, the statement and input line given by

    LINPUT N\$                                 ? Bogart, H.

would store the string value *Bogart, H.* in the string variable N$. Try this on your system if the LINPUT statement is available. Think about how this statement might be useful.

**\*32. Screen cursor location.** Use a LOCATE-type statement (see Exercise 24 on page 51) for the following:

a. Locate the three input prompts in Example 2.16 beginning at row 10 and column 5. Place the output at row 11 starting in column 40.

b. Solve Exercise 29 by printing the sample program menu beginning in row 5 and column 40. Then locate the beginning of the input prompt at row 9 and column 10.

Try running these on your system.

## 2.8 READ, DATA, AND RESTORE STATEMENTS

The use of READ and DATA statements is another approach to providing data. In this case, unlike the INPUT statement, data are supplied within the program prior to execution.

### General Form

The READ statement assigns values to variables that are initially typed onto DATA statements. The general form of the READ statement is

**READ Statement**

> **READ** *read list*
> READ CITY$,STATE$,ZIP

where the read list contains variables (separated by commas) in the same sequence as the items of data that are to be entered into memory.

The READ statement must be used with a nonexecutable statement called the DATA statement. The DATA statement contains the data items (values) that correspond to the list of variables in the READ statement. The general form of the DATA statement is

**DATA Statement**

> **DATA** *data list*
> DATA "Miami","FL",33145

where each item in the data list is either a numeric constant or a string constant, separated by a comma from the preceding data item.

The READ statement, when executed, retrieves as many values from one or more DATA statements as variables in the list of the READ statement. For example, if the list of a READ statement contains five numeric variables, then execution of this READ statement processes five numeric values from one or more DATA statements. The variables in the READ statement and the values in the DATA statement are matched in an ordered fashion—that is, the first variable with the first data value, the second variable with the second value, and so on.

**E X A M P L E   2 . 1 7**    READ/DATA Statements

Study the following program and its run.

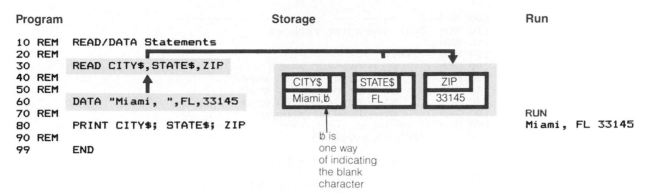

| Program | | Storage | Run |
|---|---|---|---|
| 10 REM | READ/DATA Statements | | |
| 20 REM | | | |
| 30 | READ CITY$,STATE$,ZIP | | |
| 40 REM | | | |
| 50 REM | | | |
| 60 | DATA "Miami, ",FL,33145 | | |
| 70 REM | | | RUN |
| 80 | PRINT CITY$; STATE$; ZIP | | Miami, FL 33145 |
| 90 REM | | | |
| 99 | END | | |

b is
one way
of indicating
the blank
character

Note the following:

1. When the READ statement is executed, the three successive values in the DATA statement are entered into the three respective memory locations according to the variable list in the READ statement.

2. The portion "Miami," within the DATA statement is called a quoted string, since the string constant is within quotes. In this case, it's necessary to use quotes to store the comma (which otherwise would act as a delimiter) and trailing blank.

3. The string constant FL is an unquoted string in line 60. In this case, it's not necessary to enclose the string in quotes, since it does not contain commas, leading or trailing blanks, or other special characters that could cause problems.

4. Each item in the data list is separated from the preceding item by a comma.

5. To avoid syntax errors, make sure that items in the read list and data list correspond with respect to type; that is, match a string variable with a string constant and a numeric variable with a numeric constant.

6. The DATA statement can be placed anywhere in the program, since it's nonexecutable. This is a stylistic issue that we shall take up in Section 2.9.

## Data Blocks

The data values from *all* DATA statements in a program are combined by the BASIC compiler or interpreter into a *single* sequence of data items called a **data block.** The data values are placed into the data block in the order of their appearance in the program; that is, a data value on a lower-numbered line is placed ahead of a value on a higher-numbered line, and a data value to the left is placed ahead of a data value to the right.

**E X A M P L E   2 . 1 8**     Exam Averaging Program

A simple program that will average a student's three exam scores is shown below.

```
100 REM ---------------------------------------
110 REM    Exam Averaging Program
120 REM
130 REM    Key:
140 REM       A  = Average grade
150 REM       G1 = Grade on 1st exam
160 REM       G2 = Grade on 2nd exam
170 REM       G3 = Grade on 3rd exam
180 REM       N$ = Name of student
190 REM ---------------------------------------
200        READ N$,G1,G2,G3
210 REM
220        LET A = (G1 + G2 + G3)/3
230 REM
240        PRINT "Average for "; N$; " is"; A
900 REM ---------------------------------------
901        DATA Jane Smitten,83,91,87
998 REM ---------------------------------------
999        END

RUN
Average for Jane Smitten is 87
```

The data in the DATA statements are combined into a data block that can be visualized as follows:

**Data Block**

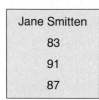

Jane Smitten
83
91
87

Even if the data were typed

| 901 DATA Jane Smitten | or | 901 DATA Jane Smitten |
| 902 DATA 83,91,87 | | 902 DATA 83 |
| | | 903 DATA 91 |
| | | 904 DATA 87 |

the computer still would combine the data into the same data block. The only thing that counts is the sequence, or order of appearance, of data items in the data lists.
    Moreover, the following READ statements could have been used:

| 200 READ N$ | or | 200 READ N$ |
| 205 READ G1,G2,G3 | | 201 READ G1 |
| | | 202 READ G2 |
| | | 203 READ G3 |

It still doesn't matter, since the only thing that counts is the order of the items, which remains N$, G1,G2,G3 in the READ statements and Jane Smitten, 83,91,87 in the data block.

**NOTE 1**    When a program with READ/DATA statements is run, the computer maintains a *pointer* to the next item of data to be read into a memory location. When the program begins execution, this pointer indicates the first item in the block of data values. Each time a READ statement is executed, values from the data block are assigned to the variables in the READ statement based on the location of the pointer. When the execution of a READ statement is completed, the pointer is advanced to the data value immediately following the last data value read in. We illustrate this process in the next section.

**NOTE 2**    Take care that the number of items in the data block at least equals the number of variables processed in the read lists; otherwise, we would get an "out of data" error.

## Restoring the Pointer

Sometimes it's necessary to reread the same data within the same program, which brings us to the RESTORE statement. A general form of this statement is

**RESTORE Statement**

RESTORE

The RESTORE statement resets the pointer back to the beginning of the data block, so that the next READ statement executed will read data from the beginning again.

**E X A M P L E   2 . 1 9**    **The RESTORE Statement**

Study the following program logic and the table on the next page.

```
100 REM--------------------------
110 REM   The RESTORE Statement
120 REM--------------------------
130        READ A,B
140        PRINT "A ="; A,  "B ="; B
150 REM--------------------------
160        RESTORE
170 REM--------------------------
180        READ C,D
190        PRINT "C ="; C,  "D ="; D
200 REM--------------------------
900        DATA 100,150
998 REM--------------------------
999        END

RUN
A = 100        B = 150
C = 100        D = 150
```

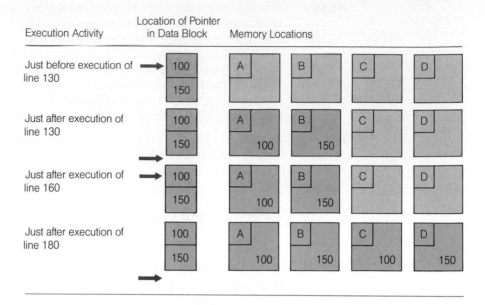

| Execution Activity | Location of Pointer in Data Block | Memory Locations | | | |
|---|---|---|---|---|---|

## Follow-Up Exercises

**33.** What do you expect will happen in Example 2.17 for each case below?
  **a.** Eliminate the quotes in line 60.
  **b.** Insert two spaces between FL and the comma in line 60.
  **c.** Reverse the read list in line 30.
  **d.** Use the following data list:
  "Kingston, ", RI,02881
  How would you correct the problem?
  **e.** Delete the portion following FL in line 60.

Try these on your system.

**34.** Indicate storage contents for D$.
  **a.** 10 READ D$
  20 PRINT D$
  90 DATA July 21, 2001
  99 END

  **b.** 10 READ D$
  20 PRINT D$
  90 DATA "July 21, 2001"
  99 END

Try running these programs.

**35.** Try running the following variations of Example 2.18 on your system.
  **a.** Change the single READ statement to

  200 READ N$
  205 READ G1,G2,G3

but leave the DATA statement alone. Does it make a difference in the output?

**b.** Change the single DATA statement to

901 DATA Jane Smitten
902 DATA 83
903 DATA 91
904 DATA 87

but leave the READ portion either as in the original or as in **a.** Is there any difference in the output?

**c.** Delete the last grade (the 87) from the data list. What happens on your system?

**d.** Use the following DATA statement but leave the READ statement alone.

901 DATA 83,91,87, Jane Smitten

What happens on your system?

**36.** What output would you expect if the RESTORE statement is removed from the program in Example 2.19?

**37.** Specify which of the indicated sets of DATA statements yield the given data block:

**a.** 100 DATA 10
102 DATA 20
104 DATA 30
106 DATA 40
108 DATA 50

**b.** 100 DATA 10,20,30,40,50

**c.** 100 DATA 50,40,30,20,10

**d.** 100 DATA 10,20
102 DATA 30,40,50

**e.** 10 DATA 10,20
20 ⎫
30 ⎬ Executable statements
40 ⎭
50
60 DATA 30,40,50

| 10 |
| 20 |
| 30 |
| 40 |
| 50 |

**38.** Consider the following READ statements:
20 READ A, B, C
30 READ D, E
For the data block in the preceding exercise, indicate the location of the pointer and contents in memory for the following:

**a.** Just before line 20 is executed.

**b.** Just after line 20 is executed.

**c.** Just after line 30 is executed.

**\*39.** Solve Exercise 30 using READ/DATA statements instead of INPUT statements.

**\*40.** Modify the tuition revenue program in Example 2.2 on page 32 by replacing LET statements with READ/DATA statements.

**\*41.** Modify the program in Example 2.18 so that exam grades are entered interactively based on the following prompts:
Student name = = = = = = = = = =>?
Grade 1 = = = = = = = = =>?
Grade 2 = = = = = = = = =>?
Grade 3 = = = = = = = = =>?

## 2.9 POINTERS

This chapter (and those that follow) concludes with a section called pointers that reinforces and summarizes design and style suggestions and highlights common errors.

### Design and Style

Methods for improving the design and style of programs are important in commercial applications for two reasons: First, good design and readability increase the reliability and facilitate the development, testing, and subsequent maintenance of programs—all of which reduce software costs. Second, programs that are easier to use because of good I/O design are more effective (and sell better!) than programs that pay scant attention to this so-called user-interface. In your program writing for this course, you should take this commercial perspective to appreciate what's happening in practice.

The following suggestions should improve the readability and reliability (and the grades!) of your programs.

1. **Variable Names.**    Choose names for variables that are descriptive of the data. It helps in following the logic of the program. If your BASIC dialect allows it, use multicharacter variable names, such as COST rather than C for the cost of an item.

2. **Uppercase vs. Lowercase Letters.**    Most systems now allow both uppercase and lowercase characters. By convention, we use uppercase for all BASIC keywords and variable names (many systems insist on this). In our documentation (REMs) and string data values, we use both uppercase and lowercase, as is natural in the written language.

3. **Use of Spaces.**    Most systems ignore blank spaces except within quoted strings. In general, we should use spaces to improve the readability and visual appeal of programs. For example, keywords and arithmetic operators are best separated from other text by at least one space, as the following illustrate:

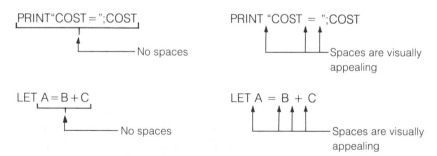

In other cases, we need to use a space to avoid potential errors. For example, the statement

LET A = 2
    └── Space to avoid error

clearly assigns the value 2 to the location A. However, if we delete all spaces, as in

```
LETA = 2
```
————— No space

then the system would most likely assign the value 2 to the location LETA. Note that the problem here is caused by the omission of a space following the keyword LET.

Finally, spaces within string constants are significant. For example,

```
PRINT "Yes"
```
————— No spaces

is not identical in its effect to

```
PRINT "  Yes"
```
——— 3 spaces

The latter prints the word *Yes* three spaces farther to the right than does the former.

**4. Output Design.** Pay attention to output design. Facilitate its readability and understanding by well-chosen labels, alignment, and spacing. Avoid clutter and unlabeled output. Use aids such as TAB functions and semicolons for compression, commas for blank zones, and PRINTs with no print list for blank print lines. Use dashes (minus signs), asterisks, and other special characters to dress up the output for improved readability. Our programs as yet don't have much output to work with, but that will change in the next chapter. (Also, by the end of the next chapter, you may want to read the PRINT USING statement in Module D.)

**5. Input Design.** Good commercial interactive programs place great emphasis on input design, since it is a key factor in ensuring correct data entry and responses. We shall come back to this issue when our programming (and I/O) becomes more sophisticated. For now we need only to point out that your programs should always prompt the user for input with a message. Also, it's good design to avoid clutter on input by the careful placement of prompt messages. Finally, it's best to request a single response or data item for each input line, as this simplifies the message and the input, thereby reducing the likelihood of input errors.

**6. Documentation.** Do a good job of documenting programs, as described in Section 2.4. Use proper indentation when REMs and other statements appear in the same section. For instance, the program of Example 2.2 on page 32 indents the LET, PRINT, and END statements, which makes it easier for a reader to focus on the execution logic when reading down a listing (the REMs along the left margin don't get in the way visually).

**7. Placement of DATA Statements.** Since DATA statements are nonexecutable, it's best for program readability to get them out of the way of the execution logic. For example, we can indent, as in

```
READ read list
DATA data list
```

or we can place both statements on the same line on systems that allow multistatement lines, as in

```
READ read list  :  DATA data list
              └──────── or \
```

In the next chapter we shall use many related DATA statements, which are best placed in a group at the end of a program. We illustrated this idea (for one DATA statement) in Example 2.18 on page 58.

**8. Numbering Lines.** It's usually best to increment line numbers by 5 or 10 at the outset. This gives room for inserting new lines of code. Then, when you're ready to turn in your "work of art," you can use your system's renumbering command to clean up the numbers. We usually give the END statement a line number such as 99 or 999. This is a stylistic preference that (psychologically for us) defines the end of a numbering scheme.

**9. Line Continuation.** What do we do if our line is too long for the screen or paper terminal? We see four alternatives:

**a.** Nothing needs to be done if the system automatically "wraps" the line to the next visual line.

**b.** Increase the line width through a system command. (Ask your instructor if this can be done on your system.)

**c.** Use a continuation symbol at the end of a line, such as ampersand (&) on the VAX-11 or the [Ctrl] [Enter] keys on the IBM PC. (Ask your instructor for the symbol for your system.)

**d.** Rework the code to shorten the line. For example, a LET statement with a super-long expression can be broken down into several LET statements, each with a portion of the overall expression. Or, a long print list can be broken down into two or more PRINT statements, in which the first and all other print lists except the last use a trailing semicolon to hold the output line. For example,

```
PRINT item 1; item 2; item 3
```

can be rewritten as

```
PRINT item 1; item 2;  ◄──────── Trailing semicolon
PRINT item 3
```

(See Example 2.13 on page 48.)

**10. Use of Multistatement Lines.** Multistatement lines originally were intended as a means to compact the code in a program, with subsequent reductions in the length of listings and in memory requirements. Unfortunately, this usually reduces readability, which increases software costs (and the frustration level of readers such as instructors). For this reason, some writers take the extreme position that multistatement lines should not be used at all. In general, assuming your system allows it, *we recommend the selective use of multistatement lines for groups of related statements*, as in item 7 above or as in

```
200 LET A = 1 : B = 1 : C = 1
            └──────┴──────── or \, depending on the system
```

In such cases, readability is actually enhanced (although, like beauty, that's in the eye of the beholder).

**11. On Providing Data.** Before designing and writing programs, we need to think carefully about the treatment of provided data. Essentially, there are five choices, as illustrated by the following examples for the data items 3.141593 (pi) and 5 (radius).[9]

**a.** As constants, for example,

```
LET AREA = 3.141593*5^2
```

**b.** As variables initialized through a LET statement, for example,

```
LET PI   = 3.141593
LET R    = 5
LET AREA = PI*R^2
```

**c.** As variables through READ/DATA statements, for example,

```
READ PI
   DATA 3.141593
READ R
   DATA 5
LET AREA = PI*R^2
```

**d.** As variables through keyboard INPUT statements, for example,

```
INPUT PI                    ? 3.141593
INPUT R                     ? 5
LET AREA = PI*R^2
```

**e.** As variables through data file input statements, which we take up in Module E.

In general, we recommend the use of variables for all data items that have descriptive meaning. In our examples, both pi and radius suggest meaning, so we would eliminate choice **a.** However, in a formula such as $C = 2\pi d$ (for the circumference of a circle), the 2 is best treated as a constant since it lacks descriptive meaning. More importantly, the choice is best determined by both the context of the problem and the likelihood that the data values change over time. For example, an interactive program that requires the user to select one of several choices from a menu necessarily must input that data item through an INPUT statement.

If a data value is likely to change from run to run, then it's best provided through a READ statement in a noninteractive application and through an INPUT statement in an interactive application. In particular, the use of INPUT reduces software maintenance costs for values that change often. In our example, we would use either LET or READ/DATA for the value in PI (since this value never changes) and INPUT for the value in R (assuming an interactive environment where the effects of R are of interest).

Data items that don't change within a computer run are usually called **parameters.** The value 2 and the variable PI are parameters in our area example.

If large amounts of data are to be provided and stored for future use, then the READ/DATA alternative is preferred to the use of INPUT statements. For

---

[9]On some systems, *pi* is a numeric function whose value is provided by the computer. Is this the case on your system?

example, if we had to type in test scores for 200 students, then READ/DATA statements (and, in particular, choice **e**) have the following advantages over the INPUT statement:

—Errors in the data list can be corrected easily.

—The same data can be processed more than once without retyping.

For either small amounts of data or the need to process interactively, the INPUT statement is preferred over the READ/DATA statements. In some cases, program design might call for the use of both INPUT and READ/DATA statements in the same program. It simply depends on the needs that the program is to fulfill.

## Common Errors

The subsections labeled *Common Errors* describe many of the errors made by beginning (and, in many cases, experienced) programmers. The following errors are common to the material in this chapter. (Also, see the errors described in Module B.)

**1. Naming Variables.**   We need to be aware of any limitations on naming variables for our system. For example, if we use the name COST on a system that doesn't allow multicharacter variable names, then we have committed a syntax error (the type of error that the compiler or interpreter detects as a violation of the BASIC language rules).

Another common error is forgetting the dollar sign as the last character in the name of a string variable.

Finally, try to get a list of keywords for your system's BASIC dialect. Using a keyword for a variable name (or sometimes even part of a variable name) causes errors. For example, NAME$ can't be used to name a string variable in Microsoft BASIC, because NAME is a command to change the name of a diskette file; CASE can't be used in VAX-11 BASIC, because it's a reserved word for a certain type of statement. If we happen to get a syntax error for *every line* that uses a certain variable name, then we are probably using a keyword as a variable name.

**2. REM Statement.**   Don't forget to use the keyword REM for lines that have only comments or remarks. If the system allows remarks to the right of a statement, then a special symbol (such as ! or ') replaces the keyword REM. The following illustrate these two errors:

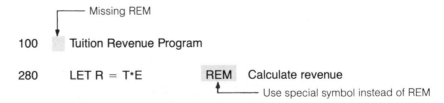

**3. LET Statement.**   Pay close attention to hierarchy, left-to-right, and parentheses rules when forming numeric expressions. Two common syntax errors are unmatched parentheses and missing numeric operators. For example, the expression in

LET F = 2*B*((C − 5) / (B + 2) ◄────── Missing right parenthesis

is missing a right parenthesis, and the expression in

────── Missing numeric operator

LET G = (P + 1)   (R − 5)

is missing a numeric operator such as * between the two parenthetic parts.

Logic errors are more insidious, since we get an answer, but it's incorrect. For example, the expression in

────── Missing parentheses

LET C = 5/9*   F − 32

incorrectly calculates degrees Celsius (see Exercise 9). Always debug your program by using test data with known answers.

Another common error is the reversal of expression and variable across an equal sign, as in

────── Single variable must be to left of =

LET   A + B   = C

which is permitted in algebra but not in BASIC.

Finally, make sure each side of the equal sign is compatible with respect to the type of value (numeric with numeric and string with string). For example,

LET R   = "yes"

────── Missing $

gives a syntax error. Use R$. Also, don't forget to include the quote marks when assigning a string value to a string variable. Thus,

LET R$ =   yes

────── Missing quote marks

would give a syntax error. Use the quoted string *"yes"* instead of the unquoted string *yes*.

**4. PRINT Statement.** Don't forget to include quotes in string constants within print lists. For example,

────── Missing quote marks

PRINT   Revenue =   , R

causes a syntax error. Also, don't forget to delimit items in a print list with commas or semicolons, although many systems allow one or more blanks or other special characters as delimiters.

**5. Input Errors.** The following errors are typical.

**a.** *Too few or too many values entered.* Make sure to enter the exact number of values required by the input list. For example, the following usually causes the system to request re-input of the values:

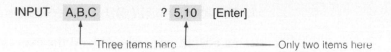

b. *Variables and values mismatched by type.* Make sure string values are paired with string variables and numeric values are paired with numeric variables. The following yields an error:

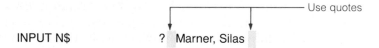

Actually, the error here (as far as the system is concerned) is caused by the attempt to store the string value F under the numeric variable R. The system would store the 3 in A$ as an unquoted string. We suggest not mixing string and numeric variables within the same input list.

c. *Use of unquoted strings.* Make sure that string values with commas, significant leading or trailing blanks, and certain other special characters (depending on the system) are enclosed in quotes. For example, the following is a common error:

The system will most likely store Marner under N$ (and ignore the ", Silas" portion). Some systems, however, may request reentry of the data.

d. *Don't use semicolons as delimiters in an input list.* Use the comma to separate items in the input list. For example, the statement

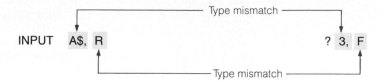

would generate a syntax error on most systems.

**6. READ/DATA Errors.** The input errors described under items **5b–d** also apply here. Additionally, note the following:

a. *Too few values in data block.* For example, suppose we run the following program:

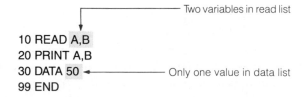

When line 10 is executed, most systems will print an "out of data" execution error message, and processing will terminate. If $n$ variables are to be read in a program, then the data block must have at least $n$ values.

**b.** *Trailing comma inserted in DATA statement.* Don't place a comma at the end of a data line. For example,

900 DATA 50, 75, ◄———Trailing comma may cause error
905 DATA 90

may cause a syntax error.

**7. Unintentional, Displeasing, or Unaligned Output.** Producing readable output that is other than trivial involves careful planning. For instance, if we have to output aligned labels and values for several variables, then we can save ourselves some grief by outlining output on a sheet of plain paper, graph paper, or print chart before we write our PRINT statements. To illustrate, consider the following layout on a print chart:

**150/10/6 PRINT CHART**  PROG. ID _____ PAGE _____

(SPACING: 150 POSITION SPAN, AT 10 CHARACTERS PER INCH, 6 LINES PER VERTICAL INCH)  DATE _____

PROGRAM TITLE _____

PROGRAMMER OR DOCUMENTALIST: _____

CHART TITLE _____

| CARRIAGE TAPE | CONTROL CHAN. | | |
|---|---|---|---|
| | | 1 | TUITION REVENUE REPORT |
| | | 2 | ------------------------ |
| | | 3 | College        Number of |
| | | 4 | Name      Tuition   Students   Revenue |
| | | 5 | ------------------------ |
| | | 6 | XXXXXXX    XXXXXXX  XXXXXXXX  XXXXXXX |
| | | 7 | |
| | | 8 | |
| | | 9 | |
| | | 10 | |
| | | 11 | |
| | | 12 | |

This layout was done *before* the PRINT statements in lines 290 through 325 on page 48 were written. (It should be done within the analysis of Step 1.) You should confirm that the PRINT lines and actual output exactly correspond to the output plan on the print chart. You might be surprised at how much effort can be saved by this practice of laying out the output design before writing the corresponding PRINT statements.

**A WORD OF CAUTION**  Please study Modules A and B following Chapter 9 before running any of this chapter's programming exercises on your computer.

**PLEASE NOTE**  End-of-chapter assignments in this and other chapters generally require you to prepare and submit the following documentation of the four-step procedure:

**1.** *Problem Analysis.* A brief description of the problem including the required output and the provided (e.g., input) data items

**2.** *Program Design.* Either pseudocode or a flowchart

**3.** *Program Code.* A listing of your BASIC program, including program documentation

**4.** *Program Test.* Sample runs showing test data and results

To be sure, ask your instructor. Also, check on the procedure for your system for obtaining *hard-copy* listings and test runs.

*Hint:* The description in Step 1 and the pseudocode in Step 2 can both be included as part of the program documentation in Step 3. See Example 2.2 on page 32 for an illustration; note that pseudocode actually appears as the REMs in lines 240, 270, 290, and 310.

**ON THE RIGHT PERSPECTIVE**   You might find it useful to take the perspective that the applications programs you develop are to be actually used by others. This will increase your awareness and appreciation of the issues that face the developers of applications software (and should improve your grade).

## ADDITIONAL EXERCISES

**42.** Define or explain the following:

| | | |
|---|---|---|
| character set | E-notation | string expression |
| alphabetic characters | precision | numeric expression |
| numeric characters | overflow | numeric operator |
| special characters | underflow | arithmetic hierarchy |
| string | string constant | multistatement lines |
| number | numeric variable | PRINT statement |
| constant | simple numeric variable | TAB function |
| variable | subscripted numeric variable | INPUT statement |
| reserved word | string variable | interactive program |
| keyword | simple string variable | conversational input |
| function | subscripted string variable | READ statement |
| expression | executable statement | DATA statement |
| statement | nonexecutable statement | data block |
| line | END statement | RESTORE statement |
| line number | REM statement | parameters |
| numeric constant | LET statement | |

**43. Revisits.** Rewrite one of the following programs to include conversational input and labeled output. Take care to ensure good I/O design.
  **a. Area Problem** (Example 2.5, page 37). Test data for radius: 4.6, 4.8, 5.0, 5.2, 5.4.
  **b. Microeconomics Problem** (Example 2.6, page 38). Test data for units: 1,2,...,10.
  **c. Temperature Conversion** (Example 2.7, page 39). Test data for degrees F: 0, 40, 80, 100, 212.

**44. Mileage Problem.** Write an interactive program to compute miles per gallon and cost per mile for an automobile. For each gas stop, enter the following data:
Beginning odometer reading
Ending odometer reading
Gallons to fill tank
Cost to fill tank

After these data are entered, the program outputs the following:

miles per gallon
cost per mile
Use the following data to test your program:

| | First Stop | Second Stop |
|---|---|---|
| Beginning odometer reading | 18763 | 19124 |
| Ending odometer reading | 19124 | 19524 |
| Gallons to fill tank | 13.4 | 14.3 |
| Cost to fill tank | 14.85 | 16.15 |

**45. Unit Pricing.** Write a program that a grocery clerk can use to compute unit prices for shelf labels. The clerk enters:
Product name
Quantity in ounces
Selling price
The computer then prints the unit cost. Unit cost is determined using the following formula:

Unit cost = selling price × 100 ÷ quantity

**a.** Process the following data in your test runs:

| Product Name | Quantity | Selling Price |
|---|---|---|
| Chips | 8 oz | $1.29 |
| Chore | 4 lb 1 oz | 1.79 |
| Sip | 67.6 oz | 2.19 |

**b.** Allow the clerk to enter the quantity in pounds and ounces and then convert to ounces before unit cost is determined.

46. **Mutual Funds.** Investors who do not wish to buy individual stocks and bonds can invest in mutual funds, which offer a portfolio of professionally managed stocks or bonds. In so-called load funds, a sales charge is levied on the amount invested. Some funds also have a redemption fee, which levies a charge on the amount withdrawn from the fund. For example, if $10,000 is invested and the sales charge is 2%, then the amount actually invested is $10,000 \times 0.98$, or $9800. If this amount grows at an annual return of 10% per year, then after, say, five years the investment is worth $(9800) \times (1.1)^5$, or $15,783. However, if the fund charges a 1% redemption fee, then the investor can withdraw $15783 \times 0.99$, or about $15,625. The amount that can be withdrawn is computed from the formula

$$W = A(1 - s)(1 + r)^t(1 - f)$$

where $W$ = amount that can be withdrawn after $t$ years

$A$ = amount originally invested
$s$ = sales charge as a proportion
$r$ = annual return as a proportion
$t$ = time in years
$f$ = redemption fee as a proportion

For our example, we have

$$W = 10000(1 - 0.02)(1 + 0.1)^5(1 - 0.01)$$
$$= 15625$$

**a.** Write a program that inputs $A$, $s$, $r$, $t$, and $f$ and prints $W$. Use the following test data:

|        | $A$   | $s$   | $r$  | $t$ | $f$  |
|--------|-------|-------|------|-----|------|
| Test 1 | 10000 | 0.020 | 0.10 | 5   | 0.01 |
| Test 2 | 10000 | 0.085 | 0.10 | 5   | 0.00 |
| Test 3 | 10000 | 0.020 | 0.10 | 25  | 0.01 |
| Test 4 | 10000 | 0.020 | 0.15 | 25  | 0.01 |

Tests 1 and 2 represent two typical types of mutual funds: one with a low front load charge with a redemption fee and one with a high front load charge and no redemption fee. Which is best for our hypothetical investor?

**b.** Also output the fees (sales and redemption) that are retained by the mutual fund.

47. **Bates Motel.** The motel owner wants to prepare a bill for each customer at check-out time. The desk clerk is to enter the following data:
Customer name
Room number
Room charge
Restaurant charges
Bar charges
The program computes the following:
Service charge ...... 5% of room and restaurant charges
Sales tax ........... 6% of room, restaurant, and bar charges
Total bill ........... Sum of room, restaurant, bar, service, and sales tax charges.

**a.** Develop a program that prepares a bill for each customer. Take some time to plan the I/O design. Use the following test data:

|                    | First Customer | Second Customer |
|--------------------|----------------|-----------------|
| Customer name      | Ada Lovelace   | Mr. Hollerith   |
| Room number        | 80             | 82              |
| Room charge        | $110.00        | $160.00         |
| Restaurant charges | 45.15          | 83.50           |
| Bar charges        | 0.00           | 15.00           |

**b.** Have the program print the following block letters across the top of the bill:

```
****        *        *****   *****   *****
*   *     *   *       *       *           *
*****     *****       *       ****    *****
*   *     *   *       *       *           *
****        *   *     *       *****   *****
```

48. **Blood Bank Inventory.** Decision making relating to the management of physical inventories is an established area in the management sciences, which in recent years has been applied increasingly in semiprivate and public organizations.

Suppose that whenever a hospital replenishes its supply of a certain type of blood, it orders from a regional blood bank the amount indicated by the formula

$$q = \sqrt{2 \cdot c \cdot d / h}$$

where $q$ is the number of pints of blood to order, $c$ is the administrative and shipping cost (in dollars) of placing the order, $d$ is the average weekly demand (usage) for this type of blood, and $h$ is the cost (dollars per pint per week) of refrigerating the blood.

Also, it can be shown that the cost per week of this inventory policy is given by the formula

$$e = \sqrt{2 \cdot c \cdot h \cdot d}$$

where $e$ is the expected cost (dollars) per week. Write a computer program that inputs values of $c$, $h$, and

$d$ and determines how much blood to order and the cost of such a policy.

Run your program and answer the following questions:

How many units of blood should be ordered if it costs $50 to place an order, weekly demand averages 3000 pints, and it costs $0.20 per week per pint of blood to refrigerate? How much should be ordered if the refrigeration cost increases to $0.30? What is the expected cost per week for each of the above?

49. **Automobile Financing.**  Many consumer automobile loans require the borrower to pay the same amount of money to the lending institution each month throughout the life of the loan. The monthly payment is based on the amount borrowed (purchase price − trade-in of used car − down payment), the time required for repayment, and the interest rate. A lending institution uses the following formula to determine the car buyer's monthly payment:

$$a = i \cdot (p - d - t) \cdot \left( \frac{(1 + i)^m}{(1 + i)^m - 1} \right)$$

where $a$ = monthly payments
  $p$ = purchase price of car
  $d$ = down payment
  $t$ = trade-in allowance
  $i$ = monthly interest rate
  $m$ = total number of monthly payments

If the interest rate is expressed on an annual basis, then $i$ in the above formula is replaced by $i/12$. Note that $(p - d - t)$ is the amount to be borrowed.

a. Write a program that determines monthly payments, given purchase price, down payment, trade-in allowance, *annual* interest rate, and total number of monthly payments as input data. Include amount borrowed, total number of months, and annual *percent* interest rate in your output, along with the monthly payment. Also include the make and model of the automobile as part of your I/O. Process the following data:

| Make | Model | Price | Down | Trade-in | Annual Interest | Months |
|------|-------|-------|------|----------|-----------------|--------|
| Lotus | 1 | $12,000 | $2,000 | $1,000 | 0.15 | 60 |
| Lotus | 2 | 12,000 | 4,000 | 1,000 | 0.15 | 60 |
| Lotus | 3 | 12,000 | 2,000 | 1,000 | 0.15 | 48 |
| Packard | Turbo | 20,000 | 3,000 | 0 | 0.14 | 36 |

b. Design your program also to calculate and print:
total amount paid over the life of the loan
total interest paid over the life of the loan
the ratio of total interest to total amount paid

50. **Retirement Contribution.** The personnel department of a large corporation is offering a new pension plan to its employees that works as follows. The employee contributes an amount $C$ that is deducted from each biweekly paycheck. The company then matches this amount (also contributes $C$) and invests the money at an annual interest rate $R$. At the end of $Y$ years, when it is time for the employee to retire, the employee can withdraw sum $S$. The necessary biweekly employee contribution to achieve $S$ after $Y$ years when the fund is compounded biweekly at rate $R$ per year is given by

$$C = \left( \frac{S}{2} \right) \cdot \left( \frac{R/26}{(1 + R/26)^{26Y} - 1} \right)$$

Thus, if the interest rate is 0.07 per year, 30 years remain until retirement, and the employee desires $40,000 at retirement, then the employee must contribute

$$C = \left( \frac{40000}{2} \right) \cdot \left( \frac{0.07/26}{(1 + 0.07/26)^{26 \cdot 30} - 1} \right)$$
$$= \$7.54$$

every two weeks. Design a program that inputs $R$ using appropriate conversation; reads employee name, $Y$, and $S$ using a READ statement; and prints the output shown at the bottom of this page. Run the program repeatedly to determine contributions for the following employees:

| Name | Y | S |
|------|---|---|
| Tahiti Joe | 30 | $ 40,000 |
| Jet-Set Sal | 40 | 200,000 |
| Too-Late Leroy | 5 | 10,000 |

What would be the effect of an increase in the interest rate to 9 percent per year?

# Control Structures and the FOR/NEXT Loop

**C H A P T E R**

# 3

Programmers often consider the programs they write their own creations without regard for others who have to modify them. The programs work, but they may include confusing or tricky logic that is understood only by the original programmer. This increases costs and creates difficulties whenever it's necessary to modify such programs. In addition, without a standard method of solving a problem, the originating programmer may spend more time than necessary in determining the appropriate solution and developing the program. To counter these problems, a concept known as structured programming is gaining widespread acceptance.

**Structured programming** is an approach to designing, coding, and testing programs that is based on a body of principles selected to promote well-thought-out, readable code and reliable execution. The basis of structured programming is that any program can be written using only three logical structures:

1. Sequence structure
2. Decision structure
3. Loop structure

These so-called **control structures** can be used to describe the logic of any program completely, as we illustrate in the next four sections.

## 3.1 SEQUENCE STRUCTURE

The **sequence structure** consists of a sequence of instructions that occur one after the other *without* any transfer of control. When transfer of control or branching occurs, the computer interrupts the normal sequential execution

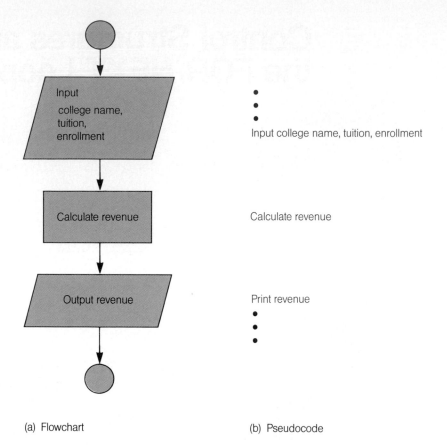

(a) Flowchart                                    (b) Pseudocode

**Figure 3.1**    Sample sequence structure[a]

[a]The connectors (circle symbols) in the flowchart allow us to focus on the structure of interest. *The first connector defines the beginning of or entry point to the structure; the second connector defines the end of or exit point from the structure.*

of a program and branches (jumps or transfers control) to some other *executable* statement in the program that is not necessarily the next instruction in the normal sequence.

Figure 3.1 illustrates a sequence structure for the tuition revenue program. The sequence structure is the only type of control structure we have presented so far.

## 3.2 DECISION STRUCTURES

**Decision,** or **selection, structures** express the logic by which one or more conditions are tested to determine which group of statements, from among alternatives, is to be executed next. In the two-alternative case, either a particular **block** (set of one or more executable statements) is to be executed if a condition is true, or an alternative block is to be executed if it is false. Figure 3.2 (a and b) illustrates the two-alternative **if–then–else structure.** Note that the pseudocode version directly incorporates the terms if, then, and else; the flowchart version uses the diamond symbol to represent the test of a stated condition.

Sometimes we have a situation in which, if a condition is true, we execute a particular block, otherwise we continue in the program sequence. This is called the single-choice or **if–then structure,** as illustrated in Figure 3.2 (c and d).

One example of an if–then–else structure is the increase in tuition needed to offset an enrollment below 5000 students. If enrollment is less than 5000

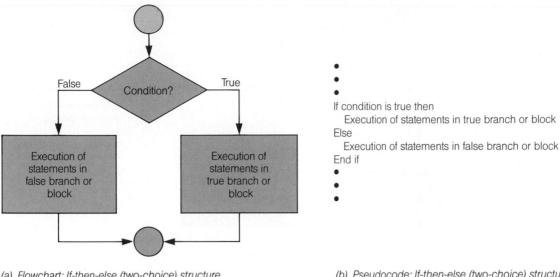

If condition is true then
   Execution of statements in true branch or block
Else
   Execution of statements in false branch or block
End if

*(a) Flowchart: If-then-else (two-choice) structure*

*(b) Pseudocode: If-then-else (two-choice) structure*

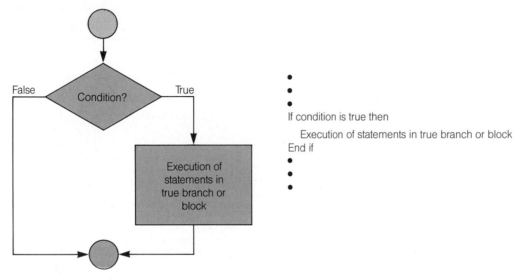

If condition is true then
   Execution of statements in true branch or block
End if

*(c) Flowchart: If-then (single-choice) structure*

*(d) Pseudocode: If-then (single-choice) structure*

**Figure 3.2**  Sample decision structures

students, we increase tuition by 10%; otherwise, we increase it by only 5%. The flowchart and pseudocode representations are shown in Figure 3.3. Note that the statements in the pseudocode version are indented in each block to improve readability.

We shall present BASIC implementations of these simple single- and two-choice selection structures in Chapter 4. More complicated decision structures are possible when there are more than two choices to be made or more than one condition to be tested. We shall discuss these decision structures in Chapter 6.

## 3.3 LOOP STRUCTURES

The **loop,** or **repetition, structure** results in the repeated execution of a set of executable statements. This structure consists of two parts.

1. **A loop body,** which is the set of executable statements that is to be repeatedly executed.

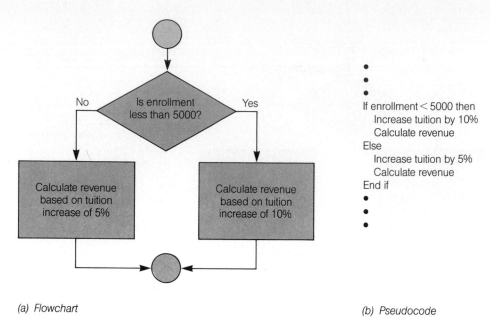

(a) Flowchart

(b) Pseudocode

**Figure 3.3**    Sample if–then–else structure for tuition revenue problem

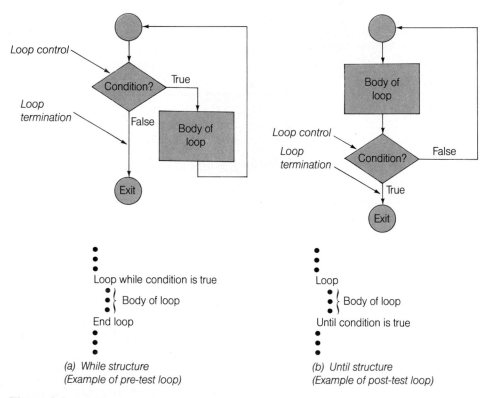

(a) While structure
(Example of pre-test loop)

(b) Until structure
(Example of post-test loop)

**Figure 3.4**    Loop structures

2. **A loop control,** which specifies either the number of times a loop is to be executed or the test (exit) condition under which the loop is to be terminated.

Figure 3.4 shows the logic of the loop structure. Part **a** is an example of a **pre-test structure.** In this structure, the first action on entering the loop structure is to test whether or not the body of the loop is to be executed. If the loop body is to be executed, control passes to the group of statements that make up the loop body. After these statements have been executed, control goes

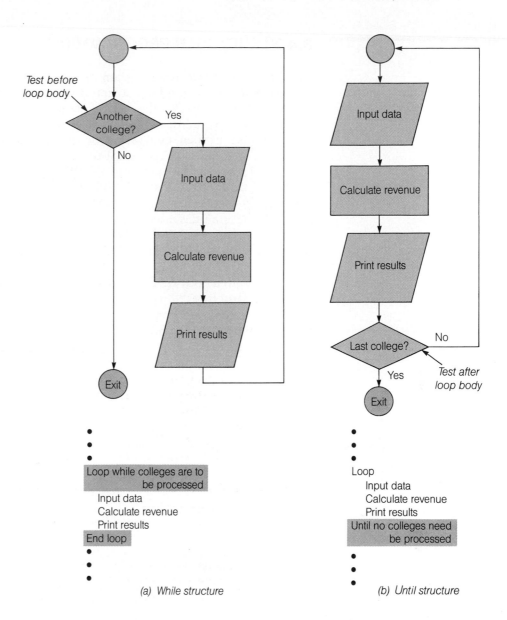

**Figure 3.5**  Loop structures
for tuition revenue problem

back to the test statement to see if the loop body is to be executed again. When the test indicates that the body is no longer to be executed, the statements in the loop body are skipped and control passes to the first executable statement following the loop structure. The **while structure** is a common pretest loop that continues looping *while* the exit condition tests true.

Another loop structure is the **post-test structure.** As seen in Figure 3.4b, this structure executes the loop body first. After each execution of the loop body, the loop control condition that *follows* the loop body is tested to determine whether or not to re-execute the loop body. The **until structure** is a common post-test loop that continues looping *until* the exit condition tests true.

Loop structures are the most powerful features of programming languages, as they enable the automatic processing of large amounts of similar data. For example, any realistic version of the tuition revenue program must include a loop for processing all institutions in the state system in one computer run, as illustrated in Figure 3.5. Note that the pseudocode version indents the body of the loop for better readability.

We shall present a popular version of BASIC coding for the pre-test loop structure in Section 3.5 and conclude the treatment of loops in Chapter 5.

## 3.4 STRUCTURED PROGRAMMING

Let's define a **structured program** as one that is written strictly in terms of sequence, decision, and loop structures. The flowchart that corresponds to a structured program is defined as a **structured flowchart.** Pseudocode itself reflects a structured design when it is based strictly on sequence, decision (if–then–else, if–then, etc.), and loop (pre-test and post-test) structures.

If you look back at Figures 3.1 to 3.5, you will see that each control structure has a single entry point and a single exit point, as denoted by the circle symbol (○). In effect, a structured program is simply a set of these control structures put together meaningfully. For example, the if–then–else structure in Figure 3.3 includes a sequence structure in each of its blocks, and the loop structure in Figure 3.5 contains a sequence structure as its body. Are you ready for this? If we replace "Calculate revenue" in Figure 3.5 with the if–then–else structure in Figure 3.3, the revised Figure 3.5 would be a loop structure with a body made up of a sequence structure with an embedded if–then–else structure.[1]

Structured programs use a concept called modular programming that breaks down a complex problem into a set of modules, each of which performs a specific function within the overall solution of the problem. In the present context, every control structure is a module.[2]

Structured programming also illustrates top-down execution, in which execution enters the top of a structure, proceeds down, and exits through the bottom of the structure. This approach to the development of programs (software) reduces the time it takes to write a program and makes it more readable and reliable.[3]

---

### Follow-Up Exercise

1.  Incorporate Figure 3.3 into Figure 3.5 by reworking the following.
    a.  Flowchart version in Figure 3.5.
    b.  Pseudocode version in Figure 3.5.

---

## 3.5 FOR/NEXT LOOPS

Each program up to now has processed a single set of data, since we have not introduced the means of looping back or returning to statements previously executed. As you have seen, this "single pass" through the program forces us to run the program separately each time we have new data.

In Section 3.3 we defined and illustrated the loop structure but did not show any of the BASIC implementations. In this section we present BASIC's traditional and direct implementation of the loop structure, the FOR/NEXT loop. In Chapter 5 we shall show other loop structure implementations.

A **FOR/NEXT loop** is defined by a FOR statement at the beginning of the loop and a NEXT statement at the end of the loop. All executable statements in between are the loop body. Loop control details are expressed in the FOR statement.

---

[1] Other legitimate decision structures are presented in Chapter 6.
[2] Modular programming is presented in Chapter 7.
[3] Top-down design is a related concept that we discuss in Chapter 4.

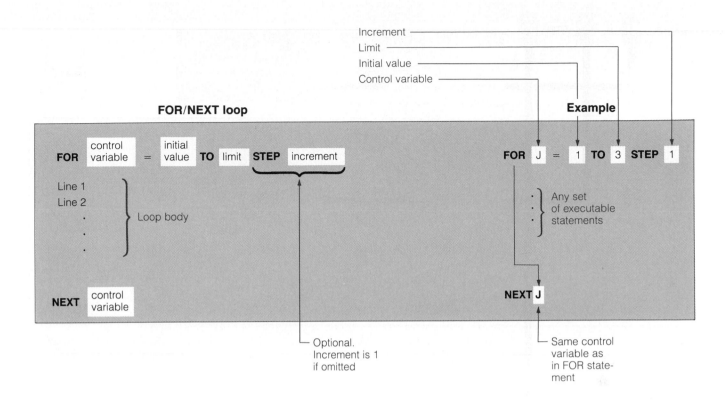

In the FOR statement we supply information that determines the number of **loop iterations,** that is, the number of times that the body of the loop is to be executed.

1. We specify the control variable, a simple numeric variable. In the preceding example, *J* is the control variable.

2. We specify the initial value of the control variable as a numeric constant, numeric variable, or, generally, any numeric expression. For example, *J* is initially set to 1 in the example, since 1 is the value found in the initial-value position.

3. We specify the limit of the control variable as a numeric constant, numeric variable, or, generally, any numeric expression. The value of the control variable must exceed (when the increment is positive) or be less than (when the increment is negative) the limit before the loop is terminated. In our example, looping continues while the value of *J* is 3 or less.

4. We specify the increment as a numeric constant, numeric variable, or, generally, any numeric expression. The value of the control variable changes by the increment at each iteration of the FOR/NEXT loop. Thus, in our example, the value of *J* increases by 1 each time the loop iterates.

In our simple example, the body of the loop is executed three times as *J* becomes 1, 2, and 3. By the way, the increment can be omitted, in which case BASIC assumes it has a value of 1. For example,

FOR J = 1 to 3        ◄——— STEP 1 can be omitted

is equivalent to

FOR J = 1 to 3    STEP 1

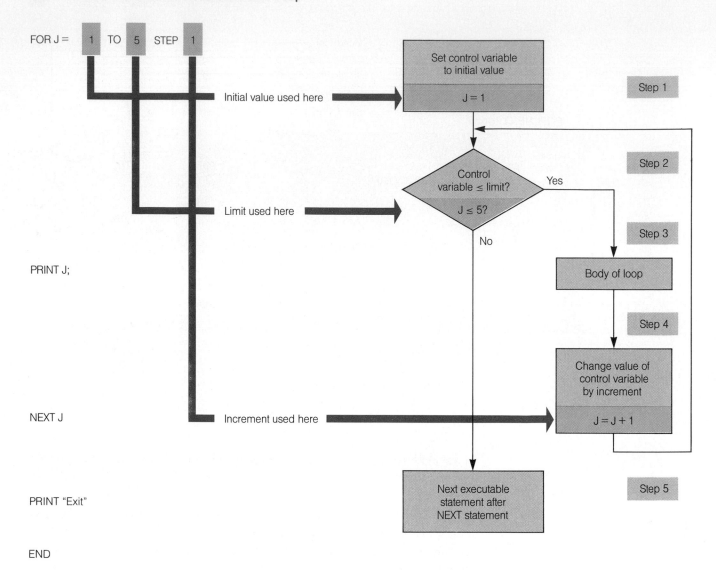

**Figure 3.6** Logic of FOR/NEXT loop for positive increment (change ≤ to ≥ for negative increment)

To better understand the mechanics of the FOR/NEXT loop consider Figure 3.6. When the FOR statement is executed, the FOR/NEXT loop is activated, whereby *J* is set to 1 (Step 1 in flowchart) and the loop-control test is made (Step 2 in flowchart). Since the current value of 1 for *J* does not exceed the limit of 5, the body of the loop is processed (Step 3) for the first time. Next, *J* is increased by its increment of 1 (Step 4) to a value of 2. Control then returns to the beginning of the loop, and the loop-control test is performed again (Step 2). *J* is again less than the limit; so the loop body is processed a second time. This process continues until the control variable has been incremented to 6. At this point the loop-control test yields a "No" response, which transfers control to the next executable statement (Step 5) following the FOR/NEXT loop. The FOR/NEXT loop is now *inactive*. Note that the loop iterates five times, which means that the body is sequentially processed five times.

**NOTE 1**  *The number of iterations in a FOR/NEXT loop is given by the limit when both the initial value and increment are 1.* In this case the control variable is said to be a *counter*, and the loop is called a *counter-controlled loop*. Figure 3.6 shows a counter-controlled loop that iterates five times, since both the initial value and the increment are 1 and the limit is 5.

**NOTE 2**  Execution of the FOR statement sets the control variable to its initial value and provides other necessary loop-control information. However, the FOR statement is never re-executed as the loop iterates; only the body gets re-executed. See the flowchart in Figure 3.6 to reinforce the fact that the loop-back point is just above the implicit loop-control test represented by the diamond but is below the box that represents the FOR statement to the left. To make sure you understand how loop iterations work, study the examples in Table 3.1.

**NOTE 3**  The increment need not have a value of 1. (See Example a in Table 3.1.)

**NOTE 4**  Increments can be negative values, in which case the initial value should be greater than the limit. Looping continues as long as the control variable equals or exceeds the limit. (See Example b in Table 3.1.) The increment, however, cannot be zero, as this implies an **infinite loop** (a loop that never terminates).

**NOTE 5**  The FOR/NEXT loop in BASIC is a pre-test structure, since the loop-control test precedes the body of the loop.[4] (See Example c in Table 3.1, which shows that the body was never executed, an impossibility for a post-test loop.)

**NOTE 6**  The control variable can take on decimal values. (See Example d in Table 3.1.)

**NOTE 7**  The *FOR/NEXT parameters*—initial value, limit, and increment—can be variables and generalized numeric expressions as well as constants. (See Example e in Table 3.1.)

**NOTE 8**  It's best to indent the loop body for better readability.

**Table 3.1**  FOR/NEXT Loop Mechanics

| Example | K | Execute Body? | Iteration | Remark |
|---|---|---|---|---|
| a. `10 FOR K = 3 TO 10 STEP 2`<br>`20    PRINT K;`<br>`30 NEXT K`<br>`40 PRINT "Exit"`<br>`99 END`<br><br>`RUN`<br>`  3  5  7  9 Exit` | 3<br>5<br>7<br>9<br>11 | Yes<br>Yes<br>Yes<br>Yes<br>No | 1<br>2<br>3<br>4<br>Exit | Initial values and increments need not be 1. The loop iterates 4 times. |

(Continued)

[4]ANS BASIC specifies the FOR/NEXT loop as a pre-test loop. However, some early BASIC dialects implement the FOR/NEXT loop as a post-test loop. Try Exercise 2c or Example c in Table 3.1 to determine the treatment on your system.

b.
```
10 FOR K = 3 TO 1 STEP -1
20   PRINT K;
30 NEXT K
40 PRINT "Exit"
99 END
```

| 3 | Yes | 1 |
| 2 | Yes | 2 |
| 1 | Yes | 3 |
| 0 | No | Exit |

The increment is negative. Note how *K* decreases. The loop iterates 3 times.

```
RUN
 3   2   1 Exit
```

c.
```
10 FOR K = 3 TO 1
20   PRINT K;
30 NEXT K
40 PRINT "Exit"
99 END
```

| 3 | No | Exit |

The loop never iterates (is inactive) since initial value exceeds limit and the step is +1.

```
RUN
Exit
```

d.
```
10 FOR K = 1.5 TO 2.5 STEP .5
20   PRINT K;
30 NEXT K
40 PRINT "Exit"
99 END
```

| 1.5 | Yes | 1 |
| 2.0 | Yes | 2 |
| 2.5 | Yes | 3 |
| 3.0 | No | Exit |

The control variable is a decimal number. The loop iterates 3 times.

```
RUN
 1.5   2   2.5 Exit
```

e.
```
5 LET U = 1
10 FOR K = U TO 2*U STEP U/2
20   PRINT K;
30 NEXT K
40 PRINT "Exit"
99 END
```

| 1.0 | Yes | 1 |
| 1.5 | Yes | 2 |
| 2.0 | Yes | 3 |
| 2.5 | No | Exit |

FOR/NEXT parameters need not be constants. Here we show use of a variable (*U*) and numeric expressions. The loop iterates 3 times.

```
RUN
 1   1.5   2 Exit
```

---

## Follow-Up Exercises

2. What values get printed for each program below? How many times does each loop iterate? Try these on your system.

a.
```
10 FOR J = 1 to 8
20   PRINT J
30 NEXT J
99 END
```

b.
```
10 FOR J = 1 to 8
30 NEXT J
40 PRINT J
99 END
```

c.
```
10 FOR J = 6 TO 0
20   PRINT J
30 NEXT J
99 END
```

d.
```
10 FOR J = 6 TO 0 STEP -2
20   PRINT J
30 NEXT J
99 END
```

e.
```
10 FOR J = 2 TO 9 STEP 3
20   PRINT J
30 NEXT J
99 END
```

f.
```
10 FOR J = 5 TO 5
20   PRINT J
30 NEXT J
99 END
```

g.
```
5 LET K = 0
10 FOR X = 5.1 TO 5.5 STEP .1
15   LET K = K + 1
20   PRINT X
30 NEXT X
40 PRINT K
99 END
```

h.
```
5 LET K = 0
10 FOR X = 5.5 TO 5.1 STEP -.1
15   LET K = K+1
20   PRINT X
30 NEXT X
40 PRINT K
99 END
```

i.
```
5 LET Y = 10
10 FOR X = Y TO 2*Y - 1 STEP Y/4
20   PRINT X
30 NEXT X
99 END
```

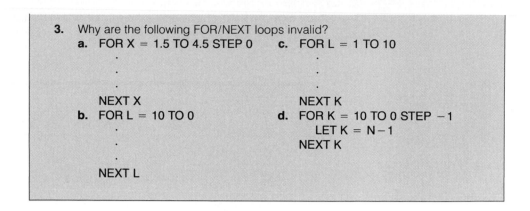

3. Why are the following FOR/NEXT loops invalid?

a. FOR X = 1.5 TO 4.5 STEP 0       c. FOR L = 1 TO 10
   .                                   .
   .                                   .
   .                                   .
   NEXT X                              NEXT K
b. FOR L = 10 TO 0                 d. FOR K = 10 TO 0 STEP −1
   .                                   LET K = N−1
   .                                   NEXT K
   .
   NEXT L

**E X A M P L E   3 . 1**   **Tuition Revenue Problem with FOR/NEXT Loop**

Consider the following version of the tuition revenue problem, which is a modification of Example 2.13 on page 48.

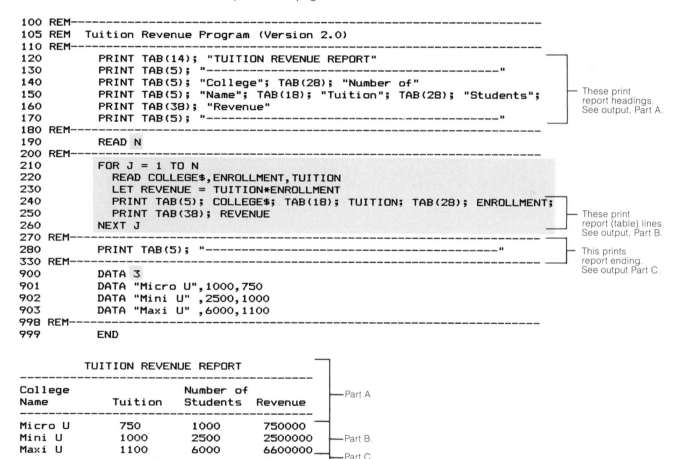

```
100 REM---------------------------------------------------------------
105 REM   Tuition Revenue Program (Version 2.0)
110 REM---------------------------------------------------------------
120         PRINT TAB(14); "TUITION REVENUE REPORT"
130         PRINT TAB(5); "--------------------------------------------"
140         PRINT TAB(5); "College"; TAB(28); "Number of"
150         PRINT TAB(5); "Name"; TAB(18); "Tuition"; TAB(28); "Students";
160         PRINT TAB(38); "Revenue"
170         PRINT TAB(5); "--------------------------------------------"
180 REM---------------------------------------------------------------
190         READ N
200 REM---------------------------------------------------------------
210         FOR J = 1 TO N
220            READ COLLEGE$,ENROLLMENT,TUITION
230            LET REVENUE = TUITION*ENROLLMENT
240            PRINT TAB(5); COLLEGE$; TAB(18); TUITION; TAB(28); ENROLLMENT;
250            PRINT TAB(38); REVENUE
260         NEXT J
270 REM---------------------------------------------------------------
280         PRINT TAB(5); "--------------------------------------------"
330 REM---------------------------------------------------------------
900         DATA 3
901         DATA "Micro U",1000,750
902         DATA "Mini U" ,2500,1000
903         DATA "Maxi U" ,6000,1100
998 REM---------------------------------------------------------------
999         END
```

These print report headings. See output, Part A.

These print report (table) lines. See output, Part B.

This prints report ending. See output Part C.

```
        TUITION REVENUE REPORT
     ----------------------------------------
     College          Number of
     Name     Tuition  Students  Revenue
     ----------------------------------------
     Micro U    750     1000      750000
     Mini U    1000     2500     2500000
     Maxi U    1100     6000     6600000
     ----------------------------------------
```

—Part A

—Part B.

—Part C.

Note the following points.

1. The number of colleges to be processed is read in under the variable *N*. Its value of 3 in the data section is consistent with the fact that three colleges are to be processed. *N* is also the limit in the FOR statement. Since this is a counter-controlled loop, the value of 3 in *N* is the number of loop iterations; that is, the loop will process three colleges.

**2.** The body of the loop iterates three times, which gives the successive values in memory that are shown in Table 3.2, as if a "snapshot" were taken just before the NEXT statement is executed.

---

**Table 3.2**  Successive Values in Memory

| N | J | COLLEGE$ | TUITION | ENROLLMENT | REVENUE |
|---|---|----------|---------|------------|---------|
| 3 | 1 | Micro U | 750 | 1000 | 750000 |
|   | 2 | Mini U | 1000 | 2500 | 2500000 |
|   | 3 | Maxi U | 1100 | 6000 | 6600000 |

Note that each execution of the READ statement in line 220 processes an entire data line. Thus, when the READ statement is executed during the first iteration ($J = 1$), all data items in line 901 are read into memory; when $J = 2$, execution of line 220 processes line 902; and when $J = 3$, the READ statement processes line 903.

**3.** The repeated execution of the PRINT statements within the loop body (see lines 240–250) gives the output a tablelike appearance (see Part B in the output). Note that line 240 has a trailing semicolon. Thus lines 240–250 behave like a single PRINT statement. PRINT statements for labels and column headings must *precede* the loop structure (see lines 120–170), so that these are printed just before the output table (see Part A in the output). Finally, PRINT statements for post-table material, such as dashed lines and summary statistics (see line 280), are placed *after* the loop structure (see Part C in the output).

**4.** There is no standard notation for specifying a FOR/NEXT loop, either in a flowchart or in pseudocode. One common flowcharting approach is to use the hexagon-shaped symbol to define the start of the loop (FOR statement) and the circle symbol to define the end of the loop (NEXT statement). Figure 3.7 illustrates this approach for Example 3.1. Note that the loop returns to the first executable statement following the FOR statement, not to the FOR statement itself. Alternative approaches to flowcharting the FOR/NEXT loop are illustrated in Figures 3.4a and 3.5.

---

**NOTE 1**  Use of the variable $N$ instead of the constant 3 in the FOR statement of Example 3.1 illustrates a style of programming whereby variables (symbols) are used in place of constants. *This promotes the generality of programs.* In our example, we need not make changes within the executable portion of the program (line 210) to process a different number of colleges. Instead, we simply change relevant data in the data section (line 900). This simplifies program maintenance, thereby reducing software cost in actual programming environments which may include changes to hundreds of data items dispersed throughout a large program.

**NOTE 2**  The data section in Example 3.1 (lines 900–903) illustrates an internal data file made up of records and fields. A **field** is a data item or attribute of some entity such as a college or person. In our example, the fields are college name, enrollment, and tuition. A **record** is a collection of related fields grouped together. In our example, the three data items for a single college define a record. Thus three records are shown in lines 901–903. **A data file,** then, is a collection of related records.

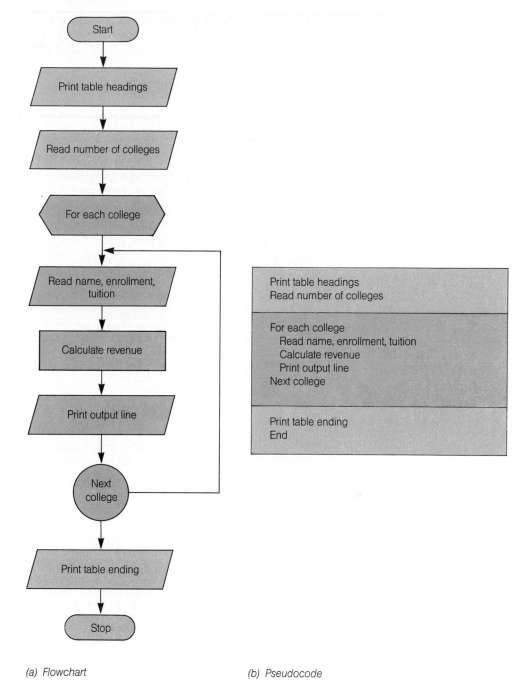

(a) Flowchart                              (b) Pseudocode

**Figure 3.7**   Flowchart and pseudocode for Example 3.1

In practice (the "real world"), data files are *external* to programs and reside in secondary storage media such as magnetic disk and tape. The processing of **external data files** is an advanced topic, which we shall delay until Module E. In the meantime we illustrate the principles of elementary file processing by using these data sections within programs, which we call **internal data files.**

**NOTE 3**   The loop structure and data files illustrate the most commercially viable aspect of computing: The ability to process automatically large data files with thousands of records. The loop structure is also a powerful construct for "number crunching," as we shall illustrate in Chapter 6. Note that each execution of the READ statement in line 220 of Example 3.1 processes an entire record. Thus the FOR/NEXT loop is set up to iterate once for each record, or a total of three times in the sample run. In general, loops that process files are designed so that the number of loop iterations equals the number of records.[5]

---

## Follow-Up Exercises

**4.** Suppose we have to process 15 institutions. What changes need to be made in the program and data of Example 3.1?

**5.** What would the output look like in Example 3.1 if
  **a.** Lines 120–170 were placed between the FOR and READ statements?
  **b.** Line 170 (or 280) were replaced by

```
170 FOR K = 1 to 41
172    PRINT "–";
174 NEXT K
176 PRINT
```

  **c.** Same as part b, except omit line 176.

---

**E X A M P L E   3 . 2**   Bank Savings

This example further illustrates both the four-step software development cycle and the FOR/NEXT loop. Note that Steps 1 and 2 are included in the program's documentation.

```
100 REM  * * * * * * * * * * * * * * * * * * * * * * * * * * * * * * * *
110 REM  *                                                            *
120 REM  *   Bank Savings Program                                     *
130 REM  *                                                            *
140 REM  *  Step 1:   Analysis                                        *
150 REM  *                                                            *
160 REM  *    This is an interactive program that prints a report showing *
170 REM  *    the accumulated funds in a savings account for different *
180 REM  *    interest percents per period (say, 1% to 3% per quarter in *
190 REM  *    steps of 0.25%) given a starting amount or principal (say, *
200 REM  *    $1000) and the number of periods over which interest is *
210 REM  *    earned (say, 20 quarters).                              *
220 REM  *                                                            *
230 REM  *    Output data:                                            *
240 REM  *      Table showing                                         *
250 REM  *        Interest percent                                    *
260 REM  *        Accumulated funds                                   *
270 REM  *                                                            *
280 REM  *    Input data:                                             *
290 REM  *     Principal                                              *
300 REM  *     Number of periods                                      *
310 REM  *     Initial interest % per period                          *
320 REM  *     Final   interest % per period                          *
330 REM  *     Step    interest % per period                          *
340 REM  *                                                            *
350 REM  *    Computations:                                           *
360 REM  *      Accum. funds = principal * (1 + interest/100)^periods *
370 REM  *                                                            *
380 REM  *                                                            *
```

(Continued)

---

[5]In Chapter 5 we shall illustrate the eof loop, which is especially designed for data file processing.

```
390 REM  *    Step 2: Design                                        *
400 REM  *                                                          *
410 REM  *      INPUT data with conversational prompts              *
420 REM  *      PRINT table headings                                *
430 REM  *      FOR each interest %                                 *
440 REM  *        Calculate accum. funds                            *
450 REM  *        PRINT interest %, accum. funds                    *
460 REM  *      NEXT interest %                                     *
470 REM  *      PRINT table ending                                  *
480 REM  *      END                                                 *
490 REM  *                                                          *
500 REM  *                                                          *
510 REM  *    Step 3:  Code                                         *
520 REM  *                                                          *
530 REM  *      Key:                                                *
540 REM  *        FUNDS ...... Accumulated funds                    *
550 REM  *        INTEREST ... Interest percent                     *
560 REM  *        INTFIRST ... First interest percent               *
570 REM  *        INTLAST .... Last  interest percent               *
580 REM  *        INTSTEP .... Step  interest percent               *
590 REM  *        PERIODS .... Number of periods                    *
600 REM  *        PRINCIPAL .. Principal                            *
610 REM  *                                                          *
620 REM  * * * * * * * * * * * * * * * * * * * * * * * * * * * * * *
630 REM-----------------------------------------------------------------
640      INPUT "Enter principal==================>"; PRINCIPAL
650      INPUT "Enter number of periods ========>"; PERIODS
660      INPUT "Enter first interest percent ===>"; INTFIRST
670      INPUT "Enter last  interest percent ===>"; INTLAST
680      INPUT "Enter step  interest percent ===>"; INTSTEP
690 REM-----------------------------------------------------------------
700      PRINT
710      PRINT ,,,"----------------------------"
720      PRINT ,,,"Interest %    Accum. Funds"
730      PRINT ,,,"----------------------------"
740 REM-----------------------------------------------------------------
750      FOR INTEREST = INTFIRST TO INTLAST STEP INTSTEP
760        LET FUNDS  = PRINCIPAL*(1 + INTEREST/100)^PERIODS
770        PRINT ,,,INTEREST, FUNDS
780      NEXT INTEREST
790 REM-----------------------------------------------------------------
800      PRINT ,,,"----------------------------"
998 REM-----------------------------------------------------------------
999      END
```

Step 4: Test

```
RUN
Enter principal==================>? 1000
Enter number of periods ========>? 20
Enter first interest percent ===>? 1
Enter last  interest percent ===>? 3
Enter step  interest percent ===>? .25
```

| Interest % | Accum. Funds |
|---|---|
| 1 | 1220.19 |
| 1.25 | 1282.039 |
| 1.5 | 1346.854 |
| 1.75 | 1414.78 |
| 2 | 1485.946 |
| 2.25 | 1560.51 |
| 2.5 | 1638.616 |
| 2.75 | 1720.43 |
| 3 | 1806.111 |

This program illustrates several points. First, observe the use of numeric variables rather than constants in all the loop parameters of the FOR statement (line 750). These are input through the execution of lines 660–680. Second, this is not a counter-controlled loop. The control variable, INTEREST, contains real values rather than integer values. In the sample run, INTEREST ranges from 1% to 3% in increments of 0.25%. Finally, the control variable, INTEREST, is used in a computation (line 760) within the loop body.

---

## Follow-Up Exercises

**6.**  Roleplay computer by filling in a memory table for the Bank Savings run, as done in Table 3.2 on page 84.

**\*7.**  Modify Example 3.2 so that annual rather than quarterly interest is input. Accumulations still must be calculated on a quarterly basis, but both the input and output should show the annual interest.

**\*8.**  Modify Example 3.2 as follows:

*Input data*

Principal
Interest % per period
Initial period
Final period
Step period

*Output data*

Table showing:
    Period
    Accumulated funds

---

## 3.6 INITIALIZATIONS AND SUMS

Accumulating sums for one or more variables is a common computation in programming. For example, a payroll program might compute gross pay, deductions, and net pay for each employee and also compute the total gross pay, total deductions, and total net pay for all employees. To illustrate how the computer can accumulate a sum, we return to our tuition revenue problem.

**E X A M P L E   3 . 3**   Tuition Revenue with Sum

The Board of Regents needs to know the total amount of money that will be collected from all the colleges within the state. Conceptually, we set aside a memory location (assign a variable) that represents the sum. Each time the computer calculates the amount of revenue expected from a college, the sum is increased by the revenue expected from that college. In effect, the sum can be thought of as a running total, the final value of which is not known until all the data are entered and processed.

For our test data in Example 3.1, the amounts from each college are $750,000, $2,500,000, and $6,600,000. As the program is computing, the sum is updated as follows.

- After the first college:                    0 +    750,000 =    750,000
- After the second college:           750,000 + 2,500,000 = 3,250,000
- After the third college:          3,250,000 + 6,600,000 = 9,850,000

Thus a running total accumulates.

The shaded portions in the pseudocode of Figure 3.8 illustrate the incorporation of a sum in the version of Figure 3.7. Note that the only changes are the initialization of the *summer* (sum variable) to zero before the loop, the incorporation of the summer in the loop to compute the running total, and the output of the summer following the loop.

In the program, SUM is the variable that stores the accumulated revenue from all colleges. Changes from the program in Example 3.1 are shaded.

```
100 REM------------------------------------------------------------
105 REM   Tuition Revenue Program (Version 2.1)
110 REM------------------------------------------------------------
120         PRINT TAB(14); "TUITION REVENUE REPORT"
130         PRINT TAB(5); "-------------------------------------------"
140         PRINT TAB(5); "College"; TAB(28); "Number of"
150         PRINT TAB(5); "Name"; TAB(18); "Tuition"; TAB(28); "Students";
160         PRINT TAB(38); "Revenue"
170         PRINT TAB(5); "-------------------------------------------"
180 REM------------------------------------------------------------
190         READ N
195         LET SUM = 0   ◄——— SUM is initialized
200 REM------------------------------------------------------------
210         FOR J = 1 TO N
220            READ COLLEGE$,ENROLLMENT,TUITION
230            LET REVENUE = TUITION*ENROLLMENT
240            PRINT TAB(5); COLLEGE$; TAB(18); TUITION; TAB(28); ENROLLMENT;
250            PRINT TAB(38); REVENUE
255            LET SUM = SUM + REVENUE  ◄——— SUM is increased by each new
260         NEXT J                              value in REVENUE
270 REM------------------------------------------------------------
280         PRINT TAB(5); "-------------------------------------------"
285         PRINT TAB(5);"Total"; TAB(38); SUM  ◄——— SUM is printed following the loop
330 REM------------------------------------------------------------
900         DATA 3
901         DATA "Micro U",1000,750
902         DATA "Mini U" ,2500,1000
903         DATA "Maxi U" ,6000,1100
998 REM------------------------------------------------------------
999         END
```

(Continued)

```
RUN
                 TUITION REVENUE REPORT
    --------------------------------------------------
    College              Number of
    Name         Tuition  Students   Revenue
    --------------------------------------------------
    Micro U        750      1000      750000
    Mini  U       1000      2500     2500000
    Maxi  U       1100      6000     6600000
    --------------------------------------------------
    Total                            9850000
```

First we initialize SUM to zero in line 195. Next we place the statement

LET SUM = SUM + REVENUE

within the loop. Thus the value stored in REVENUE is added to the value stored in SUM, and the result is stored in SUM, replacing the value previously stored in SUM.

As the program executes, the contents of memory locations for REVENUE and SUM change in the following way.

After initialization:

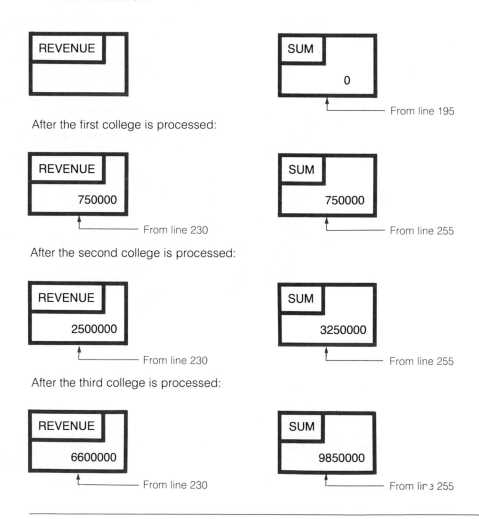

After the first college is processed:

After the second college is processed:

After the third college is processed:

---

**NOTE** Although most systems initialize all numeric variables to zero, it is good programming practice to initialize explicitly the variables that need zero initialization, as is done in line 195 of Example 3.3.

```
Print table headings
Read number of colleges
┌─────────────────────────────────┐
│ Sum = 0                         │
└─────────────────────────────────┘
For each college
      Read name, enrollment, tuition
      Calculate revenue
      Print output line
      ┌──────────────────────────┐
      │ Sum = sum + revenue      │
      └──────────────────────────┘
Next college
Print table ending
┌──────────────────┐
│ Print sum        │
└──────────────────┘
End
```

**Figure 3.8**  Pseudocode for Example 3.3

## Follow-Up Exercises

9. With respect to Example 3.3,
   a. Would the output change if the summer statement in line 255 were placed just *after* the LET statement in line 230? If so, how?
   b. Would the output change if the summer statement in line 255 were placed just *before* the LET statement in line 230? If so, how?
   c. Would the output change if the initialization in line 195 were omitted? Check this out on your system.
   d. Describe the output if the statement that prints the sum were placed just before the NEXT statement.

*10. Modify the program of Example 3.3 to print total enrollment for all colleges.

*11. Modify the program of Example 3.3 to calculate and print the average revenue, AVE. Print AVE immediately under the output for sum.

12. What would be printed by the following:
   a.  10 LET K = 0
       20 FOR J = 1 TO 3
       30    LET K = K + 5
       40    PRINT J, K
       50 NEXT J
       60 PRINT J,K
       99 END
   *b. 10 LET S = 5
       20 FOR J = 1 TO 4
       30    LET S = S + J*S
       40 NEXT J
       50 PRINT S
       99 END

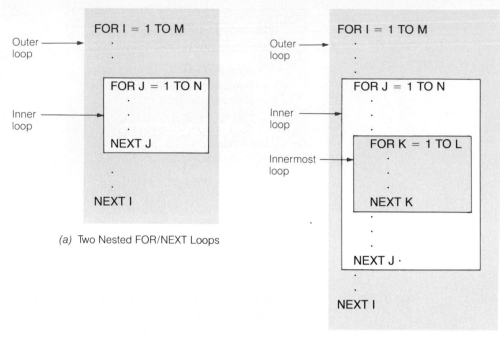

(a) Two Nested FOR/NEXT Loops

(b) Three Nested FOR/NEXT Loops

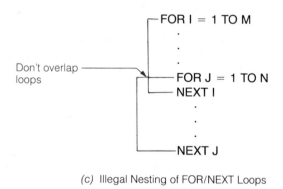

(c) Illegal Nesting of FOR/NEXT Loops

**Figure 3.9**   Nested FOR/NEXT loops

## 3.7 NESTED FOR/NEXT LOOPS

As problems become more complex, solutions may require the programmer to embed one loop inside another. For every iteration of an outside loop, the inside loop iterates through a complete cycle. The inside loop is said to be **nested** within the outside loop. FOR/NEXT loops are nested when one FOR/NEXT loop lies entirely within another FOR/NEXT loop, as illustrated in Figure 3.9.

**E X A M P L E   3 . 4**   Nested FOR/NEXT Loops

The key to understanding nested FOR/NEXT loops is careful attention to iterations and the values assigned to control variables. Consider the program and output below.

```
100 REM    Nested FOR/NEXT Loops
110 REM
120        PRINT " I", " J"
130        PRINT "-----------------"
140        FOR I = 1 TO 2
150          FOR J = 1 TO 3
160            PRINT I,J
170          NEXT J
180        NEXT I
999        END
```

```
RUN
 I                    J
-----------------
 1                    1
 1                    2
 1                    3
 2                    1
 2                    2
 2                    3
```

The inner loop (lines 150–170) is "exhausted" for each value of the outer loop's control variable $I$; that is, $J$ changes from 1 to 2 to 3 before $I$ is incremented to its next value.[6] Thus the inner loop is said to "vary the fastest." Each time the inner loop is exhausted, its control variable $J$ is reset to its initial value, since the statement

FOR J = 1 TO 3

is executed for each new value of $I$. Details on the behavior of $I$ and $J$ are shown below.

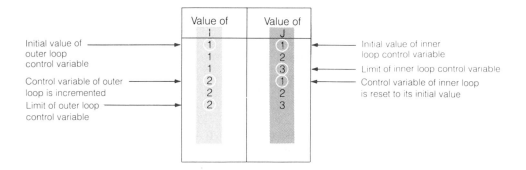

Notice that this double loop iterates a total of six times (2 × 3), or the product of the total iterations of the outer loop and the total iterations of the inner loop.

---

[6]Actually, assuming a pre-test loop structure, $J$ reaches a value of 4, at which time the inner loop becomes inactive.

**EXAMPLE 3.5**    Student Averages

This example illustrates a problem that requires the use of nested loops.

**Analysis**

We wish to develop a program that calculates the average score for each student. For example, given the data

|         | Scores    |
|-----------|-----------|
| Student 1 | Student 2 |
| 90        | 50        |
| 80        | 90        |
| 100       | 70        |

the program would compute and print an average of 90 for Student 1 and 70 for Student 2.

*Output data*

■    Name of each student

■    Average for each student

*Read data*

■    Number of students

■    Number of scores

■    Name and scores for 1st student

■    Name and scores for 2nd student

■    . . .

*Computations*

Student average = sum of scores for student ÷ number scores for student

**Design**

```
Print table headings
Read number of students, number of scores
  For each student
    Student sum = 0
    Read name of student
    For all scores of a student
      Read score
      Student sum = student sum + score
    Next score
    Student average = student sum/number of scores
    Print name of student, student average
  Next student
Print table ending
End
```

**Code**

```
100 REM-----------------------------------------------------
110 REM    Student Averages Program
120 REM
130 REM    Key:
140 REM       AVG      = Student's average
150 REM       M        = Number of students
160 REM       N        = Number of scores for a student
170 REM       SCORE    = Student's score
180 REM       SNAME$   = Student's name
190 REM       SUM      = Sum of scores for a student
200 REM-----------------------------------------------------
210         PRINT "---------------------"
220         PRINT "Name            Average"
230         PRINT "---------------------"
240 REM-----------------------------------------------------
250         READ M,N
260 REM-----------------------------------------------------
270         FOR STUDENT = 1 TO M
280           LET SUM = 0          ←————————— Initializes SUM for each student
290           READ SNAME$
300 REM
310           FOR J = 1 TO N
320             READ SCORE
330             LET SUM = SUM + SCORE   ←————— Accumulates scores for a
340           NEXT J                            student
350 REM
360           LET AVG = SUM/N        ←————————— SUM is used to calculate AVG
370           PRINT SNAME$,AVG                  following the inner loop
380         NEXT STUDENT
390 REM-----------------------------------------------------
400         PRINT "---------------------"
410 REM-----------------------------------------------------
900         DATA 4,3
901         DATA "Smith",90,80,100
902         DATA "Jones",50,90,70
903         DATA "Ellie",85,75,65
904         DATA "Budzirk",88,72,86
998 REM-----------------------------------------------------
999         END
```

**Test**

```
RUN
---------------------
Name            Average
---------------------
Smith            90
Jones            70
Ellie            75
Budzirk          82
---------------------
```

In this example the inner loop processes the scores for a specific student, and the outer loop processes each student. In particular, note that

1. The sum *must* be reinitialized each time a new student is processed, as in line 280.

2. The scores for a student are summed within the inner loop, as in line 330.

3. The student's average is calculated and printed following the inner loop, as in lines 360–370.

## Follow-Up Exercises

**13.** Roleplay the computer for Example 3.5 by filling in the following memory locations, as if a snapshot of memory were taken just before execution of each NEXT statement.

| M | N | STUDENT | SNAME$ | J | SCORE | SUM | AVG |
|---|---|---------|--------|---|-------|-----|-----|
|   |   |         |        |   |       |     |     |

**14.** What would happen in Example 3.5 if
   **a.** We were to omit the initialization of SUM in line 280? Show the output.
   **b.** We were to place the calculation of AVG just before NEXT J?

**15.** Modify the program in Example 3.5 in the following ways:
   **\*a.** Calculate and print the overall average for the class.
   **\*\*b.** Compute and print the standard deviation (a measure of variation about the average) for each student, in addition to the average.

$$s = \sqrt{\frac{n \Sigma x^2 - (\Sigma x)^2}{n(n-1)}}$$

   where $n$ = number of scores
   $x$ = score
   $\Sigma x$ = sum of scores for a student
   $\Sigma x^2$ = sum of squared scores for a student
   **\*\*c.** Allow the number of scores for each student to vary (to account for optional exams, absences, etc.). *Hint:* You need to modify the data organization as well as the program.
   **\*\*d.** Include the ability to process more than one section of a course. *Hint:* You need to add a third loop.

**16.** Specify printed output and number of iterations for each of the following nested loops.

   **a.**
```
10 FOR J = 1 TO 4
20    FOR K = 1 TO 4
30        PRINT J,K
40    NEXT K
50 NEXT J
99 END
```

   **b.**
```
10 FOR J = 1 TO 4
20    FOR K = 1 TO 2 STEP 0.5
30        PRINT J,K
40    NEXT K
50 NEXT J
99 END
```

   **\*c.**
```
10 FOR I = 1 TO 2
20    PRINT I
30    FOR J = 1 TO 3
40        PRINT ,J
50        FOR K = 1 TO 4
60            PRINT ,,K
70        NEXT K
80    NEXT J
90 NEXT I
99 END
```

   **\*d.**
```
10 LET M = 0
15 FOR I = 1 TO 10
20    LET J = I
25    FOR K = 1 TO 5
30        LET L = K
35        LET M = M + 1
40    NEXT K
45 NEXT I
50 PRINT J, L, M
55 PRINT I, K
99 END
```

\*\*Double-starred exercises are somewhat more difficult and/or tedious than other exercises. Answers to these exercises are not given in the back of the book.

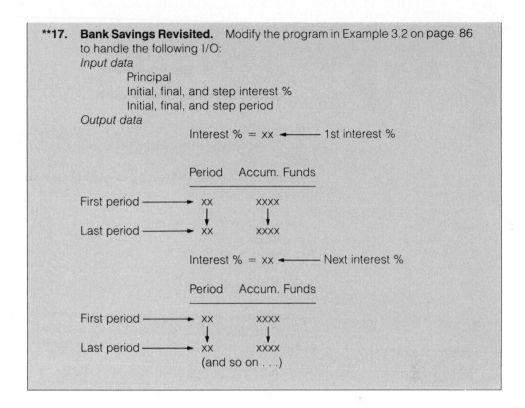

**\*\*17.  Bank Savings Revisited.**   Modify the program in Example 3.2 on page 86 to handle the following I/O:

*Input data*

       Principal

       Initial, final, and step interest %

       Initial, final, and step period

*Output data*

          Interest % = xx ◄——— 1st interest %

| | Period | Accum. Funds |
|---|---|---|
| First period ——► | xx | xxxx |
| Last period ——► | xx | xxxx |

          Interest % = xx ◄——— Next interest %

| | Period | Accum. Funds |
|---|---|---|
| First period ——► | xx | xxxx |
| Last period ——► | xx | xxxx |

          (and so on . . .)

---

## 3.8 POINTERS

### Design and Style

**1.  Indentation.**   Indent the body of the FOR/NEXT loop for better readability of the loop structure.

**2.  Generalized Loop Parameters.**   Generalize the loop parameters within the FOR statement when these values are likely to change over time. Some examples:

| Use: | Instead of: |
|---|---|
| FOR J = 1 TO N | FOR J = 1 TO 5 |
| FOR COST = C1 TO C2 STEP C3 | FOR COST = 10 TO 30 STEP 2 |

**3.  Internal Data Files.**   DATA statements that represent internal data files (see Note 2, page 84) should be placed in a group that is well removed from the visual execution logic of the program. For example, the programming logic in Example 3.5 on page 95 would be more difficult to follow if the data section (lines 900–904) were placed within the nested loops. Our preference is to place the internal data file just before the END statement.

**4.  Calculating Efficiency.**   Avoid unnecessary calculations within the loop body to improve the execution efficiency of a program. For example, many beginning programmers place the calculation of an average within the loop body, rather than following the body. To illustrate, consider the following variation of Example 3.5 on page 95:

```
FOR J = 1 TO N
    READ SCORE
    LET SUM = SUM + SCORE
    LET AVG = SUM/N
NEXT J                              Place this LET statement after the loop
```

From a practical viewpoint, AVG will store the correct value at the last iteration of this loop; however, AVG is unnecessarily calculated a total of $N-1$ times (and wrongly, at that).

Similarly, avoid constant computations within a loop body. For example, the segment

```
FOR K = 1 TO M          This gets calculated M times
    READ X
    LET Y = (A + B^2) *X
    PRINT X,Y
NEXT K
```

unnecessarily recomputes the expression $(A + B^2)$ a total of $M-1$ times. (Note that $A$ and $B$ don't change values within the loop.) A more efficient design is

```
                         Now it only gets calculated once
LET C = A + B^2
FOR K = 1 TO M
    READ X
    LET Y = C * X
    PRINT X, Y
NEXT K
```

It's also more efficient to use an integer control variable instead of the standard single precision variable. In many dialects an integer variable is specified by including a % sign as the last character in a numeric variable name. For example, K would be treated as a single precision variable and K% would be treated as an integer variable. As the number of iterations in a FOR/NEXT loop increases, the greater is the CPU-time efficiency of the loop with an integer control variable over the loop with a non-integer control variable. The following programs and runs illustrate this point on an IBM PC.

```
10 REM   Integer control variable        10 REM   Non-integer control variable
20 REM                                    20 REM
30       INPUT "Loop iterations"; M%      30       INPUT "Loop iterations"; M
40       PRINT "   Start time: ";TIME$    40       PRINT "   Start time: ";TIME$
50       FOR K% = 1 TO M%                 50       FOR K = 1 TO M
60       NEXT K%                          60       NEXT K
70       PRINT "   Stop  time: ";TIME$    70       PRINT "   Stop  time: ";TIME$
99       END                             99       END
```

```
RUN
Loop iterations? 10000
    Start time: 13:20:34
    Stop  time: 13:20:43              RUN
                                      Loop iterations? 10000
RUN                                       Start time: 13:26:31
Loop iterations? 30000                    Stop  time: 13:26:44
    Start time: 13:21:03
    Stop  time: 13:21:31              RUN
                                      Loop iterations? 30000
                                          Start time: 13:26:55
                                          Stop  time: 13:27:36
```

Time differences become more dramatic as the number of iterations increases; however, the value of an integer variable is limited to 32,767 on the IBM PC, which restricts the importance of this approach.

**5. Nesting Efficiency.**    Nest long loops within short loops. Each time an outer loop iterates, the inner-loop parameters get reinitialized, which takes time. Thus it's best to place the long loop (the one with more iterations) inside the short loop whenever possible, as this reduces the number of loop reinitializations.

**6. The Roundoff-Error Problem.**    Binary computers introduce **roundoff error** when decimal values are stored. For example, a decimal value such as 0.2 is not represented exactly in a binary (0–1) system; it's only approximated.[7] This can cause intolerable inaccuracy in certain kinds of problems, such as space-trajectory estimates and certain financial calculations. In the context of this chapter, roundoff error can give an unexpected number of loop iterations whenever loop parameters include decimal values. To illustrate, note the following program and run.

```
5   LET U = 1.6
10 FOR K = 1.2 TO U STEP .2
20    PRINT K;
30 NEXT K
40 PRINT "Exit"
99 END

RUN
 1.2  1.4 Exit
```

———— Two iterations instead of the intended three iterations

In this case, the loop iterates twice instead of the intended three times (1.6 did not get printed). A simple "fixup" is to add a small value such as 0.0001 to the upper limit, as in the following.

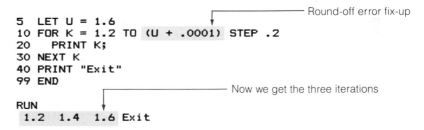

```
5   LET U = 1.6
10 FOR K = 1.2 TO (U + .0001) STEP .2
20    PRINT K;
30 NEXT K
40 PRINT "Exit"
99 END

RUN
 1.2  1.4  1.6 Exit
```

———— Round-off error fix-up

———— Now we get the three iterations

Now we obtain the expected three iterations. You might want to try these examples on your system.

**7. Control Structures as Building Blocks.**    As mentioned earlier, all programs can be written by exclusively using the three fundamental control structures: sequence, decision, and loop. Complex programs are much easier to design (and later modify) if we view each program as a set of building blocks, where each block is a control structure. The flow of execution enters each block at the top and exits through the bottom. Moreover, the flow of execution is strictly specified within the block and is independent from that of other blocks.

To illustrate this concept, consider the schematic in Figure 3.10 for the program in Example 3.1 (page 83). The building block description of this program shows that the program is made up of Blocks 1, 2, and 4 from top

---

[7]Decimal values given by ½ to an integer power are represented exactly, such as ½, ¼, ⅛, and ¹⁄₁₆. So are sums of powers of ½. For example, ¾ (or ½ + ¼) has an exact binary representation.

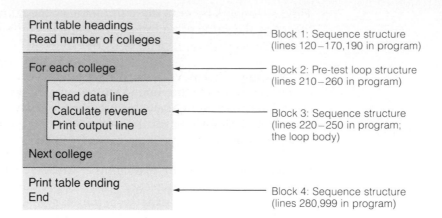

**Figure 3.10** Building blocks (control structures) in the tuition revenue program of Example 3.1 (page 83)

to bottom, forming a *stack*. Block 3 is a distinct block that resides within Block 2.

As you can see, the design issues are to decide what type of building block should be used for a particular task (such as a pre-test loop structure for processing the colleges) and how these building blocks should fit together to make up the whole. Moreover, should the program need modification in the future, we need only focus on adding new blocks, modifying existing blocks, or deleting blocks. For example, the inclusion of a summer for tuition (as in Figure 3.8, page 91) means that we need to modify Blocks 1, 3, and 4 in Figure 3.10.

It's hard to appreciate the benefits of this building block conceptualization for such simple programs. You should realize, however, that a long, complicated but structured program can be broken down into its fundamental building blocks. This not only simplifies the overall design of the program but also better isolates how we might make any needed changes.

Try to take this building block perspective. It should make your programming life easier, especially as you design more sophisticated programs.

By the way, the type of diagram shown in Figure 3.10 is a variation of what is called a **structured chart, structured diagram,** or **Nassi–Schneiderman chart.** Some writers prefer structured charts to flowcharts or pseudocode as a design tool.

**8.  Why Structured Programming?**    To underscore the importance of structured programming, consider the following quotations from "Sage of Software" by Steve Olson, which appeared in *Science*.

> Very large software systems consist of millions of separate instructions . . . written by hundreds of different people. Yet these instructions must dovetail with perfect accuracy. If even a single instruction is wrong, the software system can fail.
>
>     Then, 20 minutes before launch time [of the Columbia space shuttle], warning lights at mission control began to flash. Something was wrong with the computer system . . . [but] nothing was physically wrong with the computers. The software on board the space shuttle consists of nearly 500,000 elaborately interwoven instructions. Finding . . . a bug in that

web would be like finding a single misspelled word in an encyclopedia. The maiden flight of the space shuttle would have to be delayed.

The operating system for IBM's large 360 computer, the most important new computer of the decade, had cost hundreds of millions of dollars, was over a year late, and still contained thousands of errors. . . . In 1968 . . . NATO held a global conference on the "software crisis."

In the early 1970s a team of programmers at IBM . . . used structured programming to build an information bank for the *New York Times*. They finished in record time and then shocked the computing community when the system proved to contain almost no errors. Software developers scrambled to learn the new techniques . . . [yet] even now many programmers are staunch holdouts.[8]

A prominent computer consultant says the following about the value of structured programming and certain other software development techniques that we discuss later in the book:

. . . the new techniques *do* work—they *do* double the productivity of the average programmer, increase the reliability of his code by an order of magnitude, and decrease the difficulty of maintenance by a factor of two to ten.[9]

In short, structured programming pays off especially in the development, debugging, reliability, and subsequent maintenance of complex programs. Moreover, in our years of teaching this course, we have seen dramatic improvements in the correctness and sophistication of student programming as we switched from unstructured to structured approaches in our presentation.

## Common Errors

**1. Control Variable or Loop Parameters Redefined within Loop.**

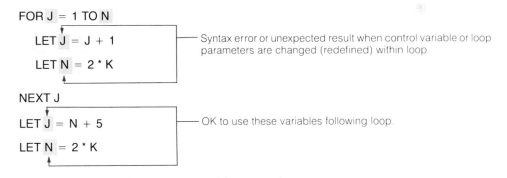

```
FOR J = 1 TO N
    LET J = J + 1 ──── Syntax error or unexpected result when control variable or loop
    LET N = 2 * K          parameters are changed (redefined) within loop.
NEXT J
LET J = N + 5 ──── OK to use these variables following loop.
LET N = 2 * K
```

**2. Improper Values for Loop Parameters.**

```
FOR K = 1 TO N ──── Execution error or inactive loop if N not explicitly assigned a
                    value and system stores zero in N.
FOR J = J1 TO J2 STEP J3 ←──── Execution error or infinite loop if J3 not explicitly assigned a
                                value and system stores zero in J3.
FOR L = 50 TO 1 ←──── Inactive loop because 50 > 1. Negative step such as − 1 needs
                      to be inserted.
```

[8] Steve Olson, "Sage of Software," *Science*, January/February 1984, pp. 75–80.

[9] Edward Yourdon, *Managing the Structured Techniques*, New York: YOURDON Press, 1979, p. 4.

**3. Incomplete FOR/NEXT Pair.**    Always make sure you pair a unique NEXT statement with a FOR statement.

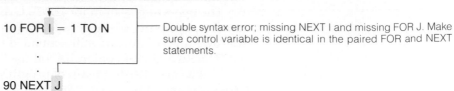

10 FOR I = 1 TO N
.
.
.
90 NEXT J

Double syntax error; missing NEXT I and missing FOR J. Make sure control variable is identical in the paired FOR and NEXT statements.

**4. Improper Nesting.**    Watch out for crossovers such as

```
┌─ FOR I = 1 TO M
│   ┌─ FOR J = 1 TO N
│   │      .
│   │      .
│   │      .
│   ├─ NEXT I
└── NEXT J
```

and the use of the same control variable for nested FOR/NEXT loops, as in

FOR K = 1 TO M
    FOR K = 1 TO N
        .
        .
        .
    NEXT K
NEXT K

Control variables must be different to avoid error.

**5. Running Out of Data.**    Watch out for situations in which the program attempts to read more data than are available, either through too many loop iterations or too little data. For example, the following program is missing data line 903, which gives an *out of data* error message when line 120 is executed at the third iteration.

```
100  READ N
110  FOR J = 1 TO N
120     READ  A,B,C
130     PRINT A;B;C
140  NEXT J
150                     REM
900  DATA 3
901  DATA 1,1,1
902  DATA 2,2,2
998                     REM
999  END
```
                              Missing DATA line 903

```
RUN
  1   1   1
  2   2   2
Out of DATA in 120
```
                              Execution error message when line 120
                              executes at the 3rd iteration

**6. Initialization Errors.**    If we forget to initialize S before the statement

500 LET S = S + X

is executed, and the system treats S as undefined, then an execution error results when this LET statement is executed (see Exercise 9c on page 91). It's good programming practice to initialize S through a statement such as

100 LET S = 0

In other situations, it's necessary to initialize certain variables (like summers) to avoid incorrect results. For example, if we were to omit

280 LET SUM = 0

in Example 3.5 on page 94, then each succeeding student benefits from the sum of all preceding students. (See Exercise 14 on page 96.)

## ADDITIONAL EXERCISES

**18.** Define or explain the following terms.

structured programming
control structures
sequence structure
decision structures
selection structures
block
if–then–else structure
if–then structure
loop structure
repetition structure

loop body
loop control
pre-test structure
while structure
until structure
post-test structure
structured program
structured flowchart
FOR/NEXT loop
FOR/NEXT statements
loop iterations
counter

counter-controlled loop
infinite loop
field
record
data file
external data file
internal data file
nested FOR/NEXT loops
roundoff error
structured chart (diagram)
Nassi–Schneiderman chart

**19. Revisits.** Modify one of the following problems from Chapter 2 by including FOR/NEXT loops as indicated. Pay attention to good I/O design.

  **a. Area.** (Example 2.5, page 37.) Use a FOR/NEXT loop to vary the radius from an initial value to a limit by a step. Treat the initial, limit, and step values as input data. The output is a table with the columns Radius and Area. Run the program twice to print two tables: The first table varies the radius from 4 to 6 inches in 0.2-inch steps; the second table varies the radius from 2 to 12 inches in 2-inch steps.

  **b. Microeconomics I.** (Example 2.6, page 38.) Use a FOR/NEXT loop to vary the units produced from an initial value to a limit by a step. Treat the initial, limit, and step values as input data. The output is a table with the columns Units and Cost. Run the program twice to print two tables: The first table varies units from 5 to 50 in 5-unit steps; the second table varies units from 5 to 15 in 1-unit steps. Use READ/DATA statements for the cost function parameters 6 and 250.

  **c. Microeconomics II.** Modify the preceding problem to print tables with the columns Units, Revenue, Cost, Profit. Revenue is given by the product of selling price and number of units sold.

Profit is revenue less cost. Cost is defined by the original cost function. Treat price as an input variable. How many units should be produced and sold to maximize profit if the price is $80 per unit? If the price is $120 per unit? Answer these questions using the data in the output tables.

  **d. Microeconomics III.** Modify the preceding problem so that an outer FOR/NEXT loop varies price from an initial value to a limit by an increment. Input the initial value, limit, and increment. Try a test run that varies price from $80 to $120 in steps of $20. (Note: This test run gives three tables as output, one for each of the three prices.)

  **e. Temperature Conversion.** (Example 2.7, page 39.) Use a FOR/NEXT loop to vary Fahrenheit temperatures from an initial value to a limit by a step. Treat the initial, limit, and step values as input data. The output is a table with the columns Fahrenheit and Celsius. Run the program twice to print two tables: The first table varies degrees F from 30 to 100 in 5-degree steps; the second table varies degrees F from −30 to 32 in 2-degree steps.

  **f. Bates Motel.** (Exercise 47, page 71.) Use a counter-controlled FOR/NEXT loop to process $N$

customers in one run. Treat *N* as an input variable. Print a summary report that shows a total for each of the following: room charge, restaurant charges, bar charges, service charge, sales taxes, and total bills.

   g. **Automobile Financing.**   (Exercise 49, page 72.) Use a counter-controlled FOR/NEXT loop to process *N* car loans in one run. Treat *N* as an input variable.

   h. **Retirement Contribution.**   (Exercise 50, page 72.) Use a counter-controlled FOR/NEXT loop to process *N* employees in one run. Treat *N* as an input variable. Print the total of all contributions.

20. **Multiplication Tables.** Consider the following multiplication table:

Multiplication Table for the Number 9

    0 times 9 =   0
    1 times 9 =   9
          .
          .
          .
    12 times 9 = 108

   a. Develop a program that prints a multiplication table. The user enters the number used for the multiplication. The table always ranges from 0 to 12.

   b. Have your program automatically generate multiplication tables for any range of numbers entered by the user. For example, if the user enters the range 2 to 11, then the program automatically generates ten multiplication tables.

21. **Individual Retirement Account (IRA).**   IRAs are an excellent means by which to build up tax-deferred retirement accounts. Essentially, a taxpayer can deduct from earned income an annual contribution to an IRA, thus reducing the federal taxes owed. The contribution is formally invested in stocks, bonds, money market account, savings account, or other approved investment vehicles. Over time, this amount increases in value (for the astute investor), with taxes still deferred. At retirement, the person can begin withdrawals, which are then taxed as if ordinary income were being earned. Develop a program that can reproduce the sample run below.

Enter current year......................... ? 1986
Enter retirement year ...................... ? 1989
Enter annual IRA contribution............. ? 2000
Enter assumed annual % return ............ ? 10

Projected IRA Accumulations

| Year | Contribution | Return | Accumulation |
|------|--------------|--------|--------------|
| 1986 | 2000 | 200 | 2200 |
| 1987 | 2000 | 420 | 4620 |
| 1988 | 2000 | 662 | 7282 |
| 1989 | 2000 | 928 | 10210 |

For simplicity, assume that all contributions are made at the beginning of the year. Thus the $2000 investment at the beginning of 1986 accumulates to $2200 by the end of 1986. In 1987 the investor contributes an additional $2000, which gives an account with $4200 at the beginning of 1987. This also earns a return of 10% for the year, or $420, which gives an accumulation of $4620 by the end of 1987 . . ., and so on. After 1989, the taxpayer can withdraw all or part of the accumulated $10,210. Of course, federal income taxes have to be paid at that time on any amount withdrawn. Debug your program with the above test run. Then try a second test run that changes the retirement year to 2026. Finally, try a third test run that generates a table from 1986 to 2026, but use an annual contribution of $1000. What's the effect of a change in the annual return to 15%?

22. **Form Letter.**   Write a program that prints the following personalized form letter.

Ms. Jane Budwick
10 North Road
Kingston, RI 02881

Dear Ms. Budwick,
   You are indeed one of the fortunate few whom we have selected for our Gala Prize Drawing. All you need to do, Jane, is fill in the enclosed handy magazine order form, which makes you eligible for one of our many Gala Prizes. Indeed, the Budwick residence at 10 North Road may be lucky enough to receive the Most Gala Prize, a free set of encyclopedias at a maintenance cost of only 10 cents per day for 30 years.

Good luck!
Hoodwink G. Fox, Manager
Dill Comic Book Co., Inc.

In one computer run, print the letter for each of the following.

| Name | Address | | |
|------|---------|---|---|
| Ms. Jane Budwick | 10 North Road | Kingston, RI 02881 |
| Mr. Al Bella Bitta | 20 Birch St. | Cincinnati, OH 44451 |
| Dr. H. Doolittle | 10 Downing | London, UK |

Make sure that each letter fits nicely within an $8\frac{1}{2}$-inch width and takes up 11 inches in length. Store all names and addresses through **READ/DATA** statements.

23. **Bank Savings with Multiple Compounding.** Consider the formula

$$A = P \cdot (1 + R/M)^{N \cdot M}$$

where  *A*  =  accumulated funds
        *P*  =  principal (amount we first invest)
        *R*  =  annual interest rate

$N$ = number of years
$M$ = number of times per year the account is compounded (for example, if the account is compounded quarterly, then $M = 4$, or interest is added in four times a year)

To illustrate, if we start with \$1000 ($P = 1000$) at 6 percent per year ($R = 0.06$) compounded once a year ($M = 1$), then after two years ($N = 2$) we have

$A = 1000 \cdot (1 + 0.06/1)^{2 \cdot 1}$
   $= \$1123.60$

However, if we compound quarterly ($M = 4$), then in two years we have

$A = 1000 \cdot (1 + 0.06/4)^{2 \cdot 4}$
   $= \$1126.49$

which is \$2.89 better than under annual compounding.

In recent years, banks have competitively increased the number of compounding periods to attract customers. For example, under daily compounding ($M = 365$) your account earns interest daily, which is preferred to, say, monthly compounding ($M = 12$).

**a.** Design and run a program that processes the following data in one run.

| $P$ | $R$ | $N$ | $M$ |
|------|------|-----|-----|
| 1000 | 0.06 | 10 | 1 |
| 1000 | 0.06 | 10 | 4 |
| 1000 | 0.06 | 10 | 12 |
| 1000 | 0.06 | 10 | 52 |
| 1000 | 0.06 | 10 | 365 |

As output, print the above table together with a new column for $A$. Comment on the behavior of $A$.

**b.** The "ultimate" account compounds continuously according to the formula

$$A = P \cdot e^{R \cdot N}$$

where $e$ is the base of natural logarithms (see Module C). For example, if we start with \$1000 and compound continuously at 6 percent per year, then after two years we have

$A = 1000 \cdot e^{(0.06) \cdot (2)}$
   $= 1000 \cdot e^{0.12}$
   $= (1000) \cdot (1.127496)$
   $= \$1127.50$

which is \$1.01 better than under quarterly compounding. Wouldn't you rather earn money even

as you read this? Modify the output in part **a** to include a last row in the table for continuous compounding. Comment on the behavior of $A$.

24. **Depreciation.** The concept of depreciation plays a prominent role in the financial accounting of organizations that report profits and pay taxes. The simplest method of depreciation is called the *straight-line method*. This method uses the following formula to determine depreciation for an asset (automobile, building, machine, etc.) in any given year:
    Depreciation = (cost − salvage value)/life

    **a.** Develop a program that inputs or reads the name of the asset and its associated cost, salvage value, and life. Output should include the type of table illustrated below.

    Depreciation Schedule
    Asset .............. Chariot
    Cost .............. \$4200
    Salvage ........... \$ 200
    Life .............. 4 years

| Year | Depreciation Expense | Accumulated Depreciation | Book Value |
|------|---------------------|--------------------------|------------|
| 1 | 1000 | 1000 | 3200 |
| 2 | 1000 | 2000 | 2200 |
| 3 | 1000 | 3000 | 1200 |
| 4 | 1000 | 4000 | 200 |

Process the following assets in your test runs.

| Asset | Cost | Salvage | Life |
|-------|------|---------|------|
| Chariot | 4,200 | 200 | 4 |
| Building | 200,000 | 0 | 15 |
| Machine | 75,000 | 5,000 | 5 |

**b.** Use a FOR/NEXT loop to process all assets in one computer run.

25. **Exponential Cumulative Distribution Function.** The function

$$p = 1 - e^{-x/a}$$

describes the probability $p$ that a random (chance) variable takes on a value less than or equal to $x$, where $a$ is the expected (average) value of the random variable and $e$ is the base of natural logarithms (see Module C). For example, if the random variable "number of hours an electronic component operates until failure (life)" is distributed exponentially, and average life is known to be 8000 hours, then the probability this component lasts 5000 hours or less is

$p = 1 - e^{-5000/8000}$
   $= 1 - e^{-0.625}$
   $= 1 - 0.5352614$
   $= 0.4647386$

that is, approximately 46 percent of these components will last 5000 hours or less.

**a.** Design a program that inputs average life $a$, initial value for $x$, terminal value for $x$, and incremental value for $x$, and outputs a table of $x$-values and corresponding probabilities. For example, if we wish to run $x$ from 1000 to 12,000 in increments of 1000, then output might appear as follows:

| LIFE | PROBABILITY |
|------|-------------|
| 1000 | 0.1175030 |
| 2000 | 0.2211992 |
| 3000 | 0.3127107 |
| . | . |
| . | . |
| . | . |
| 12000 | 0.7768698 |

Run your program for the above test data.

**b.** Include an outer loop that processes $N$ different values for average life $a$. Now, the loop in part **a** is completely within this outer loop. Run this program for the following input data.

| $a$ | Initial $x$ | Terminal $x$ | Incremental $x$ |
|------|------|------|------|
| 8000 | 1000 | 12000 | 1000 |
| 10000 | 1000 | 15000 | 1000 |
| 11000 | 1000 | 25000 | 500 |

**26. Mortgage Payments.** The formula that computes the monthly mortgage payment for a fixed-rate house loan is given by

$$P = \frac{r(1+r)^n}{(1+r)^n - 1} \times L$$

where $L$ = loan
  $r$ = monthly interest rate
  $n$ = number of months in the life of the loan
For example, a loan of $50,000 at an annual interest rate of 15% for 30 years yields the following calculations:

$r$ = 15/100 = 0.15     (to change % to rate)
  = 0.15/12 = 0.0125    (to change annual rate to monthly rate)

$n$ = 30 × 12 = 360     (to change years to months)

$$P = \frac{0.0125 \times (1.0125)^{360}}{(1.0125)^{360} - 1} \times (50000)$$

$$= \frac{0.0125 \times 87.541}{87.541 - 1} \times 50000$$

  = 0.1264 × 50000

  = 632.22

Thus the monthly mortgage payment would be $632.22.

**a.** Develop an interactive program that determines the monthly mortgage payment, given the annual interest, amount of loan, and number of years. Vary the annual interest over a range starting with an initial value and ending with a limiting value. Use the following input data: initial annual interest %, annual interest % limit, interest % increment, loan amount, and number of years in the loan. Print a table with the columns Annual Interest Percent and Mortgage Payment. Process the following input data:

| Initial % | Limiting % | Step % | Loan | Years |
|-----------|-----------|--------|--------|-------|
| 12 | 18 | 0.5 | 50,000 | 30 |
| 12 | 18 | 0.5 | 50,000 | 40 |
| 12 | 18 | 0.5 | 70,000 | 30 |
| 14 | 16 | 0.1 | 50,000 | 30 |

**b.** Include a second loop that varies the loan amount from an initial value to an ending value by an increment. These values are also entered as input data. Try reproducing the following output design:

MORTGAGE PAYMENTS
30 Year Life

| Annual Interest % | Loan Amount | | | | |
|-------------------|-------|-------|-------|-------|-------|
| | 50000 | 55000 | 60000 | 65000 | 70000 |
| 12 | | | | | |
| 13 | | | | | |
| 14 | | | | | |
| 15 | | | | | |
| 16 | | | | | |
| 17 | | | | | |
| 18 | | | | | |

Alternatively, you could simply output a table with the following columns: Annual Interest Percent, Loan Amount, Mortgage Payment.

# Simple Decisions

# 4

In this chapter we implement variations of the if-then-else decision structure first discussed in the last chapter. We also introduce two important program development tools, top-down design and stepwise refinement.

## 4.1 VARIATIONS OF THE IF-THEN-ELSE DECISION STRUCTURE

As you might recall from our introduction to structured programming in the last chapter, the **selection,** or **decision, structure** expresses the logic by which one or more conditions are tested to determine which group of statements (from among alternatives) is to be executed next. We now focus on the fundamental **if-then-else decision structure,** including two of its simple structural variations: the **if-then** and **if-else structures.** In Chapter 6 we shall con-

**Figure 4.1** Fundamental decision structures

| Type | General Flowchart | Sample Flowchart | Explanation |
|---|---|---|---|
| a. If-then-else | | | If the condition tests true (gender is female), then sum female salaries, count females, and go on to the next control structure (program segment); else sum male salaries, count males, and go on to the next control structure in the program. |
| b. If-then | | | If the condition tests true (GPA does in fact store 3.4 or greater), then increase the Dean's list counter, print the student's name and GPA, and go on to the next control structure; otherwise (false condition) go directly to the next control structure. |

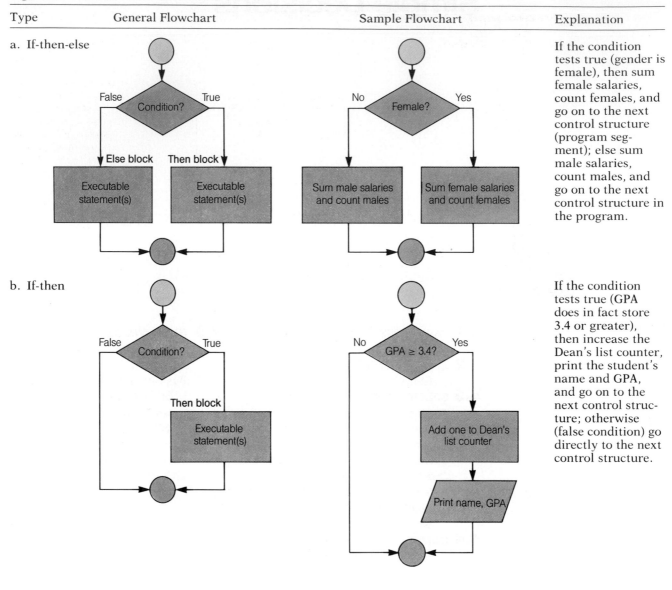

clude the treatment of decision structures by looking at some advanced selection procedures.

Figure 4.1 illustrates three simple selections. Study each selection, its terminology, and flow of control. At this time don't worry about the details of implementation. They will become clear as you read on.

**NOTE 1**    The decision (selection) structure is entered by testing a *condition* or making a decision. Then, depending on the result of this test (True or False, Yes or No), a *selection* is made regarding the next segment of the program (then block or else block) that is to be executed.

| Type | General Flowchart | Sample Flowchart | Explanation |
|---|---|---|---|
| c. If-else | 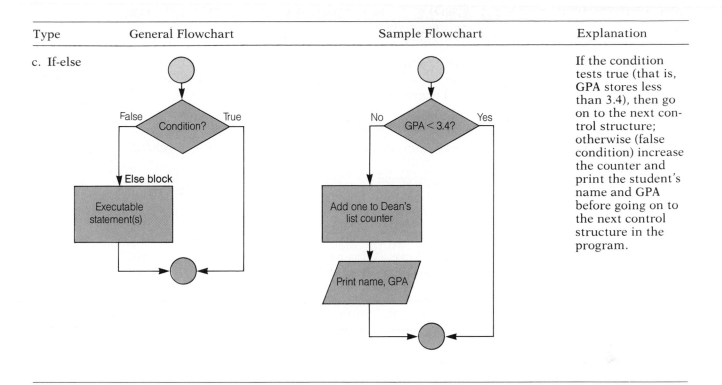 | | If the condition tests true (that is, GPA stores less than 3.4), then go on to the next control structure; otherwise (false condition) increase the counter and print the student's name and GPA before going on to the next control structure in the program. |

**NOTE 2**    The *diamond symbol* is used in the flowchart to describe the condition or decision being tested. The test is described within the diamond, and arrows show the alternate execution paths that the program may take from that decision point. The *circle symbols* indicate the beginning and end of the decision structure.

**NOTE 3**    The if-else and if-then structures are special cases of the if-then-else structure. For example, the if-then structure is the if-then-else structure with an empty else block.

**NOTE 4**    The then and else blocks are equivalent for *complementary conditions,* as shown by the two GPA examples in Figure 4.1 (GPA ≥ 3.4 is the complement of GPA < 3.4). Thus either design can be used to achieve the same end. Later we shall see that the if-then approach is preferable.

## Follow-Up Exercises

1. How would the if-then-else flowchart in Figure 4.1 change if "Female?" were replaced by "Male?"?

2. Draw flowcharts for the following conditions:
   a. If a person's last name is Smith, then print the full name and telephone number; else go on to the next portion.
   b. If a person's last name is not Smith, then go on to the next control structure; else print the full name and telephone number.
   c. If hours worked are over 40, then calculate pay based on overtime formula, keep a running sum of overtime pay, and count those who receive overtime; else calculate pay based on regular formula.

## 4.2 SIMPLE CONDITIONS BASED ON RELATIONAL OPERATORS

Implementation of the selection structure requires the formulation of a *condition that is to be tested*. A simple condition is formulated by constructing a relational expression.

**Relational Expression**

| numeric expression | relational operator | numeric expression |
|---|---|---|

| string expression | relational operator | string expression |
|---|---|---|

The relational expressions in Table 4.1 illustrate the conditions shown in Figure 4.1.

**NOTE 1** The relational expression can compare either numeric values to one another or string values to one another.

**NOTE 2** When evaluated, a relational expression will have either the value true or the value false. This determines which group of statements (then block or else block) is executed next, as shown in Figure 4.1. For example, if the string variable SEX$ stores the value M, then the relational expression SEX$ = "F" tests false, and the else block (the one for males) is executed in Figure 4.1a.

Each of the above simple examples of relational expressions shows a variable, followed by a relational operator, followed by a constant. In general, every relational expression takes the form of an expression (numeric or string), then a relational operator, and then another numeric or string expression. A **relational operator** indicates a mathematical comparison such as less than, equal to, or greater than. BASIC uses six relational operators, as indicated in

**Table 4.1** Relational Expressions for Conditions in Figure 4.1

| Condition in Figure 4.1 | Relational Expression | Type |
|---|---|---|
| a. Gender is female or equals code F? | SEX$ = "F" | String |
| b. Grade Point Average greater than or equal to 3.4? | GPA >= 3.4 | Numeric |
| c. Grade Point Average less than 3.4? | GPA < 3.4 | Numeric |

**Table 4.2** Relational Operators in BASIC

| Mathematical Comparison | Relational Operator | Meaning |
|---|---|---|
| = | = | Equal to |
| ≠ | <> | Not equal to[a] |
| < | < | Less than |
| ≤ | <= | Less than or equal to |
| > | > | Greater than |
| ≥ | >= | Greater than or equal to |

[a]Some systems use # in place of <>.

Table 4.2. To test a condition, we place one of these relational operators between the two numeric or string expressions.

As stated in Chapter 2, a numeric expression may consist of a single numeric variable, a single numeric constant, a function (Module C), or a combination of these, separated by optional parentheses and arithmetic operators. A string expression is either a string variable, a string constant, or one of the more complicated forms of strings presented in Module F.

The following examples further illustrate the use of relational expressions for testing conditions.

**E X A M P L E   4 . 1**   **Numeric Relational Expressions**

| Condition | Relational Expression | Storage Contents | Test Result |
|---|---|---|---|
| a. Hours worked 40 or less? | HOURS <= 40 | HOURS 50 | False |
| b. Is the ratio of distance to time less than the critical velocity? | D/T < CV | D 5800  T 10  CV 650 | True |
| c. Is the sex code 1? (1 = Female, 2 = Male) | SEXCODE = 1 | SEXCODE 2 | False |

A relational expression also can compare one string expression to another string expression. From a simple perspective, this comparison can be viewed alphabetically; for example, A is less than B, and g is greater than c. As you know, however, the computer internally stores all characters as coded binary numbers. Thus we can view the comparison of two strings as a comparison between the values of two coded binary numbers, in which one value (string) is less than, equal to, or greater than the other value (string).

The comparison of two strings is carried out from left to right, one character at a time. This comparison ends in one of three ways: (1) The character in one string has a lower value than the corresponding character in the other string; (2) the end of one string is reached but not the end of the other, in which case the shorter string has a lower value; or (3) the end of each string is reached, in which case the two strings have equal value.

**Table 4.3** Collating Sequence of Selected Characters[a]

| ASCII Code Values | Characters |
|---|---|
| 032 | space |
| 033–047 | ! " # $ % & ' ( ) * + , – . / |
| 048–057 | 0 1 2 3 4 5 6 7 8 9[b] |
| 065–090 | A B C ... X Y Z[b] |
| 097–122 | abc ... xyz[b] |

[a]Based on ASCII codes
[b]Numeric digits are less than alphabetic characters, and uppercase letters are less than lowercase letters.

The ordering of characters by value is called the **collating sequence.** Implementations in BASIC typically base the collating sequence on the American Standard Code for Information Interchange (**ASCII**), which officially uses 7 bits to code each of 128 characters in the sequence shown in Table 4.3.[1] For example, the code value is 48 for the digit 0, 66 for the letter $B$, and 98 for the letter $b$.

**E X A M P L E  4 . 2**   **String Relational Expressions**

| Condition | Relational Expression | Storage Contents | Test Result |
|---|---|---|---|
| a. Is gender female? | SEX$ = "F" | SEX$   M | False (M is unequal to F) |
| b. First string not equal to second string? | A$ <> B$ | A$   HAPPY    B$   happy | True (Lowercase letters are greater than uppercase letters, or h is not equal to H) |
| c. First string < second string? | A$ < B$ | A$   750A    B$   A750 | True (Numeric digits are less than alphabetic characters, or 7 is less than A) |

[1]Common enhancements include 8 bits to code 256 characters, including foreign language, graphics, and mathematical characters.

| Condition | Relational Expression | Storage Contents | Test Result |
|---|---|---|---|
| d. First string > second string? | A$ > B$ | | False (KING is less than KINGSTON; comparison ends at G) |

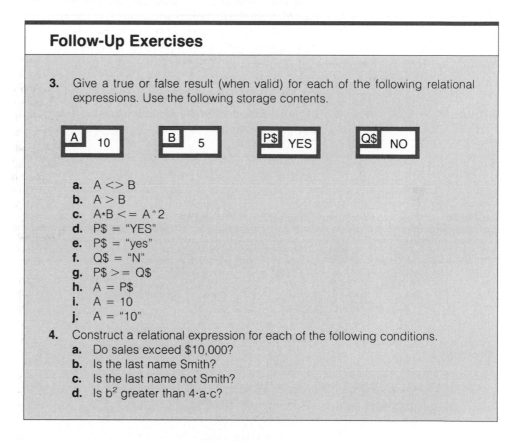

A$
KING

B$
KINGSTON

---

**NOTE 1**    Don't forget that string constants must be enclosed in quotes, as in "F" in Example 4.2a.

**NOTE 2**    Compare the equivalent conditions SEXCODE = 1 in Example 4.1c and SEX$ = "F" in Example 4.2a. Each accomplishes the same end, but the latter is more natural because gender is best described by the string code F or M than by the numeric code 1 or 2.

## Follow-Up Exercises

**3.**  Give a true or false result (when valid) for each of the following relational expressions. Use the following storage contents.

A  10        B  5        P$  YES        Q$  NO

**a.**  A <> B
**b.**  A > B
**c.**  A*B <= A^2
**d.**  P$ = "YES"
**e.**  P$ = "yes"
**f.**  Q$ = "N"
**g.**  P$ >= Q$
**h.**  A = P$
**i.**  A = 10
**j.**  A = "10"

**4.**  Construct a relational expression for each of the following conditions.
**a.**  Do sales exceed $10,000?
**b.**  Is the last name Smith?
**c.**  Is the last name not Smith?
**d.**  Is $b^2$ greater than $4 \cdot a \cdot c$?

## 4.3 SPECIFIC IMPLEMENTATIONS

The implementation of if-then-else, if-then, and if-else structures depends on the particular version or dialect of BASIC that we are using. Study the common implementations in this section and focus on those that are available on your system.

## Traditional One-Line IF/THEN Statement

The following statement is found in all BASIC dialects, including the *Minimal ANS BASIC dialect:*

**Traditional One-Line IF/THEN Statement**

> **IF** *condition*       **THEN** *line number*
>
> IF GPA < 3.4     THEN 45

The condition is tested, and the result is either true or false. If the result is true, then control is transferred to the line number specified immediately to the right of THEN (line 45 in our example). If the result is false, then the statement immediately following the IF/THEN is executed.

The traditional IF/THEN statement is often paired with the following GO TO statement:

**GO TO Statement**

> **GO TO** *line number*
>
> GO TO 230

For example, when GO TO 230 is executed, transfer of execution control goes to line 230; that is, the next statement executed is in line 230.[2]

---

**EXAMPLE 4.3** **Decision Structure Implementations Using Traditional One-Line IF/THEN and GO TO Statements**

---

Two of the decision structures first illustrated in Figure 4.1 on page 108 are implemented below.

| Type of Structure | Flowchart of Decision Structure | BASIC | Explanation |
|---|---|---|---|
| a. If-else | | ```
10 LET K = 0
15 READ M
20 FOR J=1 TO M
25    READ N$,GPA
30    IF GPA < 3.4 THEN 45
35      LET K = K + 1          ─── Else block
40      PRINT N$,GPA
45 NEXT J
50 PRINT "Number on Dean's List ="; K
90 DATA 3
91 DATA "A. Smith",3.0
92 DATA "B. Smith",3.5
93 DATA "C. Smith",2.5
99 END


RUN
B. Smith        3.5
Number on Dean's List = 1
``` | At line 30, if the value stored in GPA is in fact less than 3.4, then control immediately goes to line 45; else lines 35 and 40 are executed, followed by line 45. Lines 30–40 make up the decision structure. |

[2]Many versions of BASIC allow the variation of replacing "THEN line number" by "THEN GO TO line number" within the traditional one-line IF/THEN statement. For example,

IF GPA < 3.4 THEN GO TO 45
```

b. If-then-else

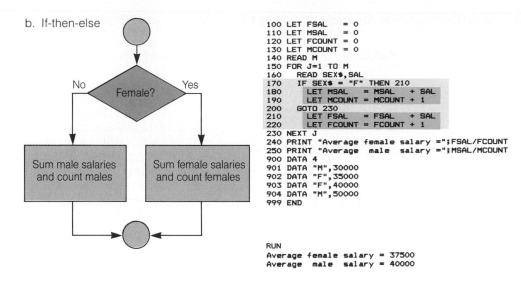

```
100 LET FSAL   = 0
110 LET MSAL   = 0
120 LET FCOUNT = 0
130 LET MCOUNT = 0
140 READ M
150 FOR J=1 TO M
160   READ SEX$,SAL
170   IF SEX$ = "F" THEN 210
180     LET MSAL   = MSAL   + SAL
190     LET MCOUNT = MCOUNT + 1
200   GOTO 230
210     LET FSAL   = FSAL   + SAL
220     LET FCOUNT = FCOUNT + 1
230 NEXT J
240 PRINT "Average female salary =";FSAL/FCOUNT
250 PRINT "Average  male  salary =";MSAL/MCOUNT
900 DATA 4
901 DATA "M",30000
902 DATA "F",35000
903 DATA "F",40000
904 DATA "M",50000
999 END
```

At line 170, if SEX$ does in fact store F, then control goes to line 210 (lines 180–200 are skipped), and lines 210–220 are executed; else control drops to line 180, and lines 180–200 are executed (lines 210–220 are skipped). Lines 170–220 implement the decision structure.

```
RUN
Average female salary = 37500
Average  male  salary = 40000
```

**NOTE 1**  The traditional IF/THEN statement cannot easily implement the IF/THEN structure, since only a line number (not a statement) is allowed in the then block just to the right of the keyword THEN. (See Exercise 5.)

**NOTE 2**  Take care that a GO TO statement separates the else and then blocks in the traditional if-then-else structure. For example, if we were to omit line 200 in Example 4.3b then lines 210 and 220 would inadvertently be executed for false conditions.

**NOTE 3**  It's good style to indent else and then blocks to improve their identification, as in Example 4.3.

**NOTE 4**  Explicit line number transfers such as THEN 210 or GO TO 230 in Example 4.3b can be hazardous to your programming health, as they increase the likelihood of "wrong line number" logic errors. It's best to avoid this style of programming if your system includes some of the statements we discuss in the remainder of this section.

### Enhanced One-Line IF/THEN Statement

Most implementations of BASIC allow the following enhanced IF/THEN statement:

**Enhanced One-Line IF/THEN Statement**

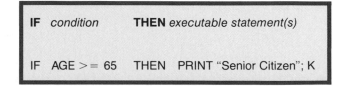

Thus, if the condition is true, then the executable statement (or multiple statements if the system allows) to the right of THEN is executed; otherwise, execution control reverts to the first executable statement immediately below the IF/THEN statement.

**E X A M P L E   4 . 4**    Decision Structure Implementations Using Enhanced One-Line IF/THEN Statement

| Type of Structure | Flowchart of Decision Structure | BASIC | Explanation |
|---|---|---|---|

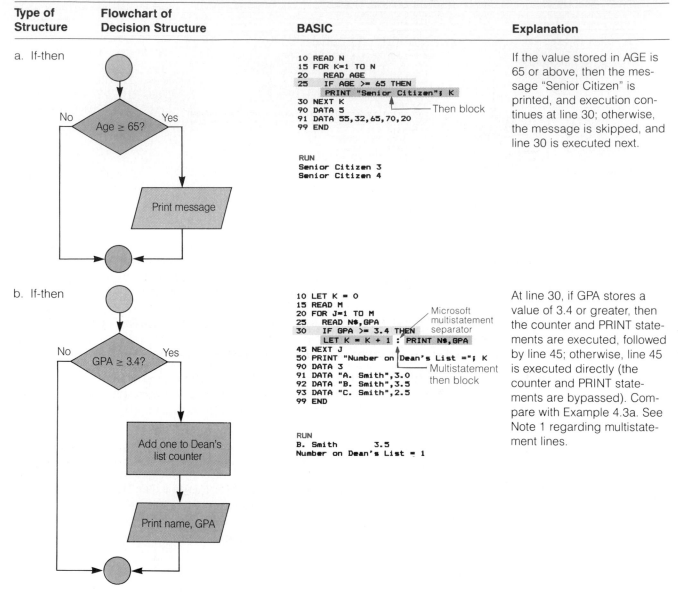

a. If-then

```
10 READ N
15 FOR K=1 TO N
20   READ AGE
25   IF AGE >= 65 THEN
       PRINT "Senior Citizen"; K
30 NEXT K
90 DATA 5
91 DATA 55,32,65,70,20
99 END
```
Then block

```
RUN
Senior Citizen 3
Senior Citizen 4
```

If the value stored in AGE is 65 or above, then the message "Senior Citizen" is printed, and execution continues at line 30; otherwise, the message is skipped, and line 30 is executed next.

Flowchart a: No / Yes — Age ≥ 65? — Print message

b. If-then

```
10 LET K = 0
15 READ M
20 FOR J=1 TO M
25   READ N$,GPA
30   IF GPA >= 3.4 THEN
       LET K = K + 1 : PRINT N$,GPA
45 NEXT J
50 PRINT "Number on Dean's List ="; K
90 DATA 3
91 DATA "A. Smith",3.0
92 DATA "B. Smith",3.5
93 DATA "C. Smith",2.5
99 END
```
Microsoft multistatement separator

Multistatement then block

```
RUN
B. Smith       3.5
Number on Dean's List = 1
```

At line 30, if GPA stores a value of 3.4 or greater, then the counter and PRINT statements are executed, followed by line 45; otherwise, line 45 is executed directly (the counter and PRINT statements are bypassed). Compare with Example 4.3a. See Note 1 regarding multistatement lines.

Flowchart b: No / Yes — GPA ≥ 3.4? — Add one to Dean's list counter — Print name, GPA

**NOTE 1**  A **multistatement line** is illustrated in Example 4.4b, which, in the example, allows us to place two statements within the then block of a single line. In the example, we used the colon as a multistatement separator, although the specific separator varies, depending on the dialect.

| Dialect | Multistatement Separator |
|---|---|
| Microsoft | Colon (:) |
| VAX-11 | Backslash (\) |
| Your system? | |

**NOTE 2**  We prefer the GPA version in Example 4.4b to that in Example 4.3a, because it avoids an explicit line number transfer; that is, "THEN 45" in Example 4.3a explicitly transfers control to line 45 when the condition is true. Explicit transfers are best avoided, because they increase the likelihood of an error that transfers to the wrong line number.

**NOTE 3**  We prefer the more direct if-then structure to the "backdoor" if-else structure. To illustrate, the if-then structure in Example 4.4b reads:

> If the student is on the Dean's list then count and print

The if-else structure in Example 4.3a states:

> If the student is *not* on the Dean's list then bypass the count and print

See what we mean?

## One-Line IF/THEN/ELSE Statements

Many versions of BASIC include one or both of the following statements:

### Older One-Line IF/THEN/ELSE Statement

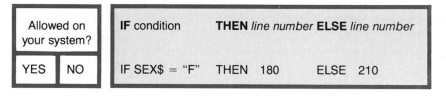

### Newer One-Line IF/THEN/ELSE Statement

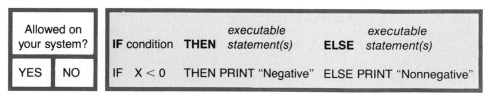

We illustrate these by example.

**E X A M P L E  4 . 5**  Decision Structure Implementations Using One-Line IF/THEN/ELSE Statements

| Type of Structure | Flowchart | BASIC | Explanation |
|---|---|---|---|

a. If-then-else

```
100 LET FSAL   = O
110 LET MSAL   = O
120 LET FCOUNT = O
130 LET MCOUNT = O
140 READ M
150 FOR J=1 TO M
160    READ SEX$,SAL
170    IF SEX$ = "F" THEN 180 ELSE 210
180       LET FSAL   = FSAL   + SAL
190       LET FCOUNT = FCOUNT + 1
200    GOTO 230
210       LET MSAL   = MSAL   + SAL
220       LET MCOUNT = MCOUNT + 1
230 NEXT J
240 PRINT "Average female salary =";FSAL/FCOUNT
250 PRINT "Average  male  salary =";MSAL/MCOUNT
900 DATA 4
901 DATA "M",30000
902 DATA "F",35000
903 DATA "F",40000
904 DATA "M",50000
999 END
RUN
Average female salary = 37500
Average  male  salary = 40000
```

Then block ← (lines 180-190)
Else block ← (lines 210-220)

If SEX$ stores F, then lines 180–200 are executed; else, lines 210–220 are executed. Compare this with the version in Example 4.3b, page 115.

b. If-then-else

```
10 READ X
15    DATA 5
20 IF X < O THEN PRINT "Negative" ELSE PRINT "Nonnegative"
99 END
```

Then block          Else block

```
10 READ X
15    DATA 5
20 IF X < O THEN PRINT "Negative"
             ELSE PRINT "Nonnegative"
99 END

RUN    Line continuation    Else block
Nonnegative
```

Then block

The second approach is more visually appealing but requires a system that allows *line continuation*. See Note 2 below.

Continuation of line indicated at this point. See Note 2.

**NOTE 1**  The ELSE portion of the one-line IF/THEN/ELSE statement (called the ELSE clause) can be omitted if we need only program an if-then structure. In this case, we simply have the enhanced one-line IF/THEN statement illustrated in Example 4.4a (page 116).

**NOTE 2**  **Line continuation** is illustrated in the second program of Example 4.5b. Visually (at the terminal), line 20 appears as two lines, but to the system it is simply program line 20. Systems can accomplish this in different ways.

| System | Method of Line Continuation |
|---|---|
| IBM PC | Simultaneously press the <Ctrl> and <Enter> keys at the end of each line that is to be continued. |
| VAX-11 | Type an ampersand (&) at the end of each line that is to be continued. |
| Your system? | |

*Warning:* Many systems limit the total length of a line to 255 characters. Check on your system's limitation.

**NOTE 3**  The approach in Example 4.5a is quite common; however, as mentioned before, explicit line number transfers are best avoided if possible. If allowed by your system, we recommend a combination of the line continuation approach in Example 4.5b (see Note 2 immediately above) and the multistatement line approach in Example 4.4b (see Note 1 on page 117):

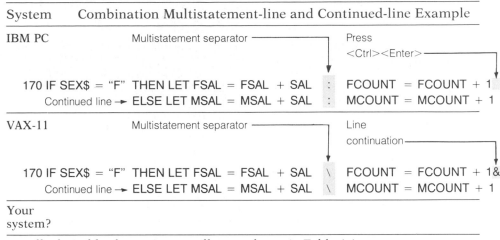

| System | Combination Multistatement-line and Continued-line Example |
|---|---|

IBM PC — Multistatement separator / Press <Ctrl><Enter>

170 IF SEX$ = "F"  THEN LET FSAL = FSAL + SAL  :  FCOUNT = FCOUNT + 1
    Continued line → ELSE LET MSAL = MSAL + SAL  :  MCOUNT = MCOUNT + 1

VAX-11 — Multistatement separator / Line continuation

170 IF SEX$ = "F"  THEN LET FSAL = FSAL + SAL  \  FCOUNT = FCOUNT + 1&
    Continued line → ELSE LET MSAL = MSAL + SAL  \  MCOUNT = MCOUNT + 1

Your system?

Equally desirable alternatives are illustrated next in Table 4.4.

## Multiline IF/THEN/ELSE Statements

Modern BASIC dialects directly implement generalized if-then-else structures, some of which are illustrated in Table 4.4. Find or fill in the one (if any) that's appropriate to your system.

**Table 4.4**  Selected Multiline If-then-else Structures

| Dialect | Structure | | Example | |
|---|---|---|---|---|
| ANS BASIC | *line no.* **IF** *condition* **THEN** | | 100 IF  SEX$ = "F" THEN | |
| | *line no.* | Group of statements executed if condition is true (then block) | 110<br>120 | LET FSAL     = FSAL + SAL<br>LET FCOUNT = FCOUNT + 1 |
| | *line no.* **ELSE** | | 130 ELSE | |
| | *line no.* | Group of statements executed if condition is false (else block) | 140<br>150 | LET MSAL     = MSAL + SAL<br>LET MCOUNT = MCOUNT + 1 |
| | *line no.* **END IF** | | 160 END IF | |
| | Note: Each statement has an associated line number. | | | |

(continued)

**Table 4.4**  Selected Multiline If-then-else Structures

| Dialect | Structure | Example |
|---|---|---|
| VAX-11 BASIC | *line no.***IF** *condition*  **THEN**<br>  Group of statements executed if condition is true (then block)<br>**ELSE**<br>  Group of statements executed if condition is false (else block)<br>**END IF**<br><br>Note: The IF statement has a line number, but the other statements do not. The VAX manual calls this "a block of program code." | 100 IF SEX\$ = "F" THEN<br>  LET FSAL  = FSAL + SAL<br>  LET FCOUNT = FCOUNT + 1<br>ELSE<br>  LET MSAL  = MSAL + SAL<br>  LET MCOUNT = MCOUNT + 1<br>END IF |
| Your system<br>(if different)* | | |

---

*****Note:** *If your system doesn't have a multiline if-then-else implementation, you must use one of the approaches illustrated in Examples 4.3, 4.4, and 4.5. Microsoft does not have a multiline if-then-else implementation.*

**NOTE 1**  Compare the if-then-else structure in Example 4.3b (page 115) or Example 4.5a (page 118) to the versions in Table 4.4. The if-then-else structure based on multiline IF/THEN/ELSE statements is clearly preferable to one-line implementations that use explicit line number transfers, for the following reasons:

**a.** The multiline version is easier to follow for us humans (it doesn't matter to the computer).

**b.** The multiline version completely avoids explicit line number transfers. Thus it's more reliable (less error-prone) than versions that explicitly use line number transfers or GO TO statements.

Multiline IF/THEN/ELSE statements are consistent with good programming style, since they reflect the "GO TO less" or "block programming" orientation of structured programs based on the well-defined control structures.

**NOTE 2**  The ELSE statement and else block are optional. For example, the ANS BASIC version

```
50  IF GPA >= 3.4 THEN
60    LET K = K + 1
70    PRINT N$, GPA
80  END IF
```

is stylistically preferable to both the traditional version in Example 4.3a (page 114) and the enhanced version in Example 4.4b (page 116).

---

## Follow-Up Exercises

**5.**  Try implementing an if-then structure for the GPA problem using the traditional approach in Example 4.3a. *Hint:* You need a GO TO statement.

6. How would you rewrite the age problem in Example 4.4a using the approach in Example 4.3?

7. **Multistatement Lines.** Rewrite the Female/Male illustration in Example 4.5a to eliminate line number transfers completely. Use a one-line IF/THEN/ELSE statement on a system that allows multistatement lines. Why is this approach better than the approach in Example 4.5a? Would you say this approach is just as good as the approaches in Table 4.4? Explain.

8. Indicate output from each program.

    **a.** 10 LET A$ = "123"
    20 LET B$ = "LOTUS"
    30 IF A$ < B$ THEN PRINT A$ ELSE PRINT B$
    99 END

    **b.** 10 LET X = 10
    20 LET Y = 5
    30 IF (X + Y/2) > 10 THEN PRINT "O.K."
    40 PRINT "BY ME"
    99 END

9. Code the given flowchart into a BASIC program using the following approaches:

    **a.** Traditional one-line IF/THEN statement
    **b.** Enhanced one-line IF/THEN statement
    **c.** One-line IF/THEN/ELSE statement
    **d.** Multiline IF/THEN/ELSE statements

    Run each version on your system (if possible) using the following earnings data: 25,900; 40,000; 20,000. Which approach is preferable and why?

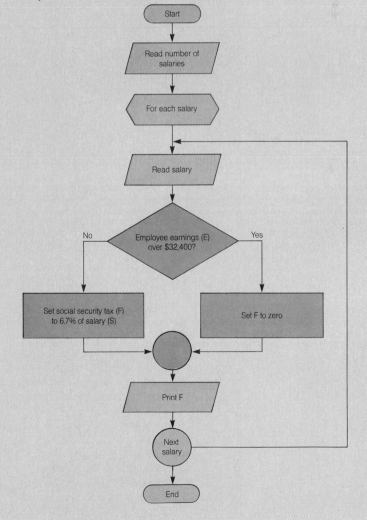

**10.** Code the given flowchart into a BASIC program using the following approaches:
   **a.** Traditional one-line IF/THEN statement
   **b.** Enhanced one-line IF/THEN statement
   **c.** One-line IF/THEN/ELSE statement
   **d.** Multiline IF/THEN/ELSE statements

   Run each version on your system (if possible) using the following data:
   2, 4, 6, 8, 10, 12. Which approach is preferable and why?

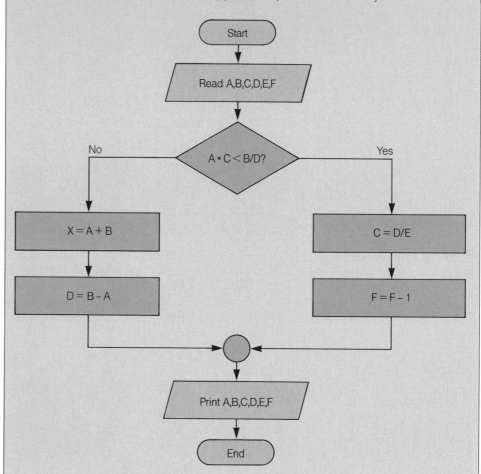

**11.** Write BASIC code for each of the pseudocode-like descriptions below. Use statements on your system that best represent good programming style.
   **a.** If sales for the week are above $10,000, add $150 to pay for the week; otherwise, go on to the next statement.
   **b.** If credits taken are 12 or more, then tuition is $1200; else, tuition is $100 times the number of credits.
   **c.** If part name equals "WRENCH", output the quantity on hand; otherwise, go on to the next statement.
   **d.** If fixed costs plus variable costs are less than sales revenue, then compute profit as sales revenue minus (fixed costs plus variable costs) and output the message PROFIT = ···; otherwise, compute loss as fixed plus variable costs minus sales revenue and output the message LOSS = ···.
   **e.** If M = N, then add 3 to *I*, 2 to *J*, and 1 to *K*; otherwise, go on to the next statement in the program.
   **\*f.** If the balance owed is under $50, the customer pays the full balance owed; else, the customer pays according to the formula $50 + 10% × (balance owed − $50). Compute and print the payment.
   **\*g.** If the response is YES, then conversationally input the date and flight number; else, continue with the next segment in the program.

Sample:

| | | |
|---|---|---|
| Flight information (YES/NO) | ? | YES |
| Enter date (month,day) | ? | 10,25 |
| Enter flight number | ? | 751 |

## E X A M P L E   4 . 6   Finding the Minimum Value

This example illustrates a common programming task: finding a minimum value.

### Analysis

The following sales order data are given:

| Customer Name | Quantity Ordered |
|---|---|
| Test 1 | 700 |
| Test 2 | 500 |
| Test 3 | 900 |
| Test 4 | 200 |
| Test 5 | 600 |

Write a general program that reads the data and prints the name of the customer who orders the least amount and the quantity ordered.

### Design

In our design we plan to use a FOR/NEXT loop to process the customer data; the body of the loop will include an if-then structure for recording a new minimum quantity and the corresponding customer's name.

Initialize minimum quantity
Read number of customers
For each customer
    Read name, quantity

    If quantity < minimum then record new minimum and note the associated name

Next customer
Print minimum and associated name
End

### Code/Test

The following program was run using the Microsoft BASIC interpreter on an IBM PC.

```
100 REM * * * * * * * * * * * * * * * * * * * * * * * * * *
110 REM *                                                 *
120 REM *     Minimum Value Program                       *
130 REM *                                                 *
140 REM *   Key:                                          *
150 REM *     N       = Number of orders                  *
160 REM *     C$      = Customer's name                   *
170 REM *     Q       = Quantity ordered                  *
180 REM *     MINQ    = Minimum quantity ordered          *
190 REM *     MINC$   = Customer with minimum order       *
200 REM *                                                 *
210 REM * * * * * * * * * * * * * * * * * * * * * * * * * *
220 REM---------------------------------------------------
230      LET MINQ = 10000
240 REM---------------------------------------------------
250      READ N
260      FOR J=1 TO N
270        READ C$,Q
280        IF Q < MINQ THEN LET MINQ = Q : LET MINC$ = C$
290      NEXT J
300 REM---------------------------------------------------
310      PRINT "Minimum quantity ordered   :"; MINQ
320      PRINT "Customer with minimum order: ";MINC$
330 REM---------------------------------------------------
900      DATA 5
901      DATA "Test 1",700
902      DATA "Test 2",500
903      DATA "Test 3",900
904      DATA "Test 4",200
905      DATA "Test 5",600
998 REM---------------------------------------------------
999      END


RUN
Minimum quantity ordered   : 200
Customer with minimum order: Test 4
```

Make sure you understand the logic in this program by working through Exercise 12.

---

**NOTE 1**　MINQ is initially set to a value that's much larger than any valid order quantity (10,000 in our example). This ensures that the first data item is a legitimate candidate for the minimum value.

**NOTE 2**　We use a multistatement line (line 280) by separating the two LET statements with a colon within the then block. Your system may use a symbol other than colon. If multistatement lines are not allowed on your system, then you could either use an else block as in Example 4.3 (which we try to avoid because of explicit line number transfers) or use two successive if-then structures as follows:

```
280 IF Q < MINQ THEN LET MINQ = Q
285 IF Q < MINQ THEN LET MINC$ = C$
```

## Follow-Up Exercises

**12.** In Example 4.6:
  **a.** Roleplay the sample run by indicating in the table below the values stored successively, where the "snapshot" of memory is taken at each loop iteration just before execution of the NEXT statement.

| N | J | C$ | Q | MINQ | MINC$ |
|---|---|----|---|------|-------|
|   | 1 |    |   |      |       |
|   | 2 |    |   |      |       |
|   | 3 |    |   |      |       |
|   | 4 |    |   |      |       |
|   | 5 |    |   |      |       |

   *b. Trace the sample values of J, C$, Q, MINQ, and MINC$ by placing an appropriate PRINT statement within the loop. Run this program on your system. (Don't bother typing in REMs for this exercise.) Try various runs with different values to make sure you understand the logic.

   *c. Rewrite Example 4.6 using the if-else structure of Example 4.3a. Why is the approach in Example 4.6 preferable to this approach?

**13.** In Example 4.6:

   a. Modify the program to also find and output the maximum order and its associated name.

   *b. Run and debug the revised program on your system. (Don't bother typing the REMs for this exercise.)

## 4.4 COMPOUND CONDITIONS BASED ON LOGICAL OPERATORS

Up to now we have tested simple conditions based on a single relational expression. In many applications it's best to combine two or more simple conditions into a compound condition. This is accomplished by using one or more of the logical operators AND, OR, and NOT to connect simple conditions according to the following scheme:

**Compound Condition**

| condition 1 | logical operator | condition 2 | logical operator | condition 3 . . . |
|-------------|------------------|-------------|------------------|-------------------|

Simple conditions based on relational expressions

As with simple conditions, the test of a compound condition yields a true or false result (logical value).

### Logical Operator AND

If all simple conditions are true within a compound condition with AND logical operators, then the compound condition itself tests true. If any condition is false, however, then the compound condition is false. For example, suppose we are looking for all females who are at least 40 years old. We might write the following compound condition:

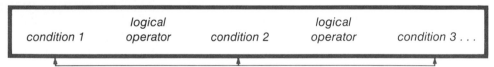

   SEX$ = "F"      AND      AGE >= 40

   condition 1    logical operator    condition 2

**Figure 4.2** Evaluation of compound conditions based on AND

| | Condition 1 Logical Value | | Logical Operator | Condition 2 Logical Value | Yields | Logical Value for Compound Condition |
|---|---|---|---|---|---|---|
| Case 1 | True | | AND | True | → | True |
| Case 2 | True | | AND | False | → | False |
| Case 3 | False | | AND | True | → | False |
| Case 4 | False | | AND | False | → | False |

Now suppose that condition 1 is true and condition 2 is true; that is, we have a person who is female and at least 40 years old. In this case the value of the compound condition is given by

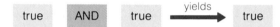

which gives the result true for the compound condition itself; however, if condition 1 is true but condition 2 is false (a female who is under 40), then we have

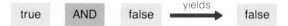

which gives the logical value false for the compound condition.

Figure 4.2 illustrates the four possible cases when two simple conditions are connected through the AND logical operator.

**E X A M P L E   4 . 7**   **Use of AND Logical Operator**

The following program prints the last name (L$), first name (F$), and age (AGE) of all female employees who are at least 40 years of age. Note how the two conditions based on gender and age are incorporated within a single IF/THEN statement through the AND operator.

```
10 READ N                          Compound condition with AND operator
15 FOR J=1 TO N
20   READ F$,L$,SEX$,AGE
25   IF SEX$ = "F" AND AGE >= 40 THEN PRINT L$,F$,AGE
40 NEXT J
90 DATA 3
91 DATA "Wendy","Brandon","F",29
92 DATA "Barbara","Lee","F",40
93 DATA "L. L.", "Bean","M",100
99 END

RUN
Lee            Barbara         40
```

## Logical Operator OR

If any condition is true in a compound condition with **OR** logical operators, then the compound condition tests true. However, if all of the simple conditions are false, then the compound condition is false.

For example, suppose an employer is interested in interviewing students with an economics (ECN) or mathematics (MTH) major. We could write the following compound condition

| MAJOR = "ECN" | OR | MAJOR = "MTH" |
|:---:|:---:|:---:|
| Condition 1 | Logical Operator | Condition 2 |

Suppose we have an economics major (that is, MAJOR stores ECN). In this case condition 1 tests true, and condition 2 is false. Thus the compound condition given by

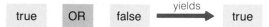

true    OR    false    yields    true

yields a true result.

Figure 4.3 illustrates the four cases for compound conditions based on OR.

**Figure 4.3**   Evaluation of compound conditions based on OR

| Condition 1 Logical Value | | Logical Operator | Condition 2 Logical Value | Yields | Logical Value for Compound Condition |
|---|---|:---:|---|:---:|---|
| Case 1 | True | OR | True | → | True |
| Case 2 | True | OR | False | → | True |
| Case 3 | False | OR | True | → | True |
| Case 4 | False | OR | False | → | False |

**E X A M P L E   4 . 8**   Use of OR Logical Operator

Suppose we wish to ask the user interactively, "Do you want the forecast" and if the response is Y or YES or YEP (let's assume upper case entries for simplicity), then we calculate and print a sales forecast. Using simple conditions we might proceed as follows:

```
100 READ S,G
110    DATA 1000,5
120 PRINT "Sales   = $"; S; "   Growth ="; G; "%"
130 PRINT TAB(35);"Do you want the forecast";
140 INPUT R$
150 IF R$ = "Y"   THEN PRINT "Forecast = $"; S*(1 + G/100)
160 IF R$ = "YES" THEN PRINT "Forecast = $"; S*(1 + G/100)
170 IF R$ = "YEP" THEN PRINT "Forecast = $"; S*(1 + G/100)
999 END
```
↑ Using sequence of three IF-THEN structures, each with a simple condition

More easily, we could write:

```
100 READ S,G
110    DATA 1000,5
120 PRINT "Sales   = $"; S; "   Growth ="; G; "%"
130 PRINT TAB(35);"Do you want the forecast";
140 INPUT R$
150 IF R$="Y" OR R$="YES" OR R$="YEP" THEN PRINT "Forecast = $"; S*(1 + G/100)
999 END
```
└ Using one IF-THEN structure with a compound condition based on OR logical operators

```
RUN
Sales      = $ 1000      Growth = 5 %
                                     Do you want the forecast? Y
Forecast = $ 1050


RUN
Sales      = $ 1000      Growth = 5 %
                                     Do you want the forecast? YES
Forecast = $ 1050


RUN
Sales      = $ 1000      Growth = 5 %
                                     Do you want the forecast? YEP
Forecast = $ 1050


RUN
Sales      = $ 1000      Growth = 5 %
                                     Do you want the forecast? N
```

Thus the use of a compound condition replaces the inefficiency of three successive if-then structures with a single if-then structure.[3]

## Logical Operator NOT

The logical operator NOT reverses the logical value of the condition on which it operates. For example, suppose we are looking for all persons 18 and under based on the test

    NOT   AGE > 18

Suppose AGE stores 21. Then the condition is evaluated according to

$$\text{NOT}\quad \underset{\substack{\uparrow\\ 21 > 18 \text{ tests true}}}{\text{true}} \quad \xrightarrow{\text{yields}} \quad \underset{\substack{\uparrow\\ \text{NOT changes true to false}}}{\text{false}}$$

On the other hand, if a person is 16, then the condition is evaluated as true according to the following:

$$\text{NOT}\quad \underset{\substack{\uparrow\\ 16 > 18 \text{ tests false}}}{\text{false}} \quad \xrightarrow{\text{yields}} \quad \underset{\substack{\uparrow\\ \text{NOT changes false to true}}}{\text{true}}$$

Figure 4.4 illustrates the general cases for evaluations based on NOT. Do you find the use of NOT unnecessarily confusing? If so, we agree with you. The logical operator NOT should be used only under special conditions, as we shall illustrate in the next chapter under the topic eof loops.

**Figure 4.4**    Evaluation of conditions based on NOT

| | Logical Operator | Condition Logical Value | Yields | Logical Value |
|---|---|---|---|---|
| Case 1 | NOT | True | | False |
| Case 2 | NOT | False | | True |

[3]In Module F we illustrate a much better method of processing YES/NO input responses.

## Hierarchy Rules

To represent more than two simple conditions we can use more than one logical operator within a compound condition. In this case there is a hierarchy among the logical operators that determines the order in which the operators are evaluated, unless the order is changed by using parentheses. Logical operators are evaluated according to the following hierarchy.

| Operator | Order |
|----------|-------|
| NOT | Highest priority |
| AND | ↓ |
| OR | Lowest priority |

**E X A M P L E   4 . 9**   **Hierarchy Rules and Use of Parentheses**

If the following values are stored,

then the compound condition in

    100 IF I = J OR I > K AND A <= 5.1 THEN LET S = S + A
    110 ...
       .
       .
       .

is true, and the then block

    LET S = S + A

is executed. This compound condition is evaluated in the following manner.

1. According to the hierarchy, AND is evaluated before OR, which means that we should focus on the shaded portion below.

   I = J OR    I > K AND A <= 5.1
                 ↓
               3 >= 5 AND 6 <= 5.1
                 ↓
               false AND false
                 ↓
               false

2. We are now left with

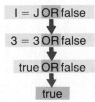

   I = J OR false
      ↓
   3 = 3 OR false
      ↓
   true OR false
      ↓
   true

Thus the compound condition itself has the value true.

*As in arithmetic expressions, parentheses can be used to modify the order of evaluation within compound conditions.* For example, if we assume the same values for I, J, K, and A, the compound condition in

100 IF   (I = J OR I > K) AND A <= 5.1 THEN LET S = S + A

110 . . .

.
.
.

is false and control goes directly to line 110 without executing the then block. Now the expression is evaluated in the following manner.

1.  Expressions enclosed within parentheses are evaluated before expressions not enclosed within parentheses. Thus the shaded portion below is evaluated first as true.

2.  We are now left with

The compound condition, therefore, is false.

*Improving readability is an alternative use of parentheses within compound conditions,* as it is in arithmetic expressions. For instance, the clarity of the original compound condition in this example can be improved as follows.

100 IF (I = J)   OR   (I > K   AND   A <= 5.1)   THEN   LET S = S + A

The value of this compound condition is true, as before; however, it is now quite clear that the operator AND is considered before the operator OR, since AND is within parentheses.

---

## Follow-Up Exercises

**14.**   Prepare a flowchart for
   **a.**   Example 4.7
   **b.**   Example 4.8

**15.**   Indicate what (if anything) is wrong for each of the following.
   **a.**   IF V > 100 AND < 200 THEN LET S = S + V
   **b.**   IF MAJOR$ = "ECN" OR "MATH" THEN PRINT N$
   **c.**   IF (A = B AND (C = D OR L < M)) THEN PRINT "Oh no!"

**16.**   Given the stored values

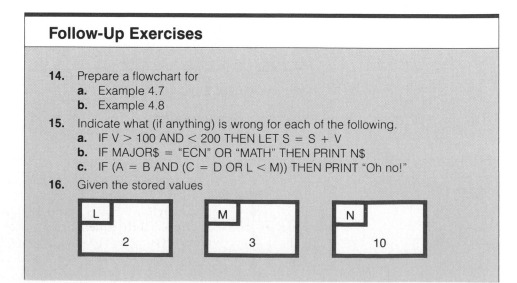

indicate whether or not the then block is executed for each of the following.
   **a.**  IF NOT (L < M) THEN . . .
   **b.**  IF L > M AND  M = N OR L <= N  AND M < 4 THEN . . .
   **c.**  IF L > M AND (M = N OR L <= N) AND M < 4 THEN . . .

**17.**  Develop BASIC code, given the following pseudocode. Use only compound conditions.
   **a.**  IF 0 < grade < 100 then print grade
                         else print "Grade out of range"
   **b.**  If gender is not equal to F or M then print "Error in gender data"
   **\*c.**  If the response is not Y or y or YES or yes
                         or N or n or NO or no
                         then print "Incorrect response. Try again."

**\*18.**  Write a short program to process the given data. Use only compound conditions.
   **a.**  Print the number of females who earn $10,000 or more.

| Income | Sex |
|--------|-----|
| 9,000 | F |
| 12,000 | M |
| 15,000 | F |
| 25,000 | F |
| 10,000 | F |

   **b.**  Print the ID of those who either earn below $5,000 or are at least 65 years old.

| Income | Age | ID |
|--------|-----|-----|
| 25,000 | 25 | 1 |
| 10,000 | 70 | 2 |
| 4,000 | 67 | 3 |
| 4,500 | 60 | 4 |
| 5,000 | 62 | 5 |

## 4.5 TOP-DOWN DESIGN AND STEPWISE REFINEMENT

Recent programming trends indicate a growing use of certain design techniques that are collectively called top-down design. This section motivates and illustrates the top-down philosophy.

### Motivation

The term **top-down design** refers to a process for simplifying and systematizing the design and development of complex programs. Strictly speaking, it is not a specific technique, but rather a philosophy that translates into a personalized process for writing programs. As such, the manner of implementing top-down design will vary from programmer to programmer or organization to organization.

Top-down design starts with an overall look at the entire problem, that is, a look from the "top." Subsequently, the problem is refined further by working "down" through successive levels of greater detail. To illustrate what we mean, consider the process of writing a textbook. First we decide the topic of the book. This is the least level of detail and the highest level of abstraction.

Then we write the titles of chapters, the next level of detail. Next we specify the main headings in each chapter, a further refinement in the level of detail. Next we state the subheadings under each main heading, and finally, we provide the greatest level of detail: each word in the body of the text.

The *implementation* of top-down design at either the design or the programming stage is often carried out by a process called **stepwise refinement,** which is an iterative (stepwise) procedure that successively refines the problem at each step. In other words, stepwise refinement is a step-by-step process that continually expands or refines the flowchart, pseudocode, or program, starting at a low level of detail and working toward a high level of detail.

As with the structured programming and other programming style guidelines, top-down design is an effort to control exploding software costs by promoting better organization and development of complex programs. In effect, top-down techniques result in lower costs for program development, debugging, and maintenance and increase program reliability.

## Illustration: Government Printing Office Orders

Let's design, write, and implement a simplified program that prints billing information for publications produced by the Government Printing Office. Stepwise refinement is illustrated under Design following Analysis of the problem.

**Analysis.**     This program determines the charge for an order of publications, prints the charge together with other data regarding the order, and finally prints summary statistics once all orders are processed. The basic charge is the unit price of the publication multiplied by the quantity ordered. This basic charge is then modified to include a 10% discount for orders between 50 and 100 copies of a single publication and a 25% discount if more than 100 copies are ordered. In addition, a surcharge of 25% is added to any order mailed to a non-U.S. address.

The data obtained from the order blank include (1) customer name, (2) customer address, (3) whether or not from a foreign country, (4) title of publication, (5) unit price of publication, and (6) quantity ordered.

At the end of each day a report is printed that lists the individual orders. In addition, a summary of the day's activities is printed that includes (1) number of orders for the day, (2) average quantity ordered, and (3) total amount billed for the day.

a. *Output data*
   For each customer:
   1. Customer name
   2. Customer address
   3. Title of publication
   4. Quantity ordered
   5. Charge for an order
   Summary:
   6. Number of orders
   7. Average quantity ordered
   8. Total amount billed (sum of all charges)
b. *Input data*
   1. Number of orders
   2. Customer name
   3. Customer address
   4. Foreign country, yes or no

    **5.** Title of publication
    **6.** Unit price of publication
    **7.** Quantity ordered
**c.** *Computations*
    **1.** Charge = unit price × quantity ordered
    **2.** Discount according to the following schedule

| Size of Order | Percent Discount |
|---|---|
| 49 or less | 0 |
| 50–99 | 10 |
| 100 or more | 25 |

    **3.** Surcharge of 25% if mailed to foreign address, after any discount. For example, consider an order quantity of 80 at a unit price of $8 per publication. The undiscounted charge would be $640 (or 8 × 80). Applying a 10% discount reduces the charge to $576 (or 0.90 × 640). If the order were foreign, then a 25% surcharge would increase the charge to $720 (or 1.25 × 576).

**Design.**    We now illustrate stepwise refinement, first through flowcharts and then through pseudocode. Figure 4.5 is an example of stepwise refinement through the "explosion" of flowcharts. Step 1, the first level of detail, describes the nature of the program. Step 2, the next level of refinement, divides the program's tasks into three segments: initial tasks, order processing, and concluding tasks. Step 3 provides a greater level of detail for each segment in Step 2. Note that the task *process order* is actually a FOR/NEXT loop. Step 4 further elaborates Step 3 by specifying the nature of the charge and identifying the specific variables to be accumulated. Finally, Step 5 gives the nitty gritty of the discount and surcharge logic, based on decision structures in this chapter.

    Figure 4.6 illustrates the same procedure by exploding the pseudocode. The flowchart and pseudocode approaches are essentially equivalent, although flowcharts are more tedious and more difficult to modify than pseudocode. In practice only one of the two is needed, according to the preference of the programmer or the organization.

    Regardless of which approach you might prefer, you should note that each iteration (or level) in stepwise refinement describes the logic of the problem in greater detail. This process of starting with the big picture followed by progressive fine tuning is conceptually appealing and consistent with the way the human mind most effectively solves complex problems.

    You should also remember that the specifics for each step in stepwise refinement are apt to vary from programmer to programmer. We ask you to consider variations of Figures 4.5 and 4.6 in Exercises 19 and 20.

    As your algorithms become more elaborate, particularly beginning with some of the problems at the end of this chapter, we advise that you practice stepwise refinement as a means of programming more effectively.[4]

**Code.**    BASIC code readily follows from either the flowchart or pseudocode version in Figures 4.5 and 4.6 as illustrated in Figure 4.7. You should confirm that the code is consistent with the flowchart and pseudocode versions.

---

[4]The explosion process takes up a lot of room, so we suggest you use printer paper. Try using the back of discarded paper, which then gives you claim to being an ecologically conscious programmer.

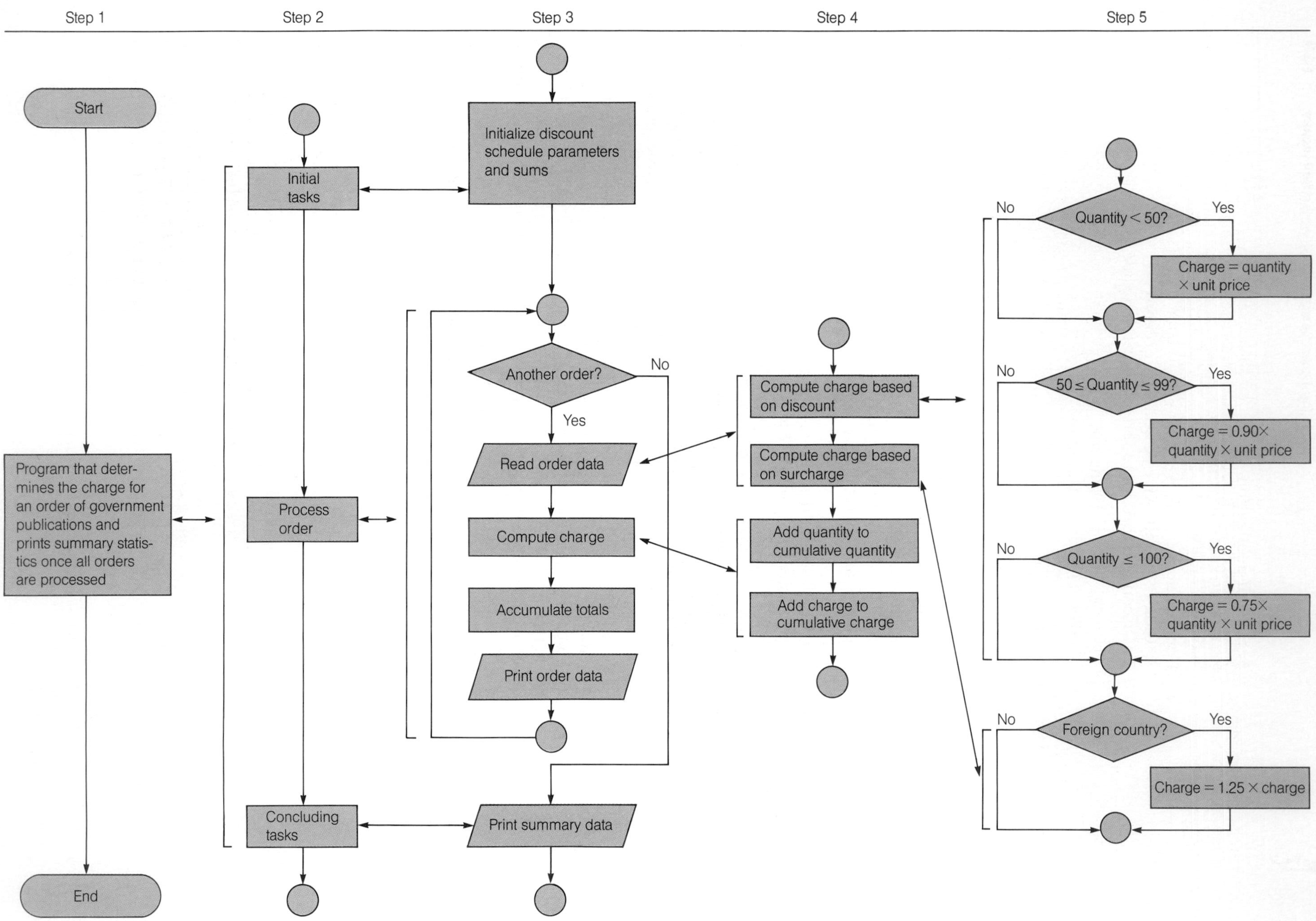

**Figure 4.5** Stepwise refinement by exploding flowcharts

**Figure 4.6** Stepwise refinement by exploding the pseudocode

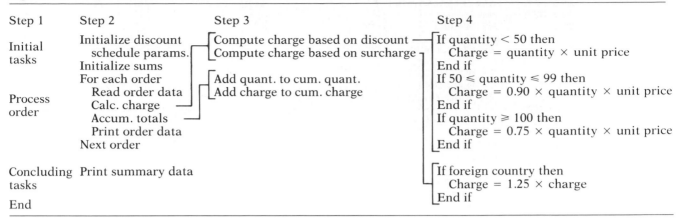

| Step 1 | Step 2 | Step 3 | Step 4 |
|--------|--------|--------|--------|

Step 1: Initial tasks / Process order / Concluding tasks / End

Step 2: Initialize discount schedule params. / Initialize sums / For each order / Read order data / Calc. charge / Accum. totals / Print order data / Next order / Print summary data

Step 3: Compute charge based on discount / Compute charge based on surcharge / Add quant. to cum. quant. / Add charge to cum. charge

Step 4:
If quantity < 50 then
    Charge = quantity × unit price
End if
If 50 ≤ quantity ≤ 99 then
    Charge = 0.90 × quantity × unit price
End if
If quantity ≥ 100 then
    Charge = 0.75 × quantity × unit price
End if

If foreign country then
    Charge = 1.25 × charge
End if

**Figure 4.7** BASIC code for Government Printing Office program

```
100 REM * * * * * * * * * * * * * * * * * * * * * * * * * * * * * * *
105 REM *                                                           *
110 REM * Government Printing Office Program          Version 1.2   *
115 REM *                                             January, 198x *
120 REM * R. Ageloff/R. Mojena                                      *
125 REM * University of Rhode Island                                *
130 REM *                                                           *
135 REM * * * * * * * * * * * * * * * * * * * * * * * * * * * * * * *
140 REM *                                                           *
145 REM * This program processes orders for publications.  It reads order *
150 REM * data, calculates the charge, and prints selected order information *
155 REM * for each order.  It prints summaries once all orders are processed. *
160 REM *                                                           *
165 REM * Output per order:                                         *
170 REM *    Customer name, address, publication title, order quantity, charge *
175 REM * Output per run:                                           *
180 REM *    Number of orders, average quantity ordered, total amount billed *
185 REM * Input:                                                    *
190 REM *    Number of orders, customer name, address, foreign (YES/NO), *
195 REM *    publication title, unit price, order quantity          *
200 REM * Parameters:                                               *
205 REM *    Discount schedule breaks and discounts, surcharge      *
210 REM *                                                           *
215 REM * * * * * * * * * * * * * * * * * * * * * * * * * * * * * * *
220 REM *                                                           *
225 REM * Key:                                      Discount Schedule *
230 REM *    N         = Number of orders              Parameters    *
235 REM *    CNAME$    = Customer name                                *
240 REM *    ADDRESS$  = Customer address           BREAK1    (=  50) *
245 REM *    FOREIGN$  = YES if foreign order       BREAK2    (= 100) *
250 REM *    TITLE$    = Title of publication       DISCOUNT1 (=0.10) *
255 REM *    PRICE     = Unit price of publication  DISCOUNT2 (=0.25) *
260 REM *    QUANTITY  = Quantity ordered                            *
265 REM *    CHARGE    = Charge for an order        Foreign Surcharge *
270 REM *    SUMQUANT  = Sum of quantities ordered                   *
275 REM *    SUMCHARGE = Sum of all charges         SURCHARGE (=0.25) *
280 REM *                                                           *
285 REM * * * * * * * * * * * * * * * * * * * * * * * * * * * * * * *
```

(Continued)

```
290 REM-----------------------------------------------------------------------
295 REM    Initializations
300 REM-------------------
305       LET BREAK1     =    50
310       LET BREAK2     =   100
315       LET DISCOUNT1 = 9.999999E-02   ◄─── This is the way our system represents 0.10
320       LET DISCOUNT2 = .25
325       LET SURCHARGE = .25
330       LET SUMQUANT  =    0
335       LET SUMCHARGE =    0
340 REM-----------------------------------------------------------------------
345 REM   Process orders
350 REM-------------------
355       READ N
360       FOR J=1 TO N
365 REM
370 REM    Read order data
375 REM    ---------------
380       READ CNAME$,ADDRESS$,FOREIGN$,TITLE$,PRICE,QUANTITY
385 REM
390 REM    Discount logic                    ┌── These lines are longer than 80 characters
395 REM    ---------------                   │
400       IF QUANTITY < BREAK1          ◄────┘
             THEN LET CHARGE = QUANTITY * PRICE
405       IF QUANTITY >= BREAK1   AND   QUANTITY < BREAK2
             THEN LET CHARGE = (1 - DISCOUNT1) * QUANTITY * PRICE
410       IF QUANTITY >= BREAK2
             THEN LET CHARGE = (1 - DISCOUNT2) * QUANTITY * PRICE
415 REM
420 REM    Surcharge logic
425 REM    ---------------
430       IF FOREIGN$ = "YES"
             THEN LET CHARGE = (1 + SURCHARGE) * CHARGE
435 REM
440 REM    Accumulate sums
445 REM    ---------------
450       LET SUMQUANT  = SUMQUANT  + QUANTITY
455       LET SUMCHARGE = SUMCHARGE + CHARGE
460 REM
465 REM    Print order data
470 REM    ---------------
475       PRINT "Name.......... "; CNAME$
480       PRINT "Address...... "; ADDRESS$
485       PRINT "Title........ "; TITLE$
490       PRINT "Quantity....." ; QUANTITY
495       PRINT "Charge................... $"; INT(CHARGE*100 + .5)/100
500       PRINT "--------------------------------------------
505 REM                                  ▲── Note use of INT function for dollar/cents
510       NEXT J                              rounding (see Module C)
515 REM-----------------------------------------------------------------------
520 REM   Concluding tasks
525 REM-------------------
530       PRINT
535       PRINT
540       PRINT "                    SUMMARY"
545       PRINT "* * * * * * * * * * * * * * * * * * * * * * * * * * *"
550       PRINT "*                                                   *"
555       PRINT "*   Number of Orders      Average Order Size    Total Billed *"
560       PRINT "*                                                   *"
565       PRINT "*           "; N,"            "; INT(SUMQUANT/N),
                        "        "; INT(SUMCHARGE*100 + .5)/100; "        *"
570       PRINT "* * * * * * * * * * * * * * * * * * * * * * * * * * *"
575 REM-----------------------------------------------------------------------
900       DATA 4
901       DATA "Adam Smith","Wall Street, NY","NO","Wealth of Nations",10,40
902       DATA "Red Brigade","Somewhere in Italy","YES","CIA Tactics",10,40
903       DATA "J. Appleseed","U. S. of A.","NO","Planting Trees",8,80
904       DATA "Benedict Arnold","West Point","NO","Devil Made Me Do It",1,500
998 REM-----------------------------------------------------------------------
999       END
```

```
Name........ Adam Smith
Address...... Wall Street, NY
Title........ Wealth of Nations
Quantity..... 40
Charge................... $ 400
------------------------------------------
Name........ Red Brigade
Address...... Somewhere in Italy
Title........ CIA Tactics
Quantity..... 40
Charge................... $ 500
------------------------------------------
Name........ J. Appleseed
Address...... U. S. of A.
Title........ Planting Trees
Quantity..... 80
Charge................... $ 576
------------------------------------------
Name........ Benedict Arnold
Address...... West Point
Title........ Devil Made Me Do It
Quantity..... 500
Charge................... $ 375
------------------------------------------
```

```
                    SUMMARY
* * * * * * * * * * * * * * * * * * * * * * * * * * *
*                                                   *
*  Number of Orders    Average Order Size   Total Billed *
*                                                   *
*        4                   165                1851     *
* * * * * * * * * * * * * * * * * * * * * * * * * * *
```

**Figure 4.8**  Test output for Government Printing Office program

**Test.**     Running the program in Figure 4.7 on an IBM PC gave the results in Figure 4.8. You should confirm that the output is correct by roleplaying the computer. Then try solving the Follow-Up Exercises.

## Loose Ends

In this section we shall tie up some loose ends by relating top-down design to structured programming and our four-step software development cycle.

**Top-Down Structured Programming.**     You should realize that structured programming is related to the stepwise refinement process in top-down design. The design illustrated in Figures 4.5 and 4.6 begins with a sequence structure and successively builds into the design additional sequence, loop, and decision structures. This approach to designing programs is often called **top-down structured programming.** Moreover, the execution of structured programs proceeds from the top to the bottom; that is, transfers of control to upper parts of the program are not possible (except for the loop structure, of course).
    Also note that execution enters each control structure from the top and exits from the bottom, which is clearly evident from the diagrams in Sections 3.1 to 3.3, pages 73–77.

**Top-Down Design and the Program Development Cycle.**     The four-step procedure introduced in Chapter 1 and used in the Government Printing Office illustration in this section (Analysis, Design, Code, Test) also utilizes top-down design ideas. The problem analysis in Step 1 is the first level of detail. Once the nature of the problem is fully defined, the process can be refined further by working down through successive levels of greater detail. The specification of the design through exploded flowcharts or pseudocode in Step 2 is the next level of detail. Step 3, specification of code, is a further refinement of the flowchart and pseudocode versions. Finally, the debugging process in Step 4 is the final level of detail.

---

### Follow-Up Exercises

19. Discuss how the process in Figures 4.5 and 4.6 might explode differently. In other words, can you think of legitimate variations in these explosions that still would be consistent with the program in Figure 4.7?

20. An alternative to the explosion scheme in Figure 4.6 is to label each task in the first step as 1, 2,..., *n*, where *n* is the number of tasks in the first step (4 in Figure 4.6); thus in place of Figure 4.6 we would write

    **1.** Initial tasks
    **2.** Process order
    **3.** Concluding tasks
    **4.** End

    Successive refinements then build on this numbering scheme by adding further digits. For example, item 1 is further refined by

    **1.1** Initialize discount schedule parameters
    **1.2** Initialize sums

    Complete this stepwise refinement scheme for the problem illustrated in Figure 4.6. Which approach do you prefer?

21. Indicate modifications to the program in Figure 4.7 as follows.
    **a.** The discount parameters change from 0.1 and 0.25 to 0.05 and 0.10, respectively. Why did we use variable names instead of constants for these parameters?
    **\*b.** Changes might either be necessary for your system or might be desirable. For example, how would you continue lines 400–410 on your system? How would you make the initializations more efficient with respect to lines of code? How might you design the output based on PRINT USING statements for your system (Module D)?

22. **Error Routine.** Let's check for correct (YES or NO) data values for foreign orders. If an incorrect response is detected, then print the error message "Incorrect YES/NO entry" just before the line that prints the customer's name and set a default value of zero for quantity.
    **a.** Modify the pseudocode in Figure 4.6.
    **\*b.** Modify the program in Figure 4.7.

**\*23.** Modify Figures 4.6 and 4.7 to include the fact that a given order can include more than one publication. For example, one order might include a quantity of 10 for a first title, 700 for a second title, and 200 for a third title.

---

## 4.6 POINTERS

The following design/style and common error pointers relate to the topics in this chapter.

### Design and Style

**1. Avoid explicit line number transfers.**    For example, try not to use statements such as

100 IF A < B THEN 150 ELSE 200

or

175 GO TO 300

This makes programs more difficult to follow, more costly to modify, and error prone with respect to unintended line number transfers.

**2. Keep on spacing.**     Indent the statements within then and else blocks. It helps to identify them. Also, use spacing (as always) to improve readability. For example, use spaces around relational and logical operators. The version

A*B  > = C  AND  A*B < = D

is more readable than

A*B> = CANDA*B< = D

Moreover, the latter version will likely cause a logic or syntax error, since the logical operator AND gets lost within CANDA.

**3. Compound conditions.**     Use compound conditions in place of multiple simple conditions to improve readability and coding efficiency, because this avoids multiple statements. Example 4.8 on page 127 is an illustration of this point.

**4. Nothing but the best.**     The best decision structure implementations are given by the choices below, none of which uses explicit line number transfers. Use only these choices if they're available on your system.

a.  **Multiline IF/THEN/ELSE.**

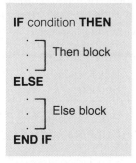

```
IF condition THEN
    .  ┐
    .  │  Then block
    .  ┘
ELSE
    .  ┐
    .  │  Else block
    .  ┘
END IF
```

This shows the ANS BASIC version, which is our preferred version. Use this for if-then-else structures that have more than one statement within the then and else blocks.

b.  **Multiline IF/THEN.**

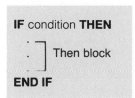

```
IF condition THEN
    .  ┐
    .  │  Then block
    .  ┘
END IF
```

This is simply a special case of the if-then-else structure with the else clause removed. Use this for an if-then structure that has more than one statement within the then block.

c. **Single-line IF/THEN/ELSE.**

> **IF** condition **THEN** statement **ELSE** statement

Use this when then and else blocks have single statements.

d. **Single-line IF/THEN.**

> **IF** condition **THEN** statement

Again, this is a special case of the if-then-else structure with no else clause. Use this for an if-then structure with just one statement in the then block.

**5. Think of control structures as building blocks.** Visualize the decision structure as a program building block that has a single entry point at the top and a single exit point at the bottom. This is consistent with both top-down and structured programming philosophies. You can't go wrong here if you use the implementations in item 4 above. Indeed, modern BASIC dialects use these implementations for precisely that reason. We tend to get in trouble when we use GO TO statements, since it's easy then to violate the single entry and single exit building-block concept. Never use a GO TO statement within the blocks of the implementations shown in item 4 above!

**6. Design of programming tasks as control structures.** Now that programs are getting more complex, spend more time on problem analysis and design before you start coding in BASIC. Always keep the sequence, decision, and loop control structures in mind, since these are the building blocks that represent programming tasks. For each programming task, decide which control structure will accomplish the task. Then build your design accordingly. For example, the overall building-block structure for the program in Figure 4.7 breaks down as follows:

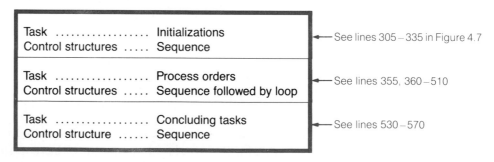

| Task ................. Initializations | See lines 305 – 335 in Figure 4.7 |
| Control structures ..... Sequence | |
| Task .................. Process orders | See lines 355, 360 – 510 |
| Control structures ..... Sequence followed by loop | |
| Task .................. Concluding tasks | See lines 530 – 570 |
| Control structure ...... Sequence | |

Within the loop body we have the following stepwise refinement:

| | |
|---|---|
| Task ................ Read order data<br>Control structure ...... Sequence | ←— See line 380 |
| Task ................ Discount logic<br>Control structures ..... Sequence of if-thens | ←— See lines 400–410 |
| Task ................ Surcharge logic<br>Control structure ...... if-then | ←— See line 430 |
| Task ................ Accumulate sum<br>Control structure ...... Sequence | ←— See lines 450–455 |
| Task ................ Print order<br>Control structure ...... Sequence | ←— See lines 475–500 |

Next we write pseudocode for each of these tasks. As you write pseudocode, don't get bogged down by the details of a complicated task. Instead, refine that task in a later step, as in Figure 4.6. Not until you're satisfied with the pseudocode version should you begin the BASIC version.

## Common Errors

**1. Explicit line transfer errors.** Here are two more reasons to avoid explicit line number transfers:

**a. Nonexistent line numbers.** A common syntax error that's fatal is to transfer control to a nonexistent line number, as when we have

```
50 GO TO 110
```

and line 110 is missing. This is an easy error to make in long programs with many transfers, particularly if you've been renumbering many lines while setting the code down on paper. For this type of error you might get an error message such as UNDEFINED LINE NUMBER.

**b. Transfer to wrong line number.** This logic error is common when we set down a long code on paper and subsequently make a series of line changes, insertions, and deletions. Make it a habit to give your program a final check to make sure your transfers are to the intended statements. Better yet, avoid GOTOs altogether if you're using a modern BASIC dialect that includes statements for directly implementing control structures.

**2. Boundary values and relational operators.** Be careful with boundary values when selecting a relational operator. For example, if we are to print the names of people who are *55 or above*, we would use

```
IF AGE  > = 55  THEN PRINT N$
```

However, if the condition reads *above 55*, we would use

```
IF AGE  > 55  THEN PRINT N$
```

In other words, pay attention to the selection of $>$ versus $> =$ and $<$ versus $< =$ operators. It's a common error to get incorrect transfers at or near boundary values such as 55 in the example above.

**3. Test data selection.** When debugging your program, consciously select test data that ensure execution flows through all decision blocks (then and else blocks) in your program. This guarantees that all segments of the program are tested. It's also a good idea to test at the boundary values (see item 2 above).

**4. Incomplete relational expressions.** Do you see what's wrong with the following?

IF ▢ K ▢ > J AND ▢ < L THEN ...
                           └── Missing K

The relational expression on the right is incomplete. We tend to make this error because of the way we would state this decision verbally: "If K is greater than J and less than L." To avoid a syntax error it must be written as follows.

IF ▢ K ▢ > J AND ▢ K ▢ < L THEN ...
                              └──K must be repeated

**5. Inattention to hierarchy rules.** Pay attention to hierarchy when using more than one logical operator. Reread Example 4.9 and make sure you understand the answers to Exercise 16.

**6. Decimal values and the = operator.** Take care in using the relational operator = when comparing real or decimal (as opposed to integer) values. Remember that the computer stores values as binary numbers; hence, many decimal numbers are stored as approximate rather than exact values.

To illustrate consider the following:

```
10 READ   A, B, C
15    DATA 9,.31,9.31
20 IF A + B = C THEN PRINT "Equal" ELSE PRINT "Unequal"
99 END

RUN
Unequal ←────── Unequal printed instead of Equal
```

Supposedly, A stores 9, B stores 0.31, and C stores 9.31, so that A + B = C should give the result *equal*. The inexact representation of real values, however, causes an *unequal* result.

The following version takes care of the problem:

```
10 READ   A, B, C
15    DATA 9,.31,9.31
20 IF ABS(A + B - C) < .00001 THEN PRINT "Equal" ELSE PRINT
   "Unequal"
99 END

RUN
Equal ←────── Correct result
```

In this case we restate the condition, from "Is A + B = C?" to "Is the absolute difference between A + B and C less than the *error tolerance* 0.00001?" (See Module C for the ABS function.) We now get the correct result.

Again, this is not a problem for integer (whole number) values. It's only a problem for certain real values. You might want to try these two programs on your system, with variations in the line 15 data values.

## ADDITIONAL EXERCISES

**24.** Define or explain the following:

| | | |
|---|---|---|
| selection structure | relational operators | multistatement lines |
| decision structure | collating sequence | simple vs. compound conditions |
| if-then-else structure | ASCII codes | logical operators |
| if-else structure | traditional one-line IF/THEN statement | top-down design |
| if-then structure | enhanced one-line IF/THEN statement | stepwise refinement |
| then block | one-line IF/THEN/ELSE statements | top-down structured programming |
| else block | multiline IF/THEN/ELSE statements | |
| relational expression | line continuation | |

**25. Revisits.** Modify one of the problems from Chapter 3 as indicated below.

  **a. Individual Retirement Account.** (Exercise 21, page 104.) Have the program check that the contribution does not exceed a maximum of $2000. If it does, print an error message to that effect and set the contribution to $2000.

  **b. Depreciation.** (Exercise 24, page 105.) Have the program check that the salvage value does not exceed the cost of the asset. If it does, print an error message to that effect and set the salvage value equal to the cost.

  **c. Exponential Cumulative Distribution Function.** (Exercise 25, page 105.) Use compound conditions to ensure that the limit exceeds the initial value whenever the increment is positive and that the limit is less than the initial value whenever the increment is negative. If either condition is violated, print an error message to that effect and set the limit equal to the initial value.

  **d. Mortgage Payments.** (Exercise 26, page 106.) Use compound conditions to ensure that the limit exceeds the initial value whenever the increment is positive and that the limit is less than the initial value whenever the increment is negative. If either condition is violated, print an error message to that effect and set the limit equal to the initial value.

**26. Parking Garage.** A parking garage has the following fees schedule:

- UNDER 3 HOURS      $2.75
- ADDITIONAL HOURS    $ .75 per hour

  **a.** Develop an interactive program whereby the parking attendant inputs the number of hours parked, and the computer outputs the charge. Process the following hourly data: 2, 3, 3.5, 5, and 36. Note: Any part of an hour counts as an entire hour. Hint: Look up the INT function in Module C.

  **b.** Build in a maximum charge of $9.00 per day.

**27. Payroll.** Consider the calculation of gross pay for hourly workers. The following test data for three workers is collected.

| Name | ID | Hourly Rate | Hours Worked |
|---|---|---|---|
| Lila | 101 | 5.50 | 35 |
| Max | 102 | 3.75 | 45 |
| Pat | 103 | 4.65 | 20 |

Gross pay is the product of hours worked and hourly pay rate. When an employee has worked over 40 hours, however, overtime is computed at time-and-a-half for all hours above 40.

  **a.** Develop a program that processes the employee data as an internal data file and prints a report table with the following column headings: Employee Name, ID, Regular Pay, Overtime Pay, and Gross Pay. Also print individual totals for regular pay, overtime pay, and gross pay.

  **b.** Include the following deductions:
- Social security is 6.85% of gross pay.
- If gross pay is less than $100, union dues are $2.00 per week; otherwise they are $4.00 per week.

This means you have to add the following three columns to the table in part **a**: SS Deduction, Union Dues, and Net Pay.

**28. Alumni File.** The Director of an MBA program wants to compute average salaries of alumni to include in a brochure of past graduates. The director collected the following data on students: name, year graduated salary on first job after graduation, and prior work experience (y or n).

Alumni File

| Name | Year of Graduation | Salary | Work Experience |
|---|---|---|---|
| Dewey | 84 | 29000 | y |
| Epcot | 85 | 43000 | y |
| Farmer | 85 | 0 | n |
| Garner | 84 | 24500 | n |
| Hu | 85 | 30000 | n |
| Jackson | 85 | 34000 | y |
| Kelley | 84 | 32500 | y |
| Moon | 85 | 23000 | n |
| Richards | 85 | 0 | y |
| Silver | 85 | 26000 | n |
| Teller | 85 | 27500 | y |

**a.** Develop an interactive query program that computes and prints the average salary for all MBA alumni in a specified graduating year. (Note: Not all MBAs have submitted salary data; to be part of the average salary computation the salary amount must be greater than 0.) Process the alumni data as an internal data file. The only input variable is the specified graduating year. Use 84 and 85 as input test data.

**b.** For graduates of the specified year, also compute and print separate average salaries by work experience vs. no work experience.

**\*\*c.** If salary data are not available for a given year, then print a message to that effect. Use 83 as test input.

29. **Inventory Reorders.** A company maintains a file on their inventory which contains the following items of data: item number, item description, quantity on hand, quantity on order, reorder point, reorder amount, supplier code, and unit cost. The file at the bottom of this page serves as test data.

**a.** Develop a program that prints a report of the inventory items to be reordered. The items to be reordered are based on the following rule: Reorder when quantity on hand plus quantity on order is less than the reorder point. The reorder report lists all items being reordered (number and description), the reorder amount, and the cost of the reorder. Include a final sum of the total cost for all items being reordered. Store the inventory file as an internal data file.

**b.** Modify the report to include a summary section that prints the number of items in the inventory file and the number of items being reordered. Also include the value of inventory for each of these two categories, and the overall inventory value.

**\*\*c.** **Control Breaks.** Modify the report so a subtotal of costs to a supplier is printed immediately following the items reordered from a particular supplier. (Hint: The data in the file have all items from the same supplier together.) When the current supplier code differs from the previous supplier code, we have a *control break*. Print the subtotal for a supplier when a control break occurs.

30. **Quadratic Roots.** A quadratic equation is defined by

$$y = ax^2 + bx + c$$

where $a$, $b$, and $c$ are constants called parameters. Many mathematical applications require the *roots* of this equation. By definition, a root is a value of $x$ that when substituted into the equation yields a value of zero for $y$. The following familiar *quadratic formula* determines the appropriate roots.

$$x = \frac{-b \pm (b^2 - 4ac)^{1/2}}{2a}$$

Run a program to calculate and print quadratic roots for the following input values of $a$, $b$, and $c$.

| $a$ | $b$ | $c$ |
|---|---|---|
| 5 | 6 | 1.35 |
| 1 | 10 | $-1$ |
| 1 | 2 | 1 |
| 7 | 4 | 2 |

Use a FOR/NEXT loop to process these values. Your program should have three decision structures within the loop, depending on the value of the expression $b^2 - 4ac$. If this expression is negative, have the computer print "COMPLEX ROOTS"; if the expression equals zero exactly, evalute the single root using $x = -b/(2a)$; if the expression is positive, use the above quadratic formula to calculate the two roots.

31. **Factorials.** The factorial of a number $N$ (written $N!$) is a useful calculation in many problems in mathematics and statistics. By definition $N!$ is given by the product

$$N \cdot (N - 1) \cdot (N - 2) \ldots 2 \cdot 1$$

For example, if the value of $N$ is 5, then

$$5! = 5 \cdot 4 \cdot 3 \cdot 2 \cdot 1 = 120$$

Inventory File for Exercise 29

| Item Number | Description | Quantity on Hand | Quantity on Order | Reorder Point | Reorder Amount | Supplier Code | Unit Cost |
|---|---|---|---|---|---|---|---|
| B100 | Ripoff belt | 500 | 0 | 200 | 400 | XX50 | 4 |
| C105 | Fake chain | 1035 | 0 | 1400 | 2000 | XX50 | 5 |
| C110 | Real chain | 115 | 200 | 400 | 200 | XX50 | 3 |
| E225 | Bone earring | 1000 | 0 | 1200 | 1500 | YZ30 | 10 |
| G100 | Iron comb | 50 | 0 | 5 | 50 | ZX80 | 1 |
| G120 | Gold comb | 150 | 300 | 400 | 300 | ZX80 | 400 |

Note that 0! is defined to have a value of 1 and $N!$ is undefined if $N < 0$.

a. Run a program that inputs $N$ and calculates and prints $N$! What are the factorials of 1, 5, 10, 25, 50, and 100?

b. Did you get overflow in part **a**? By trial and error determine the maximum value of $N$ whose factorial your computer can process. Then design your program to check each input of N to make sure it's within the allowable range of zero to the maximum value. If it's not, print a message to the user to this effect and then process the next input value.

c. Ensure that your program is capable of printing out the correct value of 0! should a user input zero for $N$.

d. Design an outer loop in your program for the purpose of processing $K$ different values of $N$. For example, the data in part **a** would require six iterations of this loop.

e. Instead of the outer loop in part **d**, design an outer loop that processes values of $N$ from some initial value ($N1$) to some terminal value ($N2$) in increments of $N3$. Print a table of $N$ values and their factorials. Try two test runs: the first processes $N$ from 1 to 10 in increments of 1; the second processes $N$ from 10 to 50 in increments of 5.

32. **Job Placement.** The Placement Office on a college campus wants a program for the computerized matching of employers and graduating seniors looking for jobs. Each student who registers with the Placement Office provides the following information.

Item
_____

Name
Student ID
Address
Major (codes 1 to 10)
Grade point average (GPA)
Willing to relocate?   (y or n)
Willing to travel? (y or n)

The test file at the bottom of this page has been constructed for debugging purposes.

a. Develop an interactive program that prints the name and address of each student who satisfies criteria that are specified by company recruiters. Define input variables based on the following criteria: (1) desired major, (2) desired minimum GPA, (3) relocation requirement, and (4) travel requirement. Once the input data are entered, have the program search the internal data file for each student who meets the criteria. Assume that those students who are willing to relocate or travel would also be willing to accept a job that does not require relocation or travel. Test your program by running the following data for inquiries on the above four variables.

| (1) | (2) | (3) | (4) |
|-----|-----|-----|-----|
| 6 | 3.25 | y | n |
| 3 | 3.00 | n | n |
| 8 | 3.70 | y | y |

**b. Include an error routine to ensure the integrity of data in the file. Specifically, check that the major code is between 1 and 10 inclusive, GPA is 2.0 or above and 4.0 or less, and relocate and travel requirements are yes or no. If an error is found, print an appropriate error messge and go on to the next student in the file. Add new data to test each of these possible errors.

Placement Office File for Exercise 32

| Name | ID | Address | Major | GPA | Relocate | Travel |
|------|-----|---------|-------|-----|----------|--------|
| Iris Abbot | 2119 | 11 Estell Drive | 6 | 3.45 | n | y |
| Calvin Budnick | 3112 | Burnside Dorm | 8 | 2.75 | y | y |
| Susan Dent | 4112 | 12 Upper College Rd. | 3 | 2.50 | y | y |
| Ken Driden | 4819 | RR3 | 4 | 2.85 | n | n |
| Flo Further | 5811 | 107 Ocean Rd. | 1 | 3.00 | n | y |
| Ben Lewis | 6237 | Heath Dorm | 3 | 3.25 | n | n |
| Bella Senate | 6331 | 71 Boston Neck Rd. | 6 | 3.75 | n | y |
| Wally Tenure | 6581 | 15 South Rd. | 8 | 3.25 | y | n |
| Alice Tillitson | 8211 | 97 North Rd. | 6 | 3.30 | y | y |
| Martin Wiener | 9112 | 10 Ballentine | 6 | 3.70 | y | n |

# More Loops

We now complete our treatment of the repetition, or loop, structure by illustrating implementations of pre-test and post-test loops. We also cover the common data processing concept of a pre-test loop that checks for end-of-data conditions, or end-of-file loops.

## 5.1 PRE-TEST LOOPS

As you know from Chapter 3, the **loop (repetition) structure** allows the repeated execution of a **loop body** based on a **loop control** test. Figure 5.1 illustrates the most fundamental loop structure variation, called a **pre-test loop structure** because the first action on entering the loop structure is to test an exit condition. The result of this test is either "execute the loop body" or "exit the loop structure." If the body is to be executed, then control passes to the set of statements that make up the loop body. In general, the loop body can be any set of executable statements. Each time the statements within the body have been executed, control returns to the exit-condition test that precedes the loop body. And so the process continues: the loop body is repeatedly executed so long as the test indicates that the body is to be executed. When the test indicates that looping is finished, control passes to the first executable statement following the loop structure.

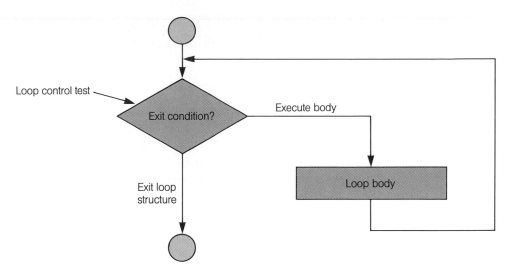

**Figure 5.1**  Flowchart of pre-test loop

**NOTE 1**   As is true in all "proper" control structures (those that reflect top-down structured programming), the flow of execution enters the loop structure through a single entry point at the "top" and exits "down" at the bottom through a single exit point.

**NOTE 2**   In general, the test result "execute body" is based on either a "true" or "false" logical value, depending on how the exit condition is formulated. The most common pre-test loop, called a **while structure,** executes the body *while* the exit condition tests true. In words, we tell the computer to "keep looping while the condition tests true."

Table 5.1 illustrates various pre-test loop implementations, depending on the BASIC dialect. The Minimal BASIC implementation is common to all BASIC dialects. The more modern while structure varies from dialect to dialect. Check out the implementation on your system and try running the given counter-controlled looping example to make sure you understand the implemementation.

**NOTE 3**   Counter-controlled looping is implemented more simply by FOR/NEXT loops. In our example, we would use

```
15 FOR J = 1 TO 5
20     PRINT J;
30 NEXT J
99 END
```

In fact, the FOR/NEXT loop is itself a pre-test loop (see Figure 3.6, page 80): The body is executed *while* the control variable ( *J* in this case) is less than or equal to the terminal value. The main examples in this chapter, however, will illustrate problems that are best implemented by other than FOR/NEXT loops.

**NOTE 4**   The Minimal BASIC implementation is weaker than the alternative implementations, because explicit line number transfers (THEN 99, GO TO 15) are required. *While implementations directly reflect the GO-TO-less spirit of structured programming.* Also note that while implementations repeatedly execute the body while the condition $J<=5$ in the example tests true. The Minimal BASIC pre-test loop implementation executes the body while the condition $J>5$ in the example is false.

**Table 5.1** Selected Pre-test Loop Implementations

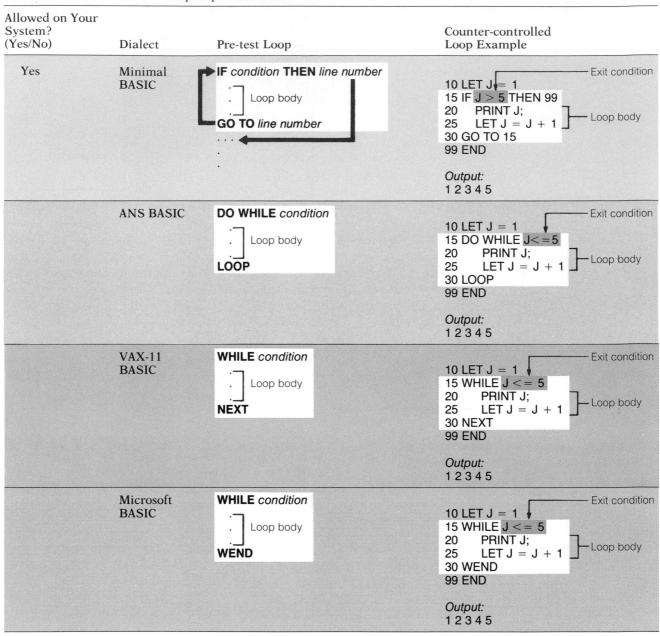

| Allowed on Your System? (Yes/No) | Dialect | Pre-test Loop | Counter-controlled Loop Example |
|---|---|---|---|
| Yes | Minimal BASIC | IF *condition* **THEN** *line number* · Loop body · **GO TO** *line number* | 10 LET J = 1 — Exit condition<br>15 IF J > 5 THEN 99<br>20   PRINT J;<br>25   LET J = J + 1 — Loop body<br>30 GO TO 15<br>99 END<br><br>*Output:*<br>1 2 3 4 5 |
|  | ANS BASIC | **DO WHILE** *condition* · Loop body · **LOOP** | 10 LET J = 1<br>15 DO WHILE J<=5 — Exit condition<br>20    PRINT J;<br>25    LET J = J + 1 — Loop body<br>30 LOOP<br>99 END<br><br>*Output:*<br>1 2 3 4 5 |
|  | VAX-11 BASIC | **WHILE** *condition* · Loop body · **NEXT** | 10 LET J = 1 — Exit condition<br>15 WHILE J <= 5<br>20    PRINT J;<br>25    LET J = J + 1 — Loop body<br>30 NEXT<br>99 END<br><br>*Output:*<br>1 2 3 4 5 |
|  | Microsoft BASIC | **WHILE** *condition* · Loop body · **WEND** | 10 LET J = 1 — Exit condition<br>15 WHILE J <= 5<br>20    PRINT J;<br>25    LET J = J + 1 — Loop body<br>30 WEND<br>99 END<br><br>*Output:*<br>1 2 3 4 5 |

Your system
(if different)*

---

**\*Note:** *If your system lacks a specific while implementation, you must use the Minimal BASIC approach.*

**E X A M P L E   5 . 1**    **The Inflation Curse: Noninteractive While Version**

### Analysis

High rates of inflation in a free-market economy can have devastating effects. For individuals, particularly those (such as retirees) who live on fixed incomes, purchasing power (the ability to buy goods and services) can erode dramatically over time. For the economy as a whole, it can lead to recession and unemployment as a result of such factors as uncertainty and high interest rates.

To illustrate, suppose an item currently costs $100 and increases in cost at a 10% rate of inflation per year. The future cost of this item one year from now would be $110, determined as follows:

$$100 + (100) \cdot (0.1)$$

or

$$100 \cdot (1 + 0.1)$$

Two years from now it would cost $110 plus an additional 10% for the price increase in the second year, or

$$110 \cdot (1 + 0.1)$$

which is $121. Thus if we define

$C$ = current cost of item
$R$ = rate of inflation
$F$ = future cost of item one year from now

then we have

$$F = C \cdot (1 + R)$$

for the cost at the end of one year and

$$F = (\text{previous year's } F) \cdot (1 + R)$$

for future costs in subsequent years.

Let's define the following data requirements.

*Output*

1. Years into future
2. Future cost

*Read*

1. Cost multiple parameter (double or 2)
2. Default % inflation rate parameter (10%)
3. Current cost
4. Percent inflation rate

### Design

The following design illustrates a nonconversational program that prints successive future costs by years *while* the future cost is less than double the current cost.

1. Initialize cost multiple and default % inflation rate
2. Read current cost, % inflation rate
3. Error routine for % inflation rate
4. Print entered data and table headings
5. Future cost = current cost
6. Year = 0
7. Calculate and print table of future years and costs
8. Print table summary
9. End

The error routine in Step 3 is further refined as follows:

3.1   If % inflation rate is out of range 1–100 then
3.2      Print error message
3.3      Set % inflation rate to default value

The table in Step 7 is generated through a while loop:

7.1   While future cost < multiple × current cost
7.2      Increment year
7.3      Future cost = previous future cost
                    × (1 + % inflation rate/100)
7.4      Print year, future cost
7.5   End loop

### Code

The code and run below were implemented in Microsoft BASIC on an IBM Personal Computer. (See Note 2 and Exercise 2.)

```
100 REM * * * * * * * * * * * * * * * * * * * * * * * * * * * * * * * * * * * * *
110 REM *                                                                     *
120 REM *      Inflation Curse Program:   Noninteractive WHILE Version        *
130 REM *                                                                     *
140 REM *    Key:                                                             *
150 REM *       CCOST     = Current cost                                      *
160 REM *       DEFAULT   = Default percent inflation rate (=10)              *
170 REM *       FCOST     = Future cost                                       *
180 REM *       MULTIPLE  = Cost multiple (=2)                                *
190 REM *       PIRATE    = Percent inflation rate                           *
200 REM *       YEAR      = Year into future                                 *
210 REM *                                                                     *
220 REM * * * * * * * * * * * * * * * * * * * * * * * * * * * * * * * * * * * * *
230 REM-----------------------------------------------------------------------
240      READ DEFAULT,MULTIPLE
250        DATA 10,2
260 REM-----------------------------------------------------------------------
270      READ CCOST,PIRATE
280        DATA 90000,.1                          ┌── Error routine
290 REM--------------------------------------------┼---------------------------
300      IF PIRATE < 1  OR  PIRATE > 100  THEN     ▼
           LET PIRATE = DEFAULT : PRINT "*** Input Error ***" :
           PRINT "Range for % inflation rate is 1-100; Default set to"; DEFAULT
310 REM-----------------------------------------------------------------------
320      PRINT "---------------------------------------------------------"
330      PRINT "Current Cost: $"; CCOST
340      PRINT "Inflation Rate:"; PIRATE; "%"
350      PRINT "---------------------------------------------------------"
360      PRINT "Future Years","Future Costs"
370      PRINT "---------------------------------------------------------"
380 REM-----------------------------------------------------------------------
390      LET FCOST = CCOST
400      LET YEAR  = 0                             ┌── While structure
410 REM--------------------------------------------┼---------------------------
420      WHILE FCOST < MULTIPLE*CCOST              ▼
430        LET YEAR  = YEAR + 1
440        LET FCOST = FCOST*(1 + PIRATE/100)
450        PRINT TAB(5);YEAR, INT(FCOST)
460      WEND
470 REM-----------------------------------------------------------------------
480      PRINT "---------------------------------------------------------"
490      PRINT "Cost increased by a factor of"; MULTIPLE; "in year"; YEAR
500 REM-----------------------------------------------------------------------
999      END
```

**Test**

```
RUN
*** Input Error ***
Range for % inflation rate is 1-100; Default set to 10
------------------------------------------------------------
Current Cost: $ 90000
Inflation Rate: 10 %
------------------------------------------------------------
Future Years  Future Costs
------------------------------------------------------------
        1         99000
        2        108900
        3        119790
        4        131769
        5        144945
        6        159440
        7        175384
        8        192923

------------------------------------------------------------
Cost increased by a factor of 2 in year 8
```

The data assumes an item (say, a house) that costs $90,000 and increases in price at the inflation rate of 10% per year. According to the output, the price of the house will double in its eighth year.

---

Look at the while structure in the program. FCOST is the loop-control variable, the value of which is tested in the WHILE statement to determine whether the loop body should or should not be executed. As long as the condition "future cost less than twice current cost" is true, the body of the loop is executed. However, the first time the condition is false, the loop body is skipped, and control is transferred to the first executable statement after the WEND statement (the PRINT in line 480). In the eighth year, the future cost exceeds double the initial cost ($192,923 > $180,000); so looping terminates, based on a false value for the relational expression in the WHILE statement.

**NOTE 1** The **error routine** in line 300 of the program and the subsequent error message in the output illustrate the usual "defensive" programming procedure of checking the data for common errors. In this case, the program requires read-in of the inflation rate as a percent in the range 1 to 100 instead of as a proportion in the range 0 to 1. Because we entered the proportion 0.1 (purposely, of course), the error routine detects the error, defaults to 10% (conveniently), prints an error message, and continues processing. If they are appropriate, we suggest the use of default values along with an error message and continuation of the run whenever an error is detected. In many situations, however, the detection of a data entry error completely invalidates any calculations that are based on that data. In these cases, it's best to print an appropriate error message and continue with the next set of data. Example 5.2 illustrates an interactive (conversational) error routine.

**NOTE 2** Remember that the WHILE/WEND statements in Example 5.1 are dialect-specific (Microsoft BASIC in Table 5.1). See Exercise 2 for this and other possible implementation differences for your system.

**E X A M P L E   5 . 2**   The Inflation Curse: Interactive While Version

### Analysis

This version is the interactive alternative to the version in Example 5.1. Now, the cost multiple, current cost, and percent inflation rate are conversationally requested from the user. The error routine is also conversational.

### Design

Only the first three steps change from Example 5.1, as indicated below by the shaded portion.

1. Input cost multiple
2. Input current cost, % inflation rate
3. Error routine for % inflation rate

   3.1 While % inflation rate is out of range
   3.2     Print error message
   3.3     Input % inflation rate
   3.4 End loop

4. Print entered data and table headings
5. Future cost = current cost
6. Year = 0
7. Calculate and print table of future years and costs
   7.1 While future cost < multiple × current cost
   7.2     Increment year
   7.3     Future cost = previous future cost
                   × (1 + % inflation rate/100)
   7.4     Print year, future cost
   7.5 End loop
8. Print table summary
9. End

### Code

The code and run below were implemented in Microsoft BASIC on an IBM Personal Computer. (See Exercise 2.)

```
100 REM * * * * * * * * * * * * * * * * * * * * * * * * * * * * * * * * * * *
110 REM *                                                                   *
120 REM *     Inflation Curse Program:   Interactive WHILE Version          *
130 REM *                                                                   *
140 REM *   Key:                                                            *
150 REM *      CCOST    = Current cost                                      *
170 REM *      FCOST    = Future cost                                       *
180 REM *      MULTIPLE = Cost multiple                                     *
190 REM *      PIRATE   = Percent inflation rate                           *
200 REM *      YEAR     = Year into future                                  *
210 REM *                                                                   *
220 REM * * * * * * * * * * * * * * * * * * * * * * * * * * * * * * * * * * *
230 REM------------------------------------------------------------------------
240     INPUT "Enter cost multiple------------>"; MULTIPLE
250     INPUT "Enter current cost------------->"; CCOST          ┌─Interactive error routine
260     INPUT "Enter % inflation rate--------->"; PIRATE         │
270 REM---------------------------------------------------------┘----------
280     WHILE PIRATE < 1  OR  PIRATE > 100
290       PRINT: PRINT "*** Percent inflation rate must be in range 1 to 100."
295       PRINT: INPUT "Enter % inflation rate--------->"; PIRATE
300     WEND
```

```
310 REM-----------------------------------------------------------------------
320        PRINT "-------------------------------------------------------------"
330        PRINT "Current Cost: $"; CCOST
340        PRINT "Inflation Rate:"; PIRATE; "%"
350        PRINT "-------------------------------------------------------------"
360        PRINT "Future Years","Future Costs"
370        PRINT "-------------------------------------------------------------"
380 REM-----------------------------------------------------------------------
390        LET FCOST = CCOST
400        LET YEAR  = 0
410 REM-----------------------------------------------------------------------
420        WHILE FCOST < MULTIPLE*CCOST
430          LET YEAR  = YEAR + 1
440          LET FCOST = FCOST*(1 + PIRATE/100)
450          PRINT TAB(5);YEAR, INT(FCOST)
460        WEND
470 REM-----------------------------------------------------------------------
480        PRINT "-------------------------------------------------------------"
490        PRINT "Cost increased by a factor of"; MULTIPLE; "in year"; YEAR
500 REM-----------------------------------------------------------------------
999        END
```

**Test**

```
RUN
Enter cost multiple-------------->? 2
Enter current cost--------------->? 90000
Enter % inflation rate----------->?  .1  ←—Incorrect entry

*** Percent inflation rate must be in range 1 to 100.

Enter % inflation rate----------->? 10
------------------------------------------------------------
Current Cost: $ 90000
Inflation Rate: 10 %
------------------------------------------------------------
Future Years   Future Costs
------------------------------------------------------------
      1          99000
      2          108900
      3          119790
      4          131769
      5          144945
      6          159440
      7          175384
      8          192923
------------------------------------------------------------
Cost increased by a factor of 2 in year 8
```

Error routine "traps" the error and requests re-entry

Correct entry

**NOTE**   Take a look at the error routine design, code (lines 280–300), and run for Example 5.2. A conversational input error routine is best designed as a while loop that repeatedly asks for the correct input response *while* the response is incorrect.

## Follow-Up Exercises

1.  Implement the example in Table 5.1 on your system. Use a while structure if it's available.

2.  Implement
    a.  Example 5.1
    b.  Example 5.2
    on your system. Be careful with any implementation differences regarding:

     **i.** While structure in lines 420–460 of Example 5.1
                        lines 280–300 of Example 5.2
                        lines 420–460 of Example 5.2
    **ii.** Line continuation in line 300 of Example 5.1
   **iii.** Multistatement lines in line 300 of Example 5.1
                        290–295 of Example 5.2
    **iv.** INPUT with prompt in lines 240–260, 295 of Example 5.2

**3.** Confirm the output in Example 5.1 or Example 5.2 by roleplaying the computer. As you do this, fill in the contents of the indicated storage locations below as if a "snapshot" of memory were taken just before execution of the WEND statement.

| CCOST | PIRATE | YEAR | FCOST |
|-------|--------|------|-------|
|       |        |      |       |
|       |        |      |       |

**4.** In Example 5.1 or Example 5.2,
    **a.** What would happen if the statement

        390 LET FCOST = CCOST

    were omitted?

    **b.** What would happen if line 440 were changed to

        440 LET FCOST = CCOST * (1 + PIRATE/100)

    **c.** What would happen if YEAR were initialized to 1? Modify the program to obtain the same output if the year is initialized to 1.
    **d.** Can you think of a way of improving the computational efficiency within the body of the loop?
    **e.** Why would it be unwise to use the loop-control test

        FCOST <> MULTIPLE * COST

    in Example 5.1 or 5.2?
    **f.** If we were to enter 0.2 as the inflation rate, what inflation rate would be used to calculate future cost in example 5.1? Example 5.2?

**5.** Modify the program in Example 5.1 or Example 5.2 to terminate looping either when future cost equals or exceeds the multiple of current cost or when ten years have passed.

**6.** **Nested Loops.** Consider the following changes in Example 5.1.
    **a.** Modify the program to incorporate an outer loop that processes *N* sets of data.
  **\*b.** Run the program for the following sets of values.

| CCOST | PIRATE |
|-------|--------|
| 90000 | 5 |
| 90000 | 10 |
| 90000 | 15 |
| 180000 | 10 |

How sensitive are the results to the percent inflation rate? To the current cost?

**\*7.   Nested Loops.** Consider the following changes in Example 5.2.
  **a.**  Modify the program to incorporate an outer while loop that processes multiple sets of input data. Prompt the user with the question

   **Do you wish to process more data (Y/N)?**

   It's not necessary to ask this question at the beginning of the run.
  **b.**  Same as part **b** in the preceding exercise.

## 5.2 POST-TEST LOOPS

The while or, more generally, the pre-test loop structure is the fundamental loop structure, but it is not necessarily preferred for all types of looping.[1] Some problems are best solved by the **post-test loop structure** discussed in Chapter 3 and illustrated in Figure 5.2.

The term *post-test loop* means that the loop-control test now follows the loop body. The first action on entering the post-test loop is to execute the loop body, which is any set of executable statements. After the statements within the loop body have been executed, the exit condition is tested. The result of this test is either "execute the body" or "exit the loop." If the body is to be executed, then control passes once again to the set of executable statements that make up the body; otherwise, loop exit is achieved.

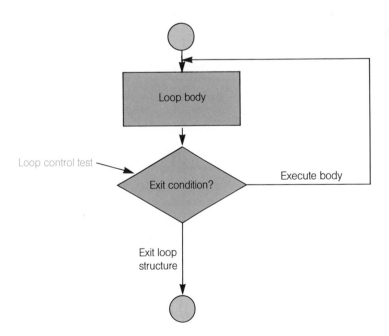

**Figure 5.2**   Flowchart of post-test loop

---

[1]The while structure is fundamental in that it can be rigorously proven that all programming tasks can be accomplished by just two control structures: sequence and while. We let you explore this conclusion in Exercise 12.

**NOTE** In general, the test result "exit loop" is based on either a "true" or "false" logical value, depending on how the exit condition is formulated. The most common post-test loop, called an **until structure,** exits the loop when the exit condition tests true. In words, we tell the computer to "keep looping *until* the condition tests true."

Table 5.2 illustrates selected post-test loop implementations. As usual, the Minimal BASIC implementation is common to all BASIC dialects. Unfortunately the preferred until version varies from dialect to dialect. Find out the available implementation on your system and try running the example to make sure you understand the implementation.

**Table 5.2**  Selected Post-test Loop Implementations

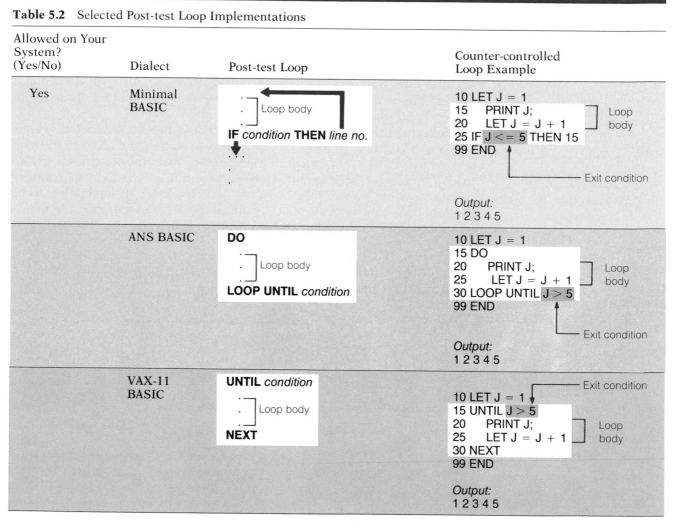

| Allowed on Your System? (Yes/No) | Dialect | Post-test Loop | Counter-controlled Loop Example |
|---|---|---|---|
| Yes | Minimal BASIC | Loop body<br>**IF** condition **THEN** line no. | 10 LET J = 1<br>15   PRINT J;<br>20   LET J = J + 1<br>25 IF J < = 5 THEN 15<br>99 END<br><br>Output:<br>1 2 3 4 5 |
| | ANS BASIC | **DO**<br>Loop body<br>**LOOP UNTIL** condition | 10 LET J = 1<br>15 DO<br>20   PRINT J;<br>25   LET J = J + 1<br>30 LOOP UNTIL J > 5<br>99 END<br><br>Output:<br>1 2 3 4 5 |
| | VAX-11 BASIC | **UNTIL** condition<br>Loop body<br>**NEXT** | 10 LET J = 1<br>15 UNTIL J > 5<br>20   PRINT J;<br>25   LET J = J + 1<br>30 NEXT<br>99 END<br><br>Output:<br>1 2 3 4 5 |
| | Your system (if different)* | | |

**Note:** *If your system lacks a specific until implementation, then you have to use the Minimal BASIC approach. Microsoft BASIC does not have an until implementation.*

**NOTE 1**    As mentioned in Note 3 on page 147, counter-controlled loops are best implemented as FOR/NEXT loops. Use the simple example in Table 5.2 to understand the mechanics of post-test loops.

**NOTE 2**    The Minimal BASIC implementation is weaker than the alternative implementations because of the explicit line number transfer in THEN 15. *Until implementations directly support the GO-TO-less spirit of structured programming.* Also note that until implementations repeatedly execute the body *until* the condition ( $J > 5$ in the example) tests true. The Minimal BASIC post-test loop implementation repeatedly executes the body *until* the condition ( $J <= 5$ ) is false.

**E X A M P L E   5 . 3**    **The Inflation Curse: Interactive Post-test Version**

### Analysis

This version is an alternative to the version in Example 5.2 on page 152. Changes include the following:

- The while loop that prints the inflation table is rewritten as a post-test loop.
- An outer post-test loop is added to allow the user the option of running different sets of data based on the prompt "Do you wish to enter new data (y/n)?"

### Design

Changes in this design from that in Example 5.2 are highlighted by shading.

```
 0. Start post-test new data loop
 1.     Input cost multiple
 2.     Input current cost, % inflation rate
 3.     Error routine for % inflation rate
        3.1 While % inflation rate is out of range
        3.2     Print error message
        3.3     Input % inflation rate
        3.4 End loop
 4.     Print input data and table headings
 5.     Future cost = current cost
 6.     Year = 0
 7.     Calculate and print table of future years and
        costs
        7.1 Start post-test table loop
        7.2     Increment year
        7.3     Future cost = previous future cost
                        × (1 + % inflation rate/100)
        7.4     Print year, future cost
        7.5 End loop when future cost ≥ multiple ×
                                    current cost
 8.     Print table summary
 9.     Input prompt for another run
10  End loop when user answers no
11. End
```

### Code

The code and run below were implemented in Microsoft BASIC on an IBM Personal Computer. (See Exercise 8.) Shaded portions of the code indicate differences between this version and that in Example 5.2.

```
100 REM * * * * * * * * * * * * * * * * * * * * * * * * * * * * * * * * *
110 REM *                                                                *
120 REM *      Inflation Curse Program:  Interactive Post-test Version    *
130 REM *                                                                *
140 REM *      Key:                                                       *
150 REM *         CCOST     = Current cost                                *
170 REM *         FCOST     = Future cost                                 *
180 REM *         MULTIPLE  = Cost multiple                               *
190 REM *         PIRATE    = Percent inflation rate                      *
195 REM *         R$        = User response to prompt                     *
200 REM *         YEAR      = Year into future                            *
210 REM *                                                                *
220 REM * * * * * * * * * * * * * * * * * * * * * * * * * * * * * * * * *
230 REM--------------------------------------------------------------------
235 REM   Start post-test new data loop
236 REM--------------------------------------------------------------------
238         PRINT : PRINT
240         INPUT "Enter cost multiple------------>"; MULTIPLE
250         INPUT "Enter current cost------------->"; CCOST
260         INPUT "Enter % inflation rate--------->"; PIRATE
270 REM--------------------------------------------------------------------
280         WHILE PIRATE < 1  OR  PIRATE > 100
290           PRINT: PRINT "*** Percent inflation rate must be in range 1 to 100"
295           PRINT: INPUT "Enter % inflation rate--------->"; PIRATE
300         WEND
310 REM--------------------------------------------------------------------
320         PRINT "------------------------------------------------------"
330         PRINT "Current Cost: $"; CCOST
340         PRINT "Inflation Rate:"; PIRATE; "%"
350         PRINT "------------------------------------------------------"
360         PRINT "Future Years","Future Costs"
370         PRINT "------------------------------------------------------"
380 REM--------------------------------------------------------------------
390         LET FCOST = CCOST
400         LET YEAR  = 0
410 REM--------------------------------------------------------------------
420 REM     Start post-test table loop
421 REM     ---------------------------
430           LET YEAR  = YEAR + 1
440           LET FCOST = FCOST*(1 + PIRATE/100)
450           PRINT TAB(5);YEAR, INT(FCOST)
460         IF FCOST < MULTIPLE*CCOST THEN 430
464 REM     ---------------------------------------------------------
465 REM     End loop when future cost >= multiple of current cost
470 REM--------------------------------------------------------------------
480         PRINT "------------------------------------------------------"
490         PRINT "Cost increased by a factor of"; MULTIPLE; "in year"; YEAR
495         PRINT : PRINT
500 REM--------------------------------------------------------------------
510         INPUT "Do you wish to enter new data (y/n)"; R$
520 REM
530       IF R$ = "Y"  OR  R$ = "y"  OR  R$ = "YES"  OR  R$ = "yes" THEN 235
540 REM     ---------------------------------
550 REM   End loop when user answers no
560 REM--------------------------------------------------------------------
570       PRINT : PRINT "Bye...Have a nice day!"
998 REM--------------------------------------------------------------------
999       END
```

Test

```
Enter cost multiple-------------->? 2
Enter current cost-------------->? 90000
Enter % inflation rate---------->? 10
--------------------------------------------------------
Current Cost: $ 90000
Inflation Rate: 10 %
--------------------------------------------------------
Future Years  Future Costs
--------------------------------------------------------
      1          99000
      2         108900
      3         119790
      4         131769
      5         144945
      6         159440
      7         175384
      8         192923
--------------------------------------------------------
Cost increased by a factor of 2 in year 8


Do you wish to enter new data (y/n)? y


Enter cost multiple-------------->? 2
Enter current cost-------------->? 90000
Enter % inflation rate---------->? 20
--------------------------------------------------------
Current Cost: $ 90000
Inflation Rate: 20 %
--------------------------------------------------------
Future Years  Future Costs
--------------------------------------------------------
      1         108000
      2         129600
      3         155520
      4         186624
--------------------------------------------------------
Cost increased by a factor of 2 in year 4


Do you wish to enter new data (y/n)? n

Bye...Have a nice day!
```

**NOTE 1**   The post-test loop implementations in Example 5.3 are in Minimal BASIC. As noted earlier, until implementations are preferable when available. If you must use the Minimal BASIC approach, it helps to clearly identify the loop body by indentation. It's also useful to clearly mark the beginning and end of the loop structure through REMs, as in lines 235 and 550, and 420 and 465.

**NOTE 2**   The outer post-test loop defined by lines 235 and 530 is a common approach to giving the user the option of either additional runs with new data or program termination. This is simply a user-friendly convenience that saves the user from having to retype RUN for each new set of data. (See Exercise 11 for an error routine on the y/n response.)

**NOTE 3**   The outer loop also illustrates the **nesting** of loops. Remember that one loop (the inner loop) is nested within another (the outer loop) when it's entirely contained within the body of the outer loop. In our example, two inner loops are nested within the outer loop as follows:

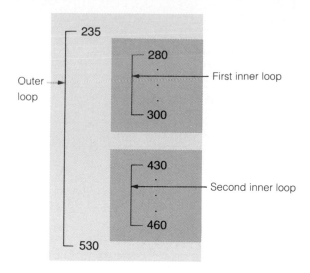

When nesting loops, take care that they don't crossover. (See the pointers in Section 5.4.)

**NOTE 4** The choice of a pre-test versus post-test loop design is often based on the programmer's preference. Note that basic input/output is identical for Examples 5.2 and 5.3. We shall give pointers on this choice in Section 5.4.

---

## Follow-Up Exercises

**8.** Implement the example in Table 5.2 on your system. Use an until structure if it's available.

**9.** Implement Example 5.3 on your system. Be careful with any implementation differences regarding:
  **i.** While structure in lines 280–300
  **ii.** Multistatement lines in lines 238, 290, 295, 495, 570
  **iii.** INPUT with prompt in lines 240–260, 295, 510
Use an until structure if it's available on your system.

**10.** Redesign the error routine in lines 280–300 as a post-test loop or until structure as follows:
  **a.** Omit the message in line 290. Just continue to request input until it's correct.
  **\*b.** Include the message in line 290 whenever input is incorrect.

**\*11.** **Code check error routine.** Modify Example 5.3 to include an error routine for the user's response to the prompt in line 510. Legitimate responses include the following: Y, y, YES, yes, N, n, NO, no. As long as the response is incorrect, print the message "Please respond y or n" and re-input the response.[2]

**\*\*12.** Reread footnote 1 on page 155. Prove by showing equivalent flowcharts that the while structure can be used to duplicate the until structure in Figure 5.2 on page 155.

---

[2] Module F shows how a string function can be used to simplify the compound condition by *stripping off* all but the first characters in the user's response. Thus the response "yep" is legitimate, since the first character, y, is acceptable.

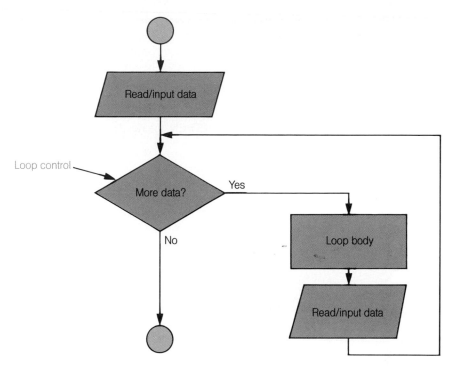

Loop control

Read/input data

More data?

Yes

No

Loop body

Read/input data

**Figure 5.3**  Flowchart of eof loop

## 5.3 END-OF-FILE (EOF) LOOPS

FOR/NEXT loops are convenient when we know the number of desired loop iterations beforehand; while and until loops are useful when exit from the loop is based on a computational result within the loop. If we don't wish to specify in advance (or if we don't know) the exact number of times the loop is to be repeated, then the **end-of-file (eof) loop** may be appropriate.

The eof loop is best implemented as a pre-test loop structure, as illustrated in Figure 5.3 and by the various implementations in Table 5.3. Take a moment now to study the eof loop structure that applies to you in the table, and trace through the execution of its corresponding example.

As you can see, the first action actually precedes the loop: a READ (or INPUT) statement is executed. Next, the loop is entered, and an **end-of-file (eof) condition** is tested. This means that a test is performed to determine whether or not the end of the data has been reached. The test, therefore, requires a special data item at the end of the data called a **trailer number,** or **sentinel.** To be special, this numeric (or string) value must never be part of the regularly provided data for the particular application. Line 90 in the example shows three legitimate ages (30, 20, and 40) and the sentinel −99. In effect, we're telling the computer to process the values 30, 20, and 40 through the loop; however, when AGE stores −99 we wish a loop exit, since −99 is the signal that all data have been processed.

Table 5.4 shows the flow of execution as we roleplay the example.

**NOTE 1**   The eof loop processes data *while* data remain to be processed; thus, it's an example of a while structure.

**Table 5.3**   Selected Eof Loop Implementations

| Allowed on Your System? (Yes/No) | Dialect | Eof Loop (as Pre-test Loop)[a] | Example |
|---|---|---|---|
| Yes | Minimal BASIC | READ list<br>If eof condition THEN line no.<br>.<br>.   ⎤ Loop<br>.   ⎥ body<br>READ list ⎦<br>GO TO line no.<br>. . .<br>.<br>. | 10 READ AGE          ⎤— Loop control<br>15 IF AGE = −99  THEN 99<br><br>20    PRINT AGE;        ⎤ Loop<br>                          ⎥ body<br>25    READ AGE        ⎦<br>30 GO TO 15<br>90 DATA 30,20,40, −99<br>99 END        ⎦— Sentinel<br><br>*Output:*<br>30 20 40 |
| | ANS BASIC | READ list<br>DO WHILE not eof condition<br>.<br>.   ⎤ Loop<br>.   ⎥ body<br>READ list ⎦<br>LOOP | 10 READ AGE          ⎤— Loop control<br>15 DO WHILE AGE <> −99<br><br>20    PRINT AGE;        ⎤ Loop<br>                          ⎥ Body<br>25    READ AGE        ⎦<br>30 LOOP<br>90 DATA 30,20,40, −99<br>99 END        ⎦— Sentinel<br><br>*Output:*<br>30 20 40 |
| | VAX-11 BASIC | READ list<br>WHILE not eof condition<br>.<br>.   ⎤ Loop<br>.   ⎥ body<br>READ list ⎦<br>NEXT | 10 READ AGE          ⎤— Loop control<br>15 WHILE AGE <> −99<br><br>20    PRINT AGE;        ⎤ Loop<br>25    READ AGE        ⎥ body<br>30 NEXT<br>90 DATA 30,20,40,−99<br>99 END        ⎦— Sentinel<br><br>*Output:*<br>30 20 40 |
| | Microsoft BASIC | READ list<br>WHILE not eof condition<br>.<br>.   ⎤ Loop<br>.   ⎥ body<br>READ list ⎦<br>WEND | 10 READ AGE          ⎤— Loop control<br>15 WHILE AGE <> −99<br><br>20    PRINT AGE;        ⎤ Loop<br>25    READ AGE        ⎥ body<br>30 WEND<br>90 DATA 30,20,40,−99<br>99 END        ⎦— Sentinel<br><br>*Output:*<br>30 20 40 |

**Table 5.3** continued

| Allowed on Your System? (Yes/No) | Dialect | Eof Loop (as Pre-test Loop)[a] | Example |
|---|---|---|---|
| | Your system (if different)[b] | | |

[a]INPUT can be substituted for READ.
[b]**Note:** *If your system lacks the while eof implementation, you must use the Minimal BASIC eof implementation.*

**Table 5.4**  Roleplay of Example in Table 5.3

| Line Executed | Comment | Action | Result |
|---|---|---|---|
| 10 | READ before loop | Read age | AGE = 30 |
| 15 | 1st loop iteration | Test for eof | False (Min BASIC); True (other dialects) |
| 20 | | Print age | 30 is printed |
| 25 | | Read age | AGE = 20 |
| 30 | | Loop back to line 15 | Line 15 is executed next |
| 15 | 2nd loop iteration | Test for eof | False (Min BASIC); True (other dialects) |
| 20 | | Print age | 20 is printed |
| 25 | | Read age | AGE = 40 |
| 30 | | Loop back to line 15 | Line 15 is executed next |
| 15 | 3rd loop iteration | Test for eof | False (Min BASIC); True (other dialects) |
| 20 | | Print age | 40 is printed |
| 25 | | Read age | AGE = −99 |
| 30 | | Loop back to line 15 | Line 15 is executed next |
| 15 | Exit loop | Test for eof | True (Min BASIC); False (other dialects) |
| 99 | | END executed | Execution ends |

**NOTE 2**   Did it occur to you that the following design might be simpler?

```
10 READ N
15 FOR J = 1 TO N
20    READ AGE
25    PRINT AGE;
30 NEXT J
90 DATA 3,30,20,40
99 END
```

True. However, many applications (especially in data processing) require the processing of large amounts of data. The FOR/NEXT approach requires an exact count of the number of data items, which introduces the likelihood of error in this count. The eof approach more simply requires a sentinel at the very end of the data. Primarily for this reason, the eof loop is the most common loop design in commercial applications that process sequential (disk and tape) data files. Module E looks at this in some detail.

**NOTE 3** Carefully note that the eof pre-test loop structure requires a READ (or INPUT) statement just before the loop and a second READ (or INPUT) statement at the very end of the loop body. Thus the eof loop itself performs all READ (or INPUT) operations except the first. This may seem strange at first, so we give you the chance to ponder some variations in Exercises 14 and 20.

**NOTE 4** As usual, the test condition in the Minimal BASIC version (AGE = $-99$) is the complement of the test condition in the while versions (AGE $<>$ $-99$). Alternatively, we could restate the while versions as NOT (AGE = $-99$).

## E X A M P L E   5 . 4   Sales Report Problem

This example illustrates a more realistic application for eof loops than the one in Table 5.3[3]

### Analysis

Consider a company with field sales personnel whose number fluctuates considerably from week to week. The weekly base salary varies from person to person; if weekly sales are above $5000, however, then a bonus of $100 is added to the weekly base salary to determine the week's pay; else, no bonus is added.

We wish to write a program that reads appropriate data and prints a sales report with the following design:

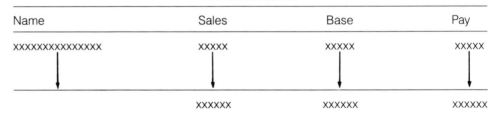

SALES REPORT
Week of xxxxxxxx

| Name | Sales | Base | Pay |
|------|-------|------|-----|
| xxxxxxxxxxxxxxx | xxxxx | xxxxx | xxxxx |
| | xxxxxx | xxxxxx | xxxxxx |

The required data are identified as follows:

*Output*

1. Name of employee
2. Sales of employee for week
3. Base salary of employee
4. Pay of employee for week
5. Total sales for week
6. Total base salaries for week
7. Total pay for week

*Read*

1. Date
2. Name of employee
3. Sales of employee for week
4. Base salary of employee

---

[3]The most realistic applications are in Module E.

*Parameters*

1. Sales cutoff ($5000)
2. Bonus ($100)

**Design**

1. Initial tasks
   1.1  Read parameters
   1.2  Initialize sums
   1.3  Read date
   1.4  Print report headings
2. Process salesperson (eof loop)
   2.1  Read name, sales, base
   2.2  While not eof
   2.3      Calculate pay
            If sales > cutoff then
               Pay = Base + Bonus
            Else
               Pay = Base
            End if
   2.4      Print name, sales, base, pay
   2.5      Accumulate sums
   2.6      Read name, sales, base
   2.7  End loop
3. Concluding tasks
   3.1  Print table summary
   3.2  End

**Code**

The program and its output in Figure 5.4 were run on an IBM PC using a Microsoft interpreter. As usual, you should note implementation differences for your system (see Exercise 17).

**Test**

Try working Exercise 15 to make sure you understand the derived output in Figure 5.4 and the mechanics of eof looping.

---

**NOTE 1**  The eof condition test in line 410 checks the contents of ENAME$ against the sentinel "eof." For the first three employees (lines 901–903), the test ENAME$ = "eof" is false; however, the NOT operator in line 410 changes each result to true. Thus, the body of the while loop (lines 420–470) is executed for each true result, or each of the three employees. In other words, *the loop body is executed while the employee name is not eof.* When the data in line 904 are processed, ENAME$ = "eof" is true and NOT (ENAME$ = "eof") is false. Thus, loop exit is achieved, and line 500 is executed next. Alternatively, we could have used the following WHILE statement:

WHILE ENAME$ <> "eof"

**NOTE 2**  The READ statement in line 400 processes line 901; the READ statement in line 470 processes lines 902–904.

**NOTE 3**  We have wide latitude in the choice of variable on which to base the sentinel and on the *value* of the sentinel itself. We chose ENAME$ for the sentinel variable and "eof" for the sentinel value. We could just as well have chosen

```
100 REM * * * * * * * * * * * * * * * * * * * * * * * * * * * * * * * * * * *
110 REM *                                                                    *
120 REM *                     Sales Report Program                           *
130 REM *                                                                    *
140 REM *      Key:                                                          *
150 REM *         BASE      = Base salary                                    *
160 REM *         BONUS     = Bonus for week (=$100 when sales > cutoff)     *
170 REM *         CUTOFF    = Sales cutoff for bonus (=$5000)                *
180 REM *         ENAME$    = Employee name                                  *
190 REM *         PAY       = Employee pay for week                          *
200 REM *         SALES     = Employee sales for week                        *
210 REM *         TOTBASE   = Total base salaries for week                   *
220 REM *         TOTPAY    = Total pay for week                             *
230 REM *         TOTSALES  = Total sales for week                           *
240 REM *         WEEK$     = Beginning week date (xx-xx-19xx)               *
250 REM *                                                                    *
260 REM * * * * * * * * * * * * * * * * * * * * * * * * * * * * * * * * * * *
270 REM---------------------------------------------------------------------
280      READ BONUS,CUTOFF : DATA 100,5000
290 REM---------------------------------------------------------------------
300      LET TOTBASE = 0 : TOTPAY = 0 : TOTSALES = 0
310 REM---------------------------------------------------------------------
320      READ WEEK$
330 REM---------------------------------------------------------------------
340      PRINT TAB(20); "SALES REPORT"     : PRINT
350      PRINT TAB(17); "Week of "; WEEK$ : PRINT
360      PRINT "---------------------------------------------"
370      PRINT "Name","Sales","Base","Pay"
380      PRINT "---------------------------------------------"
390 REM---------------------------------------------------------------------
400      READ ENAME$,SALES,BASE
410      WHILE NOT (ENAME$ = "eof")
420         IF SALES > CUTOFF THEN LET PAY = BASE + BONUS
                               ELSE LET PAY = BASE
430         PRINT ENAME$,SALES,BASE,PAY
440         LET TOTBASE  = TOTBASE  + BASE
450         LET TOTPAY   = TOTPAY   + PAY
460         LET TOTSALES = TOTSALES + SALES
470         READ ENAME$,SALES,BASE
480      WEND
490 REM---------------------------------------------------------------------
500      PRINT "---------------------------------------------"
510      PRINT ,TOTSALES,TOTBASE,TOTPAY
520 REM---------------------------------------------------------------------
900      DATA "10-15-19xx"
901      DATA "Test 1",5000,300
902      DATA "Test 2",4000,250
903      DATA "Test 3",8000,325
904      DATA "eof",0,0   ◄────These data items are required, although they need not be zeros
998 REM---------------------------------------------------------------------
999 END
           ▲
        Sentinel
```

RUN

```
                    SALES REPORT

                 Week of  10-15-19xx


-----------------------------------------------------
Name            Sales          Base           Pay
-----------------------------------------------------
Test 1          5000           300            300
Test 2          4000           250            250
Test 3          8000           325            425
-----------------------------------------------------
                17000          875            975
```

**Figure 5.4** Sales report program listing and run

some other meaningful value such as "end." Or we could have based the test on the variables SALES or BASE.

**NOTE 4** The sentinel value must be processed as part of the last READ operation of the eof loop. When line 470 processes the data in line 904, the computer not only processes the sentinel value "eof" but also processes the two zeros. Since the READ statement in line 470 has a list of three variables, we must provide three distinct values in line 904. A common "out-of-data" execution error is to forget the last two values (0,0) in line 904. We can provide any values we wish for these last two values, since they're not used for any other purpose.

**NOTE 5** This is a typical example of how internal data files (as in lines 900–904) are best processed by eof loops. We need only satisfy an eof condition at the end of the data file, without having to know beforehand how many records (data lines) are in the file. This approach is especially useful for large data files with thousands of records.

---

## Follow-Up Exercises

**13.** Implement the example in Table 5.3 on your system. Use a while structure if it's available.

**14.** What would happen in the example of Table 5.3 if
   **a.** We were to delete the READ in line 10 and move the READ in line 25 to line 18?
   **b.** We were to use the following post-test design?

```
10    READ AGE
20    PRINT AGE
30 IF AGE <> -99 THEN 10
90 DATA 30,20,40,-99
99 END
```

**15.** In Example 5.4 roleplay the given run by tracing the flow of execution as shown below.

| Line Executed | Action | Result |
| --- | --- | --- |
| | | |

**16.** What would happen in the run of Example 5.4 if line 904 had been written as
   **a.** 904 DATA "eof," 9,9
   **b.** 904 DATA "eof"
   **c.** 904 DATA "end,"0,0
   **d.** How could you change line 410 to process the DATA line given in part **c**?

**17.** Implement Example 5.4 on your system. Be careful with any implementation differences regarding
   **i.** While structure in lines 410–480
   **ii.** Multistatement lines in lines 280,300,340,350
   **iii.** Line continuation and form of if–then–else structure in line 420
   **iv.** The two omissions of LET in line 300.

*18. **Error Routine.** Modify the program in Example 5.4 to include an error routine to ensure that the base salary is less than $1000. If an error is found, print the employee's name and the message "Incorrect base salary" in place of the employee's regular table line. Then go on to the next employee.

*19. **Nested Loop.** Modify the program in Example 5.4 to include an outer eof loop that processes sales districts. The DATA section is now designed as follows:

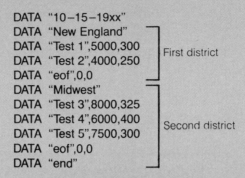

```
DATA "10-15-19xx"
DATA "New England"          ⎤
DATA "Test 1",5000,300      ⎬ First district
DATA "Test 2",4000,250      ⎥
DATA "eof",0,0              ⎦
DATA "Midwest"              ⎤
DATA "Test 3",8000,325      ⎥
DATA "Test 4",6000,400      ⎬ Second district
DATA "Test 5",7500,300      ⎥
DATA "eof",0,0             ⎦
DATA "end"
```

Now the output report has a table for each district. The heading for each table should read:

SALES REPORT FOR DISTRICT xxxxxxxxxxxxxxxxxxxxxxx

District name

Finally, include output for total company-wide sales, base salary, and pay.

*20. **Embedded-Test eof Loops.**
  a. **Minimal BASIC.** The classical Minimal-BASIC approach to eof loops uses the following embedded-test loop design:

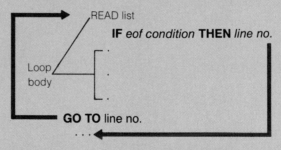

Thus this approach embeds the IF-test within the loop body immediately following the READ statement. The READ statement is now at the head of the body (which seems more natural), and an extra READ statement is eliminated; however, compared with the pre-test approach in Table 5.3, indentation is messy and the loop design is less clean. (To see what we mean, try flowcharting this design and compare it with Figure 5.1.) Rework the Minimal BASIC example in Table 5.3 using this approach. Which do you prefer? (It is a matter of preference!)

**b.** **ANS BASIC.** The embedded eof loop can be implemented in ANS BASIC as follows:

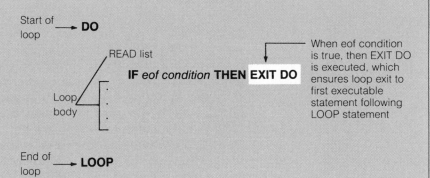

This approach is much cleaner than the Minimal BASIC approach in part **a** but is slightly messy compared with the ANS BASIC approach in Table 5.3. Rework the example in Table 5.3 using this approach. Which do you prefer?

**c.** **Your System.** If your system has an embedded eof loop similar to that in part **b**, then rework the example in Table 5.3 accordingly.

**\*21.** Rework one of the following examples by replacing the FOR/NEXT loop with an eof loop. Select an appropriate sentinel variable and test value. Indicate any changes in the pseudocode.

  **a.** Example 4.3 on page 114.

  **b.** **Minimum Value.** Example 4.6 on page 123.

  **c.** **Government Printing Office Orders.** The illustration in Section 4.5 on page 132.

## 5.4 POINTERS

Keep the following pointers in mind (and you might be a happier programmer).

### Design and Style

**1. Indentation.** Improve the readability of a loop (for us humans) by clearly indenting the loop body and identifying the *beginning* and *end* of the loop. In structured dialects such as ANS BASIC, the beginning and end of a loop are clearly identifiable by pairings such as DO/LOOP. Pre-test loops in Minimal BASIC start with an IF statement and end with a GO TO statement (with an indented body between the two). Post-test loops in Minimal BASIC begin with an indented body and end with an IF statement. It helps to use a REM statement to identify the beginning of the loop, as in line 235 of Example 5.3 on page 158.

**2. Structure of loop.** Be conscious of the correct loop structure in structured programming. Use a single entry point at the top and a single exit point at the bottom. The incorrect use of GO TO statements is one means to violate this top-down principle. It's best to use either pre-test or post-test designs exclusively, since they simplify the identification of the loop (its control and body). Some programmers use an embedded design (see Exercise 20 on page 168) for certain problems, but these must be used with care. The use of structured forms such as WHILE/WEND, WHILE/NEXT, DO WHILE/LOOP, and DO/LOOP UNTIL is preferred to the "old" Minimal BASIC approaches, for all the reasons cited.

**3.   Pre-test vs. post-test loops.**    The choice of a pre-test versus a post-test loop design is often based on the preferences of the programmer, since many problems are solvable by either approach. In other cases, the dialect determines the choice. For example, in Microsoft BASIC we prefer the while design, since the dialect does not directly support the until design (see lines 420–460 in Example 5.2 on page 153 versus the same lines in Example 5.3 on page 158). Finally, some problems are better solved by one design rather than another. For example, pre-test or while designs are best for eof loops, since the post-test design causes the processing of the data line with the sentinel as if it were a legitimate data line (see Exercise 14b).

**4.   Eof vs. FOR/NEXT loops.**    In general we should use an eof loop whenever a loop is to process many lines of data (records in an internal data file), the number of which is likely to change from run to run. This approach is convenient and reliable, since it avoids the error-prone activity of having to specify beforehand the exact number of loop iterations, as in using a FOR/NEXT loop. This is a key reason why the eof approach is the method of choice in commercial data processing applications such as payrolls, billings, and inventory control.

**5.   Loop efficiency.**    Constant computations are best removed from loop bodies. For example, the segment

```
150   READ X
160   LET Y = (A + B∧2/C) * X
170   PRINT Y
180 IF Y > 0 THEN 150
```

unnecessarily recomputes the constant expression (A + B∧2/C) for each loop iteration after the first. A more efficient design is

```
140 LET D = A + B∧2/C
150   READ X
160   LET Y = D * X
170   PRINT Y
180 IF Y > 0 THEN 150
```

Also see Exercise 4d on page 154.

**6.   Error messages.**    The design of error messages takes on rather rich dimensions in interactive user-friendly minicomputer and microcomputer environments. For example, the error routine in lines 280–300 of Example 5.2 on page 152 can be designed to alert the user to a problem by using a combination of sound, color, blinking, and reverse video (hopefully, not all at once!). At a minimum we should print clearly distinguishable error messages that alert users to the exact nature of the problem.

**7.   Screen design.**    The input/output design of interactive programs takes special care. Input requests should be stated concisely and clearly, without clutter. Likewise, output should be designed to enhance readability. It's also best to segregate input from output visually. For example, input can appear in one part of the screen and output in another. Better yet, many dialects have a special statement for clearing the screen. For example, the Microsoft BASIC statement **CLS** clears the screen and places the cursor in the *home* position (the upper-left corner). It's an especially useful statement to place at the begininng of a program so that dated or unrelated material doesn't clutter the screen.

Another common problem is the scrolling of output on a screen. For example consider a screen that fits 24 lines and a loop that prints a 30-line table. In this case, the first six lines of the table would be scrolled off the top of the screen. To view the top 24 lines of the table on the screen, we could press the proper "pause" key, or combination of keys, to freeze the output as it's scrolling. Then we can usually continue by pressing another key. Do you know how to pause output to your screen? Better yet, programs can be designed to pause execution at certain strategic points. For example, the VAX-11 BASIC statement

    SLEEP 120

would suspend execution for 120 seconds. Ask your instructor how this might be done on your system.

## Common Errors

**1. Loop iterations.** Programming an incorrect number of loop iterations is a very common mistake. One cause of this error is an incorrect description of a boundary in the construction of the loop-control condition. In particular, pay attention to $>=$ versus $>$ and $<=$ versus $<$ operators. For example, do we want $A > 5$ or $A >= 5$? Also note, for example, that $J >= K+1$ and $J > K$ are equivalent when $J$ and $K$ store integer values exclusively. Another cause of this error is incorrect or undefined variables when the loop-control condition is tested. For example, consider the following:

    110 IF  A  <= 0 THEN 200
          .
          .
          .
    180     INPUT A
    190 GO TO 110
    200 . . .
          .
          .

If $A$ is undefined (has not been explicitly assigned a value) by line 110, then one of two errors will occur: either the body will not be executed (for systems that initialize $A$ to zero, line 110 gives a true result) or an execution error terminates processing at line 110. In this example, the following statement is missing:

    100 INPUT A

**2. Infinite loop.** In designing loop structures, take care that the loop control satisfies the condition sometime during the processing of the loop. If the loop exit condition is never met, then we have committed a logic error called an **infinite loop.** In this case, the body of the loop is continually processed until execution is stopped by outside intervention (the user hits the "break" key or turns off the machine). *One cause of infinite loops is testing for equality of real values.* If the test is based on a computational result, roundoff error may prevent the resulting value from *exactly* equaling the test value. For example, in our inflation curse problem, a while condition stated as "process the loop while future cost is unequal to double the current cost" or an until condition stated as "process the loop until future cost equals double current cost" would most likely cause an infinite loop. (See Exercise 4e on page 154.)

**3.   Crossovers.**     Watch out for crossovers when nesting loops. If one loop is only partially contained within another loop, then either (1) the system detects the crossover as a syntax or execution error or (2) a logic error is committed by the programmer. For example, the following crossover should be detected by an **ANS BASIC** interpreter:

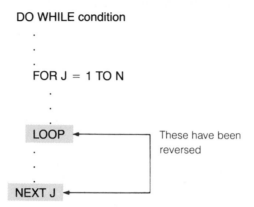

Another type of crossover is caused by inattention to proper control structure pairings. Consider the following ANS BASIC segment:

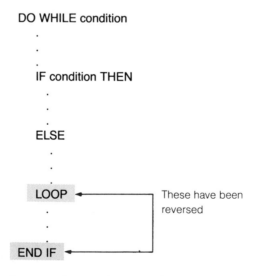

Take care that each control structure has the right beginning and end (**FOR/ NEXT, DO/LOOP, WHILE/WEND, WHILE/NEXT, UNTIL/NEXT, IF/THEN/ ELSE/END IF,** etc.) and in the right place.

**4. Incomplete sentinel data line.** Make sure that the sentinel data line for an eof loop is complete with respect to the expected number of data items:

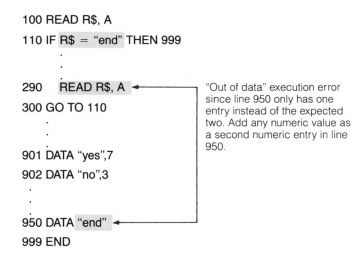

100 READ R$, A

110 IF R$ = "end" THEN 999

290 READ R$, A

300 GO TO 110

901 DATA "yes",7

902 DATA "no",3

950 DATA "end"

999 END

"Out of data" execution error since line 950 only has one entry instead of the expected two. Add any numeric value as a second numeric entry in line 950.

**5. Data validation.** If we can't find fault with our algorithm, yet computer output does not validate our hand-calculated results, then (assuming that our hand-calculated results are correct) we should look for the possibility of faulty input data. For example, sometimes we inadvertently switch two or more values in the input sequence, or mistype values, or place values improperly on the input medium.

We can visually check any input data that are part of the output to make sure that correct values are stored. Generally, we can check for read data errors by inserting an *echo print* immediately after each READ statement:

READ list

PRINT list ◄——————— Same list as READ statement

Better yet, most commercial programs anticipate data entry errors by using error routines that validate the entered data. Examples 5.1 (page 149) and 5.2 (page 152) illustrate two approaches to implementing a so-called *range check* for values in the range 1 to 100. Exercise 11 (page 160) deals with an error routine for a *code check*, whereby only legitimate entries to yes/no code responses are allowed. We shall show other approaches in the next chapter.

In general, we should program defensively by testing all parts of our program and by training ourselves to anticipate potential errors that can be overcome by good program design.

## ADDITIONAL EXERCISES

**22.** Define or explain the following:

| | | |
|---|---|---|
| loop structure | while structure | eof loop |
| loop body | post-test loop structure | eof condition |
| loop-control test | until structure | trailer number |
| repetition structure | nesting (of loops) | sentinel |
| pre-test loop structure | end-of-file loop | infinite loop |

**23. Revisits.** Modify one of the problems from Chapter 4 as indicated below.

   **a. Parking Garage.** (Exercise 26, page 143.) Use a loop design that keeps processing until zero is input for hours.

   **b. Payroll.** (Exercise 27, page 143.) Use an eof loop to process the employee file.

   **c. Alumni File.** (Exercise 28, page 143.) Use an eof loop to process the alumni file. Use a yes/no until loop to process queries from the MBA Director.

   **d. Inventory Reorders.** (Exercise 29, page 144.) Use an eof loop to process the inventory file.

   **e. Job Placement.** (Exercise 32, page 145.) Use an eof loop to process the placement office file. Also, use a while–error loop to ensure that input data are correct. Specifically, make sure the user enters codes of 1 to 10 inclusive for desired major and y or n for the relocate and travel conditions.

**24. Optimal Cost per Credit.** Suppose that the cost per credit charged by a college directly affects student enrollment according to the following *demand* curve.

$$S = D1 - D2 \cdot C$$

where

     $S$ = number of students enrolled
     $C$ = cost (\$) per credit
     $D1$ = first parameter in demand curve
     $D2$ = second parameter in demand curve

For example, if the tuition charge is \$80 per credit, $D1$ is 14,000, and $D2$ is 100, then the number of students that will enroll is estimated by

$$S = 14000 - (100) \cdot (80)$$
$$= 6000$$

If the cost per credit is increased to \$90, then the estimated enrollment drops to

$$S = 14000 - (100) \cdot (90)$$
$$= 5000$$

The average balance due the college is given by

$$B = A \cdot C + F$$

where

     $B$ = average balance due the college
     $A$ = average number of credit hours for the college
     $C$ = cost per credit
     $F$ = average fee for the college

For example, if the average number of credit hours taken by students is 14, the cost per credit is \$80, and average fees are \$250, then the average bill per student is

$$B = (14) \cdot (80) + 250$$
$$= \$1370$$

Since projected enrollment is 6000 students when the per-credit charge is \$80, it follows that the college would realize a projected revenue of (\$1370 per student) · (6000 students), or \$8,220,000.

   **a.** Develop a program that uses a FOR/NEXT loop to vary $C$ from an initial value ($C1$) to a limit ($C2$) in increments of $C3$. Process the following data:

| D1 | D2 | A | F | C1 | C2 | C3 |
|---|---|---|---|---|---|---|
| 14000 | 100 | 14 | 250 | 50 | 80 | 5 |

     Store $D1, D2, A,$ and $F$ through READ statements and interactively input $C1, C2,$ and $C3$.

     Print an output table headed by four columns: Cost per Credit, Average Bill, Expected Enrollment, and Expected Revenue. On the basis of this output, what cost per credit maximizes expected revenue for the college?

   **b.** Add a yes/no until loop that's outer to the loop in part **a**. Use this loop to better "zoom in" on the desired cost per credit. For example, the user may wish to change the values of $C1, C2,$ and $C3$. In this case, the program should ask "Do you wish to change the cost per credit range?" and should respond accordingly. Try a new range of 55 to 65 in steps of 1. Now what's the best cost per credit?

   **c.** Add an outer eof loop that processes all colleges in a state-wide system. Run the following test data.

| College Name | D1 | D2 | A | F | C1 | C2 | C3 |
|---|---|---|---|---|---|---|---|
| Test 1 | 14000 | 100 | 14 | 250 | 50 | 80 | 5 |
| Test 2 | 14000 | 25 | 14 | 250 | 200 | 300 | 5 |
| Test 3 | 30000 | 250 | 13.5 | 500 | 10 | 60 | 1 |

     Just before each output table print the name of the college, $D1, D2, A,$ and $F$.

     What tuition (cost per credit) should be charged at each college to maximize revenue? Would you say there's a flaw in the algorithmic logic if students freely change colleges within the system on the basis of tuition?

  **\*\*d.** Replace the loop in part **a** with a while loop that keeps printing the table while the current revenue exceeds the immediately preceding revenue. Only $C1$ and $C3$ need to be entered, since loop termination is not based on $C2$.

  **\*\*e.** For all you math whizzes out there: Solve this problem by calculus. Do your analytic and computer results agree?

**25. Forecasting Population Growth.** In recent years, the prediction of world population levels into the next century has been a concern of many political, environmental, and agricultural planners. The following equation can be used to predict future levels of world population:

$$p = c \cdot [1 + (b - d)]^n$$

where

$p$ = predicted level of future population
$b$ = birth rate
$c$ = current level of population
$d$ = death rate
$n$ = number of years into the future

For example, estimated data for the year 1976 show $c = 4$ (billions), $b = 0.025$ (2.5%), and $d = 0.009$ (0.9%). If $b$ and $d$ essentially remain constant over a 10-year period ($n = 10$), then we can predict the world population in 1986 as

$$p = 4 [1 + (0.025 - 0.009)]^{10}$$
$$= 4 (1.016)^{10}$$
$$= 4(1.1720)$$
$$= 4.688 \text{ billions}$$

**a.** Develop a program that processes input data for $c$, $b$, $d$, and $n$ using a yes/no until loop. Calculate and print the predicted level of future population. Use the following test data:

| c | b | d | n |
|---|---|---|---|
| 4 | 0.025 | 0.009 | 10 |
| 4 | 0.025 | 0.009 | 20 |
| 4 | 0.025 | 0.009 | 30 |
| 4 | 0.020 | 0.009 | 30 |

Does a drop in the birthrate to 0.020 make much difference?

Repeatedly change the value of $n$ to determine the number of years it would take for the population to double. Try different values for $n$ and observe the output values for $p$. Answer this question for both the 0.025 and the 0.020 birthrates.

**b.** Let $N$ be a counter for "years into future" in an "inner" loop that lies entirely within the outer loop in part **a**. This inner loop increments $N$ by 1, calculates predicted population, and prints $N$, corresponding year, and predicted population. Initialize $N$ by defining an input variable called $N1$. Exit from the loop when the ratio of predicted population to current population exceeds a desired ratio ($R$). Run the program for the following three sets of input values.

| Current Population | Base Year | b | d | N1 | R |
|---|---|---|---|---|---|
| 4 | 1976 | 0.025 | 0.009 | 10 | 2 |
| 4 | 1976 | 0.025 | 0.009 | 25 | 3 |
| 4 | 1976 | 0.020 | 0.009 | 30 | 3 |

For example, your output for the first run should look like this.

| Years into Future | Corresponding Year | Predicted Population |
|---|---|---|
| 10 | 1986 | 4.688 |
| 11 | 1987 | 4.763 |
| . | . | . |
| . | . | . |
| . | . | . |
| 43 | 2019 | 7.915 |
| 44 | 2020 | 8.042 |

Note that the counter is initialized by $N1$ and that this loop terminates when the predicted population *exceeds* (not equals) double ($R$ has a value of 2) the current population. Comment on the number of years it takes the current world population to double and triple relative to changes in the birthrate.

**26. Poisson Probability Function.** The function

$$p = \frac{a^x \cdot e^{-n}}{x!}$$

describes the probability ($p$) that a random or chance variable takes on a value equal to $x$, where $a$ is the mean or average value of the random variable, $e$ is the base of natural logarithms (see Module C), and $x!$ ($x$ factorial) is the product $1 \cdot 2 \cdot 3 \ldots (x - 1) \cdot x$. For example, if the random variable "number of electronic failures per year" is distributed according to the Poisson function above, and the average number of failures is known to be 5.2 per year ($a = 5.2$), then the probability of zero failures ($x = 0$) in a one-year period is

$$p = \frac{(5 \cdot 2)^0 \cdot e^{-5.2}}{0!}$$
$$= \frac{(1) \cdot (0.005516564)}{(1)}$$
$$= 0.0055 \text{ (or } 0.55\%)$$

and the probability of five failures per year is

$$p = \frac{(5.2)^5 \cdot e^{-5.2}}{5!}$$
$$= \frac{(3802.040) \cdot (0.005516564)}{120}$$
$$= 0.1747850 \text{ (or } 17.5\%)$$

Note that 0! is defined as 1.

The Poisson function is widely used to describe phenomena; hence published tables of probabilities for this function are common.

**a.** Design and run a program that inputs the average $a$ and outputs a table of probabilities as follows:

A = xxx.xxx

| X | PROBABILITY |
|---|---|
| 0 | .xxxx |
| 1 | .xxxx |
| 2 | .xxxx |
| ↓ | ↓ |

Terminate this table when the probability drops below 0.0001.

**b.** Include an outer loop that processes different values of *a*. Use the following input values: 2.0, 5.2, 6.0, 10.0, 20.0.

**27. Credit Billing.** Develop a program that prints monthly bills (statements) for Muster Charge, an internationally renowned credit card company. Use the internal data file below for three customers. Printout for each person should take up exactly 12 lines in order to conform to the size of the billing statement. In other words, ideally the printout should appear exactly as illustrated.

Output for these three customers would appear as shown in the chart at the bottom of the page.

Certain conditions must be reflected by the program.

1. The finance charge is 1.5% of the difference between the previous month's balance and the payments made since the previous month.
2. The minimum payment due is determined according to one of four results.
   a. If the new balance exceeds the credit limit, then the minimum payment is the difference between the new balance and the credit limit plus 10% of the credit limit. Thus, for the first statement, (903−800) + 10% · (800) gives $183.
   b. If the new balance is $100 or more and does not exceed the credit limit, then the minimum payment is 10% of the new balance. Thus, for the second statement, 10% · (675.97) gives $67.60.
   c. If the new balance is less than $100, then the minimum payment is set to the new balance (see the third statement).

| Name | Address | Credit Limit | Previous Balance | Payments | New Purchases |
|---|---|---|---|---|---|
| Napoleon B. | 19 Waterloo St. Paris, France | $ 800 | $ 300.00 | $ 100.00 | $700.00 |
| Duke Welly | 1 Thames Ave. London, UK | 1500 | 1350.70 | 1320.70 | 645.52 |
| Betsy Ross | 1776 Flag St. Boston, MA USA | 2000 | 36.49 | 36.49 | 19.15 |

```
NAPOLEON B.          PREVIOUS                FINANCE    NEW            NEW
19 WATERLOO ST       BALANCE - PAYMENTS +    CHARGE +   PURCHASES =    BALANCE
PARIS FRANCE
                      300.00 -  100.00 +      3.00 +     700.00 =       903.00

                                             MINIMUM PAYMENT DUE =      183.00
**WARNING**
YOU HAVE EXCEEDED YOUR CREDIT LIMIT
CONTROL YOURSELF, OR ELSE...



DUKE WELLY           PREVIOUS                FINANCE    NEW            NEW
1 THAMES AVE         BALANCE - PAYMENTS +    CHARGE +   PURCHASES =    BALANCE
LONDON GB
                     1350.70 - 1320.70 +      .45 +      645.52 =       675.97

                                             MINIMUM PAYMENT DUE =      67.60






BETSY ROSS           PREVIOUS                FINANCE    NEW            NEW
1776 FLAG ST         BALANCE - PAYMENTS +    CHARGE +   PURCHASES =    BALANCE
BOSTON MA USA
                      36.49 -   36.49 +      0. +        19.15 =        19.15

                                             MINIMUM PAYMENT DUE =      19.15
```

d. If the new balance is negative, then the minimum payment is zero.
3. A warning is printed if the credit limit is exceeded by the new balance (Muster Charge doesn't fool around).

28. **Police Car Replacement.** A police administrator would like to estimate the mileage at which a police cruiser should be replaced. Data analyses show that the *cost of operation* (gasoline, maintenance, and so on) is approximated by

$$c = f + v{\cdot}m + s{\cdot}m^2$$

where $f$, $v$, and $s$ are called parameters, and $m$ is the mileage reading (in thousands) on the odometer. For example, a cruiser that is driven for 30,000 miles and is characterized by $f = 1000$, $v = 200$, and $s = 2$ incurs an operating cost of approximately

$$c = 1000 + (200){\cdot}(30) + (2){\cdot}(30)^2$$
$$= \$8800.$$

The police department has an arrangement with the automaker for trade-ins of used police cruisers. The automaker has agreed to reduce the price of a new cruiser by the following amount.

$$r = pd^m$$

where $r$ is the trade-in (salvage) value of a used cruiser, $p$ is the original (new) car price, $d$ is some depreciation factor, and $m$ is defined as before. For example, if $p = \$10,000$, $d = 0.95$, and $m = 30$, then

$$r = (10,000){\cdot}(0.95)^{30}$$
$$= \$2146.$$

This means that the police department pays $10,000 for a new cruiser, drives it for 30,000 miles, and gets $2146 on a trade-in. The *depreciation cost* in this case is $7854, or the difference between the new car price and the salvage price.

Thus a cruiser driven for 30,000 miles costs $8800 to operate and $7854 in depreciation cost, for a total cost of $16,654. If this type of cruiser is replaced by a new cruiser of the same type at 30,000-mile intervals, then the total cost per 1000 miles is approximately $555 (that is, $16,654 ÷ 30).

a. Run a program that determines the mileage (to the nearest thousand) at which cruisers should be replaced. Data for each cruiser should include the following.

1. Cruiser name
2. $f$, $v$, $s$, $p$, $d$

Output for each cruiser should appear as shown in the first table below.
Thus the best mileage at which to replace a cruiser is that which gives the smallest value in column (6). Note that 100,000 miles is the maximum replacement mileage that the police administrator is willing to consider. The police administrator is evaluating several types of cruisers, one of which must be selected. Their characteristics are shown in the second table below.
At which mileage should each type be replaced, and what is the total cost per 1000 miles? Which cruiser is the cheapest on the basis of total cost per 1000 miles?

b. Design your program such that the program itself determines and outputs the best cruiser type and its associated total cost per 1000 miles.

c. As you go down column (6) in this type of table, costs typically begin high, decrease to a minimum, and begin increasing again. Design your loop to achieve exit once total cost begins to increase.

Analysis For Cruiser Name

| Miles (1000s) (1) | Operating Cost ($) (2) | Operating Cost (per 1000 miles) (3) = (2) ÷ (1) | Depreciation Cost ($) (4) | Depreciation Cost (per 1000 miles) (5) = (4) ÷ (1) | Total Cost per 1000 miles (6) = (3) + (5) |
|---|---|---|---|---|---|
| 1 | | | | | |
| 2 | | | | | |
| 3 | | | | | |
| . | | | | | |
| . | | | | | |
| . | | | | | |
| 100 | | | | | |

| Cruiser Name | $f$ | $v$ | $s$ | $p$ | $d$ |
|---|---|---|---|---|---|
| (Make | 1000 | 200 | 2·0 | 10,000 | 0.95 |
| these | 800 | 300 | 2·5 | 8,000 | 0.93 |
| up) | 1200 | 225 | 1·6 | 13,000 | 0.98 |

**29. Personnel Benefits Budget.** A budget officer for the State Agency of Education is in the process of preparing the personnel budget for the next fiscal year. One phase of this process is to prepare a budget of personnel expenditures paid by the state in addition to salaries. The additional expenditures include the following.

1. *Social Security.* The state contributes 6.7% of an employee's salary up to $32,400. No deduction is made for earnings above that amount.
2. *Retirement.* The state contributes 9.6% of total salary if the employee belongs to the state retirement plan; 9% is contributed by the state if the employee elects a private plan; and nothing is contributed by the state if the employee is not eligible for a retirement plan (for example, employees under 30 years of age are not eligible for a retirement plan).
3. *Group Life Insurance.* The state contributes $1.30 for every $1000 of salary paid to the employee. For purposes of calculation, round every salary to the next highest $1000. For example, a yearly salary of $11,150 results in a $15.60 contribution ($12 \times 1.30$).

The data for each employee consist of
1. Name
2. Social Security number
3. Annual salary
4. Code for retirement: NE = not eligible; SP = state plan; PP = private plan
a. Run a program that outputs each employee's name, Social Security number, salary, Social Security contribution, retirement contribution, group life contribution, and total contribution. After all employees have been processed, print the totals of each budget category (the four contribution columns) for all employees. Use the test data below to debug your program.

Employee File

| Name | Social Security Number | Salary ($) | Retirement Code |
|------|------------------------|-----------|-----------------|
| TEST 1 | 111-11-1111 | 17,000 | SP |
| TEST 2 | 222-22-2222 | 19,500 | PP |
| TEST 3 | 333-33-3333 | 21,300 | SP |
| TEST 4 | 444-44-4444 | 35,000 | NE |
| TEST 5 | 555-55-5555 | 32,400 | SP |
| TEST 6 | 666-66-6666 | 10,750 | NE |
| TEST 7 | 777-77-7777 | 24,375 | SP |
| TEST 8 | 888-88-8888 | 15,600 | PP |

b. Design your program to check for errors in the retirement code. If a code is in error, print an appropriate error message and bypass the employee. Change the code for the third employee to RP as a test of your logic.

**30. Checking Account Report.** Develop a program that produces a monthly checking account report for each customer. Checking charges are calculated on the basis of the following information.

1. If the ending balance is less than $200, the following service charges are assessed: a monthly fee of 80 cents plus a charge of 10 cents per honored check (withdrawal). No charges are assessed for deposits.
2. If the ending balance is $200 or more, no service charges are assessed.
3. If a check "bounces" (that is, if the balance becomes negative when the bank attempts to honor a check), a charge of $5 is assessed, and the current balance is reduced by this amount. This charge is made for each check that bounces. Checks that bounce are not honored. In other words, a withdrawal is not made from the account, since the person to whom the check was made out does not get paid. Also, the $200 limit does not apply to this bounce charge; that is, if a check bounces, the $5 charge is assessed regardless of the ending balance.

For each bank customer
1. The first line of data contains three items: bank account number, name, and beginning balance.
2. A variable number of lines follows the first line, each line representing a single transaction. If the value is negative, the transaction is a withdrawal; if the value is positive, the transaction is a deposit. A zero entry in this line indicates the end of transactions for this customer.

*Sample Customer Data*

614275, WENDY BRANDON, 741.62
50.75
−125
−260.50
0
216422, PAT LEE, 250.15
−115
−80.75
100
−236.80
0

*Sample Output*

### BANK STATEMENT

| | |
|---|---|
| WENDY BRANDON | 614275 |
| BEGINNING BALANCE | 741.62 |
| TOTAL DEPOSITS | 50.75 |
| TOTAL WITHDRAWALS | 385.50 |
| CHARGES | 0.00 |
| ENDING BALANCE | 406.87 |

11 lines

6 blank lines and then next bank statement (if any)

### BANK STATEMENT

| | |
|---|---|
| PAT LEE | 216422 |
| BEGINNING BALANCE | 250.15 |
| TOTAL DEPOSITS | 100.00 |
| TOTAL WITHDRAWALS | 195.75 |
| CHARGES | 6.00 |
| ENDING BALANCE | 148.40 |

**TOTAL NOT HONORED**

236.80

2 blank lines and then next bank statement (if any)

Debug your program using the above data and the following additional data.

| Account Number | Name | Beginning Balance | Transactions |
|---|---|---|---|
| (Make these up) | | 240.00 | − 50.00 |
| | | | − 35.00 |
| | | | − 175.00 |
| | | | + 200.00 |
| (Make these up) | | 450.00 | − 300.00 |
| | | | − 125.00 |
| | | | + 200.00 |
| | | | − 75.00 |
| | | | − 35.00 |
| | | | + 150.00 |
| | | | − 66.00 |

Before designing your program, make sure you understand the logic by solving these problems by hand. Note that each bank statement takes up exactly 17 lines of output in order to conform to a standardized form. By the way, this is a good program to use diagnostic PRINT statements (traces) for current balance and charges during the debugging phase.

# Advanced Decisions

# 6

The solutions to many problems require that the computer choose from among several alternative courses of action the one that determines which block of statements is to be executed. In this chapter we illustrate three variations of the so-called **multiple alternative decision structures:** nested, multiple-block, and CASE structures. We also present two complete programs: The first illustrates an interactive menu and table lookup procedure for price quotations; the second demonstrates user-defined functions and BASIC's ability for intricate algorithmic logic in applied mathematics. We conclude with our usual pointers on design, style, and errors.

## 6.1 NESTED DECISION STRUCTURES

A **nested decision structure** contains one or more decision structures within another decision structure. Typically, one or more *inner* if-then, if-else, or if-then-else structures are placed within the then block and/or the else block of an *outer* if-then, if-else, or if-then-else structure. We can best illustrate these by example.

**E X A M P L E   6 . 1**   **Sales Bonus Problem: Inner If-then-else Structure Nested within Then Block of Outer If-then-else Structure**

Consider the following sales force bonus plan for determining the appropriate bonus based on weekly sales and travel expenses.

| Weekly Sales | Travel Expenses | Bonus |
|---|---|---|
| Above $5000 | Below $600 | $100 |
| Above $5000 | $600 or above | $ 50 |
| $5000 or below | Any amount | $ 0 |

Study the nested design in Figure 6.1 and its implementation in Table 6.1. Then read the notes that follow.

**NOTE 1**   This program has two if-then-else structures, one nested within the other. The inner if-then-else structure in this case is within the then block of the outer if-then-else structure. If the condition "S > 5000" is true, a second condition "T < 600" is tested. If travel cost is less than $600, the statement that sets B to 100 is executed; otherwise B is set to 50. If the condition "S > 5000" is false, the else block is executed and B is set to zero.

**NOTE 2**   Indentation facilitates understanding of the nesting logic in both the pseudocode version (Figure 6.1) and the BASIC version (Table 6.1).

**NOTE 3**   "Structured" dialects such as ANS BASIC greatly increase the readability of nested decision structures over unstructured dialects such as Minimal BASIC. Convince yourself of this by (1) a visual comparison of the two examples in

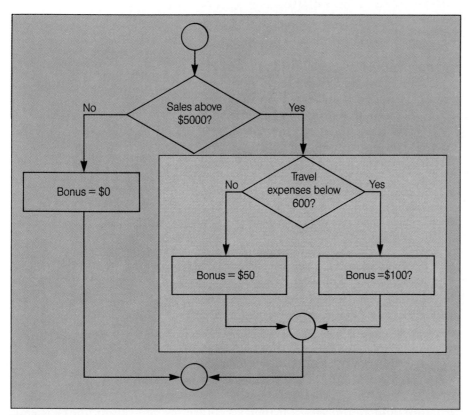

Flowchart

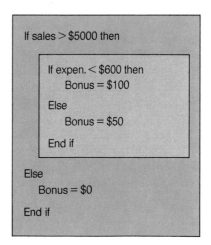

Pseudocode

**Figure 6.1**   Inner if-then-else structure within then block of outer if-then-else structure (Example 6.1)

**Table 6.1**   Implementations of Inner If-then-else Structure within Then Block of
Outer If-then-else Structure (Example 6.1)

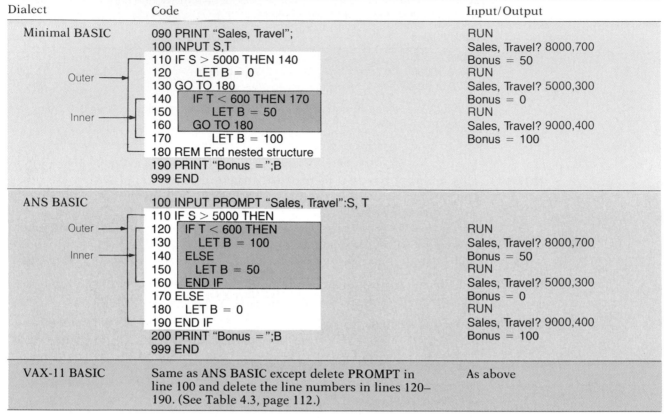

| Dialect | Code | Input/Output |
|---|---|---|
| Minimal BASIC | 090 PRINT "Sales, Travel"; <br> 100 INPUT S,T <br> 110 IF S > 5000 THEN 140 <br> 120   LET B = 0 <br> 130 GO TO 180 <br> 140   IF T < 600 THEN 170 <br> 150     LET B = 50 <br> 160   GO TO 180 <br> 170     LET B = 100 <br> 180 REM End nested structure <br> 190 PRINT "Bonus =";B <br> 999 END | RUN <br> Sales, Travel? 8000,700 <br> Bonus = 50 <br> RUN <br> Sales, Travel? 5000,300 <br> Bonus = 0 <br> RUN <br> Sales, Travel? 9000,400 <br> Bonus = 100 |
| ANS BASIC | 100 INPUT PROMPT "Sales, Travel":S, T <br> 110 IF S > 5000 THEN <br> 120   IF T < 600 THEN <br> 130     LET B = 100 <br> 140   ELSE <br> 150     LET B = 50 <br> 160   END IF <br> 170 ELSE <br> 180   LET B = 0 <br> 190 END IF <br> 200 PRINT "Bonus =";B <br> 999 END | RUN <br> Sales, Travel? 8000,700 <br> Bonus = 50 <br> RUN <br> Sales, Travel? 5000,300 <br> Bonus = 0 <br> RUN <br> Sales, Travel? 9000,400 <br> Bonus = 100 |
| VAX-11 BASIC | Same as ANS BASIC except delete PROMPT in line 100 and delete the line numbers in lines 120–190. (See Table 4.3, page 112.) | As above |

Your system
(if different)[a]

---

[a]**Note:** If your system lacks a multiline if-then-else implementation, you must use either the Minimal BASIC approach or single-line if-then-else implementations shown in Chapter 4. Microsoft BASIC does not have a multiline if-then-else implementation at this time.

Table 6.1 and (2) a vocal reading of each line in the program. Moreover, as stressed in other chapters, structured dialects are less error prone, because they avoid explicit line number transfers such as THEN 140 and GO TO 180.

**NOTE 4**   Many nested decision structure variations are possible. For example, we could nest an inner if-then structure within the then block of an outer if-then-else structure and have another inner if-then-else structure within the else block of the same outer if-then-else structure. We could also nest more than two levels. For example, we could have an outer if-then structure, an inner if-then-else structure, and an *innermost* if-then structure. As you might guess, it can get confusing. For this reason, it's often desirable to replace elaborate nested logic by a sequence of if-then structures with compound conditions (see Exercises 2 and 3a) or by the approaches in Sections 6.2 and 6.3.

## Follow-Up Exercises

1. Implement the example in Table 6.1 on your system. If possible, completely avoid explicit line number transfers.

2. **If-then Sequence as Alternative to Nesting.** Replace the nested logic in Table 6.1 with a sequence of three if-then structures (one for each bonus), two of which use compound conditions with the logical operator AND. Use the proper implementation for your system and run the program. Which approach do you prefer and why?

3. *a. Write BASIC code for your system that represents the following logic:

   If sales > $5000 and travel cost < $300, bonus is $150.
   If sales > $5000 and travel cost ≥ $300 but < $600, bonus is $100.
   If sales ≤ $5000, bonus is $0.
   If travel cost ≥ $600, bonus is $0.

   Avoid nested logic with a sequence of if-then structures that use compound conditions (based on logical operators) where appropriate.

   *b. Implement on your system a program that inputs the sales and travel cost data below and prints the appropriate bonus based on the BASIC code in part **a.**

   | Sales | Travel Cost |
   | --- | --- |
   | $6000 | $200 |
   | 6000 | 300 |
   | 5000 | 400 |
   | 7000 | 600 |

   **c. Use nested logic.
   **d. Same as part **b,** except use the nested logic from part **c.**

4. Consider the following logic:

   If status (S$) is married (M) then
     If age > 55 then
       Print "Married and over 55"
     Else
       Print "Married and not over 55"
     End if
   Else
     If age ≥ 30 then
       Print "Not married and 30 or above"
     Else
       Print "Not married and under 30"
     End if
   End if

   a. In words, describe the outer/inner nesting structure for this problem.
   *b. Flowchart this problem.
   *c. Write BASIC code for your system.
   *d. Implement on your system a program that processes the following data:

   | Status | Age |
   | --- | --- |
   | M | 56 |
   | M | 55 |
   | S | 30 |
   | S | 29 |

**5.** Code the following flowcharts.

**a.**

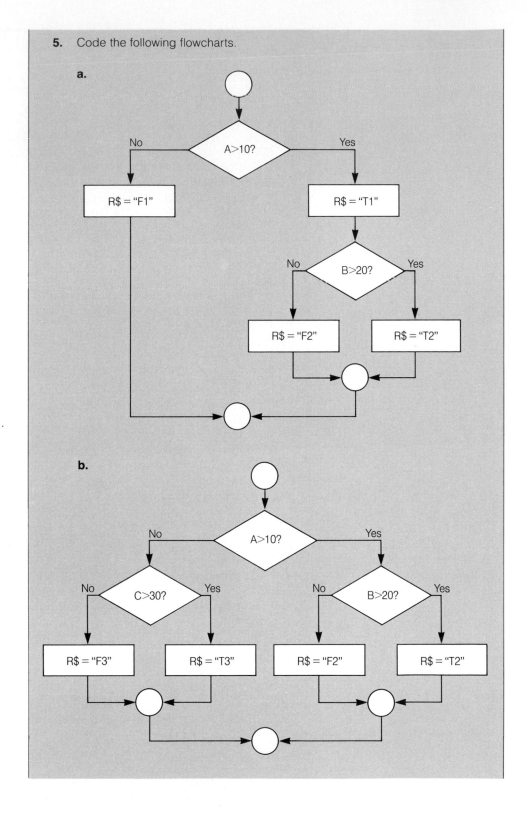

**b.**

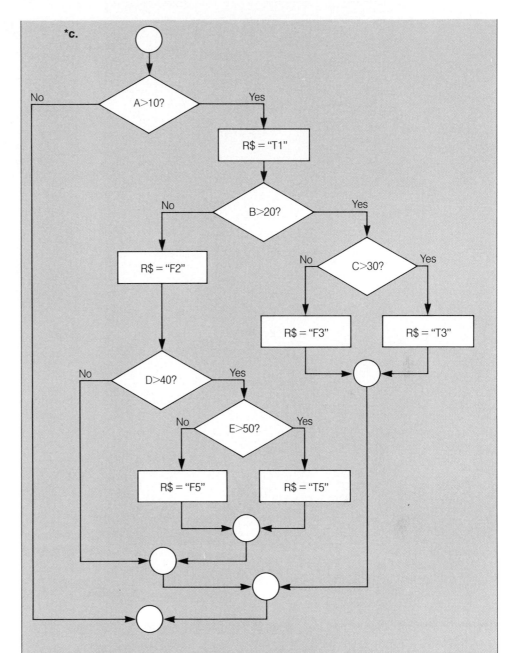

**d.** Fill in the final value in R$ if R$ initially stores the characters NULL, and the following values are stored in A, B, C, D, E.

|  | A | B | C | D | E | Final value in R$ based on | | |
|---|---|---|---|---|---|---|---|---|
|  |  |  |  |  |  | Part a | Part b | Part c |
| i. | 5 | 15 | 25 | 35 | 45 |  |  |  |
| ii. | 20 | 15 | 25 | 35 | 45 |  |  |  |
| iii. | 20 | 25 | 25 | 35 | 45 |  |  |  |
| *iv. | 20 | 20 | 35 | 50 | 45 |  |  |  |

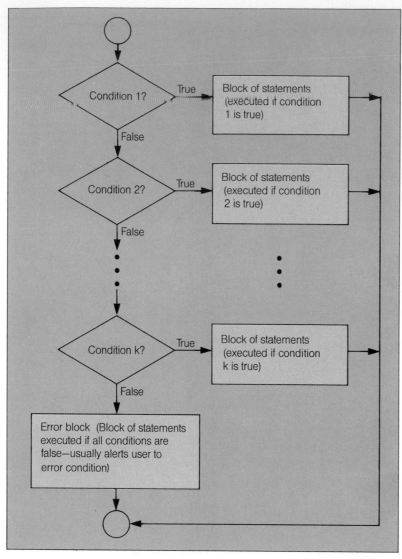

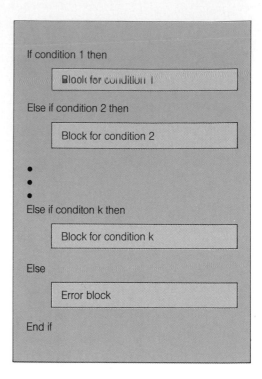

(a) Flowchart

(b) Pseudocode

**Figure 6.2**   Multiple-block (else-if) decision structure

## 6.2 MULTIPLE-BLOCK DECISION STRUCTURE

In the last section we executed a specific decision block (then block or else block) chosen from among several by using nested decision structure logic. We also mentioned that elaborate nested logic is not particularly easy to follow for us humans. In this section we present a more desirable alternative to nested logic that can be used in certain situations.

The **multiple-block decision structure** of **else-if decision structure** is illustrated in Figure 6.2. This structure evaluates a series of conditions from top to bottom until one (if any) is true. The block of statements corresponding to the first true condition is executed, after which control passes out through the bottom of the structure. If all the conditions are false, control drops to a special block that usually includes an error routine.

As you might recall from the last chapter, an **error routine** is a segment of the program that detects errors in either entered data or computational results. Typically, an error routine prints a message that alerts the user to the problem and then either continues with the normal execution sequence or terminates program execution.

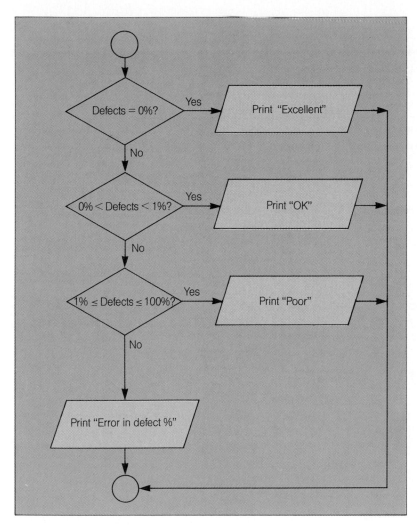

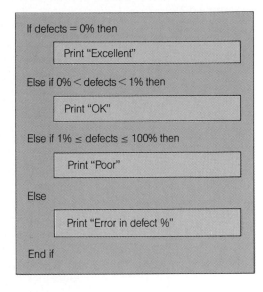

Flowchart                                                      Pseudocode

**Figure 6.3**  Example of multiple-block (else-if) decision structure (Example 6.2)

---

**E X A M P L E   6 . 2**   **Quality Control Problem: Multiple-Block (Else-if) Decision Structure**

A manufacturing company has implemented a quality control program that, among other things, prints a message based on the following criteria:

- If percent defects is exactly 0%, then performance is excellent.
- If percent defects is > 0% but < 1%, then performance is OK.
- If percent defects is ≥ 1% but ≤ 100%, then performance is poor.

The else-if design in Figure 6.3 prints the appropriate performance description based on the percent defect variable. Table 6.2 illustrates various implementations of this design.

---

**NOTE 1**   Make sure you understand the execution logic and output in Table 6.2. Try roleplaying the computer.

**NOTE 2**   The ANS BASIC example illustrates the enhanced readability of structured dialects over unstructured dialects such as Minimal BASIC. The traditional approach is messy, isn't it?

**Table 6.2**   Implementations of Multiple-Block (Else-if) Decision Structure (Example 6.2)

| Dialect | Structure/Syntax | Code |
|---|---|---|

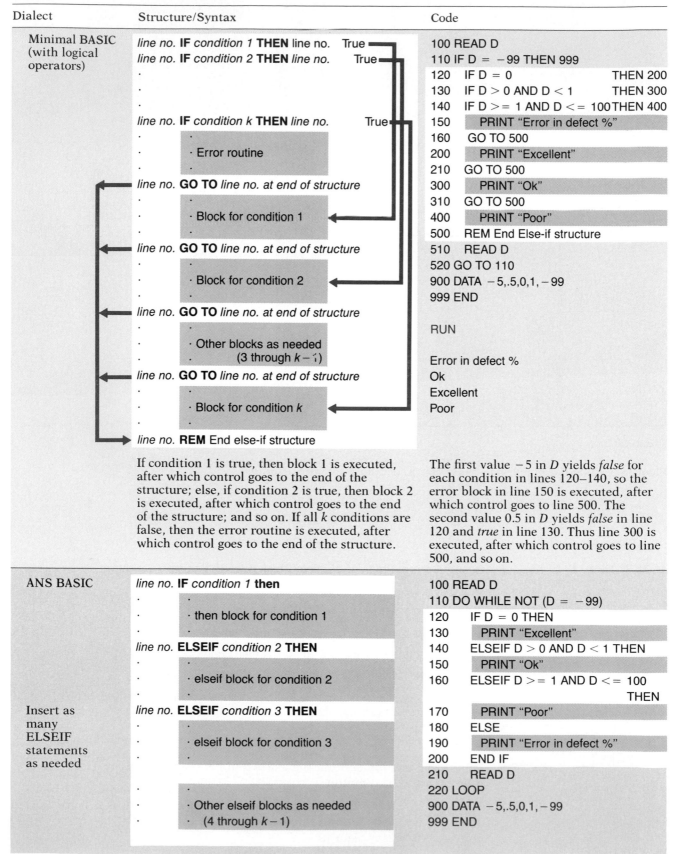

**Minimal BASIC (with logical operators)**

*line no.* **IF** *condition 1* **THEN** *line no.*   True
*line no.* **IF** *condition 2* **THEN** *line no.*   True
·
·
·
*line no.* **IF** *condition k* **THEN** *line no.*   True
    · Error routine
*line no.* **GO TO** *line no. at end of structure*
    · Block for condition 1
*line no.* **GO TO** *line no. at end of structure*
    · Block for condition 2
*line no.* **GO TO** *line no. at end of structure*
    · Other blocks as needed
        (3 through k − 1)
*line no.* **GO TO** *line no. at end of structure*
    · Block for condition k
*line no.* **REM** End else-if structure

```
100 READ D
110 IF D = −99 THEN 999
120     IF D = 0                  THEN 200
130     IF D > 0 AND D < 1        THEN 300
140     IF D >= 1 AND D <= 100    THEN 400
150        PRINT "Error in defect %"
160     GO TO 500
200        PRINT "Excellent"
210     GO TO 500
300        PRINT "Ok"
310     GO TO 500
400        PRINT "Poor"
500     REM End Else-if structure
510     READ D
520 GO TO 110
900 DATA −5,.5,0,1,−99
999 END

RUN

Error in defect %
Ok
Excellent
Poor
```

If condition 1 is true, then block 1 is executed, after which control goes to the end of the structure; else, if condition 2 is true, then block 2 is executed, after which control goes to the end of the structure; and so on. If all *k* conditions are false, then the error routine is executed, after which control goes to the end of the structure.

The first value −5 in *D* yields *false* for each condition in lines 120–140, so the error block in line 150 is executed, after which control goes to line 500. The second value 0.5 in *D* yields *false* in line 120 and *true* in line 130. Thus line 300 is executed, after which control goes to line 500, and so on.

**ANS BASIC**

*line no.* **IF** *condition 1* **then**
    · then block for condition 1
*line no.* **ELSEIF** *condition 2* **THEN**
    · elseif block for condition 2
*line no.* **ELSEIF** *condition 3* **THEN**
    · elseif block for condition 3
    · Other elseif blocks as needed
        (4 through k − 1)

**Insert as many ELSEIF statements as needed**

```
100 READ D
110 DO WHILE NOT (D = −99)
120     IF D = 0 THEN
130        PRINT "Excellent"
140     ELSEIF D > 0 AND D < 1 THEN
150        PRINT "Ok"
160     ELSEIF D >= 1 AND D <= 100
                                  THEN
170        PRINT "Poor"
180     ELSE
190        PRINT "Error in defect %"
200     END IF
210     READ D
220 LOOP
900 DATA −5,.5,0,1,−99
999 END
```

**Table 6.2** Implementations of Multiple-Block (Else-if) Decision Structure (Example 6.2) (Continued)

| Dialect | Structure/Syntax | Code |
|---|---|---|

*line no.* **ELSEIF** *condition k* **THEN**
```
·          · elseif block for last condition
·          ·
line no. ELSE
·          ·
·            · else block (optionally used for all
·                              false conditions)
line no. END IF
```

RUN

Error in defect %
Ok
Excellent
Poor

The else-if structure is simply implemented by placing the needed number of ELSEIF statements within the then block of an if-then-else structure. The block of statements between an ELSEIF statement and another ELSEIF, ELSE, or END IF statement is called an elseif block. If condition 1 is true, the then block is executed, after which control is transferred to the end of the structure (the next statement following END IF); else, if condition 2 is true, the elseif block for condition 2 is executed, followed by exit from the structure; and so on. If conditions 1 through *k* are false, the else block is executed, followed by exit from the structure.

The first value −5 in *D* yields *false* for each condition in lines 120, 140, and 160. Thus the error (else) block in line 190 is executed, after which control exits the structure at line 200. The second value 0.5 in *D* yields *false* in line 120 and *true* in line 140. Thus the block in line 150 is executed, after which control goes to line 200, and so on.

---

**VAX-11 BASIC**

Same as ANS BASIC except:
(1) Delimit ELSE from IF by at least one space;
(2) Don't use line numbers except for the IF/THEN statement (the structure is a *program block*).

This version does not have ELSEIF statements; rather the "look" of an else-if structure is simulated by nesting if-then-else structures within a program block.

Note space between ELSE and IF

```
100 READ D
110 WHILE NOT (D = −99)
120    IF D = 0 THEN
          PRINT "Excellent"
       ELSE IF D > 0 AND D < 1    THEN
          PRINT "Ok"
       ELSE IF D >= 1 AND D <= 100
                                  THEN
          PRINT "Poor"
       ELSE
          PRINT "Error in defect %"
       END IF
210    READ D
220 NEXT
900 DATA −5,.5,0,1,−99
999 END
RUN
```
Program block

Error in defect %
Ok
Excellent
Poor

This else-if structure almost looks identical to the ANS BASIC version, but it's quite different. Line 120 is a *program block* with IF/THEN/ELSE statements nested within else blocks. The illustrated approach is necessary because this version of BASIC does not have an ELSEIF statement. Otherwise, the execution flow is as in in the ANS version.

**Table 6.2** Implementations of Multiple-Block (Else-if) Decision Structure (Example 6.2) (Continued)

| Dialect | Structure/Syntax | Code |
| --- | --- | --- |
| Your system (if different)[a] | | |

[a]**Note:** *If your system lacks an else-if implementation, you must use the Minimal BASIC approach. Microsoft BASIC does not have an else-if implementation at this time.*

## Follow-Up Exercises

**6.** Implement the example in Table 6.2 on your system. If possible, completely avoid explicit line number transfers.

**7.** What output would we get in Example 6.2 if all of the following conditions were used:

```
D =  0    as before
D < 1    instead of D >  0 AND D < 1
D < = 100 instead of D > = 1 AND D < = 100
```

What type of error is this?

**8. a.** Rework the example in Table 6.2 as a nested if-then-else structure (using the approach in Table 6.1 that's appropriate to your system). Would you say that any else-if structure can be coded as a nested decision structure? Would you agree that the logic of the else-if structure is easier to follow (especially as the number of blocks increases)?

**b.** Is it desirable to replace *all* nested decision logic with else-if logic? Explain by reworking the example in Table 6.1 using the approach in Table 6.2.

**9.** Given the following logic:

```
05 INPUT "Enter value for J"; J
10 LET M = 5
```

```
15 IF J < M THEN
20    LET J = J + 5
25    LET M = M + 3
30 ELSEIF J < 8 THEN
35    LET M = M + 10
40 ELSE
45    LET M = M + 20
50 END IF
55 PRINT J,M
99 END
```

What gets printed if
**a.** $J = 2$?
**b.** $J = 7$?
**c.** $J = 10$?
**d.** $J = 5$?
**\*e.** Implement an appropriate version of this program on your system and process the given values for $J$.

**\*10.** In Example 6.1, assume that the bonus is based on the following schedule, in which travel expense does not play a role.

| | |
|---|---|
| Weekly sales under $4000 | bonus is $0 |
| Weekly sales between $4000 and $5000 | bonus is $50 |
| Weekly sales over $5000 | bonus is $100 |

Modify Example 6.1 to include this schedule. Use whatever implementation works on your system. Try each of the following variations:
**a.** Sequence of if-then structures with multiple conditions (as in Exercise 2)
**b.** Nested if-then-else structures
**c.** Else-if structure
Which approach do you prefer and why?

## 6.3 CASE STRUCTURE

The **case structure,** another variation of the multiple alternative decision structure, arises when the execution of one of many alternative blocks of code (**case blocks**) is selected on the basis of a defined value (**case item**) for a numeric or string expression. For example, in a socioeconomic study, we might define the following four cases: (1) Single (2) Married (3) Divorced (4) Widowed. If the numeric variable $C$ stores the code value 1, 2, 3, or 4, then $C$ is the expression, and the defined values 1, 2, 3, 4 are the case items. A defined value for $C$ thus identifies the marital status of a particular individual, where we assume that each marital category (case) requires unique programming tasks or treatment (case blocks).

Figure 6.4 illustrates flowchart and pseudocode for the case structure, and Example 6.3 shows selected implementations of the case structure for our marital example.

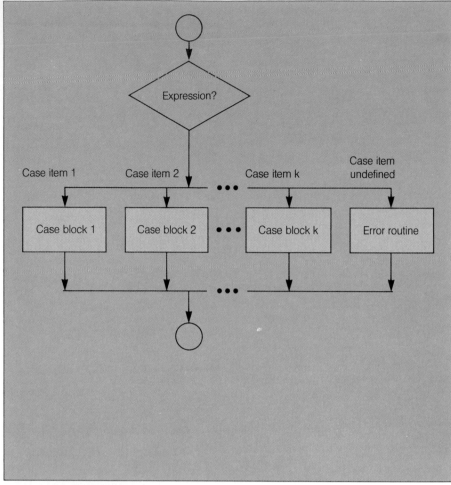

*(a) Flowchart*

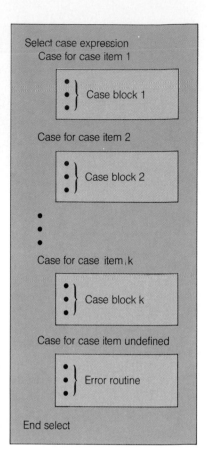

*(b) Pseudocode*

**Figure 6.4**  Case structure

---

**E X A M P L E   6 . 3**   **Marital Example: Selected Case Structure Implementations**

As usual, implementation of the case structure varies, depending on the BASIC dialect. In relating the marital example to Figure 6.4, note the following:

**1.** The expression is numeric and given by the variable $C$.

**2.** There are 4 cases ($k$ is 4) and the case items are legitimate values for the expression, or 1,2,3,4 in this example.

| Case Item | Meaning |
|-----------|---------|
| 1 | Single |
| 2 | Married |
| 3 | Divorced |
| 4 | Widowed |

**3.** If the value of the expression is not one of the case items (less than 1 or greater than 4 in our example), then an error case is implemented.

Study the implementation in Table 6.3 that's appropriate for your system, relate it to Figure 6.4, and go on to the notes and exercises that follow.

**Table 6.3**  Selected Case Structure Implementations (Example 6.3)

| Dialect | Structure/Syntax | Code |
|---|---|---|
| Minimal BASIC | | |

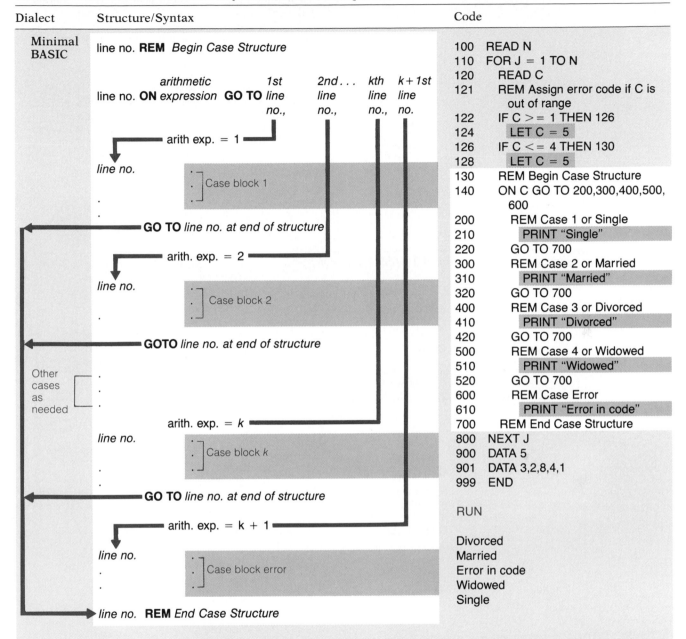

```
line no. REM Begin Case Structure

            arithmetic      1st      2nd...   kth    k+1st
line no. ON expression GO TO line    line     line   line
                              no.,    no.,     no.,   no.

            arith exp. = 1
line no.
   .        Case block 1
   .
   .

   GO TO line no. at end of structure

            arith. exp. = 2
line no.
   .        Case block 2
   .
   .

   GOTO line no. at end of structure

Other
cases
as
needed

            arith. exp. = k
line no.
   .        Case block k
   .
   .

   GO TO line no. at end of structure

            arith. exp. = k + 1
line no.
   .        Case block error
   .
   .

line no. REM End Case Structure
```

```
100   READ N
110   FOR J = 1 TO N
120     READ C
121     REM Assign error code if C is
          out of range
122     IF C >= 1 THEN 126
124     LET C = 5
126     IF C <= 4 THEN 130
128     LET C = 5
130     REM Begin Case Structure
140     ON C GO TO 200,300,400,500,
          600
200       REM Case 1 or Single
210         PRINT "Single"
220       GO TO 700
300       REM Case 2 or Married
310         PRINT "Married"
320       GO TO 700
400       REM Case 3 or Divorced
410         PRINT "Divorced"
420       GO TO 700
500       REM Case 4 or Widowed
510         PRINT "Widowed"
520       GO TO 700
600       REM Case Error
610         PRINT "Error in code"
700     REM End Case Structure
800   NEXT J
900   DATA 5
901   DATA 3,2,8,4,1
999   END

RUN

Divorced
Married
Error in code
Widowed
Single
```

The ON/GO TO statement evaluates an arithmetic expression. If its value is 1, then control goes to the 1st line number in the list of line numbers within the ON/GO TO statement; if its value is 2, then control goes to the 2nd line number in the list; and so on. A GO TO statement at the end of *each* case block must transfer control to the end of the case structure. The last line number in the ON/GO TO list should correspond to the error case; otherwise, if the value of the arithmetic expression is outside the inclusive range 1 to *k*, then a fatal execution error may occur. Also see Figure 6.4.

The first value 3 in *C* yields a transfer of control to line 400 when the decision in line 140 is evaluated. In other words, when line 140 is executed, control goes to the 3rd line number in the list (line 400), because the arithmetic expression *C* stores 3. Next, line 400 is ignored (REMs are nonexecutable), line 410 is executed ("Divorced"' is printed, which is our 3rd case), and line 420 is executed (which transfers control to the end of the case structure). The next time line 140 is executed, the value 2 in *C* causes a transfer to the 2nd line number in the list (line 300). Thus the 2nd case ("Married") is entered.

(continued)

The third value in $C$ is 8, which is out of range. The logic in lines 122–128 resets $C$ to 5, which is the error case. Now, execution of line 140 transfers control to line 600 (or the 5th line number in the list 200,300,400,500,600), and so on.

Many BASIC dialects capture the out-of-range error condition ($C$ less than 1 or greater than 4) by a special clause (ELSE, OTHERWISE, NONE, etc.) to the right of the ON/GO TO statement, depending on the dialect. For example, Waterloo BASIC has the following syntax for line 140:

140 ON C GO TO 200,300,400,500 NONE 600

This eliminates the need for the tortuous logic that captures the error in lines 122–128. Does your dialect have this type of clause?

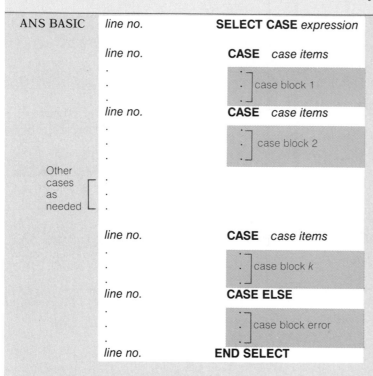

ANS BASIC

```
100   READ N
110   FOR J = 1 TO N
120   READ C
130   SELECT CASE C
200     CASE 1
210       PRINT "Single"
300     CASE 2
310       PRINT "Married"
400     CASE 3
410       PRINT "Divorced"
500     CASE 4
510       PRINT "Widowed"
600     CASE ELSE
610       PRINT "Error in code"
700   END SELECT
800   NEXT J
900   DATA 5
901   DATA 3,2,6,4,1
999   END

RUN

Divorced
Married
Error in code
Widowed
Single
```

The **SELECT CASE statement** evaluates an expression (numeric or string), the **CASE statements** define cases 1 through $k$, the **CASE ELSE statement** defines the error routine, and the **END SELECT statement** defines the end of the structure. The expression is evaluated and its value is compared with the case items until a match is found. If a match is found for a particular case, then the case block for that case is executed and control then goes to the end of the structure. If a match is not found, then the error case block is executed. Case items within a CASE statement can include (1) one or more constants separated by commas or (2) one or more **TO** or **IS ranges** separated by commas, or (3) both. See the examples to the right for case item variations and Figure 6.4 for the flow of a case structure.

The first value 3 in $C$ yields a transfer to line 400 when line 130 is executed, since line 400 contains the case item 3. Thus the 3rd case is entered, and the PRINT in line 410 is executed, after which control automatically goes to the end of the case structure (line 700). When $C$ stores 2, execution of line 130 results in a transfer to line 300 (the 2nd case), which prints the message "Married." When $C$ stores 8, the SELECT CASE statement detects an out-of-range condition and transfers control to the error case at line 600, and so on.

Additional Examples:
(a) 050 SELECT CASE M + N
    100 CASE 1,3,5
    .
    .
    .
    200 CASE 2,4,6,8
    .
    .
    .
    300 CASE 9 TO 50, 70 TO 80
    .
    .
    .
    400 CASE IS > 80
    .
    .
    .
    500 CASE ELSE
    .
    .
    .
    600 END SELECT
(b) 700 SELECT CASE COLOR$
    750 CASE "red", "white"
    .
    .
    .
    800 CASE "blue"
    .
    .
    .
    850 CASE ELSE
    .
    .
    .
    900 END SELECT

| | | |
|---|---|---|
| VAX-11 BASIC | Same as ANS BASIC except the SELECT statement does not contain the keyword CASE. The CASE statement can contain a single expression, a single relational expression, or a range. The range has the form *value* **TO** *value*. Multiple ranges separated by commas are allowable. These variations are illustrated in the examples to the right. Also see Figure 6.4 for the flow within the case structure. | The marital program is the same as the ANS version except: <br><br> Delete the keyword CASE in line 130 |

(continued)

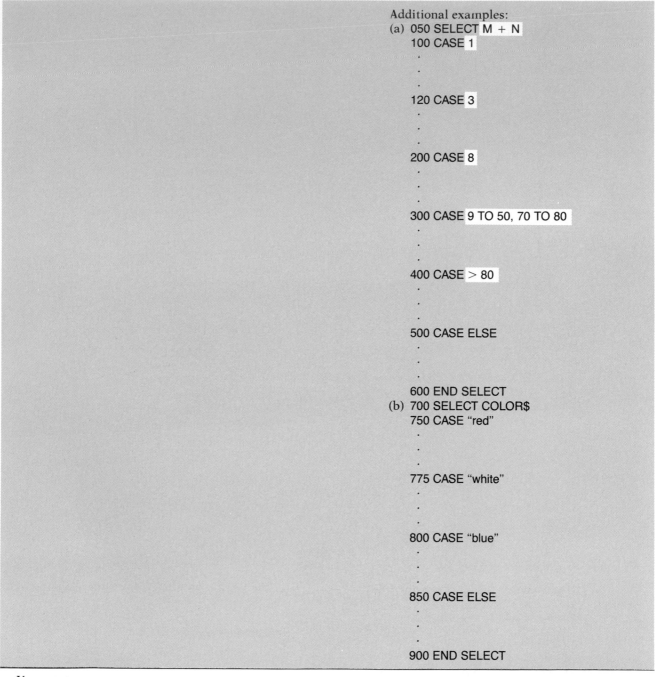

Additional examples:
(a) 050 SELECT M + N
    100 CASE 1
    .
    .
    .
    120 CASE 3
    .
    .
    .
    200 CASE 8
    .
    .
    .
    300 CASE 9 TO 50, 70 TO 80
    .
    .
    .
    400 CASE > 80
    .
    .
    .
    500 CASE ELSE
    .
    .
    .
    600 END SELECT
(b) 700 SELECT COLOR$
    750 CASE "red"
    .
    .
    .
    775 CASE "white"
    .
    .
    .
    800 CASE "blue"
    .
    .
    .
    850 CASE ELSE
    .
    .
    .
    900 END SELECT

Your system
(if different)[a]

(continued)

---

[a]**Note:** If your system lacks a case implementation, you must use the Minimal BASIC approach. Microsoft BASIC does not have a case implementation at this time.

**NOTE 1**   Make sure you understand the execution logic and output in Table 6.3 by roleplaying the computer.

**NOTE 2**   As usual, structured implementations such as ANS BASIC are more readable and less error prone than unstructured implementations like Minimal BASIC. Just compare the two examples in Table 6.3.

**NOTE 3**   Case items are not necessarily limited to integer constants; they can include one or more constants separated by commas, or a range of values. For example, see the ANS BASIC and VAX-11 implementations in Table 6.3.

**NOTE 4**   Case items can be string constants. For example, see the ANS BASIC and VAX-11 implementations in Table 6.3. Also see Exercise 13.

## Follow-Up Exercises

11. Implement the example in Table 6.3 on your system. If possible, completely avoid explicit line number transfers.

12. Rework the example in Table 6.3 as follows:
    a. A sequence of if-then structures.
    b. A nested structure.
    c. An else-if structure.

    Use whatever dialect is appropriate to your system. Which approach do you prefer and why?

13. Suppose code values for the cases in Example 6.3 are as follows:

| Case item | Meaning |
|-----------|---------|
| S | Single |
| M | Married |
| D | Divorced |
| W | Widowed |

   a. Why can't you use the Minimal BASIC case structure? What structure would be best in Minimal BASIC?
   b. Change the ANS (or VAX-11 or your system) case structure in Table 6.3 to utilize string codes directly.

*14. Design a case structure that tests the value in *X* and prints the message "Negative", "Positive", or "Zero". Use whatever dialect is available to you.

*15. The Affirmative Action Officer of a large corporation needs to determine statistics on employees in each of the following categories:

| Category Designation (CAT) | Category Description |
|---|---|
| 1 | American Indian, Alaskan Native |
| 2 | Asian, Pacific Islander |
| 3 | Black |
| 4 | Hispanic |
| 5 | White |
| 6 | Other |

Design a case structure to count the number of employees and sum salaries in each category. Salary is stored under SAL. Use NUM1, NUM2, . . . for counts and SUM1, SUM2, . . . for sums.

**\*16.** Solve Exercise 10 using a case structure (if possible on your system).

## 6.4 ILLUSTRATIONS

In this section we present two complete programs that illustrate several important applications procedures: menu selection, table lookup, algorithmic logic, and user-defined functions.

### Menus and Table Lookup: Price Quotation Program

**Step 1: Problem Analysis.**   A computer-store chain, Microland, is aggressively trying to penetrate the high-school and college market for microcomputers. As part of this strategy, it is offering the schools a discount on large orders of two popular microcomputers, as shown in Table 6.4.

For example, an order of 20 Manzana micros would cost $27,000 (1350 × 20) according to the second line in the table; the same order for EBM micros would cost $36,000 (1800 × 20).

Microland would like us to write an interactive, menu-driven, price-quotation program for these two products. Later, other products might be added.

*Output*
Report showing:
>    Type of micro
>    Order size
>    Cost of order

*Input*
Menu item selection
>    E  For EBM micro
>    M  For Manzana micro
>    S  For Stop processing

Order size

**Table 6.4**   Discount Schedule

| Order Size | Price per Manzana Micro | Price per EBM Micro |
|---|---|---|
| 1–9 micros | $1500 | $2000 |
| 10–29 | 1350 | 1800 |
| 30 or more | 1200 | 1600 |

*Parameters*

| | |
|---|---|
| Minimum order size | ( = 1) |
| First table line size cutoff | ( = 9) |
| Second table line size cutoff | ( = 29) |
| First price for Manzana | ( = $1500) |
| Second price for Manzana | ( = $1350) |
| Third price for Manzana | ( = $1200) |
| First price for EBM | ( = $2000) |
| Second price for EBM | ( = $1800) |
| Third price for EBM | ( = $1600) |

**Step 2: Design.**    The overall design indicates a while loop for processing different price quotes, with a case structure within the loop body for selecting the appropriate microcomputer:

1.  Read parameters
2.  Print menu
3.  Input menu item
4.  While menu selection is not Stop process price quote
5.      Input order size with prompt
6.      Set report error flag to no error
7.      Determine order cost for appropriate micro
      7.1   Select case menu item
      7.2     Case EBM
      7.3         Calculate order cost
      7.4         Assign EBM name to micro
      7.5     Case Manzana
      7.6         Calculate order cost
      7.7         Assign Manzana name to micro
      7.8     Case undefined
      7.9         Print error message
      7.10        Set report error flag to error
      7.11  End select
8.      If no error then print output reports
9.      Print menu
10.     Input menu item
11. End loop
12. Print farewell message
13. End

After the first selection of a menu item (E for EBM, M for Manzana, or S for Stop), the loop is entered, and a case block is selected based on the response E or M. The order cost for the appropriate micro is calculated, the right name is assigned, the case structure is exited, the output report is printed, and the menu prompt appears once again. This procedure is repeated while the menu selection is not Stop. Finally, when S is entered by the user, looping terminates and execution ends. If the user inputs a menu item other than E, M, or S, then the undefined case block prints an appropriate error message.

The calculation of order cost within the EBM and Manzana case blocks needs further refinement. The logic of finding the appropriate line or row in a table like Table 6.4 is called **table lookup.** The use of an else-if structure is one way of designing a table lookup.[1]

The design for lines 7.3 or 7.6 (Calculate order cost) is identical, as follows:

---

[1] In Chapter 8 we illustrate another popular approach to implementing table lookup logic.

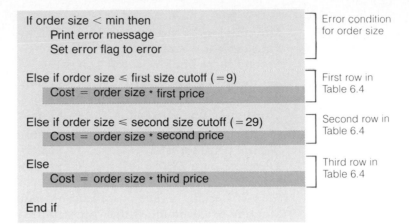

Note that the two elseif blocks and the else block respectively represent each of the three rows in Table 6.4. In this design, the then block represents an error block.

**Step 3: Code.** The program in Figure 6.5 was prepared on a DEC VAX-11 computer. As usual, you should note any implementation differences between this BASIC dialect and the one available to you (see Exercise 17).

**Figure 6.5** Listing for price quotation program

```
100 REM * * * * * * * * * * * * * * * * * * * * * * * * * * * * * * * * * * * *
105 REM *                                                                     *
110 REM *              Microcomputer Price Quotation Program                  *
115 REM *                                                                     *
120 REM *      Key:                                                           *
125 REM *        Parameters                                                   *
130 REM *          MINOR  = Minimum order                        (= 1)        *
135 REM *          CUT1   = First table line size cutoff         (= 9)        *
140 REM *          CUT2   = Second table line size cutoff        (=29)        *
145 REM *          P1MAN  = First price for Manzana              (=$1500)     *
150 REM *          P2MAN  = Second price for Manzana             (=$1350)     *
155 REM *          P3MAN  = Third price for Manzana              (=$1200)     *
160 REM *          P1EBM  = First price for EBM                  (=$2000)     *
165 REM *          P2EBM  = Second price for EBM                 (=$1800)     *
170 REM *          P3EBM  = Third price for EBM                  (=$1600)     *
175 REM *        Variables                                                    *
180 REM *          COST   = Cost of order                                     *
185 REM *          ITEM$  = Menu item selection:  E for EBM                   *
190 REM *                                         M for Manzana               *
195 REM *                                         S for Stop                  *
200 REM *          FLAG   = Error flag (0 = no error; 1 = error)              *
205 REM *          ORDER  = Order size                                        *
210 REM *          MICRO$ = Type of micro                                     *
215 REM * * * * * * * * * * * * * * * * * * * * * * * * * * * * * * * * * * * *
220 REM-----------------------------------------------------------------------
225 REM  Read  parameters
230 REM------------------
235       READ MINOR,CUT1,CUT2
240         DATA 1,9,29
245       READ P1MAN,P2MAN,P3MAN
250         DATA 1500,1350,1200
255       READ P1EBM,P2EBM,P3EBM
260         DATA 2000,1800,1600
265 REM-----------------------------------------------------------------------
270 REM  Print initial menu and input menu item
275 REM-------------------------------------------
280       PRINT TAB(11);"Select one of the following:"
285       PRINT TAB(11);"  E  for Ebm micro"
290       PRINT TAB(11);"  M  for Manzana micro"
295       PRINT TAB(11);"  S  for Stop"
300       PRINT
305       INPUT "  Selection";ITEM$
310       PRINT
```

```
315 REM-------------------------------------------------------------------
320 REM    Process price quote
325 REM--------------------
330       WHILE NOT (ITEM$ = "S")
335 REM        ---------------------------------------------------
340 REM        Input order size and set error flag to 'no error'
345 REM        ---------------------------------------------------
350           INPUT "Order size";ORDER
355           LET FLAG = 0
360 REM        ---------------------------------------------------
365 REM        Determine order cost for appropriate micro
370 REM        ---------------------------------------------------
375           SELECT ITEM$
380             CASE "E"
385               IF ORDER < MINOR THEN
                     PRINT
                     PRINT "******** Order size must be at least 1"
                     PRINT
                     LET FLAG = 1
                   ELSE IF ORDER <= CUT1 THEN
                     LET COST = ORDER*P1EBM
                   ELSE IF ORDER <= CUT2 THEN   ◄─────────────── Table look-up
                     LET COST = ORDER*P2EBM
                   ELSE
                     LET COST = ORDER*P3EBM
                   END IF
390               LET MICRO$ = "EBM"
395 REM
400             CASE "M"
405               IF ORDER < MINOR THEN
                     PRINT
                     PRINT "******** Order size must be at least 1"
                     PRINT
                     LET FLAG = 1
                   ELSE IF ORDER <= CUT1 THEN
                     LET COST = ORDER*P1MAN
                   ELSE IF ORDER <= CUT2 THEN   ◄───────────────┘
                     LET COST = ORDER*P2MAN
                   ELSE
                     LET COST = ORDER*P3MAN
                   END IF
410               LET MICRO$ = "Manzana"
415 REM
420             CASE ELSE
425               PRINT
430               PRINT "******** Please enter E, M, or S for your selection"
435               PRINT
440               LET FLAG = 1
445           END SELECT
450 REM        ------------------------
455 REM        Print report if no error
460 REM        ------------------------
465           IF FLAG = 0 THEN
                 PRINT
                 PRINT TAB(30);"======================="
                 PRINT TAB(30);"Quote for ";MICRO$
                 PRINT TAB(30);"  Order size :   ";ORDER
                 PRINT TAB(30);"  Cost        : $";COST
                 PRINT TAB(30);"======================="
               END IF
470 REM        --------------------------------
475 REM        Print menu and input menu item
480 REM        --------------------------------
485           PRINT
490           PRINT TAB(11);"Select one of the following:"  ◄─── Subsequent printings of menu
495           PRINT TAB(11);"  E   for Ebm micro"
500           PRINT TAB(11);"  M   for Manzana micro"
505           PRINT TAB(11);"  S   for Stop"
510           PRINT
515           INPUT "  Selection";ITEM$
520           PRINT
525 REM        ------------------------------
530       NEXT
535 REM-------------------------------------------------------------------
540       PRINT "Another day, another $...  Have a nice evening!"
545 REM-------------------------------------------------------------------
999       END
```

```
                       Select one of the following:
                         E   for Ebm micro
                         M   for Manzana micro
                         S   for Stop

            Selection? E

       Order size? 5


                               ========================
                               Quote for EBM
                                  Order size :    5
                                  Cost        : $ 10000
                               ========================

                       Select one of the following:
                         E   for Ebm micro
                         M   for Manzana micro
                         S   for Stop


            Selection? R

       Order size? 10


       ********* Please enter E, M, or S for your selection


                       Select one of the following:
                         E   for Ebm micro
                         M   for Manzana micro
                         S   for Stop

            Selection? M

       Order size? 10


                               ========================
                               Quote for Manzana
                                  Order size :    10
                                  Cost        : $ 13500
                               ========================
```

**Figure 6.6**   Test of price quotation program (continues on facing page)

**Step 4: Test.**    The input/output in Figure 6.6 represents a test run for this program. Try following the execution logic by tracing the given input through to its corresponding output.

**NOTE 1**   In general, a **menu** is a list of options on the screen that gives the user clearly described alternative selections (EBM Micro, Manzana Micro, or Stop processing, in our example) together with the required response (input) for making a specific selection (E, M, or S in our example). Menus are very common in commercial interactive programs, since they facilitate the correct use of programs (that is, they are user friendly). For example, many game programs include menus of available games; word processing programs include menus for tasks such as document (file) retrieval, storage, edit, print, and other tasks; spreadsheet programs such as VisiCalc and Lotus 1-2-3 not only have extensive main menus but also have submenus that give further options once main menu items are selected.

**NOTE 2**   Once a menu item is selected, the user's choice must be implemented by some decision structure, usually a case structure (as in our example) or the closely

```
        Select one of the following:
          E  for Ebm micro
          M  for Manzana micro
          S  for Stop

    Selection? M


Order size? O


******** Order size must be at least 1


        Select one of the following:
          E  for Ebm micro
          M  for Manzana micro
          S  for Stop

    Selection? M


Order size? 50


                          =========================
                          Quote for Manzana
                             Order size :    50
                             Cost       : $ 60000
                          =========================

        Select one of the following:
          E  for Ebm micro
          M  for Manzana micro
          S  for Stop

    Selection? S


Another day, another $...   Have a nice evening!
```

allied else-if structure. Also, an incorrect menu response should be detected by the program. In our test run (Figure 6.6), the incorrect menu selection R is trapped within the undefined case block (lines 420–440), normal output is bypassed at line 465, and the menu is offered once again at lines 485–515.

**NOTE 3**    The statement

**Stop Statement**

> **STOP**

is sometimes used to implement a menu choice for stopping execution. In other cases, it is used to stop execution should a serious error occur. We let you explore the use of this statement in Exercise 20; later we illustrate it ourselves in Figure 6.10.

**NOTE 4**    We treat the data in the discount schedule as parameters by assigning values through the READ/DATA statements in lines 235–260. This facilitates subsequent program updates should we need to change the discount structure (a certainty in the real world). For example, to change the prices for the EBM

Micro we need change only the third DATA statement in line 260, which avoids getting into the table lookup logic for EBM (the else-if decision structure in the block beginning at line 385) to make changes.

---

## Follow-Up Exercises

**17.** Implement the price quotation program on your system. Be careful with differences regarding if-then, case, and else-if structure implementations.

**18.** Suppose the prices for the Manzana micro change as follows: $1400, $1300, and $1100.
 **a.** Modify the program accordingly.
 **\*b.** Suppose, in addition to the above prices, that the size cutoffs for Manzana (but not EBM!) change to 24 and 49. Modify the program accordingly.
 **\*c.** Same as parts **a** and **b** except add a fourth line to the discount schedule for Manzana. Use $1000 for the price and 99 for the size cutoff.

**\*19.** Modify the program to add a third microcomputer with the following characteristics:
 Name: Lila
 Prices: $5000, $4500, $4000.

**20.** **Stop Statement.** Modify the program as follows:
 **a.** Terminate execution if the user inputs an order size that's out of range. What's the disadvantage of this approach?
 **\*b.** Incorporate the Stop menu response as a case within the case structure. *Hint:* You might want to use a FOR/NEXT loop instead of the while loop.

**\*21.** **Alternative Error Traps.** As currently designed, the error detection of both a menu item entry and an illegal order size is delayed. For example, the incorrect menu response R still forced the user to input order size before the error was detected. Redesign both error routines so that errors are detected immediately after input. Make sure the program repeatedly requests correct input while input is incorrect.

---

## Algorithmic Logic and User-Defined Functions: Root Bisection Program**

In this problem we illustrate the capability of an algebraic language such as BASIC to model intricate algorithmic logic. We also show the efficient implementation of a user-defined function.

**Step 1: Problem Analysis.**    Many mathematical applications, particularly in calculus, require values for the root(s) of a mathematical function. Given a general mathematical function of $x$, $f(x)$, a root of the function is a value of $x$ that yields a value of zero for $f(x)$. For example, the linear function

$$f(x) = -1 + 2x$$

has a root at $x = 0.5$, since this value for $x$ yields $f(0.5) = 0$. The quadratic function

$$f(x) = -2.25 - 4x + x^2$$

has two roots, one at $x = -0.5$ and another at $x = 4.5$. Figure 6.7 illustrates sketches of these functions. Note from the figure that real roots for the function

$$f(x) = 2^x$$

---

**This illustration is advanced and can be skipped without loss of continuity.

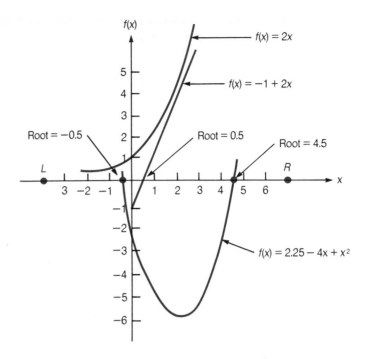

**Figure 6.7**  Sketches of sample functions

are not defined, since this function approaches the *x*-axis asymptotically (gets closer and closer to it but does not cross it).

A number of analytic procedures have been developed for finding the roots of functions. In this section we illustrate the bisection method for finding a real root (if it exists) of any function; Exercise 37 at the end of the chapter describes another procedure.

To illustrate the root bisection procedure for the linear function in Figure 6.7, study Table 6.5 and Figure 6.8 together.

Make sure you understand the bisection procedure by reworking Table 6.5 and Figure 6.8 starting with, say, $L = -1$ and $R = 5$.

The root bisection program calculates a real root of a function, if it exists within the interval specified. Output, input, and parameters are defined as follows:

*Output*

A root (if it exists) or a message stating that a root can't be found for the given interval.

*Input*

Menu item selection

    F    Function change

    R    Root search

        Left end of interval        ⎫

        Right end of interval    ⎬  If R is selected

        Error tolerance          ⎭

    S    Stop processing

*Parameters*

Within the user-defined function (see Module C) given by

$$f(x) = -1.0 + 2.0x$$

**Table 6.5**  Root Bisection Method for the Function $f(x) = -1 + 2x$ (also see Figure 6.8)

| Iteration | Interval from Left to Right (L) | (R) | Midpoint (M) or Root Estimate | Function Values f(L) | f(R) | f(M) | Half-interval or Max. Error | Comment |
|---|---|---|---|---|---|---|---|---|
| 1 | −3.0 | 1.0 | −1.0 | −7.0 | 1.0 | −3.0 | 2.0 | Root in right half-interval since $f(L)$ and $f(M)$ have same sign (both negative). Thus, set $L = M = -1.0$ to create new interval at iteration 2. |
| 2 | −1.0 | 1.0 | 0.0 | −3.0 | 1.0 | −1.0 | 1.0 | Again root in right half-interval, so set $L = M = 0.0$ at iteration 3. |
|   | 0.0 | 1.0 | 0.5 | −1.0 | 1.0 | 0.0 | 0.5 | Root found at $x = M = 0.5$ since $f(M) = 0.0$. |

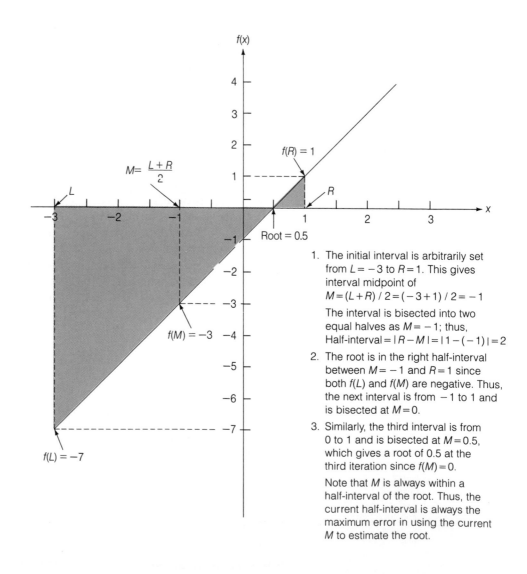

1. The initial interval is arbitrarily set from $L = -3$ to $R = 1$. This gives interval midpoint of
$M = (L + R) / 2 = (-3 + 1) / 2 = -1$
The interval is bisected into two equal halves as $M = -1$; thus,
Half-interval $= |R - M| = |1 - (-1)| = 2$

2. The root is in the right half-interval between $M = -1$ and $R = 1$ since both $f(L)$ and $f(M)$ are negative. Thus, the next interval is from $-1$ to $1$ and is bisected at $M = 0$.

3. Similarly, the third interval is from 0 to 1 and is bisected at $M = 0.5$, which gives a root of 0.5 at the third iteration since $f(M) = 0$.

Note that $M$ is always within a half-interval of the root. Thus, the current half-interval is always the maximum error in using the current $M$ to estimate the root.

**Figure 6.8**  Bisection method for $f(x) = -1 + 2x$ (also see Table 6.5)

**Step 2: Design.**    Figure 6.9 illustrates exploded pseudocode for this algorithm. Try to follow the root logic in this figure by relating the steps in Table 6.5 and Figure 6.8 to the pseudocode in Figure 6.9. Next, relate the pseudocode to the program in Figure 6.10 and the input/output in Figure 6.11 together with the notes that follow. Note that line numbers in the pseudocode correspond to line numbers in the program, so you can better relate the pseudocode, program, and discussion. Are you up to it?

**Step 3: Code.**    The program in Figure 6.10 was prepared on a DEC VAX-11 computer. As usual, you should note any implementation differences between this BASIC dialect and the one available to you. (See Exercise 22.)

**Step 4: Test.**    The input/output in Figure 6.11 shows a test run for this program. Try following the execution logic by tracing the given input through to its corresponding output. (See Exercise 23.)

The following notes relate to the pseudocode (Figure 6.9), program (Figure 6.10), and input/output (Figure 6.11):

**NOTE 1**    The program defines a single-line **user-defined function FNF(X)** in line 215 to facilitate the calculation of FNF(LEFTC) in line 470, FNF(RIGHTC) in lines 470 and 18, and FNF(MIDC) in lines 17, 18, and 33. Note the following functional notation before reading on:

*Functional equivalence between Table 6.5 and the program:*

$f(L)$ is the same as FNF(LEFTC)
$f(R)$ is the same as FNF(RIGHTC)
$f(M)$ is the same as FNF(MIDC)

This user-defined function works much like a library function. For example, FNF(MIDC) in line 33 is evaluated using FNF(X) in line 215, with $X$ replaced by MIDC. This saves us the effort of having to use $-1.0 + 2.0 * \text{MIDC}$ in place of FNF(MIDC) in lines 17, 18, and 33. The same goes for our use of FNF(LEFTC) and FNF(RIGHTC). The user-defined function also simplifies program changes

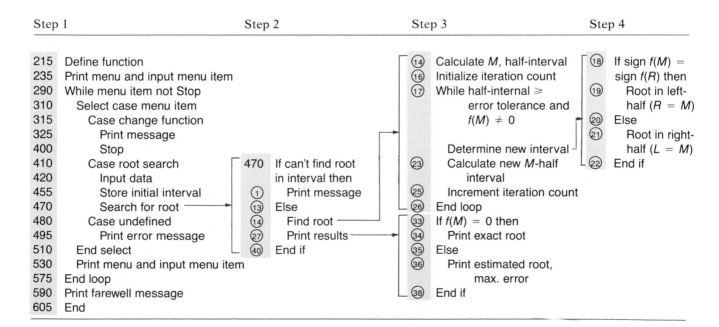

**Figure 6.9**  Stepwise refinement of pseudocode for root bisection program

**Figure 6.10**    Listing of root bisection program

```
100 REM * * * * * * * * * * * * * * * * * * * * * * * * * * * * * * *
105 REM *                                                           *
110 REM *                    Root Bisection Program                 *
115 REM *                                                           *
120 REM *        Key:                                               *
125 REM *           ERRTOL = Error tolerance                        *
130 REM *           FNF(X) = User-defined function reference (*** See line 215) *
135 REM *           HALF   = Width of half-interval                 *
140 REM *           INLEFT = Initial left end of interval           *
145 REM *           INRITE = Initial right end of interval          *
150 REM *           ITEM$  = Menu item selection:  F  for Function change *
155 REM *                                          R  for Root search *
160 REM *                                          S  for Stop processing *
165 REM *           ITER   = Iteration count                        *
170 REM *           LEFTC  = Left end of current interval           *
175 REM *           MIDC   = Middle of current interval             *
180 REM *           RIGHTC = Right end of current interval          *
185 REM *           X      = Argument in user-defined function (The abscissa) *
190 REM *                                                           *
195 REM * * * * * * * * * * * * * * * * * * * * * * * * * * * * * * *
200     !-----------------------------------------------------------
205     !  User-defined function
210     !-----------------------------------------------------------
215        DEF FNF(X) = -1.0 + 2.0*X
220     !-----------------------------------------------------------
225     !  Print initial menu and input menu item
230     !-----------------------------------------------
235        PRINT
240        PRINT TAB(11);"Select one of the following:"
245        PRINT TAB(11);"  F  for Function change"
250        PRINT TAB(11);"  R  for Root search"
255        PRINT TAB(11);"  S  for Stop"
260        PRINT
265        INPUT "  Selection";ITEM$
270        PRINT
275     !-----------------------------------------------------------
280     !  Main loop
285     !-----------
290        WHILE NOT (ITEM$ = "S")
295     !     ------------------------
300     !     Determine appropriate case
305     !     ------------------------
310           SELECT ITEM$
315             CASE "F"
320     !
325                PRINT "* * * * * * * * * * * * * * * * * * * * * * *"
330                PRINT "*                                           *"
335                PRINT "*  To change the function type the following: *"
340                PRINT "*                                           *"
345                PRINT "*     215   DEF FNF(X) = expression          *"
350                PRINT "*                                           *"
355                PRINT "*  Example:                                 *"
360                PRINT "*     215   DEF FNF(X) = -1.0 + 2.0*X        *"
365                PRINT "*                                           *"
370                PRINT "*  Then run the program once again.         *"
375                PRINT "*                                           *"
380                PRINT "*  Don't forget to save the program if you want *"
385                PRINT "*  the new function stored!                 *"
390                PRINT "*                                           *"
395                PRINT "* * * * * * * * * * * * * * * * * * * * * * *"
400                STOP
405     !
410             CASE "R"
```

```
415        !
420                   PRINT "           Enter left and right end of interval in the"
425                   PRINT "           form xx,xx"
430                   INPUT "--------->";LEFTC,RIGHTC
435                   PRINT
440                   PRINT "           Enter error tolerance"
445                   INPUT "--------->";ERRORT
450        !
455                   LET INLEFT = LEFTC
460                   LET INRITE = RIGHTC
465        !
470                   IF  FNF(LEFTC)*FNF(RIGHTC)  >  0.0   THEN
           !
           !---------- Can't find root
           !
  ①                      PRINT "============================================";
  ②                      PRINT "========="
  ③                      PRINT "Root can't be found within the interval";
  ④                      PRINT LEFTC;" TO";RIGHTC
  ⑤                      PRINT "Possible reasons:"
  ⑥                      PRINT "  1.  No roots exist"
  ⑦                      PRINT "  2.  Root outside interval (Expand interval)"
  ⑧                      PRINT "  3.  Multiple roots within interval ";
  ⑨                      PRINT "                              "(Contract interval)"
  ⑩                      PRINT "============================================";
  ⑪                      PRINT "========="
  ⑫                      PRINT
           !
  ⑬                   ELSE
           !
           !---------- Find root by bisection method
           !
  ⑭                      LET MIDC = (LEFTC + RIGHTC)/2.0
  ⑮                      LET HALF = ABS(RIGHTC - MIDC)
  ⑯                      LET ITER = 1
           !
  ⑰                      WHILE  HALF  >=  ERRORT   AND   FNF(MIDC)  <>  0.0
           !
  ⑱                         IF  FNF(MIDC)*FNF(RIGHTC)  >  0.0   THEN
           !
           !-------------- Root in left half-interval
           !
  ⑲                            LET RIGHTC = MIDC
           !
  ⑳                         ELSE
           !
           !-------------- Root in right half-interval
           !
  ㉑                            LET LEFTC  = MIDC
           !
  ㉒                         END IF
           !
  ㉓                         LET MIDC = (LEFTC + RIGHTC)/2.0
  ㉔                         LET HALF = ABS(RIGHTC - MIDC)
  ㉕                         LET ITER = ITER + 1
           !
  ㉖                      NEXT
           !
  ㉗                      PRINT
  ㉘                      PRINT "------------------------------------------------"
  ㉙                      PRINT "Initial interval: ";INLEFT;"to";INRITE
  ㉚                      PRINT "Error tolerance : ";ERRORT
  ㉛                      PRINT "Iterations      : ";ITER
  ㉜                      PRINT
           !
  ㉝                      IF FNF(MIDC)  =  0.0   THEN
  ㉞                         PRINT "Exact root      : ";MIDC
  ㉟                      ELSE
  ㊱                         PRINT "Estimated root  : ";MIDC
  ㊲                         PRINT "Maximum error   : ";HALF
  ㊳                      END IF
           !
  ㊴                      PRINT "------------------------------------------------"
           !
  ㊵                   END IF
```

**Figure 6.10** (continued)

```
475     !
480           CASE ELSE
485     !
490              PRINT
495              PRINT "******** Please enter F, R, or S for your selection"
500              PRINT
505     !
510           END SELECT
515     !    --------------------------------
520     !    Print menu and input menu item
525     !    --------------------------------
530           PRINT
535           PRINT TAB(11);"Select one of the following:"
540           PRINT TAB(11);"  F  for Function change"
545           PRINT TAB(11);"  R  for Root search"
550           PRINT TAB(11);"  S  for Stop"
555           PRINT
560           INPUT "  Selection";ITEM$
565           PRINT
570     !    --------------------------------
575        NEXT
580     !----------------------------------------------------------------------
585        PRINT
590        PRINT "You have just terminated me... I've been ROOTing for you."
595        PRINT "I hope you found your ROOTs..."
600     !----------------------------------------------------------------------
605        END
```

**Figure 6.11** Test of root bisection program

```
              Select one of the following:
                 F  for Function change
                 R  for Root search
                 S  for Stop

        Selection? R


              Enter left and right end of interval in the
              form xx,xx
         --------->? -3,1


              Enter error tolerance
         --------->? .001


         ---------------------------------------------
         Initial interval: -3 to 1
         Error tolerance :  .001
         Iterations      :  3

         Exact root      :  .5
         ---------------------------------------------

              Select one of the following:
                 F  for Function change
                 R  for Root search
                 S  for Stop

        Selection? R


              Enter left and right end of interval in the
              form xx,xx
         --------->? -50,50


              Enter error tolerance
         --------->? .001
```

**Figure 6.11**   (continued)

```
------------------------------------------------
Initial interval: -50 to 50
Error tolerance :  .001
Iterations      :  17

Estimated root  :  .499725
Maximum error   :  .762939E-03
------------------------------------------------


         Select one of the following:
            F  for Function change
            R  for Root search
            S  for Stop

   Selection? R


       Enter left and right end of interval in the
       form xx,xx
--------->? -50,50


       Enter error tolerance
--------->? .00001


------------------------------------------------
Initial interval: -50 to 50
Error tolerance :  .00001
Iterations      :  24

Estimated root  :  .500005
Maximum error   :  .596046E-05
------------------------------------------------


         Select one of the following:
            F  for Function change
            R  for Root search
            S  for Stop

   Selection? D


  ******** Please enter F, R, or S for your selection


         Select one of the following:
            F  for Function change
            R  for Root search
            S  for Stop

   Selection? R


       Enter left and right end of interval in the
       form xx,xx
--------->? 100,200


       Enter error tolerance
--------->? .001


============================================================
Root can't be found within the interval 100  TO 200
Possible reasons:
   1.  No roots exist
   2.  Root outside interval (Expand interval)
   3.  Multiple roots within interval (Contract interval)
============================================================
```

**Figure 6.11**   (continued)

```
          Select one of the following:
             F   for Function change
             R   for Root search
             S   for Stop

   Selection? S




You have just terminated me... I've been ROOTing for you.
I hope you found your ROOTs...




          Select one of the following:
             F   for Function change
             R   for Root search
             S   for Stop

   Selection? F


* * * * * * * * * * * * * * * * * * * * * * * *
*                                             *
*  To change the function type the following: *
*                                             *
*    215  DEF FNF(X) = expression             *
*                                             *
*  Example:                                   *
*    215  DEF FNF(X) = -1.0 + 2.0*X           *
*                                             *
*  Then run the program once again.           *
*                                             *
*  Don't forget to save the program if you want *
*  the new function stored!                   *
*                                             *
* * * * * * * * * * * * * * * * * * * * * * * *
%BAS-I-STO, Stop
-BAS-I-FROLINMOD,   from line 400 in module F610
Ready
```

for a new function since we need change only line 215; otherwise, we would have to change lines 470, 17, 18, and 33. Module C presents single-line user-defined functions in greater detail.

**NOTE 2**   The implementation of menus through a case structure and use of the STOP statement are discussed under Notes 1, 2, and 3 on pages 202–203. In particular, note how we use the STOP statement in line 400 to allow the user an opportunity to change the function.

**NOTE 3**   The program can't find a root if the product FNF(LEFTC) * FNF(RIGHTC) is positive in line 470. This can happen if:

1.   No root exists, as in the $2^x$ function in Figure 6.7. In this case, the interval from $L$ to $R$ gives $f(L) > 0$ and $f(R) > 0$, so that $f(L) * f(R) > 0$.

2.   The root is outside the interval. For example, the interval $L = -3$ to $L = 0$ in Figure 6.8 does not contain the root. In this case, $f(L) < 0$ and $f(R) < 0$, so that $f(L) * f(R) > 0$.

3. Multiple roots are within the interval, as in Figure 6.7 for the function $f(x) = -2.25 - 4x + x^2$. Here we have $f(L) > 0$ and $f(R) > 0$, so that $f(L) * f(R) > 0$. In these cases, the message in lines 1 through 12 is printed.

**NOTE 4** The while loop in lines 17 to 26 implements the bisection procedure for finding the root. This loop continues iterating until either the half-interval drops below the error tolerance or the exact root is found, that is, FNF(MIDC) = 0.

**NOTE 5** The test FNF(MIDC) * FNF(RIGHTC) > 0.0 in line 18 is a slick way of determining whether the root lies in the left half-interval or the right half-interval. Take a look at Figure 6.8 again, which shows the root in the right half of the interval that runs from $-3$ to 1. In this case, we have FNF(MIDC) = $-3$ and FNF(RIGHTC) = 1. Thus the test in line 18 is false, so LEFTC gets set to MIDC in line 21. In general, if FNF(MIDC) and FNF(RIGHTC) have the same sign (both negative or both positive), then the root is in the left half-interval; else, the root is in the right half-interval. You should confirm the generality of this approach by working Exercise 29.

**NOTE 6** The algorithm is not likely to find an exact root as in Table 6.7 for one of two reasons: either roundoff error may prevent locating the exact value or the root may be an irrational number such as one-third (0.3333 . . .). For these reasons, we need to specify a certain error tolerance within which the precision of the computed root is acceptable. For example, we could terminate the algorithm and print the root whenever the half-interval is less than 0.001. The test in line 17 and the output logic in lines 33 to 38 handle both situations: an exact root and an approximate root.

## Follow-Up Exercises

22. Implement the root bisection program on your system. Be careful with differences regarding if-then-else, while, and case structures.

23. Roleplay computer by processing the following data through the program:
    a. 0.0, 1.0 for the interval and 0.001 for error tolerance    (Note that $M$ = root)
    b. 0.5, 1.0 for the interval and 0.001 for error tolerance    (Note that $L$ = root)
    c. 0.0, 0.5 for the interval and 0.001 for error tolerance    (Note that $R$ = root)
    You might want to fill in a table similar to Table 6.5 as you roleplay.

24. How would you change the program to process the function $f(x) = 2^x$? (See Figure 6.7.) Roleplay this function through the program, assuming the input data $-3$, 1 for the interval and 0.001 for error tolerance.

*25. How would you change the program to process the function $f(x) = -2.25 - 4x + x^2$? (See Figure 6.7.) Roleplay this function through the program for the following input data:
    a. 4, 6, 0.01
    b. $-2$, 1, 0.01
    c. 1, 3, 0.01
    d. $-3$, 6, 0.01

*26. Convince yourself that the test in line 18 for the location of the root in the left or right half-interval is perfectly general. Pick an interval in Figure 6.8 that locates the root in the left half and evaluate the test. Next, sketch a negatively sloped linear function and repeat the test for two different intervals, one that locates the root in the left half and one that locates it in the right half.

*27. Improve the computational efficiency of the program by accounting for the possibility (as in Exercise 23b,c) that either FNF(LEFTC) or FNF(RIGHTC) is zero; that is, the initial $L$ or $R$ is at the root. (*Hint:* Make the if-then-else structure in line 470 a multiple alternative structure that includes new cases.)

## 6.5 POINTERS

The following pointers reinforce those mentioned earlier and introduce additional thoughts for improving style and avoiding error.

### Design and Style

**1. Indentation.** Don't forget to indent then blocks, else blocks, else-if blocks, and case blocks within nested, multiple-block, and case structures. As usual, this practice improves the readability of programs. (Try to picture the price quotation and root bisection programs in Section 6.4 without indentation!)

**2. Making the design choice.** As you know, various designs are possible for decision structures with multiple alternatives. Table 6.6 summarizes the pros and cons of each. Of course, the issues described in the table are not the only bases for determining just which design we would implement in practice, since the BASIC dialect we must use may restrict our choice. For example, if SELECT/CASE statements are not available but the ELSEIF statement is, then we would be inclined to use the elseif design over a case design that must use the ON/GO TO statement.

**3. GO TOs are dangerous to our programming health.** Problems caused by the excessive use of GO TO statements and explicit transfers such as THEN 100 were one motivating factor in the development of top-down structured programming concepts. Undisciplined use of this statement makes programs difficult to follow, hard to modify, and error prone. For example, the GO TO statement requires the numeric reference to which control is transferred. Subsequently, this opens the door to incorrect transfers and programs that violate top-down design and control structure principles.

Programs that eliminate the use of explicit line number transfers also greatly reduce the likelihood of certain execution errors, as when control is transferred from outside into the body of a FOR/NEXT loop or into a then block, else block, else-if block, or case block.

**Table 6.6** Alternative Designs for Multiple Alternative Decision Structures

| Name | Pseudocode Design | Comment |
|---|---|---|
| 1. Sequence of if-then structures | If condition then<br><br>· Block 1<br>·<br>End if<br><br>If condition then<br><br>· Block 2<br>·<br>End if<br><br>· More if–then<br>structures | This is readable but inefficient with respect to processing time, because each condition in the sequence is evaluated regardless of whether or not an earlier condition tested true. Typically, we design the structure so that only a single condition tests true in the sequence. Designs 2 and 3 below are CPU-efficient, because they exit the structure immediately after the first *true* block is entered. |

**Table 6.6** continued

| Name | Pseudocode Design | Comment |
|---|---|---|
| 2. Nested if-then-else structures | **If condition then**<br><br>· Block 1<br><br>**Else**<br>**If condition then**<br><br>· Block 2<br><br>**Else**<br><br>· More if-then-else structures<br><br>**End if**<br>**End if** | This design is more CPU-efficient and more appropriate when conditions are related than design 1, but readability diminishes drastically as the number of nests increases. Some organizations forbid nesting beyond two or three levels to avoid potential logic problems. We prefer design 3 to this design. (Try visualizing 20 blocks to see what we mean!) |
| 3. Else-if structure | **If condition then**<br><br>· Block 1<br><br>**Else if condition then**<br><br>· Block 2<br><br>· More ELSEIF statements and blocks<br><br>**Else**<br><br>· Optional error block<br><br>**End if** | This is our preferred approach for decision structures with nonsimple conditions and many blocks. It's more CPU-efficient than design 1 and more readable than design 2. Its implementation, however, is limited for currently available dialects. (See Table 6.2 for implementations and Exercise 9 for desirability.) |
| 4. Case structure | **Select case condition**<br>**Case one**<br><br>· Block 1<br><br>**Case two**<br><br>· Block 2<br><br>· More cases<br><br>**Case undefined**<br><br>· Optional error block<br><br>**End select** | This is our preferred approach for decision structures with simple conditions such as codes and many blocks. It's more CPU-efficient and more readable than the other three designs. Its implementation, however, is limited to specific dialects. (See Table 6.3 for implementations.) |

*When programmers first heard that they should try to program without GOTOs, many were incredulous. It seemed absurd. GOTOs were among the most commonly used instructions in a programmer's arsenal.*[2]

If we have a structured **BASIC** dialect like **ANS BASIC** available, then structures such as if-then-else, else-if, case, while, and until are implementable without a single explicit transfer of control. Given such a dialect, a statement such as

```
IF condition THEN 100 ELSE 200
```

falls under the category of "mortal programming sin."

**4. Try being friendly.**    It's useful to take the perspective that your program will be run by others. Commercial interactive programs pay close attention to having a friendly user-interface, which makes it easy for a user to learn to operate and otherwise interact with a program. (This wasn't always the case, but the widespread use of microcomputers has changed this.) For example, many commercial programs are menu-driven (as in Section 6.4), since this facilitates the selection of options and implementation of commands. Thus it pays to design the menus carefully with respect to layout, use of color, and choice of responses. It's best to avoid screen clutter by displaying a menu in isolation from preceding material or succeeding output. This is best accomplished by clearing the screen just before the menu is displayed and clearing the screen again once the menu item is selected. For example, Microsoft BASIC uses the statement

**CLS Statement**

```
CLS
```

to clear a screen. Does your dialect have such a statement? Programs with extensive menu choices are often designed with hierarchical menus, whereby the selection of one menu item generates a submenu of other choices. Also, all incorrect user input should be trapped if possible. For example, incorrect menu choices and out-of-range data input should be detected, giving the user a chance to correct the entry. (For example, see Figure 6.6). Many microcomputer programs effectively use sound and color to alert the user to incorrect responses. Finally, many commercial programs provide interactive *help* facilities to aid users when they are unsure of what response to make. For example, at the touch of a key a user can get a full explanation of a particular option, feature, procedure, or form of data input.

**5. A poorly designed algorithm is a primary factor that contributes to excessive computer time.**    This factor is so important in certain applications that professionals in applied mathematics, statistics, and computer science have devoted extensive research efforts to improving the time efficiency of many algorithms. More often than not, this involves the development of an entirely new algorithm that achieves the same end result. For example, sorting algorithms have been developed that are significantly lower in cost than traditional sorting methods such as the bubble sort described in Chapter 8. In general, we should look for economies that make a significant difference, but without degrading the readability of the program. In commercial appli-

[2]Steve Olson, "Sage of Software," *Science*, January/February 1984, p. 79.

cations, an esoteric, obscure code that saves CPU time is generally not preferred to a less efficient version that is readable, understandable, and easy to change.

## Common Errors

**1. Incorrect line number transfers.**    If you must use explicit transfers to implement a structure such as the minimal **ANSI** case structure, then take care that you transfer control to the intended statements, that you include a GO TO at the end of each block to transfer control to the end of the structure (see GO TO 700 in Table 6.3), and that you trap data errors through an error block as in Tables 6.2 and 6.3.

**2. Illegal nesting.**    Watch out for the illegal nesting of control structures. The block of one control structure must not *partially* contain another control structure. The following designs illustrate this condition:

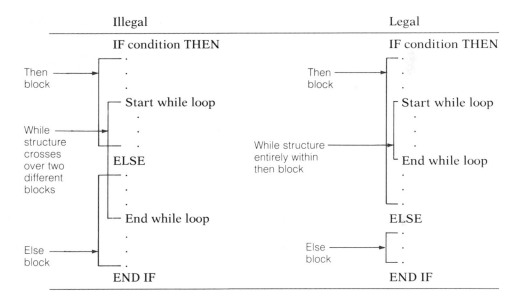

Note that the use of brackets makes it easier to keep structures from crossing over. This is true whether we nest loops, decision structures, or both. *An inner nested structure must be contained entirely within the block of its outer structure.*

**3. Algorithmic logic errors and test data selection.**    Now that you are designing more complicated algorithms, you need to validate your programs carefully and systematically during the debugging phase. *The key to this procedure is the deliberate selection of test data.* Always select test read/input data that validates each logical segment or branch in your program. For example, the data for our test runs of the price quotation program in Section 6.4 were selected to test each block of the design on page 199. Specifically, we entered the following input data:

- E to test the **EBM** case block (see Figure 6.6)
- R to test the undefined case block (see Figure 6.6)
- M to test the Manzana case block (see Figure 6.6)
- S to test loop termination (see Figure 6.6)

- 0   order sizes to test the minimum order then blocks within the two cases (done for the *M*-case in Figure 6.6).

- Various order sizes to test each block within the else-if structures (three out of six shown in Figure 6.6).

The output from the program was then checked against a set of hand-calculated results.

Where appropriate, extreme data values should be selected to test potential problems. For example, select a data item that might cause division by 0 and check the computer's reaction. If the result is unwanted, then you must program an error routine. A common cause of this type of error is incorrect input/read data, as when mistakes are made keying in data. Another example includes boundary values within tested conditions. To illustrate, the values 1, 9, and 29 in Table 6.4 and line 240 in Figure 6.5 are boundary values that should be tested to ensure intended results. (These tests were not shown in Figure 6.6.)

The use of temporary trace (diagnostic PRINT) statements within blocks is sometimes useful for uncovering logic problems in programs with complicated structures. Many systems further facilitate this process with certain diagnostic aids. For example, Microsoft **BASIC** includes **TRON** (TRace ON) and **TROFF** (TRace OFF) commands to enable and disable a trace flag that prints each line number of a program as it is executed. These line numbers typically appear in square brackets, as illustrated by the sample run below.

```
Ok

10 FOR J=1 TO 2
20    FOR K=1 TO 3
30       PRINT J;K
40    NEXT K
50 NEXT J
60 END

TRON
Ok
RUN
[10][20][30] 1   1
[40][30] 1   2
[40][30] 1   3
[40][50][20][30] 2   1
[40][30] 2   2
[40][30] 2   3
[40][50][60]
Ok

TROFF
Ok
```

Does your system have this diagnostic facility? If so, give it a try with the sample program above.

The test data we give in exercises at the ends of chapters are designed to push you in this debugging direction. You should always check the data for thoroughness, however, and add your own when warranted. To complete the validation, confirm the correctness of computer output by parallel hand calculations.

In general, you should program defensively by testing all parts of your program and by training yourself to anticipate potential errors that can be overcome by good program design.

# ADDITIONAL EXERCISES

**28.** Define or explain the following:

multiple-alternative decision structures
nested decision structures
multiple-block decision structure
else-if decision structure
error routine
ELSEIF statement

elseif block
case structure
case block
case item
ON/GO TO statement
SELECT or SELECT CASE statement
CASE statement

CASE ELSE statement
END SELECT statement
table lookup
menu
STOP statement
user-defined function
TRON/TROFF commands

**29.** **Revisits.** Modify one of the following earlier examples or exercises, as indicated.

**a.** **Government Printing Office Orders.** (Section 4.5, page 132.) Use an else-if structure for the discount logic and implement the revised program on your system. Make any other improvements or add any other features that might be worthwhile.

**b.** **Alumni File.** (Chapter 4, Exercise 28, page 143.) Use the following menu:

Report Choices

| | |
|---|---|
| 1 | Average salary report |
| 2 | Work experience count |
| 3 | Year of graduation count |
| 4 | Stop processing |

The count reports simply print frequency distributions or counts. For example, choice 3 might print the following report:

Year of Graduation Report

| Year | Count |
|---|---|
| 84 | 3 |
| 85 | 8 |
| Total | 11 |

**c.** **Inventory Reorders.** (Chapter 4, Exercise 29, page 144.) Offer the user a menu that prints various report choices. Look at the data in the inventory file and decide for yourself what choices should be offered. Some obvious choices are given in parts **a** and **b** of the exercise.

**d.** **Credit Billing.** (Chapter 5, Exercise 27, page 143.) Offer the following menu:

Select One

| | |
|---|---|
| P | Print bills |
| C | Credit limit count |
| A | Averages |
| S | Stop processing |

The credit limit count choice should print the following report based on the given internal data file:

Credit Limit Count

| Limit | Count |
|---|---|
| Under $1000 | 1 |
| $1000–$2000 | 2 |
| Over $2000 | 0 |
| Total | 3 |

Choice a prints a report that gives the average of each numeric column in the data file.

**e.** **Personnel Benefits Budget.** (Chapter 5, Exercise 29, page 177.) Offer the following menu:

Choose One

| | |
|---|---|
| F | Full report |
| A | Average salary report |
| R | Retirement breakdown report |
| S | Stop processing |

The full report is described in the exercise and the average salary report is simply the average of the salary column. Choice R prints the following report:

Retirement Breakdown Report

| Code | Count |
|---|---|
| NE | 2 |
| SP | 4 |
| PP | 2 |
| Total | 8 |

**30.** **Tuition Schedule.** The following table reflects the tuition schedule at a local college.

| | Full-time Student | Part-time Student |
|---|---|---|
| In-state resident | $1500/term | $50/credit |
| Out-of-state resident | $3000/term | $125/credit |

A program is to use the following read/output:

*Output*
1. Student name
2. Tuition

*Read*
1. Student name
2. Time status (FULL or PART)
3. Residency (IN or OUT)
4. Number of credits

The following design is proposed:

1. Read parameters
2. Read data
3. Start eof loop
4.   Determine tuition
5.   Print output
6.   Read data
7. End loop
8. End

a. Draw a flowchart or write down refined pseudocode for the tuition decision logic in step 4.
b. Write a BASIC program that's implementable on your system.
c. Test the program on your system for the following data:

Test 1,FULL,IN,15
Test 2,FULL,OUT,18
Test 3,PART,IN,6
Test 4,PART,OUT,9

31. **Student Grades.** A student is assigned a grade A, B, C, D, or F according to the following rule.

| | |
|---|---|
| test score ≥ 90 | grade is A |
| 80 ≤ test score < 90 | grade is B |
| 70 ≤ test score < 80 | grade is C |
| 60 ≤ test score < 70 | grade is D |
| test score < 60 | grade is F |

A program is to use the following read/output:

*Output*
1. Student name
2. Letter grade

*Read*
1. Student name
2. Test score

a. Design a program (flowchart or pseudocode) that uses an eof loop to process students. Use parameters to store the grade class ranges (100, 90, 80, 70, and 60). Include an error routine that prints name and error message for grades outside the range 0–100.
b. Write a BASIC program that can be implemented on your system.
c. Test the program for the following data:

Test 1,80
Test 2,75
Test 3,110
Test 4,50
Test 5,95
Test 6,64

32. **Primary Elections.** Write a program that interactively enters the number of votes for each candidate and declares a winner. Input data include the following:

State
Number of candidates
Name of each candidate and number of votes

For each candidate, print the number of votes and the percent of total votes that the candidate receives. On separate lines, print the total number of votes cast and the name of the candidate with the most votes.

Use the following test data:

| State | Candidate | Votes |
|---|---|---|
| Massachusetts | Favorite Person | 130,000 |
| | Dark Horse | 12,000 |
| | The Pol | 450,000 |
| Georgia | The Pol | 200,000 |
| | Local Guy | 250,000 |
| Colorado | King Schuss | 75,000 |
| | Local Gal | 90,000 |
| | Mountain High | 10,000 |

33. **Property Tax Assessment.** The property tax rate in a town is set at an increasing rate according to the following table.

Annual Property Tax Schedule

| *Value of Property* | *Tax Rate* |
|---|---|
| Less than $10,000 | 3% |
| $10,000 or more but under $30,000 | 4% |
| $30,000 or more but under $60,000 | 5% |
| $60,000 and over | 6% |

a. Run a program to read in the value of the property, then determine and print the tax charge. Process the following test data as an internal data file.

| Lot Number | Owner's Name | Property Value |
|---|---|---|
| 613 | A. Smith | $ 8,900 |
| 975 | A. B. Smith | 25,000 |
| 152 | B. C. Smith | 42,000 |
| 1642 | C. B. Smith | 37,000 |
| 1785 | Deaf Smith | 75,000 |

Sample Output

| Lot Number | Owner | Property Value | Tax Charge |
|---|---|---|---|
| 613 | A. Smith | 8900 | 267 |
| 975 | A. B. Smith | 25000 | 1000 |
| 152 | B. C. Smith | 42000 | 2100 |
| 1642 | C. B. Smith | 37000 | 1850 |
| 1785 | Deaf Smith | 75000 | 3750 |

**b.** Modify the program in part **a** so that it prints the sum of property values, the total tax charge, the average property value, and the average tax charge.

**c.** Check the entered data for errors by ensuring that lot numbers are greater than zero and less than 5000 and property values are greater than $1 and less than $5 million. If an error is found, print an appropriate error message, bypass the tax charge calculation, and go on to the next property. Add new data to test each of these possible errors.

**34. Traffic Court Fines.** Each week the clerk in traffic court summarizes the fines collected for traffic violations by major categories: moving violation, standing violation, and warning. The data on each violation include ticket number, traffic violation type (1 = moving violation; 2 = standing violation; 3 = warning) and amount of fine (see Figure 1).

**a.** Write a program that summarizes the traffic violations data from Figure 1 and prints a report (Figure 2) that accumulates the dollar amount (total fines) collected for moving violations and counts the number of moving violations; accumulates the total fines collected and counts the number of fines for standing violations; and counts the number of warnings (warnings do not involve a fine).

FIGURE 1
Violations Data File

| ticket number | type | amount |
|---|---|---|
| 789 | 1 | 50 |
| 790 | 2 | 15 |
| 791 | 2 | 20 |
| 793 | 25 | 2 |
| 794 | 1 | 75 |
| 795 | 3 | 0 |
| 798 | 2 | 10 |
| 799 | 2 | 15 |

FIGURE 2
Traffic Violation Summary Report

| type | number | amount |
|---|---|---|
| MOVING | 2 | 125 |
| STANDING | 4 | 60 |
| WARNING | 1 | 0 |

**b.** Build in error-checking logic to trap errors in the traffic violations type code and print the following error message before printing the summary report.

```
***************************************************************
ERROR IN CODE FOR TICKET                 4
***************************************************************
```

**c.** Print a count of the number of errors following the report.

**35. Telephone Company Billing.** "Flat rate service" charges for telephone service is a method of billing that includes some fixed amount for the main station (main telephone, switchboard, and so on) plus a variable amount per extension phone in service. Distinctions also are made between residential and business customers according to the table below. Private Branch Exchange (PBX) service uses a switchboard for the main station, off which extensions can be wired. Centrex service is for large-scale business firms and governmental agencies, which require such a large number of extensions that the telephone switching equipment is located on the customer's premises.

| Customer Type | Code | Type of Service | Monthly Flat Rates Main Station | Each Extension |
|---|---|---|---|---|
| Residential | 1 | Main phone/ extensions | $ 13 | $ 3 |
| Business | 2 | Main phone/ extensions | 50 | 10 |
| Business | 3 | PBX/ extensions | 150 | 5 |
| Business | 4 | Centrex/ extensions | 500 | 3 |

In actual practice, PBX and Centrex include many special features. For example, options include fully automatic equipment versus partly manual equipment, facilities for data transmission, private lines that ring at specific locations when the receiver is picked up (PLs), facilities for foreign exchange (FX), and many others.

To illustrate a calculation, consider a business customer with **PBX** equipment and 50 extensions. In this case, the monthly flat rate is $400 [or $150 + (50 × $5)], which, of course, excludes long-distance charges, taxes, and charges due to special features.

**a.** Design and write a program that calculates flat rate service charges and outputs customer name, telephone number, and charge. Test your program with the following data.

Telephone Data File

| Customer Name | Customer Phone Number | Code | Number of Extensions |
|---|---|---|---|
| Test 1 | 783-5123 | 2 | 5 |
| Test 2 | 792-7541 | 4 | 400 |
| Test 3 | 445-8162 | 4 | 550 |
| Test 4 | 612-6148 | 3 | 75 |
| Test 5 | 783-1235 | 1 | 0 |
| Test 6 | 445-2164 | 1 | 3 |
| Test 7 | 789-5849 | 2 | 7 |
| Test 8 | 789-7812 | 4 | 730 |
| Test 9 | 792-2674 | 1 | 1 |
| Test 10 | 615-6513 | 3 | 50 |

Terminate customer read-in based on an eof condition.

**b.** Modify the program in part **a** to include the calculation and output of the following.
  1. Total number of customers by code category
  2. Percent of customers by code category
  3. Total charges by code category
  4. Overall total charges
  Try to design your output for easy readability.

**c.** Include error detection for code. If an error is found, print an appropriate error message and go on to the next customer. Do not include that customer's data in the output of part **a** or **b**. Add new data with incorrect codes to debug your error logic.

36. **Mailing List.** A professional group of computer specialists is planning a regional meeting in New Orleans. A subgroup of information system specialists within this professional group is having a well-known computer scientist as a guest speaker. The chairperson of this subgroup plans to send meeting notices to members in two regions—southeast (code 3) and southwest (code 5)—who have an interest in information systems (code 15) or computer science (code 18).

The organization maintains the following data on each member (see sample data file below):

1. Last name
2. First name
3. Address
4. City
5. State
6. Zip
7. Region code (one digit; there are nine regions overall)
8. Interest code (two digits; there are 20 interest areas overall)

**a.** Design a menu-driven program that can be used to prepare mailing labels for any region and/or area of interest criteria. Sample menu, response, and output follow:

```
    MAILING LIST MENU
1    Specific region only
2    Specific interest area only
3    Specific region or interest area
4    Specific region and interest area
5    Stop processing
Your Selection? 2

Option 2—Specific interest area only

Enter interest code ? 15

Mailing labels

Frank Fastcode
11 Flower
Dallas, TX 75215

M.I.S. Crowley
1 Hope Rd
Atlanta, GA 30901
```

**b.** Include error detection for region and interest codes. If an error is found, then print an appropriate error message and go on to the next member. Add new data with incorrect codes to debug your error logic.

37. **Newton's Approximation Method.** This method describes a procedure for approximating the root of a function. Consider Figure 6.12, which reproduces a blown-up portion of the quadratic function in Figure 6.7. If we arbitrarily select the first root approximation at $x = 6.00$, then the second approximation is at $x = 4.78$. Graphically, the second approximation is found by constructing a tangent line on the function at $x = 6.00$ and extending this line to the

Sample Data File

| 1 | 2 | 3 | 4 | 5 | 6 | 7 | 8 |
|---|---|---|---|---|---|---|---|
| Fastcode | Frank | 11 Flower | Dallas | TX | 75215 | 5 | 15 |
| Burden | Kathy | 193 West St | Warwick | RI | 02886 | 1 | 18 |
| Peripheral | Leslie | 18 Grande | Slidell | LA | 70808 | 5 | 20 |
| Crowley | M.I.S | 1 Hope Rd | Atlanta | GA | 30901 | 3 | 15 |
| Deff | Doris | 111 High St | Hartford | CT | 06518 | 7 | 12 |
| Aipes | Clyde | 963 Main St | Orlando | FL | 32407 | 3 | 18 |
| Frick | Ford | 2 Rose Way | Boston | MA | 01906 | 9 | 18 |

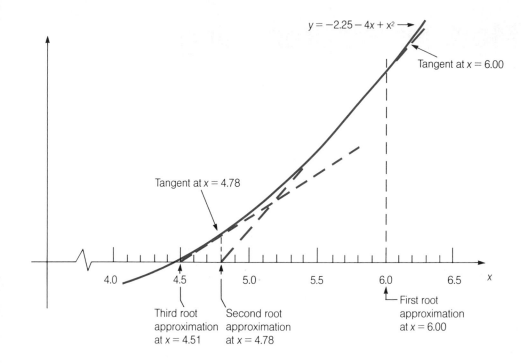

**Figure 6.12**    Newton's approximation method

*x*-axis. The intersection of the tangent line with the *x*-axis gives the next root approximation, which is 4.78 approximately. Next we construct a tangent at $x = 4.78$, and it intersects the *x*-axis at roughly 4.51. This process continues until a desired precision is achieved. Note that each successive approximation gets closer and closer to the root at $x = 4.50$.

Analytically, a tangent line is determined as the first derivative of the function, which we label $y'$ ($y$ prime). For the function

$$y = -2.25 - 4x + x^2$$

the first derivative is

$$y' = -4 + 2x$$

The next root approximation is determined from the following formula.

$$\text{Next } x = \text{current } x - \frac{y}{y'}$$

The table below illustrates three iterations of this procedure.

| Current $x$ | $y = -2.25 - 4x + x^2$ | $y' = -4 + 2x$ | Next $x$ |
|---|---|---|---|
| 6.000000 | 9.750000 | 8.000000 | 4.781250 |
| 4.781250 | 1.485351 | 5.562500 | 4.514220 |
| 4.514220 | 0.0713022 | 5.028440 | 4.500040 |
| . | . | . | . |
| . | . | . | . |
| . | . | . | . |

**a.** Design and run a program that approximates roots by this method. Terminate iterations when the difference between two successive *x*'s is less than 0.00001. Use the following test data.

| $y$ | $y'$ | Initial $x$ values |
|---|---|---|
| $-2.25 - 4x + x^2$ | $-4 + 2x$ | 6.0; 4.0; 4.5 |
| $-1 + 2x$ | 2 | 3.0; $-2.0$ |
| $2^x$ | $(2^x) \cdot (\ln 2)^*$ | 10 |
| $-20 + 108x^2 - 4x^3$ | $216x - 12x^2$ | Make up your own. Try to find multiple roots. |

*Ln 2 stands for the natural (base-*e*) logarithm of 2 (see Module C).

**\*\*b.** Incorporate logic for finding multiple roots (if any).

# Modular Programming

# 7

This chapter introduces, motivates, and implements a style of programming called modular programming. As we will see, this approach to programming is especially useful in designing and developing long, complex programs of the type encountered in commercial applications.

## 7.1 SUBROUTINES

This section defines and motivates the modular concept and illustrates modular programming implementations by means of subroutines.

### The Modular Concept

Behavioral research, not to mention our own experiences, clearly shows that the human brain best solves elaborate problems by a "divide and conquer" strategy. That is, we divide a large problem into distinct and manageable major portions, or tasks. Then we separately work on each task, generally completing one before going on to the next. Finally, when all major tasks are complete, we have a solution to the overall problem. Table 7.1 illustrates the breakdown of specific problems into major tasks.

**Table 7.1** Sample Major Tasks or Modules

| Problem | Major Tasks (Modules) |
| --- | --- |
| Write book | Front matter |
| | Chapter 1 |
| | . |
| | . |
| | . |
| | Chapter 9 |
| | Appendix A |
| | Appendix B |
| | Index |
| Build house | Excavation |
| | Foundation |
| | First floor |
| | Second floor |
| | Plumbing |
| | Electrical work |
| | Finish work |
| Develop telephone billing program | Data input and error routine |
| | Calculation of bills |
| | Printing of bills |
| | Management report |

Similarly, as programs increase in length and complexity, it's best to view the major processing tasks as groups of related statements called **modules.** The act of designing and developing a program as a set of modules is called **modular programming.**

As illustrated by the third example in Table 7.1, a module represents a processing task. But exactly what is a module and how is it implemented? Unfortunately, there is no unique definition of a module, nor is there just one way to implement modules. Moreover, the selection of good modules based on processing tasks requires study, experience, talent, and insight. So, rather than answering these questions directly, let's list some key properties of a module and then illustrate their selection and implementation through a series of examples.

**Properties of a Module**

1. **A module has a single entry point and a single exit point.** In essence, a module is like a "black box" that is uniquely activated (entered through the top), performs some assigned function, and is uniquely deactivated (exited through the bottom).
2. **A module is independent from other modules.** Essentially this means that we can design, develop, change, or modify a module without affecting other modules. In reality, absolute independence may not be achievable in many cases; however, modules should at least exhibit the type of functional independence described in the four modules of the telephone billing example in Table 7.1.
3. **A module is not too large.** The industry rule of thumb says that a module should not exceed 50 to 100 lines of code, which is one or two pages of listing. The basic idea is that the size of a module should not become so unwieldy that the programmer loses intimacy (understanding in depth) with this portion of the code. Needless to say, this property is subjective but well meaning.

## Subroutines as Modules

A **subroutine** is a uniquely identifiable group of successive statements within a program that accomplishes a specific purpose within that program. Subroutines are useful because (1) they allow a modular approach to long, complicated programs, (2) they promote shorter programs when the repeated use of a sequence of statements is needed at different points in a program, and (3) they save programming effort when a code that accomplishes a popular task can be used in more than one program.

Figure 7.1 illustrates the typical structure of a program that uses subroutines. Note that a subroutine is not used by itself; rather, it's embedded within the larger program. Also note how the scheme in Figure 7.1 effectively subdivides the program into its component modules. The first module is called

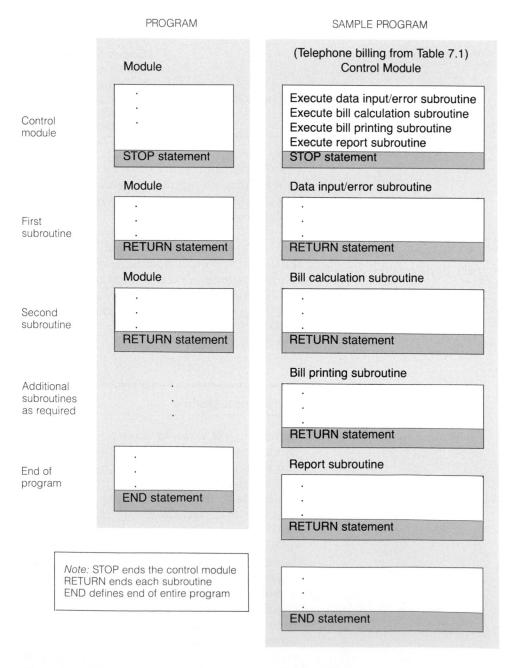

**Figure 7.1** Typical structure of programs with subroutines

the **control module.** Generally, this first module initiates the program and controls the order in which other modules within the program are executed.

The next example illustrates how we construct and execute subroutines and introduces the new BASIC statements GOSUB and RETURN.

**E X A M P L E   7 . 1**    **Bar Chart Program**

The following steps illustrate a program with just two modules, the control module and one subroutine.

### Analysis

Let's develop a noninteractive program that reads data for a frequency distribution and prints a graphical representation called a bar chart. Figure 7.2 shows a sample frequency distribution and its corresponding bar chart for final grades in an academic course.

The data requirements are as follows:

*Output*
Title of bar chart
Label for each bar
Bars
Length of each bar

*Read*
Title of bar chart
Number of bars
Label for each bar
Length of each bar

### Design

The first step in the design is a top-down look at the overall modular structure. Typically, a module has either a specialized task or a set of related tasks within the overall purpose of the program. In our example, let's design a subroutine or module that prints the elements of a bar chart as in Figure 7.2b. Thus our subroutine will specialize in printing each bar in a bar chart, together with its label and length. The control module, then, must carry out the other tasks, as described below.

| | |
|---|---|
| *Control module* | Reads all data.<br>Prints title.<br>Establishes a loop that processes a complete bar chart.<br>Stops processing. |
| *Subroutine bar print* | Prints the label, bar, and length of the bar. |

(a) Frequency Distribution          (b) Bar Chart

**Figure 7.2**  Frequency distribution and bar chart of final grades

The following pseudocode reflects this design.

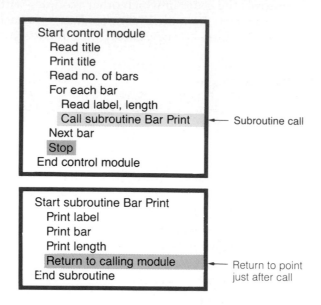

Start control module
  Read title
  Print title
  Read no. of bars
  For each bar
    Read label, length
    Call subroutine Bar Print    ◄── Subroutine call
  Next bar
  Stop
End control module

Start subroutine Bar Print
  Print label
  Print bar
  Print length
  Return to calling module    ◄── Return to point
End subroutine                     just after call

Note that the subroutine is referenced within the loop in the control module when it's time to print the label, bar, and length for any one bar. This is termed a **subroutine call.** Calling the subroutine means that we tell the computer to execute the statements within the subroutine at this time. The subroutine itself looks like any other program design we have written up to now, except that when the computer is through executing the subroutine, execution control must be "returned" to the module that called the subroutine in the first place.

Thus, from an execution point of view, the loop design in the control module works as follows:

**1.**   Read the label and length of a bar.

**2.**   Call the subroutine.

  The subroutine prints the label, bar, and length, after which it returns control to the control module.

**3.**   Go on to the next bar and repeat steps 1 and 2 as often as necessary.

The bar itself is printed as a set of special characters such as =, *, or +. The number of these special characters in the bar is equivalent to the length of the bar. Thus we can further refine the subroutine as follows:

Print bar ⎡ For each character in bar
          ⎢   Print character
          ⎣ Next character

In other words, it takes a FOR/NEXT loop to print the individual characters that make up the bar.

Figure 7.3 shows equivalent flowcharts for the given pseudocode. Note that each module is a separate flowchart and that modules are "called" using the predefined process symbol.

### Code and Test

Figure 7.4 shows the program and test run for the bar chart problem. Study the program together with its output, relate it to the pseudocode design and discussion, and then go on to the text that follows the example for further explanations.

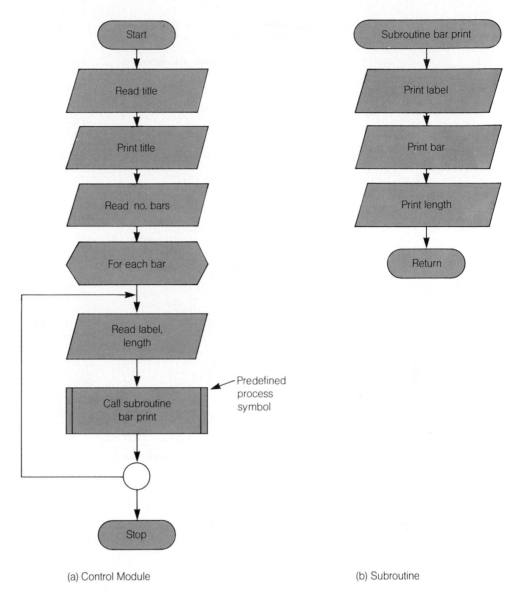

(a) Control Module                                    (b) Subroutine

**Figure 7.3**  Flowcharts for bar chart program

A subroutine is called through the execution of a GOSUB statement of the following type:[1]

**GOSUB Statement**

> **GOSUB** *line number*
> GOSUB 400

This statement transfers control to the indicated line number, which should be the first line in the subroutine. The statements within the subroutine are then executed, until a RETURN statement transfers control back to the calling module.

In the example, execution of GOSUB 400 transfers execution control to line 400. Looking at the program in Figure 7.4, we see that when line 300 is executed, control is next transferred to line 400. Since lines 400 and 410 are REM statements, the next line executed is really line 420, which prints the label A for the first bar. Next, the bar is printed within the loop defined by

---

[1]The subroutine also can be called through an ON/GOSUB statement. See Exercise 9.

```
100 REM  * * * * * * * * * * * * * * * * * * * * * * * * * *
110 REM  * Bar Chart Program                                *
120 REM  *                                                  *
130 REM  *    Control module ... Reads data and loops for each *
140 REM  *                       bar to be printed.          *
150 REM  *                       Calls subroutine bar print. *
160 REM  *                                                  *
170 REM  *    Sub. bar print ... Prints a bar, together with *
180 REM  *                       its label and length.      *
190 REM  * * * * * * * * * * * * * * * * * * * * * * * * * *
200 REM
210 REM-------------- Control Module --------------------------
220 REM
230      PRINT
240      READ TITLE$
250      PRINT TITLE$
260      PRINT
270      READ BARS
280      FOR J = 1 TO BARS
290        READ LABEL$,LENGTH
300        GOSUB 400                    ' Call subroutine bar print
310      NEXT J
320      PRINT
330      STOP
399 REM
400 REM-------------- Subroutine Bar Print ----------------------
410 REM
420      PRINT LABEL$;" ";
430      FOR K = 1 TO LENGTH
440        PRINT "=";
450      NEXT K
460      PRINT LENGTH
470      RETURN
499 REM
900 REM-------------- Data Section --------------------------
901 REM
905      DATA "Distribution of Final Grades"
910      DATA 5
911      DATA "A",8
912      DATA "B",15
913      DATA "C",20
914      DATA "D",6
915      DATA "F",3
998 REM------------------------------------------------------
999      END
```

```
RUN

Distribution of Final Grades

A ======== 8
B =============== 15
C ==================== 20
D ====== 6
F === 3

Break in 330
```

**Figure 7.4**  Bar chart program and test run

lines 430–450, the length of the bar (8) is printed in line 460, and then the RETURN statement in line 470 is executed.

The last statement in a subroutine is the RETURN statement, which has the following general form:

**RETURN statement**

```
RETURN
```

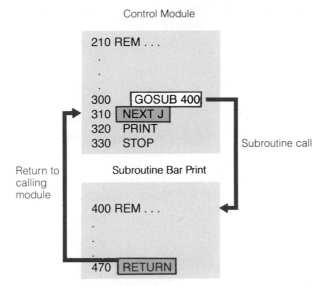

**Figure 7.5**    The call/return process for the bar chart program

*This statement transfers control back to the statement immediately following the GOSUB statement that called the subroutine.* For example, execution of line 470 in Figure 7.4 transfers execution to just after the call in line 300, which means that line 310 is executed next. This call/return process is better illustrated in Figure 7.5. Note that this process is repeated five times (once for each bar) for the data given in Figure 7.4.

**NOTE 1**    The program in Figure 7.4 reflects the generalized modular design in Figure 7.1. In particular, note that the control module ends with a STOP statement, the bar print module ends with a RETURN statement, and the remaining portion or data section ends with an END statement. Moreover, execution of each module starts at the top of the module and exits through the bottom, which is consistent with the desirability of *top-down execution*. This described structure is not syntactically necessary, however, since it's possible to place a subroutine *before* the control module or even *within* the control module without provoking a syntax error. Moreover, a subroutine can be both accessed and exited through GOTO statements. Good program design, however, dictates the modular setup we have described, together with subroutine accesses only through GOSUB statements and subroutine exits only through RETURN statements.

**NOTE 2**    A subroutine can use any BASIC statement. Also, a subroutine has access to all variables in a program. In Figure 7.4, the subroutine utilized the variables LABEL$ and LENGTH, whose values were read in by the control module.

**NOTE 3**    A subroutine does not have a unique first line, either to indicate the beginning of a subroutine or to separate it from the preceding module. Our own preference is to use a REM statement containing the name of the module as the first line of a subroutine.

**NOTE 4**    We use the STOP statement at the end of the control module to halt execution of the program. By placing the STOP statement at line 330 in Figure 7.4, we ensure that execution control does not inadvertently drop into subroutine bar print. In Exercise 3 we look at alternatives to STOP.

## Follow-Up Exercises

1. Roleplay the execution of the FOR/NEXT loop in lines 280–310 in Figure 7.4 by indicating the line executed and the action taken. We'll get you started.

| Line Executed | Action |
|---|---|
| 280 | Set FOR/NEXT parameters |
| 290 | Read in A for LABEL$ and 8 for LENGTH |
| 300 | Call subroutine |
| 420 | Print label A |
| 430 | Set FOR/NEXT parameters |
| 440 | |
| 450 | |
| 440 | |
| 450 | Print 8 = signs |
| . | |
| . | |
| . | |
| 460 | Print length 8 |
| 470 | Return |
| 310 | Next bar |

Fill in just for the 2nd bar

2. Is the coding of the program in Figure 7.4 general enough to handle any frequency distribution (except for changes in the data section)?
   a. Change the program in Figure 7.4 to process the following frequency distribution.

   Age Distribution of Employees

   | Age | Number |
   |---|---|
   | Under 20 | 5 |
   | 20–29 | 30 |
   | 30–39 | 50 |
   | 40–49 | 70 |
   | 50–59 | 40 |
   | Over 59 | 10 |

   b. Run the changed program on your system.

3. What happens in the output when the STOP statement in line 330 is executed? Can you think of alternatives to STOP that might avoid this? What's your preference?

4. **GOSUB with String Label.** Some systems allow GOSUB statements of the form

   **GOSUB** *string label*
   GOSUB bar_print

## Pseudo-local vs. Global Variables

The bar chart example illustrated how we might go about designing modules based on defined processing tasks and presented the mechanics of implementing subroutines. In many applications we need to repeatedly use a subroutine, using a different set of variables in each repetition. This brings us to the issue of local versus global variables, which is best illustrated by example.

**E X A M P L E   7 . 2**   **Combinations Program**

The following example illustrates the repeated use of three subroutines, shows calls from one subroutine to another, and raises the issue of local versus global variables.

**Analysis**

The number of combinations of $n$ objects taken $k$ at a time (where $n \geqslant k$) is a common calculation in many statistical and mathematical applications. The formula is given by

$$C = \frac{n!}{(n-k)!k!}$$

where the exclamation point represents "factorial." For example, 5! reads "the factorial of 5" or "5 factorial," which is defined by the product $1 \cdot 2 \cdot 3 \cdot 4 \cdot 5$, or 120. The number of combinations of 5 taken 2 at a time ($n = 5$ and $k = 2$) is calculated from

$$C = \frac{5!}{(5-2)!2!} = \frac{5!}{3!2!} = \frac{1 \cdot 2 \cdot 3 \cdot 4 \cdot 5}{(1 \cdot 2 \cdot 3)(1 \cdot 2)} = \frac{120}{6 \cdot 2} = \frac{120}{12} = 10$$

Combinations are defined only if $n \geqslant k$, $n > 0$, and $k \geqslant 0$. Moreover, 0! is defined as 1. Let's design an interactive program that offers the user a menu of two items:

C   Calculate combinations
S   Stop processing

If C is selected, then let's ask the user to enter values for $n$ and $k$, calculate and print the combinations, and reoffer the menu. Our data requirements follow:

*Input*
Menu selection item (C or S)

$\left. \begin{array}{l} n \text{ in formula} \\ k \text{ in formula} \end{array} \right]$ if C is chosen

*Output*
Menu description
Combinations based on formula

## Design

Let's segment this program into four processing modules.

| | |
|---|---|
| *Control module* | This module establishes the main processing loop and repeatedly calls two other modules—a combinations module and a menu module. |
| *Menu module* | This module prints the menu and inputs the selection. |
| *Combinations module* | This module inputs values for *n* and *k* in the formula, calculates combinations, and prints combinations. Each time it calculates a combination, it calls the factorial module. |
| *Factorial module* | This module calculates the factorial of a number. |

Now let's look at some of the reasoning behind the selection of these particular modules.

The most obvious module is perhaps the combinations module, since the problem revolves around the connected tasks of entering *n* and *k*, calculating *C*, and printing the result.

Looking at the combination formula, we see a subtask that must be repeated three times under slightly changed conditions—namely, the calculation of $n!$, $(n - k)!$, and $k!$. The subtask "calculate the factorial" is the same in each case. Only the value whose factorial is to be calculated changes. Thus, within the combinations module, an obvious candidate subtask for a subroutine is the calculation of a factorial; that is, let's use a subroutine that specializes in calculating factorials. Whenever the combinations module requires a factorial, it calls the factorial module.

If our control module uses a while loop to process the user's menu selections, then we might realize from our work in the last chapter that the printing of a menu and the subsequent input of the menu selection must be repeated twice: just before the loop and as the last task within the loop.[2] Thus, we can increase efficiency by relegating the menu offering and input choice to a subroutine.

The pseudocode for these four modules reads as follows.

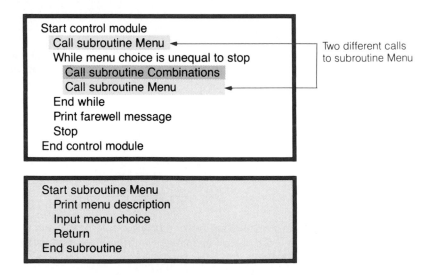

Start control module
  Call subroutine Menu
  While menu choice is unequal to stop
    Call subroutine Combinations
    Call subroutine Menu
  End while
  Print farewell message
  Stop
End control module

Two different calls
to subroutine Menu

Start subroutine Menu
  Print menu description
  Input menu choice
  Return
End subroutine

[2]For example, see the two sets of menu-related statements in the price quotation program on page 200.

```
Start subroutine Combinations
    Input n and k
    Call subroutine Factorial to calculate n!          ◄── Three different calls to subroutine
    Call subroutine Factorial to calculate (n − k)!    ◄── Factorial. Note that this subroutine
    Call subroutine Factorial to calculate k!          ◄── is calling another subroutine
    Calculate combinations
    Print combinations
    Return
End subroutine
```

```
Start subroutine Factorial
    Initialize factorial to 1
    Calculate factorial
    Return
End subroutine
```

### Code and Test

Figure 7.6 shows the Combinations program and its test run. Let's take a look at the flow of execution for the sample test run.

```
100 REM   * * * * * * * * * * * * * * * * * * * * * * * * * * * * * *
105 REM   *                                                         *
110 REM   * Interactive Combinations Program: IBM PC Version        *
115 REM   *                                                         *
120 REM   *   Control Module ..... Establishes processing loop and calls *
125 REM   *                        subroutines menu and combinations.    *
130 REM   *                                                         *
135 REM   *   Sub. Menu .......... Prints the menu and inputs the selection. *
140 REM   *                                                         *
145 REM   *   Sub. Combinations .. Inputs N and K, calculates combinations *
150 REM   *                        while calling subroutine factorial, and *
155 REM   *                        prints combinations.            *
160 REM   *                                                         *
165 REM   *   Sub. Factorial ..... Calculates the factorial of a number. *
170 REM   *                                                         *
175 REM   * * * * * * * * * * * * * * * * * * * * * * * * * * * * * *
180 '
200 '------------------------- Control Module -----------------------------
205 '
210        GOSUB 300                                  ' Call sub. Menu
215 '
220        WHILE M$ <> "S"  AND  M$ <> "s"
225 '
230          GOSUB 400                                ' Call sub. Combinations
235          GOSUB 300                                ' Call sub. Menu
240 '
245        WEND
250 '
255        PRINT : PRINT "Bye..."
260 '
265        STOP
300 '------------------------- Subroutine Menu -----------------------------
305 '    Key:
310 '      M$ = Menu selection
315 '
320        PRINT : PRINT "                          Menu Selection:"
325        PRINT : PRINT "                            C  Calculate combinations"
330              PRINT "                            S  Stop processing"
335 '
340        PRINT : INPUT "                Selection";M$
345 '
350        RETURN
```

**Figure 7.6**   Combinations program and test run                                 (continued)

```
400 '------------------------ Subroutine Combinations ------------------
405 '    Key:
410 '      C = Combinations              FACN  = Factorial of N
415 '      N = N in formula             FACNK = Factorial of N - K
420 '      K = K in formula             FACK  = Factorial of K
425 '
430     PRINT : INPUT "Enter N------>";N
435     PRINT : INPUT "Enter K------>";K
440 '
445     LET X = N     :   GOSUB 500 :  LET FACN  = F  ' Call sub. Factorial
450     LET X = N - K :   GOSUB 500 :  LET FACNK = F  ' Call sub. Factorial
455     LET X = K     :   GOSUB 500 :  LET FACK  = F  ' Call sub. Factorial
460 '
465     LET C = FACN/(FACNK*FACK)
470 '
475     PRINT : PRINT " Combinations ="; C
480 '
485     RETURN
500 '------------------------ Subroutine Factorial ------------------------
505 '    Key:
510 '      X = The number whose factorial is to be calculated
515 '      F = The factorial of X
520 '
525     LET F = 1
530 '
535     FOR J = 2 TO X
540       LET F = F*J
545     NEXT J
550 '
555     RETURN
998 '---------------------------------------------------------------------
999     END
```

```
                    Menu Selection:

                      C  Calculate combinations
                      S  Stop processing

               Selection? c

Enter N------>? 5

Enter K------>? 2

 Combinations = 10

                    Menu Selection:

                      C  Calculate combinations
                      S  Stop processing

               Selection? c

Enter N------>? 10

Enter K------>? 4

 Combinations = 210

                    Menu Selection:

                      C  Calculate combinations
                      S  Stop processing

               Selection? s

Bye...
Break in 265
```

Subroutine Menu is first called at line 210, which prints the menu options and inputs the user's response. In this case, the user chooses to calculate combinations by entering C; so program control enters the while loop, and subroutine Combinations is called at line 230. After the input of 5 for N and 2 for K through execution of lines 430–435, the program successively calls subroutine Factorial three times: to calculate the factorial of N at line 445, of N – K at line 450, and of K at line 455. This is our first example of one subroutine calling another subroutine. In this case, subroutine Factorial is a **nested subroutine** within subroutine Combinations. After the last factorial is returned at line 455, the number of combinations is calculated at line 465 and printed at line 475, giving the output 10 in Figure 7.6. Program control is then returned to the control module, just after the point of call at line 230. Now, subroutine Menu is called again, and the process repeats itself. All subsequent menu offerings and menu input choices are accomplished through GOSUB 300 at line 235.

Note that the use of subroutine Menu allows us to write the menu print/input code just once, as a module or subroutine in lines 300–350. Without the use of this subroutine, we would have to repeat twice the block of code defined by lines 320–340: once at the location given by line 210 and again at the location defined by line 235.[3]

Now let's look at the use of subroutine Factorial. Our first task at line 445 is the calculation of N factorial, or 5! for our first set of data. At line 445 we have three separate statements separated by the colon that's used on IBM PCs.[4] The first statement sets X to N, or 5 in our test data. Next, subroutine Factorial is called. Next, line 525 is executed (lines 500–520 are nonexecutable and thus ignored), which sets the factorial F to 1. The FOR/NEXT loop in lines 535–545 then calculates the proper factorial, and 120 gets stored in F for our test data (which we ask you to confirm in Exercise 5). The RETURN statement in line 555 is executed next, which transfers control to just after the point of call. Since the point of call is GOSUB 500 in line 445, the next statement executed is LET FACN = F. Thus FACN now stores the 120 that's currently in F.

In effect, the first call in line 445 calculates the factorial of 5 and stores the result 120 in FACN, which gives us the numerator value for line 465. The next two calls in lines 450 and 455 give us the required denominator values in line 465—namely, $(5 - 2)!$ or 3! or 6 in FACNK and 2! or 2 in FACK. This gives the following evaluation in line 465,

$$
\begin{aligned}
\text{LET C} = \text{FACN/(FACNK} * \text{FACK)} \\
= 120 \, / \, (6 * 2) \\
= 120 \, / \, 12 \\
= 10
\end{aligned}
$$

which is what is printed as the output for subroutine Combinations when N stores 5 and K stores 2.

Figure 7.7 illustrates the call/return process between subroutines Combinations and Factorial. In effect, the value in X is sent to subroutine Factorial, and the factorial (F) is returned.

---

In reality, all variables within BASIC programs are **global variables,** since any one variable can be used, referenced, or changed within any module.[5] For example, the variable M\$ is treated globally since it's used both within the control module in line 220 and within subroutine Menu in line 340. Conceptually, however, it's good design practice to think of certain variables as pseudo-local, as the following discussion illustrates.

The variables X and F in Example 7.2 are termed **pseudo-local variables** in the sense that they have meaning and use only within the local context of

---

[3]This is precisely what we had to do within the price quotation program on page 200.

[4]Your system might use a separator other than a colon for multistatement lines, or it may not allow multistatement lines at all. In the latter case, line 445 would simply be rewritten as three separate lines. The use of multistatement lines is desirable here, since each line clearly shows the complete three-step process for that particular call and return.

[5]We show exceptions to this in Section 7.3.

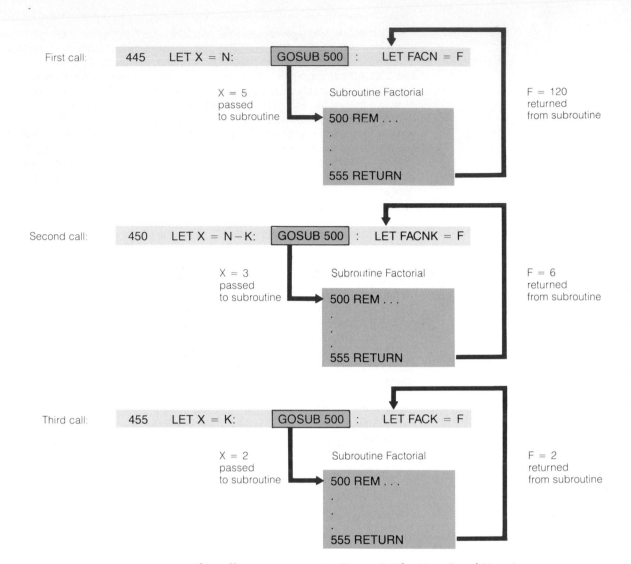

First call:

445   LET X = N:   GOSUB 500 :   LET FACN = F

X = 5 passed to subroutine

Subroutine Factorial

500 REM . . .
.
.
.
555 RETURN

F = 120 returned from subroutine

Second call:

450   LET X = N − K:   GOSUB 500 :   LET FACNK = F

X = 3 passed to subroutine

Subroutine Factorial

500 REM . . .
.
.
.
555 RETURN

F = 6 returned from subroutine

Third call:

455   LET X = K:   GOSUB 500 :   LET FACK = F

X = 2 passed to subroutine

Subroutine Factorial

500 REM . . .
.
.
.
555 RETURN

F = 2 returned from subroutine

**Figure 7.7**   The call/return process in Figure 7.6 for N = 5 and K = 2

subroutine Factorial. Of course, X and F are also used within subroutine Combinations in lines 445–455, but only as vehicles to *provide* subroutine Factorial with the value whose factorial is to be calculated (in this case X) and to return the factorial that has been calculated (in this case F) to its eventual storage location (FACN, FACNK, or FACK). From another viewpoint, we define X just before the call in lines 445–455 in order to provide the subroutine Factorial with the proper value whose factorial is to be calculated. Once the factorial is calculated and stored in F, we use F to *return* the proper factorial to the calling module. In other words, each call to subroutine Factorial sends a specific value in X to subroutine Factorial and gets back from the subroutine a specific value in F, as illustrated in Figure 7.7.

The pseudo-local variable X thus allows us to pass differently defined values to the subroutine (N, N − K, and K), and the pseudo-local variable F returns the corresponding factorials for storage within differently defined locations in subroutine Combinations (FACN, FACNK, and FACK).

Table 7.2 further illustrates the concept of variables as either pseudo-local or global with respect to their intended use. True local variables are possible only within the types of modules described in Sections 7.3 and 7.4.

**Table 7.2**  Pseudo-local and Global Variables

|  | Module | Pseudo-local Variables (Used Essentially within One Module) | Global Variables (Intended Use across More Than One Module) |
|---|---|---|---|
| Example 7.1 | Control | TITLE$<br>BARS<br>J | LABEL$<br>LENGTH |
|  | Bar Print | K | LABEL$<br>LENGTH |
| Example 7.2 | Control | None | M$ |
|  | Menu | None | M$ |
|  | Combinations | N<br>K<br>FACN<br>FACNK<br>FACK |  |
|  | Factorial | X<br>F<br>J |  |

**WARNING**  Be careful not to redefine unintentionally a pseudo-local variable within another module, since in reality all variables are accessible by any module. For example, if we had used K in place of J in lines 535–545 in Example 7.2, then K would have been unintentionally redefined (its value changed) within subroutine Factorial. This would cause the wrong value to be used for K in lines 295 and 300. Developing a table like Table 7.2 helps to avoid this potential error.

**NOTE**  The program in Example 7.2 shows two obvious advantages of modular programming:

1. The modular structure simplifies the design, coding, and understanding of the program by breaking it up into manageable segments, building blocks, or modules. This reduces the cost of developing and later modifying programs, especially those that are large and elaborate with respect to tasks.

2. Programs are shorter when the same task needs to be repeated at different points. For example, without subroutine Menu in the Combinations program, the menu logic would have to be repeated twice (at line 210 and again at line 235); without subroutine Factorial, the factorial logic in lines 525–545 would have to be repeated three times at lines 445–455. (See Exercise 8.)

We discuss other advantages in Section 7.5.

## Follow-Up Exercises

5. Roleplay the following values as lines 445 – 455 in Example 7.2 are executed.

| N | K | X | F | J | FACN | FACNK | FACK |
|---|---|---|---|---|------|-------|------|
| 10 | 4 | | | | | | |
| | | | | | | | |
| 5 | 0 | | | | | | |
| | | | | | | | |

6. Implement Example 7.2 on your system. Process the following values for N and K.

| N | K |
|-----|----|
| 5 | 2 |
| 10 | 4 |
| 5 | 0 |
| 5 | 5 |
| 4 | 10 |
| 100 | 30 |

7. **Error Routines.** Modify Example 7.2 to include the following error routines.
   a. In subroutine Combinations, print an error message and reinput N and K while N is less than K.
   b. In subroutine Menu, print an error message and reinput the menu choice while M$ is unequal to C, c, S, or s.
   c. Implement these on your system and try the test data in the preceding exercise.

*8. Rewrite the program in Example 7.2 without using subroutines. Compare the two versions and list the advantages of using modules for this application.

**9. **ON/GOSUB Statement.** It's also possible to call subroutines through execution of an ON/GOSUB statement, which is analogous to the ON/GOTO statement in Chapter 6.

**ON/GOSUB Statement**

| | | 1st line | 2nd line | kth line |
|---|---|---|---|---|
| | *arithmetic* | | | |
| **ON** *expression* **GOSUB** | | no., | no., . . . , | no. |
| ON | CHOICE GOSUB | 400, | 900 | |

In the example, if CHOICE stores 1, then the subroutine beginning at line 400 is called. If CHOICE stores 2, then the subroutine beginning at line 900 is called.
   a. Rewrite Example 7.2. by adding subroutine Bye, starting at line 900, which prints the farewell message and stops processing. Change the menu choices to 1 and 2 instead of C and S. Use the ON/GOSUB statement illustrated above to call the subroutines from the control module.
   b. Compare the merits of this approach to that in Example 7.2.
   c. Run this program on your system. Use the test data in Exercise 6.

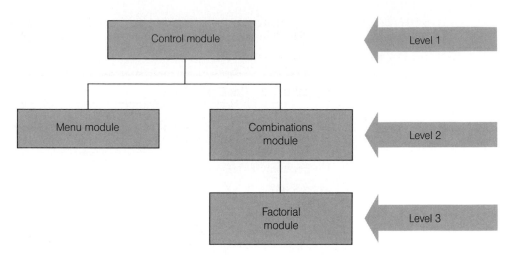

**Figure 7.8**  Hierarchy chart for combinations program (Example 7.2)

## 7.2 HIERARCHY CHARTS

As the number of modules and their interrelationships increases, a need for additional design and documentation tools becomes evident. One such tool is the **hierarchy chart, structure chart,** or **top-down chart** illustrated in Figure 7.8. This chart expresses the relationships among modules in a manner similar to that of organization charts of companies. Note that each module is represented by a box and that these boxes appear at different levels, or hierarchies. If a subroutine call is made by a particular module, then the called module is shown at the next level below the calling module. In Figure 7.8, the control module calls both the menu module and the combinations module; hence, these appear below the control module within Level 2 in the hierarchy chart. The combinations module calls the factorial module, which gives a hierarchy chart with three levels.

Note that the hierarchy chart clearly shows not only the modular breakdown of the program, but also the structure or relationships among modules with respect to which modules are called and which modules do the calling.

Elaborate programs generally have three or more hierarchy levels, with many modules at each level. Our next example is a hierarchy chart with four levels and seven modules.

**E X A M P L E   7 . 3**    **Car Rental Decision Program**

### Analysis

Hartz Rent-Some-Wheels, the largest and most progressive car-rental company, has decided to improve customer service by designing an interactive computer program to be used by its agents to quote projected rental fees. Basically, the program is to compute projected total cost for each of its two rental plans: the daily plan and the weekly plan. A customer who rents a car under the daily plan pays a fixed cost per day plus a charge per mile but does not pay for gasoline expenses. Under the weekly plan, the customer pays both a fixed cost per week and buys gasoline but does not pay a mileage charge. Which plan is cheaper for a customer depends on factors such as the various costs for the specific type of automobile, the projected number of miles to be driven, the number of days that the car is to be rented, the price of gasoline, the efficiency of the automobile, and (of course) the driving habits of the customer.

Currently, the company rents cars from the three car groups shown in Table 7.3. Other car groups may be added in the future, however.

**Table 7.3**   Car-Group Data

| Car Group | Code | Daily Fixed Cost | Charge per Mile | Weekly Fixed Cost | Price per Gallon of Gasoline | Miles per Gallon (EPA Rating) |
|-----------|------|------------------|-----------------|-------------------|------------------------------|-------------------------------|
| Economy | E | $17 | $0.15 | $145 | $1.15 | 42 |
| Midsize | M | 25 | 0.20 | 200 | 1.15 | 25 |
| Luxury | L | 49 | 0.35 | 400 | 1.40 | 13 |

To illustrate the cost calculations for each plan, consider a customer who plans to rent a car from the Economy group and estimates 800 miles of driving over a 12-day period.

$$
\begin{aligned}
\text{Cost of daily plan} &= \left(\begin{array}{c}\text{Daily}\\\text{fixed cost}\end{array}\right) \times \left(\begin{array}{c}\text{Days in}\\\text{rental}\end{array}\right) + \left(\begin{array}{c}\text{Charge}\\\text{per mile}\end{array}\right) \times \left(\begin{array}{c}\text{Miles of}\\\text{driving}\end{array}\right)\\
&= (17) \times (12) + (0.15) \times (800)\\
&= \$324
\end{aligned}
$$

$$
\begin{aligned}
\text{Cost of weekly plan} &= \left(\begin{array}{c}\text{Weekly}\\\text{fixed cost}\end{array}\right) \times \left(\begin{array}{c}\text{Weeks in}\\\text{rental}\end{array}\right) + \left[\left(\begin{array}{c}\text{Miles of}\\\text{driving}\end{array}\right) \times \left(\begin{array}{c}\text{Price per}\\\text{gallon}\end{array}\right) \div \left(\begin{array}{c}\text{Miles}\\\text{per}\\\text{gallon}\end{array}\right)\right]\\
&= (145) \times (2) + [(800) \times (1.15) \div (42)]\\
&= \$312
\end{aligned}
$$

Thus this customer should select the weekly plan, since it's $12 cheaper than the daily plan. (Did you notice that 12 days counts as 2 weeks in the weekly plan calculation? Any part of a week counts as a whole week.)

The data requirements for this problem are described below:

*Output*
Cost of daily plan
Cost of weekly plan

*Input*
Car group code choice
Miles of driving
Days in rental
Menu choice:
    P   Process customer
    S   Stop processing

*RECORD LAYOUT FOR INTERNAL DATA FILE (DATA SECTION)*

| Field | Type |
|-------|------|
| Car group code | String |
| Daily fixed cost ($) | Numeric |
| Charge per mile ($) | Numeric |
| Weekly fixed cost($) | Numeric |
| Price per gallon ($) | Numeric |
| Miles per gallon | Numeric |

**Design**

Design considerations include the following:

1.   The program is interactive.

2. It's to be used by unsophisticated users, which implies that:
   a. Screen design should be uncluttered
   b. Input errors should be trapped
   c. Menu should be offered
3. Car rental plans should be easily added, deleted, or modified, which suggests the use of a module for each car plan.
4. Car groups should be easily added, deleted, or modified, which implies the need for treatment of car groups as records in a data file. Also, car group codes in these records can be matched to the code chosen by the user.

The primary programming tasks are divided into the seven modules described within the hierarchy chart of Figure 7.9. Pseudocode for these modules is shown in Figure 7.10.

### Code

Figure 7.11 shows code in Microsoft BASIC for the IBM PC. Study each module and relate its code to the pseudocode version. In particular, note the following:

*Module 1.* We assume at the start that a customer is to be processed; hence, the menu choice is initialized to P. Alternatively, we could have offered the menu first (see

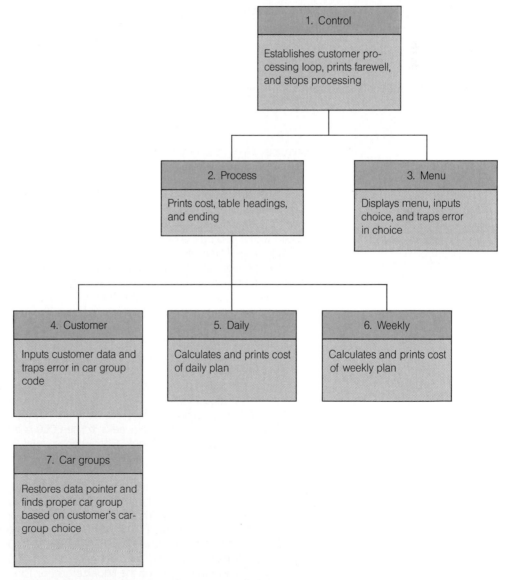

**Figure 7.9**  Hierarchy chart for car rental decision program

Start control module
  Initialize menu choice
    to process customer
  While menu choice ≠ Stop
    Call subroutine Process
    Call subroutine Menu
  End while
  Clear screen
  Print farewell message
  Stop
End control module

a. Module 1

Start subroutine process
  Clear screen
  Call subroutine Customer
  Print cost table headings
  Call subroutine Daily
  Call subroutine Weekly
  Return
End subroutine

b. Module 2

Start subroutine Menu
  Print menu
  Input choice
  While choice incorrect
    Beep the user
    Clear screen
    Print error message
    Input choice
  End while
  Return
End subroutine

c. Module 3

Start subroutine Customer
  Input car group choice
  While choice incorrect
    Beep the user
    Print error message
    Input choice
  End while
  Input miles
  Input days
  Call subroutine Car Groups
  Return
End subroutine

d. Module 4

Start subroutine Daily
  Calculate cost
  Print cost
  Return
End subroutine

e. Module 5

Start subroutine Weekly
  Calculate weeks
  Calculate cost
  Print cost
  Return
End subroutine

f. Module 6

Start subroutine Car Groups
  Restore data pointer
  Read data for first car group
  While car-group choice ≠ car group code
    Read data for next car group
  End while
  Return
End subroutine

g. Module 7

**Figure 7.10**  Pseudocode for modules in car rental decision program

Exercise 16). CLS in line 1600 is the Microsoft statement for clearing the screen. This may differ for your system (see Exercise 12).

*Module 2.* This subroutine is another example of calls from one subroutine to another. In this case, three calls are made to separate subroutines. The first call (to subroutine Customer) obtains the necessary data for the cost calculations in the next two calls (to subroutines Daily and Weekly). Subroutines Customer, Daily, and Weekly are nested within subroutine Process.

*Module 3.* The while loop traps incorrect menu choices by using the same design as an earlier version (see Example 5.2, page 152, lines 280–300). Thus the error routine insists on a correct choice before proceeding, since it keeps requesting a choice while the choice is incorrect. BEEP in line 3160 is the Microsoft statement for making a single beeping sound through the computer's speaker. This is a commonly used audio alert to incorrect user responses.

*Module 4.* This subroutine provides all of the data needed for the cost calculations. The subroutine itself interactively inputs the customer's data (car-group choice with error trap, miles of driving, and days in rental). Then it calls subroutine Car Groups to provide the correct car-group data, that is, the daily fixed cost, charge per mile, and so on, for the chosen car group.

*Module 5.* The printout of daily cost is to the nearest integer.

*Module 6.* The calculation of weeks in line 6060 is a bit tricky. Remember that any part of a week counts as one week. Check for yourself that the calculation in line 6060 gives one week for days in the range 1–7; two weeks for days in the range 8–14; and so on.

*Module 7.* This module is slick! Its purpose is to find the correct car group (record) within the internal data file in lines 9010–9030. It's best to roleplay this logic. Suppose a customer wants to rent a car within the Luxury car group; then the variable CAR.GROUP.CHOICE\$ stores L. The READ in line 7070 processes the first car group, or the Economy record in line 9010. Thus CAR.GROUP.CODE\$ stores E. Next, the while test in line 7080 gives true, since L is in fact unequal to E. This means that line 7090 is executed next, which processes the Midsize group. The while test again gives true, since L is unequal to M. Line 7090 is executed again, which means that the Luxury

```
1000 REM   * * * * * * * * * * * * * * * * * * * * * * * * * * * * * * * *
1010 REM   *                                                             *
1020 REM   *               CAR RENTAL DECISION PROGRAM                   *
1025 REM   *                    (IBM PC Version)                         *
1030 REM   *                                                             *
1040 REM   *   This program processes customer requests for comparing the *
1050 REM   *   costs of different car plans.                             *
1060 REM   *                                                             *
1070 REM   *   Description of modules:                                   *
1080 REM   *                                                             *
1090 REM   *      1.   Control ........ Establishes customer processing loop, *
1100 REM   *                            calls subroutines process and menu, *
1110 REM   *                            prints farewell message, and stops *
1120 REM   *                            processing.                      *
1130 REM   *      2.   Process ........ Processes customer by printing cost *
1140 REM   *                            table heading, calling subroutines *
1150 REM   *                            customer, daily, and weekly, and *
1160 REM   *                            printing table ending.           *
1170 REM   *      3.   Menu ........... Displays menu, inputs choice, and *
1180 REM   *                            checks that the choice is legitimate. *
1190 REM   *      4.   Customer ....... Inputs car-group choice, projected *
1200 REM   *                            miles of driving, and number of  *
1210 REM   *                            rental days, and calls subroutine *
1220 REM   *                            car groups.                      *
1230 REM   *      5.   Daily .......... Calculates and prints cost of daily *
1240 REM   *                            plan.                            *
1250 REM   *      6.   Weekly ........ Calculates and prints cost of weekly *
1260 REM   *                            plan.                            *
1270 REM   *      7.   Car groups ..... Restores the data pointer and finds *
1280 REM   *                            the proper car group based on the *
1290 REM   *                            customer's car-group choice.     *
1496 REM   *                                                             *
1497 REM   * * * * * * * * * * * * * * * * * * * * * * * * * * * * * * * *
1498 REM
1499 REM===============================================================
1500 REM               MODULE 1:   CONTROL MODULE
1510 REM
1520 REM          Programming notes:
1530 REM             1.   Variables are self-descriptive
1540 REM
1550      LET MENU.CHOICE$ = "P"
1560      WHILE MENU.CHOICE$ <> "S"
1565 '
1570          GOSUB 2000                        '  Call sub. process
1580          GOSUB 3000                        '  Call sub. menu
1585 '
1590      WEND
1595 '
1600      CLS                                   '  Clear screen
1605 '
1610      PRINT "Another day ... Another $"
1630      STOP
1997 REM
1999 REM===============================================================
2000 REM               MODULE 2:   SUBROUTINE PROCESS
2010 REM
2020 REM          Programming notes:
2030 REM             1.   Variables are self-descriptive
2040 REM             2.   GOSUBs for new plans inserted within this module
2050 REM
2055 '
2060      CLS                                   '  Clear screen
2065 '
2070          GOSUB 4000                        '  Call sub. customer
2075 '
2080      PRINT "Cost Estimates"
2090      PRINT "--------------------"
2100      PRINT "Plan","Cost"
2110      PRINT "--------------------"
2115 '
2130          GOSUB 5000                        '  Call sub. daily
```

**Figure 7.11**   BASIC program for car rental decision                (continued)

```
2140      GOSUB 6000                            ' Call sub. weekly
2150 '
2160      PRINT "----------------------"
2180 '
2190      RETURN
2997 REM
2999 REM==============================================================
3000 REM                    MODULE 3:   SUBROUTINE MENU
3010 REM
3020 REM          Programming notes:
3030 REM             1.   Variables are self-descriptive
3040 REM             2.   Upper case user choices assumed
3050 REM
3055 '
3060      PRINT TAB(40); " _____ "
3070      PRINT TAB(40); "| Select one:             |"
3080      PRINT TAB(40); "|                         |"
3090      PRINT TAB(40); "|   P  Process customer   |"
3100      PRINT TAB(40); "|   S  Stop processing    |"
3110      PRINT TAB(40); "|_____|"
3120      PRINT TAB(36); "Choice";
3130      INPUT MENU.CHOICE$
3140 '
3150      WHILE MENU.CHOICE$ <> "P"  AND  MENU.CHOICE$ <> "S"
3155 '
3160        BEEP                                ' Guess what this does
3162        CLS                                 ' Clear screen
3165 '
3170        PRINT TAB(36); "* * * * * * * * * * * * * * * *"
3180        PRINT TAB(36); "*                             *"
3190        PRINT TAB(36); "*       Please enter P or S   *"
3200        PRINT TAB(36); "*                             *"
3210        PRINT TAB(36); "* * * * * * * * * * * * * * * *"
3215 '
3220        PRINT
3225        PRINT TAB(36); "Choice";
3230        INPUT MENU.CHOICE$
3235 '
3240      WEND
3245 '
3250      RETURN
3997 REM
3999 REM==============================================================
4000 REM                    MODULE 4:   SUBROUTINE CUSTOMER
4010 REM
4020 REM          Programming notes:
4030 REM             1.   Variables are self-descriptive
4040 REM             2.   Upper case car-group choices assumed
4042 REM                   E   Economy group
4044 REM                   M   Midsize group
4046 REM                   L   Luxury group
4050 REM
4055 '
4070      PRINT TAB(36); "Enter car group (E, M or L) ===>";
4080      INPUT CAR.GROUP.CHOICE$
4085 '
4090      WHILE CAR.GROUP.CHOICE$ <> "E"  AND CAR.GROUP.CHOICE$ <> "M"
                                          AND CAR.GROUP.CHOICE$ <> "L"
4095 '
4100        BEEP                                ' Guess what this does
4105 '
4110        PRINT TAB(36); "* * * * * * * * * * * * * * * *"
4120        PRINT TAB(36); "*                             *"
4130        PRINT TAB(36); "*     Please enter E, M or L   *"
4140        PRINT TAB(36); "*                             *"
4150        PRINT TAB(36); "* * * * * * * * * * * * * * * *"
4155 '
4160        PRINT
4170        PRINT TAB(36); "Enter car group (E, M or L) ===>";
4180        INPUT CAR.GROUP.CHOICE$
4185 '
4190      WEND
4195 '
4200      PRINT TAB(36); "Enter estimated miles ========>";
4210      INPUT MILES
```

```
4215 '
4220        PRINT TAB(36); "Enter rental days =============>";
4230        INPUT DAYS
4235 '
4240        GOSUB 7000                                ' Call sub. car groups
4245 '
4250        RETURN
4997 REM
4999 REM==================================================================
5000 REM                MODULE 5:   SUBROUTINE DAILY
5010 REM
5020 REM        Programming notes:
5030 REM           1.  Variables are self-descriptive
5040 REM
5045 '
5050        LET COST.DAILY = DAILY.FIX.COST * DAYS  +  CHARGE.PER.MILE * MILES
5055 '
5060        PRINT "Daily", INT( COST.DAILY + .5 )
5065 '
5070        RETURN
5997 REM
5999 REM==================================================================
6000 REM                MODULE 6:   SUBROUTINE WEEKLY
6010 REM
6020 REM        Programming notes:
6030 REM           1.  Variables are self-descriptive
6040 REM           2.  Any part of a week counts as an entire week
6050 REM
6055 '
6060        LET WEEKS = INT((DAYS - 1)/7) + 1
6065 '
6070        LET COST.WEEKLY = WEEK.FIX.COST*WEEKS  +  MILES*PRICE.PER.GAL/MPG
6075 '
6080        PRINT "Weekly", INT( COST.WEEKLY + .5 )
6085 '
6090        RETURN
6997 REM
6999 REM==================================================================
7000 REM                MODULE 7:   SUBROUTINE CAR GROUPS
7010 REM
7020 REM        Programming notes:
7030 REM           1.  Variables are self-descriptive
7040 REM           2.  See data section for car group data
7050 REM
7055 '
7060        RESTORE
7065 '
7070        READ CAR.GROUP.CODE$,DAILY.FIX.COST,CHARGE.PER.MILE,WEEK.FIX.COST,
                PRICE.PER.GAL,MPG
7075 '
7080        WHILE CAR.GROUP.CHOICE$ <> CAR.GROUP.CODE$
7085 '
7090          READ CAR.GROUP.CODE$,DAILY.FIX.COST,CHARGE.PER.MILE,WEEK.FIX.COST,
                  PRICE.PER.GAL,MPG
7095 '
7100        WEND
7105 '
7110        RETURN
7997 REM
7999 REM==================================================================
9000 REM                DATA SECTION
9005 '
9010        DATA E,17,.15,145,1.15,42
9020        DATA M,25,.20,200,1.15,25
9030        DATA L,49,.35,400,1.40,13
9996 '
9998 REM----------------------------------------------------------------
9999        END
```

group data now have been read into the appropriate variables in primary memory. Now the while test gives false (the user choice L now matches the car-group code L); so execution drops out of the loop, and control returns to the calling module (subroutine Customer) with the appropriate car-group data. Roleplay customer choices E and M to convince yourself that this routine works as it should.

**Test**

Figure 7.12 illustrates a sample run. In particular, note the following points regarding a friendly user-interface.

1. The I/O has a screen orientation, which means that we pay attention to the fact that screens have a fixed number of lines (24 in this case). This means that we want to fit relevant I/O within one screen. More importantly, we don't want to "roll off the top" or clear any information that might be needed.

2. The cost table is visually segregated from the customer input and subsequent menu selection (see Screen 1). The menu clearly shows the proper selections, and the input choice is aligned under the alternatives P and S. Color can also be used effectively to segregate portions of the screen visually.

3. The screen is cleared for each new customer, which gives us Screen 2 when P is selected at the bottom of Screen 1.

4. The user is alerted to input errors both by sound (a beep) and visually (starred boxes enclosing an error message). See Screens 2 and 3.

To *really* understand this program, try working the following exercises.

---

## Follow-Up Exercises

**10.** Confirm the output for the first customer processed in Figure 7.12 by role-playing. In doing so, finish filling in the table below.

| Line Executed | Action/Result |
|---|---|
| 1550 | P stored in MENU.CHOICE$ |
| 1560 | True |
| 1570 | Subroutine Process called |
| 2060 | Screen cleared |

What costs get printed for a customer who chooses L and drives 800 miles over 12 days? Suppose the customer drives 300 miles over 5 days?

**\*11.** Modify the program in Figure 7.11 to print a count of the number of customers processed just before the farewell message.

**\*12. Clearing the Screen.** Does CLS work on your system? If not, design a subroutine that clears the screen. This subroutine simply prints 24 blank lines (if that's your screen size). Ideally, it should also locate the cursor in the "Home" position, or upper-left corner. For example, in Microsoft BASIC we can do this with the statement LOCATE 1,1.
   **a.** Modify the hierarchy chart in Figure 7.9 and the pseudocode in Figure 7.10.
   **b.** Modify the program in Figure 7.11.
   **c.** Run the revised program on your system. (To save typing time, forget all REMs except those that segregate modules.)

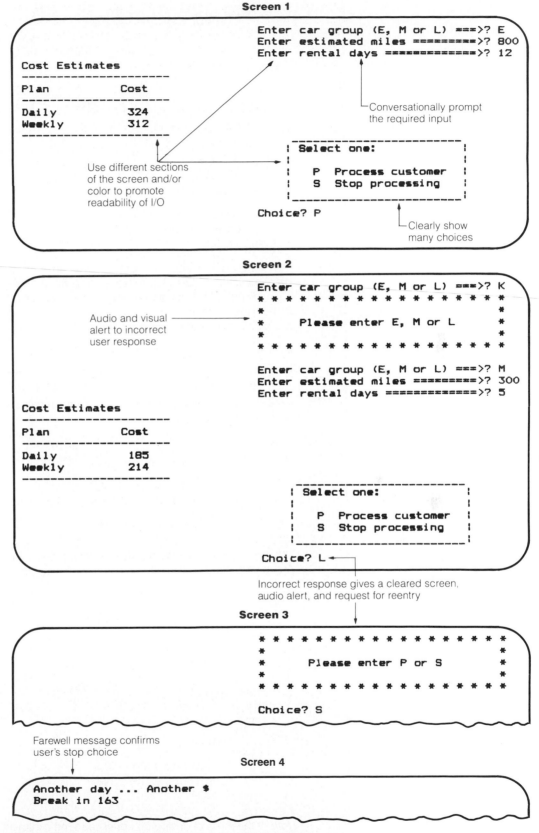

**Figure 7.12**  Test run for car rental decision program

**\*13.** Consider the following new car groups:

| Car group | Code | Daily Fixed Cost | Charge per Mile | Weekly Fixed Cost | Price per Gallon | MPG |
|---|---|---|---|---|---|---|
| Super Luxury | S | 70 | 0.70 | 600 | 1.40 | 15 |
| Recreational | R | 100 | 0.80 | 800 | 1.15 | 20 |

**a.** Modify the program in Figure 7.11 to include these. Don't forget to include these codes in the error trap.

**b.** Run the revised program on your system. (To save typing time, forget all REMs except those that segregate modules.)

**\*14.** Redesign the car rental program to include a revised menu:

P   Process customer
V   View car group data
S   Stop processing

The selection V results in the printing of a table that displays the car-group data (the internal data file). Achieve this through a new subroutine called View. *Hint:* Subroutine view includes either a FOR/NEXT loop, or better yet, an eof loop.

**a.** Modify the hierarchy chart in Figure 7.9 and the pseudocode in Figure 7.10.

**b.** Modify the program in Figure 7.11.

**c.** Run the revised program on your system. (To save typing time, forget all REMs except those that segregate modules.)

**\*\*15.** Consider a new car plan called Special, which calculates cost as follows:

$$\text{Cost of special plan} = \left( \begin{array}{c} \text{Daily fixed cost} \\ + \\ \text{daily surcharge} \end{array} \right) \times \left( \begin{array}{c} \text{Days in} \\ \text{rental} \end{array} \right)$$

$$+ \left( \begin{array}{c} \text{Charge} \\ \text{per mile} \end{array} \right) \times \left( \begin{array}{c} \text{Miles of} \\ \text{driving} \end{array} - \text{Allotment} \right)$$

$$+ \ (\text{Gasoline expenses})$$

where Allotment = (Miles per day) × (Days in rental). The table of car-group data now has two new fields for each car group:

| Car Group | Daily Surcharge | Miles per Day |
|---|---|---|
| Economy | $4 | 50 |
| Midsize | 5 | 100 |
| Luxury | 6 | 150 |

To illustrate, consider the first customer in Figure 7.12, who wants an Economy car and plans to drive 800 miles in 12 days.

$$\begin{aligned} \text{Cost of special plan} &= (17 + 4) \times (12) \\ &\quad + (0.15) \times (800 - 50 \times 12) \\ &\quad + (800) \times (1.15) \div (42) \\ &= \$304 \end{aligned}$$

*Note:* If the miles of driving do not exceed the allotment—that is, (Miles of driving − Allotment) is negative—then no charge per mile is incurred.

a. Modify the hierarchy chart in Figure 7.9 and the pseudocode in Figure 7.10.
b. Modify the program in Figure 7.11.
c. Run the revised program on your system. (To save typing time, forget all REMs except those that segregate modules.)

**\*\*16. The Pause That Refreshes.**   Modify the program in Figure 7.11 so that each screen starts with the menu and ends with the cost table. Immediately after the cost table is printed, print the message

Strike any key to continue . . .

which indicates a pause condition. Can you pause this way on your system? *Hint:* In Microsoft BASIC we can pause by writing a procedure that continues looping (with no action in the loop body) while the user does not strike a key. Look up the INKEY$ variable and check out the program in Example E.5 in Module E. If your system doesn't have an INKEY$ variable, then look up statements like SLEEP, WAIT, and PAUSE.

## 7.3 EXTERNAL FUNCTIONS\*\*

This section introduces a type of module called an external function, but first let's define some new terms.

### Program Units

User-defined functions (the DEF functions in Module C) and subroutines are classified as **internal modules,** since they appear within a single program unit. A **program unit** is a segment of the overall program that is independently compiled or interpreted, so that it is like a separate program. One consequence of independent compilation or interpretation is that all variables within a program unit are considered *local* to that program unit; that is, they are **local variables** having unique memory locations that are independent from any identically named variables in other program units.

Up to now we have dealt with just a single type of program unit called the **main program,** which terminates with an END statement. Recent versions of BASIC allow three other types of program units: external functions, subprograms, and chained modules. These are called **external modules,** since they are external to or do not appear in the main program.

Figure 7.13 shows the structure of BASIC programs based on program units. Note that up to now we have dealt only with main programs. In this section we illustrate how to implement external functions.

### Structure of External Functions

An **external function** is an external module that *returns a single value* to the calling program unit. Its general structure is shown in Table 7.4. The next example shows a specific implementation.

---

\*\*This section may be skipped without loss of continuity.

PROGRAM

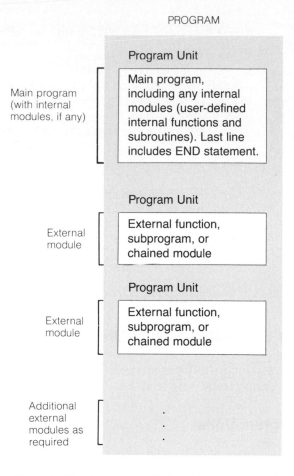

**Figure 7.13** Structure of BASIC programs with program units

**Table 7.4** General Structure of External Function

| Dialect[a] | Structure | Comment |
|---|---|---|
| ANS BASIC | EXTERNAL FUNCTION statement<br><br>.<br>. ] Body of function<br>.<br><br>END FUNCTION statement | Must include LET statement that assigns value to function name. Can include EXIT FUNCTION statement. |
| VAX-11 BASIC | Same as ANS BASIC except delete EXTERNAL | |
| Your System (if different) | | |

[a]External functions are not available in Microsoft BASIC at this time.

**E X A M P L E   7 . 4**     **Combination Program with VAX-11 External Function**

Let's rework the program in Example 7.2 on page 233 to show the specific syntax and implementation of an external function. In this case, the listing in Figure 7.14 shows module Factorial as an external function in the VAX-11 BASIC dialect. I/O for this program is essentially the same as on page 236.

Note that the structure of this program conforms to that in Figure 7.13. In this case, we have a main program with three internal modules: a control module and two

**Main Program**

```
100 REM   * * * * * * * * * * * * * * * * * * * * * * * * * * * * * * *
105 REM   *                                                           *
110 REM   * Interactive Combinations Program: VAX-11 Version          *
115 REM   *                                                           *
120 REM   *    Control Module ..... Establishes processing loop and calls  *
125 REM   *                         subroutines menu and combinations.     *
130 REM   *                                                           *
135 REM   *    Sub. Menu ......... Prints the menu and inputs the selection. *
140 REM   *                                                           *
145 REM   *    Sub. Combinations .. Inputs N and K, calculates combinations  *
150 REM   *                         while calling function factorial, and   *
155 REM   *                         prints combinations.                    *
160 REM   *                                                           *
165 REM   *    Func. Factorial .... Calculates the factorial of a number. *
170 REM   *                                                           *
175 REM   * * * * * * * * * * * * * * * * * * * * * * * * * * * * * * *
180 !
200 !------------------------- Control Module -------------------------
205 !
210     GOSUB Menu                                    ! Call sub. Menu
215 !
220     WHILE M$ <> "S"  AND  M$ <> "s"
225 !
230       GOSUB Combinations  ◄── Note use of        ! Call sub. Combinations
235       GOSUB Menu              string labels       ! Call sub. Menu
240 !
245     NEXT
250 !
255     PRINT \ PRINT "Bye..."
260 !
265     STOP
300 !------------------------- Subroutine Menu -------------------------
301 !
302   Menu: ◄── Control transfer point
303 !
305 !    Key:
310 !      M$ = Menu selection
315 !
320     PRINT \ PRINT "                        Menu Selection:"
325     PRINT \ PRINT "                          C  Calculate combinations"
330           PRINT "                          S  Stop processing"
335 !
340     PRINT \ INPUT "                    Selection";M$
345 !
350     RETURN
400 !------------------------- Subroutine Combinations -------------------------
401 !
402   Combinations: ◄── Control transfer point
403 !
405 !    Key:
410 !      C = Combinations
415 !      N = N in formula
420 !      K = K in formula
425 !
426     EXTERNAL INTEGER FUNCTION FACTORIAL           ! Define external function
427 !
430     PRINT \ INPUT "Enter N------>";N
435     PRINT \ INPUT "Enter K------>";K
440 !
465     LET C = FACTORIAL(N) / (FACTORIAL(N-K) * FACTORIAL(K))
470 !
475     PRINT \ PRINT " Combinations ="; C
480 !
485     RETURN
998 !------------------------------------------------------------------
999     END
```

**External Function**

```
500   FUNCTION INTEGER FACTORIAL (X)
504 !
505 !    Key:
510 !      X        = The number whose factorial is to be calculated
515 !      F        = The factorial of X
518 !      FACTORIAL = Name of function
520 !
525     LET F = 1
530 !
535     FOR J = 2 TO X
540       LET F = F*J
545     NEXT J
550 !
555     LET FACTORIAL = F
560 !
599     END FUNCTION
```

**Figure 7.14**  Listing of program with external function

subroutines. The main program is followed by an external function.

The external function is executed by referencing the function name within the calling module. For example, line 465 within the main program references the function named FACTORIAL three times. Each reference transfers execution control to the function. For example, FACTORIAL (N) is the first function reference in line 465. This means that the value in N is passed to the function, the function is evaluated, and its value is returned. If N stores 5, the factorial value 120 is returned. Note that the mechanics of this procedure are essentially the same as references to BASIC-supplied functions such as SQR or INT. Figure 7.15 summarizes the call/return process for this example.

**Figure 7.15**   The call/return process: evaluation of C in Example 7.4 (N = 5, K = 2)

465 LET C = FACTORIAL (N) / (FACTORIAL (N − K) * FACTORIAL (K))

$\quad$ = FACTORIAL (5) / (FACTORIAL (5 − 2)   * (FACTORIAL (2) )

Actual parameter value 5 passed to function FACTORIAL and matched to formal parameter X

```
500 FUNCTION INTEGER FACTORIAL (X)
525   LET F = 1
535   FOR J = 2 to X
540     LET F = F * J
545   NEXT J
555   LET FACTORIAL = F
599 END FUNCTION
```

External function FACTORIAL

Value in FACTORIAL returned

$\quad$ = 120 / ( FACTORIAL (3)   * FACTORIAL (2) )

Actual parameter value passed to function and result returned

$\quad$ = 120 / ( 6 * FACTORIAL (2) )

Actual parameter value passed to function and result returned

$\quad$ = 120 / ( 6 * 2 )

$\quad$ = 120 / 12

$\quad$ = 10

*Note:* The actual order of evaluation is
$\qquad$ FACTORIAL (3), giving 6
$\qquad$ FACTORIAL (2), giving 2
$\qquad$ 6 * 2, giving 12
$\qquad$ FACTORIAL (5), giving 120
$\qquad$ 120/12, giving 10.

In general, external functions are evaluated as described below.

**Function Reference, Call, or Evaluation**

> function name (actual parameter list)
> FACTORIAL (N)

The **actual parameter list** is a list of variables or expressions separated by commas. It represents the set of values that gets passed to the function. In the first reference (Figure 7.15), the actual parameter list is simply N. This gets matched to the **formal parameter list** within the external FUNCTION statement, or X in the example. The formal parameter list is thus used within the external function to calculate the value returned by the function.

The **external FUNCTION statement** is the first statement within the external function (line 500 in Figure 7.14). This statement defines the beginning of the external function, names the function, and provides the formal parameter list that gets matched to the actual parameter list within the calling module. Table 7.5 gives the syntax of this statement, together with the statement that defines the end of the external function, the **END FUNCTION statement.** Execution of the END FUNCTION statement terminates execution of the external function, at which time control returns to the calling module just after the point of call.

**Table 7.5**  Syntax of External FUNCTION Statement and END FUNCTION Statement

| Dialect[a] | Syntax | Examples |
|---|---|---|
| ANS BASIC | **EXTERNAL FUNCTION** *function name (formal parameter list)* <br> Optional <br> **END FUNCTION** | EXTERNAL FUNCTION FACTORIAL (X) ← Function name <br> EXTERNAL FUNCTION AREA (HEIGHT, WIDTH) <br> EXTERNAL FUNCTION ANSWER\$ (R1,R2,R3) <br> Formal parameter <br> END FUNCTION |
| VAX-11 BASIC | **FUNCTION** *data type function name (formal parameter list)* <br> Optional <br> **END FUNCTION** <br><br> *Notes:* <br> 1. Common data type keywords are INTEGER for storage of whole numeric values <br> REAL for storage of numeric values with decimals <br> STRING for storage of string values <br> 2. Function names can be up to 30 characters <br> 3. Each formal parameter can be preceded by a data type keyword. | FUNCTION INTEGER FACTORIAL (X) <br> FUNCTION REAL AREA (HEIGHT, WIDTH) <br> FUNCTION STRING ANSWER\$ (R1,R2,R3) <br><br> END FUNCTION |
| Your System (if different) | | |

[a]These statements are not available in Microsoft BASIC at this time.

**NOTE 1** The actual and formal parameter lists must agree with respect to the number of items (arguments) and type of data (for example, numeric matched with numeric and string matched with string).

**NOTE 2** Make sure that the body of the external function has at least one LET statement that assigns a value to the function name. For example, the function named FACTORIAL in Example 7.4 uses the following:

```
555 LET FACTORIAL = F
```

**NOTE 3** Avoid the use of REM statements following the END statement in the main program and before the FUNCTION statement in the external function, as these may cause unusual error conditions.

**NOTE 4** External functions offer certain advantages over internal modules such as subroutines:

1.  All variables within the external function are *local* to that function. Thus variables within the external module (J, K, etc.) that have the same names as variables in other modules don't cause errors of inadvertently reassigned values. If any variable within the formal parameter list is assigned a value within the external function, however, then the corresponding actual variable also gets reassigned. Thus, *make sure that the values for formal parameters are not changed within the external function.*

2.  The external function can be invoked, called, or referenced by any other module, whether internal or external. In contrast, subroutines can be called only from within the same program unit. Some BASIC dialects also may allow **recursive calling,** in which a function calls itself (see Exercise 21).

3.  Certain common programming tasks are widely used by different programs. These include, for example, common mathematical and statistical calculations (matrix manipulations, descriptive statistics such as mean, range, and standard deviation), graphics (bar charts, X–Y graphs, etc.), and data processing procedures (sorting names, numbers, etc.). In these cases, it may be cost efficient to code these tasks as external modules, which can then be used by assorted programs. These are often called **utility modules,** because of their general usefulness in the programming environment. The Factorial module in Example 7.4 is a good utility module. So is the Bar Print module from Example 7.1 (see Exercise 24).

## Implementation of External Functions

Implementation of an external function may require a **declarative statement** within the calling module. This statement declares to the compiler/interpreter that the module will require a particular external function (see line 426 in Example 7.4). It also provides certain other implementation-defined information, such as the length of a string parameter. Table 7.6 shows the syntax for implementation-defined declarative statements.

The procedure for running programs that use external functions varies from implementation to implementation. Table 7.7 describes the procedure that was used in Example 7.4.

**Table 7.6** Syntax of Declarative Statements

| Dialect[a] | Syntax | Examples |
|---|---|---|
| ANS BASIC | **EXTERNAL FUNCTION** *function name(s)* | EXTERNAL FUNCTION FACTORIAL<br>EXTERNAL FUNCTION AREA, ANSWER$ |
| VAX-11 BASIC | **EXTERNAL** *data type* **FUNCTION** *function name (external parameters)*<br>└─────────┘<br>Optional | EXTERNAL INTEGER FUNCTION FACTORIAL<br>EXTERNAL REAL FUNCTION AREA (REAL)<br>EXTERNAL STRING FUNCTION ANSWER$(INTEGER) |

*Notes:*
1. Data type keywords and function name as in Table 7.5.
2. External parameters allow data typing of actual parameters within the function call, and other options beyond the scope of this chapter.

Your System
(if different)

[a]This statement is not available in Microsoft BASIC at this time.

**Table 7.7** Execution of Programs with External Functions

| Dialect | Procedure | Example |
|---|---|---|
| VAX-11 BASIC | Assume that the main program and external function have been written and stored as *separate* program files. Also assume that we are operating within the BASIC environment. | Assume that the external function has been stored as file FACT and that the main program has been stored as file COMBO. |
| | 1. Load the external function into the work area.<br>    **OLD** *function program file* | OLD FACT |
| | 2. Compile the external function to create an object-code version.<br>    **COMPILE** | COMPILE |
| | 3. Load the object-code external function into the work area.<br>    **LOAD** *function program file* | LOAD FACT |
| | 4. Load the main program into the work area.<br>    **OLD** *main program file* | OLD COMBO |
| | 5. Execute the main program.<br>    **RUN** | RUN |
| | *Note:* Once the external function has been compiled, there is no need to repeat Steps 1 and 2 for subsequent runs of the main program during other sessions. | |

Your System
(if different)

## Follow-Up Exercises

**17.** With respect to Example 7.4:
   **a.** Identify each variable as pseudo-local, pseudo-global, local, or global.
   **b.** Is there any problem if we change J to N in lines 535–545?
   **c.** Is there any problem if we insert the following?

   558 LET X = F

   **d.** Is there any problem if we delete line 555?
   **e.** Try implementing the example on your system.

**18.** **EXIT FUNCTION Statement.** The statement

   **EXIT FUNCTION**

   can be used within the body of the function in the ANS and VAX-11 dialects to exit the function (return back to the point of call). Revise the external function in Example 7.4 so that exit from the function is achieved (after F has been initialized) whenever X is 1 or less.

**\*19.** **Volume Function.** The volume of a sphere with radius $r$ is given by the formula

   $$\text{Volume of sphere} = \tfrac{4}{3}r^3$$

   **a.** Write an external function called VOLUME.SPHERE that receives the radius (which can be a decimal number) and returns the volume of a sphere.
   **b.** Write a short main program that tests the function for the following radii: 0.5, 1, 10.3, 100.

**\*20.** Consider the task in which one of four messages gets printed depending on the sum of three binary (0–1) variables given by B1, B2, B3.

| Sum B1 + B2 + B3 | Message |
|---|---|
| 0 | All are off |
| 1 | One is on |
| 2 | Two are on |
| 3 | All three are on |

If the sum is outside the given range, then print the message

   "Error in binary data."

   **a.** Write a string external function called MESSAGE$ that returns the appropriate message after receiving the binary variables.
   **b.** Write a short main program that returns the appropriate message given the following data:

| B1 | B2 | B3 |
|---|---|---|
| 0 | 0 | 5 |
| 0 | 0 | 0 |
| 0 | 1 | 0 |
| 0 | 1 | 1 |
| 1 | 1 | 1 |

**\*\*21.** **Multiline Internal Function.** Review the multiline internal functions described in Module C.
  **a.** Rewrite the factorial function in Example 7.4 as a multiline internal module, if available on your system.
  **b.** Is there any advantage to this approach? Any disadvantage?
  **c.** Run this version of the program on your system.

**\*\*22.** **Recursive Calls.** If a module calls itself, it's termed a *recursive call*. Some versions of BASIC allow recursive calls for external functions. These are useful for certain applications that require recursive calculations, in which the final calculated value is determined in part by a past sequence of similarly calculated values. The factorial problem is a good illustration of this, since we can recursively define $x!$ as follows:

$$x! = 1 \qquad \text{if } x = 0$$
$$x! = x*(x-1)! \qquad \text{if } x > 0$$

  **a.** Try replacing the logic in lines 525–555 of Example 7.4 with an IF/THEN/ELSE structure that reflects the above recursive definition for $x$. *Hint:* The structure tests X and assigns a value to FACTORIAL depending on the result. Do you find this approach more readable? Do you see why we couldn't simply replace F with FACTORIAL in lines 525 and 540 of the original? The VAX-11 compiler would expect a recursive call to the right of the $=$ sign in line 540 and would therefore give a syntax error because of the missing actual parameter X.
  **b.** Run this revised program on your system.

## 7.4 OTHER EXTERNAL MODULES**

This section concludes the presentation of the types of external modules by briefly describing external subprograms and chained modules.

### External Subprograms

An external **subprogram** has a structure and syntax as indicated in Table 7.8. Study the structure, syntax, and calling procedure, as applied to the factorial example. Then read the notes that follow.

Note the following regarding the use of subprograms.

**NOTE 1**   The structure and syntax of the external subprogram are similar to those of the external function. In this case, the external SUB statement identifies the start of the subprogram, and the END SUB or SUBEND statement identifies its end and terminates its execution.

**NOTE 2**   The **subprogram call** is initiated by a CALL statement. The actual and formal parameter lists behave identically to those in external functions. Unlike external functions, however, *the external subprogram is designed to return any number of values*. The mechanisms for returning values is through the parameter lists. Thus the parameter lists include a set of values for passing and another set of values for returning. In some applications, however, the subprogram may not return any values. For example, a subprogram may simply print a lengthy report.

\*\*This section can be skipped without loss of continuity.

**Table 7.8** Structure, Syntax, and Call of External Subprograms

| Dialect[a] | Structure, Syntax, and Call | Example |
|---|---|---|
| ANS BASIC | Calling module | . |
| | | . |
| | | CALL FACTORIAL (N, FACN) |
| | **CALL** *subprogram name* (*actual parameter list*) | CALL FACTORIAL (N − K, FACNK) |
| | └─────────┬─────────┘ | CALL FACTORIAL (K, FACK) |
| | Optional | |
| | | LET C = FACN/(FACNK∗FACK) |
| | | . |
| | | . |
| | | . |
| | Subprogram | |
| | **External SUB** *subprogram name* (*formal parameter list*) | EXTERNAL SUB FACTORIAL (X,F) |
| | └─────────┬─────────┘ |    LET F = 1 |
| | Optional |    FOR J = 2 TO X |
| | . Body of |      LET F = F∗J |
| | . subprogram |    NEXT J |
| | . | END SUB |
| | **END SUB** | |

*Note:* If the keyword EXTERNAL is ommitted, then the subprogram is *internal* to a program unit, as is the subroutine.

| VAX-11 BASIC | This is the same as ANS BASIC, except delete the keyword **EXTERNAL** and use the keyword **SUBEND** instead of END SUB. |

Your System
(if different)

[a]Subprograms are not available in Microsoft BASIC at this time.

**NOTE 3**   Operationally, the external subprogram is similar to the subroutine. Convince yourself of this by comparing the example in Table 7.8 to the listing in Example 7.2 and the call/return process in Figure 7.7. Unlike subroutines, however, the external subprogram is an independent program unit with local variables and with the other advantages of external modules discussed on page 256. Note, however, that *formal parameters whose values have been changed within the subprogram also change the values of the corresponding actual parameters.*

**NOTE 4**   The external subprogram is preferable to the external function when the external module returns either no values (as in printing a bar chart) or more than one value. The external function is best for returning a single value, primarily because the function is easily referenced.

**Follow-Up Exercises**

**\*23.** Rework Example 7.2 as follows:
   **a.** Use a subprogram instead of a subroutine for the calculation of factorials.
   **b.** Use a subprogram for printing the menu.
   **c.** If possible, run this revised program on your system.

**24.** **EXIT SUB or SUBEXIT Statement.** One of the statements described below can be used within the body to exit the subprogram (return to the point of call). Revise the subprogram example in Table 7.8 so that exit from the subprogram is achieved (after F has been initialized) whenever X is 1 or less.

| Dialect | Statement |
| --- | --- |
| ANS BASIC | EXIT SUB |
| VAX-11 BASIC | SUBEXIT |
| Your System (if different) | |

**\*25.** Rework Example 7.1 as follows:
   **a.** Use a subprogram to print the bars, labels, and lengths.
   **b.** If possible, run this revised program on your system.

**\*26.** **Volume Subprogram.** Rework Exercise 19 as a subprogram called VOL-UME. In addition to the volume of a sphere, return the volume of a cylinder, as given by the following formula:

Volume of cylinder $= r^2 h$

where $r$ is its radius and $h$ is its height.

**\*27.** Rework Exercise 20 as a subprogram. In this case, the subprogram itself prints the messages.

## Chained Modules

A third approach to external modules is to write the external modules as if they were separate main programs. Then, **CHAIN statements** can be used to execute the separate main programs serially. Each separate program is a **chained module** that contains a CHAIN statement for executing the next module in the sequence. Table 7.9 shows one implementation of the CHAIN statement.

Note the following regarding the use of chained modules.

**NOTE 1**  Each module is a main program with its proper END statement. All properties of main programs apply, such as calls to internal modules, calls to external modules, and all variables local.

**NOTE 2**  Dialects that allow chaining usually provide the option of passing all or some subset of values from the chaining (calling) program to the chained program. For example, Microsoft BASIC provides the ALL option in the CHAIN statement and the COMMON statement for specific variables that are to be shared among chained modules.

**NOTE 3**  Chained modules have the following unique advantages in addition to those described earlier for external modules:

**Table 7.9**   Chained Modules

| Dialect | Structure, Syntax, and Calls | Examples |
|---|---|---|

Microsoft BASIC (IBM PC)

Main program 1

```
.
.
.
CHAIN MERGE next program name options
          ⌐     ⌐
        Optional            Optional
.
.
.
END
```

Main program 2

```
.
.
.
CHAIN statement
.
.
.
END
.
.  ⎤  Other main programs as required
.  ⎦
```

*Note:* The *next program name* is
the name of the program file
that is to be executed next.
See the examples for **MERGE** and other options.

**Examples**

**Stored in Drive B as File ONE**
```
10 '  Main program 1
50     PRINT "Prog. 1 executed"
90     CHAIN "B:TWO"
99     END
```

**Stored in Drive B as File TWO**
```
10 '  Main program 2
15     PRINT "Prog. 2 executed"
20     LET P$ = "B:THREE"
95     CHAIN P$
99     END
```

**Stored in Drive B as File THREE**
```
10 '  Main program 3
95     PRINT "Prog. 3 executed"
99     END
```

```
LOAD"b:one
Ok
RUN
Prog. 1 executed
Prog. 2 executed
Prog. 3 executed
Ok
```

*Other examples:*
a.  Revise program ONE as follows:

    90 CHAIN "B: TWO", 20

    This starts execution of main
    program 2 at line 20, thus
    bypassing the PRINT in line 15.

b.  Revise program TWO as
    follows:

    95 CHAIN P$, ALL

    This passes all variables in
    program 2 to the chained
    module called program THREE.
c.  Revise program TWO as
    follows:

    95 CHAIN MERGE P$

    This merges or overlays
    program THREE with program
    TWO. The merged program
    (THREE) must be saved as an
    ASCII file. (See Exercise 28.)

**Your System**
(if different)

**a.** Very large programs that might otherwise exceed available primary memory are candidates for chaining.

**b.** Some environments allow a chained module to be in a different programming language from the calling or chaining module. Thus, for example, a utility module already written in FORTRAN would not need to be rewritten in BASIC for use with a BASIC program.

---

### Follow-Up Exercises

**28.** Regarding the examples in Table 7.9.
  **a.** What would the output look like if we were to use

  90 CHAIN "B: TWO", 20

  in file ONE?
  **b.** Show the listing and output of the program that is executed if

  95 CHAIN MERGE P$

  were used in file TWO.

**\*29.** Take a program that you have already written and break it into chained modules. Try implementing this on your system.

---

## 7.5 POINTERS

The following pointers summarize those mentioned earlier and introduce additional ones for improving design/style and avoiding errors.

**1. On Using Modular Programming.** The *bottom line* in using modular programming is lower software development and maintenance costs. Therefore, we take here the perspective that we are dealing with the development, testing, and maintenance of large commercial programs.

**a.** The assignment of sets of related tasks to modules makes large programs more manageable (the *divide-and-conquer* strategy).

**b.** Tasks that need to be repeated at different points in a program are best implemented as modules, as this reduces the amount of coding. Our factorial module is a good example of this.

**c.** A program may use a task that has already been programmed. Assigning this task to a *utility module* makes it unnecessary to *reinvent the wheel.*

**d.** The development of large programs requires a team of programmers. The use of modules facilitates the management of the project: one can assign specific modules to specific programmers. This *specialization and division of labor* is an established principle of managerial economics.

**e.** Modular programming is a form of stepwise refinement, in which we need not refine a particular task at the point of call. For example, suppose the control module requires the use of five separate, elaborate tasks, among other things. As we design the control module (that is, write pseudocode), we need not provide the details for those tasks at that time. Rather, we simply indicate five calls to those modules. Later we can refine each module in turn.

**f.** Modular programming facilitates the debugging process, since bugs are more easily isolated in modules for diagnosis and correction. Moreover, modules can be debugged one-at-a-time by a procedure called **top-down testing.** To illustrate, open the book to Figure 7.10 on page 244 (without losing this page). We could first code and debug the control module before coding the other modules. In this case dummy modules (also called program stubs) are used in place of modules 2–7. Each dummy module might be nothing more than a PRINT statement that gives a message like "Module 3 is not ready yet" and a RETURN statement. Once the control module is debugged, we can proceed to the next level of detail: the writing and debugging of modules 2 and 3 . . . and so on.

**g.** The subsequent maintenance of modular programs is easier, since tasks are more clearly defined and isolated. For example, adding, dropping, or revising a car plan in our car rental program simply requires the addition of a new module, the deletion of a module, or changes within a module.

**2. On Designing Modular Programs.**    Start with the overall (top down) modular design of the program. The hierarchy chart is especially useful here. In designing modules, keep in mind the desirable properties of single entry/ single exit, independence, and manageable size. Don't forget the proper structure for modular programs, as described in Figure 7.1 and Figure 7.14. In particular, access modules only through proper calls (for example, GOSUB statements for subroutines) and terminate the execution of modules through proper returns (such as RETURN statements in subroutines). It's also best not to *overmodularize* a program, since too much modular detail also causes confusion and increases execution-time "overhead." (We're in danger of this in Example 7.3.)

**3. On Selecting and Implementing Modules.**    As you know there are many types of modules, which we now summarize:

**a.** *Internal modules*
　　User-defined functions
　　　　Single-line (Module C in the back of the text)
　　　　Multiline (Module C in the back of the text)
　　Subroutines (Sections 7.1–7.2)
　　Internal subprograms (note in Table 7.8)
**b.** *External modules*
　　External functions (Section 7.3)
　　External subprograms (Section 7.4)
　　Chained modules (Section 7.4)

The selection and implementation of a specific type depends on the particular task being modularized, the BASIC dialect being used, and other considerations such as the size of the program relative to the available primary memory. For example, a universal task such as sorting numbers in increasing order is best programmed as an external utility module, since such modules are more easily utilized by different programs. On the other hand, the available BASIC dialect may not support external modules, in which case we are left with a subroutine for this particular task. As another example, a complicated one-line mathematical calculation that is unique to one program, but which is repeated several times within that program, is best programmed as a single-line DEF function (See Module C).

A module that needs to be used by more than one program unit within the same run needs to be an external module, since internal modules can be called only within the same program unit. If the module needs to return only a single value, it's best programmed as a function rather than a subroutine or subprogram, since functions are more conveniently referenced for that purpose.

Finally, a large program that might otherwise exceed the available primary memory can be executed by serially calling chained modules (see Section 7.4); then, only a single chained module takes up primary memory at any one time. For instance, the SAMPLES program on the DOS diskette for the IBM PC is a control module that offers a main menu of ten demonstration programs (MUSIC, ART, MORTGAGE, etc.). Each demo program is a chained module that's called from the control module according to the user's menu choice. If all modules were to be combined into one main program, then its size would be about 36KB. By using chained modules, IBM reduced the maximum RAM required to about 8KB.[6]

**4. Program Documentation.** Internal modules should be visually segmented to improve their visual identification in listings. For example, we can use dashes or equal signs to separate modules. Use a REM statement to identify the name of a module, especially if the first BASIC statement within the module does not include its name (as in a subroutine). Describe the purpose of each module, either at the beginning of the module itself or within the control module. Provide a variable key within each module if variables are not self-descriptive. It's also useful to identify variables by local and global categories, as in Table 7.2 on page 239. Programming notes within each module (as in Example 7.3) are also useful, especially within commercial environments where programs change over time. Finally, provide a hierarchy chart that clearly shows the interrelationships among modules. With some effort, it's even possible to include the hierarchy chart as part of the documentation within the control module. Try it! Your instructor will be impressed, if not by your programming ability, at least by your perseverance.

**5. Transportability.** This term refers to the ease with which a particular program can be transported or ported to different computers or different operating systems. The fewer changes that need to be made to a ported program, the more transportable it is. This, of course, translates into lower software costs in commercial environments that change systems over time (a virtual certainty) and within software houses that develop different versions of programs to use in various systems. As you can imagine, the babble of BASIC dialects makes a severe transportability problem. No dialect is universally dominant (as in FORTRAN or COBOL), although some guidelines are clear. For example, Minimal BASIC is the most transportable dialect, but it's also the least powerful. Within the microcomputer business market, Microsoft BASIC is the most transportable, primarily because of the IBM PC's popularity. Our intent here is to make you aware that this issue is of great concern within certain programming environments. To the extent that the recent ANS BASIC dialect is accepted, this should somewhat ease the transportability problem for programs written in BASIC.

---

[6]If an IBM PC is available, and you want to see examples of technically good programs that are unstructured, stylistic nightmares, then take a look at the listings of these programs.

## Common Errors

**1. Subroutine Errors.**    Two errors seem to occur often in the use of subroutines.

**a.**  If a programmer doesn't precede a subroutine by a STOP statement (at the end of the preceding control module) or a RETURN statement (at the end of the preceding subroutine), then execution drops into that subroutine, causing a logic error or an execution error.

**b.**  If a pseudo-local variable is inadvertently used outside its proper subroutine and reassigned a value, then a logic or execution error might occur. For example, see the warning on page 239.

**2. External Module Errors.**\*\*    We have seen four common errors here (in addition to the usual errors from inattention to the syntax or proper form of a statement).

**a.**  Mismatches between the actual and formal parameter lists with respect to the number, ordering, and data typing of parameters. Make sure that each parameter list has the same number of items, that the items are in the intended sequence, and that numeric matches numeric and string matches string.

**b.**  Unintentional redefinition of a formal parameter, which changes the value of its corresponding actual parameter. For example, consider the following:

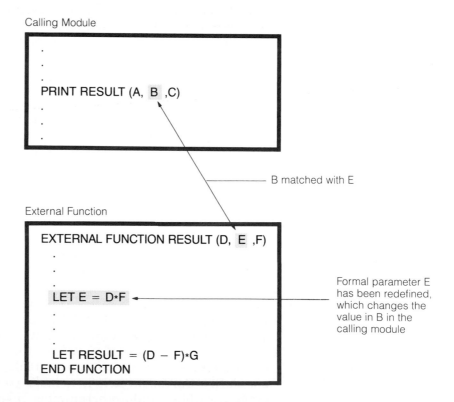

In this case, the value in formal parameter E is redefined within the function (as D\*F), which thus changes the value in the corresponding actual parameter B. This is most likely unintentional, since the value in B is supposedly passed to the function for the sole purpose of returning the single value in RESULT.

c. Omission of the function name assignment within the body of an external function. For example, this error would occur if we were to omit the assignment

LET RESULT = (D − F)*G

in the preceding example. (Also see Exercise 19d, page **000**.)

d. Use of REMs after the END statement in the main program or before the EXTERNAL FUNCTION or SUB statement in the external module. This can cause confounding execution error messages on some systems (we speak from personal experience!).

## ADDITIONAL EXERCISES

33. Define or explain each of the following:

| | | |
|---|---|---|
| modules | top-down chart | EXTERNAL statement |
| modular programming | internal modules | EXIT FUNCTION statement |
| subroutine | program units | recursive calls |
| control module | main program | external subprogram |
| subroutine call | external modules | external SUB statement |
| GOSUB statement | external function | END SUB or SUBEND statement |
| RETURN statement | local variables | CALL statement |
| nested subroutines | function reference | subprogram call |
| pseudo-local variables | actual parameter list | EXIT sub |
| global variables | formal parameter list | chained module |
| ON/GOSUB statement | external FUNCTION statement | CHAIN statement |
| hierarchy chart | END FUNCTION statement | top-down testing |
| structure chart | declarative statement | |

34. **Revisits.** Rework one of the following earlier problems according to the prescribed modular design.
   a. **Government Printing Office.** (Figure 4.7, page 135.) Use four separate modules for initialization, calculation of charge/sums, order print, and summary print.
   b. **Inflation Curse.** (Example 5.2, page 152.) Use two separate modules for input/error check and print heading.
   c. Modularize one of your previous assignments from Chapters 4–6.

35. **Population.** A staff member of the Rhode Island statewide planning division has collected population data on the five counties in the state (see Figure 1).

Write a menu-driven, modular program that allows the planner to choose from the following options:
1 Print population change report (see Figure 2)
2 Print bar graph (see Figure 3)
3 Stop processing

**Figure 1** Population for Five RI Counties

| | 1970 | 1980 |
|---|---|---|
| Bristol | 45,900 | 43,200 |
| Kent | 142,400 | 152,000 |
| Newport | 94,200 | 82,700 |
| Providence | 581,500 | 561,300 |
| Washington | 85,700 | 87,600 |

**Figure 2** Population Change

| | 1970 | 1980 | % Change |
|---|---|---|---|
| Bristol | 45,900 | 43,200 | − 5.9 |
| Kent | 142,400 | 152,000 | 6.7 |
| Newport | 94,200 | 82,700 | − 12.2 |
| Providence | 581,500 | 561,300 | − 3.4 |
| Washington | 85,700 | 87,600 | 2.2 |

**Figure 3** Population 1970

| | | |
|---|---|---|
| Bristol | ***** | 45,900 |
| Kent | *************** | 142,400 |
| Newport | ********* | 94,200 |
| Providence | *********************************************************** | 581,500 |
| Washington | ********* | 85,700 |

**36. Exam Reports.** A class of students has the following grades on four examinations taken in a BASIC programming course.

| Name | Exam Scores | | | |
|------|----|----|----|----|
| Affrick | 45 | 80 | 80 | 95 |
| Bubble | 60 | 50 | 70 | 75 |
| Crandell | 65 | 40 | 44 | 55 |
| Fleck | 90 | 85 | 95 | 100 |
| Linus | 75 | 60 | 85 | 70 |

**a.** Develop a modular program that can be used by an instructor for record-keeping. The data collected for each student include name and scores on each of four exams. The program should allow the instructor to choose from the following report options:

1 Print student names
2 Print names and exam scores
3 Print names and averages
4 Print average for the class

**b.** Assign letter grades to each student and include in option 3. Use the following logic to assign grades:

| Grade | Range |
|-------|-------|
| A | Above 90 |
| B | 80–89 |
| C | 70–79 |
| D | 60–69 |
| F | Below 60 |

**c.** Build in a bar-chart option that plots the frequency of each letter grade.

**37. Crew Selection.** An oceanic food firm is planning extensive underwater experiments in aquaculture (sea farming). These experiments require people to live together in an isolated underwater environment for extended periods of time. To avoid problems associated with incompatibility, the firm has decided to run isolation tests to judge compatibility. In these tests people will live together for two weeks in a monitored, above-ground capsule that is cut off from the outside world.

Suppose that four people are available for the experiments but only two are required to live together underwater. How many subgroups of two persons are possible from among four? If we let *P1* represent the first person, *P2* the second person, and so on, then we have the following six subgroups of two persons each: (*P1*, *P2*), (*P1*, *P3*), (*P1*, *P4*), (*P2*, *P3*), (*P2*, *P4*), (*P3*, *P4*). Right? Thus six separate isolation tests would have to be conducted in the capsule to select the most compatible two persons.

This approach of listing groups works fine when we are dealing with small numbers, but it becomes impractical when the numbers get large. For instance, if 10 people are available, and we need four for the experiments, then we have 210 subgroups of four

each. If you have had a course in statistics, then most likely you realized that this is a so-called combination problem.

**a.** Design and write an interactive program that calculates combinations of *n* people taken *k* at a time. Output should include combinations and the total number of days required for all isolation experiments, given that each experiment takes 14 days. Run the following data through your program:

| n | k |
|----|----|
| 6 | 2 |
| 10 | 4 |
| 10 | 6 |
| 10 | 10 |
| 20 | 4 |
| 40 | 4 |
| 60 | 6 |

**b.** Did you have numeric overflow when $n = 60$ and $k = 6$? Certain efficiencies can be realized in the calculation of $C$ by dividing terms in the numerator by terms in the denominator. For example, for $n = 60$ and $k = 6$, we can write

$$C = \frac{60 \cdot 59 \cdot 58 \cdot 57 \cdot 56 \cdot 55}{6 \cdot 5 \cdot 4 \cdot 3 \cdot 2 \cdot 1}$$

Design your program to take advantage of this efficiency.

**38. Craps Simulation.** A front line bet in a game of craps works as follows:

*First roll of dice*

1. You win what you bet if on the first toss you roll 7 or 11 (a natural).
2. You lose what you bet if on the first toss you roll a 2, 3, or 12 (a crap).
3. If you roll a 4, 5, 6, 8, 9, or 10 on the first toss, then this number becomes your *point* for subsequent rolls.

*Subsequent rolls of dice*

4. To win, you must roll your point again *before* you roll a 7.
5. If you roll a 7 while trying to get your point, then you lose.
6. If neither your point nor 7 is rolled, then roll again.

**a.** Write a modular program that simulates the roll of dice. Note that you need two random numbers for each roll—one for the first die and one for the second die. *Hint:* Uniform digits between 1 and 6 can be simulated using

    INT(RND*6 + 1)

See Module C for the functions INT and RND.

**b.** Design a loop that simulates a single game of craps as described in items 1 through 6 above. The outcome of this loop is either "won" or "lost."

**c.** Add a second loop that simulates N games. Assume $1 is bet on each game. Keep track of wins and losses. Debug your program by simulating five games. In your output for each roll, print the point on the first die, the point on the second die, and the overall point (sum of the two dice). At the end of a game print "won" or "lost." At the end of the five games print the following summaries: number of games won, number of games lost, your total dollar winnings (or losses), and the percent (of the total amount bet) dollar winnings (or losses).

**d.** Provide an option in the program to suppress the output for each roll and the "won" or "lost" output at the end of each game. For each of the following runs just print the summary statistics:

(1)  N = 100
(2)  N = 500
(3)  N = 1000
(4)  N = 5000

Based on your output, estimate the expected (percent) loss by betting the front line in craps.

**39. Depreciation.**   The concept of depreciation plays a prominent role in the financial accounting of organizations that report profits and pay taxes. The simplest method of depreciation is called the straight-line method. This method uses the following formula to determine depreciation for an asset (automobile, building, machine, etc.) in any given year:

$$\text{Depreciation} = \frac{(\text{Cost} - \text{Salvage value})}{\text{Life}}$$

A second method is the double-declining balance method (a method used to increase the amount of depreciation in early years). This method uses the formulas:

$$\text{Book value of asset} = \left(\begin{array}{c}\text{Cost of}\\\text{asset}\end{array}\right) - \left(\begin{array}{c}\text{Accumulated}\\\text{depreciation}\\\text{from all prior years}\end{array}\right)$$

$$\text{Depreciation} = \left(\begin{array}{c}\text{Book value}\\\text{of asset}\end{array}\right) \cdot (2) \cdot \left(\frac{1}{\text{Life of asset}}\right)$$

**a.** Develop a menu-driven, modular program that has the following options:

1  Data entry
2  Straight-line depreciation schedule
3  Double-declining balance depreciation schedule
4  Stop processing

Enter the data for each asset using the following screen design.

Asset type  = = = = = = = =>
Cost        = = = = = = = =>
Salvage     = = = = = = = =>
Life        = = = = = = = =>

Sample output for menu-choice 2 might look as follows:

DEPRECIATION SCHEDULE
Method: Straight Line

Asset ......... Chariot
Cost .......... $4200
Salvage ....... $ 200
Life .......... 4 years

| Year | Depreciation Expense | Accumulated Depreciation | Book Value |
|------|----------------------|--------------------------|------------|
| 1 | 1000 | 1000 | 3200 |
| 2 | 1000 | 2000 | 2200 |
| 3 | 1000 | 3000 | 1200 |
| 4 | 1000 | 4000 | 200 |

Process the following assets in your test runs:

| Asset | Cost | Salvage | Life |
|-------|------|---------|------|
| Chariot | 4,200 | 200 | 4 |
| Building | 200,000 | 0 | 15 |
| Machine | 75,000 | 5,000 | 5 |

**b.** At the end of each schedule print the present value of tax savings, based on the following description:

Let present value (pv) = 0
For each year
   Let pv = pv + depreciation/(1 + discount rate)^ year
Next year

   Let tax savings = tax rate * pv

Some definitions:

■  Present value   The present worth (in today's dollar) of some future amount. For example, a dollar received one year from now is worth today about 91 cents (1/1.1) if we assume a discount rate equivalent to a 0.1 (or 10%) rate of inflation. Put another way, what might cost $1 a year from now would cost $0.91 today, assuming a 10% rate of inflation.

■  Tax rate   The corporate income tax rate. Currently this is 0.25.

In our straight-line example from part **a**, the present value of depreciation-flows over four years is $3170, assuming a discount rate of 0.1 per year. This gives a tax savings of $792. In your test runs, compare the tax savings generated by each depreciation method. Which method is best with respect to tax savings?

c. Include a third depreciation method called sum of the years digits. Check any introductory accounting text for a description of this method.

40. **Electric Bill.** Gotham City Electric Company wishes to redesign the computerized bills that it sends to commercial and residential customers. It has announced a city-wide contest to determine the best design and BASIC program for this purpose.

a. Read data include the following.

*Date data*

1. Month (three letters) and day (two digits) for beginning date of monthly billing cycle
2. Month and day for ending date of monthly billing cycle
3. Year (two digits)

*Customer data*

4. Previous meter reading in kilowatt-hours (up to seven digits)
5. New meter reading in kilowatt-hours
6. Customer rate code (one digit)
7. Past due amount (dollars and cents)
8. Payment since last bill (dollars and cents)
9. Name of customer (up to 20 characters)
10. Street address of customer (up to 20 characters)
11. City, state, and ZIP (up to 24 characters)
12. Account number of customer (up to eight digits)

Use the following sample data for the computer run.

Billing Cycle

| From | To | Year |
|------|------|------|
| SEP 19 | OCT 18 | 1985 |

Use the following sample data per customer.

Rate codes and their corresponding rates per kilowatt-hour (kWh) are explained by the following table.

| Rate Code | Rate per kWh (cents) | Comment |
|------|------|------|
| 1 | 10.25 | Residential, partly electric home |
| 2 | 9.85 | Residential, all electric home |
| 3 | 8.50 | Commercial, usage under 50,000 kWh |
| 3 | 7.50 | Commercial, usage between 50,000 kWh and 100,000 kWh |
| 3 | 6.50 | Commercial, usage above 100,000 kWh |

If past due amount less payment is more than zero, then a 1% per month charge on this difference is added to the customer's bill. For example, the last customer in the input data is commercial and used 225,000 kWh (1,025,500 − 800,500). Thus the customer is charged at 6.5 cents per kWh, which amounts to a current bill of $14,625.00. This customer, however, has a $3000 past due account and payments of only $1000. At an interest rate of 1% per month, the interest charge is $20, that is, (3000 − 1000) × 0.01; hence, the total now due from this customer is $16,645.00, that is, 2000 + 20 + 14,625.

Output from your program should include the following.

1. Name of customer
2. Street address of customer
3. City, state, and ZIP
4. Account number
5. Billing cycle: from (month, day) to (month, day, year)
6. Kilowatt-hours
7. Current amount owed
8. Past due amount
9. Interest charge
10. Total amount due

| Previous Reading | New Reading | Rate Code | Past Due Amount | Payment | Name | Street Address | City, State, Zip | Account Number |
|------|------|------|------|------|------|------|------|------|
| 27648 | 28648 | 1 | 60.10 | 60.10 | Make these up | ............................ | | |
| 42615 | 45115 | 2 | 45.20 | 0.00 | Make these up | ............................ | | |
| 314625 | 354625 | 3 | 3110.00 | 3110.00 | Make these up | ............................ | | |
| 615700 | 695700 | 3 | 8000.00 | 8000.00 | Make these up | ............................ | | |
| 800500 | 1025500 | 3 | 3000.00 | 1000.00 | Make these up | ............................ | | |

Label your output and design it to fit within a 3-by 5-inch image, since these statements must fit in a standard size envelope.

**b.** Include error detection to ensure that the rate code is 1, 2, or 3 and that the new meter reading is greater than the previous meter reading. If an error is encountered, print an appropriate error message that includes the customer's name, complete address, and account number; bypass the calculations and printout for this customer; space down to the next statement; and go on to the next customer. Add new data to test each of the possible input errors.

Use a modular design for your program. By the way, the winner of the contest gets to ride the Batmobile, which recently was retrofitted with an all-electric power plant.

# One-Dimensional Arrays

# 8

Most of the programs that we have written or studied have had the following structure:

1. Read in or input data
2. Process the data
3. Print the results
4. Return to Step 1 if necessary

In some problems we may want to store large quantities of related data (such as a table of numbers) before the processing step (Step 2 above). This was not practical in our earlier programs, because read-in or input of new data automatically replaced the previously stored values. The alternative was either reentry of data for interactive programs or restoration of the data pointer for programs using DATA statements as internal data files. In this and the next chapters we offer the array alternative, which allows the storage of and access to all related data.

## 8.1 MOTIVATION

An **array** is a group of consecutive memory locations that have the same name. The use of arrays

1. Permits access to any data item that has been stored.

2. Provides simple yet powerful capabilities to name and manipulate a large number of related storage locations.

To help you visualize this concept, the illustration below shows three storage locations for an array named DEPOSITS.

DEPOSITS

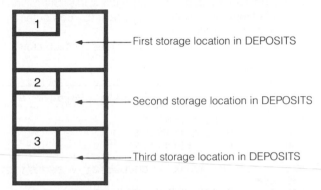

First storage location in DEPOSITS

Second storage location in DEPOSITS

Third storage location in DEPOSITS

Just how we specify and manipulate arrays will become clear in the next two sections. First, however, we motivate their use by the following example.

## E X A M P L E   8 . 1   Analysis of Bank Deposits

The vice-president of a bank wants to compare the percent of deposits that each branch contributes to the bank's total deposits. The number of deposits for each of the three test bank branches is given below.

| Bank | Number of Deposits |
|------|--------------------|
| 1 | 3500 |
| 2 | 5000 |
| 3 | 4000 |

Let's first try to solve this problem using approaches from previous chapters. A program such as the following might be written.

```
100 REM-------------------------------------
110 REM        Bank Deposits, Version A
120 REM
130        LET TOTAL = 0
140 REM
150        READ N
160        FOR J = 1 TO N
170          READ DEPOSITS
180          LET TOTAL = TOTAL + DEPOSITS
190        NEXT J
200 REM
210        RESTORE
220 REM
230        PRINT "Bank","Deposits","Percent"
240        READ N
250        FOR J = 1 TO N
260          READ DEPOSITS
270          LET PERCENT = DEPOSITS*100/TOTAL
280          PRINT J,DEPOSITS,PERCENT
290        NEXT J
300 REM
900        DATA 3
901        DATA 3500,5000,4000
998 REM
999        END


RUN
Bank           Deposits     Percent
 1             3500          28
 2             5000          40
 3             4000          32
```

In the first loop (lines 160–190), each of the three data items is read in, and total deposits (TOTAL) are accumulated. Next, the RESTORE statement moves the data block pointer back to the beginning of the data block, which subsequently allows us to reread the data within the second loop (lines 250–290). This loop requires each data item once more in order to calculate and print the required percentages.

Note that each value stored in the variable DEPOSITS is replaced by the next value read in. Thus, never does the entire set of related data (the deposits 3500, 5000, and 4000) appear at one time in primary memory. That's why we needed to reread the data within the second loop. This approach works, but it's inefficient because the reading of data is a time-consuming machine task (by computer standards!); and this version reads the same set of data twice.

Now consider the following approach, which stores the entire set of data within primary memory.

```
100 REM------------------------------------------------
110 REM          Bank Deposits, Version B
120 REM
130          READ DEPOSITS1
140          READ DEPOSITS2
150          READ DEPOSITS3
160 REM
170          LET TOTAL = DEPOSITS1 + DEPOSITS2 + DEPOSITS3
180 REM
190          PRINT "Bank","Deposits","Percent"
200 REM
210          LET PERCENT = DEPOSITS1*100/TOTAL
220          PRINT 1,DEPOSITS1,PERCENT
230 REM
240          LET PERCENT = DEPOSITS2*100/TOTAL
250          PRINT 2,DEPOSITS2,PERCENT
260 REM
270          LET PERCENT = DEPOSITS3*100/TOTAL
280          PRINT 3,DEPOSITS3,PERCENT
290 REM
00           DATA 3500,5000,4000
10 REM
20           END

RUN
Bank          Deposits     Percent
 1            3500         28
 2            5000         40
 3            4000         32
```

*This program works, but* it's very rigid and inefficient. It works for three branches, but if we wish to add a fourth branch, the program will have to be rewritten extensively. Worse yet, visualize this program written for the hundreds of Chase Manhattan branch banks in New York City. What a long and tedious program it would be for such a simple problem! A simpler solution to this problem is to use an array.

```
100 REM------------------------------------------------
110 REM          Bank Deposits, Version C
120 REM
130          DIM DEPOSITS(3)
140 REM
150          LET TOTAL = 0
160 REM
170          READ N
180 REM
190          FOR J = 1 TO N
200             READ DEPOSITS(J)
210             LET TOTAL = TOTAL + DEPOSITS(J)
220          NEXT J
230 REM
240          PRINT "Bank","Deposits","Percent"
250 REM
260          FOR J = 1 TO N
270             LET PERCENT = DEPOSITS(J)*100/TOTAL
280             PRINT J,DEPOSITS(J),PERCENT
290          NEXT J
```

```
300 REM
900        DATA 3
901        DATA 3500,5000,4000
998 REM
999        END


RUN
Bank              Deposits        Percent
  1                3500             28
  2                5000             40
  3                4000             32
```

In this program the first loop reads the number of deposits for each branch bank, storing them in an array called DEPOSITS, and accumulates the total deposits for all branches in TOTAL. The second loop references, or recalls, each element in the array DEPOSITS in the expression that calculates percentages and prints the number of deposits and the relative percent of total deposits for each branch bank. At this point, don't worry about the exact nature of the array or about the DIM statement. We discuss this topic next.

You should realize, however, that after the first loop the entire set of deposit data resides within primary memory in array DEPOSITS. This is precisely why we did not need to reread the data within the second loop, as we did in Version A. Moreover, the addition of a fourth branch bank simply requires changing the 3 to a 4 in line 130 (besides the usual data line changes). If we were to use, say, 100 in line 130, then this version of the program would handle *any number* of branch banks up to 100.

## 8.2 ARRAY NAMES AND SUBSCRIPTS

An array is used to store a collection of related data items, as illustrated by array DEPOSITS in Example 8.1. An **array element** is the memory location within which a data item is stored. In our earlier example, we used the following array elements.

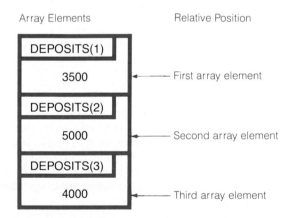

Each array element is accessed or referenced by an **array-element name** that has two distinct parts: an array name and a subscript enclosed within parentheses.

**Array-Element Name**

**Array name (subscript)**

DEPOSITS (J)

The **array name** is simply the variable name that identifies the array: DEPOS-ITS in our example. The same rules that apply to naming simple variable names also apply to naming array variable names. The **subscript** is a *numeric expression*, within parentheses, that follows the array name. It acts as an index or pointer for locating the array element. In our example the subscript is J. If J stores the value 1, then the first array element in DEPOSITS is referenced, as illustrated below.

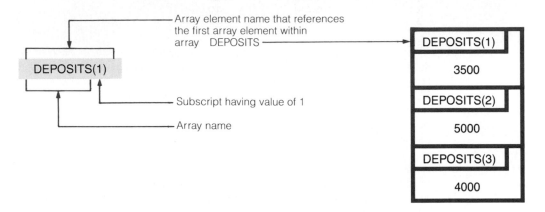

Array element name that references the first array element within array   DEPOSITS ──→ DEPOSITS(1) 3500

DEPOSITS(1)

Subscript having value of 1

Array name

DEPOSITS(1)   3500
DEPOSITS(2)   5000
DEPOSITS(3)   4000

**E X A M P L E   8 . 2**   **Subscripted Variables: Algebra vs. BASIC**

The use of subscripts in BASIC gives the language great ease and flexibility in naming and manipulating a large number of *related* variables. This feature is "borrowed" from algebra.

| Stock Number | Price of Stock ($) | Subscripted Variables in Algebra | Array-Element Names (Subscripted Variables) in BASIC |
|---|---|---|---|
| 1 | 75 | $x_1$ | X(1) |
| 2 | 42 | $x_2$ | X(2) |
| 3 | 24 | $x_3$ | X(3) |
| . | . | . | . |
| . | . | . | . |
| . | . | . | . |
| 500 | 105 | $x_{500}$ | X(500) |

For example, if we have a series of 500 numbers, and each number represents the price of a stock at the end of a given day on the New York Stock Exchange, then the algebraic notation $x_3$ refers to the price of the third stock, and $x_{75}$ refers to the price of the 75th stock. Similarly in BASIC, X(3) refers to the storage location for the price of the third stock, and X(75) identifies the storage location for the price of the 75th stock. Array-element names are often called **subscripted variables,** since this is the formal term used in algebra.

Naming so many related variables would be quite tedious and impractical without subscripts. For example, you wouldn't recommend a scheme such as A, B, C, . . . to name 500 variables, would you? These names are cumbersome, difficult to manipulate, cause inefficient coding, and do not suggest contextual meaning. As you will see, the use of arrays overcomes each of these difficulties.

You should keep in mind the following points when working with subscripts.

**1.**   An array-element name with a single subscript references a **one-dimensional array.**

**2.**   Subscripts must have *non-negative values*. Usually they are either *positive integer constants* or variables that store positive (nonzero) integer values. For example,

COST(K)
          └──── Variable as subscript

uses the *variable* K as a subscript.

When we use a variable as a subscript we can reference any element in the array on the basis of the value we assign that variable. For example, the program segment

DIM SALE(20)
.
.
.
LET K = 3
LET SALE(K) = 500

results in the storage of 500 in the third location of the array SALE.

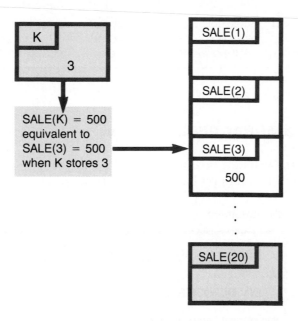

**3.** Generally the subscript can be any numeric expression. The computer determines which array element is referenced by evaluating the subscript and using this result to identify the specific array element. For example, if K stores 4, then LOAD(K + 3) and LOAD(2*K + 1) are legitimate array-element names that reference the seventh and ninth elements of the array LOAD.

**4.** Subscripts can store *real* (fractional) values; however, any subscript with a fractional value is either truncated (as in VAX-11 BASIC) or rounded (as in Microsoft BASIC) before the array element is retrieved. For example, WEIGHT(5.7) would reference the fifth array element of WEIGHT on some systems and the sixth on others. *Does your system truncate or round real subscript values?*

**5.** Many programmers prefer using *integer* values for subscripts, since this practice promotes faster processing times. On many systems, we declare integer values by adding a % sign to a numeric constant or variable. For example, the array element name SALE(K) would be written as SALE(K%). *Can you declare integer constants and variables on your system? If so, how?*

**6.** We can use the same variable name as a subscript to reference corresponding elements in different arrays. For example, the program segment

LET K = 2

LET PROFITS(K) = SALES(K) − COSTS(K)

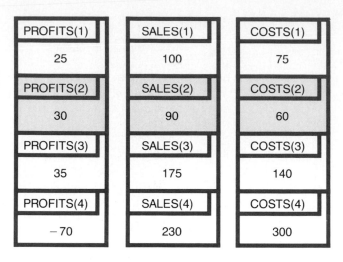

subtracts the second array element in COSTS from the second array element in SALES and stores the result in the second array element of PROFITS.

7. Subscripts are not part of the array name; thus LAB(J) and LAB(I) both reference the array LAB. In addition, if I and J are equal, then LAB(J) and LAB(I) reference the same element in LAB.

## 8.3 ARRAY DECLARATION

Arrays should be *declared* for the computer to reserve a specific number of multiple memory locations. The DIM statement is used for this purpose.

**DIM Statement**

> **DIM** $^{array}_{name}$ (array size), $^{array}_{name}$ (array name) , . . .
>
> DIM DEPOSITS(3)

This statement declares to the compiler or interpreter which variable names are array names and defines their size (total number of array elements). In the example, the DIM statement reserves three memory locations (array elements) for the array named DEPOSITS, which we can illustrate in the usual way.[1]

---

[1]Most versions of **BASIC** use a *lower bound* of zero instead of one for the value of the subscript. Thus, the statement DIM DEPOSITS(3) would actually reserve four locations: DEPOSITS(0), DEPOSITS(1), DEPOSITS(2), and DEPOSITS(3). In this case, it is best to conceptualize the integer value in the DIM statement as the *upper bound* on the value of the subscript. As a compromise on the issue of a lower bound, the statements

| Most BASIC Dialects | ANS BASIC | Your Dialect |
|---|---|---|
| **OPTION BASE 0** | **BASE 0** | |
| or | or | |
| **OPTION BASE 1** | **BASE 1** | |

explicitly declare the lower bound of the subscript. For our purposes, *we shall assume a lower bound of one throughout the chapter* (as does ANS BASIC).

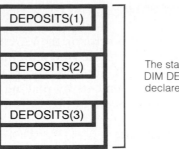

The statement
DIM DEPOSITS(3)
declares array size of 3

Note that the contents (stored values) of these locations are left blank;[2] they are filled in with the appropriate values when the READ statement is executed three times in the FOR/NEXT loop. If we had used

DIM DEPOSITS(5)

then five memory locations would have been reserved for DEPOSITS.

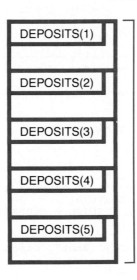

The statement
DIM DEPOSITS(5)
gives array size of 5

However, the program of Example 8.1, Version C, still would use only the first three of these locations.

More than one array can be dimensioned in a single DIM statement by using commas to separate each array specification. For example,

DIM COST(80),REV(50),PROFIT(50)

reserves 80 locations for an array named COST, 50 locations for array REV, and 50 locations for array PROFIT.

Here are some additional points to keep in mind when working with DIM statements.

1.  The DIM statement is a *nonexecutable* statement that normally is placed at the beginning of a program, but it may appear anywhere in the program before the array is used.[3]

2.  For compiled BASICs, the constant that specifies the size of the array *must* be an integer constant. For example.

---

[2] Most versions of BASIC automatically initialize all numeric array elements to zero.
[3] Some versions of BASIC may treat the DIM statement as an executable statement.

DIM DEPOSITS(N)

would yield a syntax error on the VAX-11, since a variable is *not* permitted within parentheses in the DIM statement.

On many BASIC interpreters, however, we can reserve a variable number of array elements by placing a simple numeric variable in the DIM statement as an array-size parameter. For example,

DIM DEPOSITS(N)
        ┗━━━━━━ Numeric variable instead of numeric constant

is permitted in Microsoft BASIC. *Is this permitted on your system?*

The actual size of the array is entered during the execution of the program, as illustrated in Example 8.3. The ability to change the array size from run to run is called **dynamic storage allocation,** or **dynamic arrays.** This allows greater programming flexibility, because it avoids wasted storage space and eliminates some program modification.

---

**E X A M P L E  8 . 3**  Dynamic Arrays

---

```
100 REM----------------------------------------------------
110 REM         Bank Deposits:  Dynamic Array Version
120 REM
130         INPUT "Number of banks"; N ◄──────── Defines size of dynamic array
140         PRINT
150 REM
160         DIM DEPOSITS(N) ◄──────── Dynamic array, with size defined
170 REM                                by the value stored in N
180         LET TOTAL = 0
190 REM
200         FOR J = 1 TO N
210           PRINT "Bank"; J; "deposits ";
220           INPUT DEPOSITS(J)
230           LET TOTAL = TOTAL + DEPOSITS(J)
240         NEXT J
250 REM
260         PRINT TAB(35); "Bank","Deposits","Percent"
270 REM
280         FOR J = 1 TO N
290           LET PERCENT = DEPOSITS(J)*100/TOTAL
300           PRINT TAB(35); J,DEPOSITS(J),PERCENT
310         NEXT J
998 REM
999         END
```

```
RUN
Number of banks? 3 ◄──────── Dynamic allocation of 3 array elements

Bank 1 deposits ? 3500
Bank 2 deposits ? 5000
Bank 3 deposits ? 4000
```

|  | Bank | Deposits | Percent |
|---|------|----------|---------|
|  | 1 | 3500 | 28 |
|  | 2 | 5000 | 40 |
|  | 3 | 4000 | 32 |

---

3.  We can reserve more locations for an array than are actually used in a particular program; however, if we reserve only 15 locations for an array and need 17, an error message will occur during execution of the program

when the value of the subscript exceeds 15. For this reason it's a good defensive programming practice to ensure that the subscript value does not exceed the upper dimension bound.

4. On some systems, the DIM statement may be omitted, in which case a one-dimensional array is automatically assigned an upper dimension of 10. Thus it is not always necessary to define arrays with DIM statements. However, *we recommend you use the DIM statement even if its use is optional.* This way you avoid the error of forgetting the DIM statement when it's needed, and your programs identify arrays more clearly.

5. What size array should we declare? In general, the size of a declared array is a trade-off between wasted storage costs and the software cost of updating the array declaration, taking into consideration actual and projected data needs. For example, if we have 75 branch banks and over the next 10 years expect at most 25 more branch banks, then it is reasonable to declare DEPOSITS as a 100-element array, since it is certain that the cost of updating the declaration in the program each time a branch bank is added far exceeds the cost of keeping 25 empty storage locations. However, if an array generally requires no more than 5000 elements, but once in a great while it needs 100,000 elements, then it may be less costly to occasionally change the program itself by updating the array size from 5000 to 100,000 when needed. Unfortunately, an array with 100,000 elements could easily exceed the available primary memory. For example, on most systems each element in DEPOSITS would require four bytes of storage. Thus, 400,000 bytes would be needed just to allocate storage for 100,000 elements!

## Follow-Up Exercises

1. How clear are you on the intricate terminology of the last two sections? For example, can you distinguish between
   a. An array and an array name?
   b. An array name and an array-element name?
   c. An array element and an array-element name?
   d. An array element and a storage location?
   e. The value of a subscript and the $j$th array element?

2. Which of the following references to array A are valid if A is dimensioned as follows:

   DIM A(500)

   a. A(−3)
   b. A(10)
   c. A(510)
   d. A(0)

3. Indicate what is wrong, if anything, with each of the following program segments.
   a. 10 READ K,X(K)
      20 DIM X(K)

      .
      .
      .

**b.** 10 LET M = 5
20 LET N = 8
30 LET A(0) = 100
40 LET A(15) = 500
50 LET A(M − 2*N) = M*N
.
.
.

**c.** 10 DIM D(10),E(10)
20 FOR J = 1 TO 26
30    LET D(J) = J ˆ 2
40 NEXT J
50 FOR J = 1 TO 19
60    LET E(J + 1) = D(J)*D(J + 1)
70 NEXT J
.
.
.

What would be stored in E(3) once the program is corrected?

** **4.**    Indicate the storage contents of specific array elements for the following.

```
010 DIM R(5),S(5),T(5)
020 READ N
030 FOR J = 1 TO N
040   LET R(J) = J
050   LET L = N + 1 − J
060   LET S(L) = L
070 NEXT J
080 LET T(5) = 0
090 FOR K = 1 TO N
100   LET T(K) = R(K)*S(K)
110   LET T(5) = T(5) + T(K)
120 NEXT K
    .
    .
    .
900 DATA 4
999 END
```

| R(1) | S(1) | T(1) |
| R(2) | S(2) | T(2) |
| R(3) | S(3) | T(3) |
| R(4) | S(4) | T(4) |
| R(5) | S(5) | T(5) |

## 8.4 READ, INPUT, AND OUTPUT

In the discussions that follow, assume that we wish to read, input, or print every element in the array, beginning with the first element and moving sequentially through the array to the last element.

### Read/Input

The FOR/NEXT loop is a convenient means to read in or input array values. In this case, the control variable in the FOR statement can be used as a subscript that takes on values that coincide with each element in the array. The program segment

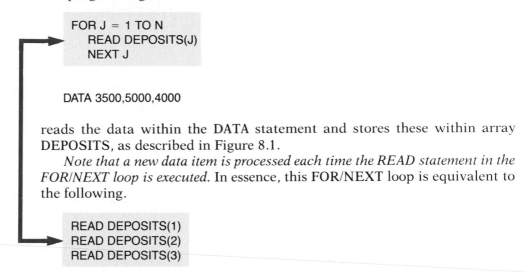

```
FOR J = 1 TO N
    READ DEPOSITS(J)
NEXT J
```

DATA 3500,5000,4000

reads the data within the DATA statement and stores these within array DEPOSITS, as described in Figure 8.1.

*Note that a new data item is processed each time the READ statement in the FOR/NEXT loop is executed.* In essence, this FOR/NEXT loop is equivalent to the following.

```
READ DEPOSITS(1)
READ DEPOSITS(2)
READ DEPOSITS(3)
```

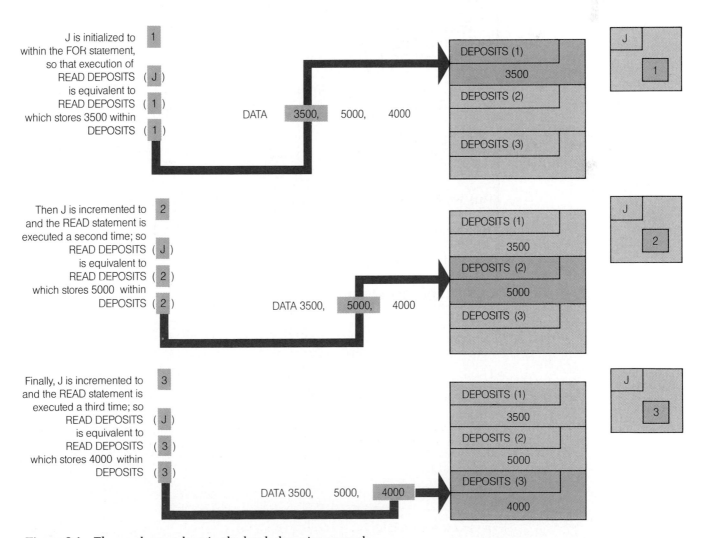

**Figure 8.1**   The read procedure in the bank deposits example

In other words, identical results would be obtained if the FOR/NEXT loop were replaced with the above three statements. If we were reading in deposits for 200 banks, the power of the FOR/NEXT loop approach would be apparent.

## Output

This looping technique using the FOR/NEXT statements also can be used for output. For example, the statements

```
FOR J = 1 TO 3
      PRINT DEPOSITS(J)
NEXT J
```

give *column output* for the contents of array DEPOSITS as follows:

```
3500
5000
4000
```

*Note that a new output line is written each time the* PRINT *statement is executed.* In effect, this FOR/NEXT loop is equivalent to the following:

```
PRINT DEPOSITS(1)
PRINT DEPOSITS(2)
PRINT DEPOSITS(3)
```

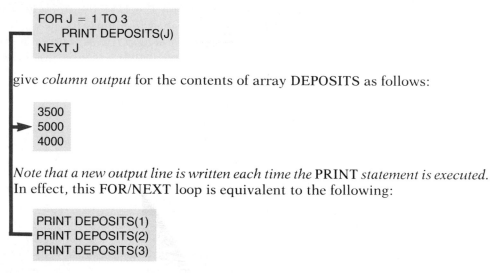

If *row output* rather than column output is desired, then a trailing comma or semicolon should be used in the PRINT statement, as follows:

```
FOR J = 1 TO 3
      PRINT DEPOSITS(J);          Note trailing semicolon
NEXT J
```

This would give the row output

```
3500      5000      4000
```

which is equivalent to

```
PRINT DEPOSITS(1); DEPOSITS(2); DEPOSITS(3);
```

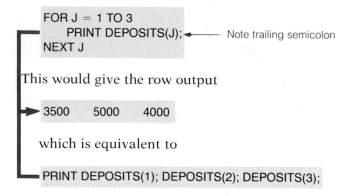

## Follow-Up Exercises

**5.** With respect to Version C of Example 8.1 on page 274:

   **a.** Change the program to process 100 branch banks. How many more statements would be needed in the Version B program to accomplish the same task? How about the length of the statement that calculates TOTAL? Do you now see why arrays are such a powerful means of naming and manipulating a large number of *related* storage locations?

\*  **b.** Modify the program so that the output appears as follows:

| Bank | 1 | 2 | 3 |
|------|------|------|------|
| Deposits | 3500 | 5000 | 4000 |
| Percentage | 28 | 40 | 32 |

**6.** Consider the following program segment for the input of 50 values into an array named B:

```
100 DIM B(50)
110 INPUT B(1)
120 INPUT B(2)
130 INPUT B(3)
        .
        .
        .
600 INPUT B(50)
```

Rewrite this segment using the FOR/NEXT loop. In general, which approach is more efficient?

**\*7.** Given the following data:

| Cost | Sales |
|------|-------|
| 40 | 100 |
| 20 | 125 |
| 75 | 95 |

   **a.** Write an efficient program segment to read these data into the arrays C and S. What might be the most logical way of placing data on DATA statements?

   **b.** Write the code to output these data so they appear as presented in the above table.

   **c.** Write the code to output these data as follows:

| COST | 40 | 20 | 75 |
|-------|------|------|------|
| SALES | 100 | 125 | 95 |

## 8.5 MANIPULATING ARRAYS

This section presents four short examples that illustrate techniques of manipulation for one-dimensional arrays.

**E X A M P L E   8 . 4**    **Initialization**

Often it is necessary to set each element in an array to some initial value. For example, to initialize all values in a 100-element array to 50, we could write the following instructions:

```
10 FOR K = 1 TO 100
20     LET S(K) = 50
30 NEXT K
```

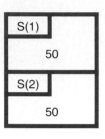

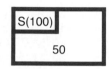

As the value in K changes from 1 to 100, each of the 100 locations in the array S is set to 50. After this segment of the program is executed, array S appears as illustrated.

**E X A M P L E   8 . 5**    **Accumulation of a Sum**

Quite often it's necessary to perform arithmetic operations on all the elements in an array. The following segment from Example 8.1, Version C, illustrates the accumulation of a sum.

```
LET TOTAL = 0
FOR J = 1 TO N
  READ DEPOSITS(J)
  LET TOTAL = TOTAL + DEPOSITS(J)
NEXT J
```

As the value of J changes from 1 to 3, each element of the array DEPOSITS is added to the accumulator TOTAL. When J = 1 we actually are executing

TOTAL = TOTAL + DEPOSITS(1)    or    TOTAL =    0 + 3500;

when J = 2 we are executing

TOTAL = TOTAL + DEPOSITS(2)    or    TOTAL = 3500 + 5000;

and when J = 3 we are executing

TOTAL = TOTAL + DEPOSITS(3)    or    TOTAL = 8500 + 4000.

Thus 12500 gets stored in TOTAL.

**E X A M P L E   8 . 6**   **Correspondence among Arrays and Direct Access of Array Elements**

Sometimes we need to perform operations among *corresponding elements* of different (parallel) arrays. For example, assume that a department store analysis program computes profits for each department in the store. Sales are stored in the array SALES, and costs are stored in the array COSTS. A third array, PROFITS, is used to store profits for each department based on the following computations.

```
FOR K = 1 TO N
    LET PROFITS(K) = SALES(K) – COSTS(K)
NEXT K
```
Corresponding elements

where N is the number of departments to process and K is the *k*th department.

When K equals 1, the first element in array COSTS is subtracted from the first array element in SALES, and the difference is stored in the first array element of PROFITS. The calculation of profits continues for all N array elements as illustrated in the following diagram of the array contents.

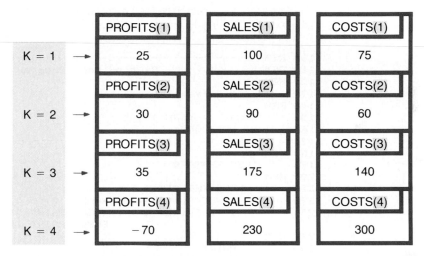

Sometimes we don't need to manipulate all the elements in an array. For example, the store manager can inquire about sales, costs, and profits for a specific department by using the following program.

```
100 REM--------------------------------------------------
110 REM           Departmental Query Program
120 REM
130      DIM SALES(100),COSTS(100)
140 REM
150      READ N
160 REM
170      FOR K = 1 TO N
180        READ SALES(K),COSTS(K)
190      NEXT K
200 REM
210      INPUT "Department Number"; DEPT
220 REM
230      IF DEPT < 1 OR DEPT > N THEN
             PRINT "Error in department number!" :
             STOP
240 REM
250      LET PROFIT = SALES(DEPT) - COSTS(DEPT)
260 REM
270      PRINT TAB(10);"Sales .......... $"; SALES(DEPT)
280      PRINT TAB(10);"Costs .......... $"; COSTS(DEPT)
290      PRINT TAB(10);"Profits ........ $"; PROFIT
300 REM
900      DATA 4
901      DATA 100,75
902      DATA 90,60
903      DATA 175,140
904      DATA 230,300
998 REM
999      END


RUN
Department Number? 3
       Sales .......... $ 175
       Costs .......... $ 140
       Profits ........ $ 35
```

Directly accesses or points to desired array element.

Note that the value entered for DEPT through line 210 *directly accesses* or *points* to the desired array element in lines 250, 270, and 280. The sample run queries financial data for department 3, which effectively means that line 250 reads as follows:

```
250    LET PROFIT = SALES(DEPT) − COSTS(DEPT)
              = SALES( 3 )   − COSTS( 3 )
              = 175          − 140
              =  35
```

Also note the error test in line 230, which ensures that the departmental entry does not exceed the number of departments (see Exercise 8).

---

## E X A M P L E   8 . 7    String Arrays

String arrays are particularly useful when we need to store and manipulate a set of data with related string values, such as days of the week, months of the year, or names of employees. In this example we retrieve a specific day from an array that stores names for all the days of the week.

```
100 REM-------------------------------------------------------------
110 REM                    Days of Week Program
120 REM
130     DIM DAY$(7)
140 REM
150     FOR I = 1 TO 7
160       READ DAY$(I)
170     NEXT I
180 REM
190     LET REPEAT$ = "Y"
200 REM
210     WHILE REPEAT$ = "Y"
220       INPUT "ith day of week"; I
230       IF I < 1 OR I > 7 THEN  PRINT "***"; I; "out of range"
                            ELSE  PRINT TAB(18); DAY$(I)
240 REM
250       PRINT
260       INPUT "Another day(Y/N)"; REPEAT$
270       PRINT
280     WEND
290 REM
900     DATA "MONDAY","TUESDAY","WEDNESDAY","THURSDAY"
905     DATA "FRIDAY","SATURDAY","SUNDAY"
998 REM
999     END
```

— Direct access to *ith* array element

```
RUN
ith day of week? 3
               WEDNESDAY

Another day(Y/N)? Y

ith day of week? 7
               SUNDAY

Another day(Y/N)? N
```

Again we illustrate the common procedure of *directly accessing* an array element without having to process any other element. For example, the entry of 3 when line 220 is executed results in a direct access to element DAY$(3) in line 230, which prints the string value WEDNESDAY.

Finally, note that the test in line 230 is a defensive programming technique that ensures the avoidance of a "subscript-out-of-bound" execution error message. For example, an entry of 9 for the *i*th day of the week would exceed the upper bound of 7 for the array DAY$, as declared in line 130. Line 230, however, would trap this error, thereby avoiding a fatal execution error. (See Exercise 9.)

---

## Follow-Up Exercises

**8.** With respect to Example 8.6,
  **a.** Could we have replaced lines 901–904 with

    901    DATA 100,75,90,60,175,140,230,300

  If so, why might the original approach be preferable?
  **b.** Roleplay the output for departmental number entries of 3 and 5.
  **\*c.** Modify the error test so that the user can input a new departmental number if an error occurs.

**9.** With respect to Example 8.7,
  **a.** What gets stored in DAY$(1), DAY$(2), . . . , DAY$(7)?
  **b.** Indicate output for the numeric input 5, 10, and 0.

**10.** A student, wishing to initialize an array with 200 elements to 0, wrote the following:

```
10 DIM T(200)
20 T(K) = 0
```

On seeing this, a friend (who also takes BASIC programming) says that the above doesn't make sense because K is undefined. Perhaps, they reason, we can try the following approach:

```
10 DIM T(200)
20 T = 0
```

Explain why each approach would be incorrect. Correct this segment of the program.

**11.** Describe output for the following program.

```
100 DIM A(15)
105 READ N
110 FOR I = 1 TO N
115    READ A(I)
120 NEXT I
125 FOR I = N TO 1 STEP − 1
130    PRINT A(I)
135 NEXT I
901 DATA 4
902 DATA 5,10,15,20
999 END
```

**12.** Assume that a banking program has stored the current month's total dollar deposits in array DEPA and the total dollar withdrawals in array WITA. A third array can be used to accumulate the new balance (BAL), as follows.

```
300 FOR K = 1 TO N
310    LET BAL(K) = BAL(K) + DEPA(K) − WITA(K)
320 NEXT K
```

where N represents the number of customers to be processed.

**a.** Suppose that before running the program segment, memory appears as follows:

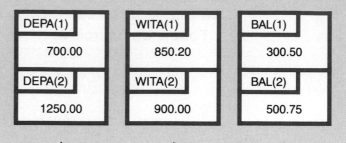

| DEPA(1) | WITA(1) | BAL(1) |
|---------|---------|--------|
| 700.00 | 850.20 | 300.50 |

| DEPA(2) | WITA(2) | BAL(2) |
|---------|---------|--------|
| 1250.00 | 900.00 | 500.75 |

What changes would occur for the first two customer accounts following execution of the given program segment?

**\*b.** Modify the loop body to print the account number, ACCNO(K), and new balance whenever the new balance is less than zero.

**13.** Assume that the array VALUE has the following contents.

VALUE

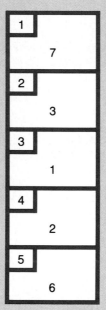

| 1 | 7 |
|---|---|
| 2 | 3 |
| 3 | 1 |
| 4 | 2 |
| 5 | 6 |

What values are stored in X, Y, and VALUE after the following segment is executed?

```
10 LET N = 1
15 LET M = 3
20 LET X = VALUE(M + N)
25 LET Y = VALUE(M) + VALUE(N)
30 LET VALUE(M) = M
35 LET VALUE(N + M) = N
```

**\*14.** Describe output for the following:

    **a.**
```
100 DIM A(100),B(100),C(100)
110 READ M
120 FOR J = 1 TO M
130    READ A(J),B(J)
140    LET C(J) = A(J)/B(J)*100
150 NEXT J
160 FOR K = 1 TO M
170    PRINT A(K);B(K);C(K)
180 NEXT K
900 DATA 4
901 DATA 10,20
902 DATA 15,20
903 DATA 10,40
904 DATA 20,50
999 END
```

    **b.** Change line 170 to

```
170 PRINT A(K);B(K);C(K)
```

    **c.** How would you change the program to get the following output?

| | | | |
|---|---|---|---|
| 10 | 15 | 10 | 20 |
| 20 | 20 | 40 | 50 |
| 50 | 75 | 25 | 40 |

**\*15.** Suppose the input

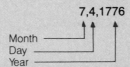

```
        7,4,1776
```

Month ——
Day ——
Year ——

    results in the output
    JULY 4, 1776

    **a.** Write a program to accomplish this. Terminate input if the year is zero or less. Print an error message if data input for either the month or the day is out of range.

    **b.** Describe how storage appears for the month data.

**\*\*16.** Write code for the following manipulations of the 25-element array LIST.

    **a.** Input N values in reverse order; that is, the first value gets stored in LIST(N), the second in LIST(N−1), and so on.

    **b.** Find and print the largest value in the array.

    **c.** Print locations of array elements (values of subscripts) that store values of zero.

    **d.** Create a second array, LIST2, consisting of all nonzero elements in LIST.

    **e.** Move all values in the array up one position; that is, the value in LIST(1) is eliminated, LIST(2) is moved to LIST(1), LIST(3) to LIST(2), and so on. Insert −99 in the last array element.

## 8.6 SELECTED APPLICATIONS

This section illustrates three common applications of one-dimensional arrays.

### Table Lookup

The term **table lookup** refers to procedures for accessing data that are stored in a table. These procedures satisfy a very common need across a wide variety of professional fields and occupational areas. In this example we work with one-dimensional tables; in the next chapter, we discuss two-dimensional tables.

**Table 8.1**    Premium Schedule

| Upper Age Limit | Annual Premium ($) |
|-----------------|--------------------|
| 25              | 277                |
| 35              | 287                |
| 45              | 307                |
| 55              | 327                |
| 65              | 357                |

**Analysis.**    Suppose that a life insurance company uses the premium schedule shown in Table 8.1 to quote insurance costs over the phone. The annual premium is based on the age of the policyholder. For example, a policyholder who is 47 years old would pay a premium of $327 per year.

When looking up information in a table, three basic elements are required. First, there is the search key, which is the item of information that helps us locate the right place in the table. In the case of the life insurance company, each policyholder's age is the search key.

The table that is to be searched usually makes up the other two sets of elements needed for the search: (1) the set of keys used to access the proper location and (2) the set of function values. In the premium schedule, the set of keys is the limits on the various age classes, and the corresponding premiums are the function values. The required output, input, and read data are specified as follows for an interactive premium quotation program:

*Output*
Cost quotation for annual insurance premium

*Input*
Name of policyholder
Age of policyholder

*Read*
Premium schedule (Table 8.1) as two arrays: one for the age limits and another for the corresponding premiums

**Design.**    Refined pseudocode for this program reads as follows:

1.  Initial tasks

    1.1  Read premium schedule
         For each row
             Read agelimit, premium    ◄——— Each array is a column
         Next row                            in Table 8.1
    1.2 Initialize processing flag

2.  Process quotation

    2.1 While more quotations
    2.2     Input name, age
    2.3     Determine premium: table lookup logic
                Initialize table index (row) to one
                While age > agelimit                    ◄——— This logic finds the proper row
                    Increment index or row                   (or index value) in Table 8.1.
                End loop

2.4    Output cost of premium
          If index = 6 then
             Print uninsurable message  ◄──────── Is printed if entered age is greater than
          Else                                     the maximum age limit
             Print cost of premium  ◄──────────── Based on the index value
                                                   found in Step 2.3
          End if
2.5    Input processing flag (Another quotation?)
2.6 End loop


3.  Concluding tasks


3.1 Print farewell message
3.2 End


This design is self-descriptive, except perhaps for the table lookup logic. To understand this logic, consider the person aged 47 with an annual premium of $327. Confirm this premium from Table 8.1 right now. OK, how did you do this? Most likely you visually scanned down the age limit column until the age 47 showed less than the age limit of 55. This means that the fourth row is the correct row or category, with a corresponding premium of $327.

The shaded logic in the pseudocode essentially does the same thing, except that we continue scanning down the column while the age is greater than the age limit. Note that the scan begins at row 1 (the index is set to 1) and continues (the index is incremented) while the age is greater than the age limit. Also note that if we scan off the table (for example, someone aged 73), then the index would have a value of 6. In this case, the print logic in Step 2.4 of the pseudocode would print a message to the effect that this person is uninsurable.

**Code.**    The following code was written in Microsoft BASIC for the IBM PC.

```
100 REM * * * * * * * * * * * * * * * * * * * * * * * * * * * * * *
110 REM *                                                         *
120 REM *    TABLE LOOK-UP: LIFE INSURANCE PREMIUM QUOTATIONS     *
130 REM *                                                         *
140 REM *    KEY:                                                 *
150 REM *       ROWS       = Number of rows in premium schedule   *
160 REM *       AGELIMIT   = Array containing upper age limits    *
170 REM *       PREMIUM    = Array containing insurance premiums  *
180 REM *       AGAIN$     = Flag to indicate whether processing is *
190 REM *                    to continue or not                   *
200 REM *       FULLNAME$  = Name of policyholder                 *
210 REM *       AGE        = Age of policyholder                  *
220 REM *       INDEX      = Pointer to location within array     *
230 REM *                                                         *
240 REM * * * * * * * * * * * * * * * * * * * * * * * * * * * * * *
250 '
260 '------------------------------------------------------------
270     DIM AGELIMIT(6),PREMIUM(6)
280 '-------------------- Read premium schedule ----------------
290     READ ROWS
300     FOR J = 1 TO ROWS
310       READ AGELIMIT(J),PREMIUM(J) ◄─────── Premium schedule stored as
320     NEXT J                                  two separate arrays (columns)
330 '------------------------------------------------------------
340     LET AGAIN$ = "y"
350 '
```

```
360 '------------------- Begin processing loop --------------------
370 '
380     WHILE AGAIN$ = "y"
390       INPUT "Name      :"; FULLNAME$
400       INPUT "Age       :"; AGE
410 '
420 '       ----------------- Table look-up logic ------------------
430 '
440       LET INDEX = 1
450       WHILE AGE > AGELIMIT(INDEX)
460         LET INDEX = INDEX + 1
470       WEND
480 '
490 '       ---------------- Output results of table look-up --------------
500 '
510       IF INDEX = ROWS THEN PRINT "Uninsurable-- over"; AGELIMIT(ROWS-1)
                          ELSE PRINT "Premium is:$"; PREMIUM(INDEX)
520       PRINT
530       PRINT
540 '       -------------------------------------------------------
550       INPUT "Another quotation (y/n)"; AGAIN$
560       PRINT
570       PRINT
580 '
590     WEND
600 '
610 '------------------- End processing loop --------------------
620 '
630     PRINT "See you tomorrow at 8 sharp!"
640 '
650 '------------------- Data Section ----------------------------
660 '
900     DATA 6
901     DATA 25,277
902     DATA 35,287
903     DATA 45,307
904     DATA 55,327
905     DATA 65,357
906     DATA 1E30,0
998 '-------------------------------------------------------------
999     END
```

*Annotations:*

INDEX is equivalent to the row or category being checked within the premium schedule

Stores the maximum legitimate age limit

Correct premium

**Test.**    The following test run represents a partial debugging of the program (see Exercise 17).

```
RUN
Name       :? Clark S. Kent
Age        :? 42
Premium is:$ 307


Another quotation (y/n)? y


Name       :? Lois S. Lane
Age        :? 28
Premium is:$ 287


Another quotation (y/n)? n


See you tomorrow at 8 sharp!
```

**Discussion.**    First, the premium schedule is read into two one-dimensional arrays: AGELIMIT and PREMIUM. Memory locations for these arrays appear as follows *after* lines 290–320 are completed:

| AGELIMIT(1) | | PREMIUM(1) |
|:---:|:---:|:---:|
| 25 | | 277 |

| AGELIMIT(2) | | PREMIUM(2) |
|:---:|:---:|:---:|
| 35 | | 287 |

| AGELIMIT(3) | | PREMIUM(3) |
|:---:|:---:|:---:|
| 45 | | 307 |

| AGELIMIT(4) | | PREMIUM(4) |
|:---:|:---:|:---:|
| 55 | | 327 |

| AGELIMIT(5) | | PREMIUM(5) |
|:---:|:---:|:---:|
| 65 | | 357 |

| AGELIMIT(6) | | PREMIUM(6) |
|:---:|:---:|:---:|
| 1E30 | | 0 |

Notice that there are six array elements in each array. The sixth array element is used for the case in which the policyholder's age is greater than 65.

Next, we enter the loop that processes quotations. After the entry of name and age, the next segment contains the table lookup logic. In this case the search key is the value stored in AGE, and the set of keys is the set of array elements in AGELIMIT. Starting with the first element (when INDEX = 1), the loop test sequentially evaluates each element of AGELIMIT until the proper age class is found; that is, until the age of the policyholder (search key) is less than or equal to an age limit value in array AGELIMIT. When this condition is satisfied (the while-loop test gives a false result), the appropriate premium (function value) is identified as the array element of PREMIUM that corresponds to the matching age class. For example, when 42 is stored in AGE, the while loop operates as follows.

**Table Lookup Logic**

| INDEX | Is AGE Greater Than AGELIMIT(INDEX)? | Result |
|:---:|---|---|
| 1 | True; 42 is greater than 25 | Continue looping |
| 2 | True; 42 is greater than 35 | Continue looping |
| 3 | False; 42 is not greater than 45 | Exit from loop |

Thus, when loop exit is achieved, the statement

PRINT "Premium is:$"; PREMIUM(INDEX)

is executed, and the correct value of 3 in INDEX (age class) is used as the value of the subscript for PREMIUM. In this case, the contents of PREMIUM(3) are printed, which gives a premium of $307 for someone aged 42. If, however, the index value is 6, then the message that the policyholder is over 65 and uninsurable is printed.

---

## Follow-Up Exercises

**17.** What would the output look like if we were to process a quotation for Rip Van Winkle, aged 99? Also roleplay the output for ages 55, 63, and 20.

**18.** Modify the program so that AGELIMIT and PREMIUM are dynamic arrays.

**19.** Modify the program to add a new row in the table with an age limit of 75 and a premium of $500. Do you see why we used the variable ROWS in lines 290–300 and 510?

**20.** Do you see anything wrong with the following table lookup logic as a replacement to lines 440–510?

```
440 FOR J = 1 TO 5
450    IF AGE <= AGELIMIT(J) GO TO 470
460 NEXT J
470 PRINT "Premium is:$"; PREMIUM(J)
```

**\*21.** We need not artificially create a sixth row in the table to catch those ages that are over 65. Instead, we could use the following if/then/else structure to replace lines 440–510:

```
If age > agelimit then
    Print uninsurable message
Else
    Implement table lookup
    Print premium
End if
```

Rewrite the program based on this logic. Which approach do you prefer and why?

**\*22.** Rewrite the program to eliminate entirely the use of arrays. Try using either a sequence of if/then structures or a multiple-block decision structure to implement the table lookup logic. Which approach do you prefer and why?

**\*23.** Implement this program on your system, after making any necessary dialect changes.

---

## Sorting

Sorting is the sequential ordering of numeric or alphabetic data. It is one of the most common operations performed in computer-based information systems.

**Analysis.**    A student file contains a number of records; there is one for each student. Each record contains student name and identification number and other data. We could sort the file either by ascending or descending ID numbers or by alphabetized student names. In either case, the item in the record that is used to sort the file is known as the sort key.

Let's assume we want a listing of students in ascending order of ID numbers. For simplicity, let's assume we have only four students.

The required data are identified as follows:

*Output*
Sorted IDs

*Read*
Unsorted IDs

*Parameters*
Array limit ( = 500)
Switch to indicate whether sort is finished ($=0$) or unfinished ($=1$)

We assume that the unsorted IDs are to be stored within array ID. The sort routine will rearrange the array elements within array ID in ascending numeric order. The following design reflects these requirements.

**Design.**    Consider the following pseudocode.

```
Start control module

1. Initial tasks
      1.1 Initialize sort switch
      1.2 Initialize array limit
      1.3 Read number of items to be sorted

2. Array upper bound error routine
      2.1 If number of items to be sorted > array limit then
            Print error message
            Stop
          End if

3. Read unsorted IDs

4. Sort IDs by calling subroutine Sort

5. Concluding tasks
      5.1 Print sorted elements
      5.2 Stop processing

End control module
```

```
Start subroutine Sort                    Sorting procedure
                                                ↓
      4.1 While sort unfinished
      4.2     Set sort switch to finished
      4.3     For each element in array
      4.4          If two adjacent elements are out of sequence then
                        Exchange or swap these two elements
                        Set sort switch to unfinished
                     End if
                  Next element

              End loop

      4.5 Return

End subroutine
```

You should be aware of the following design considerations. First, in Step 2 we use the defensive programming technique of trapping cases for which the upper bound of the array (the array limit) is exceeded. Second, the use of a subroutine call to sort IDs in Step 4 illustrates the use of top-down design. In this case, subroutine Sort is a stepwise refinement of Step 4.

The task of sorting within computer-based environments is very often required. As a result, sorting procedures are commonly written and stored within libraries as utility modules. We shall shortly discuss in detail the particular sorting procedure shown above. For now you should realize that the procedure successively compares adjacent elements within the array. If any two elements are out of sequence, they are exchanged, or swapped. This process continues until a complete pass of the array shows that no swaps took place.

**Code.** The following code was written in Microsoft BASIC for the IBM PC.

```
100 REM * * * * * * * * * * * * * * * * * * * * * * * * * * * * *
110 REM *                                                       *
120 REM * SORT PROGRAM IN ASCENDING NUMERIC ORDER               *
130 REM *                                                       *
140 REM *    Control module ... Reads data into array ID        *
150 REM *                       Calls subroutine sort           *
160 REM *                       Prints sorted elements in ID    *
170 REM *                                                       *
180 REM *    Subroutine sort .. Rearranges values of array in   *
190 REM *                       ascending order                 *
200 REM *                                                       *
210 REM * * * * * * * * * * * * * * * * * * * * * * * * * * * * *
220 '
230 '----------------------- Control Module -----------------------
240 '
250     DIM ID(500)                       ' Declare array
260 '
270     LET SWITCH      = 1               ' Initialize
280     LET ARRAY.LIMIT = 500
290 '
300     READ NUM.ITEMS
310                                       ' Test for upper bound error
320     IF NUM.ITEMS > ARRAY.LIMIT THEN
           PRINT NUM.ITEMS; " exceeds maximum number of items" :
           STOP
330 '
340     FOR J = 1 TO NUM.ITEMS
350        READ ID(J)                     ' Read unsorted values
360     NEXT J
370 '
380     GOSUB 500                         ' Call subroutine sort
390 '
395     PRINT
400     PRINT "Sorted IDs:"
410     FOR J = 1 TO NUM.ITEMS
420        PRINT ID(J)                    ' Output sorted values
430     NEXT J
440     PRINT
450 '                                                    | Bubble sort
460     STOP
470 '
500 '----------------------- Subroutine Sort -----------------------
510 '
520     WHILE SWITCH = 1
530 '
540        LET SWITCH = 0
550 '
560        FOR J = 2 TO NUM.ITEMS         Swap of elements
570 '
580           IF ID(J) < ID(J-1) THEN
                 LET TEMP   = ID(J) : ID(J) = ID(J-1) : ID(J-1) = TEMP :
                 LET SWITCH = 1
590 '
600        NEXT J          Step 1          Step 2          Step 3
610 '
620     WEND
630                 ' Note: Sort completed when no elements have been swapped
640                 '       (SWITCH = 0) in one complete pass of array.
650     RETURN
897 '
898 '----------------------- Data Section -----------------------
899 '
900     DATA 4
901     DATA 8321,3076,2501,7771
998 '-------------------------------------------------------------
999     END
```

**Test.**    The following test run is a partial debugging of the program (see Exercise 25).

```
RUN

Sorted IDs:
 2501
 3076
 7771
 8321

Break in 460
```

**Discussion.**    The DIM statement in line 250 sets an upper bound or array limit of 500 on array ID. Line 280 assigns this value to the variable ARRAY.LIMIT. The error routine in line 320 thus avoids an execution-time error by checking the number of items to be sorted against the array limit. If this number exceeds 500, then an error message is printed, and execution stops. (See Exercise 26 for the dynamic array alternative.)

The one-dimensional array called ID is used to store and then sort the ID numbers. The array is read in using the FOR/NEXT loop in lines 340–360, which gives the following contents for the *unsorted* array ID:

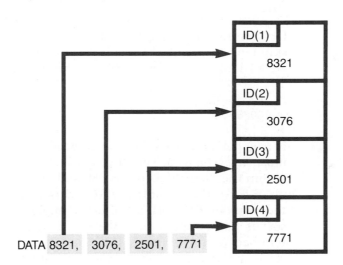

For this problem, we use the **exchange method** of sorting. On each pass through the array, the first element is compared with the second: The smaller number is stored in this first position, and the larger number is stored in the second position. Then the second element of the array is compared with the third: The smaller number is placed in the second position, and the larger number is placed in the third position. This process of comparison and rearranging continues throughout the entire array. When this first pass through the array is complete, the array is processed again, from beginning to end. This procedure continues until no exchanges take place in a pass through the entire array. The exchange method is also called a **bubble sort,** since items that are below their correct positions in the array tend to move upward, like bubbles in a carbonated drink.

The logic within the subroutine (lines 520–620) illustrates the bubble sort. The subscripts $J$ and $J - 1$ are used to compare values stored in adjacent array elements. When an exchange (or swap) takes place between two adjacent elements, a separate memory location (TEMP) serves as a temporary

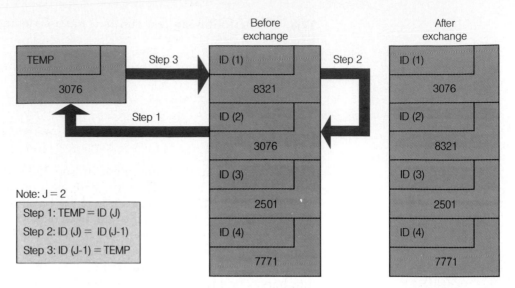

**Figure 8.2**  Exchange method for $J = 2$

location to hold one of the values while the exchange takes place. To understand exactly what's happening, consider the case for $J = 2$ within the FOR/NEXT loop in lines 560–600. The test in line 580, or

ID(2) < ID(1)
3076 < 8321

is true, which means that the adjacent elements defined by ID(2) and ID(1) must be exchanged. The three distinct steps in the exchange logic are given within the then block in line 580 and are explained within Figure 8.2.

Finally, the variable SWITCH acts as a switch by storing either 0 or 1. If the value in SWITCH is 1 after a complete pass through the array, then the sort is not complete, and the entire array must be scanned again for the numbers out of sequence. If the value in SWITCH is 0 after a complete pass through the array, then the sort is complete.

## Follow-Up Exercises

**24.** Fill in the following table based on the data in the example.

| | | Contents When Control Is at NEXT J in Line 600 | | | | |
|---|---|---|---|---|---|---|
| J | TEMP | ID(1) | ID(2) | ID(3) | ID(4) | SWITCH |
| 2 | 3076 | 3076 | 8321 | 2501 | 7771 | 1 |
| 3 | | | | | | |
| 4 | | | | | | |
| 2 | | | | | | |
| 3 | | | | | | |
| 4 | | | | | | |
| 2 | | | | | | |
| 3 | | | | | | |
| 4 | | | | | | |

**a.** How many passes through the entire array does it take to sort the array? How many passes does it take to terminate execution?

**\*b.** Implement this program on your system.

**25.** What would happen if we were to try a sort of 3000 items? Make the necessary changes to implement a 3000-item sort.

**\*26. Dynamic Arrays.** Modify the program so that ID is a dynamic array. Do we need the error routine now?

**\*27.** Make appropriate changes in the program for a numeric sort in descending order. Test your program by roleplaying the given data or implement the program on your system.

**\*28. SWAP Statement.** Microsoft BASIC has a statement that simplifies the sort logic. The purpose of this statement, the SWAP statement, is to exchange the values of two variables. Its syntax is given by

**SWAP Statement**

> **SWAP** *variable1, variable2*
>
> SWAP A,B

where variable1 and variable2 can be simple variables or array-element names. If A stores the value 5 and B stores the value 10, then after execution of the SWAP statement A stores 10 and B stores 5.

**a.** Rework the program to incorporate the SWAP statement.

**b.** Implement this program on your system, if possible.

**\*29.** Suppose the DATA statements included student names, as follows:

```
901 DATA 8321,"Jones"
902 DATA 3076,"Smith"
903 DATA 2501,"Meyer"
904 DATA 7771,"Adams"
```

**a.** Modify the program so that these names are printed beside the numerically sorted data. *Hint:* Each time there's an ID swap, there must also be a name swap.

**b.** Implement this program on your system.

**\*30. Alphabetic Sort.** Rework the preceding exercise so that the sort key is the student's name rather than the ID.

**\*31. External Modules.** If it's possible on your system, try implementing our sorting example by treating the sorting module as an external module (as described in Sections 7.4 and 7.5). Use array X as the formal parameter within the external module. Check your system's user manual or ask your instructor regarding the pass/return process for arrays.

## Polynomial Plot

Computerized graphics are playing an increasingly important role in software applications. The use of high-resolution color monitors and printers, the availability of sophisticated graphics commands and specialized graphics software packages, and the implementation of drawing aids such as light pens, mice, and graphics tablets have led to presentation-quality graphics that previously could have been generated only by commercial artists.

The following example illustrates a very simple statistical graphics application, without the use of any specialized hardware or specialized graphics commands in BASIC. To get a better idea of the graphics/color capabilities of your system, take a look at the *BASIC Users Manual* and look up graphics statements such as CIRCLE, COLOR, DRAW, LINE, and PAINT. Are any of these (or others) available on your system?

**Analysis.**    Consider the commonly used polynomial function of degree $d$

$$y = b_0 + b_1 x + b_2 x^2 + \cdots + b_d x^d$$

where the $b_i$ are coefficients of the function. For example,

$$y = 25 + 8x - x^2$$

is a polynomial function of degree 2 (also called a quadratic function), where $b_0 = 25$, $b_1 = 8$, and $b_2 = -1$.

Let's develop a program that generates an $x$–$y$ graph of any polynomial function of degree 2 over a user-defined $x$-range. For example, given an $x$-range of 1 to 10 in steps of 1 and the above polynomial function, the following coordinates would be calculated and plotted by the program:

| $y$-value | $x$-value |
|---|---|
| 32 | 1 |
| 37 | 2 |
| 40 | 3 |
| 41 | 4 |
| 40 | 5 |
| 37 | 6 |
| 32 | 7 |
| 25 | 8 |
| 16 | 9 |
| 5 | 10 |

*Note:* Try confirming a couple of these values by entering $x$-values into the function and calculating the corresponding $y$-values.

Let's define the following data requirements:

*Output*
$y$-values for polynomial function of degree 2 (stored as array)
$x$-values
$x$–$y$ graph

*Input*
Plot symbol (such as * or +)
Second-degree polynomial coefficients ($b_0$, $b_1$ $b_2$ stored as array)
$x$-range (first value, last value, and step)

*Parameters*
Array-$y$ limit (= 100)
Polynomial degree (= 2)
Maximum $y$-scale (= 50, defines the character-width of the graph)

In the follow-up exercises we shall have you generalize the requirements to a polynomial of any degree.

**Design.**    We see four distinctly separate tasks for this program, as defined by the following modules:

*Control module*            Establishes the main processing loop and calls the other modules.

| | |
|---|---|
| *Subroutine input* | Inputs the data defined above. |
| *Subroutine y-array* | Generates a degree-2 polynomial *y*-array based on the entered *x*-range. |
| *Subroutine plot* | Plots the *x–y* graph of *any y*-array based on the entered *x*-range. |

The following pseudocode reflects this design.

```
Start control module
     Initialize y-limit (array size) and user's looping response
     Establish processing loop that calls each module and terminates based on a "no"
          response from user
     Print farewell message
     Stop processing
End control module
```

```
Start subroutine Input
     Input plot symbol
     Set polynomial degree to 2
     Input polynomial coefficients into array using FOR/NEXT loop
     Input x-range
     Return
End subroutine
```

```
Start subroutine Y-array
     Initialize y-array subscript
     For each x
          Increment subscript
          If subscript exceeds y-limit then
             Print error message
             Stop
          Else
             Calculate y-value
          End if
     Next x
     Return
End subroutine
```

```
Start subroutine Plot
     Initialize maximum y-scale
     Print graph headings
     Initialize y-array subscript
     For each x
        Increment subscript
        Print y- and x-values
        If y-value <= max y-scale then
           Print plot symbol
        Else
           Don't print plot symbol
        End if
     Next x
     Print graph footing
     Return
End subroutine
```

Take some time right now to study each module; then go on to the program listing for the coding refinements, confirm the given output, and read the discussion that follows.

**Code.**    The following program was written in Microsoft BASIC for the IBM PC.

```
100 REM * * * * * * * * * * * * * * * * * * * * * * * * * * * * * * * * *
110 REM *                                                               *
120 REM *                POLYNOMIAL PLOT PROGRAM                        *
130 REM *                                                               *
140 REM *    Control module .... Establishes  processing loop          *
150 REM *                        Calls subroutines input, Y-array       *
160 REM *                        and plot                               *
170 REM *    Sub. input ........ Inputs plot symbol, polynomial         *
180 REM *                        coefficients, and X-range              *
190 REM *    Sub. Y-array        Generates polynomial Y-array based     *
195 REM *                        on X-range                             *
200 REM *    Sub. plot ........ Plots graph of any Y-array based        *
210 REM *                        on X-range                             *
220 REM *                                                               *
230 REM * * * * * * * * * * * * * * * * * * * * * * * * * * * * * * * * *
240 '
250 '--------------------- Control Module ---------------------
260 '
270     DIM Y(100),B(2)  ◄——————— Arrays for y-values and polynomial coefficients
275 '
280     LET YLIMIT = 100  ◄——————— Upper bound on Array Y
290     LET AGAIN$ = "y"
295 '
300     WHILE AGAIN$ = "y"
305 '
310       GOSUB 400                                   ' Call sub. input
320       GOSUB 600                                   ' Call sub. Y-array
330       GOSUB 800                                   ' Call sub. plot
335 '
340       INPUT "Another plot (y/n)"; AGAIN$
345 '
350     WEND
355 '
360     PRINT : PRINT "Sorry to see you go ..." : PRINT
365 '
370     STOP
399 '
400 '--------------------- Subroutine Input ---------------------
405 '
410     PRINT
420     INPUT "Enter plot symbol such as * or +"; SYMBOL$
430     PRINT
435 '
440     LET DEGREE = 2  ◄——————— Polynomial of degree 2 assumed
445 '
450     FOR K = 0 TO DEGREE
460       PRINT "Enter polynomial coefficient"; K;
470       INPUT B(K)  ◄——————— Note storage of polynomial coefficients within Array B
480     NEXT K
485 '
490     PRINT
500     INPUT "Enter first X-value"; XFIRST
510     INPUT "Enter last  X-value"; XLAST
520     INPUT "Enter step  X-value"; XSTEP
530     PRINT
535 '
540     RETURN
599 '
600 '--------------------- Subroutine Y-array ---------------------
605 '
610     LET J = 0
615 '
620     FOR X = XFIRST TO XLAST STEP XSTEP
```

```
625  '
630      LET J = J + 1
640      IF J > YLIMIT THEN PRINT "*** Too many Y-values.  Reduce X-range.":
                             STOP
                           ELSE LET Y(J) = B(0) + B(1)*X + B(2)*X^2
650      NEXT X
655  '
660      RETURN
799  '
800  '--------------------------- Subroutine Plot ---------------------------
805  '
810      LET MAX.SCALE = 50
815  '
820      PRINT : PRINT TAB(35);"GRAPH OF Y-FUNCTION" : PRINT
830      PRINT TAB(20);"Y-scale ====>"
840      PRINT " Y";TAB(12);"X";TAB(20);
850      PRINT "+----+----+----+----+----+----+----+----+----+----+"
855  '
860      LET J = 0
865  '
870      FOR X = XFIRST TO XLAST STEP XSTEP
875  '
880        LET J = J + 1
885  '
890        PRINT Y(J);TAB(11);X;TAB(19);"¦";
895  '
900        IF Y(J) <= MAX.SCALE THEN PRINT TAB(20 + Y(J)); SYMBOL$;TAB(71);"¦"
                               ELSE PRINT TAB(71);"¦"
905  '
910      NEXT X
915  '
920      PRINT TAB(20);"+----+----+----+----+----+----+----+----+----+----+"
930      PRINT
935  '
940      RETURN
998  '--------------------------------------------------------------------
999      END
```

- LET J = J + 1
- IF J > YLIMIT: If true, then upper bound of Y-array is exceeded
- ELSE LET Y(J) = B(0) + B(1)*X + B(2)*X^2 : Calculates value of polynomial function and stores as *Jth* array element
- LET MAX.SCALE = 50 : Y-scale range of 0 to 50 is assumed
- Prints plot symbol at proper y-coordinate
- If false, then plot symbol is off the graph, so we bypass printing it

**Test.**    The following test run is a partial debugging of the program. (Also see the follow-up exercises.)

```
RUN

Enter plot symbol such as * or +? *

Enter polynomial coefficient 0 ? 25
Enter polynomial coefficient 1 ? 8
Enter polynomial coefficient 2 ? -1

Enter first X-value? 1
Enter last  X-value? 10
Enter step  X-value? 1
```

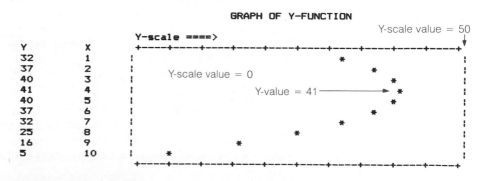

```
Another plot (y/n)? n

Sorry to see you go ...

Break in 370
```

**Discussion.**    The control and input modules are rather straightforward, so let's go on to the other modules. Note the following regarding subroutine *Y*-array:

1. The subscript *J* is a counter that takes on the subscript values 1, 2, . . . , number of *x*-values. In the sample run, the *x*-range had 10 values; hence, the *y*-array must have 10 elements, or one *y*-value for each corresponding *x*-value.

2. The subscript *J* is tested against the *y*-array limit in line 640. Without this test, we would get a "subscript out of bounds" execution error when we try to plot more than 100 values. (See Exercise 33.)

Consider the following regarding subroutine Plot:

1. The graph runs from columns 20 to 70 on the screen, since the early columns are reserved for the *y* and *x* output values. This gives a *y*-scale that runs from 0 (at column 20) to 50 (at column 70). This is why the variable MAX.SCALE is set to 50 in line 810.

2. The test in line 900 ensures that we don't print a plot symbol if the *y*-value exceeds 50, since this would otherwise print the plot symbol off the screen to the right (actually, it would "wrap around" the * to the next line and spoil the look of the graph). Exercise 38 explores the scaling alternative to this problem, and Exercise 35 looks at what happens when we have negative *y*-values.

3. Did you notice the cunning use of the TAB function in line 900 for printing the plot symbol? (Actually, we can't take credit for this bit of programming, since it's old stuff in BASIC.) To illustrate, consider the case in which Y(4) = 41. The PRINT statement in line 900 thus reads as follows:

```
PRINT TAB(20 + Y(4)); SYMBOL$;TAB(71);"|"
PRINT TAB(20 + 41 ); SYMBOL$;TAB(71);"|"
PRINT TAB(   61   ); SYMBOL$;TAB(71);"|"
```

Thus a * is printed in column 61, which is equivalent to a *y*-value of 41 after accounting for the fact that the graph actually starts in column 20 (which is why we have the 20 within the argument of the TAB function in the first place!). Take a look at the graph to confirm that the * is, in fact, at position 41 on the *y*-scale (the + symbols along the top of the scale are in increments of 5 for easy counting).

## Follow-Up Exercises

32. Indicate I/O for plotting the first-degree polynomial (straight line)

$$y = 1 + 4x$$

over the *x*-range 1 to 5 in steps of 1.

33. Describe what happens if the entered *x*-range results in more than 100 *y*-values.

34. Describe what happens in the output should the *y*-value exceed 50.

35. Describe what happens when the program tries to plot a negative *y*-value. Specifically, where is the * plotted if *x* = 11 (which gives *y* = −8)? Correct this problem by modifying the test in line 900.

**\*36.** Implement the sample program on your system, after making any necessary changes for your BASIC dialect.

**\*37.** Modify the program to process a polynomial function of any degree. *Hint:* You need a FOR/NEXT loop to calculate Y(J), which now is calculated as the sum of its parts.

**\*\*38.** **Scaling Alternative.** The current version of subroutine Plot does not scale values of *y*, which means, for example, that a value of 200 for *y* would exceed the width of a print line.

**a.** Modify the subroutine to scale the *y*-scale so that the plot symbol is always printed between print positions 20 to 70. For example, if the maximum value of *y* is 200 and the minimum is 7, then the asterisk corresponding to a value of 100 for *y* is printed at print position 44, as calculated from the integer part of

$$20 + \left(\frac{100 - 7}{200 - 7}\right) \cdot (70 - 20)$$

*Hint:* Adapt subroutine Sort on page 298 as another subroutine that determines the minimum and maximum values of *y*. The plotting subroutine calls the Sort subroutine. *Warning:* Create a second one-dimensional array for the sort to avoid altering the original Y-array.

**b.** Show that this scaling technique always prints the * between columns 20 and 70. Suppose the minimum *y*-value is −8 and the maximum *y*-value is 41. Where do these values get plotted along the *y*-scale?

**c.** Implement this revised program on your system.

## 8.7 POINTERS

### Design and Style

**1. Array Declarations.** Declare all arrays through DIM statements, even though most systems automatically dimension arrays if there are ten or fewer array elements. This also clearly identifies the arrays for anyone reading a listing of the program. The placement of DIM statements at the beginning of the program also facilitates the identification of arrays. It's also best to identify the arrays within the program's documentation.

**2. The Array Size/Storage Trade-Off.** Make sure that the array-size parameter that defines the number of array elements is large enough to handle all normal situations. Remember, it's better to waste storage space than to have execution-time errors resulting from a subscript value above the upper dimension bound.

**3. Defensive Programming.** Don't forget to include an error routine that catches a subscript value that exceeds its upper dimension bound. This avoids "subscript out of bound" execution errors. The sample programs in Section 8.6 illustrate this style of programming.

**4. Generalized Programming.** Use simple variables rather than constants to define the number of repetitions in FOR/NEXT loops used to read, manipulate, and print arrays. This avoids program modification when the number of repetitions changes. To illustrate, we need not change the FOR statement in lines 190 and 260 of Example 8.1, Version C, when there's a change in the number of branch banks. We simply change the data item in line 900.

**5. Array Names.** Avoid using the same name to represent an array and a simple variable. For example, SUM(J) is treated as an array element and SUM as a simple variable in the statement

    PRINT SUM, SUM(J)

We don't recommend this practice, however, as it makes programs more difficult to follow. Worse yet, some systems prohibit this practice.

## Common Errors

Arrays are great for giving a lot of practice in debugging. Often one small error will result in an avalanche of error messages. Pay attention to the following, and you might avoid apoplexy.

**1. Declaration of Array.** Don't forget to declare your array by using the DIM statement. Some systems allow you to omit the DIM statement for arrays that use 10 or less elements. In this case, you will get an execution error if the subscript of an array exceeds 10 during execution. On other systems, if you forget to dimension an array, then you will get a syntax error message for each line containing a subscripted variable. So, if you get an error message such as "Undefined array" or "Undefined function" for each line in which the subscripted variable appears, then check whether you dimensioned the array.

**2. Subscripts.** If you get an execution error message such as "Subscript out of bounds" or "Subscript out of range," then a subscript is negative, zero (in systems that don't allow this lower bound), or greater than the upper bound specified in the DIM statement. Two kinds of mistakes are possible here: either you reserved too few locations for your array, or you made a logic error in assigning values to subscripts. In the latter case, you might want to diagnose the error by using a *trace* to print subscript values, as illustrated by the following simple example.

```
10 REM   Subscript-out-of-bounds example
15 REM
20       DIM X(5)
25       FOR J = 1 TO 6         Execution error
30         LET X(J) = J^2       when J reaches 6,
35         PRINT J;X(J)         which exceeds the
40       NEXT J                 upper bound of 5
99       END                    in the DIM statement

RUN
 1   1
 2   4
 3   9
 4   16
 5   25
Subscript out of range in 30
```

**3. Array Names.** A common point of confusion among beginning programmers is just what represents the array name. For example, are B(J) and B(I) one and the same array? Yes. In this case, the array name is B, not B(J) or B(I). B(J) and B(I) are called array-element names, which simply reference specific elements in array B.

**4. Initialization.** Most systems use implicit initialization—the automatic initialization of all numeric storage locations to zero. If your system does not use implicit initialization, you will get an execution error the first time your program attempts to process an uninitialized counter or summer.

Even if a specific system provides implicit initialization, it's a good programming practice to use explicit initialization, for two reasons: The program is transportable to systems that don't implicitly initialize, and certain types of logic and execution errors are avoided. To illustrate the latter, consider the explicit initialization of J in line 610 on page 304. If we were to omit this line, subscript J in lines 630 and 640 would still store the proper values 1, 2, . . . 10 for our sample run, since our system implicitly initializes J to zero. If we also delete the explicit initialization in line 860, then subscript J in lines 880, 890, and 900 would run from 11 to 20, instead of from 1 to 10. This would be a logic error because array elements 11 through 20 store zero. Moreover, subsequent plots would give the wrong subscript values in line 630. Given enough plots, J would eventually exceed its limit in line 640.

**5. Data Entry and Output.**   Don't forget to use a loop to enter or output an array. We often see the following approaches as attempts to output the entire contents of an array:

```
PRINT A(K)
PRINT A
```

The first either prints one element (if a positive integer within the bounds of the array is stored for K) or results in an execution error. The second either gives an execution error or prints the stored value of a simple numeric variable A.

## ADDITIONAL EXERCISES

**39.**   Define or explain each of the following.

array  
array element  
array-element name  
array name  
subscript  

subscripted variable  
one-dimensional array  
DIM statement  
OPTION BASE statements  
dynamic storage allocation  

dynamic arrays  
table lookup  
sorting  
exchange method  
bubble sort  

**40. Revisits.**   Modify an earlier problem as indicated below.

**a. Microcomputer Price Quotation Program.** (Section 6.4, page 198.) Use a table lookup procedure to determine the proper prices according to the discount schedule (Table 6.4).

**b. Property Tax Assessment.** (Chapter 6, Exercise 33, page 220.) Use a table lookup procedure to determine the proper tax rate.

**c. Exam Reports.** (Chapter 7, Exercise 36, page 307.) Add a menu option that prints sorted averages in descending order.

**41. Crime Data Summary.** The data below represent the number of arrests for felony crimes in a state over a three-year period.

|  | Arrest Data by Year | | |
|---|---|---|---|
| Felony | 1 | 2 | 3 |
| Homicide | 1,000 | 1,000 | 1,000 |
| Robbery | 10,000 | 9,000 | 11,000 |
| Burglary | 27,000 | 24,000 | 28,000 |
| Assault | 13,000 | 15,000 | 16,000 |
| Theft | 19,000 | 20,000 | 23,000 |
| Forgery | 10,000 | 9,000 | 10,000 |

**a.** Design and write a program to read the data into several one-dimensional arrays. Print out the data in a table format that includes a new row for total arrests in each year and a new column for average arrests for each crime over the past three years. There is no need to label rows and columns here.

**b.** In the output of part **a**, label your columns 1, 2, 3, and AVERAGE. Label your rows according to the felony names in the above table, the last row being TOTALS. Store felony names in a one-dimensional string array.

**c.** Print a second table that gives the ratio of arrests for each crime to the total number of arrests in that year.

**42. SAT Scores.** Every year State College prints a fact book that includes average combined (math plus verbal) SAT scores of students categorized as freshmen, sophomore, junior, and senior.

**a.** Write a program that reads a student data file (Figure 1) that includes student name, college code (1 = humanities, 2 = sciences), class code (1 = freshmen, 2 = sophomore, . . .), math SAT score, and verbal SAT score.

**Figure 1** Student File

| Student name | College code | Class code | SAT Math | SAT Verbal |
|---|---|---|---|---|
| Hicks | 2 | 2 | 580 | 640 |
| Garfolo | 1 | 3 | 720 | 680 |
| Beck | 2 | 2 | 610 | 560 |
| Thuki | 1 | 2 | 580 | 420 |
| Vasu | 1 | 4 | 495 | 505 |

Figure 2 shows how the report should appear.

**Figure 2** SAT Data

| Code | Count | Average |
|---|---|---|
| Freshmen | 0 | 0 |
| Sophomore | 3 | 1130 |
| Junior | 1 | 1400 |
| Senior | 1 | 1000 |

Use the direct access concept to calculate counts and averages for each class.

**b.** Modify the program to print a separate report for each college. Include a printout of the overall average for each college.

**43. Support Facility for Oil-Drilling Platforms.** Consider the coordinate system below, where the plotted points 1 through 5 represent the coordinate locations of offshore oil-drilling platforms, and the plotted point labeled $(x_0, y_0)$ is a possible location for a support facility. The figure

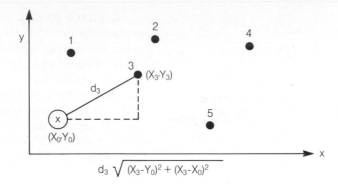

$$d_3 \sqrt{(X_3 - Y_0)^2 + (X_3 - X_0)^2}$$

also illustrates the distance $d_3$ between the support facility and platform 3. The formula for calculating $d_3$ is called the Euclidian distance formula. The coordinates in miles are given below.

| Platform $i$ | $x_i$ | $y_i$ |
|---|---|---|
| 1 | 5 | 20 |
| 2 | 15 | 22 |
| 3 | 12 | 15 |
| 4 | 25 | 21 |
| 5 | 21 | 5 |

**a.** Design and write a (preferably interactive) program that calculates and prints distances between each platform and the following proposed locations for the support facility.

| $x_0$ | $y_0$ |
|---|---|
| 4 | 6 |
| 20 | 14 |
| 20 | 18 |
| 23 | 20 |

Include the *total* distance $(d_1 + d_2 + \cdots + d_5)$ as part of your output.

**b.** Use your program (interactively) to determine the coordinate (to the nearest mile) for the support facility that minimizes total distance. In other words, by trial and error input a proposed location and, based on the output, make a judgment regarding your next proposed coordinate. Repeat this procedure until you're satisfied you have converged on the coordinate that minimizes total distance.

**\*\*c.** Instead of the trial-and-error search in part **b**, design your program systematically to vary $x_0$ and $y_0$ between chosen ranges. Include $x_0$, $y_0$, and total distance in your output. Also, have the program print the coordinate, of the ones considered, that minimizes total distance.

44. **Sales Forecasts.** Design and write an interactive program that calculates and prints sales forecasts by quarters for future years based on current sales and projected annual growth rate. For example, if currently we are at the end of the second quarter in the year 1985, and sales this quarter were $1.2 million with a projected growth rate of 2% per quarter, then forecasts through 1987 should appear as follows:

Sales Forecast for Ouija Board

| Current Year 1985 | Quarter 2 | Sales $1.2 M |
|---|---|---|

| Year | Quarter | Sales |
|---|---|---|
| 1985 | 3 | 1.224 |
| 1985 | 4 | 1.248 |
| 1986 | 1 | 1.273 |
| 1986 | 2 | 1.299 |
| 1986 | 3 | 1.325 |
| 1986 | 4 | 1.351 |
| 1987 | 1 | 1.378 |
| 1987 | 2 | 1.406 |
| 1987 | 3 | 1.434 |
| 1987 | 4 | 1.463 |

Note that the next forecast is always the last forecast increased by the growth rate.

**a.** Run your program for the following data.

| Product Name | Current Sales | Growth Rate | Years into Future |
|---|---|---|---|
| OUIJA BOARD | 1.20 | 0.02 | 2 |
| STAR TREK CHARM | 0.85 | 0.05 | 4 |

Note that the sample output is based on the first set of data. Your program should allow input for a variable number of products.

**b. Graphical Output.** To the right of each sales forecast, print the asterisk character in a graph format. Do this as follows: Reserve columns 30 through 70 for graphical output. In this case, column 30 represents 0 on a graph, and column 70 represents 40 (that is, there are 40 print columns between 30 and 70). This means that all sales forecasts must be scaled to a range between 0 and 40; that is,

$$\text{Scaled forecast} = \left(\frac{\text{Forecast}}{\text{Maximum forecast}}\right) \cdot 40$$

For example, the scaled forecast for the fourth quarter in 1986 is (1.351/1.463) · 40, or 36.9.

This means that we want an asterisk printed in column 66 (or 30 + 36) of the print line where 1.351 is printed for sales.

**c. Numeric Sort.** Print a table that summarizes total sales over the next four quarters by product. Entries in this table should be arranged in descending order of total sales.

**d. Alphabetic Sort.** Same as part **c**, except that the table should list the results in alphabetical order by product name.

45. **Revenue Sharing.** Consider the allocation program whereby the federal government apportions certain federal funds to the states on the basis of a ratio of each state's population to the total U.S. population. The table below provides population figures for all 50 states according to a recent census.

Population by State (in Thousands)

| | | | |
|---|---|---|---|
| ME | 1,059 | NC | 5,451 |
| NH | 808 | SC | 2,818 |
| VT | 468 | GA | 4,926 |
| MA | 5,199 | FL | 8,327 |
| RI | 938 | KY | 3,396 |
| CT | 3,080 | TN | 4,188 |
| NY | 18,101 | AL | 3,614 |
| NJ | 7,322 | MS | 2,364 |
| PA | 11,841 | AR | 2,068 |
| OH | 10,745 | LA | 3,762 |
| IN | 5,313 | OK | 2,681 |
| IL | 11,160 | TX | 12,017 |
| MI | 9,117 | MT | 748 |
| WI | 4,566 | ID | 820 |
| MN | 3,905 | WY | 374 |
| IA | 2,857 | CO | 2,534 |
| MO | 4,772 | NM | 1,147 |
| ND | 636 | AZ | 2,224 |
| SD | 681 | UT | 1,206 |
| NB | 1,541 | NV | 592 |
| KS | 2,266 | WA | 3,544 |
| DE | 577 | OR | 2,288 |
| MD | 4,089 | CA | 20,876 |
| VA | 4,967 | AK | 341 |
| WV | 1,803 | HI | 854 |

**a.** Write a program that uses one array for the names of the states and another array for the population figures. Read these arrays, calculate how much revenue should go to each state if $380 million is available for allocation, and output a table with appropriate labels that lists each state and its allocated amount. Include a flowchart or pseudocode.

**b.** Modify the preceding program to include a loop that processes more than one allocation. For example, if three allocation programs are to be run, then the output should appear as follows:

---

Dollar Amounts Allocated Under Each Program

| State | 1 | 2 | 3 | Totals |
|-------|-------|-------|-------|--------|
| ME | xxxxxxx | xxxxxxx | xxxxxxx | xxxxxxx |
| NH | xxxxxxx | xxxxxxx | xxxxxxx | xxxxxxx |

The number of allocations to be made (three in the above example) should be a variable. Note that the total amount that is to be allocated to each state is given by row sums and output under the column labeled "Totals." Test your program by processing the following funds available for allocation under three programs: $380 million, $800 million, $500 million.

c. Modify your output in either part **a** or part **b** so that the states are listed in alphabetical order. *Hint:* The bubble sort can be used for alphabetic data.

46. **Exam Grading.** Consider an N-question multiple choice exam, in which only one answer is correct for each question.

a. Design and write a program to grade the exam and print the student's name, the number right, the number wrong, and the final grade. The final grade is the percent number right. The data consist of
1. One line for N
2. One line containing N integers representing the N correct answers (answer key)
3. One line for each student, containing the student's name and N answers.

Use two one-dimensional numeric arrays to store the answer key and a student's answers. Test your program with the following test data:

```
20
1,3,5,4,4,1,1,2,3,5,5,1,2,3,4,4,5,3,2,1
"Petrocelli",1,3,4,4,4,1,1,2,3,3,5,1,2,3,4,4,5,1,1,1
"Baker",1,3,5,4,3,2,1,2,3,4,3,2,2,3,3,3,5,1,2,1
"Valentino",1,3,5,4,4,1,1,2,3,5,5,1,2,3,4,4,4,3,2,1
"Simpson",1,2,5,4,4,2,2,3,3,1,2,1,3,3,3,5,5,3,1,1
"Carter",2,3,5,4,4,1,1,3,3,5,4,1,5,4,4,4,5,2,1,3
"eof"
```

b. Print the name and grade of the student with the highest grade.
c. Modify your output in part **a** so that the required output is in alphabetical order according to last name. *Hint:* The bubble sort can be used for alphabetic data.
d. Print a frequency distribution of final grades for the exam, as follows:

| | |
|---|---|
| 90 or above | xx |
| 80 but under 90 | xx |
| 70 but under 80 | xx |
| 60 but under 70 | xx |
| 50 but under 60 | xx |
| below 50 | xx |

--------------------------------

xx

AVERAGE GRADE FOR EXAM = xx.x

**e. Incorporate parts **a–d** into a menu-driven program.

**47. **Statistical Analysis Program.** Large programs that give options for various statistical analyses are common in commercial applications. For example, UCLA's BMD, North Carolina State's SAS, and the University of Chicago's SPSS are all widely used packages for implementing a variety of statistical analyses across many disciplines.

a. **Measures of Central Tendency and Dispersion.** Design and write an interactive modular program that calculates and prints the statistics described below for analyzing a set of $n$ data items given by $x_1, x_2, \ldots, x_n$. In the descriptions below, assume the following set of values for $x$: 7, 14, 10, 6, 3.

1. Mean, given by

$$\bar{x} = \frac{x_1 + x_2 + \cdots + x_n}{n} = \frac{\sum_{i=1}^{n} x_i}{n} = \frac{40}{5} = 8$$

2. Median, a value such that one-half of the values are above it and one-half are below it. First sort the data in ascending order, and then find the *position* of the median using the formula $(n + 1)/2$. For example, if the sorted values of $x$ are

3    6    7    10    14

location of median

then the median is found in position $(5 + 1)/2$, or third position. Thus the median is 7. If $n$ is an even number, however, then the median is defined as halfway between the two adjacent positions in the center. For example, in the six-item sequence

3    6    7    10    14    16

location of median in position

$$\frac{6 + 1}{2}$$

the median is in position 3.5, or midway between the third item (7) and the fourth item (10). Thus the median is 8.5.

3. Minimum value of $x$, or 3 for the given data.
4. Maximum value of $x$, or 14 for the given data.
5. Range, the difference between max $x$ and min $x$, or 11 for the given data.
6. Mean absolute deviation (MAD), given by

$$MAD = \frac{\sum_{i=1}^{n} |x_i - \bar{x}|}{n} = \frac{16}{5} = 3.2$$

7. Variance, given by

$$s^2 = \frac{\sum_{i=1}^{n} (x_i - \bar{x})^2}{n-1} = \frac{70}{4} = 17.5$$

8. Standard deviation, given by

$$s = \sqrt{s^2} = \sqrt{17.5} = 4.1833$$

Offer the user a menu that includes data entry and two other choices: central tendency measures (items 1 and 2 above) and dispersion measures (items 3–8 above).

**b. Frequency Distribution.** Add a second option to the program to print a frequency distribution. Let the user specify one of two suboptions here: (1) enter number of classes and upper class limits, or (2) just enter number of classes and let the computer determine class limits. For example, in the first suboption we might want to group the data into four classes with upper limits 5, 10, and 15 for the first three classes.

In this case, the frequency distribution is given by

| Class limits | Frequency |
|---|---|
| under 5 | 1 |
| 5 but under 10 | 2 |
| 10 but under 15 | 2 |
| 15 or above | $\frac{0}{5}$ |

Thus, for the five data items, one was under 5, two were at least 5 but under 10, two were in the range 10 but under 15, and none were 15 or above. In the second suboption, a four-class frequency distribution would be given by

| min $x$ —————⟍ | Class Limits | Frequency |
|---|---|---|
| Width of each class | 3.00 but under 5.75 | 1 |
| is 2.75, or range | 5.75 but under 8.50 | 2 |
| divided by number | 8.50 but under 11.25 | 1 |
| of classes | 11.25 but under 14.01 | 1 |
| | max $x$ + .01 ——⟶ | 5 |

**c. Bar Chart.** Add a third option that prints a bar chart, as illustrated for the second frequency distribution in part **b**:

CLASS + FREQUENCIES

| 1 | + * 1 |
|---|---|
| 2 | + ** 2 |
| 3 | + * 1 |
| 4 | + * 1 |

**\*\*d. Histogram.** Instead of the bar chart in part **c**, print a histogram as follows:

```
                2
   1           ***        1           1
  ***          ***       ***         ***
--------------------------------------------------
  5.75         8.50      11.25       14.01
```

# Two-Dimensional Arrays

# 9

In many situations it's convenient to store data in arrays with more than one dimension. Some computer systems allow several dimensions, but we focus here on the more common two-dimensional arrays.[1]

## 9.1 MOTIVATION

Generally, it's desirable to use two-dimensional (2-D) arrays when we wish to store and manipulate data that are characterized by two attributes, as the following examples illustrate.

- Occupied beds in a hospital are tabulated by *day* of the week and by *ward*.
- Deposits for a major bank are recorded for all *branch banks* on a *monthly* basis.
- Enrollments at a college are tabulated by *major* and *class standing*.
- Five *exam scores* for a course are recorded for all *students*.
- Ten *financial ratios* from the Fortune 500 list of major U.S. corporations are recorded for all 500 *corporations*.

## 9.2 ARRAY NAMES AND SUBSCRIPTS

It's easier to understand a **matrix,** or **two-dimensional array** (an array with two subscripts), if we visualize a group of memory locations as a grid of boxes (table) arranged in rows and columns.

[1] For example, VAX-11 BASIC allows up to 32 dimensions and ANS BASIC includes 3-dimensional arrays.

**3 × 5 Array**

Column

| | 1 | 2 | 3 | 4 | 5 |
|---|---|---|---|---|---|
| 1 | | | | | |
| Row 2 | | | | | |
| 3 | | | | | |

An array element within a two-dimensional array is referenced by specifying two subscripts: one for row number and one for column number. For example, in the three-row by four-column array below, called DEPOSITS, the memory location that is marked with an **X** is found by looking at row 2, column 3; the memory location marked with **XX** is found in row 3, column 2.

**3 × 4 Array DEPOSITS**

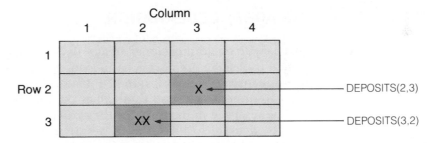

As you can see, two subscripts are needed when we use two-dimensional arrays. In BASIC, the subscripts must be enclosed in parentheses and separated by a comma. For example, in the above array named DEPOSITS, the location of the X is referenced as DEPOSITS(2,3), and the location of the XX is referenced as DEPOSITS(3,2). Notice that, in accordance with mathematical convention, the subscripts of the array-element name are always given in the following order: row subscript followed by column subscript.

**Array-Element Name**

> **array name (row subscript, column subscript)**
> DEPOSITS(I,J)

Except for the use of two subscripts, according to the above convention, *subscripts for two-dimensional arrays are treated in the same manner as for one-dimensional arrays.*

We can also illustrate array locations by using array-element names as follows:

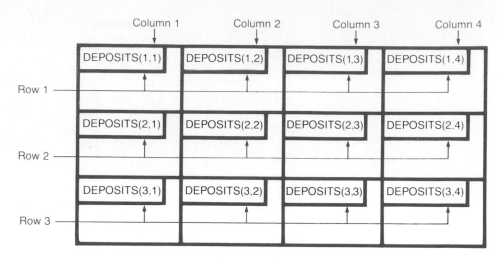

In actual practice, storage locations for two-dimensional arrays don't physically resemble a table in memory, but that need not concern us since the BASIC convention treats them like a table.

## 9.3 ARRAY DECLARATION

Just as with one-dimensional arrays, two-dimensional arrays must be dimensioned to reserve memory locations for the array. In addition to identifying one-dimensional variables, the DIM statement can indicate which variables are two-dimensional and establishes the number of rows and columns that will be reserved in memory for the array.

The general form of the DIM statement for use with two-dimensional arrays is

**DIM Statement**

$$\text{DIM} \quad \begin{matrix} array \\ name \end{matrix} \left( \begin{matrix} row & column \\ size, & size \end{matrix} \right) \begin{matrix} array \\ , name \end{matrix} \left( \begin{matrix} row & column \\ size, & size \end{matrix} \right) \dots$$

DIM DEPOSITS(3,4)

For example, we might store the number of deposits for three branch banks in each of four quarters in a three-row by four-column (3 × 4) two-dimensional array named **DEPOSITS**, where each row stores the quarterly data for one branch. The DIM statement would be specified as

DIM DEPOSITS(3,4)

If we wanted **DEPOSITS** to store branch deposits for each month of the year, then we could set up an array with 3 rows and 12 columns. In this case, the DIM statement would be given by

DIM DEPOSITS(3,12)

In the first case, **DEPOSITS** has 12 elements in memory, whereas in the second case, 36 locations are reserved in memory.[2]

---

[2]As in one-dimensional arrays, some versions of BASIC use a zero subscript; thus DIM D(3,12) would reserve 4 rows and 13 columns, or 52 locations, including the element D(0,0).

It's often useful to consider any attribute represented by the second subscript to be *within* the attribute represented by the first subscript. For example, we can use a two-dimensional array named SALES to store sales by states and counties within states. To properly dimension this array we need to know the number of states for the first dimension and the number of counties within the state with the most counties for the second dimension. If we assume the entire United States, then we have 50 for the row size. The state with the most counties turns out to be Texas, with 254. Thus, we can dimension SALES using the statement[3]

DIM SALES(50,254)

Both one- and two-dimensional arrays can be dimensioned in a single DIM statement by using commas to separate each array specification. For example,

DIM LOAD(5,10),EXP(10,8),TOT(5)

This results in the reservation of 50 locations for the 2-D array LOAD, 80 locations for the 2-D array EXP, and 5 locations for the 1-D array TOT.[4]

**NOTE 1**   As with 1-D arrays, the size declarations within the DIM statement must be numeric constants, unless your system allows *dynamic storage allocation* as described on page 280.

**NOTE 2**   Be aware that large row and column sizes can easily exceed available primary memory. For example, the 50 × 254 array SALES described earlier takes up 12,700 storage locations or array elements. On most systems single precision numeric arrays use four bytes per storage location. Thus, array SALES would require 50,800 bytes of primary memory. This could exceed the remaining memory in a 64KB microcomputer after accounting for the memory taken up by the BASIC interpreter and the program. *How much primary memory is available for your program and its data on your system?*

## 9.4 READ, INPUT, AND OUTPUT

The read, input, and output of two-dimensional arrays are best accomplished by the use of two FOR/NEXT loops, one nested within the other, as the next example illustrates.

---

[3]We thank Professor L. E. Harvey from DeAnza College for this example.

[4]As in one-dimensional arrays, the omission of the DIM statement on some systems causes the implicit assignment of an upper bound of 10 on each subscript. As stated in the last chapter, however, the omission of the DIM statement, even when allowed, is not a good programming practice.

**E X A M P L E   9 . 1**    **Read/Output with FOR/NEXT Loops**

Let's assume that the two-dimensional array DEPOSITS stores the following data on the number of deposits by branch name and by quarter.

|  | Quarter | | | |
|---|---|---|---|---|
| Bank | 1 | 2 | 3 | 4 |
| 1 | 1000 | 800 | 500 | 1200 |
| 2 | 500 | 2000 | 2000 | 500 |
| 3 | 1500 | 300 | 700 | 1500 |

Consider the following program which reads the bank data into the array DEPOSITS and then outputs this array. First, let's review the shaded segment of code, which reads the data into the array.

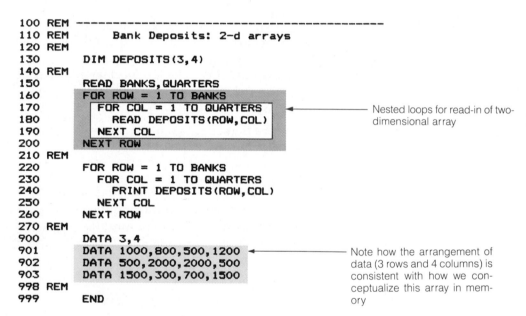

```
100 REM ------------------------------------------------
110 REM         Bank Deposits: 2-d arrays
120 REM
130       DIM DEPOSITS(3,4)
140 REM
150       READ BANKS,QUARTERS
160       FOR ROW = 1 TO BANKS
170           FOR COL = 1 TO QUARTERS
180               READ DEPOSITS(ROW,COL)
190           NEXT COL
200       NEXT ROW
210 REM
220       FOR ROW = 1 TO BANKS
230           FOR COL = 1 TO QUARTERS
240               PRINT DEPOSITS(ROW,COL)
250           NEXT COL
260       NEXT ROW
270 REM
900       DATA 3,4
901       DATA 1000,800,500,1200
902       DATA 500,2000,2000,500
903       DATA 1500,300,700,1500
998 REM
999       END
```

Nested loops for read-in of two-dimensional array

Note how the arrangement of data (3 rows and 4 columns) is consistent with how we conceptualize this array in memory

The flowchart in Figure 9.1 should help you visualize how the nesting of FOR/NEXT loops works. The key concept that you need to understand here is the exact manner in which the subscripts change values. Carefully look at the program and the flowchart to confirm that the subscripts of array DEPOSITS change values as follows:

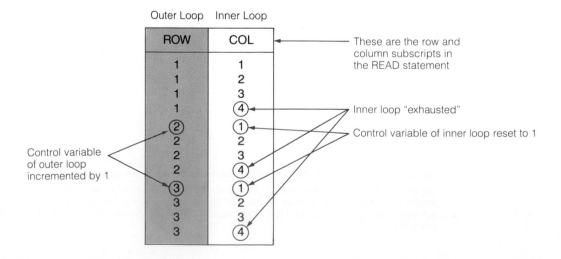

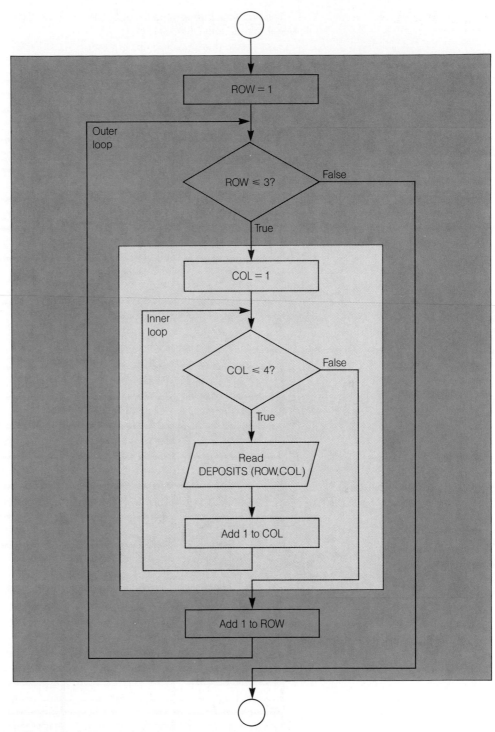

**Figure 9.1** Nested FOR/NEXT loops for read-in

The first time through the loops, ROW = 1 and COL = 1, so the first data item in line 901 is read into DEPOSITS(1,1).

After execution of READ DEPOSITS(1,1)

| DEPOSITS(1,1) | DEPOSITS(1,2) | DEPOSITS(1,3) | DEPOSITS(1,4) |
| 1000 | | | |
| DEPOSITS(2,1) | DEPOSITS(2,2) | DEPOSITS(2,3) | DEPOSITS(2,4) |
| | | | |
| DEPOSITS(3,1) | DEPOSITS(3,2) | DEPOSITS(3,3) | DEPOSITS(3,4) |
| | | | |

The second time through the inner loop, ROW = 1 and COL = 2, so the second item in line 901 is read into DEPOSITS(1,2).

After execution of READ DEPOSITS(1,2)

| DEPOSITS(1,1) | DEPOSITS(1,2) | DEPOSITS(1,3) | DEPOSITS(1,4) |
| 1000 | 800 | | |
| DEPOSITS(2,1) | DEPOSITS(2,2) | DEPOSITS(2,3) | DEPOSITS(2,4) |
| | | | |
| DEPOSITS(3,1) | DEPOSITS(3,2) | DEPOSITS(3,3) | DEPOSITS(3,4) |
| | | | |

The third time through the inner loop, ROW = 1 and COL = 3, so the third item in line 901 is read into DEPOSITS(1,3).

After execution of READ DEPOSITS(1,3)

| DEPOSITS(1,1) | DEPOSITS(1,2) | DEPOSITS(1,3) | DEPOSITS(1,4) |
| 1000 | 800 | 500 | |
| DEPOSITS(2,1) | DEPOSITS(2,2) | DEPOSITS(2,3) | DEPOSITS(2,4) |
| | | | |
| DEPOSITS(3,1) | DEPOSITS(3,2) | DEPOSITS(3,3) | DEPOSITS(3,4) |
| | | | |

The fourth time through the inner loop, ROW = 1 and COL = 4, so the fourth item in line 901 is read into DEPOSITS(1,4).

┌─After execution of READ DEPOSITS(1,4)

| DEPOSITS(1,1) | DEPOSITS(1,2) | DEPOSITS(1,3) | DEPOSITS(1,4) |
|---|---|---|---|
| ──1000── | ──800── | ──500── | ──▶1200 |
| DEPOSITS(2,1) | DEPOSITS(2,2) | DEPOSITS(2,3) | DEPOSITS(2,4) |
| | | | |
| DEPOSITS(3,1) | DEPOSITS(3,2) | DEPOSITS(3,3) | DEPOSITS(3,4) |
| | | | |

At this point COL gets incremented to 5, and the inner loop tests false (see Figure 9.1). Then, ROW is incremented to 2 and again COL varies from 1 to 4. This results in the following sequence.

Read Operations for Second Row

| ROW | COL | |
|---|---|---|
| 2 | 1 | READ DEPOSITS(2,1) |
| 2 | 2 | READ DEPOSITS(2,2) |
| 2 | 3 | READ DEPOSITS(2,3) |
| 2 | 4 | READ DEPOSITS(2,4) |

Now the array appears as follows in memory.

───── After completion of inner FOR/NEXT loop with ROW = 2

| DEPOSITS(1,1) | DEPOSITS(1,2) | DEPOSITS(1,3) | DEPOSITS(1,4) |
|---|---|---|---|
| 1000 | 800 | 500 | 1200 |
| DEPOSITS(2,1) | DEPOSITS(2,2) | DEPOSITS(2,3) | DEPOSITS(2,4) |
| 500 | 2000 | 2000 | 500 |
| DEPOSITS(3,1) | DEPOSITS(3,2) | DEPOSITS(3,3) | DEPOSITS(3,4) |
| | | | |

Finally, ROW is set equal to 3, and COL varies from 1 to 4. This results in the sequence:

Read Operations for Third Row

| ROW | COL | |
|---|---|---|
| 3 | 1 | READ DEPOSITS(3,1) |
| 3 | 2 | READ DEPOSITS(3,2) |
| 3 | 3 | READ DEPOSITS(3,3) |
| 3 | 4 | READ DEPOSITS(3,4) |

At this point, read-in of the array is complete, yielding the following configuration in memory.

After completion of inner FOR/NEXT loop with ROW = 3

| DEPOSITS(1,1) | DEPOSITS(1,2) | DEPOSITS(1,3) | DEPOSITS(1,4) |
| 1000 | 800 | 500 | 1200 |
| DEPOSITS(2,1) | DEPOSITS(2,2) | DEPOSITS(2,3) | DEPOSITS(2,4) |
| 500 | 2000 | 2000 | 500 |
| DEPOSITS(3,1) | DEPOSITS(3,2) | DEPOSITS(3,3) | DEPOSITS(3,4) |
| 1500 | 300 | 700 | 1500 |

Note that the READ statement is executed exactly 12 times. *Since there is only one variable in the list of the READ statement, this means that 12 data items are required,* as given in lines 901–903 within the program on page 318.

Nested loops are likewise used to print two-dimensional arrays. For example, the statements

```
220     FOR ROW = 1 TO BANKS
230       FOR COL = 1 TO QUARTERS
240         PRINT DEPOSITS(ROW,COL)
250       NEXT COL
260     NEXT ROW
```

print array DEPOSITS as follows:

```
1000
800
500
1200
500
2000
2000
500
1500
300
700
1500
```

To print the two-dimensional array in the desirable table format requires a trailing comma or semicolon and a blank print line. For example,

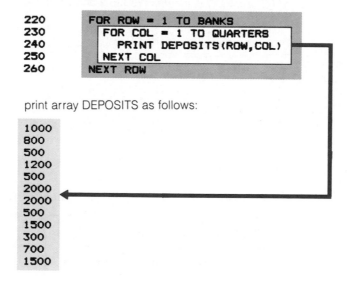

```
220     FOR ROW = 1 TO BANKS
230       FOR COL = 1 TO QUARTERS
240         PRINT DEPOSITS(ROW,COL);
250       NEXT COL
255     PRINT
260     NEXT ROW
```

Trailing semicolon holds the row

Spaces down to next row (by filling the remainder of the current row with blanks)

Note how the output is consistent with the row by column table format

results in

```
1000    800    500   1200
500    2000   2000    500
1500    300    700   1500
```

**NOTE**    We cannot overemphasize the need for you to concentrate on the manner in which the subscripts of two-dimensional arrays in **READ, INPUT,** or **PRINT** statements change values. Again, *the inner loop must be exhausted (the control variable must exceed its limit) for each iteration (loop) of the outer loop. Once the inner loop is exhausted, then the control variable of the outer loop is incremented and the control variable of the inner loop is reset to its initial value.*

## Follow-Up Exercises

1. How would the output appear if the PRINT statement in line 255 on page 322 were omitted?

2. How would the output appear if the loop ROW were the inner loop and loop COL were the outer loop (that is, interchange statements 220 and 230 and 250 and 260 on page 322)?

3. Suppose the following arrangement of DATA statements is used:

   901 DATA 1000
   902 DATA 800
   903 DATA 500
   904 DATA 1200
   905 DATA 500

   .
   .
   .

   912 DATA 1500

   How does memory appear after execution of lines 160 to 200 on page 318?

4. Suppose the following program segment is executed using the DATA statements in Example 9.1.

   ```
   160 FOR COL = 1 TO QUARTERS
   170    FOR ROW = 1 TO BANKS
   180       READ DEPOSITS(ROW,COL)
   190    NEXT ROW
   200 NEXT COL
   ```

   How would DEPOSITS appear in memory? Does DEPOSITS get filled in row by row or column by column? How should we place the data on the DATA statements so we store the values in DEPOSITS exactly as they appear on page 322?

*5. The array L is to be stored in memory as follows:

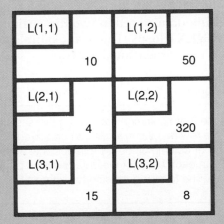

   Prepare program segments that could be used to input these six values into the array L in one of two ways:
   a. Row-by-row input (that is, in the sequence 10, 50, 4, 320, 15, 8).
   b. Column-by-column input (that is, in the sequence 10, 4, 15, 50, 320, 8).

*6. Indicate how the output of array L in Exercise 5 would appear for each segment below.

**a.** 100 FOR K = 1 TO 3
    110   FOR J = 1 TO 2
    120     PRINT L(K,J)
    130   NEXT J
    140 NEXT K

**b.** 100 FOR K = 1 TO 3
    110   FOR J = 1 TO 2
    120     PRINT L(K,J);
    130   NEXT J
    140 NEXT K

**c.** 100 FOR K = 1 TO 3
    110   FOR J = 1 TO 2
    120     PRINT L(K,J);
    130   NEXT J
    135   PRINT
    140 NEXT K

**\*7.** Modify Example 9.1 to check that the number of banks and number of quarters do not exceed the array boundaries. If they do print an error message and stop processing.

**\*\*8.** Given memory as on page 322:

**a.** Write code to print the values stored in DEPOSITS so the output appears as follows:

### DEPOSITS AT BANK

|  | 1 | 2 | 3 |
|---|---|---|---|
| Quarter 1 | 1000 | 500 | 1500 |
| Quarter 2 | 800 | 2000 | 300 |
| Quarter 3 | 500 | 2000 | 700 |
| Quarter 4 | 1200 | 500 | 1500 |

**b.** Implement this program on your system.

## 9.5 MANIPULATING ARRAYS

Processing data stored in two-dimensional arrays normally involves nesting of FOR/NEXT loops. The next example illustrates some common manipulations of two-dimensional arrays.

**E X A M P L E   9 . 2**   Row Totals

One of the more common processing tasks is finding totals of each row or column in an array. The row or column totals can be stored either in one-dimensional arrays or in an extra row or column of the two-dimensional array. For example, to find the annual bank deposits in each bank for the data given on page 318, we need to sum the entries in each row. The following revision to Example 9.1 determines row sums.

```
100 REM------------------------------------------------------------
110 REM        Bank Deposits: Row Totals
120 REM
130     DIM DEPOSITS(3,4), SUM(3)          ── Declaration
140 REM                                        of 1-D array SUM
150     READ BANKS,QUARTERS
160     FOR ROW = 1 TO BANKS
170       FOR COL = 1 TO QUARTERS
180         READ DEPOSITS(ROW,COL)
190       NEXT COL
200     NEXT ROW
210 REM
```

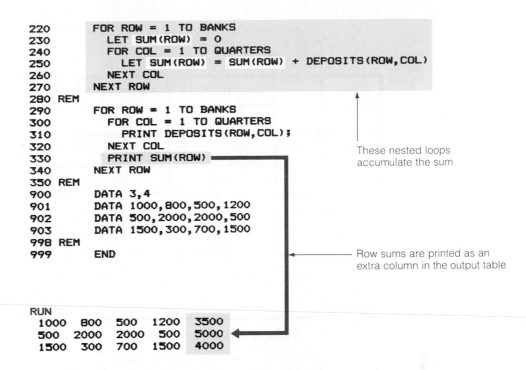

```
220        FOR ROW = 1 TO BANKS
230          LET SUM(ROW) = 0
240          FOR COL = 1 TO QUARTERS
250            LET SUM(ROW) = SUM(ROW) + DEPOSITS(ROW,COL)
260          NEXT COL
270        NEXT ROW
280 REM
290        FOR ROW = 1 TO BANKS
300          FOR COL = 1 TO QUARTERS
310            PRINT DEPOSITS(ROW,COL);
320          NEXT COL
330          PRINT SUM(ROW)
340        NEXT ROW
350 REM
900        DATA 3,4
901        DATA 1000,800,500,1200
902        DATA 500,2000,2000,500
903        DATA 1500,300,700,1500
998 REM
999        END
```

These nested loops accumulate the sum

Row sums are printed as an extra column in the output table

```
RUN
 1000    800    500   1200   3500
  500   2000   2000    500   5000
 1500    300    700   1500   4000
```

When ROW = 1, SUM(1) is initialized to zero in line 230; the inner or column loop then sums the values in the first row given by DEPOSITS(1,1), DEPOSITS(1,2), DEPOSITS(1,3), and DEPOSITS(1,4) and stores this sum in the first element of the array SUM.

| SUM(1) | DEPOSITS(1,1) | DEPOSITS(1,2) | DEPOSITS(1,3) | DEPOSITS(1,4) |
|---|---|---|---|---|
| 3500 | 1000 | 800 | 500 | 1200 |
| SUM(2) | DEPOSITS(2,1) | DEPOSITS(2,2) | DEPOSITS(2,3) | DEPOSITS(2,4) |
| | 500 | 2000 | 2000 | 500 |
| SUM(3) | DEPOSITS(3,1) | DEPOSITS(3,2) | DEPOSITS(3,3) | DEPOSITS(3,4) |
| | 1500 | 300 | 700 | 1500 |

When the outer loop is incremented (ROW = 2), SUM(2) is initialized to zero, and the values in row 2 are accumulated and stored in the second element of array SUM.

| SUM(1) | DEPOSITS(1,1) | DEPOSITS(1,2) | DEPOSITS(1,3) | DEPOSITS(1,4) |
|---|---|---|---|---|
| 3500 | 1000 | 800 | 500 | 1200 |
| SUM(2) | DEPOSITS(2,1) | DEPOSITS(2,2) | DEPOSITS(2,3) | DEPOSITS(2,4) |
| 5000 | 500 | 2000 | 2000 | 500 |
| SUM(3) | DEPOSITS(3,1) | DEPOSITS(3,2) | DEPOSITS(3,3) | DEPOSITS(3,4) |
| | 1500 | 300 | 700 | 1500 |

Finally, the outer loop iterates for the last time (ROW = 3), and the values of the third row are added to the third element in the array SUM.

| SUM(1) | | DEPOSITS(1,1) | DEPOSITS(1,2) | DEPOSITS(1,3) | DEPOSITS(1,4) |
|---|---|---|---|---|---|
| 3500 | | 1000 | 800 | 500 | 1200 |
| SUM(2) | | DEPOSITS(2,1) | DEPOSITS(2,2) | DEPOSITS(2,3) | DEPOSITS(2,4) |
| 5000 | | 500 | 2000 | 2000 | 500 |
| SUM(3) | | DEPOSITS(3,1) | DEPOSITS(3,2) | DEPOSITS(3,3) | DEPOSITS(3,4) |
| 4000 | | 1500 | 300 | 700 | 1500 |

## Follow-Up Exercises

**9.** Add program segments to Example 9.2 that accumulate and print the bank's total deposits for each quarter. Store these results in a one-dimensional array called TOTAL.

**\*\*10.** Consider the following output:

### DEPOSITS AT BANK

| | Quarter | | | | |
|---|---|---|---|---|---|
| | 1 | 2 | 3 | 4 | Bank Totals |
| Bank 1 | 1000 | 800 | 500 | 1200 | 3500 |
| Bank 2 | 500 | 2000 | 2000 | 500 | 5000 |
| Bank 3 | 1500 | 300 | 700 | 1500 | 4000 |
| Totals for Quarter | 3000 | 3100 | 3200 | 3200 | |

   **a.** Revise the program in Example 9.2 accordingly.
   **b.** Implement this program on your system.

**\*11.** Assume that DEPOSITS has been dimensioned to four rows and five columns. Instead of using SUM as in the example and TOTAL as in Exercise 9, use the fourth row of DEPOSITS to store column totals and the fifth column to store row totals.

   **a.** Write program segments that accomplish this. Don't forget to initialize your summers to zero.
   **b.** Implement this program on your system.

**\*12.** Consider the following variation to Example 9.2.

   **a.** Write a program segment that calculates the percentage of each quarter's deposit to the annual number of deposits for each branch. Store these percentages in the two-dimensional array PERCENT. After processing, PERCENT should have the stored values shown. Can you fill in the third row? Note that, except for possible rounding error, rows of PERCENT sum to 100.

| PERCENT(1,1) | PERCENT(1,2) | PERCENT(1,3) | PERCENT(1,4) |
|---|---|---|---|
| 28.57143 | 22.85714 | 14.28571 | 34.28571 |
| PERCENT(2,1) | PERCENT(2,2) | PERCENT(2,3) | PERCENT(2,4) |
| 10.00000 | 40.00000 | 40.00000 | 10.00000 |
| PERCENT(3,1) | PERCENT(3,2) | PERCENT(3,3) | PERCENT(3,4) |
| | | | |

**b.** Implement this program on your system.

**13.** Suppose an array has been dimensioned as follows:

DIM WEIGHT(100,50)

Write a program segment that initializes each element in WEIGHT to 100.

**14.** Write a program segment that initializes the (4 × 4) array X in the following manner.

```
1  0  0  0
0  1  0  0
0  0  1  0
0  0  0  1
```

**15.** Suppose we want the following memory for arrays A and B.

|   | A 1 | A 2 | A 3 |   | B 1 | B 2 | B 3 |
|---|---|---|---|---|---|---|---|
| 1 | 5 | 10 | 15 | 1 | 75 | 76 | 77 |
| 2 | 20 | 25 | 30 | 2 | 78 | 79 | 80 |

Specify input code if the data are to be input as follows.
**a.** Enter number of rows . . . . . . ? 2
Enter number of columns . . . ? 3

Now enter each row in array A:

Row 1, Column 1 ? 5
Row 1, Column 2 ? 10
.
.
.
Row 2, Column 3 ? 30

Now enter each row in array B:

Row 1, Column 1? 75
.
.
.
Row 2, Column 3 ? 80

**b.**   Enter number of rows . . . . . . ? 2
Enter number of columns . . . ? 3

Now enter corresponding elements in arrays A and B:

Row 1, Column 1 ? 5,75
Row 1, Column 2 ? 10,76
.
.
.
Row 2, Column 3 ? 30,80

**\*c.**   Same as part **b** except use column-by-column instead of row-by-row input.

**\*\* 16.   Input Error Routine.**   Consider the following input procedure for array A in the preceding exercise.

Enter number of rows . . . . . . ? 2
Enter number of columns . . . ? 4

Rows    = 2
Columns = 4
Are these correct (y/n)? n

Enter number of rows . . . . . . ? 2
Enter number of columns . . . ? 3

Rows    = 2
Columns = 3
Are these correct (y/n)? y

Now enter each row in array:

| Row | Col | |
|-----|-----|------|
| 1 | 1 | ? 5 |
| 1 | 2 | ? 19 |
| 1 | 3 | ? 15 |
| 2 | 1 | ? 29 |
| 2 | 2 | ? 25 |
| 2 | 3 | ? 30 |

Array: 5      19      15
       29     25      30
Are these correct (y/n)? n

For each line of input enter row,col,value. End with 0,0,0.

?   1,2,10
?   2,1,29
?   0,0,0

Array: 5      10      15
       29     25      30
Are these correct (y/n)? n

**DID YOU HAVE A TOUGH NIGHT!**

For each line of input enter row,col,value. End with 0,0,0.

   ?  2,1,20
   ?  0,0,0

Array: 5     10    15
       20    25    30
Are these correct (y/n)? y

**OK . . . NOW WE'RE COOKING!**

  **a.** Develop code that reproduces this input procedure.
  **b.** Test this procedure on your system.

**\*17.** Suppose a 10 × 20 array X already exists in memory. Write code to
  **a.** Interchange the values of corresponding array elements in column 3 and column 1.
  **b.** Print out the smallest value in X and its location (row and column).

**\*18.** Given a 5 × 5 array A, write code to
  **a.** Print the lower triangle and main diagonal as shown below.

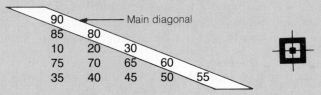

  **b.** Fill in the upper triangle symmetrically; that is, assuming only the lower triangle and main diagonal have been input as above, fill in the upper triangle to give the following symmetric matrix.

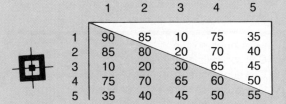

|   | 1 | 2 | 3 | 4 | 5 |
|---|----|----|----|----|----|
| 1 | 90 | 85 | 10 | 75 | 35 |
| 2 | 85 | 80 | 20 | 70 | 40 |
| 3 | 10 | 20 | 30 | 65 | 45 |
| 4 | 75 | 70 | 65 | 60 | 50 |
| 5 | 35 | 40 | 45 | 50 | 55 |

*Note:* In a symmetric matrix, the first row is the same as the first column; the second row is identical to the second column; and so on.

# 9.6 SELECTED APPLICATIONS

This section illustrates two common applications of two-dimensional arrays.

## Financial Report

**Analysis.**    The sales (revenue) and cost data for each region and model line of the Effete Automotive Corporation have been collected. Data for the most recent quarter are as follows.

| | Sales ($ Millions) | | Costs ($ Millions) | |
|---|---|---|---|---|
| | *Model 1* | *Model 2* | *Model 1* | *Model 2* |
| Region 1 | 100 | 150 | 50 | 100 |
| Region 2 | 60 | 40 | 40 | 10 |
| Region 3 | 30 | 70 | 25 | 75 |

The controller needs a report that presents sales, costs, and profits, with totals for each region and model line. We have been hired as consultants (@ $1000 per day) to develop a noninteractive program with the following data requirements:

*Output*
Sales revenue with totals by region and model
Costs with totals by region and model
Profits with totals by region and model

*Read*
Number of regions and number of models
Sales by region and model (a regions × models array)
Costs by region and model (a regions × models array)

*Parameters*
Row and column array upper boundaries

**Design.** A control module calls five processing modules. These include initialization, array entry, profit calculation, accumulation of totals, and printing of summary reports. The pseudocode for these modules follows:

```
Start control module
   Call subroutine Initialization
   Call subroutine Array Entry
   Call subroutine Profit Calculation
   Call subroutine Totals
   Call subroutine Reports
   Stop
End control module
```

```
Start subroutine Initialization
   Initialize array upper boundaries
   Read no. of regions, no. of models
   If no. of regions or no. of models > upper boundary then
      Print error message
      Stop
   End if
   Return
End subroutine
```

```
Start subroutine Array Entry
   Read sales, costs (into 2-D arrays)
   Return
End subroutine
```

Start subroutine Profit Calculation
   Let profit = sales − costs (into 2-D array)
   Return
End subroutine

Start subroutine Totals
   Calculate total sales, costs, and profits for each region
   Calculate total sales, costs, and profits for each model
   Return
End subroutine

Start subroutine Reports
   Print sales report
   Print cost report
   Print profit report
   Return
End subroutine

**Code.**    The following code was written in Microsoft BASIC for the IBM PC.

```
1000 REM * * * * * * * * * * * * * * * * * * * * * * * * * * * * * *
1020 REM *                                                         *
1040 REM *                    FINANCIAL REPORT                     *
1060 REM *                                                         *
1080 REM *    Control module ....... Calls each subroutine         *
1100 REM *                                                         *
1120 REM *    Sub. initialization .. Sets array limits             *
1140 REM *                           Reads number of regions & models *
1160 REM *                           Verifies region & models within *
1180 REM *                              array limits               *
1200 REM *                                                         *
1220 REM *    Sub. array entry ..... Reads sales & costs into arrays *
1240 REM *                                                         *
1260 REM *    Sub. profit calc ..... Calculates profit for each    *
1280 REM *                              region & model             *
1300 REM *                                                         *
1320 REM *    Sub. totals .......... Calculates total sales, costs *
1340 REM *                              & profits by region & model *
1360 REM *                                                         *
1380 REM *    Sub. reports ......... Prints reports for sales,     *
1400 REM *                              costs & profits            *
1420 REM *                                                         *
1440 REM * * * * * * * * * * * * * * * * * * * * * * * * * * * * * *
1460 '
2000 ' ================= Control Module =================
2020 '
2040     DIM SALES(10,10),COSTS(10,10),PROFITS(10,10)
2060 '
2080     GOSUB 3000               'Call subroutine initialization
2100     GOSUB 4000               'Call subroutine array entry
2120     GOSUB 5000               'Call subroutine profit calculation
2140     GOSUB 6000               'Call subroutine totals
2160     GOSUB 7000               'Call subroutine reports
2180 '
2200     STOP
2220 '
3000 ' ================= Subroutine Initialization =================
3020 '
3040     LET ROW.LIMIT    = 9
3060     LET COLUMN.LIMIT = 9
3080 '
3100     READ REGIONS,MODELS
3120 '
3140     IF REGIONS > ROW.LIMIT OR MODELS > COLUMN.LIMIT THEN
         PRINT "Upper array boundary exceeded. Check Line 9000." :
         PRINT "Limits:   Regions =";ROW.LIMIT; "Models ="COLUMN.LIMIT :
         STOP
3160 '
3180     RETURN
```

```
3200 '
4000 ' ================== Subroutine Array Entry =====================
4020 '
4040    FOR I = 1 TO REGIONS
4060      FOR J = 1 TO MODELS
4080        READ SALES(I,J)
4100      NEXT J
4120    NEXT I
4140 '
4160    FOR I = 1 TO REGIONS
4180      FOR J = 1 TO MODELS
4200        READ COSTS(I,J)
4220      NEXT J
4240    NEXT I
4260 '
4280    RETURN
4300 '
5000 ' ================== Subroutine Profit Calculation =================
5020 '
5040    FOR I = 1 TO REGIONS
5060      FOR J = 1 TO MODELS
5080        LET PROFITS(I,J) = SALES(I,J) - COSTS(I,J)
5100      NEXT J
5120    NEXT I
5140 '
5160    RETURN
5180 '
6000 ' ================== Subroutine Totals =========================
6020 '
6040    FOR I = 1 TO REGIONS                ' Calculate totals for each
6060      LET SALES(I,MODELS+1)    = 0      ' region and store as last
6080      LET COSTS(I,MODELS+1)    = 0      ' column in array
6100      LET PROFITS(I,MODELS+1) = 0
6120      FOR J = 1 TO MODELS
6140        LET SALES(I,MODELS+1)   = SALES(I,MODELS+1)   + SALES(I,J)
6160        LET COSTS(I,MODELS+1)   = COSTS(I,MODELS+1)   + COSTS(I,J)
6180        LET PROFITS(I,MODELS+1) = PROFITS(I,MODELS+1) + PROFITS(I,J)
6200      NEXT J
6220    NEXT I
6240 '
6260    FOR J = 1 TO MODELS                 ' Calculate totals for each
6280      LET SALES(REGIONS+1,J)    = 0     ' model and store as last
6300      LET COSTS(REGIONS+1,J)    = 0     ' row in array
6320      LET PROFITS(REGIONS+1,J) = 0
6340      FOR I = 1 TO REGIONS
6360        LET SALES(REGIONS+1,J)   = SALES(REGIONS+1,J)   + SALES(I,J)
6380        LET COSTS(REGIONS+1,J)   = COSTS(REGIONS+1,J)   + COSTS(I,J)
6400        LET PROFITS(REGIONS+1,J) = PROFITS(REGIONS+1,J) + PROFITS(I,J)
6420      NEXT I
6440    NEXT J
6460 '
6480    RETURN
6500 '
7000 ' ================== Subroutine Reports =======================
7020 '
7040    PRINT "SALES"
7060    PRINT,
7080    FOR J = 1 TO MODELS
7100      PRINT J,
7120    NEXT J
7140    PRINT "Region totals"
7160 '
7180    PRINT "----------------------------------------------------------"
7200 '
7220    FOR I = 1 TO REGIONS
7240      PRINT I,
7260      FOR J = 1 TO MODELS+1
7280        PRINT SALES(I,J),
7300      NEXT J
7320      PRINT
7340    NEXT I
7360 '
7380    PRINT "----------------------------------------------------------"
7400 '
7420    PRINT "Model totals",
7440    FOR J = 1 TO MODELS
7460      PRINT SALES(REGIONS+1,J),     ◄────── Last-row output
7480    NEXT J
```

```
7500 '
7520     PRINT
7540     PRINT
7560 '
7580     PRINT "COSTS"
7600     PRINT ,
7620     FOR J = 1 TO MODELS
7640       PRINT J,
7660     NEXT J
7680     PRINT "Region totals"
7700 '
7720     PRINT "----------------------------------------------------------"
7740 '
7760     FOR I = 1 TO REGIONS
7780       PRINT I,
7800       FOR J = 1 TO MODELS+1
7820         PRINT COSTS(I,J),
7840       NEXT J
7860       PRINT
7880     NEXT I
7900 '
7920     PRINT "----------------------------------------------------------"
7940 '
7960     PRINT "Model totals",
7980     FOR J = 1 TO MODELS
8000       PRINT COSTS(REGIONS+1,J),          ◄──────── Last-row output
8020     NEXT J
8040 '
8060     PRINT
8080     PRINT
8100 '
8120     PRINT "PROFITS"
8140     PRINT ,
8160     FOR J = 1 TO MODELS
8180       PRINT J,
8200     NEXT J
8220     PRINT "Region totals"
8240 '
8260     PRINT "----------------------------------------------------------"
8280 '
8300     FOR I = 1 TO REGIONS
8320       PRINT I,
8340       FOR J = 1 TO MODELS+1
8360         PRINT PROFITS(I,J),
8380       NEXT J
8400       PRINT
8420     NEXT I
8440 '
8460     PRINT "----------------------------------------------------------"
8480 '
8500     PRINT "Model totals",
8520     FOR J = 1 TO MODELS
8540       PRINT PROFITS(REGIONS+1,J),       ◄──────── Last-row output
8560     NEXT J
8580 '
8600     PRINT
8620     PRINT
8640 '
8660     RETURN
8997 '
8998 ' ===================== Data Section =============================
8999                                          ' Regions,Models
9000     DATA 3,2
9005                                          ' Sales array
9011     DATA 100,150
9012     DATA 60,40
9013     DATA 30,70
9500                                          ' Costs array
9501     DATA 50,100
9502     DATA 40,10
9503     DATA 25,75
9996 '
9997 ' ===============================================================
9998 '
9999     END
```

**Test.**   The following test run is a partial debugging of the program (see Exercise 22).

```
SALES
                    1              2              Region totals
-----------------------------------------------------------------------
    1              100            150            250
    2              60             40             100
    3              30             70             100
-----------------------------------------------------------------------
Model totals       190            260

COSTS
                    1              2              Region totals
-----------------------------------------------------------------------
    1              50             100            150
    2              40             10             50
    3              25             75             100
-----------------------------------------------------------------------
Model totals       115            185

PROFITS
                    1              2              Region totals
-----------------------------------------------------------------------
    1              50             50             100
    2              20             30             50
    3              5              -5             0
-----------------------------------------------------------------------
Model totals       75             75
```

**Discussion.**   Take some time right now to relate the pseudocode and program on a module by module basis. As you study subroutine Reports, confirm the output. The program itself is fairly descriptive, but pay special attention to the shaded segments.

The program uses procedures that we have already seen in examples and follow-up exercises, so we shall restrict our discussion to the following points.

The sums for each region and model line are stored within each of the two-dimensional arrays (SALES, COSTS, and PROFITS). For example, the statement

6140    LET SALES(I,MODELS + 1) = SALES(I,MODELS + 1) + SALES(I,J)

stores row totals (region totals) in the column immediately after the last model-line. The statement

6360    LET SALES (REGIONS + 1,J) = SALES(REGIONS + 1,J) + SALES(I,J)

stores column totals (model-line totals) in the row immediately following the last row that stores sales.

We can visualize the structure of the array SALES as follows.

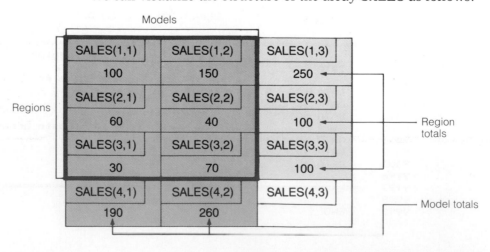

A similar structure applies to arrays COSTS and PROFITS.

---

### Follow-Up Exercises

**19.** Roleplay the computer by processing the data. In particular, notice how the program stores row and column sums. Confirm the output, paying close attention to spacing and the methods used to output headings and labels.

**20.** Why are the variables ROW.LIMIT and COLUMN.LIMIT not set to the upper boundaries of the arrays?

**21.** Draw a hierarchy chart for this program.

**22.** Indicate output if line 9000 were to read as follows:

    9000    DATA 3,20

**\*\*23.** The program does not accumulate overall (grand) totals for sales, costs, and profits.
  **a.** Modify the program so these totals are accumulated and printed. Use the bottom right (4th row, 3rd column) element within each array to store each grand total.
  **b.** Implement this program on your system.

**\*\*24.** Suppose one additional row and one additional column are to be used within each array. The new row contains each model's contribution to overall sales, costs, and profits (each column total as a percentage of the overall total). The new column contains each region's contribution to overall sales, costs, and profits (each row total as a percentage of the overall total).
  **a.** Modify the program accordingly.
  **b.** Implement this program on your system.

---

## Income Tax Form

**Analysis.**    Paying taxes is one of life's certainties (for most of us), and filing tax returns is one of our annual rituals (and headaches). In its efforts to increase compliance and reduce mistakes, the federal government has developed the 1040EZ income tax return for single taxpayers whose tax liabilities are minimal. Most college students fit this model. Figure 9.2 is a sample 1040EZ tax form.

A taxpayer's income can consist of wages and interest; however, if interest exceeds $400 the 1040EZ form can't be used. Adjusted gross income is the sum of wages and interest. Taxable income is determined as adjusted gross income less charitable contributions (not to exceed $25), less the $1000 personal exemption. The income tax is determined by taking the taxpayer's taxable income and looking up the correct tax bracket according to the tax rate schedule in Figure 9.3. Once the tax bracket is determined, the table entries are used to compute the income tax liability.

To illustrate the computations, consider a college student who has earned $6500 in wages and $300 in interest income. Adjusted gross income is $6800 ($6500 + $300), and taxable income is $5800 ($6800 − $1000). From Schedule X in Figure 9.3 the tax is determined to be

$$\$251 + 0.15 \times (\$5800 - \$4400) = \$461$$

If the taxpayer has paid $500 in withholding taxes during the year, then the taxpayer will receive a welcome refund of $39.

Department of the Treasury · Internal Revenue Service

**Form 1040EZ Income Tax Return for**

**1983    Single filers with no dependents** (X)

OMB No. 1545-0675

**Name & address**

If you don't have a label, please print:

Please write your numbers like this.

| 1 | 2 | 3 | 4 | 5 | 6 | 7 | 8 | 9 | 0 |

► Write your name above (first, initial, last)

Present home address (number and street)

City, town, or post office, state, and ZIP code

Social security number

**Presidential Election Campaign Fund**
Check box if you want $1 of your tax to go to this fund. ►

**Dollars    Cents**

**Figure your tax**

1   Wages, salaries, and tips. Attach your W-2 form(s).    1

2   Interest income of $400 or less. If more than $400, you cannot use Form 1040EZ.    2

Attach Copy B of Form(s) W-2 here

3   Add line 1 and line 2. This is your **adjusted gross income.**    3

4   Allowable part of your charitable contributions. Complete the worksheet on page 19. Do not write more than $25.    4

5   Subtract line 4 from line 3.    5

6   Amount of your personal exemption.    6    1,000.00

7   Subtract line 6 from line 5. This is your **taxable income.**    7

8   Enter your Federal income tax withheld. This should be shown in Box 9 of your W-2 form(s).    8

9   Use the tax table on pages 29-34 to find the **tax** on your taxable income on line 7. Write the amount of tax.    9

**Refund or amount you owe**

10   If line 8 is larger than line 9, subtract line 9 from line 8. Enter the **amount of your refund.**    10

11   If line 9 is larger than line 8, subtract line 8 from line 9. Enter the **amount you owe.** Attach check or money order for the full amount, payable to "Internal Revenue Service."    11

Attach tax payment here

**Sign your return**

I have read this return. Under penalties of perjury, I declare that to the best of my knowledge and belief, the return is true, correct, and complete.

Your signature                                        Date

X

For IRS Use Only—Please do not write in boxes below.

For Privacy Act and Paperwork Reduction Act Notice, see page 38.

**Figure 9.2**   Form 1040EZ income tax return

Let's develop an interactive program that acts as a substitute for the 1040EZ Income Tax Form.[5] The data requirements are as follows:

*Output*
Adjusted gross income
Taxable income
Tax liability
Tax owed/refund

[5]Many programs of this type, some elaborate (and expensive), are available for microcomputers.

**Figure 9.3**   Schedule X

**Schedule X**
**Single Taxpayers**
Use this Schedule if you checked **Filing Status Box 1** on
Form 1040—

| If the amount on Form 1040, line 37 is: | | Enter on Form 1040, line 38 | | of the amount over— |
|---|---|---|---|---|
| Over— | But not over— | | | |
| COL. 1 | COL.2 | COL. 3 | COL. 4 | COL. 5 |
| $0 | $2,300 | —0— | | |
| 2,300 | 3,400 | . . . . . . 11% | | $2,300 |
| 3,400 | 4,400 | $121 + | 13% | 3,400 |
| 4,400 | 8,500 | 251 + | 15% | 4,400 |
| 8,500 | 10,800 | 886 + | 17% | 8,500 |
| 10,800 | 12,900 | 1,257 + | 19% | 10,800 |
| 12,900 | 15,000 | 1,656 + | 21% | 12,900 |
| 15,000 | 18,200 | 2,097 + | 24% | 15,000 |
| 18,200 | 23,500 | 2,865 + | 28% | 18,200 |
| 23,500 | 28,800 | 4,349 + | 32% | 23,500 |
| 28,800 | 34,100 | 6,045 + | 36% | 28,800 |
| 34,100 | 41,500 | 7,953 + | 40% | 34,100 |
| 41,500 | 55,300 | 10,913 + | 45% | 41,500 |
| 55,300 | . . . . . . | 17,123 + | 50% | 55,300 |

*Input*
Full name
Home address
City-State-Zip
Social Security Number
Combined wages, salaries, and tips
Interest income
Charitable contributions
Federal income tax withheld

*Read*
Rows and columns in Tax Schedule X
Tax Schedule X (as two-dimensional array)

*Parameters*
Exemption ($1000)
Upper array boundaries (14 rows and 3 columns)
Maximum interest income ($400)
Maximum charitable contributions ($25)

**Design.**    The program follows the steps of the 1040EZ tax form in Figure 9.2. A control module calls four processing modules. These include initialization, taxpayer data, tax liability, and tax owed/refund. The pseudocode for each module describes the necessary tasks, as illustrated next.

```
Start control module
    Call subroutine Initialization
    Call subroutine Taxpayer Data
    Call subroutine Tax Liability
    Call subroutine Tax Owed/Refund
    Stop
End control module
```

Start subroutine Initialization
   Initialize other data
   Read array limits for tax schedule
   Verify array limits with upper array bounds
   Read tax schedule X
   Return
End subroutine

Start subroutine Taxpayer Data
   Input name, address, city-state-zip, ssn
   Input wages                            (Line 1 in 1040EZ)
   Input interest                        (Line 2 in 1040EZ)

   If interest > max then
     Print message
     Stop
   End if

   Compute and print adjusted gross income  (Line 3 in 1040EZ)
   Input charitable contributions       (Line 4 in 1040EZ)

   If contributions > max then
     Let contributions = max
     Print message
   End if

   Print Line 3 minus Line 4         (Line 5 in 1040EZ)
   Print personal exemption          (Line 6 in 1040EZ)
   Determine taxable income

   If taxable income <= 0 then
     Print message
   End if

   Print taxable income             (Line 7 in 1040EZ)
   Input income tax withheld        (Line 8 in 1040EZ)
   Return
End subroutine

Start subroutine Tax Liability
   Find proper tax bracket in Schedule X (Table lookup logic)
   Compute tax liability
   Print tax liability              (Line 9 in 1040EZ)
   Return
End subroutine

```
Start subroutine Tax Owed/Refund

  If tax liability < = tax withheld then
    Calculate refund
    Print refund                          (Line 10 in 1040EZ)
  End if

  If tax liability > tax withheld then
    Calculate tax owed
    Print amount owed                     (Line 11 in 1040EZ)
  End if


  Return
End subroutine
```

**Code.**   The following code was written in Microsoft BASIC for the IBM PC.

```
100 REM * * * * * * * * * * * * * * * * * * * * * * * * * * * * * * * * * *
105 REM *                    INCOME TAX PROGRAM                           *
110 REM *                                                                 *
115 REM *       Control Module ................... Calls each subroutine  *
120 REM *                                                                 *
125 REM *       Sub. Initialization .............. Initializes exemptions *
130 REM *                                          Sets array boundaries  *
135 REM *                                          Reads table limits     *
140 REM *                                          Verifies array bounds  *
145 REM *                                          Reads Tax Schedule X   *
150 REM *                                                                 *
155 REM *       Sub. Taxpayer Data ............... Inputs/prints through  *
160 REM *                                          line 8 in Form 1040EZ  *
165 REM *                                                                 *
170 REM *       Sub. Tax Liability ............... Determines/prints tax  *
175 REM *                                                                 *
180 REM *       Sub. Tax Owed/Refund ............. Determines and prints  *
185 REM *                                          amount owed or refunded *
190 REM * * * * * * * * * * * * * * * * * * * * * * * * * * * * * * * * * *
195 '
200 ' =============== Main Program ================================
205 '
210     DIM TAXTABLE (14,3)
215 '
220     GOSUB 300               'Call subroutine initalization
225     GOSUB 400               'Call subroutine taxpayer data
230     GOSUB 700               'Call subroutine tax liability
235     GOSUB 800               'Call subroutine tax owed/refund
240 '
245     STOP
250 '
300 ' =============== Subroutine Initialization ===================
305 '
310     LET EXEMPTION          = 1000
315     LET ROW.LIMIT          = 14
320     LET COLUMN.LIMIT       = 3
325     LET MAX.INTEREST       = 400
330     LET MAX.CONTRIBUTIONS  = 25
335 '
340     READ M,N
345     IF M > ROW.LIMIT OR N > COLUMN.LIMIT THEN
          PRINT TAB(35);"Tax schedule is too large!  Check line 900." :
          PRINT TAB(40);"Max rows =";ROW.LIMIT; " Max columns =";COLUMN.LIMIT:
          STOP
350 '
355     FOR I = 1 TO M
360       FOR J = 1 TO N
365         READ TAXTABLE(I,J)
370       NEXT J
375     NEXT I
380 '
385     RETURN
390 '
```

```
400 ' ============== Subroutine Taxpayer Data ===============================
405 '
410     PRINT " _____ "
415     PRINT "¦                                   ¦"
420     PRINT "¦ Form 1040EZ tax return for        ¦"
425     PRINT "¦ single filers with no dependents  ¦"
430     PRINT "¦_____¦"
435     PRINT
437 '
440     INPUT "Full Name                 :"; FULL.NAME$
445     INPUT "Home Address              :"; HOME.ADDR$
450     INPUT "City, State, Zip          :"; CITY.STATE.ZIP$
455     INPUT "Social Security Number    :"; SSN$
460 '
470     PRINT
475 '
480     INPUT "1  Wages, Salaries & Tips     :"; WAGES            ' Line 1
485 '
490     INPUT "2  Interest income            :"; INTEREST         ' Line 2
495 '
500     IF INTEREST > MAX.INTEREST THEN
          PRINT TAB(40); "Interest above $"; MAX.INTEREST :
          PRINT TAB(40); "We can't use 1040EZ" :
          STOP
505 '
510     LET ADJ.GROSS.INCOME = WAGES + INTEREST
515 '
520     PRINT "3  Adjusted gross income        "; ADJ.GROSS.INCOME    ' Line 3
525 '
530     INPUT "4  Charitable contributions   :" ; CONTRIBUTIONS     ' Line 4
535 '
540     IF CONTRIBUTIONS > MAX.CONTRIBUTIONS THEN
          LET CONTRIBUTIONS = MAX.CONTRIBUTIONS :
          PRINT TAB(40); "Contributions adjusted to $"; MAX.CONTRIBUTIONS
545 '
550     PRINT "5  Subtract line 4 from line 3  ";
555     PRINT                ADJ.GROSS.INCOME - CONTRIBUTIONS       ' Line 5
560 '
565     PRINT "6  Personal exemption           "; EXEMPTION         ' Line 6
570 '
575     LET TAX.INCOME = ADJ.GROSS.INCOME - ( CONTRIBUTIONS + EXEMPTION )
580 '
585     IF TAX.INCOME <= 0 THEN
          PRINT TAB(40); "Taxable income is zero or less." :
          PRINT TAB(40); "Double check your financial data."
590 '
595     PRINT "7  Taxable income               "; TAX.INCOME        ' Line 7
600 '
605     INPUT "8  Federal income tax withheld:" ; WITHHELD          ' Line 8
610 '
615     RETURN
620 '
700 ' ============== Subroutine Tax Liability==============================
705 '
710     LET I = 1
715     WHILE TAX.INCOME > TAXTABLE(I,1)      ← Table look-up logic
720       LET I = I + 1
725     WEND
730 '
735     LET TAX = TAXTABLE(I,2)+ TAXTABLE(I,3)*(TAX.INCOME - TAXTABLE(I-1,1))
740 '
745     PRINT "9  Tax                          "; INT(TAX)          ' Line 9
750 '
755     RETURN
760 '
800 ' ============== Subroutine Tax Owed/Refund =============================
805 '
810     IF TAX <= WITHHELD THEN
          LET REFUND = WITHHELD - TAX :
          PRINT "10 Amount of your refund.     "; REFUND           ' Line 10
815 '
820     IF TAX > WITHHELD THEN
          LET TAX.OWED = TAX - WITHHELD :
          PRINT : PRINT "11 Amount you owe.             "; TAX.OWED ' Line 11
825 '
830     RETURN
897 '
```

```
898 '  =============== Data Section:  Tax Schedule X =============================
899 '
900      DATA 14,3
901      DATA 2300,0,0
902      DATA 3400,0,.11
903      DATA 4400,121,.13
904      DATA 8500,251,.15
905      DATA 10800,866,.17
906      DATA 12900,1257,.19
907      DATA 15000,1656,.21
908      DATA 18200,2097,.24
909      DATA 23500,2865,.28
910      DATA 28800,4349,.32
911      DATA 34100,6045,.36
912      DATA 41500,7953,.40
913      DATA 55300,10913,.45
914      DATA 1E30,17123,.5
996 '
997 '  =========================================================================
998 '
999      END
```

**Test.**   The following test run is a partial debugging of the program (see Exercise 25).

```
------------------------------------
!                                  !
! Form 1040EZ tax return for       !
! single filers with no dependents !
!                                  !
------------------------------------

Full Name                 :? Adam Smith Jr
Home Address              :? 1 Wall Street
City, State, Zip          :? New York  NY   10007
Social Security Number    :? 000-00-0001

1  Wages, Salaries & Tips    :? 6500
2  Interest income           :? 300
3  Adjusted gross income        6800
4  Charitable contributions  :? 0
5  Subtract line 4 from line 3  6800
6  Personal exemption           1000
7  Taxable income               5800
8  Federal income tax withheld:? 500
9  Tax                          461
10 Amount of your refund.       39
Break in 245
```

**Discussion.**   The program is reasonably easy to understand, especially if we relate it to its pseudocode and to Form 1040EZ in Figure 9.2. Note how the line numbers in the tax form are identified in both the pseudocode and the program for easy cross-referencing. In looking at the I/O for the test run, keep in mind that the purpose of this program is to provide a set of figures that will act as an acceptable substitute for Form 1040EZ. This purpose itself raises certain issues that we shall ask you to look at in Exercise 32.

The most difficult part of this program is the two-dimensional table look-up procedure (Lines 710–725 in the program) and the subsequent tax bracket calculation (Line 735).

First, we must clearly understand that the two-dimensional array TAX-TABLE stores the necessary columns from Schedule X in Figure 9.3. *A source of confusion is that we only need to store columns 2, 3, and 4 from Schedule X. These columns then are stored, respectively, as columns 1, 2, and 3 within array TAXTABLE.*

We use a while loop in lines 710–725 to lookup the taxpayer's tax bracket. This bracket is found when taxable income (search key) is less than or equal to the upper limit of a tax bracket (Column 1 in array TAXTABLE and column 2 in Figure 9.3).

Once the correct row entry in TAXTABLE is determined (as the value in I when loop exit is achieved), the tax computation is executed. This computation is based on the formula

$$\text{Tax} = \text{Base tax} + (\text{Marginal tax rate}) \times (\text{Taxable income} - \text{Lower limit of tax bracket})$$

| Column 2 in TAXTABLE | Column 3 in TAXTABLE | Column 1 in TAXTABLE |
|---|---|---|
| or | or | or |
| Column 1 in Figure 9.3 | Column 4 in Figure 9.3 | Column 2 in Figure 9.3 |

Line 735 in the program reproduces this logic.

To illustrate the calculation, the taxable income (TAX.INCOME) in our sample run is \$5800, so the table lookup in lines 710–725 determines that the proper tax bracket is the 4th row (I = 4 at loop exit). Thus we have

```
735 LET TAX = TAXTABLE(I,2) + TAXTABLE(I,3) *(TAX.INCOME − TAXTABLE(I − 1,1))
            = TAXTABLE(4,2) + (TAXTABLE(4,3)*(TAX.INCOME − TAXTABLE(4 − 1,1))
            =      251     +    0.15   *  (5800    −    4400)
            = 461
```

Notice that the *lower* limit of the tax bracket (Column 1 in Figure 9.3) is the *upper* limit of the *previous* tax bracket (Column 2 in Figure 9.3). That's precisely why we need not store the first column in Figure 9.3 and why we use the subscript I − 1 in line 735.

## Follow-Up Exercises

**\*25.** Roleplay computer to determine the output for the following test cases:

|     | Wages | Interest | Contributions | Tax Withheld |
|-----|-------|----------|---------------|--------------|
| a.  | 16500 | 400      | 25            | 600          |
| b.  | 16500 | 600      | 25            | 600          |
| c.  | 16500 | 400      | 75            | 600          |
| d.  | 0     | 300      | 0             | 0            |

**\*\*e.** Implement these test runs on your system.

**26.** The last row in column 1 of array TAXTABLE contains a value of 1E30. Why?

**27.** Suppose a new tax law changes maximum charitable contributions to \$50 and the personal exemption to \$1500. Make necessary program changes, and comment on the design issue that facilitates these changes.

**28.** Consider the following input:

City, State, Zip         :? New York, NY 10007

Any potential problems? How might we revise the program to avoid any potential problem?

**\*29.** Indicate output if line 900 were to read as follows:

900     DATA 15,3

**\*30.** Modify the tax program so that lines 10 and 11 are always printed. In our sample run, for instance, the following would be printed just after line 10:

11  Amount you owe.              0

**\*31.** Rework the tax program as follows:
  **a.** Use 1-D arrays for table look-up, as in Chapter 8.
  **b.** Implement this version on your system.

**\*\*32.** As the program stands, it has some 1040EZ gaps and some shortcomings for commercial distribution and implementation. For example, the control module does not have a processing loop for additional runs, a screen versus line-printer versus external-file[6] output option is missing, the Presidential election campaign fund section and the signature section are missing, and other "bells and whistles" are lacking (such as audio error alerts and use of color to, say, highlight the input lines and error messages). Try your hand at improving, redesigning, and otherwise changing the program with these and, perhaps, other issues in mind. Then offer your program to commercial software publishers, and live happily thereafter on your royalties.

## 9.7 POINTERS

Design, style, and error issues that apply to one-dimensional arrays also apply to two-dimensional arrays. So review once more the pointers discussed on pages 307–309, and mentally modify them for two-dimensional arrays.

Use the concept of visual tables for better readability of two-dimensional array data. Specifically, set up array data in DATA statements in a row by row (a table) manner, as in lines 9011–9503 on page 333 for the sales and costs arrays (tables) and lines 901–914 on page 341 for the Schedule X array (table).

The output of two-dimensional arrays should also look like tables. Typically we use a trailing semicolon or comma and extra PRINT statement, as illustrated in lines 220–260 of Example 9.1 on page 322.

Remember that the processing of two-dimensional arrays typically requires one loop nested within another loop. When using nested loops, keep in mind that the inner-loop control variable varies faster than the outer-loop control variable. We usually let the inner-loop control variable represent the column subscript and the outer loop-control variable the row subscript. This means that the array is read, input, or output in a row-by-row manner (Right?), which is conceptually consistent with the usual way we treat tables.

## ADDITIONAL EXERCISES

**33.** Define or explain each of the following:
matrix
two-dimensional array

**34.** **Revisits.** Modify an earlier problem as indicated below.
  **a.** **Table Lookup.** (Section 8.6, page **292**.) Rewrite the example by storing the Premium Schedule (Table 8.1) as a two-dimensional array. Implement the revised program on your system using the original test data in the example and in Exercise 17 of that chapter. Improve the program in any other manner you see fit.
  **b.** **Property Tax Assessment.** (Chapter 6, Exercise 33, page **220**.) Store the tax schedule as a two-dimensional array, and use a table lookup procedure to find the appropriate tax rate.
  **c.** **Mailing List.** (Chapter 6, Exercise 36, page **222**.) Store the data file within a two-dimensional string array.
  **d.** **Crime Data Summary.** (Chapter 8, Exercise 41, page **309**.) Store the arrest data as a $6 \times 3$ array and the crime descriptions as a one-dimensional string array.

**35.** **Stock-Portfolio Valuation.** Companies, universities, banks, pension funds, and other organizations routinely invest funds in the stock market. The set of stocks in which the organization invests its funds is called a *stock portfolio*. The table below illustrates

[6]External files are covered in Module E at the end of the text.

a sample stock portfolio, including the number of shares owned of each stock, the purchase price per share, and the latest price per share quoted by the stock exchange.

Stock Portfolio

| Stock | Number of Shares | Purchase Price ($/share) | Current Price ($/share) |
|---|---|---|---|
| Allegh Airls | 40,000 | $5\frac{7}{8}$ | $7\frac{1}{4}$ |
| Boeing | 5,000 | $61\frac{1}{2}$ | 56 |
| EastmKo | 10,000 | 60 | $64\frac{1}{2}$ |
| Hewlett P | 15,000 | 80 | $100\frac{1}{8}$ |
| IBM | 2,500 | $77\frac{1}{8}$ | $80\frac{3}{4}$ |
| Texaco | 8,000 | $23\frac{1}{2}$ | 19 |
| Tex Inst | 12,000 | 80 | $85\frac{7}{8}$ |

a. Design and run a program to calculate the initial (purchase) value of the portfolio, the current value of the portfolio, and the net change in the value. Store number of shares, purchase prices, and current prices in a two-dimensional array. *Hint:* The value of the portfolio is found by multiplying shares by corresponding prices and summing.

b. Output the portfolio before printing the items in part **a**. Store the stock name in a one-dimensional string array.

c. Include a loop in the program for processing more than one portfolio. Find two copies of a newspaper that were published at least two weeks apart. Select a portfolio, make up shares owned, and use the two sets of prices for purchase and current prices. Process the given portfolio and the new portfolio in one run, and include the output of combined value of all portfolios.

36. **State Taxes.** The state budget office has collected the following data on state tax collections for the past year.

Tax Dollars Collected (in millions)

| Tax Type | QTR 1 | QTR 2 | QTR 3 | QTR 4 |
|---|---|---|---|---|
| Motor vehicle | 2 | 3 | 4 | 3 |
| Gasoline | 1 | 2 | 4 | 3 |
| Cigarette | 1 | 1 | 1 | 2 |
| Sales | 15 | 20 | 20 | 50 |
| Corporate income | 25 | 12 | 10 | 8 |
| Personal income | 25 | 75 | 12 | 20 |

Prepare a menu-driven program that has the following options:
1. *Tax Collection Report.* Report shows annual tax collected for each tax type
2. *Percentage Report 1.* Contribution of each tax's quarterly receipts in relation to the total taxes received from all sources during the quarter
3. *Percentage Report 2.* Contribution of each tax's quarterly receipts in relation to total dollars received for that tax during the year
4. *Stop Processing.*

Store the quarterly data within a two-dimensional numeric array; store the tax type description within a one-dimensional string array.

37. **Interactive Airline Reservation System.** All major airlines have automated their systems for handling seat reservations. A central computer keeps a record in storage of all relevant information describing the services being sold: flight numbers, flight schedules, seats available, prices, and other data.

A reservation agent can request information on seat availability, can sell seats to passengers (providing seats are available), can cancel reservations (which increases available seats), and, if a flight is full, can put individuals on a waiting list.

a. Design and develop an interactive program to incorporate the following menu options.

1. Update the accompanying flight information table. For example, if a customer requests one tourist reservation on flight number 4, the program should check for available tourist seats. Since one is available, it should then adjust the available tourist seats to zero and print a message such as RESERVATION ALLOWED. If the passenger had requested two seats, however, the program should print RESERVATION DISALLOWED. SORRY, OUR HIGH ETHICAL STANDARDS DO NOT PERMIT US TO OVERBOOK.

2. Retrieve status on a particular flight by printing the appropriate row in the flight information table.

3. Print entire flight information table.

4. Terminate the run.

Remember to read the flight information data into arrays at the start of the program.

Current Table of Flight Information

| Flight Number | Departing Airport | Arriving Airport | Time of Departure | Time of Arrival | Available Seats First Class | Available Seats Tourist | Seats Sold First Class | Seats Sold Tourist |
|---|---|---|---|---|---|---|---|---|
| 1 | BOS | CHI | 0730 | 0855 | 20 | 8 | 10 | 75 |
| 2 | BOS | CHI | 1200 | 1357 | 20 | 20 | 10 | 50 |
| 3 | BOS | TOR | 0810 | 1111 | 30 | 10 | 0 | 120 |
| 4 | ATL | SF | 1145 | 1604 | 15 | 1 | 25 | 129 |
| 5 | CHI | BOS | 0645 | 0948 | 30 | 25 | 5 | 90 |
| 6 | CHI | NY | 0945 | 1237 | 30 | 8 | 0 | 120 |
| 7 | CHI | LA | 1530 | 1851 | 20 | 10 | 30 | 60 |
| 8 | CHI | TOR | 1955 | 2114 | 5 | 5 | 25 | 85 |
| 9 | TOR | DEN | 1025 | 1611 | 10 | 6 | 60 | 60 |
| 10 | TOR | SF | 1435 | 1556 | 20 | 10 | 10 | 89 |

Process the following requests in your computer run on an interactive basis.

| Option Request | Flight Number | Seat Type | Number of Tickets | Reservation Request |
|---|---|---|---|---|
| 1 | 4 | Tourist | 1 | Reserve |
| 1 | 6 | Tourist | 4 | Reserve |
| 2 | 3 | — | — | — |
| 1 | 9 | Tourist | 2 | Cancel |
| 1 | 9 | 1st Class | 4 | Cancel |
| 1 | 4 | Tourist | 2 | Reserve |
| 3 | — | — | — | — |

**\*\*b.** Besides the options in part **a,** give your program the capability to retrieve and print flight information on all flights between two specified airports. Test your program for flights from Boston to Chicago and Chicago to Los Angeles. In the first case, you should get a printout of the first two rows; in the second case, the seventh row should be printed.

**38. Personnel Salary Budget.** The personnel office for a state government agency is in the process of developing a salary budget for the next fiscal year. The personnel file contains the following information on each employee:

1. Employee name
2. Social security number
3. Current annual salary
4. Union code (1 = clerical, 2 = teacher, 3 = electrical)
5. Current step in pay schedule (1 through 5)
6. Year hired

The state agency deals with three labor unions: clerical, teacher, and electrical. Each union has negotiated a separate salary schedule that entitles each employee to an annual step increase. The salary schedules are listed in the table below. Each employee is hired at the lowest step in the salary schedule for their union and moves up one step each year. The field "current step in pay schedule" indicates the employee's step prior to the new salary for the coming year; that is, "current annual salary" is consistent with this step. The salary for the upcoming year is to be based on the next highest step. Employees who have reached Step 5 are at the maximum salary level for that job. Thus next year's step salary is the same as their current annual salary.

In addition to the salary step increase, employees who have been employed by the state for 10 years or more are entitled to a longevity increase. A longevity increase is a 5% increment added to the employee's *new* step salary.

Salary Schedules

| Step | Clerical | Teacher | Electrical |
|---|---|---|---|
| 1 | 10176 | 9133 | 12170 |
| 2 | 10592 | 10433 | 14260 |
| 3 | 10956 | 11833 | 16668 |
| 4 | 11320 | 13333 | 19501 |
| 5 | 11921 | 14893 | 22801 |

Personnel File

| | | | | | |
|---|---|---|---|---|---|
| Smythie Smile | 032166789 | 10956 | 1 | 3 | 71 |
| Alfred Alfredo | 123454321 | 13333 | 2 | 4 | 68 |
| Mendal Mickey | 987654345 | 22801 | 3 | 5 | 67 |
| Field Flora | 543297541 | 12170 | 3 | 1 | 76 |
| Curran Current | 045811222 | 10176 | 1 | 1 | 76 |
| Handel Halo | 315791123 | 11320 | 1 | 4 | 70 |
| Unkind Cora | 129834765 | 9133 | 2 | 1 | 75 |

a. Design and write a program that prints a budget report for the personnel office. Output from the report includes employee's name, current salary, increase in salary due to step, increase in salary due to longevity, and new salary. Following the output table, print totals for the four numeric columns. Treat the salary schedules as a two-dimensional (5 × 3) array that is to be read in. Data in the personnel file and in the output table need not be treated as arrays.

b. Print a table that summarizes the salary budgets as follows:

SALARY BUDGETS

| | | |
|---|---|---|
| Clerical | $ | xxxxxx |
| Teacher | $ | xxxxxx |
| Electrical | $ | xxxxxx |
| | $ | xxxxxx |

**c. Print the table of part **b** *prior* to the output in part **a**. *Hint:* Unlike part **a**, now you must subscript both the variables in the personnel file and the output in the report of part **a**. Do you see why? Use two-dimensional arrays.

39. **Poisson-Distributed Electronic Failures.** The likelihoods (probabilities) of failures for many electronic processes can be described by the Poisson probability function

$$f(x) = \frac{\lambda^x \cdot e^{-x}}{x!}$$

where

$f(x)$ = probability of $x$ failures per time period

$\lambda$ = average number of failures per time period (lambda)

$e$ = base of natural logarithm (the irrational number 2.71828 . . .)

$x$ = number of failures per time period

$x!$ = $x$ factorial, or the product $1 \cdot 2 \cdot 3 \cdots (x - 1) \cdot (x)$

(*Note:* 0! is defined as 1.)

For example, suppose that malfunctions of onboard navigation systems for a large squadron of aircraft are Poisson-distributed with a failure rate of 20 per month (that is, $\lambda = 20$). In this case, the probability of 15 failures (that is, $x = 15$) in a month is

$$f(15) = \frac{(20)^{15} \cdot e^{-20}}{15!} = 0.0516$$

or about 5.16 percent.

a. Print a table of Poisson probabilities in which rows represent values of $x$ from 0 to 40 in increments of 1 and columns represent values of $\lambda$ from 10 to 20 in increments of 2. Use a two-dimensional array to store probabilities. *Note:* You might want to use the exponential function described in Module C.

b. Print a table of cumulative probabilities in which rows represent the same values of $x$ and columns represent the same values of $\lambda$, as described in part **a**. The cumulative probability of $x$ for a given $\lambda$ is defined as the probability of $x$ or less failures, or

$$F(x) = f(0) + f(1) + f(2) + \cdots + f(x)$$
$$= \sum_{i=0}^{x} f(i)$$

For example, the probability of three or *fewer* failures during a month when $\pi = 10$ is

$$F(3) = f(0) + f(1) + f(2) + f(3)$$
$$= 0.0000 + 0.0005 + 0.0023 + 0.0076$$
$$= 0.0104$$

or just over 1%.

c. Use your tables to find the following probabilities.
1. The probability of exactly 20 failures given $\lambda = 20$
2. The probability of 20 or fewer failures given $\lambda = 20$
3. The probability of exactly 0 failures given $\lambda = 10$
4. The probability of exactly 10 failures given $\lambda = 10$
5. The probability of exactly 20 failures given $\lambda = 10$
6. The probability of 20 or fewer failures given $\lambda = 10$
7. The probability of 20 or fewer failures given $\lambda = 16$
8. The probability of more than 20 failures given $\lambda = 16$

**40. Questionnaire Analysis.** A university is conducting a survey to determine its undergraduates' "attitudes toward and experiences with the consumption of alcoholic beverages." The following questionnaire has been designed for this survey:

___1. What is your sex? 1. male ___ 2. female ___
___2. Where do you live? 1. on campus ___ 2. off campus with parents ___ 3. off campus alone/with roommates ___

__3. What is your class standing? 1. fresh-
man __ 2. sophomore __ 3. junior __
4. senior __ 5. other __

__4. How often on the average do you drink
alcoholic beverages? 1. never __ 2. less than
once a week __ 3. one to three times per
week __ 4. four to five times per week __
5. more than five times per week __

__5. Do you feel other people's drinking has any
adverse effects on your life? 1. frequently
__ 2. occasionally __ 3. rarely __ 4. never
__

__6. Do your drinking habits affect your aca-
demic life? 1. frequently __ 2. occasionally
__3. rarely __ 4. never __

__7. Do you ever feel guilty about your drink-
ing? 1. frequently __ 2. occasionally __ 3.
rarely __ 4. never __

__8. Do you feel you drink primarily because of
1. boredom __ 2. peer pressure __ 3. ten-
sion __4. other __ (specify)

Before conducting the full survey, it has been
decided to pretest the questionnaire on 10 students. The results are shown below.

| Student | Answer to Question No. | | | | | | | |
|---|---|---|---|---|---|---|---|---|
| | *1* | *2* | *3* | *4* | *5* | *6* | *7* | *8* |
| 1 | 1 | 1 | 3 | 3 | 4 | 4 | 2 | 3 |
| 2 | 1 | 1 | 3 | 1 | 2 | 2 | 1 | 1 |
| 3 | 2 | 2 | 2 | 2 | 1 | 3 | 3 | 2 |
| 4 | 2 | 3 | 1 | 4 | 3 | 1 | 3 | 3 |
| 5 | 1 | 1 | 4 | 4 | 1 | 1 | 2 | 3 |
| 6 | 1 | 2 | 2 | 2 | 1 | 1 | 2 | 3 |
| 7 | 2 | 3 | 4 | 1 | 3 | 2 | 1 | 2 |
| 8 | 2 | 1 | 1 | 2 | 4 | 4 | 2 | 1 |
| 9 | 1 | 2 | 3 | 3 | 1 | 1 | 1 | 1 |
| 10 | 2 | 2 | 1 | 4 | 2 | 3 | 2 | 1 |

a. Design and write a program that reads questionnaire data into a two-dimensional array and
outputs a frequency distribution for each question. For example, the frequency distribution
for the first question and the above data would
be

| | Responses | |
|---|---|---|
| Question | *1* | *2* |
| 1 | 5 | 5 |

For the second question, we have

| | Responses | | |
|---|---|---|---|
| Question | *1* | *2* | *3* |
| 2 | 4 | 4 | 2 |

Label your output and try to make it as efficient
as possible.

**b. Modify your program to provide cross-tabula-
tion of responses for any two questions that are
specified by the user. For example, if we wish
to assess differences between the drinking frequencies of men and women, then our output
might appear as follows:

| | Question 1 | |
|---|---|---|
| | 1 | 2 |
| Question 4  1— | 1 | 1 |
| 2— | 1 | 2 |
| 3— | 2 | 0 |
| 4— | 1 | 2 |
| 5— | 0 | 0 |

To make sure you understand this cross-tabu-
lation, confirm the numbers based on the data.

**41. Matrix Multiplication.** Let's define a matrix, **A**,
as having dimensions (rows and columns) $m_1$ by
$n_1$ or ($m_1 \times n_1$). Another matrix, **B**, has dimensions ($m_2 \times n_2$). Two matrices can be multiplied
if and only if they are *compatible*, that is, the number of columns in the first matrix equals the number of rows in the second matrix. As an example,
the multiplication of matrix **A** times matrix **B**,
defined by **AB**, is possible if and only if $n_1 = m_2$.
Similarly, the product **BA** is possible if and only
if $n_2 = m_1$.

If two matrices are compatible, then the
resulting matrix will have dimensions ($m \times n$),
where $m$ equals the number of rows in the first
matrix, and $n$ equals the number of columns in
the second matrix. Referring to the matrices **A**
and **B**, we see that if **AB** is possible and

**AB = C**

then the product matrix, **C**, will have dimensions
($m_1 \times n_2$). Similarly, if **BA** is possible and

**BA = D**

then **D** will have dimensions ($m_2 \times n_1$).

To compute the product matrix, consider the
product

**AB = C**

Let $c_{ij}$ be a generalized element that is located
in row $i$ and column $j$ of the product matrix. To
compute any $c_{ij}$, the elements in row $i$ of matrix
**A** are multiplied by the respective elements in column $j$ of matrix **B** and are algebraically summed.

For example, if

$$A = \begin{pmatrix} 1 & 4 \\ 5 & -3 \end{pmatrix}$$

and

$$\mathbf{B} = \begin{pmatrix} 1 \\ 4 \end{pmatrix}$$

then **A** is a (2 × 2) matrix, and **B** is a (2 × 1) matrix. If we wish to find the product **AB**, then we must first examine the dimensions of the matrices. The product **AB** involves multiplying matrices with dimensions

Inner dimensions
$$\downarrow \qquad \downarrow$$
(2 × 2) times (2 × 1)
$$| \qquad\qquad\qquad |$$
Outer dimensions

This product is defined because the inner dimensions are equal; that is, the number of columns of **A** equals the number of rows of **B**. The product matrix **C** will have dimensions equal to the outer dimensions indicated above, that is, (2 × 1). Thus the product will be of the form

**AB = C**

or

$$\begin{pmatrix} 1 & 4 \\ 5 & -3 \end{pmatrix} \begin{pmatrix} 1 \\ 4 \end{pmatrix} = \begin{pmatrix} c_{11} \\ c_{21} \end{pmatrix}$$

To compute the elements of **C**, we have

$$c_{11} = (1 \quad 4) \begin{pmatrix} 1 \\ 4 \end{pmatrix} = (1)(1) + (4)(4)$$
$$= 17$$

and

$$c_{21} = (5 \quad -3) \begin{pmatrix} 1 \\ 4 \end{pmatrix} = (5)(1) + (-3)(4)$$
$$= -7$$

or

$$\mathbf{C} = \begin{pmatrix} 17 \\ -7 \end{pmatrix}$$

The product **BA** is not defined because the inner dimensions do not match; that is, it involves multiplying a (2 × 1) matrix times a (2 × 2) matrix, and the number of columns of **B** *does not equal* the number of rows of **A** (1 ≠ 2).

Design an algorithm and write a program to input two matrices and print the two matrices together with their matrix product (if defined).

Process the following to debug your program.
  **a.** Find **AB** given **A** and **B** as in the example.
  **b.** Find **BA** given **A** and **B** as in the example.
  **c.** Find **AB** given

$$\mathbf{A} = \begin{pmatrix} 1 & 0 & 6 \\ 2 & -3 & 1 \end{pmatrix}$$

$$\mathbf{B} = \begin{pmatrix} 1 & 0 & 0 \\ 0 & 1 & 0 \\ 0 & 0 & 1 \end{pmatrix}$$

# Running BASIC Programs

Figure A.1 illustrates the process of running BASIC programs. This process assumes that we are using either a time-sharing or a microcomputer system. On those systems we enter our program at a terminal or keyboard directly into the computer.

On a time-sharing system, the log-in procedure includes turning on the terminal, establishing contact with the computer, and providing valid identification. Each user has a unique identification code which usually has two parts: a user name, user number, or user id (which may include letters) and a password. The user number is used by the computer center for controlling access to the computer system and for accounting purposes; the password is a means of maintaining security and privacy. *The exact log-in procedure for your system will be detailed by your instructor.*

On a microcomputer, logging in includes the act of inserting the disk operating system (DOS) diskette and turning on the computer. *The exact procedure for your system will be explained by your instructor (and User Manual).*

The components and logic of the process in Figure A.1 are mostly self-explanatory, but they will vary somewhat from system to system. Study the figure before reading on. In the remainder of this section this process is further explained and illustrated.

---

*This module is best assigned just before, during, or just after Chapter 2.

## A.1 SYSTEM COMMANDS

We communicate with the operating system through a language that we call **system commands**, although the exact term for this language varies from system to system.[1] Among other things, system commands allow us to run (execute) the program, obtain a listing of the program code, and save the program in secondary storage for recall. Therefore, when we run programs in an interactive environment, we have to learn a set of system commands in addition to the BASIC statements that appear within the programs.

Unfortunately, system commands are not universal, which means that they differ from one system to another. *Your instructor (and User Manual), therefore, must provide you with system commands that are specific to your system.*

## A.2 WORKSPACE VERSUS LIBRARY

After logging in, each user in a time-sharing system gets a separate portion of primary memory called the **workspace**. The purpose of the workspace is to store both the BASIC program and the data the program is to work with. On a microcomputer, the workspace is the portion of RAM that's available for the program and its data.

When we log out from a computer system, the program in the workspace is erased. For this reason, each user on a time-sharing system has an assigned secondary storage area (on magnetic disk) called a **library** that stores programs and data for recall. Storing programs in secondary storage avoids having to retype programs. On microcomputers, diskettes are normally the secondary storage areas for programs and data.

A program within a library is often called a **program file**. We can also store data within libraries for use as input to one or more programs. A set of data stored in this manner is called a **data file**. We discuss this topic in Module E.

## A.3 ILLUSTRATIONS

In this section we illustrate the process of running the program in Example 2.16 (page 54) on two computer systems: Digital's VAX-11 minicomputer (Example A.1) and the IBM PC (Example A.2). *If you use a different system, then your system will not operate exactly as shown in the illustration.* In this case, just pay attention to the principles, since these are universal. *Your instructor will discuss the appropriate modifications for your system.*

In these examples, boxed segments indicate the computer run, and marginal notes describe the corresponding boxed segment. The numbers to the left of the boxed segments correspond to the numbers within symbols in Figure A.1. As you read the illustration, relate each boxed segment to the appropriate symbol in Figure A.1.

To clearly point out the interactions between the user and the computer, all text typed by the user is in color; *text typed by the computer is in black.*

**NOTE 1** As you study the examples, *keep in mind the very important distinction between a BASIC **statement** and a system **command**.* This distinction seems to give beginning students much grief. System commands such as LIST and RUN

---

[1]For example, the system commands are called Digital Command Language on the VAX-11 computer system and DOS commands and BASIC commands on the IBM PC. The word command is fairly common across all systems.

are used strictly to communicate with the operating system. In our illustrations, system commands are not found *within* the BASIC programs; only BASIC statements are found within the BASIC programs.

**NOTE 2**  Remember that these examples are for two systems: VAX-11 and IBM PC. If you use a different system, then your system commands will differ. (See Exercise 2.) As you study the illustration, *write in the appropriate system commands for your system,* and relate the illustration to Figure A.1. Note that numbered boxes in the illustration correspond to numbered boxes in the flowchart of Figure A.1. Errors that occur in this process are discussed in detail in Module B.

## E X A M P L E   A . 1   Sample Session on the VAX-11 Minicomputer

**1.**
```
Username: ANSI
Password:


Welcome to VAX/VMS version V3.3
01:45 P.M. Monday, March 5, 1984
```
Entry of user name and password for logging in. Each time we finish typing a line, we must press the Carriage Return or Enter key on the keyboard. ANSI is the user name, but the password that was entered is not displayed by the computer for security reasons.

**2.**
```
$ BASIC
```
The **$** symbol is the VAX-11's Digital Command Language (DCL) prompt, which means that the operating system (OS) is waiting for us to give it a system or DCL command. **BASIC** is the DCL command for using the BASIC compiler.

**3.**
```
VAX-11 BASIC V2.1

Ready
```
This now takes us to the BASIC environment, which is a subset of the OS. The response **Ready** indicates that we have successfully completed the command. The BASIC environment is now waiting for us to do something.

**4.**  (No visible action here)

We need some housekeeping to create a new program in the workspace.

**5.**
```
100 REM   Tuition Revenue Program (Version 1.4)
110 REM-------------------------------------------------
250         INPUT "Enter college name --->"; COLLEGE$
255         INPUT "Enter tuition -------->"; TUITION
260         INPUT "Enter enrollment ----->"; ENROLLMENT
265 REM-------------------------------------------------
280         LET REVENUE = TUITION*ENROLLMENT
285 REM-------------------------------------------------
290         PRINT
300         PRINT "Revenue ..............$"; REVENUE
325 REM-------------------------------------------------
999         END
```
Entry of program into workspace. *These are* BASIC statements. Note that the system does not respond "Ready" here, since these are not system commands. Also note that each line has a unique line number.

Session is not over.

We need to run the program.

**14.**  (No visible action here)

**4.**  (No visible action here)

**6.**
```
RUN
```
**RUN** is a BASIC (system) command that first compiles and then executes the program. Note that within the BASIC environment we use BASIC commands, but within the OS environment we use DCL commands. Thus two sets of commands need to be learned for working within these two environments.

**7.**
```
NONAME        5-MAR-1984  13:49
```
The computer first prints a header (program name, date, and time). Next it compiles the program.

**8.**  (No visible action here)

No syntax errors are found, so execution begins with line 250 in the program.

**9.**
```
Enter college name --->? Micro U
Enter tuition -------->? 750
Enter enrollment ----->? 1000

Revenue ..............$ 750000
Ready
```
During execution, the computer prompts for three input values (college name, enrollment, and tuition). We enter these values, and then the program displays the output (revenue) on the screen. Execution of lines 250–260 yields the input prompts, and execution of line 300 gives the output.

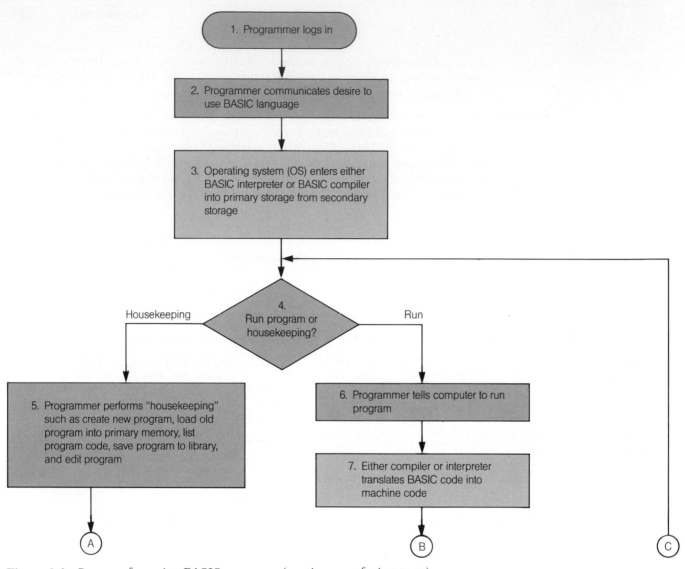

**Figure A.1**  Process of running BASIC programs (continues on facing page).

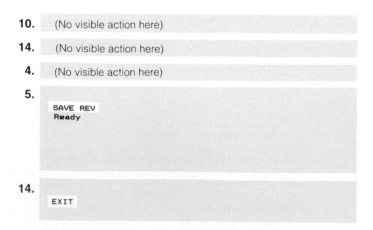

| 10. | (No visible action here) | Results are correct. |
| 14. | (No visible action here) | Session is not over. |
| 4. | (No visible action here) | We need to save the program. |
| 5. | `SAVE REV`<br>`Ready` | **SAVE** is the BASIC command for creating in the library a copy of the program in the workspace. The program has now been saved for recall at a later date under the name REV. The response Ready indicates that we have successfully completed the SAVE command. |
| 14. | `EXIT` | **EXIT** is the BASIC command for leaving the BASIC environment and returning to the operating system. |

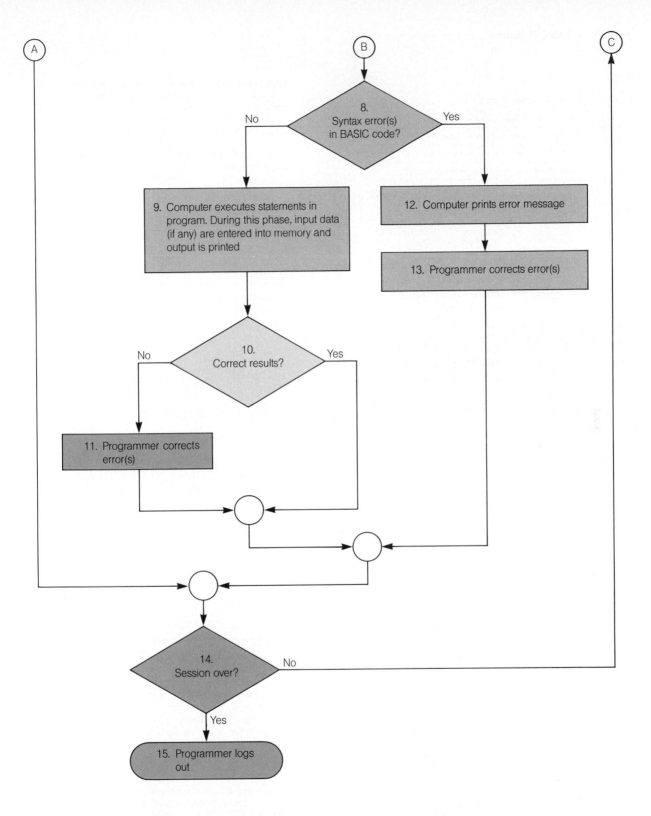

**15.**

```
$ LOGOFF
```

•
•
•

**4.** (No visible action here)

**5.**

```
OLD REV
Ready
```

**LOGOFF** is the DCL command for logging out of the computer.

Let's assume that we get back onto the computer the next day by completing Steps 1–3.

We need to do some housekeeping.

**OLD** is the BASIC command for retrieving a previously saved program from the library into the workspace (a copy of the program still remains in the library).

**5.**

```
LIST
REV            5-MAR-1984  13:53

100 REM   Tuition Revenue Program (Version 1.4)
110 REM------------------------------------------
250         INPUT "Enter college name --->"; COLLEGE$
255         INPUT "Enter tuition -------->"; TUITION
260         INPUT "Enter enrollment ----->"; ENROLLMENT
265 REM------------------------------------------
280         LET REVENUE = TUITION*ENROLLMENT
285 REM------------------------------------------
290         PRINT
300         PRINT "Revenue ..............$"; REVENUE
325 REM------------------------------------------
999         END

Ready
```

**LIST** is the BASIC command that displays the program currently in the workspace. This command does not execute the program; thus no results are displayed other than the listing of the program. *Note:* To obtain a hard-copy listing, use the DCL systems command **PRINT** REV.BAS; this spools the BASIC program named REV to a line printer.

**14,4.** (No visible action here)

Let's run the program again.

**6–10.**

```
RUN
REV            5-MAR-1984  13:55


Enter college name --->? Micro U
Enter tuition -------->? 750
Enter enrollment ----->? 1000

Revenue ..............$ 750000


Ready
```

Run of the program in the workspace. Same input/output as before.

**14.** (No visible action here)

Let's key in a new program.

**4.** (No visible action here)

Housekeeping is needed.

**5.**

```
NEW EXAM
```

**NEW** is the BASIC command for clearing the workspace and starting fresh with a new program. Here we gave the new program the name EXAM.

•
•
•

And so on . . .

---

# E X A M P L E   A . 2   Sample Session on the IBM PC

**1.**

```
Current date is Tue 1-01-1980
Enter new date: 3/05/84
Current time is  0:00:14:66
Enter new time:


The IBM Personal Computer DOS
Version 1.10 (C) Copyright IBM Corp 1981, 1982
```

Insert the Disk Operating System (DOS) diskette in drive A and turn on the IBM PC. (*Note:* In this illustration we assume the use of two diskette drives; the DOS diskette is in drive A, and the user's file (library) diskette is in drive B.) The system prompts for the date and time, which we enter. Don't forget to press the Enter key whenever you're through typing a line.

**2.**

```
A>BASIC
```

The *prompt* **A**> on the screen indicates we have successfully loaded the operating system (DOS). DOS now waits for us to type a DOS command. **BASIC** or **BASICA** is the DOS command we use to load the BASIC interpreter.

**3.**

```
The IBM Personal Computer Basic
Version A1.10 Copyright IBM Corp. 1981, 1982
61066 Bytes free
Ok
```

This now takes us to the BASIC environment. The response **Ok** indicates that we have successfully completed the command. The BASIC environment is now waiting for us to do something.

**4.** (No visible action here)

We need some housekeeping to create a new program in the workspace.

5.

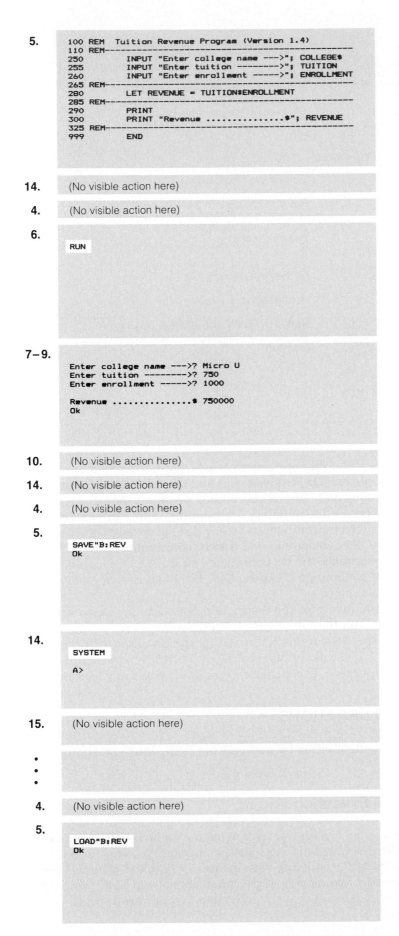

```
100 REM   Tuition Revenue Program (Version 1.4)
110 REM--------------------------------------------------------
250        INPUT "Enter college name --->"; COLLEGE$
255        INPUT "Enter tuition --------->"; TUITION
260        INPUT "Enter enrollment ----->"; ENROLLMENT
265 REM--------------------------------------------------------
280        LET REVENUE = TUITION*ENROLLMENT
285 REM--------------------------------------------------------
290        PRINT
300        PRINT "Revenue ...............$"; REVENUE
325 REM--------------------------------------------------------
999        END
```

Entry of program into workspace. *These are* BASIC statements. Note that the system does not respond "Ready" here, since these are not system commands. Also note that each line has a unique line number.

14.  (No visible action here)

Session is not over.

4.  (No visible action here)

We need to run the program.

6.

```
RUN
```

**RUN** is the BASIC (system) command for interpreting/executing the program. Note that within the BASIC environment we use BASIC commands, but within the DOS environment we use DOS commands. Thus two sets of commands need to be learned for working within these two environments. *Note:* Instead of typing **RUN** we could press the function key **F2**.

7–9.

```
Enter college name --->? Micro U
Enter tuition --------->? 750
Enter enrollment ----->? 1000

Revenue ...............$ 750000
Ok
```

During execution, the computer prompts for three input values (college name, tuition, and enrollment). We enter these values, and then the program displays the output (revenue) on the screen. Execution of lines 250–260 yields the input prompts, and execution of line 300 gives the output.

10.  (No visible action here)

Results are correct.

14.  (No visible action here)

Session is not over.

4.  (No visible action here)

We need to save the program.

5.

```
SAVE"B:REV
Ok
```

**SAVE**" is the BASIC command that stores a copy of the program in the workspace onto the disk. The program is saved on the diskette in drive B for recall at a later date using the name REV. The Ok indicates successful completion of the SAVE command. *Note:* Instead of typing SAVE"B:REV we could press the **F4** key and type B:REV.

14.

```
SYSTEM

A>
```

**SYSTEM** is the BASIC command for leaving BASIC and returning to the operating system (DOS). We can carry out other housekeeping chores from DOS, such as backing up files with the **COPY** command and listing diskette directories with the **DIR** command.

15.  (No visible action here)

We log out by removing the diskettes and turning off the power.

•
•
•

Let's assume that we get back onto the microcomputer the next day by completing Steps 1–3.

4.  (No visible action here)

We need to do some housekeeping.

5.

```
LOAD"B:REV
Ok
```

**LOAD**" is the BASIC command for retrieving a previously saved program from a diskette into the workspace in RAM. In this case, we retrieve a copy of the program REV from the diskette in drive B. A copy of this program still remains on the diskette. *Note:* Instead of typing LOAD"B:REV we could press key **F3** followed by B:REV.

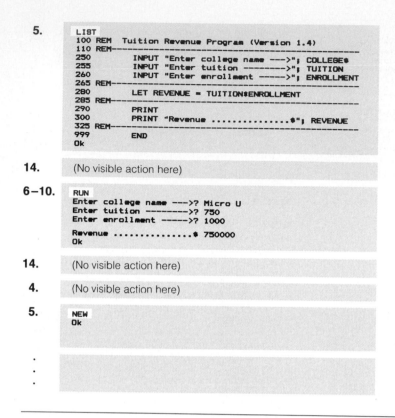

5.

```
LIST
100 REM   Tuition Revenue Program (Version 1.4)
110 REM-------------------------------------------------
250       INPUT "Enter college name --->"; COLLEGE$
255       INPUT "Enter tuition --------->"; TUITION
260       INPUT "Enter enrollment ----->"; ENROLLMENT
265 REM-------------------------------------------------
280       LET REVENUE = TUITION$ENROLLMENT
285 REM-------------------------------------------------
290       PRINT
300       PRINT "Revenue ...............$"; REVENUE
325 REM-------------------------------------------------
999       END
Ok
```

**LIST** is the BASIC command that displays the program currently in the workspace. This command does not execute the program; thus no results are displayed other than the listing of the program. *Note:* Instead of typing LIST we could press the function key **F1**. To obtain a hard-copy listing off the line printer, use the command **LLIST**.

14. (No visible action here)

Let's run the program again.

6–10.

```
RUN
Enter college name --->? Micro U
Enter tuition --------->? 750
Enter enrollment ----->? 1000

Revenue ...............$ 750000
Ok
```

Run of the program in the workspace. Same input/output as before. *Note:* To obtain a hard copy of the input/output on the screen press the **PrtSc** key.

14. (No visible action here)

Let's key in a new program.

4. (No visible action here)

Housekeeping is needed.

5.

```
NEW
Ok
```

**NEW** is the BASIC command for clearing the workspace and starting fresh with a new program.

.
.
.

And so on . . .

---

The two examples show that we generally operate within two environments: The **operating system (OS) environment** and the **BASIC environment**. Typically, the BASIC environment is a specialized subset of the OS environment and has the purpose of developing, maintaining, and running BASIC programs. Moreover, each environment has its own set of system commands: **OS commands** for the OS environment and **BASIC commands** for the BASIC environment. In our examples, the OS commands are called DCL commands on the VAX-11 and DOS commands on the IBM PC. *What are they called on your system?*

We need to be quite aware of the distinction between these two sets of commands, since they usually don't "travel" well between the two environments. For example, the OS command for listing the directory of program names in our library is most likely different from the BASIC command that accomplishes the same purpose. This is a good example of system unfriendliness.

## A.4 OTHER CONSIDERATIONS

This section concludes the module by noting other items that you should be aware of.

### Translation versus Execution

As you know from Chapter 1, a high-level language such as BASIC must first be translated into the machine language of the computer. If translation is by an interpreter, then each line (starting with the lowest numbered line) is first interpreted and then (if a syntax rule of the language has not been violated) executed. By executed we mean that the indicated action (input, print, etc.) is carried out.

If translation is by a compiler, then all lines in the source program are translated (starting with the lowest line number), yielding an object program. The object program is then executed, if there are no syntax errors.

In our sample program, the first executable statement is the INPUT statement in line 250 (the REMs serve only to document programs for us humans). The execution sequence thus starts at line 250 and proceeds to lines 255, 260, 280, 290, 300, and 999. The only evidence of execution we see visually is execution of the INPUT statements in lines 250–260 and of the PRINT statements in lines 290–300.

## Additional System Commands

The system commands that we have illustrated are a small subset of the many commands available for a typical system. For example, commands exist for displaying the names and other characteristics of files within our library, for deleting files from the library, for copying files, for renaming files, for resequencing the line numbers within programs, and for altering or editing programs. Ask your instructor about other useful commands on your system (and check your system's *User Manual*).

## Editors

Editors are powerful tools that enable a user to enter, alter, and store programs. There are two types of editors: line-oriented and screen-oriented.

A line-oriented editor[2] has a set of commands that typically operate on one line at a time (or a range of lines) within the program in the workspace. For example, suppose the program in Example A.1 had a typographical error within the keyword INPUT in line 255.

```
100 REM  Tuition Revenue Program (Version 1.4)
110 REM---------------------------------------------------
250        INPUT "Enter college name --->"; COLLEGE$
255        INPIT "Enter tuition -------->"; TUITION
                ▲
                └─────────── typo
```

The following general description indicates one approach (of many) to correcting line 255 with a typical line editor.

**Step 1.** Invoke the line editor by typing a system command that puts us under control of the line editor. The line editor conceptually points to the first line in the program (line 100), and offers an edit prompt as it waits for us to type an edit command.

**Step 2.** We type a special edit command that moves the pointer to line 255.

**Step 3.** We type a special edit command that substitutes the string INPUT for thc string INPIT.

[2]The VAX-11 EDT editor in line mode and the IBM-PC EDLIN editor are examples of line editors.

**Step 4.**    We end the editing session by typing a special edit command that files or stores the revised program in our library.

A screen-oriented editor[3] allows movement of the cursor to any point on a screen that shows a listing of the program. Text is then altered through straightforward typing, including the use of any special keys for insertions, deletions, and other tasks. For example, suppose we wish to correct line 255 as before, and lines 100–255 are listed on the screen. The following describes a typical screen-oriented approach to correcting this error. The cursor initially resides at the 1 in line 100.

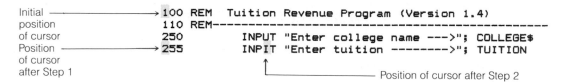

**Step 1.**    Move the cursor straight down to line 255 by striking the appropriate cursor control key three times.

**Step 2.**    Move the cursor to the right along line 255 until it reaches the second I in INPIT.

**Step 3.**    Type the letter U.

**Step 4.**    Strike the "Enter" key. This enters our changed line into the program in the workspace.[4]

As you can see, the process of editing with a screen-oriented editor is much simpler than with a line-oriented editor.

By the way, the ultimate screen-oriented editors are the wordprocessors commonly available for microcomputers. These allow not only the full-screen movements illustrated above but also the use of powerful commands for copying, moving, searching, and replacing text. You might want to try a wordprocessor if one is available to you, especially if you're developing long programs.

You will be doing a lot of editing in this course, *so check out the editor on your system and invest some time in learning how to use it.* Of course, you could just "brute force" your editing by simply retyping entire lines (we could easily have retyped line 255 entirely in our sample illustration); for extensive editing, however, this approach doesn't help your productivity (unless you have nothing better to do!).

**NOTE**    On many systems it's possible to work strictly within the OS environment, thereby bypassing the BASIC environment. In this case, programs are developed and modified using the OS editor, and OS commands are used for housekeeping tasks. *Is this possible on your system?*

---

[3]The VAX-11 EDT editor in keypad mode and the IBM-PC BASIC editor are examples of screen-oriented editors.

[4]The listing shown on the screen actually resides in a special storage area called the screen buffer. Thus, changing a line on the screen changes the corresponding line within the screen buffer, not the corresponding line within the workspace. The act of striking the "Enter" key copies the line from the screen buffer to the workspace.

# EXERCISES

**1.** Define or explain each of the following:

system commands   OS environment
workspace         BASIC environment
library            OS commands
program file       BASIC commands
data file          editors

**2.** Try the following on your system.

   **a.** Duplicate our illustrative run on your system. If you make a mistake typing a line, simply retype the line. The newly typed line will replace the old, incorrect line in your workspace. Better yet, learn to use your system's editor.

   **b.** Experiment. Try different things. Be bold. For example, it's OK to type lines out of numeric sequence, since the BASIC system rearranges lines numerically in your workspace. In other words, we could have typed lines 250, 255, 100, 110, 260, . . . , 999, and they would be stored in the correct numeric sequence. Try it, and then list the program. Try some system commands we haven't illustrated, such as the command that lists your library directory.

   *Note 1:* Make sure that the syntax in the INPUT statements (lines 250–260) is appropriate for your system. If not, make any necessary changes. (The Minimal BASIC approach in Table 2.8, page 41, will work on any system.)

   *Note 2:* Does your system allow multicharacter variable names such as COLLEGE$, TUITION, ENROLLMENT, and REVENUE? If not, change these to C$, T, E, and R.

**3.** Try separate runs of the tuition revenue program in the preceding exercise to answer the following questions.

   **a.** What revenue will be generated if the tuition is increased to $875?

   **b.** What revenue will be generated if the tuition is increased to $875, and enrollment drops to 8500?

   **c.** Validate each of your computer results by hand calculation. Validation is an important part of testing programs.

# Debugging Programs

**Debugging** is the process of detecting and correcting errors.[1] Much of your time, in fact, will be spent on this process. To help you along, we now define types of errors, illustrate them in actual computer runs, and indicate how you go about debugging such errors.

## B.1 ERROR DETECTION AND CORRECTION

The process of uncovering and correcting errors requires an understanding of the possible types of errors and some classic techniques for their debugging.

### Types of Errors

Any programming error will be one of the following:

**1.** Syntax error

**2.** Execution error

**3.** Logic error

   A **syntax error** occurs when a BASIC statement violates a rule of the BASIC language. When we make this type of error, our program will fail to run, and

---

*This module is best assigned immediately after Module A is assigned.

[1]According to computer lore, the term *bug* was born when the Mark I computer at Harvard University stopped working one day in 1945. It seems that a moth got crushed between a set of relay contacts, thereby causing the malfunction. The computer was "debugged" by removing the moth with tweezers.

the translator (compiler/interpreter) will identify the incorrect statement by an appropriate diagnostic message. Thus syntax errors are detected by the translator during the translation of the program.

An error that aborts execution of the program is said to be a **fatal error**. Virtually all syntax errors are fatal; that is, the program never enters the execution phase of a run.

Some syntax errors that are common when one is learning to program are described in the Common Errors section of Chapter 2. In particular, see items 1–4 on pages 66–67. Other syntax errors include the following.

1. **Typographical errors.**　Take care with typos; the computer isn't very permissive. For example, typing PRONT instead of PRINT yields a fatal error.

2. **Inattention to syntax.**　BASIC lives by the rules, and so must you. Pay attention to the rules that govern a particular statement. For example, note the correct spelling of keywords (such as RESTORE) and special punctuation (such as the commas that separate items in a read list).

3. **Key confusion.**　Don't confuse the letter–O key and the zero key. To help with this issue, many computer systems slash the zero. Also, those of you who are accustomed to using typewriters may have a tendency to substitute lower case L for the digit 1, since these often look the same. This kind of mistake can be very difficult to debug and can cause any of the three types of errors (syntax, execution, or logic).

Once we determine the exact nature of our syntax error (with the help of error messages printed by the system), we simply replace the incorrect statement with a syntactically correct statement. This can be done either by entirely retyping the line that contains the error (the brute-force approach) or by using an editor (as described in Module A).

Our program executes completely only after it is free of syntax errors. Unfortunately, a second type of error can occur after the translation phase: An **execution error** is one that takes place during the execution of the program. Typically, when an execution error is encountered, an error message or code is printed, and the computer terminates execution (the error proves fatal). Common execution errors relating to the material in Chapter 2 include the following.

1. **Improper numeric condition during the evaluation of a numeric expression.**　For example, we might attempt to divide by a variable that has the value *zero* in its storage location, or we might attempt to raise a negative number to a noninteger power, or the evaluation might exceed the range of values allowed. If a computed value is larger than that allowed by the system, then an overflow error occurs; if smaller, then an underflow error message is printed. Many systems continue execution by assigning machine infinity (largest possible value) to the value that overflows and machine zero to the value that underflows.

2. **Initialization of variables.**　The act of giving a variable an initial value is called **initialization**. Just before execution most systems initialize all *numeric* variables to zero, but others don't. To illustrate the possible difficulties we might encounter, consider the following statement:

```
200 LET K = K + 1
```

Now, suppose that earlier in the program we did not *explicitly* assign a value to $K$. Usually one of two things will happen when the system executes this statement.

**a.** A value of zero is used for the $K$ to the right of the equal sign. Thus the system itself initialized $K$ to zero. This works fine if we want $K$ to have an initial value of zero; otherwise, we have committed a logic error. In general, it's best to assign explicitly the initial values we want by LET, READ, or INPUT statements.

**b.** The system treats the initial contents of $K$ as undefined and aborts execution due to a fatal execution error. Thus a variable used in a numeric expression must have been previously defined (assigned an explicit value) either through a LET statement or through input/read statements. For example, if we want $K$ to have an initial value of zero before the execution of line 200, then earlier in the program we could write

```
10 LET K = 0
```

Systems that access the contents of an uninitialized *string* variable usually behave in a manner similar to uninitialized numeric variables; that is, either the system initializes the variable to a blank (instead of zero) or the system treats the contents as undefined. The former is more common.

**3. Input/read errors.**  See items 5 and 6 in Section 2.9, pages 67–68.

Generally, it's more difficult to determine the exact location and nature of an execution error than of a syntax error, for several reasons: execution errors tend to be system-dependent; execution-error messages may be more ambiguous than syntax-error messages in locating and diagnosing errors; and the cause of an execution error may be due to faulty program logic, which is related to the third category of errors.

If our program runs but gives us unexpected, unwanted, or erroneous output, then we may assume that a **logic error** exists. Common logic errors include the following:

**1. No output.**  Did you forget to include PRINT statements?

**2. Wrong numeric results.**

**a.** Are the provided data correct?

**b.** Are the numeric expressions and LET statements correct? In particular, check the sequence of arithmetic calculations in numeric expressions based on hierarchy rules.

**c.** Is the program logic correct? For example, are the statements in proper sequence?

**d.** Have any statements been omitted?

**3. Wrong sequence of statements.**  Sometimes an execution action is attempted before the appropriate value has been stored in a memory location. For example,

```
10 PRINT A  ◄── PRINT precedes READ
20 READ A
30 DATA 50
99 END
```

either yields a logic error when a system initializes all variables to zero (the output will be 0 instead of 50) or yields an execution error because the value in A is undefined when line 10 is executed.

Here is some emphatic advice: *Just because your program runs (that is, you get results) does not mean your program is correct—check your results for logic errors against a set of known results.* We cannot overemphasize the importance of this advice. In Step 4 of the four-step procedure, *always* validate your program under varying conditions using a set of test data for which you already know the correct results.

## Classic Debugging Techniques

In your efforts to debug execution and logic errors, you might try the following classic debugging techniques.

1. **Roleplaying the computer.**    Pretend that you're the computer and begin "executing" your program line by line. As you do this, enter data into boxes that represent storage locations. You will be surprised at how many errors you can find this way. Really. You should do this with every program you write. In practice, roleplaying is carried out by small groups of programmers and is called the **group walkthrough**, or **structured walkthrough**.

2. **Data validation techniques.**    To check your data for read/input errors, place a PRINT statement immediately after each READ statement. The paired statements must have identical variable lists. Once you have confirmed that the data are correct, remove these statements. This technique is called **mirror**, or **echo**, **printing**. Other data validation techniques include **error routines** that trap user input errors and otherwise check for incorrect data types and values. We take a look at these approaches in Chapters 4–6.

3. **Diagnostic PRINT (trace) statements.**    Place temporary PRINT statements at strategic points in your program. These should print the values of important variables as the calculating sequence evolves. In other words, these PRINT statements provide intermediate results that may be helpful in tracing what, where, and when something went wrong. When the error is corrected, remove these PRINT statements. Alternatively, we can halt or break program execution at strategic points either through a "break" key at the keyboard or by using **STOP statements** within the program. Then we can type

    PRINT list of important variables

    in **immediate mode**; that is, use a PRINT statement without a line number. The computer thus prints the current values of these variables. Finally, we can resume execution by typing the BASIC command **CONT**, which continues execution from the point at which the break occurred. *Will this approach work on your system?*

4. **Execution traces.**    The display of line numbers as lines within a program are executed is called an *execution trace*. This can be useful when debugging programs that have complicated execution flows. We illustrate this technique in Chapter 6 by using the TRON (TRace ON) and TROFF (TRace OFF) commands.

5. **BASIC error-handling routines.**    Special segments of code can be written that trap execution and syntax errors and follow with a programmer-specified action. These BASIC error-handling routines utilize the ON ERROR/GO TO statement, which we illustrate in Module E.

6. **Programming technique.**    You will avoid many errors if you carefully practice the first three steps of our four-step program development cycle. Get in the habit now.

7. **Experience.**    Learn by your mistakes. Experience is the classic teacher.

8. **Attitude.** Time and again we have seen students become frustrated and upset during the process of correcting errors. This is a good time to practice detachment. Actually, debugging can be fun. Finding and correcting errors can be a very satisfying experience. Perhaps you will become the greatest debugging sleuth in computer history.

Once we realize the exact nature of our errors, we can correct them by either typing new lines to replace old lines, by deleting certain lines, by adding new lines, or by changing lines using the system's editing capabilities. We illustrate this process next.

## B.2 ILLUSTRATIONS

In this section we run the tuition revenue program once more, with syntax, execution, and logic errors purposely included. *Keep in mind that the specifics in these illustrations relate to the VAX-11 system (Example B.1) or the IBM PC system (Example B.2).* If your system is different, pay attention to the general procedures and concepts, and then duplicate our run on your system.

In these illustrations we shade the error messages printed by the computer. *To distinguish clearly what the computer prints from what the user types, all user-typed text is in color.*

### EXAMPLE B.1 VAX-11 Debugging Illustration

1.
```
100 REM   Tuition Revenue Program (Version 1.4)
110 REM-----------------------------------------------
250        INPUT "Enter college name --->"; COLLEGE$
255      · INPIT "Enter tuition --------->"; TUITION
260        INPUT "Enter enrollment ----->"; ENROLLMENT
265 REM-----------------------------------------------
280        LET TUITION$ENROLLMENT = REVENUE
285 REM-----------------------------------------------
290        PRINT
300        PRINT "Revenue ..............$"; REVENUE
325 REM-----------------------------------------------
999        END
```
This program was entered with syntax errors in lines 255 and 280.

2.
```
RUN
NONAME        6-MAR-1984  14:24


Error on line 255

      255           INPIT "Enter tuition --------->"; TUITION



Error on line 280

      280           LET TUITION$ENROLLMENT = REVENUE

Ready
```
The BASIC compiler in the VAX-11 first compiles the entire source program. Execution is aborted because fatal **syntax errors** are encountered. These are listed one by one. We realize that INPIT should be INPUT in line 255 and that REVENUE must appear to the left of = in line 280.

3.
```
255           INPUT "Enter tuition --------->"; TUITION
280           LET REVENUE = TUITION^ENROLLMENT
```
The syntax errors are corrected by retyping the incorrect lines. Sometimes it's easier to retype lines entirely (if they're short), but usually it's best to use the system's editor (the screen-oriented one, ideally).

4.
```
RUN
NONAME        6-MAR-1984  14:30

Enter college name --->? Micro U
Enter tuition --------->? 750
Enter enrollment ----->? 1000
%BAS-F-FLOPOIERR, Floating point error or overflow
-BAS-I-USEPC_PSL,  at user PC=00074B00, PSL=03C00000
-BAS-I-FROLINMOD,  from line 280 in module NONAME
-MTH-F-FLOOVEMAT, floating overflow in math library
   user PC 0013BFED
Ready
```
The program is executed again. This time no syntax errors exist, since the program begins execution by prompting for input data; however, we use exponentiation (^) instead of multiplication (*) in line 280. This causes an **execution error** called overflow (result of calculation is larger than $10^{38}$, the maximum for this system). On the VAX-11, this error is fatal, and execution terminates.

5.
```
280           LET REVENUE = TUITION$ENROLLMENT
```
Correction of line 280 by retyping the line.

**6.**

```
RUN
NONAME            6-MAR-1984   14:34



Enter college name --->? Micro U
Enter tuition --------->? 750
Enter enrollment ----->? 2000

Revenue .............$ .15E+07
Ready
```

The program is run again. Previously calculated test data gave us revenue of $750,000, not the .15E + 07 ($1,500,000) that the computer prints. Thus a **logic error** exists. The reason for the logic error is incorrect entry of enrollment data. It should be 1000, not 2000. To correct, we run the program again and enter the correct data.

**7.**

```
RUN
NONAME            6-MAR-1984   14:36

Enter college name --->? Micro U
Enter tuition --------->? 750
Enter enrollment ----->? 1000

Revenue .............$ 750000
Ready
```

The program is executed again. Finally, we get the correct results.

---

# E X A M P L E   B . 2    IBM PC Debugging Illustration

**1.**

```
100 REM   Tuition Revenue Program (Version 1.4)
110 REM---------------------------------------------
250        INPUT "Enter college name --->"; COLLEGE$
255        INPIT "Enter tuition --------->"; TUITION
260        INPUT "Enter enrollment ----->"; ENROLLMENT
265 REM---------------------------------------------
280        LET TUITION$ENROLLMENT = REVENUE
285 REM---------------------------------------------
290        PRINT
300        PRINT "Revenue .............$"; REVENUE
325 REM---------------------------------------------
999        END
```

This program was entered with syntax errors in lines 255 and 280.

**2.**

```
RUN
Enter college name --->? Micro U
Syntax error in 255
Ok
255        INPIT "Enter tuition --------->"; TUITION
```

The IBM PC interpreter first interprets a line and then executes it. Line 250 interprets without errors and then executes, so we enter the college name following the conversational prompt; however, a **syntax error** is encountered in line 255. The system aborts execution at this point and displays line 255 for review and full-screen editing.

**3.**

```
255        INPUT "Enter tuition --------->"; TUITION

LIST 255
255        INPUT "Enter tuition --------->"; TUITION
Ok
```

The syntax error is corrected by simply moving the cursor to the second I in INPIT and typing U. Next we press the "Enter" key and list the line to show that it stands corrected. *Note:* A corrected line on the screen is not corrected in the workspace until the "Enter" key is pressed while the cursor is on that line.

**4.**

```
RUN
Enter college name --->? Micro U
Enter tuition --------->? 750
Enter enrollment ----->? 1000
Syntax error in 280
Ok
280        LET TUITION$ENROLLMENT = REVENUE
```

The program is again executed, and another syntax error is detected, this time in line 280. We realize that REVENUE must be to the left of the = sign.

**5.**

```
280        LET REVENUE = TUITION^ENROLLMENT
```

The syntax error is corrected by retyping line 280.

**6.**

```
RUN
Enter college name --->? Micro U
Enter tuition --------->? 750
Enter enrollment ----->? 1000
Overflow


Revenue .............$ 1.701412E+38
Ok
```

The program is executed again. This time no syntax errors exist; however, we used exponentiation (^) instead of multiplication (*) in line 280. This causes an **execution error** called overflow (result of calculation is greater than $1.7E + 38$, the maximum value for this system). The error is not fatal on this system. Thus REVENUE is set to the maximum value in line 280, the overflow message is printed, and an incorrect value for REVENUE gets printed as part of the output.

**7.**

```
280        LET REVENUE = TUITION$ENROLLMENT
```

Correction of line 280 by retyping the line.

**8.**
```
RUN
Enter college name --->? Micro U
Enter tuition -------->? 750
Enter enrollment ----->? 2000

Revenue ..............$ 1500000
Ok
```

The program is executed again. Previously calculated test data gave us revenue of $750,000, not the $1,500,000 that the computer prints. Thus a **logic error** exists.

The reason for the logic error is incorrect entry of enrollment data. It should be 1000, not 2000. To correct, we run the program again and enter the correct data.

**9.**
```
RUN
Enter college name --->? Micro U
Enter tuition -------->? 750
Enter enrollment ----->? 1000

Revenue ..............$ 750000
Ok
```

The program is executed again. Finally, we get the correct results.

---

**NOTE 1** BASIC compilers (as in Example B.1) print all syntax error messages in one place following the RUN command. BASIC interpreters print only one syntax error at a time (as in Example B.2). *Are you using a compiler or an interpreter?*

**NOTE 2** The compiler or interpreter will identify syntax errors, and the operating system will print execution error messages; but *we* must identify any logic errors by validating the output.

**NOTE 3** *Any time we edit a line, replace an old line with a new line, delete a line, or insert a line, the change is made in the workspace, not in the library.* So if we want to use the corrected program at a later date, we must type the system command that replaces the incorrect program in the library with the correct program in the workspace.

---

## EXERCISES

**1.** Define or explain each of the following:

| | | |
|---|---|---|
| syntax error | group or structured walkthrough | STOP statements |
| fatal error | data validation techniques | immediate mode |
| execution error | mirror or echo printing | CONT command |
| initialization | error routines | execution traces |
| logic error | diagnostic PRINT statements | BASIC error-handling routines |
| roleplaying | trace statements | |

**2.** With respect to our debugging illustration:
   **a.** Duplicate it on your system, noting any differences. Practice line changes using your system's editor.
   **b.** Once your program is error-free, try deleting line 255 and see what happens. Do you get an execution error in line 280 (undefined variable TUITION) or do you get a logic error (as shown by the output value for REVENUE) because TUITION is initialized to zero?
   **c.** Practice some of the classic debugging techniques discussed on pages 363–364.

# Built-In and User-Defined Functions

## M O D U L E

# C*

**C.1** BUILT-IN FUNCTIONS
**C.2** USER-DEFINED FUNCTIONS
  **Single-line Functions**
  **Multiline Functions**
**C.3** POINTERS
  **Design and Style**
  **Common Errors**

This module defines built-in functions and user-defined functions and illustrates their use.

## C.1 BUILT-IN FUNCTIONS

Suppose we wish to determine the square root of the arithmetic expression

$$b^2 - 4ac$$

and to store it in the address labeled Y. As you know, we could simply use the statement

    LET Y = (B^2 − 4*A*C)^0.5

An alternative approach is to use the following SQR (SQuare Root) function:

    LET Y = SQR(B^2 − 4*A*C)

The right-hand side of this statement is called a **built-in function**,[1] which can be generalized as follows:

---

*This module can be covered anytime after Chapter 3, except for the last example which uses the if–then structure implementation found in Chapter 4.

[1] Other commonly used terms are **BASIC-supplied function, implementation-supplied function**, and **library function**.

**Built-in Function**

```
function name (argument)
              └─────┘
                    ↑
SQR (B^2 − 4*A*C)
```
— Not always required,
depending on the function

The **function name** is a keyword of three letters. In our example, SQR is the function name. The **argument** is any valid numeric expression in the case of numeric functions and any valid string expression in the case of string functions. In our example, the numeric argument is B^2 − 4*A*C. The purpose of the SQR function, of course, is to determine the square root of the argument. For example, if A stores 10, B stores 7, and C stores 1, then the argument is evaluated as 9, and the SQR function returns the value 3.

Built-in functions in BASIC can be grouped into the five categories shown in Table C.1. We might note that Table C.1 just shows some of the more popular built-in functions. Any BASIC dialect includes additional functions as well, which you should check out in your system's BASIC manual. The algebraic, arithmetic, and utility functions are broadly used across disciplines like business, the social and physical sciences, and engineering. The trigonometric functions are used mostly in engineering and physical science applications, whereas the string functions are popular in business, social science, and the arts. The built-in string functions comprise a numerous and important class of specialized functions, which are best treated in a separate module (see Module F). The string functions can be studied any time after this module.

Study the examples in Table C.1 and note the following points.

1. **Function call.**    The built-in function is implemented, referenced, or called by using its function name followed by the parenthetically enclosed argument, if required.

2. **Whence came the function?**    The machine-language instructions for evaluating the function are provided by the translator (interpreter or compiler). For example, to find the natural logarithm of a number, we would use the LOG function. When the translator processes the LOG function, it provides a set of prewritten instructions that calculates the natural logarithm of the argument.

3. **Motivation for use.**    The use of built-in functions within our programs has several advantages.

    a.   For certain standardized tasks, as in calculating logarithms, it saves us programming effort by not having to "reinvent the wheel" (write these instructions ourselves) each time we wish to perform the same task.

    b.   Prewritten systems instructions for evaluating functions are more computationally efficient than those that might be written by the programmer in a high-level language such as BASIC. For example, an SQR function requires less processing time than raising an expression to the 0.5 power.

    c.   The use of a built-in function is stylistically preferred, since the task suggested by the function name is well understood by any programmer that might read a listing of the program.

In the next two examples, we illustrate some common uses of the EXP, INT, and RND functions.

**E X A M P L E   C . 1**    **Continuous Compounding Using the EXP Function**

The following formula determines the accumulated savings $A$ in a bank account, given the initial amount or principal $P$, the annual interest rate $R$, the number of years over which interest is earned $N$, and the number of times $M$ in a year the account earns interest (365 for daily, 12 for monthly, and so on):

$$A = P (1 + R/M)^{NM}$$

For example, if we start with \$5000 ($P = 5000$) at an annual interest rate of 6% ($R = 0.06$), and the account compounds quarterly ($M = 4$); then after 5 years ($N = 5$) our savings account will have grown to

$$
\begin{aligned}
A &= 5000 (1 + 0.06/4)^{5 \cdot 4} \\
&= 5000 (1.015)^{20} \\
&= 5000 (1.34686) \\
&= \$6734.28
\end{aligned}
$$

This calculation illustrates *quarterly compounding,* which means that our money earns interest once every quarter. It should make sense to you that compounding as often as possible is to our monetary benefit. For example, if our savings were to be compounded monthly ($M = 12$) instead of quarterly, then we would end up with

$$A = 5000 (1 + 0.06/12)^{5 \cdot 12} = \$6744.25$$

or \$9.97 richer.

In recent years, banks have offered *continuous compounding.* In this case the ultimate in compounding is achieved: Our money earns interest continuously, even as we sit here thinking about it. The appropriate formula for continuous compounding is

$$A = Pe^{RN}$$

where $e$ is the base of natural logarithms, or the irrational number 2.71828 . . . . For our sample data, we would end up with

$$
\begin{aligned}
A &= 5000e^{(0.06)(5)} \\
&= 5000e^{0.3} \\
&= 5000(1.34986) \\
&= \$6749.29
\end{aligned}
$$

which is a not-so-impressive \$15.01 better than under quarterly compounding.

The following program illustrates continuous compounding by using the EXP function. Output is expressed in whole dollars by using the INT function.

```
100 REM      Continuous Compounding
110 REM
120          INPUT "Principal        : "; P
130          INPUT "Interest rate %   : "; R
140          INPUT "Number of years   : "; N
150 REM
160          LET A = P * EXP(R/100*N)
170 REM
180          PRINT
190          PRINT "Accumulated savings: $"; INT(A)
200 REM
999          END


RUN
Principal        : ? 5000
Interest rate %   : ? 6
Number of years   : ? 5

Accumulated savings: $ 6749
```

**Table C.1** Selected Built-in Functions

| Category | Function[a] | Dialects[b] | Purpose | Algebraic Example | BASIC Example | Argument | Result |
|---|---|---|---|---|---|---|---|
| Algebraic | 1. **EXP(X)** | 1, 2, 3 | Exponential of $X$, or antilog of $X$, or base $e$ raised to $X$th power | $y = ae^{-2t}$ | LET Y = A*EXP(-2*T) | Numeric value | A 10 — T 0.5 — Y 3.678795 |
| | 2. **LOG(X)** | 1, 2, 3 | Natural (base $e$) logarithm of $X$ | $p = q \ln 5$ | LET P = Q*LOG(5) | Positive numeric value | Q 1 — P 1.609438 |
| | 3. **SQR(X)** | 1, 2, 3 | Square root of $X$ | $r = (\sqrt{s})(t + 1)^2$ | LET R = SQR(S)*(T + 1)^2 | Positive numeric value | S 9 — T 4 — R 75 |
| Arithmetic | 4. **ABS(X)** | 1, 2, 3 | Absolute value of $X$ | $z = |x - y|$ | LET Z = ABS(X - Y) | Numeric value | X 4 — Y 10 — Z 6 |
| | 5. **INT(X)** | 1, 2, 3 | Greatest integer less than or equal to $X$ | $k = [a/b]$ | LET K = INT(A/B) | Numeric value | A -8 — B 3 — K -3 |
| | 6. **IP(X)** or **FIX(X)** | 1 / 2, 3 | Integer part of $X$ | $k = [a/b]$ | LET K = IP(A/B) or LET K = FIX(A/B) | Numeric value | A -8 — B 3 — K -2 |
| | 7. **SGN(X)** | 1, 2, 3 | Algebraic sign of $X$ | $y = \begin{cases} -1 & \text{if } X < 0 \\ 0 & \text{if } X = 0 \\ +1 & \text{if } X > 0 \end{cases}$ | LET Y = SGN(X) | Numeric value | X -10 — Y -1 |
| Utility | 8. **RND** | 1, 2, 3 | Uniformly distributed random real number between 0.0 and 1.0 | $y = 0 \leqslant m < 1$ | LET Y = RND | Not required | Y .6291626 |

|  | Function | Version[b] | Description | Argument | Example | Result |
|---|---|---|---|---|---|---|
| 9. | | | Returns current date in form of: | | | |
| | DATE$ | 1, 2 | mm-dd-yyyy | Not required | PRINT DATE$ | 07-27-1984 |
| | or | | | | | |
| | DATE$(0) | 3 | dd-Mmm-yy | Integer value | PRINT DATE$(0) | 27-Jul-84 |
| 10. | | | Returns current time in form of: | | | |
| | TIME$ | 1, 2 | hh:mm:ss | Not required | PRINT TIME$ | 13:55:31 |
| | or | | | | | |
| | TIME$(0) | 3 | hh:mm AM or PM | Integer value | PRINT TIME$(0) | 01:56 PM |
| Trigono-metric | 11. ATN(X) | 1, 2, 3 | Arctangent of X | Expression in radians | PRINT ATN(1) | .7853983 |
| | 12. COS(X) | 1, 2, 3 | Cosine of X | Expression in radians | PRINT COS(0.7854) | .7071055 |
| | 13. SIN(X) | 1, 2, 3 | Sine of X | Expression in radians | PRINT SIN(0.7854) | .7071081 |
| | 14. TAN(X) | 1, 2, 3 | Tangent of X | Expression in radians | PRINT TAN(0.7854) | 1.000004 |
| Strings | See Module F, Table F.1. | | | | | |

[a] The symbol X refers to any expression, including a single numeric variable or single numeric constant.

[b] 1 = ANS BASIC    2 = IBM PC (Microsoft) BASIC    3 = VAX-11 BASIC    4 = your system

**E X A M P L E    C . 2**    **State Lottery Numbers Using the RND Function**

The RND function is used to generate a uniform real number between 0.0 and 1.0 (including 0.0 but less than 1.0). By *uniform* we mean that every decimal value between 0.0 and 1.0 has an equal chance of occurring. This function is particularly useful in computer simulation models.

To illustrate the RND function, we consider a program for simulating a state lottery that generates a three-digit winning number each day. To select the winning number, many states use a machine with 10 "whirling" balls numbered 0, 1, 2, 3, 4, 5, 6, 7, 8, 9. These balls are randomly whirled by air streams, so that the machine selection of any one ball is as likely as the selection of any other ball. Thus, digits between 0 and 9 have an equal chance of occurring. To generate a three-digit random number, the lottery commission simply uses three different machines of the type described.

We simulate the lottery drawing with the following program:

```
100 REM   State lottery drawing
110 REM
120       INPUT "Enter number of digits in lottery"; N
130       PRINT
140       PRINT "The winning number for tonight is ";
150 REM
160       FOR J = 1 TO N
170          LET DIGIT = INT(10*RND)
180          PRINT DIGIT;
190       NEXT J
200 REM
999       END


RUN
Enter number of digits in lottery? 3

The winning number for tonight is  6  1  6
```

The variable DIGIT stores an integer number between 0 and 9 inclusive. We guarantee that each number (0 to 9) has an equal chance of being generated by using the random number function RND. Several steps are needed to produce each random digit, as illustrated in line 170. First, a random number between 0 and 1, but less than 1, is generated using the function RND. Then the random number is scaled into the range 0 to 10, but less than 10, using the expression 10*RND. Finally, the INT function is used to create a random digit between 0 and 9. Thus, for the given run we obtain the sequence:

| RND | 10*RND | INT(10*RND) | |
|-----|--------|-------------|---|
| .6291626 | 6.291626 | 6 | ◄——— first random digit |
| .1948297 | 1.948297 | 1 | ◄——— second random digit |
| .6305799 | 6.305799 | 6 | ◄——— third random digit |

which gives 616, the winning lottery number.

On most systems, this program will generate the same lottery number, or sequence of random digits, each time the lottery program is run. This undesirable result occurs in systems that generate random numbers from the same internal value called a seed. Unless the seed is changed for each run, the sequence of random numbers is the same. The following program illustrates this behavior.

```
100 REM   Sequence of 5 random numbers
110 REM
120       FOR J = 1 TO 5
130          PRINT RND;
140       NEXT J
150 REM
999       END

RUN
 .6291626   .1948297   .6305799   .8625749   .736353

RUN
 .6291626   .1948297   .6305799   .8625749   .736353
```

Same sequence
of 5 random numbers

The ability to generate identical sequences of random numbers is useful for debugging simulation models and for other statistical purposes, but for some situations such as the lottery example, it's undesirable. The RANDOMIZE statement can be used to generate different sequences of random numbers each time the program is run. The general form of this statement is

**RANDOMIZE Statement**

> RANDOMIZE

For example, the program

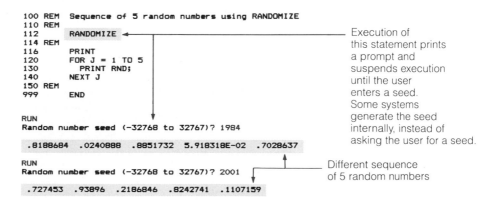

```
100 REM   Sequence of 5 random numbers using RANDOMIZE
110 REM
112       RANDOMIZE
114 REM
116       PRINT
120       FOR J = 1 TO 5
130         PRINT RND;
140       NEXT J
150 REM
999       END
```

Execution of this statement prints a prompt and suspends execution until the user enters a seed. Some systems generate the seed internally, instead of asking the user for a seed.

```
RUN
Random number seed (-32768 to 32767)? 1984

 .8188684   .0240888   .8851732   5.918318E-02   .7028637
```

```
RUN
Random number seed (-32768 to 32767)? 2001

 .727453   .93896   .2186846   .8242741   .1107159
```

Different sequence of 5 random numbers

generates a different sequence of random numbers each time the user enters a different seed. This particular example illustrates the approach taken in Microsoft BASIC on the IBM PC. Other systems, however, may internally generate their own unpredictable seed each time the RANDOMIZE statement is executed (as on the VAX-11, for example). *How does your system implement the RANDOMIZE statement?*

## Follow-Up Exercises

1. In Table C.1 look at the column labeled *BASIC Example* and answer the following:
   **a.** Example 1. What is stored in Y if 2 is stored in A and 4 is in T?
   **b.** Example 2. What is stored in P if 10 is stored in Q?
   **c.** Example 3. What is stored in R if 25 is in S and 3 is in T?
   **d.** Example 4. What is stored in Z if 5.4 is in X and 2.1 is in Y? If 5.4 is in X and 7.4 is in Y?
   **e.** Example 5. What is stored in K if 7 is in A and 2 is in B? If 7.6 is in A and 2 is in B? If 6 is in A and 2 is in B? If −7.6 is in A and 2 is in B?
   **f.** Example 6. Answer the same questions as in part **e**.
   **g.** Example 7. What is stored in Y if −73.2 is stored in X? If 105 is in X? If 0 is in X?

2. Revise the INT function in Example C.1 to
   **a.** Round to the nearest whole dollar. For example, the original approach would truncate $325.75 to $325; we wish to round this figure to the nearest dollar, or $326.

**b.** Round to dollars and cents.

**\*c.** Implement each of the three versions on your system (the original version, and those in parts **a** and **b**).

**\*3.** Write a short program that compares compounding effects based on the formulas in Example C.1. Specifically, compare values of A for the following data:

| P | R | N | M |
|---|---|---|---|
| $10,000 | 0.06 | 10 | 1 |
| 10,000 | 0.06 | 10 | 4 |
| 10,000 | 0.06 | 10 | 12 |
| 10,000 | 0.06 | 10 | 52 |
| 10,000 | 0.06 | 10 | 365 |
| 10,000 | 0.06 | 10 | Continuous |
| 10,000 | 0.08 | 10 | Continuous |

**\*4.** With respect to the first program in Example C.2:
   **a.** Modify the program to generate seven three-digit lottery numbers, one for each day of the week. Print the three digits of a lottery number on the same line as its corresponding day. Each lottery number is to appear on a separate line. This program is to be used week after week by a lottery commission, so make sure you don't generate the same numbers each week.
   **b.** Implement this program on your system.

**\*5.** **Coin-flip simulation.** Write and run a program that simulates N flips of a coin, where N is input by the user. Remember that a fair, or balanced, coin will theoretically result in 50% heads and 50% tails over the long run (which none of us is destined to witness). Consider a random number between 0 and less than 0.5 to be a head and one between 0.5 and less than 1.0 to be a tail.
   **a.** Simulate 10, then 50, then 100, and finally 1000 flips of a coin. Visually count the number of heads and tails. Any interesting results?
   **b.** Use the IF/THEN statement from Chapter 4 to count the number of heads and tails for you. Next to each random number that is printed, print whether it represents a head or a tail. Then print each count and the proportion of heads and tails that were simulated.

**\*6.** **Baseball simulation.** A ballplayer's batting average can be used to simulate a *time at bat.* For example, if the batting average is 273, then we can say that 0.273 is the probability of getting a hit. This is the same as saying that this batter gets a hit 27.3% of the time.
   **a.** Write and run a program to simulate 10, then 50, then 100, then 200 times at bat. Visually count the number of hits. Any interesting results?
   **b.** Use the IF/THEN statement from Chapter 4 to count the number of hits and outs for you. Next to each random number that gets printed, print whether it represents a hit or an out. Then print each count and the proportion of hits and outs that were simulated.

**\*7.** Write the code which would generate N random numbers within the interval A to B, where values for A and B are to be input by the user. Run this program on your system such that
   **a.** Twenty random numbers are generated between 10 and 20.
   **b.** Eight random numbers are generated between $-0.5$ and 2.5.

## C.2 USER-DEFINED FUNCTIONS

At times we need access to a function that is not included in the computer's set of built-in functions, in which case we can define our own function. Functions defined by programmers are called **user-defined functions** and are easily identified by the DEF statement. We shall illustrate this approach in our next example.

**E X A M P L E   C . 3**    **Rounding Function**

A procedure for rounding a number to any number of decimal places is useful when using the PRINT statement to output results. A general expression for rounding a number is

$$FIX(V * 10^{\wedge}P + SGN(V) * 0.5) / 10^{\wedge}P$$

where $V$ is the value to be rounded, and $P$ is the number of decimal places.

In the payroll program which follows, gross pay and net pay for each employee are output. In the first run the results are rounded to two decimal places; in the second run the results are rounded to whole numbers.

```
100 REM    Payroll program with user-defined rounding function
110 REM ----------------------------------------------------------
120        DEF FNROUND(V,P) = FIX (V*10^P + SGN(V)*.5) / 10^P        User-defined
                                                                    function
130 REM ----------------------------------------------------------
140        LET FICA.TAX.RATE = .0685
150 REM
160        INPUT "Number of decimal places :"; PLACES
170 REM ----------------------------------------------------------
180        PRINT
190        PRINT TAB(10); "PAYROLL REPORT"
200        PRINT TAB(12); DATE$                           Note use of
                                                          DATE function
210        PRINT
220        PRINT "------------------------------------"
230        PRINT "Name            Gross Pay      Net Pay"
240        PRINT "------------------------------------"
250 REM ----------------------------------------------------------
260        READ N
270        FOR J = 1 TO N
280          READ FULL.NAME$,GROSS.PAY
290          LET FICA.TAX = GROSS.PAY * FICA.TAX.RATE
300          LET NET.PAY  = GROSS.PAY - FICA.TAX
310          PRINT FULL.NAME$,FNROUND(GROSS.PAY,PLACES),FNROUND(NET.PAY,PLACES)
320        NEXT J                                                   Function
330        PRINT "------------------------------------"            calls
340 REM ----------------------------------------------------------
900        DATA 3
901        DATA "A. Buckles",325.78
902        DATA "B. Frankle",405.49
903        DATA "C. Hinkle ",250.29
998 REM ----------------------------------------------------------
999        END
```

```
RUN
Number of decimal places :? 2
```

```
            PAYROLL REPORT
              07-28-1984 ◄──────────────────── Output from
                                               DATE function
        ----------------------------------
        Name         Gross Pay     Net Pay
        ----------------------------------
        A. Buckles     325.78      303.46 ◄──────────── Rounded to
        B. Frankle     405.49      377.71               2 places
        C. Hinkle      250.29      233.15
        ----------------------------------


        RUN
        Number of decimal places :? 0

            PAYROLL REPORT
              07-28-1984

        ----------------------------------
        Name         Gross Pay     Net Pay
        ----------------------------------
        A. Buckles     326          303 ◄──────────────── Rounded
        B. Frankle     405          378                   to zero places
        C. Hinkle      250          233
        ----------------------------------
```

Note that the user-defined function is defined in line 120 and called twice in line 310. At this time, don't worry about the exact details of how this function works, as we will discuss it throughout this section.

---

There are two categories of user-defined functions: those consisting of one line and those consisting of multiple lines. Each of these is different enough to warrant separate presentations.

## Single-line Functions

The **DEF statement** defines the user-defined single-line function. The general form of the DEF statement for a **single-line function** is

**DEF Statement (for Single-line Function)**

> **DEF** *function name (formal parameter list)* = *expression*
>
> DEF FNY(A,B,X) = A + B*X

The keyword DEF is a signal to BASIC that we are defining a user-defined function. For some dialects (such as Microsoft BASIC) the function name must begin with the letters FN, followed by any valid variable name. For example, FNY, FNROUND, and FNTITLE$ are all function names. The name FNTITLE$ defines a string function, while the other names define numeric functions. In certain other dialects (such as VAX-11 and ANS BASIC) the function name need not begin with the letters FN. Thus, Y, ROUND, and TITLE$ are legitimate function names in these dialects. *Must the function name in your dialect begin with FN?* Following the function name comes a list of formal parameters, separated by commas and enclosed in parentheses. The formal parameters are variables (often called dummy variables) that act as placeholders for the actual values supplied each time the function is used. In our FNY sample function above, the formal parameter list is A,B,X. When the function is referenced or called (much as our function calls for built-in functions), values for the dummy variables A, B, and X are supplied to the function. These values are then used to evaluate the expression to the right of the equal sign. The expression is any valid expression, numeric in the case of numeric functions and string in the case of string functions. This expression includes the dummy variables from the formal parameter list, and it may also use other variables, constants, and functions as well.

In example C.3, the function

$$120 \text{ DEF FNROUND(V,P)} = \text{FIX(V} * 10\,\hat{}\,\text{P} + \text{SGN(V)} * 0.5) / 10\,\hat{}\,\text{P}$$

is a user-defined function that rounds a number *V* to the specified number of decimal places *P*. In this case, FNROUND is the (numeric) function name, *V* and *P* are the formal parameters, and

$$\text{FIX( V} * 10\,\hat{}\,\text{P} + \text{SGN(V)} * 0.5) / 10\,\hat{}\,\text{P}$$

is the numeric expression. This numeric expression is evaluated as follows (assuming *V* stores 5.748 and *P* stores 2):

1. The value 5.748 is multiplied by 100 (or $10^2$) to give 574.8.
2. The built-in function SGN(5.748) returns the value $+1$ (see Table C.1). This gives the result $+0.5$ when SGN(5.748) $*$ 0.5 is evaluated.
3. The values 574.8 (from Step 1) and 0.5 (from Step 2) are added, giving 575.3.
4. The integer part of 575.3 is taken by the built-in FIX function, giving 575.
5. The value 575 is divided by 100 (or $10^2$), giving 5.75. Thus, the original value 5.748 has been rounded (not truncated) to two decimal places, as required.

Note that the addition of 0.5 in Step 3 assured rounding to the nearest integer value in Step 4. To understand this function better, go through each step for each of the following: round 5.742 to two places, giving 5.74; round $-6.7$ to zero places, giving $-7$.

The following points should further help you understand single-line functions.

1. **Placement.**   The function definition or DEF statement can be placed anywhere before its use within the program; however, it's good programming practice to define all user-defined functions at the beginning of a program. This is because the DEF statement is *nonexecutable*, and programs are more readable if nonexecutable statements are out of the way when we read program listings. It also ensures that we don't call the function before we define it.

2. **Size.**   The particular form of the DEF statement shown earlier restricts the size of the function to a single line. A long formal parameter list and an elaborate evaluation may require a multiline user-defined function (next subsection), a subroutine (Chapter 7), or an external function (Chapter 7).

3. **Nested calls.**   A function definition can reference other built-in functions and user-defined functions. For example, the function FNROUND references two built-in functions: FIX and SGN.

4. **Optional formal parameters.**   Inclusion of the formal parameter list is optional and can be omitted if it is not needed. For example,

DEF FNPI = 3.14159

defines a function whose value is $\pi$.

**Calling the User-Defined Function.**    Once the function is defined by its DEF statement, it can be used (called or referenced) anywhere in the program by specifying its function name and listing in parentheses the actual values we want the function to use. The following general form describes the **function call**.

Function Call or Reference

> **Function name (actual parameter list)**
> FNROUND(NET.PAY,PLACES)

where the actual parameter list is a list of variables, constants, or expressions that are separated by commas. The actual parameters are the set of values that gets passed to the user-defined function; that is, the user-defined function uses the actual values in place of the corresponding dummy variables defined by the formal parameter list.

In Example C.3 the function is called two separate times within the PRINT statement in line 310. When the function is called, control is transferred to the user-defined function, where the numeric expression is executed using the values from the actual parameter list in place of the variables in the formal parameter list. For example, during the first call to function FNROUND, the actual values in GROSS.PAY and PLACES are *passed* or sent to the numeric expression within function FNROUND via the formal parameters *V* and *P*. The call and function evaluation can be visualized as follows.

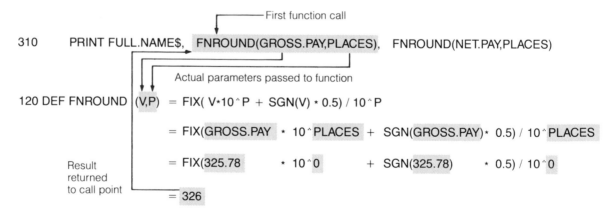

Note that GROSS.PAY is matched with V and PLACES is matched with P, since corresponding parameters within the actual and formal parameter lists are matched according to their ordering. If 325.78 is stored in GROSS.PAY and 0 is stored in PLACES, then the DEF statement is evaluated as shown. Then the result 326 is *returned* to line 310 and printed.

The second call works similarly, except that the actual parameters NET.PAY and PLACES are used in place of the formal parameters V and P to evaluate the function.

**Additional Considerations.**    Some additional points regarding user-defined functions follow:

1. The order and number of actual parameters in a function reference must correspond to the order and number of formal parameters in the definition of the function.

2. The names of actual and formal parameters are not usually the same. For example, the names of the actual parameters GROSS.PAY and PLACES in the function call FNROUND(GROSS.PAY,PLACES) are not the same names used as formal parameters (V and P). The formal parameter is a way to generalize the use of the function for more than one call to the function within the same program. For example, the function FNROUND is called twice in Example C.3. In both cases, the variable for the first parameter is different, that is, GROSS.PAY and NET.PAY both correspond to the formal parameter V.

3. The formal parameters are local to the function definition. That means these variables represent memory locations that are separate from variables with the same name that are used elsewhere in the program. If the function in Example C.3 were written as

   ```
   120 DEF FNROUND (N,P) = FIX( N * 10^P + SGN(N) * 0.5) / 10^P
   ```

   then N within the function would represent a different variable than does N in line 260. The value 3 is stored in N when line 260 is executed, but N in line 120 is not affected by this statement and does not store the value 3. We mention this point so that you can understand the local nature of formal parameters; however, from a style standpoint, we don't recommend using names for formal parameters that are used elsewhere in the program.

4. The numeric expression in the DEF statement can contain variables that are not found in the parameter list but are found elsewhere in the program. For example, the function in Example C.3 could be rewritten as

   ```
   120 DEF FNROUND(V) = FIX( V * 10^PLACES + SGN(V) * 0.5) / 10^PLACES
   ```
   └─One formal parameter

   in which case the variable PLACES in line 160 is the same variable as in line 120. Thus, when the number of decimal places is entered in line 160, the variable PLACES in line 120 is automatically assigned the same value, since PLACES is a single storage location. Also note that the function calls in line 310 would now have to be changed to reflect a single actual parameter, as follows:

   ```
   310 PRINT FULL.NAME$, FNROUND(GROSS.PAY), FNROUND(NET.PAY)
   ```
   └─One actual parameter─┘

5. The main motivation for using single-line functions is coding efficiency. Not using the rounding function in Example C.3, for instance, would require in line 310 two repetitions of the rather complicated numeric expression that rounds numbers. This coding efficiency can be better appreciated if the function were to be called 20 or 30 times within a long program. A secondary motivation is style. It's easier to read program listings with multiple function calls than program listings that otherwise would have complicated numeric expressions in place of every call.

## Follow-Up Exercises

**8.** Describe output for the following program:

   **a.** 10 DEF FNC(Y) = Y^3 + Y + 3 − 2*SQR(2*Y − 1)
      20 PRINT FNC(1), FNC(3), FNC(5)
      30 END

   **b.** Rewrite this program without the DEF statement. Which version is preferable and why?

**9.** What does the following program output?

    10 DEF FNB(X) = X + 3*ABS(X − 2)
    20 READ A,B,C
    30 PRINT FNB(A), FNB(INT(B)), FNB(C)
    40 DATA 3, 1.25,3.5
    50 END

**10.** Create a user-defined function named FNA for the following expressions. In each case treat $n$ and $i$ as formal parameters.
   **a.** $1/n^2 + 1/\sqrt{n}$
  **\*b.** $|p(1 + i)^n − e^{in}|$

**11.** Indicate what is wrong, if anything, with each of the following:

| Function | Calling Statement |
|---|---|
| a. 10 DEF FNE1 = (A + B + C)/3 | 50 LET D = FNE1 |
| b. 15 DEF FNE(A,B,C) = (A + B + C)/3 | 55 LET D = FNB(X,Y,Z) |
| c. 20 DEF FNE(N) = (A + B + C)^N | 10 LET D = 4*FNE(8) + A^2 + 10 |
| d. 25 DEF FNE(A(K)) = A(K)*B | 60 PRINT FNE(B(J)) |
| e. 25 DEF FN5(A) = A*B*C | 65 PRINT FN5(A + 5*X − 7) |
| f. 30 DEF FNTITLE$ = "EBM CO." | 70 PRINT FNTITLE$ |

**12.** A simpler function than that used in Example C.3 to round a number to any number of decimal places is shown below.

    DEF FNROUND(V,P) = INT( V *10^P + 0.5) / 10^P

   Does this function return the same results as the rounding function used in example C.3? To answer the question, try roleplaying the following 2 sets of values for V and P: 5.748 for V and 2 for P; −6.7 for V and 0 for P.

**\*13.** With respect to Example C.3:
   **a.** Modify the program to add FICA taxes to the report rounded to the same number of decimal places as gross pay and net pay.
   **b.** Implement this program on your system.

**\*14.** With respect to Example C.3:
   **a.** Modify the program so that the values for GROSS.PAY and NET.PAY are rounded to the specified number of places before the PRINT statement.
   **b.** Implement this program on your system.

**Table C.2** Multiline User-Defined Functions

| Dialect | Structure/Syntax | Code |
|---|---|---|
| ANS BASIC | **FUNCTION** *function name (formal parameter list)*<br><br>] Body of function<br><br>**END FUNCTION** | FUNCTION PRICE(ITEM$)<br>IF ITEM$ = "C" THEN LET PRICE = 5<br>IF ITEM$ = "P" THEN LET PRICE = 4<br>IF ITEM$ = "R" THEN LET PRICE = 4.5<br>END FUNCTION |
| VAX-11 BASIC | **DEF** *function name (formal parameter list)*<br><br>] Body of function<br><br>**END DEF** | DEF PRICE(ITEM$)<br>IF ITEM$ = "C" THEN LET PRICE = 5<br>IF ITEM$ = "P" THEN LET PRICE = 4<br>IF ITEM$ = "R" THEN LET PRICE = 4.5<br>END DEF |
| Your system (if different)[a] | | |

[a]Minimal BASIC and Microsoft BASIC do not have multiline user-defined functions.

## **Multiline Functions

Multiline user-defined functions are used instead of single-line functions when more complex functions need to be defined. The general forms of the multiline function are defined in Table C.2, where the function name and formal parameter list are defined as in single-line functions.

Consider the following points regarding multiline user-defined functions.

1. Either the **FUNCTION statement** or the **DEF Statement** indicates the beginning of the function, depending on the dialect.

2. The function is evaluated within its body. The body of the function typically contains the necessary executable statements for evaluating the function.

3. The function body must have at least one statement of the form

   LET function name = expression

4. The end of the function is signaled by either the **END FUNCTION statement** or the **END DEF statement**, depending on the dialect.

5. Multiline functions are called or referenced in the same way that single-line functions are referenced.

6. Not all BASIC dialects have multiline user-defined functions. *Does yours? If so, is it one of the forms shown in Table C.2?*

7. As in the case of single-line functions, our focus here is on numeric functions. Multiline string functions are taken up in Module F.

**E X A M P L E   C . 4**   Billing Program

| Brand | Brand Code | Unit Price |
|---|---|---|
| Coca Cola | C | $5 |
| Pepsi | P | $4 |
| Royal Crown | R | $4.50 |

A softdrink distributor has its truck drivers give a bill to each retail dealer on delivery of soda to the store. On their pocket micros the truck drivers enter the dealer's name, code for brand of soda, and number of cases sold. The program looks-up the correct unit price and then prints out the total amount owed (unit price times number of cases sold).

The program uses a multiline function to determine the unit price for the brand of soda sold. The prices for the three brands sold by the distributor are shown at left.

**This section requires knowledge of the IF/THEN statement from Chapter 4.

```
100 REM   Billing program with multi-line function
110 REM
120       DEF PRICE(ITEM$)
130          IF ITEM$ = "C" THEN   LET PRICE = 5
140          IF ITEM$ = "P" THEN   LET PRICE = 4
150          IF ITEM$ = "R" THEN   LET PRICE = 4.5
160       END DEF
170 REM
180       INPUT "Dealer name      "; DEALER$
190       INPUT "Drink code       "; BRAND$
200       INPUT "Cases purchased"; NUMBER
210 REM
220       LET BILL = PRICE(BRAND$) * NUMBER
230 REM
240       PRINT "Amount owed     $"; BILL
250 REM
999       END
```

——— Multi-line function

——— Note use of function name

——— Function call

```
RUNNH


Dealer name      ? ART'S SODA SHOP

Drink code       ? R

Cases purchased? 20


Amount owed    $ 90
Ready
```

In the multiline function, the formal parameter ITEM$ represents the brand code whose soft drink was sold. The function determines the correct price and returns a single value: the unit price for the brand of soda sold. Note that a string parameter was used in both the function definition (formal parameter ITEM$) and the reference to the function (actual parameter BRAND$).

In the sample run, R is entered for BRAND$. The function call in line 220 then transfers control to function PRICE in line 120, which uses the actual value R for the dummy variable ITEM$. Next, the sequence of if–then structures in lines 130–150 determines the correct unit price of $4.50. *Note that the result 4.50 is assigned to variable PRICE in line 150, which is identical to the name of the function in line 120.* Execution of the END DEF statement then returns the result 4.50 to the point of call in line 220. Finally, the bill calculation is completed, and the bill is printed. In essence, line 220 gets evaluated as follows.

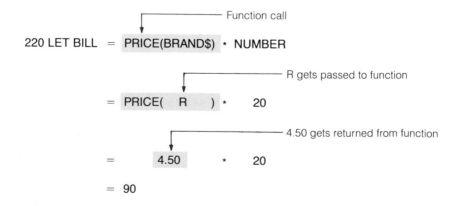

## Follow-Up Exercises

15. In Example C.4:
    a. Modify the program to add a new brand, Dr. Pepper with code D, at a price of $6 a case.
    *b. Implement this program on your system.

*16. a. Write a multiline function to return the maximum of two numbers.
    b. Implement this function on your system.

**17. **Baseball simulation revisit.** Rework Exercise 6 as follows:
    a. Simulate a time at bat according to the following probability distribution:

| Probability | Result | Meaning |
|---|---|---|
| 0.727 | 0 | Out |
| 0.200 | 1 | Single |
| 0.050 | 2 | Double |
| 0.020 | 3 | Triple |
| 0.003 | 4 | Homerun |

Design a multiline function to return the result.
    b. Implement the simulations described in Exercise 6 on your system.

## C.3 POINTERS

### Design and Style

1. **Use built-in functions.** Don't write your own code to accomplish what a built-in function can accomplish. It's more efficient and stylistically preferred to use built-in functions, as explained on page 368.

2. **Placement of user-defined functions.** Locate user-defined functions at the beginning of the program. This improves readability and guards against the error of making a function call without first having defined the function.

3. **Naming formal parameters.** To prevent confusion, variables used as formal parameters should not appear elsewhere in our program.

### Common Errors

1. **Incorrect function call.** To execute a user-defined function don't branch to a DEF or FUNCTION statement; instead we reference the function in the statement where the calculation is performed.

2. **Parameter lists mismatch.** Make sure that the order and number of the actual parameters in a function call correspond to the order and number of formal parameters in the DEF or FUNCTION statement.

## ADDITIONAL EXERCISES

**18.** Define or explain each of the following terms:

| | |
|---|---|
| built-in functions | formal parameter list |
| RANDOMIZE statement | actual parameter list |
| user-defined functions | multiline functions |
| DEF statement | FUNCTION statement |
| single-line functions | END FUNCTION statement |
| function call or reference | END DEF statement |

# Print Using Statement and Formatted Output

MODULE

# D*

Many computerized reports require more precise control and more features than PRINT statements can provide. The statements in this module allow us to implement **formatted output**, which means that the output line is printed precisely according to an image that we provide.

## D.1 PRINT USING STATEMENT AND FORMAT STRINGS

Compare the two sets of output below. The first version uses PRINT statements, while the second version uses PRINT USING statements. Notice that version B is easier to read and more attractive than version A.

*This module can be covered anytime after Chapter 2, except for Section D.3, which requires Chapter 3.

**Version A: Based on PRINTs.**

```
                    PAYROLL REPORT

      -----------------------------------------------------
        Name        Hours         Rate          Pay
      -----------------------------------------------------
        Phil Murray   15           6.35          95.25
        Hilda Snark   30.25        5.85          176.9625
        Margo Barker  32           6.8           217.6
        Ralph Kiner   20.75        6.25          129.6875
        Mark Fargo    35           6             210
        Anna AlDente  38           7.78          295.64
      -----------------------------------------------------
        Totals                                   1125.14
```

**Version B: Based on PRINT USINGs.**

```
                    PAYROLL REPORT

      -----------------------------------------------------
        Name              Hours      Rate        Pay
      -----------------------------------------------------
        Phil Murray       15.00      6.35         95.25
        Hilda Snark       30.25      5.85        176.96
        Margo Barker      32.00      6.80        217.60
        Ralph Kiner       20.75      6.25        129.69
        Mark Fargo        35.00      6.00        210.00
        Anna AlDente      38.00      7.78        295.64
      -----------------------------------------------------
        Totals                               $1,125.14
```

In general the **PRINT USING statement** allows us to conveniently implement the following features:

1. *Right-justify* (align on the right) rather than left-justify numeric output
2. Round numbers to a specified number of decimal places
3. Align a column of numbers so that decimal points appear one below the other
4. Insert commas into a number
5. Assign a fixed or floating dollar sign to a number
6. Output numeric values in exponential notation
7. Insert blanks and other characters at any location

As usual in life, we pay a price for our benefits: the PRINT USING statement includes demanding detail, and BASIC dialects vary in their implementation. The general form of this statement for several systems is illustrated in Table D.1.

For either version of the PRINT USING statement an image of the output line is written using a format string that describes how the items in the output line are to be printed. The **format string** is a string expression containing one or more **format fields (format items)**. A format field controls the output of a single value. There are three types of format fields: **numeric format fields** for printing numeric values, **string format fields** for printing string values, and **literal format fields** for printing unquoted string constants as labels, headings, and so on. Numeric and string format fields contain one or more consecutive **format characters (format symbols)**. In Table D.1,

- ###.# is a numeric format field or item
- # is the format character or symbol for printing digits
- . is the format character or symbol for locating the decimal point

**Table D.1**    Variations of the PRINT USING Statement

| Dialect | Structure | Examples |
|---------|-----------|----------|
| VAX-11 | **PRINT USING** *format string ; output list* | *Note:* Assume VALUE stores 50.76. All three examples print the output value 50.8 in columns 2–5.<br>1. PRINT USING "###.#" ; VALUE |
| IBM PC<br>Microsoft | | 2. LET F$ = "###.#"<br>PRINT USING F$ ; VALUE |
| | where<br>*format string* is a string expression that provides an image of how the items in the output list are to be printed. The format string can be either a string constant (Example 1) or a string variable (Example 2).<br>*output list* is a list of constants, variables, and/or expressions whose values are to be printed according to the format string. | |
| ANS | *Version 1:*<br>The same as VAX-11 and IBM PC, except use a colon (:) instead of a semicolon (;) to separate the format string from the output list.<br>*Version 2:*<br>    **PRINT USING** *image line no: output list*<br>*image line no.* **IMAGE** *:format string* | 3. 40 PRINT USING 50 : VALUE<br>50 IMAGE :###.# |
| | where<br>*image line number* is a numeric constant that identifies the IMAGE statement with the format string<br>*output list* is defined above<br>*format string* is an unquoted string constant beginning immediately to the right of the colon (:) that provides an image of how the items in the output list are to be printed. (See Example 3.) | |

Your system
(if different)

**Table D.2** Selected Format Characters or Symbols

| Format Symbol | Description (Note any differences between this table and your system) |
|---|---|
| # | Each pound sign (#) represents a digit position within a numeric format field. |
| . | The decimal point (.) represents an actual decimal point inserted into the printed output. |
| , | The comma (,) prints a comma between every third digit to the left of the decimal point. |
| $ | A single dollar sign as the first character in a numeric format field prints a dollar sign in that position. |
| $$ | A double dollar sign at the beginning of a numeric format field prints a dollar sign to the immediate left of the most significant digit. |
| ** | A double asterisk at the beginning of a numeric format field inserts asterisks in place of leading spaces. |
| ^ ^ ^ ^ | A numeric field followed immediately by four caret symbols indicates that the number is displayed in exponential notation. |
| \ \ | Two back-slash symbols separating $n$ spaces indicate the starting and ending positions of a string format field for printing string values (the field width or length is $n+2$ character positions).[a] |

[a]ANS BASIC uses the pound symbol (#) instead of back-slashes to print string values.

Table D.2 identifies a popular subset of format symbols that are used in ANS, VAX, and Microsoft versions of BASIC.

## D.2 FORMAT FIELDS AND SYMBOLS

This section illustrates how we can design some common format fields.

### Printing Numeric Values

Numeric values are printed by using the pound symbol (#) as a format symbol. The symbol is repeated for each numeric digit of the field. For example, study the following program and its output.

**EXAMPLE D.1** Numeric Values

| Program | Output | Comments |
|---|---|---|

```
100 REM   Numeric values
105 REM
110       LET X = 10
120       LET Y = -3
125 REM
130       PRINT USING "##" ; X            10      ──── Printed in columns 1 and 2
140       PRINT USING "###"; X            10      ──── Printed in columns 2 and 3 (see note 1)
150       PRINT USING "#"  ; X           %10      ──── Insufficient field width (see note 2)
160       PRINT USING "###"; Y            -3      ──── Printed in columns 2 and 3 (see note 3)
170       PRINT USING "###   ##"; X,Y     10   -3  ──── X is printed in columns 2 and 3, and Y is printed in columns 6 and 7 (see note 4)
180       PRINT USING "###  ##"; X        10      ──── X is printed in columns 2 and 3 (see note 5)
190       PRINT USING "##" ; X,Y        10-3      ──── X is printed in columns 1 and 2, and Y is printed in columns 3 and 4 (see note 6)
998 REM
999       END
```

Consider the following points concerning the # symbol:

1.  If the number of # symbols is greater than the number of digits stored in the variable, then the numeric value is right-justified within the format field. See line 140 in Example D.1.

2.  If the value stored in the variable is larger than the number of digits in the format field, then the value is displayed with a percent sign (%) before the value to indicate an insufficient field width. See line 150 in Example D.1.

3.  A # symbol reserves space for a digit or a minus sign (if the number is negative). See line 160 in Example D.1.

4.  Two or more items in the output list imply the use of multiple format fields within the format string. Multiple format fields are separated by spaces, as follows:

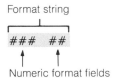

See line 170 in Example D.1.

5.  *If the number of items in the output list is less than the number of format fields within the format string, then the extra format fields are ignored.* See the output for line 180 in Example D.1. In this case, the single output-list item X is printed based on the first numeric field ###. The second numeric field ## is ignored.

6.  *If more items are in the output list than in the format fields within the format string, then the format string is repeatedly used to output the remaining items.* See the output for line 190 in Example D.1. Here we have two items in the output list (X and Y), but only one numeric field within the format string (##). Thus, the 10 in *X* is printed in columns 1 and 2 using ##; then the −3 in *Y* is printed in columns 3 and 4 again using the same ##.

## Printing Numeric Values with a Decimal Point

Decimal or real values are printed by using the # symbol and a single decimal point as a format symbol. The placement of the decimal point indicates its precise location, and the number of # symbols to the right of the decimal point specifies the number of decimal places to be output. For example, study the following program and its output.

**E X A M P L E   D . 2**   **Numeric Values with a Decimal Point**

| Program | Output | Comments |
|---|---|---|
| 100 REM  Numeric values with decimal point | | |
| 105 REM | | |
| 110      LET X = 57.183 | | |
| 115 REM | | |
| 120      PRINT USING "##.###" ; X | 57.183 | Printed as stored |
| 130      PRINT USING "##.##" ; X | 57.18 | Rounded to 2 places (see note 1) |
| 140      PRINT USING "##.#" ; X | 57.2 | Rounded to 1 place |
| 150      PRINT USING "##.####"; X | 57.1830 | Unused position filled with zero (see note 2) |
| 998 REM | | |
| 999      END | | |

Note the following concerning the decimal point symbol:

1. When the value stored in the variable contains more decimal positions than the width of the format field, then the printed value is rounded to the number of decimal places shown in the format field. See lines 130 and 140 in Example D.2.

2. When the fractional part to be output has fewer decimal positions than specified in the format field, then the unused symbols are filled with zeros. See line 150 in Example D.2.

## Printing Numeric Values with a Comma

To make larger numbers more readable, a comma can be inserted in the format field. This symbol causes a comma to be printed between every third digit to the left of the decimal point.

**E X A M P L E   D . 3**   Numeric Values with a Comma

| Program | Output | Comments |
|---|---|---|

```
100 REM    Numeric values with comma
105 REM
110        LET X = 16032
120        LET Y = 478
125 REM
130        PRINT USING "##,###" ; X      16,032  ◄── Field width is 6 since comma takes up a space
140        PRINT USING "##,###" ; Y         478  ◄── A leading comma is not printed
998 REM
999        END
```

## Printing Numeric Values with a Dollar Sign

To print the currency symbol in the output, the dollar sign($) format symbol is placed in the format field. There are two ways the $ symbol can be used: in either a fixed position or a floating position. When the format field begins with two dollars signs ($$), the $ sign is printed to the immediate left of the number. This is often called a floating dollar sign. If the format field begins with a single dollar sign ($), then the $ sign is printed in the exact position found in the format field. This is sometimes called a fixed dollar sign.

**E X A M P L E   D . 4**   Numeric Values with a Dollar Sign

| Program | Output | Comments |
|---|---|---|

```
100 REM    Numeric values with $
105 REM
110        LET X = 6.03
120        LET Y = .57
130        LET Z = 4327.52
135 REM
140        PRINT USING "$###.##"; X      $  6.03  ◄──── Fixed dollar sign
150        PRINT USING "$$##.##"; X         $6.03  ◄──── Floating dollar sign
160        PRINT USING "$$##.##"; Y         $0.57  ◄──── Floating dollar sign. Note zero before decimal point
170        PRINT USING "$$##.##"; Z      %$4327.52 ◄──── Field width is not large enough
998 REM
999        END
```

## Printing Numeric Values with Asterisks

Two asterisks placed at the beginning of a format field result in the replacement of leading spaces with asterisks. The asterisk symbol is often used to protect a field amount from being tampered with. For this reason, the asterisk is called a check protection symbol in check writing applications, as the following example illustrates.

**E X A M P L E   D . 5**    **Numeric Values with Asterisks**

| Program | Output | Comments |
|---|---|---|

```
100 REM   Numeric values with *s
105 REM
110       LET X = 5.57
115 REM
120       PRINT USING "$#####.##" ; X    $    5.57    ◄──── This number could be tampered with by inserting, say, 9999 just before the 5
130       PRINT USING "$**###.##" ; X    $****5.57    ◄──── Asterisks make it difficult to change the number
140       PRINT USING "$**,###.##"; X    $*****5.57   ◄──── Position for comma replaced with asterisk
998 REM
999       END
```

## Printing Numeric Values in Exponential Form

The output of very large or small numbers can be printed in exponential (scientific) form. For example, the value 9100000 can be expressed in E-notation as $9.1E+06$. Exponential notation is indicated by supplying four carat symbols ($^^^$) after the digit positions are specified. The system fits as much of the number as it can within the numeric format field and determines the appropriate exponent, as the following example illustrates.

**E X A M P L E   D . 6**    **Numeric Values in Exponential Form**

| Program | Output | Comments |
|---|---|---|

```
100 REM   Numeric values in E form
105 REM
110       LET X = 12345
115 REM
120       PRINT USING "#.##^^^^"  ; X    0.12E+05
130       PRINT USING "#.#####^^^^"; X   0.12345E+05
140       PRINT USING "##.##^^^^"  ; X   1.23E+04
998 REM
999       END
```

Note the variations on what precedes the decimal point, the number of digits printed to the right of the decimal point, and the system's adjustment of the exponent

## Printing String Variables

Data stored in string variables can be output with a string field. A pair of backslash (\) symbols are used to specify the beginning and end of the string format field. Blank spaces are included between the backslashes to determine the width of the field.

**E X A M P L E   D . 7**   String Variables

| Program | Output | Comments |
|---|---|---|

```
100 REM   String variables
105 REM
110       LET N$ = "HELP"
115 REM        ──────
120       PRINT USING "\    \"; N$      HELP ◄────────── Field width is 6. Value printed in columns 1–4 (see note 2).
130       PRINT USING "\  \" ; N$      HELP ◄────────── Field width is 4. Value printed in columns 1–4.
140       PRINT USING "\ \" ; N$      HEL ◄──────────── Field width is 3. Lose rightmost character (see note 3).
998 REM
999       END
```

Consider the following points concerning the backslash (\) symbol.

1. The two backslashes define the beginning and end of the string format field. If *n* spaces appear between the two backslashes, then the field width is *n* + 2. In our example, field widths of 6, 4, and 3 were used.

2. When the number of characters in the string value is fewer than the field width, then the characters are printed left-justified in the field, and the remaining positions are filled with blanks. See line 120 in Example D.7.

3. When the number of characters in the string value is greater than the field width, then the rightmost characters are truncated. See line 140 in Example D.7.

## Printing String Constants (Literals)

Messages, titles, and labeled output can also be printed with the PRINT USING statement. A **literal format field** is a set of characters other than format characters that is to be printed exactly (literally) as it appears in the format string. The following example illustrates the labeling of output with literal fields.

**E X A M P L E   D . 8**   String Constants (Literals)

| Program | Output | Comments |
|---|---|---|

```
100 REM   Literal fields
105 REM
110       LET FMT1$ = "REVENUES:   $###.##"      Note how each format string has a literal field that
120       LET FMT2$ = "COSTS    :  $###.##"      labels the numeric field to its right. Also note how
130       LET FMT3$ = "PROFITS  :  $###.##"      format strings are stored within the string variables
135 REM                                          FMT1$, FMT2$, and FMT3$ in lines 110–130. These string
140       READ REVENUE,COST                      variables are then referenced in lines 170–190.
150          DATA 40.05,45.20
155 REM
160       LET PROFIT = REVENUE - COST
165 REM
170       PRINT USING FMT1$; REVENUE      REVENUES:   $ 40.05
180       PRINT USING FMT2$; COST         COSTS    :  $ 45.20
190       PRINT USING FMT3$; PROFIT       PROFITS  :  $ -5.15
998 REM
999       END
```

The following points are illustrated in Example D.8.

1. Each format string is stored in a special string variable which is referenced by the appropriate PRINT USING statement. For example, the string variable FMT1$ stores the first format string in line 110. Then this variable is used in line 170 to print the revenue. Note that the format string in line 110 contains two fields: the literal field REVENUES: and the numeric field $###.##.

2. All format strings are placed in a group to facilitate the alignment of output. (See lines 110–130.)

3. All format strings are placed at the beginning of the program to get them visually out of the way of the execution logic.

---

## Follow-Up Exercises

1. Indicate the output if

   X stores 4645.8184
   Y stores    3.2

   a. PRINT USING "####.#"          ; X
   b. PRINT USING "#,###.##"         ; X
   c. PRINT USING "#,###.##"         ; Y
   d. PRINT USING "$$,###.##"        ; Y
   e. PRINT USING "$**,###.##"       ; Y
   f. PRINT USING "**$,###.##"       ; Y
   g. PRINT USING "#.##^^^^"         ; X
   h. PRINT USING "###    #####"   ; X
   i. PRINT USING "###    #####"   ; Y,X
   j. PRINT USING "#######"          ; Y,X

   Try these on your system.

2. Assume 500 is stored in B and 25.75 in C. Indicate the PRINT USING statements necessary to output the following:

   ```
   Column
        1 2 3 4 5 6 7 8 9
   a.                 5 0 0
   b.  B =      5 0 0
   c.  5 0 0    2 5 . 7 5
   ```

3. Assume 3.283 is stored in X. Write code and make the following successive changes to output X right-justified in column 8. First output X to zero decimal places without printing a decimal point; then output X to zero decimal places printing the decimal point; then to one decimal place; then to three decimal places; and finally to five decimal places.

4. Assume "GOOFUS" is stored in A$. Develop PRINT USING statements that output GOOFUS, GOOF, and GO, beginning in output column 5.

5. Assume the following values are stored:

   ```
   X                Y               Z$
           -50              15.32           INCHES
   ```

   Given the following format strings:

   ```
                               ┌── Two spaces
   LET FMT1$ = "###   ##.#"
                         ┌── One space
   LET FMT2$ = "Number = ####"
       One space ──────────┘
   LET FMT3$ = "###.###  \          \"
       Field width = 10
       Field width = 8
   LET FMT4$ = " \        \ \        \"
       One space ──┘                Field width = 10
   ```
   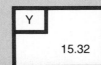
   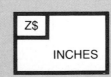

Indicate the exact output for each of the following:
a. PRINT USING FMT1$; X,Y
b. PRINT USING FMT2$; X
c. PRINT USING FMT3$; Y,Z$
d. PRINT USING FMT4$; "scale in",Z$
e. PRINT USING FMT3$; Z$,Y

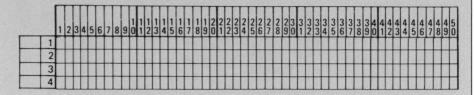

**6.** Specify PRINT USING and format strings as string variables to output.

a. The integer values of the variables *A* and *B* and the real value of *C* in scientific notation. The value of *A* ranges from 0 to 9999, the value of *B* ranges from $-100$ to 999, and the value of *C* ranges from $-1.00$ to $9.99 \times 10^{35}$.

b. The label and the value of the variable *B*, whose value ranges from 0.00 to 999.99.

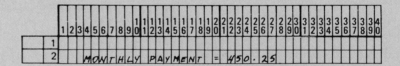

c. The heading

d. The column headings and the values of variables N$ (14 characters or less), S$ (11 characters), R (positive real numbers less than 10 to two decimal places with dollar sign), and P (positive real numbers less than 1000 to two decimal places with floating dollar sign).

| | 1 | EMPLOYEE | SOCIAL | | PAY | | |
| | 2 | NAME | SEC. NO. | | RATE | | GROSS PAY |
| | 3 | | | | | | |
| | 4 | SMITH ADAM | 199-31-0716 | | $5.72 | | $275.23 |

*7. Run Examples D.1 through D.8 on your system. Any differences in the output?

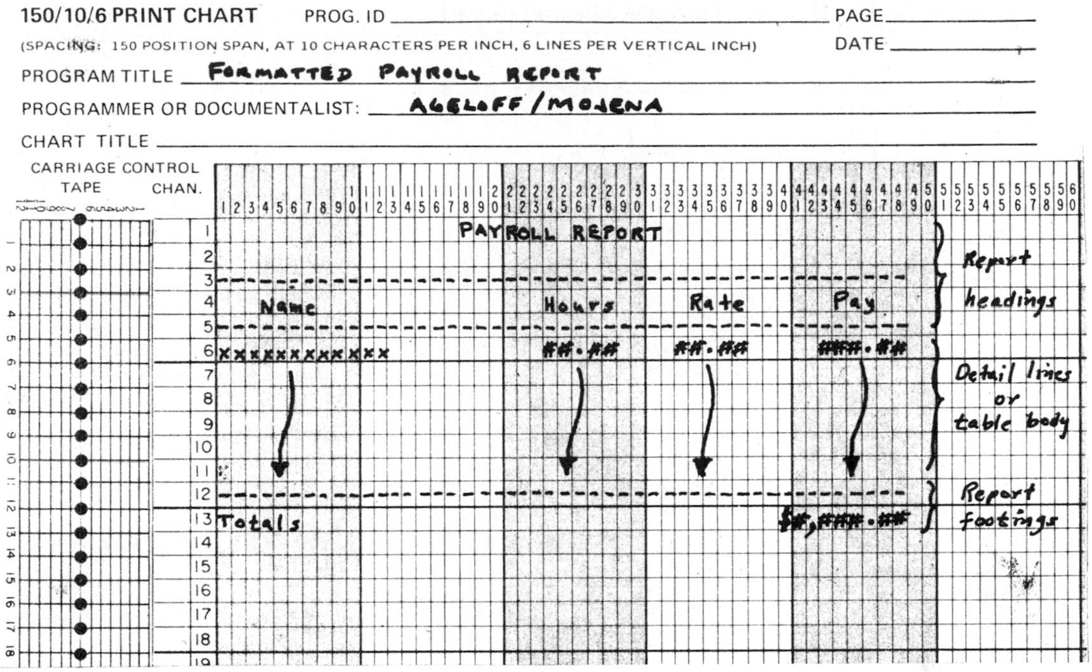

**Figure D.1**   Print Chart for Payroll Report Layout.

# D.3 BUILDING A COMPLETE REPORT

The real value of the PRINT USING statement becomes evident when we format an entire report. To illustrate this point, let's consider a payroll program that calculates gross pay and prints the employee name, hours worked, rate of pay, and gross pay.

Before we encode format strings for a report, it's best to design the actual layout of the report on a sheet of paper. Ideally, the paper should have column and row markings, such as quadrille paper or special computer forms called print charts.

A sample payroll report layout is illustrated by the print chart in Fig. D.1. In the report layout, report headings such as titles and column labels are aligned above the detail lines that appear within the body of the output table. Numeric values using the # symbol (including any decimal points) and string values using the x (or some other) symbol are placed exactly where they would appear on the printed line. Spacing between fields is designated by blank spaces on the layout sheet. Finally, the report footing, or ending, is designated by appropriate labels and field values.

The following program demonstrates the use of PRINT USING statements for building the formatted report described in Fig. D.1.

**E X A M P L E   D . 9**   Formatted Payroll Report

```
100 REM   Formatted payroll report                              | Format strings
110 REM
120       LET FMT1$ = "                    \            \                    "
130       LET FMT2$ = "\                                              \"
140       LET FMT3$ = "    \    \              \    \      \    \      \   \  "
150       LET FMT4$ = "\              \        ##.##    ##.##      ###.##"
160       LET FMT5$ = "Totals                                    $#,###.##"
170 REM
180       PRINT USING FMT1$; "PAYROLL REPORT "
185       PRINT
190       PRINT USING FMT2$; "----------------------------------------------------"
200       PRINT USING FMT3$; "Name","Hours","Rate","Pay"
210       PRINT USING FMT2$; "----------------------------------------------------"
220 REM
230       READ N                                          | Prints report headings.
240       FOR J = 1 TO N
250         READ FULL.NAME$,HOURS,RATE
260         LET PAY   = HOURS * RATE
270         LET TOTAL = TOTAL + PAY
280         PRINT USING FMT4$; FULL.NAME$,HOURS,RATE,PAY  <---- Prints body of table
290       NEXT J
300 REM
310       PRINT USING FMT2$; "----------------------------------------------------"
320       PRINT USING FMT5$; TOTAL
330 REM
900       DATA 6
901       DATA Phil Murray,15,6.35                        | Prints report footings
902       DATA Hilda Snark,30.25,5.85
903       DATA Margo Barker,32,6.80
904       DATA Ralph Kiner,20.75,6.25
905       DATA Mark Fargo,35,6
906       DATA Anna AlDente,38,7.78
998 REM
999       END
```

```
RUN
                      PAYROLL REPORT

    -------------------------------------------------
      Name            Hours     Rate      Pay
    -------------------------------------------------
    Phil Murray       15.00     6.35       95.25
    Hilda Snark       30.25     5.85      176.96
    Margo Barker      32.00     6.80      217.60
    Ralph Kiner       20.75     6.25      129.69
    Mark Fargo        35.00     6.00      210.00
    Anna AlDente      38.00     7.78      295.64
    -------------------------------------------------
    Totals                              $1,125.14
```

Let's note the following points.

1.  The format strings are stored within special string variables and grouped together in lines 120–160. This design is consistent with the print chart in Fig. D.1.

2.  The same format string can be referenced more than once. See lines 190, 210, and 310.

### Follow-Up Exercises

**8.** Make the following changes in Example D.9.
   **a.** Insert two dashed lines (equal sign) after the totals line is printed.
   **b.** Use floating dollar signs in the Rate and Pay columns.
   **c.** Allow up to 20 characters in an employee's name, without affecting the positions of the other fields.

**\*9.** Implement Example D.9 on your system. Try making improvements in the (almost perfect!) output design.

**\*10.** The actual report headings in Example D.9 are included within the PRINT USING statements in lines 180–210. It would be easier to code these as literals within the format strings. Agree? For example, the dashed lines would not have to be repeated twice, and the labels *Name, Hours, Rate,* and *Pay* would not have to be enclosed in quotes or separated by commas. Try the following on your system.
   **a.** Incorporate as literal fields the title within FMT1$, the dashes within FMT2$, and the column labels within FMT3$. Don't use backslashes. The PRINT USING statements in lines 180–210 now don't have an output list. *Does this work on your system?*
   **b.** Use IMAGE statements (if available) that directly incorporate the title, dashes, and column labels as literal fields.

## D.4 POINTERS

### Design and Style

1. **Report design.**    Use a sheet of paper or (preferably) print chart to design the output report. This report layout facilitates the coding of format strings.

2. **Format strings within string variables.**    For output other than simple output, use string variables to store format strings rather than including the format strings in **PRINT USING** statements. Place these format strings together at the beginning or end of the program, as done in Examples D.8 and D.9. The use and grouping of these special string variables aid in the alignment of output and make programs more readable.

### Common Errors

1. **Unaligned or unintended output.**    This logic error is often the result of spending insufficient time in designing output reports. Use a report layout to design the output and then encode the format strings according to this design.

2. **Field overflow.**    Make sure field widths are sufficiently large to handle the output data. If the width of the format field is not large enough for a numeric field to print properly, then the system usually widens the field to accommodate the value and prints a leading % sign. *Is this the way your system handles field overflow?* (See Example D.1. on page 388.) Field overflow for *string* fields results in a truncated string value. (See Note 3 on page 392.)

3. **Format string inconsistencies.**    We may get unintended output results if the number of items in an output list is different from the number of numeric and string fields in a format string. For example, see notes 5 and 6 on page 389. Another potential error is type mismatch between the items

in the output list and the fields in the format string, as the following illustrates on an IBM PC.

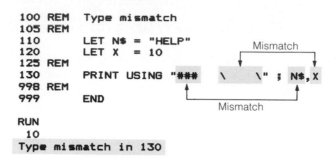

```
100 REM    Type mismatch
105 REM
110        LET N$ = "HELP"
120        LET X  = 10
125 REM
130        PRINT USING "###    \     \" ; N$,X
998 REM
999        END

RUN
 10
Type mismatch in 130
```

```
130        PRINT USING "###    \      \" ; X,N$

RUN
 10    HELP
```

Here we tried to output the string variable N$ using the numeric field ###, and the numeric variable X using the string field \      \. The system ignored the type mismatch N$ with ###, printed the value 10 in X using the numeric field, and then printed the error message. We then got the right result after correcting the error. *How does your system handle type mismatch?*

## Follow-up Exercise

**\*11.**   Implement the type mismatch example on your system.

---

## ADDITIONAL EXERCISES

12.  Apply PRINT USING statements to a previously written program. Try improving your earlier output design.

13.  Define or explain each of the following terms:

formatted output              format string                   numeric format field
PRINT USING statement         format fields or format items   string format field
IMAGE statement               format characters or format symbols   literal format field

# External Data Files and Transaction Processing

# E*

Many applications, particularly those with large amounts of data, require the processing of data files that reside within secondary storage media. For example, customer files are typically carried on either magnetic tape or magnetic disk in mainframe and minicomputer environments, and within either diskettes or hard disks in microcomputer environments. This module motivates and illustrates the storage of data within external media.

## E.1 MOTIVATION

Until now we have entered data into storage locations in three ways.

1. **LET statements.** This approach works for data that change infrequently from run to run (parameters); however, it's far too inefficient for large amounts of data, it's cumbersome to change values when necessary, it does not make the data available to other programs, and it's inappropriate for data values that change during a computer run.

2. **INPUT statements.** This approach is needed for entering choices and data values interactively, but it's inefficient for large amounts of data.

---

*This module can be covered anytime after Chapter 5.

Moreover, the data have to be reentered if they are needed by another program.

3. **READ/DATA statements.** This approach is good for storing parameters and data values that change during a computer run (especially the *internal data files* described in Chapter 3). For large internal data files, however, the maintenance of data (changing, adding, or deleting lines) is tedious. Also, it's cumbersome to merge or append the internal data file should another program require the same data.

An **external data file** stores data within a secondary storage medium such as magnetic disk, diskette, or magnetic tape. External data files are uniquely referenced by names (as are the program files we have been working with), which means that programs can either place data in the files or retrieve data from them for processing and viewing.

The advantages of external data files include the following.

1. **Cheaper maintenance.** The task of adding, deleting, or changing records (lines of data within the data file) in large files is less costly than for the three storage approaches discussed above.

2. **Multiprogram access.** A file is easily accessible by different programs that require its data. For example, an employee file might be processed weekly by a payroll program and daily by a personnel query program. The savings in storage and maintenance costs by avoiding use of identical multiple files are obvious.

3. **Multifile access.** A program can process more than one file within a computer run. For example, a bank checking-statement program might process the following three files: a file that contains monthly transactions such as deposits, cleared checks, and withdrawals; a file that shows customer data such as name, address, and last month's balance; and a file that updates the customer's account with the new balance. Try doing this with an internal data file!

4. **Output storage.** Programs can store the results of processing within an external data file that is subsequently used by the same or other programs. For example, a sales program might output a monthly sales report to a data file. At a later time the report can be viewed on a screen or printed. Moreover, the same report file might be processed by another specialized program that prints graphs on color slides for a sales presentation. These procedures were not possible with our earlier data storage methods.

Before going on to the next section, let's take a look at two very simple programs that use the same external data file.

**E X A M P L E   E . 1**    **Creating and Viewing a Simple Grade File**

Suppose we wish to store the exam scores 90, 75, 85, 95, and 70 within an external data file called "grades" for later viewing. Table E.1 shows two typical programs for these purposes. (Your instructor will provide the necessary changes if your system's implementation differs.) The programs and their brief explanations should give you a good idea of the following fundamental steps for using external data files:

1. **Open the data file.** This step uses the OPEN statement to tell the operating system the name of the file, its intended use (we plan either to output *to* the file or input *from* the file), and relates the *file name* ("grades" in our example) to a *file*

**Table E.1**  Creation/Display of Grade File (Example E.1)

| Implementation | Program/Execution | Comments |
|---|---|---|
| **IBM PC**<br>**VAX-11** | *File creation program:* | This program takes the number of grades and the five grades within the internal data file in lines 90–95 and places them within the external data file called "grades." File "grades" resides within the diskette in drive A (IBM PC) or within your private library (VAX-11). The OPEN statement ties in the file name "grades" to the file #1 and opens the file for output (since we plan to output data from primary memory storage locations to the external file). The PRINT # statement is used to output data to file #1 (i.e., file grades). The CLOSE statement completes the process by closing the file. |

```
10        OPEN "grades" FOR OUTPUT AS #1
15 REM
20        READ N
25        PRINT #1, N
30 REM
35        FOR J = 1 TO N
40          READ SCORE
45          PRINT #1, SCORE
50        NEXT J
55 REM
60        CLOSE #1
65 REM
70        PRINT "File grades has been created"
75 REM
90        DATA 5
95        DATA 90,75,85,95,70
98 REM
99        END


RUN
File grades has been created
```

*File display program:*

This program accesses the grades within the file named "grades" and displays them on the screen. Note that line 10 now opens this file as an input file; i.e., we plan to input the data into primary memory from the external file. The INPUT # statement is used for this purpose.

```
10        OPEN "grades" FOR INPUT AS #1
15 REM
20        PRINT "Scores: ";
25 REM
30        INPUT #1, N
35        FOR J = 1 TO N
40          INPUT #1, SCORE
45          PRINT SCORE;
50        NEXT J
55 REM
60        CLOSE #1
65 REM
70        PRINT
75        PRINT "File grades has been displayed"
98 REM
99        END


RUN
Scores:  90  75  85  95  70
File grades has been displayed
```

Your system
(if different)

*number* (#1 in our example) for subsequent use within the PRINT # and INPUT # statements.

2. **Output to the file or input from the file.**    In the first program, the PRINT # statement is used to output the number of scores and the individual scores to the file. In the second program, the INPUT # statement is used to retrieve the same data for viewing on the screen.

3. **Close the data file when finished.**    This step uses the CLOSE statement.

At this time, don't worry about the details of using the OPEN, PRINT #, INPUT #, and CLOSE statements. We shall discuss these shortly. For now, all you need to understand is that we have placed data on an external file called "grades" with one program and subsequently have viewed that file with another program. And both tasks were accomplished by the same three fundamental steps.

---

### Follow-Up Exercises

1. Try running the two programs in Table E.1 on your system.
2. Change the two programs in Table E.1 as follows:
   a. Use the file name mgs207.
   b. Use file #3. Do you think we could use #1 in the first program and #3 in the second program?
   c. Store the two additional scores 65 and 95.

## E.2 FIELDS, RECORDS, AND FILES

There are many variations on the uses and types of external files. This section covers the necessary foundation material for our work with external files.

### Some Definitions

Let's review some definitions from our work with internal data files.

**Field.**    A fact or attribute (data item) about some entity such as a person, place, thing, or event. For example, an employer might maintain data on employees' attributes such as name, identification number, salary, and sex. Each of these attributes is considered a field. The variables that appear within the lists of input and output statements are used to process fields; i.e., each variable in the list corresponds to a field.

**Record.**    A group of related fields, retrievable as a unit. For example, all of the data items relating to one employee are a record. Typically, the execution of a file input or output statement processes a single record. The fields that make up a record are usually described by a **record layout**. For example, the record layout for an employee record might appear as follows.

Record Layout for Employee Record

| Field | Type | Length (Bytes) |
|-------|------|----------------|
| Full name | String | 20 |
| ID number | Numeric | 4 |
| Salary | Numeric | 4 |
| Sex | String | 1 |

**File.** A collection of related records. Each record is a logical part of the file, because it contains the same data items (fields, not data values) as all the other records in the file. For example, an *employee file* contains all employee records.

Figure E.1 illustrates this relationship among fields, records, and a file. This file contains three records, and each record contains four fields.

**Internal and External Files.** An **internal file** is a collection of records stored within the program's DATA statements. Chapters 3–9 use this type of data file.

An **external file** is a collection of records stored on a medium external to primary memory. For example, files stored on an I/O medium such as magnetic tape (reel or cassette) or magnetic disk (hard or floppy) are called external files. The typical storage medium within BASIC environments is magnetic disk. For example, diskettes ("floppies") are used in microcomputers; hard disks are used in minicomputers. In the latter case, we usually don't see the hard disk since it resides at the computer center; however, we have used it all along to store program files (and soon data files) within our library.

**Unformatted and Formatted Files.** An **unformatted record** does not explicitly specify field lengths, whereas a **formatted record** indicates the number of bytes to be used by each field. The record layout illustrated above shows a formatted record. An **unformatted file** uses unformatted records, whereas a **formatted file** is made up of formatted records. We shall illustrate both of these approaches shortly.

**ASCII and Binary Files.** An **ASCII file** stores data according to the ASCII coding scheme first discussed on page 112. A **binary file** stores data directly in machine form as bits. Binary files are processed more rapidly because the computer does not need to convert data from ASCII form to binary form during input operations, or from binary to ASCII during output operations.

| | | Fields | | |
|---|---|---|---|---|
| | | Name | Employee ID | Salary | Sex |
| | Record 1 | Abatar Jane A. | 1 | 20000 | f |
| File | Record 2 | Bomberg Bo B. | 3 | 15800 | m |
| | Record 3 | Drury David D. | 6 | 18000 | m |

**Figure E.1** Relationship among fields, records, and file.

Binary files, however, are processor-dependent. Thus, if a particular file is likely to be used or transmitted from one computer to another, it's best to store it as an ASCII file. We shall focus on ASCII files in this text.

**Sequential and Relative Files.**      The records in a **sequential file** are processed only sequentially; that is, the records cannot be processed any way except in the order of storage, one after the other. For example, if a sequential personnel file contains 1000 records (employees), then sequential processing means that we can process the 900th record if and only if we first process the first 899 records.

A record in a **relative file** (also called **random file** or **direct access file**) can be processed (input or written) without the need to process any other record in the file. For example, in a 1000-record relative file, we can directly input the 900th record without having to input the preceding 899 records.

Figure E.2 conceptually illustrates sequential and relative files for our personnel illustration. In part (a), note that sequential files always terminate with an **end-of-file (eof)** mark. This signals the processor that the physical end of the file has been reached. In part (b), note that records in a relative file are numbered 1 to 6. These **record numbers** uniquely identify records for storage and retrieval. Also note that a record location either stores a record or is empty. For example, a relative employee file with 1000 record locations (numbered 1–1000) and 850 employees would contain 150 empty records.

Sequential files can be stored on media such as magnetic tape and disk, but relative files can be stored only within a direct access medium such as magnetic disk (but not a sequential medium such as tape). The "grades" file used in Example E.1 illustrates a sequential file with six records on a magnetic disk medium, as conceptually shown in Figure E.3. Note that the exe-

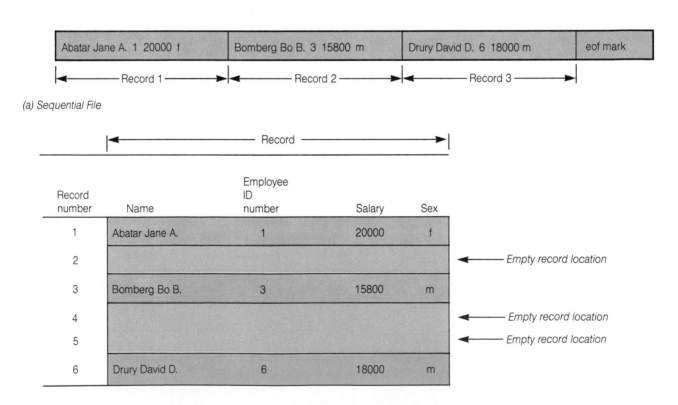

(a) Sequential File

(b) Relative File

**Figure E.2**   Conceptual representation of sequential and relative files.

cution of each PRINT # statement within the first program in Table E.1 places a carriage return or <cr> mark after each data item, which effectively terminates a record. In other words, each PRINT # statement generates a single record by placing a <cr> mark on the disk.

## Follow-Up Exercises

**3.** Briefly describe the possible makeup of a student grade file for a large (say, 500 students) academic course. What kind of storage medium might be used? Suppose this file is to be used by a menu-driven interactive query program to answer questions such as "What are the current grades for Bob Meyer?" Which type of file would be best, sequential or relative? Suppose the application is a program that calculates and assigns final grades and prints a report at the end of each term. Which file type might be best?

**4.** Suppose we have to add the following record to the employee file:

Clark   G.W.   2   24000   m

From the standpoint of processing efficiency, which file type do you think would be easier to update, sequential or relative? (Use Figure E.2 to help you.)

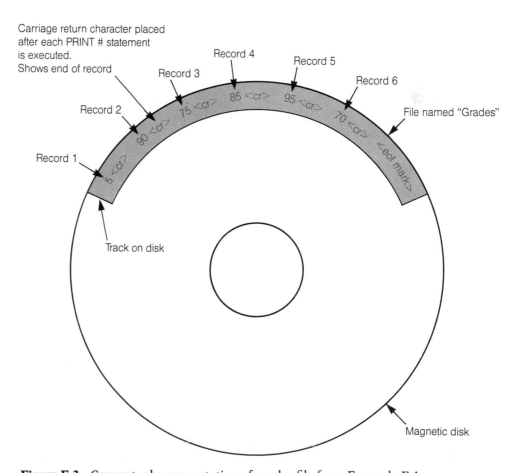

**Figure E.3** Conceptual representation of grades file from Example E.1.

## E.3 SEQUENTIAL FILES

We now turn to the details of processing sequential files. As indicated earlier in Example E.1, the general operations for processing sequential files include the following: opening, output to or input from, and closing the file. Additionally, there are some specialized operations.

Not surprisingly, the statements for accomplishing these operations vary from system to system. We shall focus on the IBM PC (Microsoft) and VAX-11 implementations, with emphasis on the former. If your system is not illustrated, then you should focus on the general principles of file processing as discussed in the text and illustrated in the examples. Then make any necessary changes within the tables and examples according to your system's manual or your instructor.

### Opening a File

A program must first inform the computer that a certain external data file is to be used in a particular manner. The **OPEN statement** is typically used to communicate the following information:

1. The sequential data file to be processed is identified by name.
2. One of the following purposes is indicated: write (output) records to the file, append records at the end of the file, or read (input) records from the file.
3. A file number is indicated for subsequent use by other file-related statements like PRINT # and INPUT #.
4. The system sets the file pointer to either the beginning of the file (if the purpose is input or output) or the end of the file (if the purpose is to append new records).

The OPEN statement and some examples are illustrated in Table E.2. Study this table and make any necessary changes for your system.

**NOTE 1** The OPEN statement must precede any other statements in the program that use the file.

**NOTE 2** If more than one file is open at once, make sure that the same file number is not assigned to more than one file.

**NOTE 3** Opening a file for input implies that we want to read from an *existing* file; opening a file for output implies that we want to *create* a new file; opening a file for append implies that we want to add, or append, new records to an existing file.

**WARNING** If a file is opened for output, and it already exists, then its previous contents are deleted. If we had really meant to open for input but instead opened for output, then we have inadvertently erased an existing file.

### Output to a File

The creation of a file implies that we wish to output or print data to the file. Up to now we have used either the PRINT or the PRINT USING statement to output data to a screen. Similarly, we can use either a PRINT # or a PRINT # USING statement to output data to a sequential file. A third approach, the WRITE # statement, is also available on some systems. The first program in Example E.1 on page 401 illustrates the creation of a complete sequential file

**Table E.2**  Opening a Sequential File

| Implementation | Statement Syntax | Examples |
|---|---|---|

IBM PC

*Version 1:*

**OPEN** *filespec* **FOR** *mode* **AS** *#filenum*

where

*filespec* is the following file specification

*device:filename*

such as B:F$ or "grades"

where
*device* indicates where to look for the file

such as A for disk drive A
          B for disk drive B

*Note:* Drive A is assumed if "device:" is omitted.

*filename* is the name of the file to look for on that particular device. Filename can be either a string constant such as "grades" or "employee.dat" or a string variable such as F$ or FILE.NAME$ whose value must conform to the following:

*name.extension*

where

*name* is 1 to 8 characters
*extension* is 1 to 3 characters

*Note:*  Extensions are useful to distinguish among different types of files. The following file name extensions are common:
   name.DAT  ← To distinguish data files from BASIC program files that often have the .BAS extension
   name.BAK  ← To indicate a backup file

*mode* is one of the following

*OUTPUT*  to output data onto the file
*INPUT*  to input data from the file
*APPEND*  to position the file pointer at the end of the file

Examples:

1. OPEN "grades" FOR OUTPUT AS #1

2. OPEN "GRADES" FOR INPUT AS #1
      ← Identical

3. OPEN "A:GRADES" FOR INPUT AS #1

4. OPEN FILE.NAME$ FOR OUTPUT AS #1
      ← Identical if FILE.NAME$ stores employee

5. OPEN "employee" FOR OUTPUT AS #1

6. OPEN F$ FOR INPUT AS #3
      ← Identical if F$ stores B:SALES.DAT

7. OPEN "B:SALES.DAT" FOR INPUT AS #3
      The # symbol is optional →

8. OPEN "B:SALES.DAT" FOR INPUT AS 3
      Identical if N stores 2 →

9. OPEN "B:SALES.DAT" FOR INPUT AS N+1

10. OPEN FOLDER$ FOR APPEND AS #1

*filenum* is an integer expression whose value is 1 to 3.
This value is used to associate the file number with the filespec, so that PRINT #, WRITE #, PRINT # USING, INPUT #, and CLOSE statements can use the file number in place of the file specification.

*Version 2:*

**OPEN** *mode2*, #*filenum,filespec*

where

    *mode2* is one of the following string constants

        *"O"*  to output data onto the file
        *"I"*  to input data from the file

    *filenum* is defined above

    *filespec* is defined above

11. OPEN "I",#1,"GRADES"

12. OPEN "O",#1,FILE.NAME$

13. OPEN "I",#3,F$

VAX-11      The same as version 1 for the IBM PC in its most simple form, except for the following:

1. The "device:" portion within the filespec is omitted.
2. APPEND is handled as an access clause rather than a mode. Thus, the tenth example above would be rewritten as

10. OPEN FOLDER$ FOR OUTPUT AS #1,ACCESS APPEND

The complete form is rather involved, as it includes various file type, record, security, and other parameters. See the **VAX-11 BASIC USER'S GUIDE** (if you dare).

Your system
(if different)

using the PRINT # statement. Take a look at this program once more to get the overall picture.

     The syntax and examples of the PRINT #, PRINT # USING, and WRITE # statements are shown in Table E.3. Study these, make any necessary modifications for your system, and be aware of the following notes.

**NOTE 1**      The first use of a PRINT #, WRITE #, or PRINT # USING statement must be preceded by an OPEN statement that opens the file for *output*.

**NOTE 2**      The file number used in the output statement must correspond to the file number used in the OPEN statement. For example, if #2 is used in the OPEN statement, then #2 must be used in the PRINT # or related statement.

**Table E.3** Output to a Sequential File

| Implementation | Statement Syntax | Examples |
|---|---|---|
| IBM PC | **PRINT** #*filenum, list* | |

**PRINT** #*filenum, list*

where
    *filenum* is the corresponding fiie number used in the **OPEN** statement
    *list* is the list of numeric and/or string expressions whose values will be written to the file. As usual, items in the list are separated by commas and/or semicolons.

*Note 1:* This statement writes a record image to the data file just as it would be displayed on the screen with a PRINT statement. Thus, it's best to use semicolon rather than comma delimiters in the list of items, so as to avoid unnecessary blank spaces between data values in the file.

*Note 2:* Items in a record within the file must be separated or *delimited* by at least one blank space or comma. For this reason, it's necessary to place a comma after the output of a string value by printing the string constant ",". This is not necessary for numeric values since these are printed with trailing spaces. Remember that items within the file must be delimited properly for successful processing by the INPUT # statement. A carriage return/line feed mark (which we show as <cr>) is placed on the file following the last item in the list, which effectively terminates a record. See Examples 1–4 to the right.

**Examples**

1. PRINT #1, SCORE

This places the record

    ƀ90ƀ<cr>

on file #1 when SCORE stores 90 in primary memory. (ƀ is our way of showing a blank space.)

2. PRINT #2, X;Y;Z

This places the record

    ƀ5ƀ–10ƀƀ15ƀ<cr>

on file #2 when X,Y,Z store 5,–10,15. Note the trailing space after the 5, which serves to delimit the 5 from the –10 on input. The two spaces between –10 and 15 are due to the trailing space for –10 and the suppressed + sign for +15.

3. PRINT #1, A$;",";B$

This places the record

    Captain,Kirk<cr>

on file #1 when A$ and B$ store Captain and Kirk. Note the need for "," to delimit the two values in the file; otherwise, they would appear as the one value.

    CaptainKirk<cr>

which could not be input as two separate string values.

4. PRINT A$;",";B$;",";Y;X

This places the record

    Captain,Kirk,–10ƀƀ5ƀ<cr>

on file #1. *Note the need to place a comma after each string value* Captain and Kirk. A comma could be used to delimit $-10$ from 5, but the trailing space following the numeric value $-10$ makes this unnecessary.

**WRITE** #*filenum, list*

where
*filenum* and *list* are defined above.

*Note:* This statement is more convenient to use than the **PRINT #** statement because it automatically inserts commas between data items in the file. It also encloses string values within quotation marks and eliminates spaces around numeric values. The visual look of records done by this method is the same as the usual way we prepare records within **DATA** statements. See Examples 5–8 to the right.

5. WRITE #1, SCORE

This places the record

90<cr>

on file #1. Compare with Example 1 above.

6. WRITE #2, X,Y,Z

This places the record

5, $-10$,15<cr>

on file #2. Compare with Example 2.

7. WRITE #1, A$,B$

This places the record

"Captain","Kirk"<cr>

on file #1. Compare with Example 3.

8. WRITE #1, A$,B$,Y,X

This places the record

"Captain","Kirk", $-10$,5<cr>

on file #1. Compare with Example 4.

**PRINT** #*filenum,* **USING** *image string; list*

where
*filenum* and *list* are defined above
*image string* is the string expression that contains the special formatting characters (as described in Module D)

*Note:* This statement is used to explicitly format records within the file. See Module D for formatting details and Examples 9 and 10 to the right.

9. PRINT #1, USING"###.##",";R;S

This places the record

ƀ10.35, $-15.50$,<cr>

on file #1 when R and S store 10.35 and $-15.50$. Note how the comma within the image string acts as an explicit delimiter between items in the record.

10. LET IS$ = "Average cost is $###.##"
    PRINT #2, USING IS$; C

This places the record

Average cost is $125.55<cr>

on file #2 when C stores 125.548.

VAX-11    This is the same as the **IBM PC** except for the following.

1. The WRITE # statement is not available.
2. A comma instead of a semicolon separates the image string from the list in the PRINT # USING statement.
3. A PUT statement (which we don't cover here) is available for sequential output.

Your system
(if different)

**NOTE 3**   Remember that the field values within records placed on a file must be delimited as if we were entering data values in response to the execution of an INPUT statement. This means that we must make sure that at least one space or a comma follows each field value (except for the carriage return/line feed that follows the last value). Especially, see Examples 7 and 8 in Table E.3.

**NOTE 4**   Sequential files can be created in ways other than the OPEN/PRINT # approach. For example, on the IBM PC we can use any of the following alternatives: The COPY command that's normally used to backup files can be used to copy data from the console (keyboard) to a file specification; the DOS line editor (EDLIN) can be used to create an ASCII file; or a word processor that uses ASCII files can be used. Of these, the last is the most versatile, especially for correcting any mistakes in the file. What's available on your system? (See Exercise 13.)

### Input from a File

In our earlier work we entered data from the keyboard to primary memory by using the INPUT statement, or we entered data from the data block to primary memory by using the READ statement. Similarly, we can read data from a sequential file to primary memory by using either the INPUT # or the LINE INPUT # statement.

The syntax and examples of the INPUT # and LINE INPUT # statements are shown in Table E.4. Study these, make any necessary modifications for your system, and be aware of the following notes.

**NOTE 1**   Do we really need to say this? We can't input from a file that has not been created earlier by one of the methods described in the preceding section.

**NOTE 2**   The first use of an INPUT # or LINE INPUT # statement must be preceded by an OPEN statement that opens the file for input.

**NOTE 3**   The file number used in the input statement must correspond to the file number used in the OPEN statement. For example, if #1 is used in the OPEN statement, then #1 must be used in the INPUT # or related statement.

**NOTE 4**   Each pair of items within the file must be delimited properly by one or more spaces, a comma, or a <cr> mark. In other words, data items within the file must be delimited, just as we need to delimit data items within DATA statements or in responses to INPUT statements. Otherwise, the data items cannot be processed (input) by the INPUT # statement.

**Table E.4** Input from a Sequential File

| Implementation | Statement Syntax | Examples |
|---|---|---|

IBM PC

*Version 1:*

   **INPUT** #*filenum, list*

where
*filenum* is the corresponding file number used in the OPEN statement
*list* is the list of variables whose values are to be input from the file. As usual, variables in the input list are separated by commas.

*Version 2:*

   **LINE INPUT** #*filenum, string variable*

*Note:* This statement reads an entire line (up to the first <cr> or up to 254 characters), without regard for delimiters, from a file to the storage location in primary memory that corresponds to the *string variable*. This is the statement of choice for accessing reports that have been written to sequential files. See Example 10 to the right. This statement also can be used to input an entire record for subsequent viewing; however, it's not an alternative to the INPUT # statement, since it makes no distinctions among fields.

*Note:* These examples correspond to those in Table E.3. Assume the file pointer is at the beginning of each record.

| Record/INPUT # Statement | Contents in Primary Memory |
|---|---|

1.  b90b<cr>
    INPUT #1, SCORE

    SCORE
    90

2.  b5b – 10bb15b<cr>
    INPUT #2, X, Y, Z

    X    Y    Z
    5    – 10    15

3.  Captain,Kirk<cr>
    INPUT #1, A$,B$

    A$    B$
    Captain    Kirk

4.  Captain,Kirk, – 10bb5b<cr>
    INPUT #1, A$,B$,Y,X

    X    Y
    5    – 10

    A$    B$
    Captain    Kirk

5.  b90b<cr>
    INPUT #1, SCORE

    SCORE
    90

6.  5, – 10,15<cr>
    INPUT #2, X,Y,Z
    See also Example 2

    X    Y    Z
    5    – 10    15

7.  "Captain","Kirk"<cr>
    INPUT #1, A$,B$
    See also Example 3

    A$    B$
    Captain    Kirk

8.  "Captain","Kirk", – 10,5<cr>
    INPUT #1, A$,B$,Y,X
    See also Example 4.

    X    Y
    5    – 10

    A$    B$
    Captain    Kirk

9.  b10.35, – 15.50,<cr>
    INPUT #1, R,S

    R    S
    10.35    – 15.50

10. Average cost is $125.55<cr>
    LINE INPUT #2, C$

    C$
    Average cost is $125.55

| VAX-11 | This is the same as the IBM PC except that the LINE INPUT statement becomes the INPUT LINE statement. |

Your system
(if different)

---

**NOTE 5**   As in our earlier understanding of the relationship between READ operations and the data block, the concept of a *pointer* is useful. Whenever a file is opened for input, the file pointer is placed at the first data item in the file. Thereafter, it advances according to the number of variables processed within the input lists of INPUT # statements. For example, if the pointer currently resides at data item 50, and the next INPUT # statement executed has five variables within the input list, then items 50–54 are processed and the pointer ends up at item 55. *Note that each execution of an INPUT # statement reads an entire record from the file.*

**NOTE 6**   As usual we need to make sure that variables within the input list correspond to data items within the file with respect to type and number. Thus, the input of a string variable requires a matching string value within the file; the input of a numeric variable requires a corresponding numeric value within the file; and the total number of individual input operations must not exceed the total number of data items within the file.

## Closing a File

All files that have been opened during the execution of a program should be explicitly closed through a CLOSE statement, for any of the following reasons.

1. If a file is left open, the system may not print the last record to the file.
2. Systems allow a maximum number of files to be opened at one time. If we need new files after reaching this maximum during any computer run, then we must close some files.
3. If a particular file is to be used first as an input file and then as an output file (or vice versa) within the same program, then the file must be closed before it is reopened.

The syntax and examples of the CLOSE statement are shown in Table E.5. Study these, make any necessary modifications for your system, and be aware of the following note.

**NOTE**   The CLOSE statement is often overlooked, because execution of an END statement automatically closes all open files. If execution terminates through a run-time error or a STOP statement, however, then the sequential file may end up missing the last record and an eof mark. So, as a matter of safety (not

**Table E.5** Closing a Sequential File

| Implementation | Statement Syntax | Examples |
|---|---|---|
| IBM PC | **CLOSE** *list of filenums* | CLOSE #1 |
| | *Note:* This statement concludes I/O to a file as follows. | CLOSE #1,#2,#3 |
| | 1. It terminates the association between a named file and its file number (as defined in the OPEN statement). | CLOSE 1,2,3 |
| | 2. It writes any remaining record to the file (from an area of primary memory called the *buffer*). | CLOSE |
| | 3. It places an eof mark at the end of the file. The list of file numbers is optional. If omitted, then all previously opened files are closed. | |
| VAX-11 | This is the same as the IBM PC, except that the list of file numbers is not optional. | |

Your system
(if different)

to mention good programming style), we should explicitly close any opened files when we are finished with them.

## Other File Operations

All systems include special statements and functions for implementing specialized sequential file operations. For example, specific statements, functions, or procedures exist, depending on the system, for detecting end-of-file conditions, rewinding a file, and maintaining a file. Table E.6 illustrates three approaches to testing for an end-of-file (eof) condition. Table E.7 shows procedures for file rewinding, which allows us to reprocess a file from the first record. The examples that follow and Section E.5 illustrate file maintenance procedures.

**Table E.6** Sequential File Eof Procedures

| Implementation | General Procedures | Examples |
| --- | --- | --- |

**IBM PC**

*Procedure 1:* **EOF function**

Open file for input

```
100  OPEN F$ FOR INPUT AS #1
```

WHILE NOT **EOF(filenum)**

```
200  WHILE NOT EOF(1)
210      INPUT #1, A,B,C
```

] Body of loop, including INPUT # statement

WEND

```
300  WEND
```

*Note:* If an eof condition or mark is encountered for the indicated file number, then the EOF function returns a true value. Thus, NOT EOF(filenum) would be false, and exit from the while loop would be achieved.

*Procedure 2:* **ON ERROR statement**

Open file for input

```
100  OPEN F$ FOR INPUT AS #1
110  ON ERROR GOTO 310
```

**ON ERROR GOTO** *line no.*

Body of loop, including INPUT # statement

GO TO line no.

```
210      INPUT #1, A,B,C
```

```
300      GO TO 210
```

IF **ERR = 62** THEN CLOSE filenum ELSE **ON ERROR GOTO 0**

eof error routine

```
310      IF ERR = 62  THEN CLOSE #1
                      ELSE ON ERROR GOTO 0
320  . . .
```

*Note:* The ON ERROR statement traps run-time errors by transferring control to an error routine. Within the error routine, a special system variable called **ERR** is assigned an *error number code* when a run-time error occurs. (See Appendix A in the *IBM PC BASIC User Manual* and note that the error number code for an eof condition is *62*.) Within the while loop, when the program attempts to input past the end of the file, a run-time error is committed and the system assigns a value of 62 to ERR. Control is then transferred to the eof error routine, which closes the file and resumes execution with the first executable statement following the error routine. If the run-time error is other than 62, the ON ERROR GOTO 0 statement is executed, which instructs the system to stop execution and print the error message corresponding to the error that caused the trap. The ON ERROR statement must precede the point where an error might occur. In the example to the right, the ON ERROR statement is in line 110, and the eof condition would occur at line 210. Control is transferred to line 310 as soon as the eof condition is encountered. Procedure 1 is preferable to procedure 2. Right?

*Procedure 3: eof record/sentinel*

Here we assume that the file was created with a special *eof record* that contains a *sentinel*, as first described for eof loops in Chapter 5. In effect, this procedure is the same as our earlier eof-loop procedure that processed internal data files. In the example to the right, loop exit is achieved as soon as variable A stores the sentinel −99. When the file is created the eof record might read as follows:

$$-99,0,0<cr>$$

We recommend the more natural and straightforward procedure 1 over this procedure.

```
100  OPEN F$ FOR INPUT AS #1
       .
       .
       .
190  INPUT #1, A,B,C
200  WHILE A<> −99
       .
       .
       .
290      INPUT #1, A,B,C
300  WEND
```

| VAX-11 | The EOF function procedure is not available |

The ON ERROR statement procedure is the same as the IBM PC, except that the eof condition error code is 11.

The eof condition/sentinel procedure is the same as the IBM PC, except for using NEXT in place of WEND.

Your system
(if different)

**Table E.7**  Rewinding a Sequential File

| Implementation | General Procedure | Example |
|---|---|---|
| IBM PC | Close the file | CLOSE #1 |
| | Reopen the file | OPEN F$ FOR INPUT AS #1 |
| | | or |
| | | OPEN F$ FOR OUTPUT AS #1 |
| | *Note:* Execution of an OPEN statement for either input or output resets the file pointer to the beginning of the file. This is comparable to the execution of a RESTORE statement when working with an internal data file. | |
| VAX-11 | *Procedure 1* | |
| | Same as the IBM PC | |
| | *Procedure 2* | |
| | **RESTORE** #*filenum* | RESTORE #1 |
| | or | |
| | **RESET** #*filenum* | RESET #1 |
| | *Note:* These statements work the same way as the RESTORE statement worked within a data-block internal file— namely, the pointer gets reset to the beginning of the file. | |

Your system
(if different)

## Follow-Up Exercises

5. Go back to Example E.1 on page 400.
   a. How would the file look if we were to use the following?

   45    PRINT #1, SCORE;

**b.** Same as part **a**, except use (if available on your system)

   45    WRITE #1, SCORE

**c.** Would the second program have to change to read the revised file?

**6.** Consider the following program:

```
10 OPEN "SALES.DAT" FOR OUTPUT AS #1
20 READ N
30 PRINT #1, N
40 FOR J = 1 TO N
50    READ R$,S
60    PRINT #1, R$;S
70 NEXT J
80 CLOSE #1
90    DATA 2
91    DATA "East",5000
92    DATA "West",4000
99 END
```

**a.** Write the exact appearance of each record in the file.

**b.** Same as part **a** except use

   60 PRINT #1, R$;",";S

**c.** Same as part **a** except use

   60 PRINT #1, S;R$

**d.** Same as part **a** except use (if available on your system)

   60 WRITE #1, R$,S

**\*e.** Same as part **a** except use

   60 PRINT #1, S;R$;

**\*f.** Same as part **a** except use

   60 PRINT #1, R$
   65 PRINT #1, S

**\*\*g.** Same as part **a** except use

   91    DATA "East,Boston",5000
   92    DATA "West,Phoenix",4000

**\*h.** Run each of these variations on your system and display the files.

**7.** Consider the files created in the preceding exercise. For each part, write a program that displays the following report:

Number of regions = 2

| Region | Sales |
| --- | --- |
| East | 5000 |
| West | 4000 |

**\*8.** Rewrite the programs in Example E.1 as follows.
  **a.** Use an eof loop within the create program, but don't place an eof record within the external file.
  **b.** Use an EOF function within the display program (if available on your system).
  **c.** Use an ON ERROR statement approach within the display program.
  **d.** Use an eof loop (eof/sentinel approach) within the display program. How would we have to change the program in part **a**?

**E X A M P L E   E . 2**    **Creation and Display of Sequential Personnel File**

Now that we have the necessary tools, let's put it all together and illustrate the creation and display of the sequential personnel file shown in Figure E.2a on page 404.

### Analysis

Let's develop an interactive program that conversationally inputs employee records, writes the records to a sequential file, and then displays the file.
  Data requirements include the following:

*Output*

**1.** Unformatted records to a sequential file according to the record layout shown on page 403 (ignoring the length of each field).

**2.** Display of file on the screen, including the total number of records in the file.

*Input*

**1.** Name of file entered from keyboard.

**2.** Each record entered from keyboard.

**3.** Each record input from file once file is created (for display on screen).

### Design

This program has two primary tasks: file creation and file display. The file-creation logic inputs a record into primary memory from the keyboard; then the record is copied or written to the file medium (tape or disk) from primary memory. After all records have been written to the file, the file is closed, which places an endfile mark at the end of the file. The file-display logic first inputs a record from the file and stores this record in primary memory; then this record is copied from primary memory to the screen. Figure E.4 illustrates these data flows for both file creation and display.

The pseudocode below describes the design in more detail.

File-creation logic
```
Input file name
Open sequential file for output
Print reminders message to operator
Input employee name
While name not eof
    Input remaining fields in record
    Write record to file
    Input employee name
End while
Close file
Print file creation message to operator
```

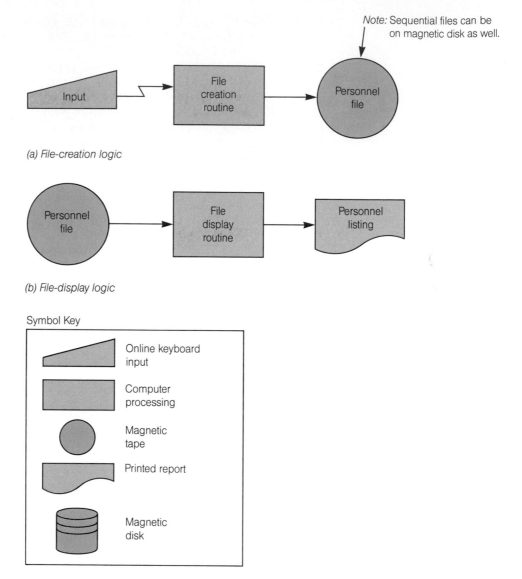

(a) File-creation logic

(b) File-display logic

**Figure E.4**  Data movement to and from sequential personnel file.

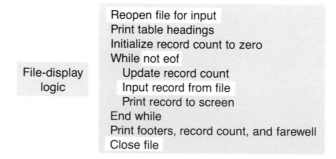

### Code and Test

The following program and run were implemented in Microsoft BASIC on an IBM PC. Note the following as you study the program and its I/O.

1. *The filename is treated as a string variable in lines 340, 360, and 730 for greater generality.* For example, this program can be used unaltered for different personnel files, if the same record layout is used in each.

2. The EOF function is used in line 820. This approach is cleaner than the alternative approaches described in Table E.6. Does your BASIC implementation have an EOF function?

3. Keep in mind that primary memory always acts as a temporary intermediary medium for each record. Looking at Figure E.4, each record in the file-creation process is entered at the keyboard, resides temporarily in memory locations as the variables FULL.NAME$, ID, SALARY, and SEX$ (until the next record overwrites it), and finally stays permanently on tape or disk. Each record in the file-display process is stored on tape or disk, temporarily is read to primary memory, and then is displayed on the screen or paper. (We show tape as the secondary storage medium in Figure E.4, although the actual computer run uses a diskette.)

```
100 '-----------------------------------------------------------------------
110 '
120 '   Personnel File Creation/Display Program:   Sequential File Version
130 '
140 '      Record Layout (Unformatted):
150 '      ----------------------------
160 '      Field                 Type
170 '      ----------------------------
180 '      FULL.NAME$            String
190 '      ID                    Numeric
200 '      SALARY                Numeric
210 '      SEX$                  String
220 '      ----------------------------
230 '
240 '-----------------------------------------------------------------------
300 ' File creation logic
310 '-------------------
320     PRINT TAB(10); "FILE CREATION ROUTINE"
330     PRINT
340     INPUT "Enter file name"; FILE.NAME$
350 '
360     OPEN FILE.NAME$ FOR OUTPUT AS #1
370 '
380     PRINT
390     PRINT TAB(10); "Reminders:"
400     PRINT TAB(12); "Don't use commas"
410     PRINT TAB(12); "Enter last name first"
420     PRINT TAB(12); "Terminate input with eof for name"
430     PRINT
440     PRINT TAB(10); "Now enter data for each employee."
450     PRINT
460 '
470     INPUT "Full name ======>"; FULL.NAME$
480 '
490     WHILE FULL.NAME$ <> "eof"
500 '
510       INPUT "ID number ======>"; ID
520       INPUT "Salary =========>"; SALARY
530       INPUT "Sex (f or m) ===>"; SEX$
540 '
550       WRITE #1, FULL.NAME$,ID,SALARY,SEX$
560 '
570       PRINT
580       INPUT "Full name ======>"; FULL.NAME$
590 '
600     WEND
610 '
620     CLOSE #1
630 '
640     PRINT : PRINT TAB(10); "File "; FILE.NAME$; " has been created.": PRINT
700 '-----------------------------------------------------------------------
```

Note use of string variable for file name (→ line 340)

File opened as output file (→ line 360)

Must close output file in order to reopen as input file (→ line 620)

```
710 '  File Display Logic                                    ─── File reopened as input file
720 '──────────────────
730      OPEN FILE.NAME$ FOR INPUT AS #1
740 '
750      PRINT : PRINT TAB(10); "FILE DISPLAY ROUTINE" : PRINT
760      PRINT TAB(10); "──────────────────────────────────────────────"
770      PRINT TAB(10); "Name";TAB(30);"ID";TAB(40);"Salary";TAB(50);"Sex"
780      PRINT TAB(10); "──────────────────────────────────────────────"
790 '
800      LET COUNT = 0
810 '                                  ─── Note use of end-of-file function
820      WHILE NOT EOF(1)
830 '
840        LET COUNT = COUNT + 1
850 '
860        INPUT #1, FULL.NAME$,ID,SALARY,SEX$
870 '
880        PRINT TAB(10); FULL.NAME$;TAB(30);ID;TAB(40);SALARY;TAB(50);SEX$
890 '
900      WEND
910 '
920      PRINT TAB(10); "──────────────────────────────────────────────"
930      PRINT TAB(10); "Number of employees ="; COUNT
940      PRINT
950      PRINT TAB(10); "End of job."
960 '
970      CLOSE #1
998 '
999      END

         RUN
                      FILE CREATION ROUTINE

         Enter file name? employee

                  Reminders:
                      Don't use commas
                      Enter last name first
                      Terminate input with eof for name

                  Now enter data for each employee.

         Full name ======>? Abatar     Jane A.
         ID number ======>? 1
         Salary =========>? 20000
         Sex (f or m) ===>? f

         Full name ======>? Bomberg    Bo B.
         ID number ======>? 3
         Salary =========>? 15800
         Sex (f or m) ===>? m


         Full name ======>? Drury      David D.
         ID number ======>? 6
         Salary =========>? 18000
         Sex (f or m) ===>? m

         Full name ======>? eof

                  File employee has been created.
                  FILE DISPLAY ROUTINE

                  ──────────────────────────────────────────────
                  Name              ID       Salary   Sex
                  ──────────────────────────────────────────────
                  Abatar    Jane A.  1         20000   f
                  Bomberg   Bo B.    3         15800   m
                  Drury     David D. 6         18000   m
                  ──────────────────────────────────────────────
                  Number of employees = 3

                  End of job.
```

## Follow-Up Exercises

**\*9.** Make any necessary changes to the program in Example E.2 and implement it on your system.

**\*10.** Change the program in Example E.2 to create a formatted file according to the record layout on page 403. Use a PRINT USING statement.

**\*11.** Modify the program in Example E.2 to create a backup copy of the personnel file. Use the file name employee.bak and the following pseudocode.

> While not eof on file 1
> > Input record from file 1
> > Write record to file 2
> End while

**\*\*12.** Change the program in Example E.2 to allow the entry and storage of commas within a person's full name.

**\*\*13.** Use your system's editor, word processor, or other specialized procedure to create the sequential personnel file. Then display this file (a) through an operating system command and (b) through a BASIC display program.

---

**\*\*EXAMPLE E.3**    **File Maintenance: Deletion of Records in Sequential Personnel File**

**File maintenance** refers to a collection of procedures for creating files, backing up files, and changing files by adding, deleting, or modifying records. This example illustrates a procedure for deleting records from the personnel file created in the preceding example. Records within a sequential file are deleted by writing all records, except those selected for deletion, to a new file. Thus, when the deletion procedure is completed, two files exist: the original file and the revised or new file. This procedure is illustrated in Fig. E.5. In Section E.5 we shall show more generalized procedures for maintaining files.

### Analysis

Let's develop an interactive program that enters, from the keyboard, the names of the original and revised employee files, and the ID numbers of employees that are to be dropped from the revised file. The program then creates and displays the revised file.

*Output*

**1.** All records except deleted records printed to revised file.

**2.** Revised file displayed on screen together with its record count.

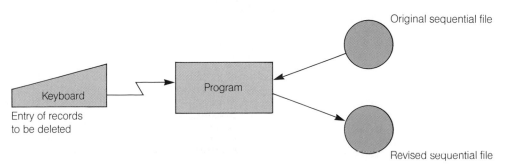

**Figure E.5**  Deletion of records from sequential files.

*Input*

1. Name of original file entered from keyboard.
2. Name of revised file entered from keyboard.
3. IDs of records to be deleted entered from keyboard.
4. All records from original file.
5. All records from revised file (to display on screen).

Design

Based on our description above, we plan to first use the original file as input. As each record is placed in primary memory, we check its ID to see if this record is to be deleted. If not, the undeleted record is written to the revised file. When we're through deleting records, the revised file is the most current employee file.

This updating procedure leaves an audit trail of past files. For example, if we use the file-name extensions 1, 2, 3, . . . to represent weekly updates for week 1, week 2, week 3, . . . , then files EMPLOYEE.1, EMPLOYEE.2, EMPLOYEE.3, . . . are an historical record of weekly employee files that can be examined if some subsequent problem arises regarding the integrity of data. An alternative approach that requires only one file is described in Exercise 17.

The following refined pseudocode describes the program's design.

1. Preliminaries

   1.1 Print title
   1.2 Input original file name                        This color denotes original file
   1.3 Input revised file name
   1.4 Open original file for input                    This color denotes revised file
   1.5 Open revised file for output
   1.6 Print reminders message                         This color denotes both files

2. Drop records

   2.1 Input drop ID (in ascending order)
   2.2 While drop ID unequal to zero
   2.3   Input records from original file and write undeleted
         records to revised file up to but not including record
         with drop id
   2.4   Input drop ID (in ascending order)
       End while

3. Write remaining records from original to revised file

   3.1 While not eof on original file
   3.2   Input record from original file
   3.3   Write record to revised file
       End while
   3.4 Close files

4. Display revised file
   This logic is the same as the display-file logic in the preceding example.

The tricky logic in this design is at Step 2.3: "Input records from original file and write undeleted records to revised file up to but not including record with drop ID." This step is further refined as follows:

Input record from original file
While ID < drop ID
    Write record to revised file
    Input record from original file
End while

To better understand the logic, let's consider the following three records within the original file employee created in Example E.2.

| Name | | ID | Salary | Sex |
|------|------|----|--------|-----|
| Abatar | Jane A. | 1 | 20000 | f |
| Bomberg | Bo B. | 3 | 15800 | m |
| Drury | David D. | 6 | 18000 | m |

First, notice that the file is sorted in ascending order by ID. Typically, sequential files are sorted according to a selected field called the **key field**, or simply **key**. Our logic relies on the fact that ID is the key. Now, suppose we wish to delete the record that contains ID = 3. This means that the drop ID is 3. The above design first inputs the record containing ID = 1. Since 1 is in fact less than 3, the while test is true, and the loop body is executed. Thus, the record containing ID = 1 is written to the revised file EMPLOYEE.2, and the next record (containing ID = 3) is input from the original file EMPLOYEE. The test ID < drop ID is now false since both variables store ID = 3. Thus, we drop out of the loop and the record containing ID = 3 is effectively deleted since it's not written to the revised file EMPLOYEE.2.

    Step 2.4 is executed next. Let's say we're through, so that we enter a drop ID of zero. This means we drop out of the while loop defined by Step 2.2 and proceed to Step 3. This step writes out the remaining record (containing ID = 6) to the revised file. Thus, the delete procedure is complete, since the revised file now contains all undeleted records. The file EMPLOYEE still contains the original three records, but the file EMPLOYEE.2 contains two records. When the update procedure is carried out in week 3, the original file will be EMPLOYEE.2 (the preceding week's file), and the revised file will be EMPLOYEE.3.

    If the delete logic is still unclear, reread the last two paragraphs, and then try roleplaying a delete of record 6. Then go on to the program and run.

### Code/Test

The following program was written in Microsoft BASIC and run on an IBM PC. Relate the code to the pseudocode and I/O, and then try your hand at the follow-up exercises to really understand what's going on.

```
100  '-------------------------------------------------------------------
105  '
110  '   Personnel Sequential File Maintenance: Record Deletion
115  '
120  '      Programming notes:
125  '        1. File #1 is the original file
130  '        2. File #2 is the revised file
135  '        3. This program does not create a backup file
140  '
145  '
150  '
155  '-------------------------------------------------------------------
```

```
160 ' Preliminaries
165 '---------------
170      PRINT TAB(10); "RECORD DELETION ROUTINE" : PRINT
175      INPUT "Enter original file name"; ORIGINAL$
180      INPUT "Enter revised  file name"; REVISED$
185 '
190      OPEN ORIGINAL$ FOR INPUT  AS #1
195      OPEN REVISED$  FOR OUTPUT AS #2
200 '
205      PRINT
210      PRINT TAB(10); "Reminders:"
215      PRINT TAB(12); "Enter IDs in ascending order"
220      PRINT TAB(12); "Terminate with an ID of zero"
225      PRINT
230 '------------------------------------------------------------------
235 ' Drop records
240 ' -----------------
245      INPUT "Enter ID for employee to be deleted"; DROP.ID
250 '
255      WHILE DROP.ID <> 0
260        INPUT #1, FULL.NAME$,ID,SALARY,SEX$
265        WHILE ID < DROP.ID
270          WRITE #2, FULL.NAME$,ID,SALARY,SEX$
275          INPUT #1, FULL.NAME$,ID,SALARY,SEX$
280        WEND
285        INPUT "Enter ID for employee to be deleted"; DROP.ID
290      WEND
295 '------------------------------------------------------------------
300 ' Write remaining records from original to revised file
305 ' ----------------------------------------------------
310      WHILE NOT EOF(1)
315        INPUT #1, FULL.NAME$,ID,SALARY,SEX$
320        WRITE #2, FULL.NAME$,ID,SALARY,SEX$
325      WEND
330 '
335      CLOSE #1,#2
340 '
700 '------------------------------------------------------------------
710 ' Display revised original file
720 '-------------------
730      OPEN REVISED$ FOR INPUT AS #2
740 '
750      PRINT : PRINT TAB(10); "Revised file "; REVISED$ : PRINT
760      PRINT TAB(10); "--------------------------------------------"
770      PRINT TAB(10); "Name";TAB(30);"ID";TAB(40);"Salary";TAB(50);"Sex"
780      PRINT TAB(10); "--------------------------------------------"
790 '
800      LET COUNT = 0
810 '
820      WHILE NOT EOF(2)
830 '
840        LET COUNT = COUNT + 1
850 '
860        INPUT #2, FULL.NAME$,ID,SALARY,SEX$
870 '
880        PRINT TAB(10); FULL.NAME$;TAB(30);ID;TAB(40);SALARY;TAB(50);SEX$
890 '
900      WEND
910 '
920      PRINT TAB(10); "--------------------------------------------"
930      PRINT TAB(10); "Number of employees ="; COUNT
940      PRINT
950      PRINT TAB(10); "End of job."
960 '
970      CLOSE #2
998 '
999      END
```

Lines 270–275 annotation: When ID = DROP.ID, we skip this section. Thus, record is not written to file

```
RUN
            RECORD DELETION ROUTINE


Enter original file name? employee
Enter revised  file name? employee.2

        Reminders:
           Enter IDs in ascending order
           Terminate with an ID of zero

Enter ID for employee to be deleted? 3
Enter ID for employee to be deleted? 0

        Revised file employee.2

        ------------------------------------------
        Name                 ID       Salary    Sex
        ------------------------------------------
        Abatar    Jane A.     1        20000    f
        Drury     David D.    6        18000    m
        ------------------------------------------
        Number of employees = 2

        End of job.
```

## Follow-Up Exercises

**14.** Start with the original file and roleplay a delete of records with IDs of 1 and 6 in the same run. Use the following table.

| Line | Result/Action |
|------|---------------|
| 245 | Enter 1 for DROP.ID |
| 255 | True |

**\*15.** Implement the program in Example E.3 on your system.

**16. Backup file.** Revise the program in Example E.3 so that the revised employee file is backed up as file EMPLOYEE.BAK.

**\*17. Program alternative 2.** Within our design description, we mentioned a second approach to this problem that inputs a single file name (say, EMPLOYEE) for the original file and creates the revised file using a programmer-assigned name (say, REVISED). System commands then can be used to rename the revised file as the original file (from REVISED to EMPLOYEE) and to rename the original file as an old file (from EMPLOYEE to EMPLOYEE.OLD). This approach makes naming a file easier, since the operator works with only one file name (EMPLOYEE); however, an audit trail does not exist since only the most recent historical file is retained (EMPLOYEE.OLD).

**a.** Rewrite the program accordingly. Can you invoke the rename command from within the program? Which approach do you prefer and why?

**b.** Implement this program on your system.

**\*18.** The following input would uncover some bugs within the present program. In each case, describe what happens and perform a fixup on the program.

**a.** Enter a 2 for drop ID.

**b.** Enter 3 then 1 within the same run for drop ID.

**c.** Enter 7 for drop ID.

**\*\*19.** **The works.** Completely rewrite Example E.3 as a full-feature maintenance program. Offer the following choices in a menu:

D   Delete employee
A   Add employee
M   Modify data for employee
B   Backup file
V   View file
S   Stop processing

Make sure any added employees are placed in the proper sequence according to the ID key. Use a modular design (if you've studied Chapter 7). Start with the original file and carry out the following choices.

| Action | ------- Fields ----------- | | | |
|--------|--------|---|-------|---|
| A | Test 1 | 2 | 30000 | f |
| D | | 3 | | |
| M | | 6 | 22000 | |
| B | | | | |
| V | Backup file | | | |
| V | Revised file | | | |
| V | Original file | | | |

# E.4 RELATIVE FILES

Relative, random, or direct-access files were defined earlier in Section E.2. Remember that relative files allow us to find a record directly by its number instead of having to search for it sequentially. Relative files can also be processed sequentially. As with sequential files, the general operations for processing relative files include the following: opening, output to or input from, and closing the file. See Table E.8.

As usual, the statements for accomplishing these operations vary from system to system. In our discussion we shall focus on the IBM PC (Microsoft) and VAX-11 implementations, with emphasis on the former. If your system is not illustrated, then you should focus on the general principles of relative file processing as presented in the text and illustrated in the examples. Then make any necessary changes within the tables and examples.

**Table E.8**  Relative File Operations

| Implementation | Operations and Syntax | Examples |
|---|---|---|
| IBM PC | *1. Opening the file* | |

**OPEN** *filespec* **AS** #*filenum* **LEN** = *reclen*
or
**OPEN "R"**, #*filenum,filespec,reclen*

where *filespec* and *filenum* were defined in Table E.2 and *reclen* is an integer expression that sets the record length.

Note 1:  The *record length* is the total number of characters or bytes within one record. The record layout on page 403 shows a record length of 29 bytes. A record length between 1 and 32,767 is allowed. If the record length is omitted, then the system assigns a length of 128 bytes.

Note 2:  The file is opened for both input and output.

*2. Allocating the buffer*

The **buffer** is a special storage area within primary memory that holds the contents of a single record. The maximum length of the buffer is defined by the record length in the OPEN statement. Records are copied from the file to the buffer during input and from the buffer to the file during output. (See Fig. E.6.) The size of the buffer and its record layout are defined by the executable **FIELD statement.**

**FIELD** #*filenum,width* **AS** *stringvar, width* **AS** *stringvar* . . .

where *filenum* is defined in Table E.2
*width*  is a numeric expression giving the *field width* or *field length* in bytes. Use a width of 4 for fields that store *single-precision numeric values*. (We assume single precision for numeric values throughout this chapter.)
*stringvar*  is a string variable that defines a field.

Note 1:  The FIELD statement must follow the corresponding OPEN statement.

Note 2:  The FIELD statement allocates the size of the buffer and defines its record layout. In Example 5, to the right, the first 20 characters (bytes) within the buffer are allocated to the variable FULL.NAMEB$; the next 4 bytes to ID$; the next 4 to SALARY$; and finally 1 byte to SEXB$.

Note 3:  The total number of bytes allocated in the FIELD statement must not exceed the record length in the corresponding OPEN statement.

**Examples (right column):**

1.  OPEN FILE.NAME$ AS #1 LEN = 29 ← constant

2.  OPEN "R",#1,FILE.NAME$,29

3.  OPEN "B:SALES" AS #2 LEN = RECLEN ← variable

4.  OPEN F$ AS #3 ← Default reclen of 128 used

This is associated with Examples 1 and 2 above

5.  FIELD #1, 20 AS FULL.NAMEB$,
      4 AS ID$,
      4 AS SALARY$,
      1 AS SEXB$

*Note 4:* More than one FIELD statement can be executed for the same file, as when the file has more than one type of record.

*Warning:* Each string variable within the buffer should be unique to the program; that is, no other string variable should have the same name as any string variable within the buffer. Otherwise, INPUT, LET, or READ statements within the program may incorrectly alter the pointer within the buffer.

*3. Moving data from regular memory locations to the buffer*

Data values are moved into the buffer from regular memory locations *only* through **LSET** or **RSET statements** (and never through LET, INPUT, or READ statements). This must be accomplished before the record is written to the relative file through a PUT statement. (See Fig. E.6.)

Examples 6 and 7 correspond to Example 5 above

**LSET** *stringvar = string expression*
**RSET** *stringvar = string expression*

6. LSET FULL.NAMEB$ = FULL.NAME$
7. LSET SEXB$          = SEX$

where *stringvar* is defined within the FIELD statement
LSET  left-justifies the string value within stringvar
RSET right-justifies the string value

8. RSET AB$ = A$
9. LSET AB$ = A$

If A$ stores yes and AB$ is a buffer variable with width 5, then AB$ stores ␢␢yes in Example 8 and yes␢␢ in Example 9

*Note:* Each string variable within the buffer has a corresponding variable that defines a regular memory location. Thus, if SEX$ is a string variable in regular memory, then we suggest SEX*B*$ as the corresponding string variable within the buffer, where we simply add the letter *B* (for *B*uffer) to the end of the name. If ID is a numeric variable within regular memory, then we suggest ID$ as the corresponding buffer variable.

Variables within the buffer must be string variables. If the corresponding variable within regular memory is a numeric variable, then the **MKS$ function** must be used to convert the single-precision numeric value to an equivalent 4-byte string value. In this case, the LSET and RSET statements will then have the following forms:

Examples 10 and 11 correspond to Example 5 above

LSET  *stringvar =* **MKS$** *(numeric expression)*
RSET  *stringvar =* **MKS$** *(numeric expression)*

10. LSET ID$        = MKS$(ID)
11. LSET SALARY$ = MKS$(SALARY)

*4. Output to the file*

**PUT** *#filenum, recnum*

where *filenum* is defined in Table E.2 and *recnum* is the record number that identifies the record being written to.

12. PUT #1, ID
13. PUT #2, 99
14. PUT #3

*Note:* This statement copies a record from the buffer to the record in the file specified by the *record number*; that is, it puts a record from the buffer to the file. If the record number is omitted, then the next available number is assigned by the system.

5. *Input from the file*

   **GET** #*filenum, recnum*

   where *filenum* and *recnum* have been defined in item 4 above.

   15. GET #1, RECORD.NUM
   16. GET #2, 99
   17. GET #3

   *Note 1:* This statement copies the record specified by *recnum* from the file to the buffer; that is, it "gets" the record from the file and places it in the buffer. If the record number is omitted, then the next record following the last GET operation is read into the buffer.

   *Note 2:* Once the record is read into the buffer, then the contents of the buffer can be used elsewhere within the program by referencing the *buffer variables* defined within the FIELD statement. If a particular string variable within the buffer actually stores numeric values in string form, then the string value must be converted back to numeric form by using the **CVS function**, as in the following generalized examples:

   These are buffer variables that store numeric values. See Examples 5,10,11 above.

   LET numeric variable = **CVS**(string variable within buffer)

   18. LET TAX = 0.1 * CVS(SALARY$)

   PRINT **CVS**(string variable within buffer)

   19. PRINT CVS(ID$),FULL.NAME$

6. *Closing the file*

   20. CLOSE #1,2,3

   Relative files use the CLOSE statement as do sequential files. See Table E.5.

---

**VAX-11**

1. *Allocating the buffer*

   The buffer is defined under item 2 in the IBM PC description. The nonexecutable **MAP statement** defines the record layout within the buffer. (See Figure E.7.)

   MAP (*mapname*) *datatype mapitem, datatype mapitem . . .*

   optional

   $ used since datatype not specified

   21. MAP (PERSON) FULL.NAME$ = 20, SINGLE ID, SALARY, STRING SEX = 1

   $ not used since datatype specified

   Also single precision

   where

   *mapname* is a name that the programmer gives the buffer
   *datatype* is one of the usual datatype designations such as **STRING** or **SINGLE** (for single-precision numeric variables)

*mapitem* in its simplest form either defines each string field as
    *string variable = length in bytes*
or defines each numeric field as
    *numeric variable*

*Note 1:* When a datatype is specified, all following mapitems are of that datatype until a new datatype is specified. If the STRING datatype is used, then the affected string variables must not end in a $ sign.

*Note 2:* Single-precision numeric variables take up 4 bytes of storage.

2. *Opening the file*

In its simplest form, the OPEN statement for relative files appears as follows:

**OPEN** *filespec* **AS #***filenum*, **ORGANIZATION RELATIVE, RECORDSIZE** *reclen*, **MAP** *mapname*

where *filespec* and *filenum* were defined in Table E.2
    *reclen* is the length in bytes of the record defined by the buffer
    *mapname* is the same name that's used in the corresponding MAP statement.

**Note:** The MAP statement must precede its corresponding OPEN statement, since the OPEN statement references a particular mapname.

*Reclen* is consistent with the 29 bytes defined in Example 21

22. OPEN FILE.NAME$ AS #1, ORGANIZATION RELATIVE, RECORDSIZE 29, MAP PERSON

Corresponds to *mapname* in Example 21

3. *Output to the file*
The PUT statement is the same as the IBM PC version except that the keyword **RECORD** precedes the record number. (See Figure E.7.)

23. PUT #1, RECORD ID
24. PUT #2, RECORD 99
25. PUT #3

4. *Input from the file*
The GET statement is the same as the IBM PC version except that the keyword **RECORD** precedes the record number. (See Figure E.7.)

26. GET #1, RECORD ID
27. GET #2, RECORD 99
28. GET #3

5. *Closing the file*
Relative files use the CLOSE statement as do sequential files. See Table E.5.

29. CLOSE #1,2,3

Your system
(if different)

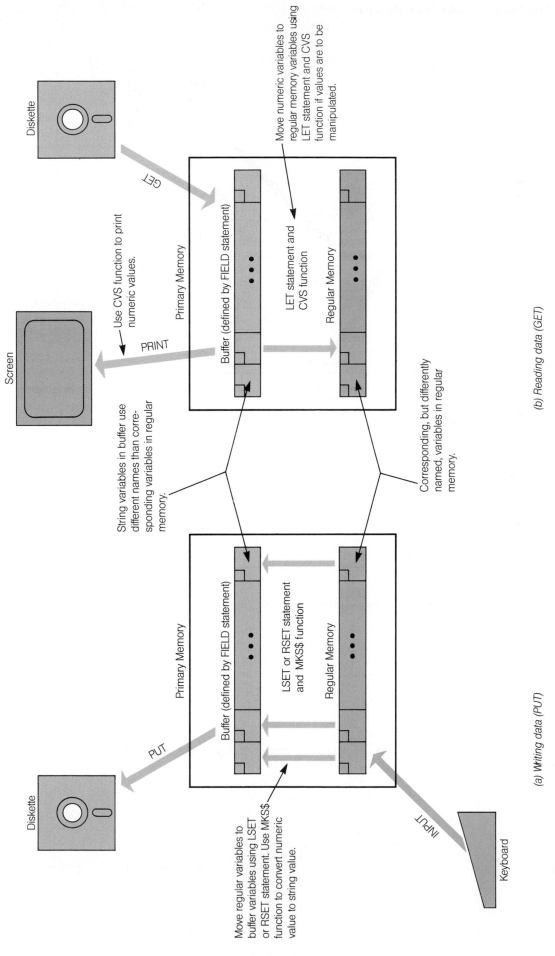

**Figure E.6**  Writing data to and reading data from a relative file: IBM PC approach.

(a) *Writing data (PUT)*

(b) *Reading data (GET)*

Move regular variables to buffer variables using LSET or RSET statement. Use MKS$ function to convert numeric value to string value.

String variables in buffer use different names than corresponding variables in regular memory.

Corresponding, but differently named, variables in regular memory.

Move numeric variables to regular memory variables using LET statement and CVS function if values are to be manipulated.

Use CVS function to print numeric values.

LET statement and CVS function

LSET or RSET statement and MKS$ function

Buffer (defined by FIELD statement)

Regular Memory

Primary Memory

Diskette

Screen

Keyboard

PUT

GET

PRINT

INPUT

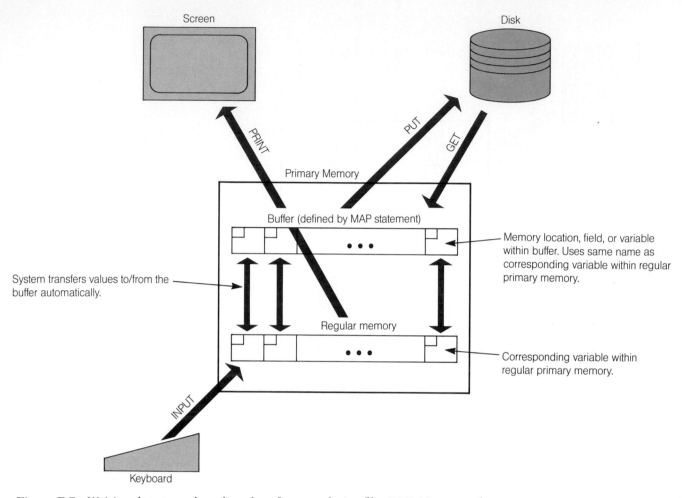

**Figure E.7** Writing data to and reading data from a relative file: VAX-11 approach.

**E X A M P L E   E . 4**   Creation and Display of Relative Personnel File

If we use a relative file instead of a sequential file in Example E.2, the analysis of the problem and the design of the program are similar to that in Example E.2, so let's go directly to the code and run on an IBM PC. If your system is different, then note the similarities and differences in the example and try implementing the program on your system (as suggested in Exercise 21).

```
100 '-------------------------------------------------------------------
110 '
120 '   Personnel File Creation/Display Program:  Relative File Version
130 '
140 '     Record Layout:
150 '     -------------------------------------------------------------
160 '     Field           Type         Buffer        Width (Bytes)
170 '     -------------------------------------------------------------
180 '     FULL.NAME$      String       FULL.NAMEB$      20
190 '     ID              Numeric      ID$               4
200 '     SALARY          Numeric      SALARY$           4
210 '     SEX$            String       SEXB$             1
220 '     -------------------------------------------------------------
230 '                                                   29
```

```
240  '-----------------------------------------------------------------------
300  ' File creation logic
310  '--------------------
320      PRINT TAB(10); "FILE CREATION ROUTINE"
330      PRINT
340      INPUT "Enter file name"; FILE.NAME$
350  '                                          ┌─ Record length in buffer (see line 230 above)
360      OPEN FILE.NAME$ AS #1 LEN=29
365      FIELD #1, 20 AS FULL.NAMEB$, 4 AS ID$, 4 AS SALARY$, 1 AS SEXB$
370  '       └──── Defines record layout in buffer (see lines 180-210 above)
380      PRINT
390      PRINT TAB(10); "Reminders:"
400      PRINT TAB(12); "Don't use commas"
410      PRINT TAB(12); "Enter last name first"
420      PRINT TAB(12); "Terminate input with eof for name"
430      PRINT
440      PRINT TAB(10); "Now enter data for each employee."
450      PRINT
460  '
470      INPUT "Full name ======>"; FULL.NAME$
480  '
490      WHILE FULL.NAME$ <> "eof"
500  '
510        INPUT "ID number ======>"; ID
520        INPUT "Salary =========>"; SALARY
530        INPUT "Sex (f or m) ===>"; SEX$
540  '
542        LSET FULL.NAMEB$ = FULL.NAME$    ◄── LSET statements copy values from
544        LSET ID$         = MKS$(ID)          memory locations to buffer
546        LSET SALARY$     = MKS$(SALARY)
548        LSET SEXB$       = SEX$
549  '                          └─ MKS$ function converts single precision numeric value to string value
550        PUT #1, ID
560  '       ↑
570        PRINT   Copies record from buffer to file as record number ID
580        INPUT "Full name ======>"; FULL.NAME$
590  '
600      WEND
610  '
620  '      CLOSE statement deleted here since file doesn't need reopening
630  '
640      PRINT : PRINT TAB(10); "File "; FILE.NAME$; " has been created.": PRINT
700  '-----------------------------------------------------------------------
710  ' File Display Logic
720  '--------------------
730  '      OPEN statement not needed since relative files are open for both
740  '      input and output
745  '
750      PRINT : PRINT TAB(10); "FILE DISPLAY ROUTINE" : PRINT
760      PRINT TAB(10); "---------------------------------------------"
770      PRINT TAB(10); "Name";TAB(30);"ID";TAB(40);"Salary";TAB(50);"Sex"
780      PRINT TAB(10); "---------------------------------------------"
790  '
800      FOR RECORD.NUM = 1 TO LOC(1) ◄── LOC function returns record number of last record read or written
810  '
820        GET #1, RECORD.NUM ◄────── Copies specific record from file to buffer
830  '
840        PRINT TAB(10); FULL.NAMEB$; TAB(30); CVS(ID$); TAB(40); CVS(SALARY$);
                  TAB(50); SEXB$
850  '                              ↑
860      NEXT RECORD.NUM          CVS function converts string values to
870  '                            single precision numeric values
920      PRINT TAB(10); "---------------------------------------------"
930      PRINT TAB(10); "Number of records ="; LOC(1)
940      PRINT
950      PRINT TAB(10); "End of job."
960  '
970      CLOSE #1 ◄──────── Close file at end of run
998  '
999      END
```

```
RUN
            FILE CREATION ROUTINE

Enter file name? personnel

          Reminders:
            Don't use commas
            Enter last name first
            Terminate input with eof for name

          Now enter data for each employee.

Full name ======>? Abatar    Jane A.
ID number ======>? 1
Salary ========>? 20000
Sex (f or m) ===>? f

Full name ======>? Bomberg  Bo B.
ID number ======>? 3
Salary ========>? 15800
Sex (f or m) ===>? m

Full name ======>? Drury     David D.
ID number ======>? 6
Salary ========>? 18000
Sex (f or m) ===>? m

Full name ======>? eof



          File personnel has been created.

          FILE DISPLAY ROUTINE

          --------------------------------------------------
          Name                 ID         Salary      Sex
          --------------------------------------------------
          Abatar    Jane A.     1          20000       f
                                0          0
          Bomberg   Bo B.       3          15800       m
                                0          0
                                0          0
          Drury     David D.    6          18000       m
          --------------------------------------------------
          Number of records = 6

          End of job.
```

We might note the following points.

1.  The OPEN statement in line 360 corresponds to Step 1 in Table E.8. The file called personnel is opened as relative file #1 with a defined record length of 29 characters.

2.  The FIELD statement in line 365 corresponds to Step 2 in Table E.8. This statement defines the record layout within the buffer that's described in lines 180–210.[1]

3.  Lines 542–548 in the program correspond to Step 3 in Table E.8.[2] Values for the variables FULL.NAME\$, ID, SALARY, and SEX\$ are entered at the keyboard through the execution of INPUT statements. Consequently, these values are stored in what we're calling *regular* memory. Lines 542–548 then move these values (the record) into the buffer. Within the buffer, all values are stored as string values under variable names that are unique to the buffer. Thus, the regular string variable FULL.NAME\$

---

[1]VAX-11 users would reverse Steps 1 and 2 and substitute the MAP statement for the FIELD statement.

[2]VAX-11 users mercifully can skip this step since VAX-11 BASIC makes no distinction between buffer variables and other variables.

corresponds to the buffer string variable FULL.NAMEB$, the regular numeric variable ID corresponds to the buffer string variable ID$ (note the use of the MKS$ function), and so on. Now that the record within the buffer has proper values, we're ready to write or output the record to the file.

4.  Line 550 in the program corresponds to Step 4 in Table E.8. Thus, the record within the buffer is written to the file by using the PUT statement, as shown in Fig. E.6. Note how the numeric variable ID is conveniently used to define the record number being written. In this case, ID is called the **record key**, since its value is used by the system as a record number for locating records within the relative file. See Exercises 23 and 24 for issues regarding this record key. The while loop defined by lines 490 – 600 thus creates the relative file.

5.  The loop defined by lines 800 – 860 sequentially inputs each record into the buffer and displays its contents on the screen, thereby displaying the entire file. The **LOC function** in lines 800 and 930 returns the most recently used record number, which is 6 (ID = 6) according to the input for the last employee. Thus, six records are displayed by the loop. Note that the task of displaying a record first requires getting the record from the file to the buffer (using the GET statement) and then printing the record to the screen using the PRINT statement. (See Fig. E.6.) Further note that ID$ and SALARY$ actually store numeric values in string form, so that the display of these numeric values first requires a string to numeric conversion using the *CVS function*, as done in line 840.[3]

6.  **Empty records.** Look at the output and note that records 2, 4, and 5 are empty. Empty records on the IBM PC system store zeros for numeric fields and blanks for string fields. The GET statement in line 820 accessed these empty records and the PRINT statement in line 840 displayed them on the screen. Some systems, however, will give a fatal execution error if a program attempts to access an undefined or empty record. On the VAX-11 computer, for example, this problem is overcome by simply using the GET statement without a record number (as in GET #1). In this case, only the three filled records would be accessed and subsequently printed. *How does your system treat empty records?*

7.  Once a relative file is opened, unlike a sequential file, it can be used for both input and output. In our example, we first used the file for output (to create it) and then we used it for input (to display it). If this were a sequential file, we would first have to open it for output; then we would have to close it and reopen it for input. Compare lines 620 and 730 of the programs in Examples E.2 and E.4.

## Follow-Up Exercises

20.  How would you suggest correcting an input error for ID that places the wrong ID number on the file, as when an ID number of 4 is used for Bomberg?

*21.  Make any necessary changes and implement Example E.4 on your system.

*22.  Revise the program in Example E.4 so that only nonempty records are printed. (Hint: You need to test a field for a value of zero.)

23.  **Index File.** Consider the following issues regarding the simplified way we treated IDs as record numbers in Example E.4.
     a.  Assume the ID field is the nine-digit Social Security Number (SSN), which is more realistic than the ID numbers we used in the example. Modify the program accordingly. Can you think of a practical problem regarding the use of SSN in place of our simpler ID?

---

[3]Happily, VAX-11 users need not worry about the CVS conversion, since the buffer directly defines **ID** and **SALARY** as numeric variables. (See Example 21 in Table E.8.)

**\*\*b.** To overcome the disk storage problem in part **a**, we can set up a sequential **index file** with the following records:

| SSN | Record Number |
|-----|---------------|
| 266629885 | 6 |
| 267683142 | 1 |
| 269712345 | 3 |

Now suppose that we wish to access the record of the employee with an SSN of 267683142. To locate this record, the index file is searched until a match is found for the desired SSN. The corresponding record number of the matched SSN is then used to locate the proper record (record number 1 in this case) within the relative employee file. SSN is called the **key**, which is typically sorted in ascending order. Modify our earlier program as follows:

1. Within the file-creation logic section, replace ID with SSN and also input the record number (RECORD.NUM). Enter SSNs in ascending order and use the same record numbers as before (as shown above). In addition to creating the relative personnel file, this section also creates the sequential index file shown above.

2. Rewrite the file-display logic to display only the selected records specified by the user. Use the following design:

Print table headings (as before)
Open index file for input
Input desired SSN (in ascending order)
While SSN <> 0
    Find record no. in index file
    Get record from personnel file
    Print record
    Input desired SSN (in ascending order)
End while
Close files

How would this logic change if we did not require the entry of SSN in ascending order?

**\*\*c.** Same as part **b**, except use the person's name as the key within another index file. Enter names in alphabetical order, which is what we did in the example.

**\*\*24. Hashing algorithm.** Hashing is a common technique used to access records in a direct-access file where the record key has more digits than the number of records (storage positions) in the file. For example, the direct use of SS numbers as record numbers would require a file of the order of one billion records, since SS number is a nine-digit number.

The hashing algorithm converts the record key to a "relative record number" having a value within the range of the number of records reserved for the file. The location of each record is determined as follows:

1. Convert the record key, via a hashing algorithm, to a relative record number that is within the range 1 to $n$, where $n$ is the number of records stored in the file. One hashing algorithm divides the record key by the *prime number*[4]

---

\*\*This example is somewhat advanced and requires knowledge of subroutines from Chapter 7.

closest to *n* and uses the remainder from the division as the relative record number (the quotient is ignored).[5]

2. Use the relative record number to write the record to (or read the record from) the direct-access file.

Modify the program in Example E.4 using a hashing algorithm. Assume the employee file contains no more than 100 employees and the Social Security number is the record key. (*Hint:* Convert the Social Security number to a two-digit record number using the hashing algorithm described above. The prime number closest to 100 is 97.)

[4]For you non-mathematical wizards, a prime number is a positive integer that is *not* evenly divisible by any positive integer except 1 and itself. For example 2, 3, 5, 7, and 11 are the first five prime numbers.

[5]Remaindering in BASIC is best accomplished by a special operator that performs modulo arithmetic. For example, in Microsoft BASIC the **MOD operator** within the expression

*numvar1* **MOD** *numvar2*

gives the remainder when numeric variable 1 is divided by numeric variable 2. Thus

100   MOD   97

would yield the remainder 3.

---

# E X A M P L E   E . 5    File Maintenance: Relative Files**

In Example E.3 we illustrated some file maintenance procedures for sequential files. Here we illustrate similar approaches to maintaining relative files.

### Analysis

Let's develop a modular menu-driven program that allows us to view the personnel file created in Example E.4 and delete unwanted records. In the follow-up exercises, we (or rather, you) shall extend its features to adding records, changing records, and backing up the file.

The following modules describe the overall structure of the program.

*Control module*
This module defines the file, establishes the primary processing loop that calls the *main menu* module and then calls the proper module (either *view* or *delete records*) based on the menu choice, and concludes processing.

*Main menu module*
This module offers the following menu

V    View records
D    Delete records
S    Stop processing

and inputs the choice.

*View module*
This module prints the following submenu

E    Entire file
I    Indicated records

and inputs the choice. A choice error is trapped by offering the menu until the choice is correct. Then either the module *view entire file* or *view indicated records* is called, depending on the choice.

*View entire file module*
This module displays the entire employee file, including counts of the number of records and the number of employees.

*View indicated records module*
This module prints selected records based on ID input by the user. As many records as desired are printed.

*Delete records module*
This module deletes selected records based on ID input by the user. As many records as desired are deleted.

*Pause module*
This module pauses output to the screen. It's a handy utility module that allows a more user-friendly screen orientation, especially when coupled with the ability to clear the screen. This module is called by the *view entire file* and *view indicated records* modules.

Finally, we should note that this program adopts the following *screen design features*:

The program starts by clearing the screen.
Each menu is printed to a cleared screen.
The display of records starts on a cleared screen and ends in a pause.
The procedure that deletes records starts on a cleared screen.
The farewell message starts on a cleared screen.

Design

The following pseudocode gives greater design detail than the modular descriptions above.

```
Start control module
    Clear screen
    Print title
    Input personnel file name
    Open personnel file as relative file
    Define the buffer
    Call main menu module
    While choice is not equal stop
        If choice is view then call view module
        If choice is delete then call delete records module
        Call main menu module
    End while
    Clear screen
    Print farewell
    Close file
    Stop
End module
```

```
Start main menu module
    Clear screen
    Print menu
    Input choice
    Return
End module
```

```
Start view module
    Until choice is correct
        Clear screen
        Print submenu
        Input choice
    End until
    If choice is E then call view entire file module
    If choice is I then call view indicated records module
    Return
End module
```

```
Start view entire file module
    Clear screen
    Print table headings
    Initialize employee count
    For each record
        Get record
        If record is nonempty then print record and count employee
    Next record
    Print table footing, number of records and number of employees
    Call pause module
    Return
End module
```

```
Start view indicated records module
    Clear screen
    Print headings
    Input ID
    While ID unequal to zero
        Get record
        Print record
        Input ID
    End while
    Print footing
    Call pause module
    Return
End module
```

```
Start delete records module
    Clear screen
    Print message
    Create empty buffer record
    Input ID
    While ID unequal to zero
        Put empty record to file
        Input ID
    End while
    Return
End module
```

*Note:* Records are not really deleted; rather, they are filled with blanks (or some other special symbol) to signify *deleted records*. Thus, we empty the buffer by placing blanks within string fields and zeros within numeric fields. This *null* buffer then is written to the *deleted record* within the file.

```
Start pause module
    Print message
    While no key is pressed
        Do nothing
    End while
    Return
End module
```

*Note:* This module establishes a loop that does nothing while the user does nothing (fair enough). As soon as any key is pressed, the loop is exited, and control returns to the calling module.

Code

The following code and run were implemented on an IBM PC in Microsoft BASIC. If your system is different, note the similarities and differences in the example and try implementing the program on your system (see Exercise 27).

```
1000 ' * * * * * * * * * * * * * * * * * * * * * * * * * * * * * * * * *
1010 ' *                                                               *
1020 ' *  Personnel File Maintenance Program:  Relative File Version   *
1030 ' *                                                               *
1040 ' *  Record Layout:                                               *
1050 ' *  ----------------------------------------------------------   *
1060 ' *  Field           Type         Buffer        Width (Bytes)     *
1070 ' *  ----------------------------------------------------------   *
1080 ' *  FULL.NAME$      String       FULL.NAMEB$      20             *
1090 ' *  ID              Numeric      ID$               4             *
1100 ' *  SALARY          Numeric      SALARY$           4             *
1110 ' *  SEX$            String       SEXB$             1             *
1120 ' *  ----------------------------------------------------------   *
1130 ' *                                               29              *
1140 ' *  Description of modules:                                      *
1150 ' *    1.   Control ......... Sets file characteristics, offers main *
1160 ' *                           menu, establishes main processing loop *
1170 ' *                           calls sub. view or delete based on  *
1180 ' *                           choice, closes file, and stops.     *
1190 ' *    2.   Main menu ....... Displays main menu and inputs choice. *
1200 ' *    3.   View ........... Offers view menu and inputs choice   *
1210 ' *                           within an incorrect choice loop, and *
1220 ' *                           calls sub. view entire file or view *
1230 ' *                           indicated records based on choice.  *
1240 ' *    4.   View ent. file .. Displays entire file and calls sub. *
1250 ' *                           pause.                              *
1260 ' *    5.   View ind. rec. .. Displays any number of desired records *
1270 ' *                           and calls sub. pause.               *
1280 ' *    6.   Delete records .. Deletes any number of desired records. *
1290 ' *    7.   Pause .......... Utility subroutine for pausing output *
1300 ' *                           to the screen.                      *
1310 ' *                                                               *
1320 ' * * * * * * * * * * * * * * * * * * * * * * * * * * * * * * * * *
2000 ' ==================== Control module =====================================
2010 '
2020      CLS                                                ' Clear screen
2030 '
2035      PRINT TAB(10);"PERSONNEL FILE MAINTENANCE PROGRAM" : PRINT
2040      INPUT "Enter file name"; FILE.NAME$
2050 '
2060      OPEN FILE.NAME$ AS #1 LEN=29
2070      FIELD #1, 20 AS FULL.NAMEB$, 4 AS ID$, 4 AS SALARY$, 1 AS SEXB$
2080 '
2090      GOSUB 2500                                         ' Call main menu
2095 '
2100      WHILE CHOICE$ <> "s"  AND CHOICE$ <> "S"
2105 '
2110        IF CHOICE$ = "v" OR CHOICE$ = "V" THEN GOSUB 3000  ' Call view
2120        IF CHOICE$ = "d" OR CHOICE$ = "D" THEN GOSUB 6000  ' Call delete
2125 '
2130        GOSUB 2500                                       ' Call main menu
2135 '
2140      WEND
2150 '
2160      CLS
2170 '
2180      PRINT "END OF JOB"
2190 '
2200      CLOSE #1
2210 '
2220      STOP
```

```
2230 '
2500 ' =================== Subroutine main menu =============================
2510 '
2520      CLS                                                    ' Clear screen
2530 '
2540      PRINT "* * * * * * * * * * * * * * * *"
2550      PRINT "*                              *"
2560      PRINT "*          MAIN MENU           *"
2570      PRINT "*                              *"
2580      PRINT "*      V  View records         *"
2590      PRINT "*      D  Delete records       *"
2600      PRINT "*      S  Stop processing      *"
2610      PRINT "*                              *"
2620      PRINT "* * * * * * * * * * * * * * * *"
2630 '
2640      INPUT "Choice"; CHOICE$
2650 '
2660      RETURN
2670 '
3000 ' =================== Subroutine view ===============================
3010 '
3020      CLS                                                    ' Clear screen
3030 '
3040      PRINT "* * * * * * * * * * * * * * * *"
3050      PRINT "*                              *"
3060      PRINT "*         VIEW PROCEDURE       *"
3070      PRINT "*                              *"
3080      PRINT "*    Do you wish to view       *"
3090      PRINT "*       E  Entire file         *"
3100      PRINT "*       I  Indicated records   *"
3110      PRINT "*                              *"
3120      PRINT "* * * * * * * * * * * * * * * *"
3130 '
3140      INPUT "  Choice"; CHOICE$
3150 '
3160      IF (CHOICE$ <> "E" AND CHOICE$ <> "e") AND
             (CHOICE$ <> "I" AND CHOICE$ <> "i") THEN 3020    ' Loop until
3170 '                                                         choice is correct
3175 '
3180      IF CHOICE$ = "E" OR CHOICE$ = "e" THEN GOSUB 4000  ' Call view entire
3190      IF CHOICE$ = "I" OR CHOICE$ = "i" THEN GOSUB 5000  ' Call view indica.
3200 '
3210      RETURN
3220 '
4000 ' =================== Subroutine view entire file ==================
4010 '
4020      CLS                                                    ' Clear screen
4030 '
4040      PRINT : PRINT TAB(10); "VIEW ENTIRE FILE PROCEDURE" : PRINT
4050      PRINT TAB(10); "File name: "; FILE.NAME$
4060      PRINT TAB(10); "--------------------------------------------"
4070      PRINT TAB(10); "Name";TAB(30);"ID";TAB(40);"Salary";TAB(50);"Sex"
4080      PRINT TAB(10); "--------------------------------------------"
4085 '
4090      LET COUNT = 0
4100 '
4110      FOR RECORD.NUM = 1 TO LOF(1)/29
4120 '
4130          GET #1, RECORD.NUM
4140 '
4150          IF CVS(ID$) <> 0 THEN PRINT TAB(10); FULL.NAMEB$; TAB(30); CVS(ID$);
                                     TAB(40); CVS(SALARY$); TAB(50); SEXB$ :
                                     LET COUNT = COUNT + 1
4160 '
4170      NEXT RECORD.NUM
4180 '
4190      PRINT TAB(10); "--------------------------------------------"
4200      PRINT TAB(10); "Number of records    ="; LOC(1)
4205      PRINT TAB(10); "Number of employees ="; COUNT
4210      PRINT
```

Annotations:
- (4090) Each record is retrieved
- (4110) Length of file in bytes returned by LOF function which when divided by 29 bytes per record gives total number of records in file
- (4160) The ID field is used to test whether or not each record is filled. If filled, then it gets printed and counted.
- (4200) Last record read, which is same as total number of records in FOR/NEXT loop
- (4205) Number of employees

```
4220  '
4230      GOSUB 9900  ◄————————— Output to screen is paused          ' Call pause
4240  '                          right after the file is printed
4250      RETURN
4260  '
5000  ' =================== Subroutine view indicated records ================
5010  '
5020      CLS                                                   ' Clear screen
5030  '
5040      PRINT : PRINT TAB(10); "VIEW INDICATED RECORDS PROCEDURE"   : PRINT
5050      PRINT TAB(10); "Reminders:   Enter ID after each ? mark."
5055      PRINT TAB(10); "            Enter zero to stop procedure." : PRINT
5060      PRINT TAB(10); "File name: "; FILE.NAME$
5070      PRINT TAB(10); "------------------------------------------------"
5080      PRINT TAB(10); "Name";TAB(30);"ID";TAB(40);"Salary";TAB(50);"Sex"
5090      PRINT TAB(10); "------------------------------------------------"
5100  '
5110      INPUT "ID"; ID  ◄
5120  '
5130      WHILE ID <> 0
5140  '
5150        GET #1, ID  ◄—————————————————————————— Only selected records
5160  '                                              are retrieved
5170        PRINT TAB(10); FULL.NAMEB$; TAB(30); CVS(ID$);
                  TAB(40); CVS(SALARY$); TAB(50); SEXB$
5180  '
5190        INPUT "ID"; ID  ◄
5200  '
5210      WEND
5220  '
5230      PRINT TAB(10); "------------------------------------------------"
5240  '
5250      GOSUB 9900  ◄————— Pause before printing main menu          ' Call pause
5260  '
5270      RETURN
5280  '
6000  ' =================== Subroutine delete records ===================
6010  '
6020      CLS                                                   ' Clear screen
6030  '
6040      PRINT : PRINT TAB(10); "DELETE RECORDS PROCEDURE" : PRINT
6050      PRINT TAB(10); "Reminders:   Enter the ID of employee to be deleted."
6060      PRINT TAB(10); "            Terminate with zero for ID."
6070      PRINT
6080  '
6090      LSET FULL.NAMEB$ = ""            '  A record is deleted by placing
6100      LSET ID$        = MKS$(0)        '  a blank in each string field
6110      LSET SALARY$    = MKS$(0)        '  and a zero in each numeric field
6120      LSET SEXB$      = ""
6130  '
6140      INPUT "ID"; ID  ◄
6150  '
6160      WHILE ID <> 0
6165  '
6170        PUT #1, ID  ◄—————————————— Selected records are "deleted"
6180        INPUT "ID"; ID  ◄
6190  '
6200      WEND
6210  '
6220      RETURN
6230  '
9900  ' =================== Subroutine pause ===========================
9910  '
9920      PRINT
9930      PRINT "Strike any key to continue ..."
9940  '
9960      WHILE INKEY$ = ""  ◄————————————— INKEY$ stores null value as
9970  '     This keeps looping while no key is pressed     long as a character is not
9980      WEND                                             entered at the keyboard
9985  '
9990      RETURN
9995  '
9998  ' ================================================================
9999      END
```

**Test**

Screen 1

```
        PERSONNEL FILE MAINTENANCE PROGRAM

Enter file name? personnel
```

Screen 2

```
* * * * * * * * * * * * * * * *
*                              *
*        MAIN MENU             *
*                              *
*    V  View records          *
*    D  Delete records        *
*    S  Stop processing       *
*                              *
* * * * * * * * * * * * * * * *
Choice? v
```

Selection V from main menu has a submenu of two choices

Screen 3

```
* * * * * * * * * * * * * * * * *
*                               *
*      VIEW PROCEDURE           *
*                               *
*   Do you wish to view         *
*      E  Entire file           *
*      I  Indicated records     *
*                               *
* * * * * * * * * * * * * * * *
  Choice? i
```

Screen 4

```
     VIEW INDICATED RECORDS PROCEDURE

     Reminders:  Enter ID after each ? mark.
                 Enter zero to stop procedure.

     File name: personnel
     ------------------------------------------
     Name              ID       Salary    Sex
     ------------------------------------------
ID? 3
     Bomberg  Bo B.     3        15800      m
ID? 0
     ------------------------------------------

Strike any key to continue ...
```

Note screen pause to allow user viewing time, or time to print the screen

**Screen 5**

```
* * * * * * * * * * * * * * * *
*                              *
*         MAIN MENU            *
*                              *
*     V   View records         *
*     D   Delete records       *
*     S   Stop processing      *
*                              *
* * * * * * * * * * * * * * * *
Choice? d
```

**Screen 6**

```
DELETE RECORDS PROCEDURE

   Reminders:  Enter the ID of employee to be deleted.
               Terminate with zero for ID.
```

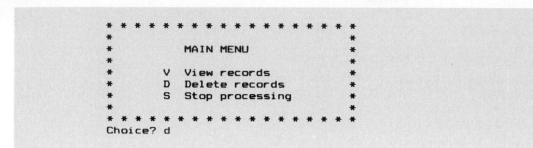

```
ID? 3  ◄──── Let's delete the employee with ID = 3
ID? 0
```

**Screen 7**

```
* * * * * * * * * * * * * * * *
*                              *
*         MAIN MENU            *
*                              *
*     V   View records         *
*     D   Delete records       *
*     S   Stop processing      *
*                              *
* * * * * * * * * * * * * * * *
Choice? v
```

**Screen 8**

```
* * * * * * * * * * * * * * * *
*                              *
*        VIEW PROCEDURE        *
*                              *
*    Do you wish to view       *
*        E   Entire file       *
*        I   Indicated records *
*                              *
* * * * * * * * * * * * * * * *
  Choice? e
```

**Screen 9**

```
VIEW ENTIRE FILE PROCEDURE

File name: personnel
-------------------------------------------------
Name                ID        Salary    Sex
-------------------------------------------------
Abatar   Jane A.    1         20000     f
Drury    David D.   6         18000     m
-------------------------------------------------
```

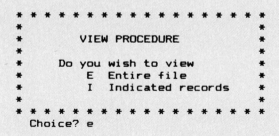

No more employee with ID = 3

```
Number of records   = 8
Number of employees = 2
```

System allocates 8 records, but only 2 are filled

```
Strike any key to continue ...
```

Screen 10

```
* * * * * * * * * * * * * * * * *
*                               *
*        MAIN MENU              *
*                               *
*      V  View records          *
*      D  Delete records        *
*      S  Stop processing       *
*                               *
* * * * * * * * * * * * * * * * *
Choice? s
```

Screen 11

```
END OF JOB
Break in 2220
```

Let's note the following points.

1. Screen clears and pauses promote easier-to-use programs, since different procedures, menus, and text don't get mixed up within the same view. See each of the screens in the output. Find out how you can pause output to the screen on your system. In our version, the **INKEY$ variable** is a special variable that stores a single character from the keyboard. As long as we don't strike a key, a null or empty string is returned to INKEY$. This repeatedly yields a true result for the while test in line 9960, thus effectively creating a pause. As soon as any key on the keyboard is pressed, its character is returned to INKEY$, the while loop is terminated, and processing continues.

2. The space for the deleted record is not actually deleted; rather, a null record is created by blanking out the deleted record. Thus, the space can be reused for a new record at a later time. Reread the procedures and notes in the pseudocode on page 441 and lines 6090–6120 of the program.

3. The FOR statement in line 4110 uses the **LOF function** to return the length of the file. In Microsoft BASIC, returned length is expressed in bytes to the next 128-increment. For example, our file uses 6 records of 29 bytes each, for a total of 174 bytes; however, the LOF function returns 256 bytes, since file sizes are allocated in increments of 128 bytes. When 256 is divided by the record length of 29 in line 4110, we get about 8.8, which is why eight records were processed within the loop, as indicated by the output in screen 9. Does your system include a LOF function, and if so, what does it return?

## Follow-Up Exercises

25. Draw a hierarchy chart for the design in Example E.5.
26. Roleplay the following entries by indicating what happens in the output of Example E.5:
    a. E for a main menu entry
    b. 3 and 2 between the 6 and 0 in screen 4.
    c. 1 between the 3 and 0 in screen 6. (How would screen 9 look?)
*27. Make any necessary changes and implement the program in Example E.5 on your system.
*28. Modify the view entire file module so that there is a pause every 15 records. Why is this approach more realistic than just pausing at the end of the file?

**\*29.** Modify the delete records module to give the user the opportunity to stop a deletion before it occurs. After the record ID is entered and the record is retrieved, print the employee's name and ID and ask the user if this is the record to be deleted. If it is, delete the record and print a message to that effect; otherwise, request a new ID.

**\*\*30.** Add the following menu items (and corresponding modules) to the program in Example E.5:

A Add record
C Change record
B Backup file

Within the add record module, it's best to ensure that the record to be added isn't already in the file, or else the user may inadvertently overwrite a good record. Within the change record module, it's best not to force the user to change *all* fields when a record needs to be altered.

## E.5 TRANSACTION PROCESSING APPLICATIONS

**Computer-based information system (CBIS)** is a term that embraces a wide range of computerized information support for an organization. For example, a CBIS can include each of the following computer-based systems.

1. **Transaction processing systems.** These systems primarily capture, store, maintain, and process data that describe *transactions* within an organization. For example, transactions in a payroll application include the number of hours worked during a given week by each nonsalaried employee; monthly transactions in a bank checking-statement application include the processed checks, deposits, and withdrawals from the checking account of each customer; and transactions in an inventory application include the daily shipments and receipts of inventory items. Transaction processing systems generally accomplish procedural tasks such as payroll, inventory control, reservations (such as airline and hotel), and billing applications. The traditional term for a transaction processing system is **data processing system**.

2. **Management information systems (MIS).** An MIS also carries out the functions of capturing, storing, maintaining, and processing data. Unlike transaction processing systems, however, it has the primary task of generating reports and answering queries that provide information to support the traditional management activities of planning, organizing, and controlling. For example, MIS applications might include reports that provide financial information for a corporate merger, sales reports that aid in the reorganization of sales regions, and quality control reports that analyze the performance of work stations in an automated factory. In recent years, MIS applications have been increasingly interactive, so that managers themselves sit at a terminal or microcomputer and generate the needed reports. This has the advantage of interactive "What if . . . ?" processing, whereby the information from one query suggests a variation on the query that provides a basis for the next report.

3. **Decision support systems (DSS).** In the literature and in practice the distinction between a DSS and an MIS is rather blurred. The distinction

is one more of emphasis than of kind. A DSS has a decision rather than an information focus and is more associated with the use of analytic modeling techniques such as forecasting, linear programming, simulation, and other models in statistics and operations research. In some cases, the decision process is automated, as in automated inventory reordering systems and in process control systems such as steelmaking and petroleum blending. These automated systems are sometimes called **programmed decision systems** and are related to the work in artificial intelligence. An **expert system** is another form of decision support system with roots in artificial intelligence research. In this case the software mimics the decision making behavior of an expert human, as in medical diagnosis.

The above systems may also include a **data base management system (DBMS)**. A DBMS manages an integrated collection of files (a database) and allows access to these files by other applications programs and end users by means of query-like or fourth-generation languages. Managing the database includes such tasks as creating, maintaining, accessing, and protecting (for security purposes) the database.

All of the applications in this text are examples of transaction processing, MIS, or DSS. Up to this module, however, we have been missing one very realistic ingredient: external files. Most real-world applications use external files. At the end of the chapter, we suggest programming assignments that revisit some earlier problems that are best implemented with external files. In the remainder of this section, we further illustrate some transaction processing concepts that use two file types called master files and transaction files.

A **master file** contains data items that are central to continued operation of the organization. These files are relatively permanent collections of records containing informational, historical, and current-status items. For example, the master file for bank checking accounts might contain a record, for each customer account, that includes the customer's name, account number, address, telephone, and last month's ending balance.

A **transaction file** is a relatively temporary collection of records containing data about transactions that have occurred during the most recent operating period of time. This type of file is used to process data against the master file. For example, a transaction file for bank checking accounts might contain data on all checks processed during the current month. At the end of the current month, data from both the transaction file and the master file are processed into a new master file that updates the current status of ending balance for each account.

Records in a sequential file (transaction or master) are typically organized for easy access through a record key. As mentioned earlier, a record key is one or more fields in each record that distinguish it from all others. For example, in the banking illustration, the customer account number might serve as the record key. Data on the bank file would be arranged (sorted) by customer account number; the customer record with the lowest account number is first, followed by the customer with the next account number, and so on until the last record is the customer with the highest account number.

---

**E X A M P L E   E . 6**   **Computerized Blood Donor System**

---

A local hospital is developing a computerized blood donor system. This system will be used to contact donors when certain types of blood are needed and to develop statistics about donor usage.

A blood donor master file consisting of one record for each donor has been created, as described by the following record layout.

Record Layout for Blood Donor Master File

| Field | Type | Length |
|---|---|---|
| Donor ID number | Numeric | 4 |
| Donor name | String | 20 |
| Address | String | 40 |
| Phone | String | 11 |
| Blood type | String | 3 |
| Date of last donation | String | 8 |

Let's simplify this example by working strictly with existing donors. In the exercises, we extend the approach to new donors.

### Method 1: Batch Processing System

One approach for updating the blood donor file is **periodic (batch) processing.** In this approach, every time a donor gives blood, the donor's ID and date of donation are recorded in a sequential transaction file. Periodically, weekly perhaps, the records in the transaction file are used to update the "date of last donation" field in the sequential master file.

The process of updating is illustrated by the system flowchart in Figure E.8. A **system flowchart** presents a general overview of an entire system, the sequence of major processing operations, and the data flow to and from files. The type of flowchart that we illustrated in other chapters is technically called a **program flowchart**.

In our blood donor illustration, each donor's contribution is recorded by a data entry operator on the same day that the blood is donated. The DATA ENTRY/EDIT program checks the validity of the date and ID before storing the blood donation transaction in a sequential transaction file. A few sample transactions might appear as follows:

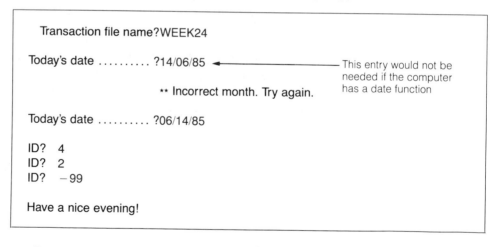

```
   Transaction file name?WEEK24

   Today's date .........?14/06/85  ◄────────── This entry would not be
                                                 needed if the computer
                ** Incorrect month. Try again.  has a date function

   Today's date .........?06/14/85

   ID?  4
   ID?  2
   ID?  −99

   Have a nice evening!
```

Transactions are appended to the end of the weekly sequential transaction file every day. At the end of the week the transaction file might contain the following four transactions:

**Transaction File**

| Donor ID | Date of Last Donation | |
|---|---|---|
| 4 | 06/14/85 | These are the transactions |
| 2 | 06/14/85 | from the sample run above |
| 3 | 06/15/85 | |
| 6 | 06/16/85 | |
| eof mark | | |

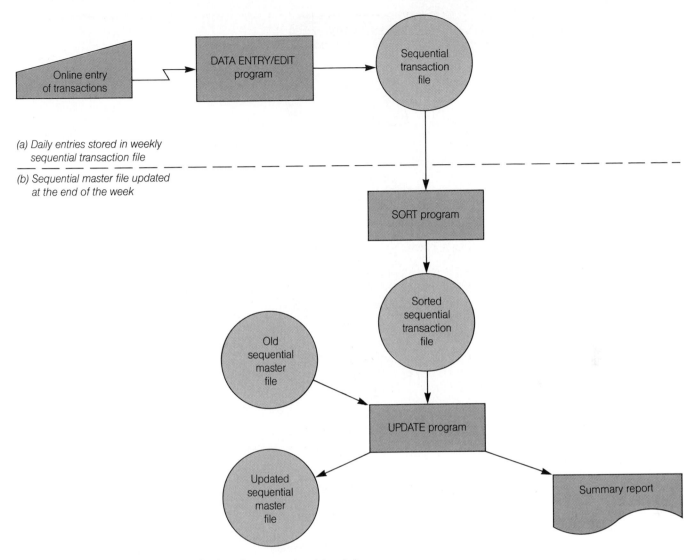

*(a) Daily entries stored in weekly sequential transaction file*

*(b) Sequential master file updated at the end of the week*

**Figure E.8**  Systems flowchart for batch processing blood donor system.

At the end of every week the sequential master file is updated. First, we create a temporary sort file that contains all the records in the transaction file, but in ascending order of ID. Records in this file appear as follows:

**Sorted Transaction File**

| Donor ID | Date of Last Donation |
|----------|----------------------|
| 2 | 06/14/85 |
| 3 | 06/15/85 |
| 4 | 06/14/85 |
| 6 | 06/16/85 |
| eof mark | |

The UPDATE program next uses the sorted transaction file and the *sequential old master file* to create a *sequential updated master file*. The purpose of this program is to update the "date of last donation" field. Additionally, the UPDATE program prints a report showing the donor name, date, and blood type for each donor during that week. If the old master file contains the data shown below before the update.

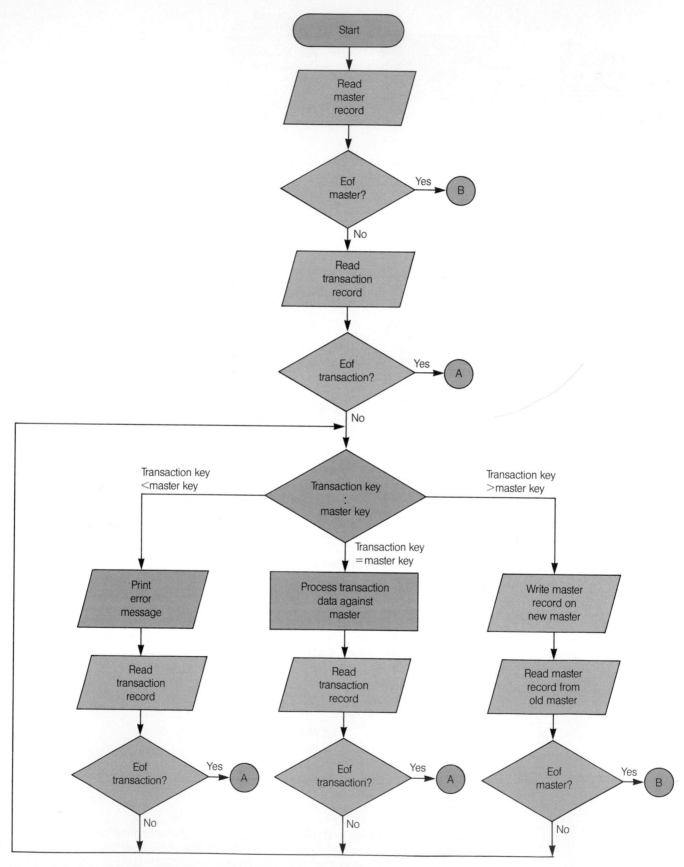

**Figure E.9**   Program flowchart for sequential file update program.

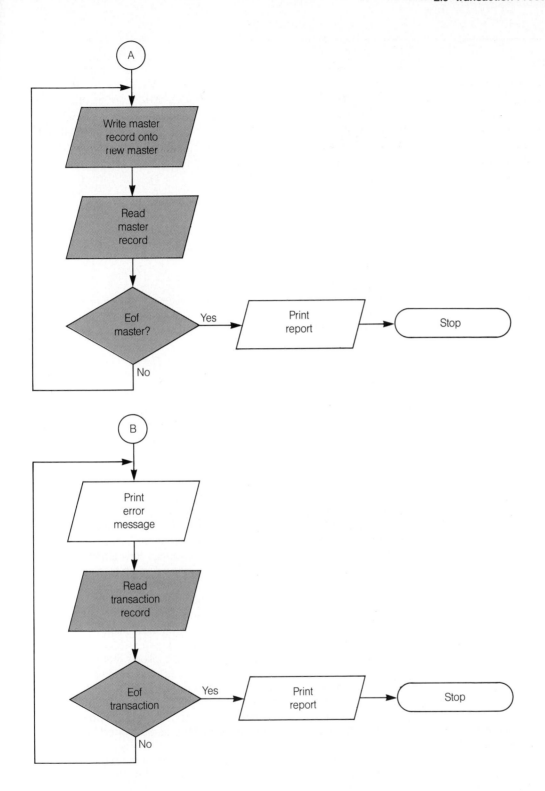

**Old Master File**

| 1 | Smith, A. | 125 Halpern Ave. | Kingston, RI | 792-4091 | A + | 01/03/83 |
|---|-----------|------------------|--------------|----------|-----|----------|
| 2 | Jones, J. | 25 Elmire Rd. | Cranston, RI | 731-2067 | B + | 11/12/81 |
| 3 | Nagel, T. | Estelle Rd. | Warwick, RI | 331-6022 | O + | 05/22/83 |
| 4 | Bosworth, B. | 106 Broad St. | Westerly, RI | 348-9021 | A − | 10/07/84 |
| 5 | Bobick, D. D. | 1 Main St. | Woonsocket, RI | 861-2221 | AB + | 08/17/84 |
| 6 | Regae, J. | 97 Sinker Dr. | Kingston, RI | 401-1111 | O + | 07/16/82 |
| 7 | Myer, B. | 2 Fort St. | Wakefield, RI | 789-1702 | O − | 03/11/85 |
| 8 | Fips, B. B. | 1036 Indian Rd. | Narragansett, RI | 783-2173 | B + | 02/12/82 |

Eof mark

the processing of the transaction file against the master file would result in the following updated master file.

**Updated Master File**

| 1 | Smith, A. | . . . | A + | 01/03/83 |
|---|-----------|-------|-----|----------|
| 2 | Jones, J. | . . . | B + | 06/14/85 |
| 3 | Nagel, T. | . . . | O + | 06/15/85 |
| 4 | Bosworth, B. | . . . | A − | 06/14/85 |
| 5 | Bobick, D. D. | . . . | AB + | 08/17/82 |
| 6 | Regae, J. | . . . | O + | 06/16/85 |
| 7 | Myer, B. | . . . | O − | 03/11/83 |
| 8 | Fips, B. B. | . . . | B + | 02/12/82 |

Eof mark    . . .

A program flowchart for the UPDATE program is illustrated in Figure E.9. The transaction key is the blood donor ID read from a record of the transaction file, and the master key is the blood donor ID from a record of the master file. In the discussion that follows, keep in mind that records in both the transaction and master files are in ascending order according to blood donor ID. Also, we assume that both files are processed by sequential access.

The update program compares the key of the transaction record with the corresponding data item (key) in the master record. If a match occurs (keys of both files are equal), the transaction data are used to update the "date of last donation" field for that master record as illustrated by the middle branch in Fig. E.9.

When the transaction key tests greater than the master key, it follows that processing of the current blood donor on the master file has been completed. Thus, the updated record for this blood donor can now be written onto the new master file. For example, when the second record in the sorted transaction file on page 451 is processed, the transaction key will test greater than the master key (4 > 3). At this time the updated record for Nagel (ID = 3) on the new master file can be written, as described in the third (rightmost) branch of Fig. E.9.

A transaction key greater than the master key may also indicate that no transaction (activity) occurred for that record. This is particularly common when master files have many records. In such cases, the master record is copied unchanged onto the new master file, as in the third branch. For example, the first record of the master file is copied unchanged, since the first transaction ID is 2.

Depending on the situation, however, an error may be indicated by the mismatch of keys. In this case, an error message is printed, as illustrated by the first branch in Fig. E.9.

**Figure E.10**
Online processing blood donor system (relative master file).

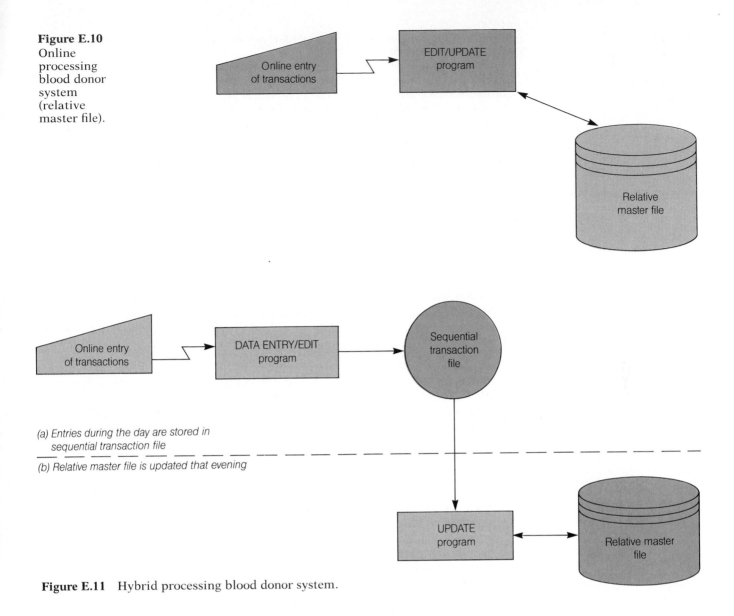

(a) Entries during the day are stored in
  sequential transaction file

(b) Relative master file is updated that evening

**Figure E.11**  Hybrid processing blood donor system.

### Method 2: Online Processing System

Alternatively, and more simply, we could design an **online processing** system that updates a relative master file as transactions are keyed in daily, as illustrated in the system flowchart of Fig. E.10. In this case, transactions are usually entered from a terminal under the control of an EDIT/UPDATE program. This program edits the input data for a valid date and record number (ID). If valid, it then directly updates the proper record in the relative master file. If invalid, it prompts the user for a correct entry.

Compared to the batch processing approach, the online system results in a more current master file and facilitates interactive applications such as record queries from the master file. Unlike the batch processing system, however, it does not maintain a separate file of transactions, which can be useful for archiving (maintaining a historical record) and processing by other programs.

### Method 3: Hybrid Processing System

A third approach to the blood donor system is a combination of batch and online processing. In this case, as transactions occur, they are edited and stored in a sequential transaction file by a DATA ENTRY/EDIT program [see Fig. E.11(a)]. Then, at a later date (say, that night) an UPDATE program processes the transaction file against a relative master file [see Fig. E.11(b)].

Note that this approach uses elements of online processing to capture the transactions [compare Figs. E.10 and E.11(a)] and features of batch processing to update the master file [compare Figs. E.8(b) and E.11(b)]. This approach is less current than the online approach, since the master file is not updated in real time, or immediately; however, it provides a separate transaction file for archiving and use by other programs.

## E.6 POINTERS

### Design and Style

1.  **Record layout.** Don't forget to specify the record layout when you analyze the problem and to include this as part of the program's documentation. In BASIC, we need only specify the length or width of each field when working with relative files. It's also useful to conceptualize a record as a line in a table, in which the column headings represent the fields in the record. For example, see the output table (file employee) in Example E.2 on page 422.

2.  **Backup files.** The greatest worry in computer installations is the complete loss of a database. The loss of a database through fire, theft, sabotage, or some other disaster is more damaging than the loss of the hardware system. Hardware is easily replaced, but a database is not easily reconstructed. An integral part of database protection is the backup (duplication) of all existing files. In large organizations, this is not a trivial task. For example, the TWA airline reservation system has 144 magnetic disk spindles for its more than one million customer records. Half of these are a backup of the other half. Moreover, on a daily basis, these files are dumped to magnetic tape and stored offsite.[6] For your purposes, it's best either to back up files using your system's copy or save command or to build backup file procedures in programs that manage files (as in Exercises 16, 19, and 30) and to ensure that you have both backup *data* files and backup *program* files. If you have yet to lose any files, you may not be as nervous as those of us who have been around computers for a while.

3.  **Sequential versus relative files.** Issues regarding which type of file medium and access method to use relate to factors such as speed, cost, the particular application, and the processing environment. For example, a payroll application for a large company within a mainframe environment would typically use sequential files on magnetic tape media; an airline reservation inquiry system within a time-shared environment would use relative files on magnetic disk media. Generally, we can show that sequential files are best for applications with high file activity, in which all or most records in the file are processed, as in the payroll example; relative files are best used for applications requiring low file activity and speedy response, as in airline reservation systems. We might also note that sequential files are easier to create and program than relative files (their BASIC syntax is simpler), but they take up more file space (they use an ASCII format whereas relative files use a *packed* binary format). To further complicate matters, other ways of organizing files have been developed for varying needs. Indexed files are a popular alternative, which we describe in Exercise 23.

[6]David Gifford and Alfred Spector, "The TWA Reservation System," *Communications of the acm,* July 1984, pp. 650–665.

### Common Errors

1. **Mis-opening files.**    Make sure that the OPEN statement precedes I/O statements, that file numbers are unique if more than one file is to be open at once, and that you don't inadvertently open an existing file for output (unless you like to see the destruction of file contents). Also, pay attention to the syntax in OPEN statements, especially how they differ with respect to the file types sequential and relative.

2. **Record mishaps.**    Make sure that sequential I/O statements (PRINT # and INPUT #) and buffer record definitions (FIELD in Microsoft BASIC and MAP in VAX-11 BASIC) reflect the record layout with respect to the type (numeric or string) and ordering of variables. In creating sequential files, take care that each field value is properly delimited from the next by blanks or a comma.

3. **Eof errors.**    If we get an error message like "Input past end" or "Not enough data in record," then we have committed an eof error. These occur either when an INPUT # statement is executed that attempts to read beyond the last data item in a sequential file or when we attempt to input from a file that's been opened for output or append. This error is fatal to execution and is best avoided by the use of an eof function. If your system lacks this function, then use one of the other procedures described in Table E.6 on page 415.

---

## ADDITIONAL EXERCISES

**31.**   Define or explain each of the following terms.

| | | |
|---|---|---|
| field | CLOSE statement | LOF function |
| record | EOF function | CBIS |
| record layout | ON ERROR statement | transaction processing system |
| file | ERR variable | data processing system |
| internal and external file | rewinding a file | MIS |
| unformatted and formatted record | file maintenance | DSS |
| ASCII and binary file | key field | programmed decision system |
| sequential and relative file | key | expert system |
| random and direct-access file | buffer | DBMS |
| eof mark | FIELD statement | master file |
| record number | LSET and RSET statements | transaction file |
| OPEN statement | MKS$ function | system flowchart |
| PRINT # statement | CVS function | program flowchart |
| PRINT # USING statement | MAP statement | batch processing system |
| WRITE statement | record key | online processing system |
| INPUT statement | LOC function | |
| LINE INPUT # (or INPUT LINE #) statement | | |

**32.   Revisits.**    Rework one of the following problems.

a. Select a program that you have already written and revise it to give the option of output to the screen, line printer (if available), or a file. Make sure you output to the file. Then display this file as a report through another program.

b. **Alumni file.** (Exercise 28, Chapter 4, page 143.) Use a sequential file for the alumni file.

c. **Inventory reorders.** (Exercise 29, Chapter 4, page 144.) Use a sequential file for the inventory file.

d. **Job placement.** (Exercise 32, Chapter 4, page 144.) Use a sequential file for the placement office file.

e. **Personnel benefits budget.** (Exercise 29, Chapter 5, page 177.) Use a sequential file for the employee file.

f. **Property tax assessment.** (Exercise 33, Chapter 6, page 220.) Use a sequential file to store the property owner's data.

g. **Traffic court fines.** (Exercise 34, Chapter 6, page 221.) Use a sequential file to store the violations data file.

**h. Telephone company billing.** (Exercise 35, Chapter 6, page 221.) Use a sequential file to store the telephone data.

**i. Mailing list.** (Exercise 36, Chapter 6, page 222.) Use a sequential file to store the sample data file.

**j. Population.** (Exercise 35, Chapter 7, page 267.) Use a sequential file to store the county population data. Also see the suggestion in part **a** above. Apply this to the population change report.

**k. Exam reports.** (Exercise 36, Chapter 7, page 268.) Use a sequential file to store the student records. Add a menu item that displays the grades for a particular student.

**l. Crime data summary.** (Exercise 41, Chapter 8, page 309.) Use a sequential file to store the arrest data. Also see part **a** above.

**m. SAT scores.** (Exercise 42, Chapter 8, page 310.) Use a sequential file to store the student file. Also see part **a** above.

**n. Revenue sharing.** (Exercise 45, Chapter 8, page 311.) Use a sequential file to store the population by state data. Also see part **a** above.

**o. Exam grading.** (Exercise 46, Chapter 8, page 312.) Use a sequential file to store the exam data.

**p. Stock portfolio valuation.** (Exercise 35, Chapter 9, page 343.) Use a sequential file to store the stock portfolio.

**q. State taxes.** (Exercise 36, Chapter 9, page 344.) Use a sequential file to store the tax-dollars-collected data.

**r. Personnel salary budget.** (Exercise 38, Chapter 9, page 345.) Use two sequential files to store the salary schedules and the personnel file.

**s. Questionnaire analysis.** (Exercise 40, Chapter 9, page 346.) Use a sequential file to store the answers.

**33. Checking account report revisited.** Design the program of Exercise 30 in Chapter 5 on page 178 so that master and transaction files are used. The master file contains bank account number, name, and last month's ending balance (called the beginning balance in the original problem). The transaction file contains account number and the monthly checking transactions for each customer. Make sure that last month's ending balance is updated on the master file.

**34. Credit billing revisited.** Design the program of Exercise 27 in Chapter 5 on page 176 so that master and transaction files are used. The master file contains name, address, credit limit , and last billing period's ending (previous) balance for each customer. The transaction file contains name, payments, and new purchases.

**a.** Run your program for the data given in the problem so that bills are printed and the master file is updated.

**\*\*b.** Include the following action codes in the transaction file and program logic.

1. Change in address
2. Change in credit limit
3. Delete customer from master file
4. Add customer to master file

Make up data to test each of these action codes.

**35. Electric bill revisited.** Design the program of Exercise 40 in Chapter 7 on page 270 so that master and transaction files are used. The master file contains previous reading, rate code, past due amount, name, street address, city, state, zip code, and account number for each customer. In addition to dates, the transaction file contains account number, name, new meter reading, and payments since last bill.

**a.** Run your program for the data given in the program so that bills are printed and the master file is updated.

**\*\*b.** Include the following action codes in the transaction file and program logic.

1. Change of address
2. Delete customer from master file
3. Add customer to master file

Make up data to test each of these action codes.

**36. Interactive airline reservation system revisited.** Modify Exercise 37 of Chapter 9 on page 344 as follows.

**a.** Use a relative file instead of an array for the current table of flight information. Each table (file) of flight information is based on a specific week for the coming year. Use flight number as the record number.

**b.** Instead of the record numbers in part **a**, use a record number based on the sum of flight number and day code. If the ten flights in the table are numbered 240, 250, 260, 810, 100, 110, 120, 130, 950, and 960 and the days in the week (Monday, Tuesday, . . . , Sunday) are coded 1, 2, . . . , 7, a request for flight 950 on Wednesday would access record number 953, whereas the same flight on Sunday would access record number 957.

**\*\*c.** Add other useful features. For example, you might want to allow 1% overbooking of seats (a common practice); create a file that stores reservations information such as customer's name, address, and telephone number; create a waiting list file that periodically is processed against the flight table (master) file.

**\*\*37. Exam reports revisited.** Rework the program of Exercise 36 in Chapter 7 on page 268 to use a relative file. Also, include the following additional menu options:

5. Display grades for any student
6. Change grades for any student
7. Add a new exam score for the class
8. Add a new student
9. Drop a student

Assume that the maximum number of scores for each student is six. Make up some IDs for record numbers.

38. **Bond issue.**   Write a program that offers the following menu:

C   Create file
A   Append to file
D   Display file
P   Print report
S   Stop processing

a. Create a sequential file called BOND with the following records:

| County | Yes votes | No votes |
|--------|-----------|----------|
| Dade | 300,000 | 400,000 |
| Cuyahoga | 100,000 | 75,000 |
| Washington | 50,000 | 30,000 |

b. Append the following records to the file:

| Orange | 250,000 | 100,000 |
|--------|---------|---------|
| Broward | 150,000 | 75,000 |

c. Display the revised file.
d. Print a report. You decide what might be nice to include in this report.

39. **Blood donor batch processing system.**   Write and run the following programs for the batch processing system described in Example E.6. Use the data given in the example.
a. DATA ENTRY/EDIT. Use the following menu:

C   Create new file
A   Append to existing file
S   Stop processing

Don't forget to design the error routine for valid dates and IDs (max = 999). *Hint:* If you use string values for dates (as shown in the example), then you need to strip off month, date, and year using the methods in Module F; otherwise, use separate numeric values for month, day, and year.
b. SORT. Create the sorted transaction file described earlier. *Hint:* See Section 8.6, page 296.
c. UPDATE. Include output of a report of your own choosing. At a minimum, include a summary of transactions by blood type.
d. Add other useful features. For example, UPDATE could include an option to echo print all records in the transaction and master files;

DATA ENTRY/EDIT could include the entry of new donors.

40. **Blood donor online processing system.**   Consider Method 2 in Example E.6.
a. Write and run the EDIT/UPDATE program. Use the data given in the example. Don't forget to edit the input data for valid dates and record numbers. If an entry is incorrect, prompt the user for a correct entry. See the hint in part **a** of the preceding exercise for the treatment of dates.
b. Include a report as described in part **c** of the preceding exercise.
c. Add other useful features, such as display of the entire master file or selected records or the addition of new donors to the master file.

41. **Blood donor hybrid processing system.**   Consider Method 3 in Example E.6.
a. Write and run the DATA ENTRY/EDIT program, as in Exercise 39a.
b. Write and run the UPDATE program. Include the report described in Exercise 39c.
c. Add other useful features, such as display of either the entire master file or selected records or the addition of new donors to the master file.

**\*\*42. Payroll.**   Each week a small firm processes its weekly payroll for hourly employees. The following file input is necessary to process the payroll.

---
Master Employee File Record Description
---
Employee ID
Name
Hourly rate of pay
Number of dependents
Cumulative gross pay thus far this year
Cumulative FICA tax thus far this year
Cumulative withholding (income) tax thus far this year
Cumulative group health contribution thus far this year
---

---
Transaction File Record Description
---
Employee ID
Date
Number of hours worked
---

Develop a program that
a. Generates a "wage summary report" consisting of a line for each employee: the line contains employee name, employee number, hourly rate, hours worked, gross pay, FICA, income tax, group health, and net pay. After

individual figures are printed, the program is to print totals for gross pay, each deduction, and net pay. Include appropriate report and column headings.

To determine the pay for each employee, the following facts must be included in your program:

1. Gross pay is defined as pay for regular time plus pay for overtime. Overtime pay is 1.5 times the regular rate for each hour above 40.
2. Social Security tax (FICA) is 6.65% of gross pay. The deduction is made until the employee's cumulative earnings are above $29,700, after which there is no deduction.
3. Deduction for withholding tax and group health plan are tied to the number of dependents as follows.

| Dependents | Income Tax (% of gross pay) | Group Health ($ per week) |
|---|---|---|
| 1 | 22 | 2.50 |
| 2 | 20 | 3.60 |
| 3 | 18 | 5.10 |
| 4 | 16 | 6.00 |
| 5 or more | 13 | 6.50 |

4. Net pay is defined as gross pay less FICA deduction less income tax deduction less group health deduction. Use the data below to test your program.

Transaction File for (date, which you supply)

| | |
|---|---|
| 1 | 60 |
| 2 | 40 |
| 61 | 45 |
| 92 | 35 |

b. Updates cumulative gross pay, cumulative FICA tax, cumulative withholding tax, and cumulative group health contribution for each employee in the master file.

c. Run parts a and b again for the next week using the data below.

Transaction file for (date one week after preceding transaction file)

| | |
|---|---|
| 1 | 32 |
| 2 | 45 |
| 61 | 35 |
| 92 | 42 |

d. Design a routine that edits the data for errors. Specifically it ensures that the

1. Numbers of dependents is greater than zero and less than 15.
2. Rate of pay is greater than $3.30 and less than $10.00.
3. Number of hours worked is greater than zero and less than 65.
4. Total earnings thus far this year is zero or greater or less than $40,000.

If an error is detected, print an appropriate error message that includes the employee's name and number, bypass the calculations and printout for this employee, and go on to the next employee. Add new data to test each of these four possible input errors.

**e. Design your program to include the following menu:

1 Change in hourly rate of pay
2 Change in number of dependents
3 Delete employee from master file
4 Add employee to master file
5 Wage summary report
6 Print transaction file
7 Print master file
8 Stop processing

Make up data to test each of these action codes.

**43. Class grades.** Design a comprehensive program that maintains and processes student grades for an academic course. You might include features such as file creation, file modifications (e.g., change a grade, add a grade, delete a grade, delete a record, add a record), file display, record display, calculation of final numeric grade based on weights for individual grades (including the assignment of a letter grade if applicable), .... If a student is added to the file, make sure this student is placed in the correct alphabetic position. Once your program is debugged, hire yourself a marketing major and pedal your program to faculty members for an exorbitant software fee.

Master File

| | | | | | | | |
|---|---|---|---|---|---|---|---|
| 1 | Bella Bitta, Al | 2.50 | 4 | 1500.00 | 99.75 | 240.00 | 180.00 |
| 2 | Budget, Frank | 8.25 | 5 | 30000.00 | 1975.05 | 3900.00 | 195.00 |
| 61 | Manicotti, Diane | 6.00 | 1 | 12300.00 | 817.95 | 2706.00 | 75.00 |
| 92 | Saintvi, Arun | 8.00 | 3 | 29600.00 | 1968.40 | 5328.00 | 153.00 |

# String Functions and Text Processing

In earlier chapters we liberally used string constants, variables, and arrays to store, test, and print character data such as names, addresses, and descriptions. Simple string processing of the type we have described is used routinely in practice but is not suggestive of more sophisticated manipulative requirements in such applications as text editing, text analysis, linguistics analysis, and the encoding/decoding of secret messages. In this chapter, following a review of string-related terminology and statements, we shall describe how BASIC can be used to manipulate string data.

## F.1 REVIEW

A **character string**, or simply **string**, is a sequence of characters, including letters, numbers, and symbols. The **length** of a string is the number of characters in the string.

A **string constant** is called a quoted string if it is enclosed within quotation marks or an unquoted string if it is not. Thus, "I LOVE BASIC" is a string constant in the form of a quoted string with a length of 12 characters.

We can store **string values** within **string variables** by using LET, READ, or INPUT statements, as shown in Example F.1.

---

*This module can be read anytime after Chapter 5, except for Section F.5, which requires Chapters 7 and 8.

**E X A M P L E   F . 1**　**Reading String Values into String Variables**

The following program reads and prints the string values for names and sex codes into the string variables FULL.NAME\$ and SEX.CODE\$. Note that string variables are data typed by using the \$ symbol as the last character in the name.[1]

```
100 REM    Reading string values into string variables
105 REM
110        READ N                              ── String variables
115 REM
120        FOR I = 1 TO N
130           READ  FULL.NAME$,SEX.CODE$,SALARY
140           PRINT FULL.NAME$,SEX.CODE$,SALARY
150        NEXT I
155 REM                                        ── String values
900        DATA 2
901        DATA Dave Hemple,M,32450
902        DATA Marge Bold,F,34000
998 REM
999        END

RUN
Dave Hemple    M                 32450
Marge Bold     F                 34000
```

A **string expression** is a string constant, string variable, string function, or some combination of these. For example, the statement

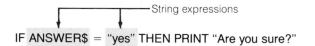

IF ANSWER\$ = "yes" THEN PRINT "Are you sure?"

illustrates a logical expression that compares two string expressions. The string expression to the left of the relational operator is the string variable, ANSWER\$; the string expression to the right is the string constant "yes." We shall show more complicated string expressions in the remaining sections of this module.

The LET statement is another way of assigning a string value to a string variable. A string LET statement has the following general form.

**String LET Statement**

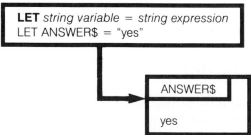

LET *string variable* = *string expression*
LET ANSWER\$ = "yes"

ANSWER\$

yes

Arrays that store string values also are commonly used in string processing, as the following example illustrates.

---

[1]Some systems allow the data typing of string variables by other means. For example, on the VAX-11 system we can use the following statement to data type FULL.NAME and SEX.CODE as string variables:

DECLARE STRING FULL.NAME, SEX.CODE

**E X A M P L E   F . 2**   Subscripted String Variables*

**String array element names** or **subscripted string variables** store a string value within each **array element**, or memory location. For example, the following program stores the months of the year within the *one-dimensional* string array MONTH$ and prints the name of the third month.

```
100 REM   Subscripted string variables
105 REM
110       DIM  MONTH$(12)  ◄──────────── Array declaration
115 REM
120       FOR J = 1 TO 12  ┌─── Storage of string values within array elements
130         READ MONTH$(J) ◄─┘
140       NEXT J           ┌─── Subscripted string variable
150 REM                    │    or
160       PRINT MONTH$(3) ◄┘    string array element name
170 REM
901       DATA January,February,March
902       DATA April,May,June
903       DATA July,August,September
904       DATA October,November,December
998 REM
999       END

RUN
March
```

Storage within array MONTH$ would appear as follows.

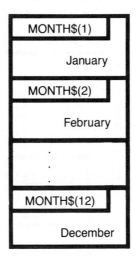

In our example, each of the 12 memory locations is an **array element**, the **string array name** is MONTH$, and MONTH(3) is a *string array element name*, or *subscripted string variable*, that references the third array element in array MONTH$.

---

Before leaving this section let's introduce one new term that is frequently used in string processing. A **substring** is a group of one or more adjacent characters in a string. A substring can include a single character, an entire string, or any adjacent part in the string. For example, the string *bc* is a substring of the string *abcde*, as is *d* and *abcde* itself; however, *ac* is not a substring in *abcde*, since the characters *a* and *c* are not adjacent in *abcde*.

*Skip this example if you haven't studied Chapter 8.

This ends a review of the string-related topics scattered throughout the text. In the next several sections we shall show, among other things, BASIC's capability to join strings, remove substrings, search a string for the occurrence of a substring, code strings, and edit strings.

---

### Follow-Up Exercises

1.   Is LVE a substring in LOVE? Explain.
2.   What is the maximum length of a string on your system?

---

## F.2 CONCATENATION

**Concatenation** is the act of joining two or more strings to form one longer string. This is accomplished by using the **concatenation operator**[2] **+** to join any two strings, as follows.

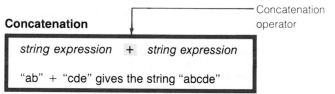

**Concatenation**

*string expression*   **+**   *string expression*

"ab" + "cde" gives the string "abcde"

---

**E X A M P L E   F . 3**   Concatenation Examples

Assume the following values are stored.

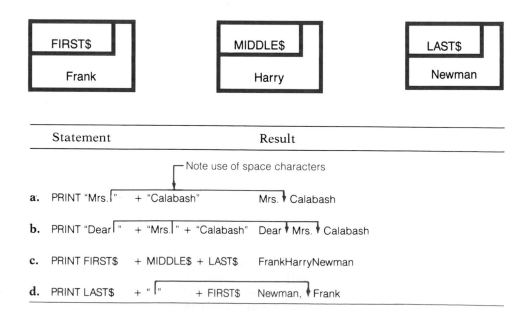

FIRST$

Frank

MIDDLE$

Harry

LAST$

Newman

| | Statement | Result |
|---|---|---|
| | | ┌ Note use of space characters |
| **a.** | PRINT "Mrs. " + "Calabash" | Mrs. ▼ Calabash |
| **b.** | PRINT "Dear " + "Mrs. " + "Calabash" | Dear ▼ Mrs. ▼ Calabash |
| **c.** | PRINT FIRST$ + MIDDLE$ + LAST$ | FrankHarryNewman |
| **d.** | PRINT LAST$ + ", " + FIRST$ | Newman, ▼ Frank |

---

[2]The ampersand (&) is used as the concatenation operator in ANS BASIC.

**E X A M P L E   F . 4**    Mailing Labels

In the following mailing label program, the variables CITY\$, STATE\$, and ZIP\$ are three separate string variables. The concatenation operator is used to join these string values and the appropriate punctuation to form the third or city–state–zip line of the mailing label.

```
100 REM    Mailing labels
105 REM
110        READ FULL.NAME$,ADDRESS$,CITY$,STATE$,ZIP$
120          DATA Rory Calhoun,117 Macintosh Drive,Cranston,RI,02878
125 REM
130        LET CTY.ST.ZP$ = CITY$ + "," + STATE$ + " " + ZIP$
135 REM
140        PRINT FULL.NAME$
150        PRINT ADDRESS$
160        PRINT CTY.ST.ZP$              Concatenation operator
165 REM
999        END

RUN
Rory Calhoun
117 Macintosh Drive
 Cranston,RI 02878
```

Note that the string expression

CITY\$ + "," + STATE\$ + " " + ZIP\$

is evaluated as the string value

Cranston, RI 02878

and is stored in the string variable CTY.ST.ZP\$

---

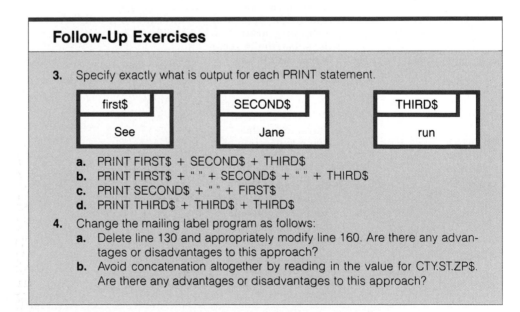

## Follow-Up Exercises

**3.**  Specify exactly what is output for each PRINT statement.

| first\$ | SECOND\$ | THIRD\$ |
|---|---|---|
| See | Jane | run |

**a.**  PRINT FIRST\$ + SECOND\$ + THIRD\$
**b.**  PRINT FIRST\$ + " " + SECOND\$ + " " + THIRD\$
**c.**  PRINT SECOND\$ + " " + FIRST\$
**d.**  PRINT THIRD\$ + THIRD\$ + THIRD\$

**4.**  Change the mailing label program as follows:
**a.**  Delete line 130 and appropriately modify line 160. Are there any advantages or disadvantages to this approach?
**b.**  Avoid concatenation altogether by reading in the value for CTY.ST.ZP\$. Are there any advantages or disadvantages to this approach?

### F.3 BUILT-IN STRING FUNCTIONS

By this time you have probably used some of the built-in functions presented in Module C, most of which relate to numeric data. BASIC also includes several **built-in string functions** that specifically process and manipulate string data, as summarized in Table F.1.

**Table F.1**    Built-in String Functions

| Function | Dialects[a] | Meaning | Examples | Results |
|---|---|---|---|---|
| **LEN(e$)** | 1,2,3 | Returns the number of characters in the string expression e$ | LEN("I LOVE BASIC")<br>LEN(" ")<br>LEN("") | 12<br>1<br>0 |
| **LEFT$(e$,n)** | 2,3 | Returns the first $n$ characters of the string expression e$ | LEFT$("I LOVE BASIC",5)<br>LEFT$("I LOVE BASIC",1)<br>LEFT$("I LOVE BASIC",0) | I LOVE<br>I<br>null or empty value |
| **RIGHT(e$,n)** | 2 | Returns the last $n$ characters of the string expression e$ | RIGHT$("I LOVE BASIC",5)<br>RIGHT$("I LOVE BASIC",12) | BASIC<br>I LOVE BASIC |
|  | or<br><br>3 | Returns the characters starting in position $n$ of the string expression e$ and ending in the rightmost character | RIGHT$("I LOVE BASIC",5)<br>RIGHT$("I LOVE BASIC",12) | VE BASIC<br>C |
| **MID$(e$,p,n)** | 2,3 | Returns $n$ characters starting at position $p$ in the string expression e$ | MID$("I LOVE BASIC",3,4)<br>LEFT$(MID$("I LOVE BASIC",8,5),2) | LOVE<br>BA |
| **INSTR(e$,s$)**<br><br>or<br><br>**POS(e$,s$)** | 2,3<br><br><br><br>1 | Searches the string expression e$ for the occurrence of a substring s$ and returns the beginning position of the substring. A zero is returned if no match occurs | INSTR("I LOVE BASIC","BASIC")<br>INSTR("I LOVE BASIC","basic")<br><br>POS("I LOVE BASIC","BASIC")<br>POS("I LOVE BASIC","basic") | 8<br>0<br><br>8<br>0 |
| **ASC(e$)**<br><br>or<br><br>**ORD(e$)** | 2,3<br><br><br><br>1 | Returns ASCII code (integer in the range 0–255) of the first character in the string expression e$ | ASC("A")<br>ASC("a")<br>ASC("Aa")<br><br>ORD("A")<br>ORD("a")<br>ORD("Aa") | 65<br>97<br>65<br><br>65<br>97<br>65 |
| **CHR$(n)** | 1,2,3 | Returns the character or graphic symbol equivalent to the internal or ASCII code $n$ | CHR$(65)<br>CHR$(97) | A<br>a |
| **VAL(e$)** | 1,2,3 | Returns numeric value of a numeric string; otherwise returns zero | VAL("55")<br>VAL("−55")<br>VAL("A") | 55<br>−55<br>0 |

**Table F.1** *(continued)*

| Function | Dialects[a] | Meaning | Examples | Results |
|----------|-------------|---------|----------|---------|
| **STR$(n)** | 1,2,3 | Converts a numeric constant or variable to a string expression representing the numeric characters | STR$(55)<br>STR$(−55) | 55<br>−55 |

(Use this space for describing other string functions that are of interest on your system)

[a]Dialects: 1 = ANS BASIC; 2 = Microsoft BASIC on the IBM PC; 3 = VAX-11 BASIC; 4 = your system (if different)

## E X A M P L E   F . 5    Line Centering with the LEN Function

We can use the following formula to center a title or heading on a report line:

$$\text{Starting print position} = \frac{\text{total length of line} - \text{length of heading}}{2}$$

In line 130 of the program below, the LEN function is used to find the length or number of characters in the title PAYROLL REPORT. This number is used in the formula on line 140 to determine the starting print position for the title. Finally, the starting print position is used as the argument of the TAB function in line 150.

```
100 REM   Line centering using the LEN function
105 REM
110       LET HEAD$      = "PAYROLL REPORT"
120       LET LINE.LENGTH = 80                          Length function
130       LET HEAD.LENGTH = LEN(HEAD$)
140       LET START      = INT( (LINE.LENGTH - HEAD.LENGTH)/2 )
145 REM
150       PRINT TAB(START); HEAD$
155 REM
999       END

RUN
                                              Start column = 33 (see lines 140-150)

              PAYROLL REPORT

                                        Head length = 14 (see line 130)

                                        Line length = 80 (see line 120)
```

**E X A M P L E   F . 6**   **User Entry Stripping with the LEFT$ Function**

In an interactive program it's best to anticipate various entries a user may give in response to a prompt. In the following program the responses *yes*, *ye*, and *y* are treated as acceptable responses by a user to continue execution of the program.

```
100 REM   Stripping using the LEFT$ function
105 REM
110       LET ANSWER$ = "yes"        ┌─ LEFT$ function strips all characters but the leftmost
115 REM                              │  or first
120       WHILE LEFT$(ANSWER$,1) = "y"
130         PRINT "Hello"
140         PRINT
150         INPUT "Do you want another run (y/n) "; ANSWER$
160       WEND
165 REM
170       PRINT
180       PRINT "End of run."
185 REM
999       END

RUN
Hello

Do you want another run (y/n) ? yes
Hello

Do you want another run (y/n) ? ye
Hello

Do you want another run (y/n) ? n

End of run.
```

Line 120 uses the LEFT$ function to strip off or ignore all but the first character of the user's response.

**E X A M P L E   F . 7**   **Date Substrings with the MID$ and RIGHT$ Functions**

In the United States the date is often expressed as a string in the form

*mm*/*dd*/*yy*

where *mm* is a two-digit month, *dd* is a two-digit day of the month, and *yy* is the last two digits of the year. Sometimes we need to extract the year, month, or day to use separately in some other part of the program, as the following illustrates.

```
100 REM   Date substrings using the RIGHT$ and MID$ functions
105 REM
110       INPUT "Date of sale"; SALES.DATE$
115 REM
120       LET YEAR$ = RIGHT$(SALES.DATE$,2) ◄── RIGHT$ function finds the year substring
130       PRINT "  Year of sale: "; YEAR$
135 REM
140       LET DAY$  = MID$(SALES.DATE$,4,2) ◄── MID$ function finds the day substring
150       PRINT "  Day  of sale: "; DAY$
155 REM
999       END

RUN
Date of sale? 08/03/85
  Year of sale: 85
  Day  of sale: 03
```

In line 120 the RIGHT$ function is used to find the year substring by assigning the last two digits of the variable SALES.DATE$ to the variable YEAR$. In line 140 the MID$ function is used to extract the day of the sale. The MID$ function extracts two characters beginning with the fourth position in SALES.DATE$ and stores the day substring in the variable DAY$.

**E X A M P L E   F . 8**   Valid Codes with the INSTR Function

In this example we use the INSTR function to search through a string of valid codes to verify that a valid code has been entered by the user.

```
100 REM    Searching for a substring with the INSTR function
110 REM
120        LET VALID.CODES$ = "RPC"                Valid codes string
130 REM                                            INSTR function looks for user
140        INPUT "Brand code"; BRAND.CODE$          code entry as a substring within
150 REM                                            the valid codes string
160        IF INSTR (VALID.CODES$,BRAND.CODE$) = O THEN
             PRINT "***" + BRAND.CODE$ + " is an invalid code."
170 REM
180        PRINT "Program completed."              Note use of concatenation
190 REM                                            operators within the print list
999        END

RUN
Brand code? D
***D is an invalid code.
Program completed.

RUN
Brand code? C
Program completed.
```

If the code entered via line 140 is not one of the valid codes (R, P, or C), then the function returns a zero in line 160; any other value returned by the INSTR function implies that the entered code is valid.

---

**E X A M P L E   F . 9**   String to Numeric Data Conversion with the VAL Function[†]

In this example we use the LEFT$ and VAL functions in line 160 to extract and convert the month to a numeric value, as entered in the date string mm/dd/yy. In line 170 this numeric value is edited to verify that its value is between 1 and 12 inclusive. If the variable MONTH$ contains a valid month, then the value is used as a subscript in the MONTH.LIST$ array to look up the correct month; otherwise an error message is printed.

```
100 REM    String to numeric data conversion
105 REM
110        DIM MONTH.LIST$(12)
115 REM
120        FOR J = 1 TO 12
130          READ MONTH.LIST$(J)          Stores months in string array
140        NEXT J
145 REM
150        INPUT "Enter sales date"; SALES.DATE$
155 REM                                        LEFT$ strips off all but first
160        LET MONTH = VAL(LEFT$(SALES.DATE$,2))   two characters and VAL
165 REM                                        converts to numeric value
170        IF MONTH >= 1 AND MONTH <= 12
             THEN PRINT "   Sales month is " + MONTH.LIST$(MONTH)
             ELSE PRINT "   Sales month is invalid"
175 REM
901        DATA January,February,March,April,May,June
902        DATA July,August,September,October,November,December
998 REM
999        END                    Numeric string value gets
                                   converted to numeric value that's
                                   used as a subscript value
RUN
Enter sales date? 08/03/85
    Sales month is August
                                   Numeric month directly accesses
RUN                                or points to specific array
Enter sales date? 25/08/85         element
    Sales month is invalid
```

---

[†]This example requires knowledge of Chapter 8.

## Follow-Up Exercises

5. In Example F.5:
   a. In what column or print position is the *P* in PAYROLL? Show by hand how this is calculated.
   b. Modify the program so that dashed lines are centered under the report title.

6. In Example F.6:
   a. Is the response *yep* acceptable?
   b. Suppose the user were to mistakenly hit the *t* key instead of the *y* key. What happens?
   *c. Correct the problem in part **b** by modifying the program to trap any entries that don't begin with *y* or *n*.

7. Modify Example F.7 so:
   a. The month is extracted and printed.
   b. The year is printed in the form 19yy.

*8. Error trap the wrong code in Example F.8 by having the program repeatedly request the code while it is incorrect.

*9. Modify Example F.9 to verify that the day entered is within the range 1 and 31 inclusive.

*10. Write a short program that enters product *id* as a four-digit string value. Then use the LEN function to verify that the product *id* is valid by not being more than four digits. If the product *id* is valid, then print the message *valid*; else print *invalid*. Use the following test data: 1234, 123, 12345.

*11. Write a short program that uses the DATE$ function on your system along with built-in string functions to print dates in the following formats:
   a. yymmdd          Example:   861225
   b. dd–mm–yyyy      Example:   25–12–1986
   c. mmm dd, yyyy    Example:   Dec 25, 1986

*12. A person's name is stored in the string variable FULL.NAME$ in the format

   first name <space> last name

   Write a short program that manipulates the string and prints the name in the following format:

   last name, <space> first name

   Use the following test data:   Harvey Core
                                  H. Core

**13. Write the code for a routine that inputs numeric data as a string value, confirms that each character in the entered value is numeric (its ASCII code is in the range 48 to 57 inclusive), and converts the string value to a numeric representation. If the string value is not numeric, then print an error message and request reentry while the value is not numeric. Reproduce the following sample run:

   Enter product code number? 123
   Enter product code number? i90
      No, dummy!   Enter a numeric code? 89o
      No, dummy!   Enter a numeric code? 890
   Enter product code number? 0
      End of run.

   What would happen without a routine that traps this type of error?

## F.4 USER-DEFINED STRING FUNCTIONS

*User-defined functions* were introduced in Module C. In that module the examples concentrated on numeric functions; however, **user-defined string functions** are also permitted, as illustrated next.

**E X A M P L E   F . 1 0**    **User Entry Stripping with a User-Defined String Function**

The program below is a modification of Example F.6, where the stripping of all characters but the first is accomplished by a user-defined function.

```
100 REM   Stripping with a user-defined string function
101 REM   (Compare to Example F.6)
105 REM                                    User-defined string function named
107       DEF FNSTRIP$(A$) = LEFT$(A$,1) ←─ FNSTRIP$
108 REM
110       LET ANSWER$ = "yes"             ──── Function FNSTRIP$ is referenced here
115 REM
120       WHILE FNSTRIP$(ANSWER$) = "y"
130         PRINT "Hello"
140         PRINT
150         INPUT "Do you want another run (y/n) "; ANSWER$
160       WEND
165 REM
170       PRINT
180       PRINT "End of run."
185 REM
999       END

RUN
Hello

Do you want another run (y/n) ? yes
Hello

Do you want another run (y/n) ? ye
Hello

Do you want another run (y/n)    n

End of run.
```

The only differences between this program and the original are shown by the shaded portions. In line 107, the string function is defined using the DEF statement. In line 120, the function is referenced.

There is no advantage to using a user-defined string function in this example. As with numeric user-defined functions, however, the user-defined string function is desirable for complicated expressions that are used in several places within a program.

## Follow-Up Exercises

14. Rework Example F.7 such that YEAR$ and DAY$ are the names of user-defined string functions.

**\*\*15.** **Baseball simulation revisit.** Rework Exercise 17 in Module C on page 383 to use a multiline string function that returns the "time at bat" result as one of the following string values: out, single, double, triple, homerun.

## F.5 SELECTED APPLICATIONS

In this section we illustrate simple applications within two areas of string processing: cryptography and text editing. We let you explore these applications in greater depth in the exercises.

### Cryptography[†]

Cryptography is the science of transforming messages for the purpose of making them unintelligible to all but the intended receiver of the message. A message is transformed either by encoding or decoding. Encoding is the process of transforming a message into code; decoding is the translation of the code into its message form. The encoding and decoding of messages usually includes a transformation algorithm for transforming the messages and a key that controls the process.

**Analysis.** One category of secret messages is called ciphers. In this approach the transformation algorithm either rearranges or replaces the letters of each word. Substitution ciphers code messages by replacing one letter with another. The following illustrates a straightforward substitution cipher:

**THE ALPHABET SHIFT CIPHER** Encode each letter by replacing it with a letter that falls a given number of positions after the actual letter. The *increment key* provides the number of positions that the letter is shifted. If the shift takes us beyond the end of the alphabet, then wrap around the alphabet by continuing at the beginning.

*Example:* If the increment key is 10, then A would be replaced by K since K is 10 positions from A. Similarly, B would be replaced by L, C would be replaced by M, and so on. If S is to be encoded, we note that a shift of 10 positions would take us three positions beyond Z. Thus, we would wrap around to C. The following shows the encoding of an entire message.

*Actual message:* HELP IS ON THE WAY
*Encoded message:* ROVZ SC YX DRO GKI

Let's design and write a program that encodes messages using the alphabet shift cipher. The data requirements are as follows.

*Output*
Encoded message (in upper case letters)

*Input*
Increment key
Actual message (in upper case letters)

**Design.** The transformation algorithm converts the message, one character at a time, to the *ASCII numeric code* representing the letter. Then we add the increment key to the ASCII code (making sure we keep within the ASCII range 65–90 for the uppercase letters A–Z). This gives us a new or shifted ASCII numeric code that we convert back to an encoded letter. Note that our example only encodes uppercase letters. In the follow-up exercises we consider messages that include lowercase letters and punctuation.

The pseudocode below describes the design in more detail.

---

[†]This example requires knowledge of Chapter 7. It's also a good idea to keep handy the ASCII character codes. Look in your system's User Manual.

```
Start control module
    Initialize ASCII codes for A and Z
    Input increment key
    Input actual message
    For each character in the message
        If character not = blank then call subroutine encode
    Next character
    Print encoded message
    Stop
End module
```

```
Start subroutine encode
    Convert letter to encoded ASCII number
    If encoded ASCII number > end of alphabet then
        Adjust ASCII number to wrap around alphabet
    End if
    Convert ASCII number to encoded letter
    Return
End subroutine
```

**Code and Test.**    The following program was written in Microsoft BASIC and run on an IBM PC computer.

```
100 '===============================================================
101 '
102 '                    MESSAGE ENCODING PROGRAM
103 '
104 '===============================================================
110 '
120 '================== Control module ========================
125 '
130         LET ASC.LOW   = 65 ◄————ASCII number for upper case A
140         LET ASC.HIGH = 90 ◄————ASCII number for upper case Z
150         LET BLANK$    = " "
160 '
170         INPUT "Enter increment key (1-26)"; INCREMENT
180         PRINT
190         INPUT " Actual message "; TEXT$
200 '
210         FOR J = 1 TO LEN(TEXT$) ◄———— Number of characters in message
220           IF MID$(TEXT$,J,1) <> BLANK$ THEN GOSUB 300 ◄——Only encodes
230         NEXT J        ▲                                    nonblanks
240 '                     └———————— Examines Jth letter in message
250         PRINT " Encoded message: "; TEXT$
260         PRINT
270 '
280         STOP
290 '
300 '================== Subroutine Encode ========================
310 '                           ╱—Converts Jth letter to ASCII numeric code
320         LET ASCII.VAL = ASC(MID$(TEXT$,J,1)) + INCREMENT
325 '                                           └—Note use of increment key
330         IF ASCII.VAL  >  ASC.HIGH THEN
              LET ASCII.VAL = ASC.LOW + (ASCII.VAL  -  ASC.HIGH) - 1
335 '                                    └— Adjusts ASCII code if its value exceeds
340         MID$(TEXT$,J,1) = CHR$(ASCII.VAL)  90 (alphabet wrap around Z)
345 '                 ▲            └———— Converts ASCII code to encoded letter
350         RETURN └———— Actual letter replaced by encoded letter
998 '===============================================================
999         END

RUN
Enter increment key (1-26)? 10

 Actual message ? HELP IS ON THE WAY
 Encoded message: ROVZ SC YX DRO GKI


Break in 280
```

**Discussion.** Note the following points:

1. The LEN function is used in line 210 to determine the length of the message, or the number of characters to process in the FOR/NEXT loop.

2. The MID$ function is a convenient means to examine each character in a string. As used in line 220, MID$(TEXT$,J,1) returns the Jth character (that is, one character starting in position J) in TEXT$.

3. Line 320 converts the Jth letter to its ASCII numeric code equivalent by using the ASC function. This ASCII number is then increased by the increment key (10 in our sample run).

4. Line 330 shows our alphabet wrap-around logic: It adjusts the ASCII value if the number goes beyond 90 (the letter Z). For example, the ASCII code for S is 83, which gives 93 after the increment key of 10 is added. Line 330 thus adjusts the value to 67, which corresponds to the encoded letter C; otherwise, the encoded letter would be three positions beyond Z, which happens to be the ASCII right bracket (]) character! (See the actual letter S and its corresponding encoded letter C in our sample run.)

5. Line 340 uses the CHR$ function to change the ASCII value to the encoded letter. Then the MID$ function is used to replace the original letter in TEXT$ with the encoded letter. Thus, the form

MID$(TEXT$,J,1) = encoded letter

replaces the Jth letter in TEXT$ by the encoded letter.

To understand the encoding transformation algorithm better, let's role-play the encoding of THE in our sample run.

| J | MID$(TEXT$,J,1) in lines 220, 320 | Line 220 test result | ASCII.VAL in line 320 | Line 330 test result | ASCII.VAL in line 330 | CHR$(ASCII.VAL) and MID$(TEXT$,J,1) in line 340 |
|---|---|---|---|---|---|---|
| 12 | T | True | 94 | True | 68 | D |
| 13 | H | True | 82 | False | 82 | R |
| 14 | E | True | 79 | False | 79 | O |

---

## Follow-Up Exercises

16. With respect to our cryptography program.
    a. What happens if we enter the message:

    HELP ISN'T ON THE WAY

    b. Modify the program so any punctuation in the message is ignored.
    *c. Implement this program on your system.

17. With respect to our cryptography program.
    a. Modify the program to input the day of the week; Monday is 1, Tuesday is 2, and so on. This number is used as the increment key for coding the message. What is the encoded message in our example for Tuesday? For Friday?
    *b. Implement this program on your system.

> **\*18.** With respect to our cryptography program.
>    **a.** Modify the program so an encoded message is entered, decoded, and printed.
>    **\*b.** Implement this program on your system.
> **\*\*19.** With respect to our cryptography program.
>    **a.** Modify the program to allow the encoding of messages with lower case letters, upper case letters, and punctuation characters.
>    **b.** Implement this program on your system. Encode the actual message:
>
>    SS Pierce: Help isn't on the way!

## Text Editor[†]

A text editor is a computer-based tool to create, revise, and maintain text. Many of you may be using a text editor to prepare term reports or to type programs. A line-oriented editor has a set of commands that typically operates on one line of text at a time. See Module A, Section A.4 for a more detailed description of text editors.

**Analysis.**    Let's develop a simple line-oriented editor with three functions: changing a line, adding a new line, and deleting a line. Here we illustrate the procedure for changing a line and leave the other two functions as an end-of-chapter exercise.

Our editor will first read in a complete text as a one-dimensional array, in which each element stores a line of text. Then it will display one line at a time, starting with the first. To correct or otherwise change a line, we respond to the editor's input prompt (\*?) by typing a command line with the following syntax:

**Change Command Line**

```
*? chg/old substring/new substring/
```
                Substring to be inserted
                Substring to be deleted
                Change command
                Editor's input prompt

Note that the *slashes* separate or delimit the three portions of the command line: the change command (chg), the old substring being replaced, and the new substring that acts as the replacement. To illustrate, suppose we are working on the *current line*

Old substring

Jack or Jill

and we want to replace the word *or* with the word *and*. Immediately after the prompt we type the following command line:

---

[†]This example requires knowledge of Chapters 7 and 8.

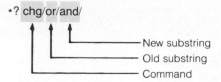

The editor then performs the indicated substitution and displays the *revised line*

┌─New substring
Jack and Jill

To delete a current line we use the delete (del) command. The form of this command is

**Delete Command Line**

> del

To insert a new line following the current line, we use the insert (ins) command. The form of this command is

**Insert Command Line**

> ins/new line/

where *new line* is the string for the new line that is to be inserted just after the current line.

The data requirements for this program are described as follows.

*Output*
Entire original text
Individual line of original text just before command line prompt
Revised or new text line following the command line
Entire revised text

*Read*
Entire original text into one-dimensional array

*Input*
Command line

**Design.**   The following pseudocode gives details of the modular design for our text editor. Again, we shall only develop the change command in our example and leave the delete and insert commands as exercises. Note that each command is a module, which simplifies the addition, deletion, and modification of commands in the program. Also note that the delete and insert modules are included within the pseudocode as unfinished program stubs or dummy modules. Their use is consistent with the ideas behind stepwise refinement (see page 132) and topdown testing (see page 264).

```
Start control module
    Call Subroutine Read Complete Text
    Call Subroutine Print Complete Text
    For each text line
        Call Subroutine Parse
        If command = "chg" then call Subroutine Change
        If command = "ins" then call Subroutine Insert
        If command = "del" then call Subroutine Delete
    Next line
    Call Subroutine Print Complete Text
    Stop
End module
```

```
Start Subroutine Read Complete Text
    Read number of text lines
    For each text line
        Read text line
    Next line
    Return
End subroutine
```

```
Start Subroutine Print Complete Text
    For each text line
        Print text line
    Next line
    Return
End subroutine
```

```
Start Subroutine Parse
    Print text line
    Input command line
    Extract command from command line
    Find position of slashes in command line
    Extract old substring
    Extract new substring
    Return
End subroutine
```

```
Start Subroutine Change
    Find position in text line where old substring begins
    Calculate total length of text line
    Calculate length of right substring
    Join left substring + new substring + right substring
    Print revised line
    Return
End subroutine
```

```
Start Subroutine Insert
    Program stub: module not completed
    Return
End subroutine
```

```
Start Subroutine Delete
    Program stub: module not completed
    Return
End subroutine
```

**Code and Test.**    The following code and run were implemented on an IBM PC in Microsoft BASIC.

```
100 '===============================================================================
101 '
102 '                         LINE-ORIENTED TEXT EDITOR
103 '
104 '===============================================================================
105 '
110 '====================== Control module ===================================
115 '
120     DIM LOC.SLASH(3),TEXT$(100)
125 '
130     GOSUB 300                                   'read complete text
135 '
140     PRINT "Original text"
145     PRINT "-------------"
150     GOSUB 400                                   'print complete text
155 '
160     PRINT "Edit process"
165     PRINT "------------"
170 '
175     FOR J = 1 TO N
180 '
185        GOSUB 500                                'parse command line
190 '
195        IF COMMAND$ = "chg" THEN GOSUB 600       'replace old with new string
200        IF COMMAND$ = "ins" THEN GOSUB 700       'insert a new line
205        IF COMMAND$ = "del" THEN GOSUB 800       'delete line from text
210 '
215     NEXT J
220 '
225     PRINT
230     PRINT
235     PRINT "Revised text"
240     PRINT "------------"
245     GOSUB 400                                   'print complete text
250 '
255     STOP
260 '
300 '====================== Read complete text module ========================
305 '
310     READ N
315     FOR J = 1 TO N
320        READ TEXT$(J)
325     NEXT J
330     RETURN
335 '
400 '====================== Print complete text module =======================
405 '
410     PRINT
415     FOR J = 1 TO N
420        PRINT TEXT$(J)
425     NEXT J
430     PRINT
435     RETURN
440 '
500 '====================== Parse module =====================================
505 '
510     PRINT
515     PRINT "Current line:   " + TEXT$(J)
520     PRINT
525     INPUT "*"; COMMAND.LINE$
530     PRINT
535 '
540     LET COMMAND$ = LEFT$(COMMAND.LINE$,3)    ◄────── Extracts command
545 '
550     LET P = 0
555     FOR I = 1 TO LEN(COMMAND.LINE$)
560        IF MID$(COMMAND.LINE$,I,1) = "/" THEN ◄────── Finds location of slashes
              LET P = P + 1  :
              LET LOC.SLASH(P) = I
565     NEXT I                                   ┌─────── Extracts old substring
570 '                                            │
575     LET LEN.OLD      = LOC.SLASH(2) - LOC.SLASH(1) - 1
580     LET OLD.STRING$ = MID$(COMMAND.LINE$, LOC.SLASH(1) + 1, LEN.OLD)
582 '
```

```
585          LET LEN.NEW        = LOC.SLASH(3) - LOC.SLASH(2) - 1
590          LET NEW.STRING$ = MID$(COMMAND.LINE$, LOC.SLASH(2) + 1, LEN.NEW)
592 '                                                                    └── Extracts new substring
595          RETURN
597 '
600 '==================== Change module ====================
605 '
610          LET FIRST.POS = INSTR(TEXT$(J), OLD.STRING$) ◄──── Calculates first position of
615          LET TOTLEN      = LEN(TEXT$(J))                       old (or new) substring
620          LET LEN.RIGHT = TOTLEN - ((FIRST.POS - 1) + LEN.OLD) ◄── Calculates length of
625 '                                                                   right substring
630          LET TEXT$(J)   =  LEFT$(TEXT$(J), FIRST.POS-1)
                              + NEW.STRING$
                              + RIGHT$(TEXT$(J), LEN.RIGHT)
635 '
640          PRINT "Revised line:   " + TEXT$(J)
645 '                                                    Concatenates left substring, new substring,
650          RETURN                                       and right substring
655 '
700 '==================== Insert module ====================
705 '
710          PRINT
715          PRINT "Program stub -- module not completed"
720          PRINT "See end of chapter assignment"
725          RETURN
730 '
800 '==================== Delete module ====================
805 '
810          PRINT
815          PRINT "Program stub -- module not completed"
820          PRINT "See end of chapter assignment"
825          RETURN
897 '
898 '==================== Data section ====================
899 '
900          DATA 3
901          DATA Jack or jill
902          DATA Went up the wall
903          DATA To fitch a pail of water
998 '====================================================
999          END
```

```
RUN
Original text
-------------

Jack or jill
Went up the wall
To fitch a pail of water

Edit process
-------------
                                    Command Line

Current line:  Jack or jill ──────── Change command
                                 ──── Old substring
*? chg/or/and/                    ──── New substring

Revised line:  Jack and jill

Current line:  Went up the wall

*? chg/wall/hill/

Current line:  To fitch a pail of water

*? chg/fitch/fetch/

Revised line:  To fetch a pail of water


Revised text
-------------

Jack and jill
Went up the hill
To fetch a pail of water

Break in 255
```

**Discussion.**    Let's discuss the features within the three key modules.

*Control module.* The control module first calls a subroutine to read the complete text into the string array TEXT$. Then it calls another subroutine to display the complete text. Note that each array element in TEXT$ is a line of text, as illustrated by the following array locations.

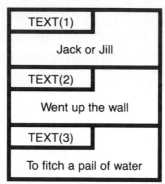

| TEXT(1) |
| Jack or Jill |
| TEXT(2) |
| Went up the wall |
| TEXT(3) |
| To fitch a pail of water |

The editing process now begins with the FOR/NEXT loop in lines 175–215. The first task within the loop includes the input and analysis of the command line, which is done by subroutine Parse. The if/then logic that follows then calls the appropriate editing module.

*Parse module.* This module prints the current line of text and waits for the user to enter the command line. Then it breaks up the command line into its three components. The process of breaking up the command line into its syntactical components is called parsing.[2] To better understand the parsing process, let's roleplay the first command line in our sample run. The INPUT statement in line 525 stores the command line in the following storage location.

| COMMAND.LINES$ |
| c h g / o r / a n d / |

Position ➝ 1 2 3 4 5 6 7 8 9 10 11

Line 540 then parses the command line to extract the command from the first three positions. Thus, the variable COMMAND$ stores *chg*. The FOR/NEXT loop in lines 555–565 locates the position of each slash. This loop examines the command line one character at a time. As in our cryptography example, the MID$ function is used to extract single characters. If the character is a slash, then it stores its position in the array LOC.SLASH. For example, when I = 4, the if-test in line 560 yields true, P is incremented to 1, and LOC.SLASH(1) stores 4. Thus, the first slash is in position 4. Once the slashes are located, it's straightforward to parse the remaining parts of the command line. Lines 575–580 extract the old substring, and lines 585–590 extract the new substring. As the parse module returns control back to the control module, we have the following breakdown of the command line.

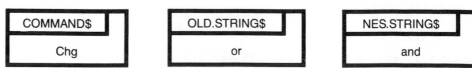

| COMMAND$ |   | OLD.STRING$ |   | NES.STRING$ |
| Chg |   | or |   | and |

*Change module.* This module changes the current text line by replacing the old substring with the new substring. To visualize this procedure, consider the first text line.

---

[2]Parsing plays an important role in the specialization called *natural language processing* in the field of *artificial intelligence*. The idea is to allow nontraditional computer users (older business executives, secretaries, and others) the entry of commands or tasks as they would in their everyday (natural) language. Parsing algorithms then extract the essentials. Mazelike computer games are another good example of the progress in parsing. For example, the original game called *Adventure* was limited in its parsing abilities. Newer versions like *Zork* are very good at parsing. Both of these games are available on the IBM PC and compatibles.

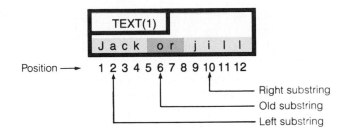

TEXT$(1) is conceptually divided into three substrings: *left substring* (all characters to the left of the old substring), *old substring*, and *right substring* (all characters to the right of the old substring). Line 610 uses the INSTR function to calculate 6 as the starting or first position of the old (which will also be the new) substring. (See the TEXT(1) box above.) Line 615 uses the LEN function to return 12 as the total length of the first line. Line 620 calculates the length of the right substring as 5. Line 630 then revises this line of text by concatenating the left, old, and right substrings. This can be visualized as follows:

| LEFT$(TEXT(J),FIRST.POS − 1) | + | NEW.STRING$ | + | RIGHT$(TEXT(J),LEN.RIGHT) |
|---|---|---|---|---|
| LEFT$(Jack or jill, 5) | + | and | | RIGHT$(Jack or jill, 5) |
| Jackb | + | and | + | bjill |

The revised first line is thus stored as follows.

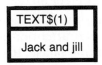

---

## Follow-Up Exercises

**20.** Answer the following:
  **a.** What happens if the user enters an invalid command? For example,

  chj/or/and/

  **\*b.** Modify the program so an invalid command is trapped, a message is printed, and the user is allowed to reenter the command line.
  **\*\*c.** Implement this program on your system.

**21.** Answer the following.
  **a.** What happens if the user enters an old substring that is not part of the string being edited? For example,

  chg/ir/and/

  **\*b.** Design a procedure that traps this error and requests a new command line.
  **\*\*c.** Implement this program on your system.

**22.** Answer the following.
  **a.** What happens if the user leaves off the final slash in the command line? For example,

  chg/or/and

> **\*b.** Design a procedure that traps this error and requests a new command line.
> **\*\*c.** Implement this program on your system.
> **23.** Answer the following.
>     **a.** If a line is correct, how might we move to the next line?
>     **\*b.** Add a new command to the text editor (skp) that skips the current line and goes on to the next text line.
>     **\*\*c.** Implement this program on your system.

## F.6 POINTERS

The following pointers describe some common errors.

1. **Transportability.**   String built-in functions are more dialect-specific than their numeric counterparts. If a program is to be used on more than one system or is to be ported to another system at a later date, then particular attention must be given to any differences in the built-in string functions. For example, the RIGHT$ function will return a substring in Microsoft BASIC that's different from the substring returned in VAX-11 BASIC (see Table F.1), which would give a logic error if the program is ported from one system to the other; or a program that uses the INSTR function on one system may require the POS function on another system, which would give a syntax error on one system if this fact goes unnoticed.

2. **Logic errors.**   These are the most common errors in string processing, so it pays to devote special attention to test data selection and output validation during the testing phase. It's especially important to roleplay difficult logic, as in our cryptography (page 472) and text editor (page 475) examples.

3. **Numeric strings.**   Beginners often forget that a numeric value assigned to a string variable is actually a string value and not a number. Thus, arithmetic calculations are not possible. For example, if the string variable AGE$ stores 32, then the 32 is a string value rather than a numeric value. A summation statement like

$$\text{LET SUM} = \text{SUM} + \text{AGE\$} \longleftarrow \text{Can't add numeric and string variables}$$

would thus give a syntax error. Either the age attribute would have to be stored in a numeric variable like **AGE** or the VAL function would have to be used as follows.

$$\text{LET SUM} = \text{SUM} + \text{VAL(AGE\$)} \longleftarrow \text{VAL function converts string numeric value to equivalent numeric value}$$

4. **Returned numeric versus string values.**   Pay attention to whether a built-in string function returns a numeric value or a string value. *If the name of the function ends in a $ sign, then we can be sure the function returns a string value.* For example, LEN(A$) returns a numeric value, and LEFT$(A$,N) returns a string value. Thus, each of the following would yield a syntax error.

```
                              Use LENGTH
10 LET LENGTH$ = LEN(A$)
                              Use ANS$
20 LET ANS      = LEFT$(A$,N)
```

## ADDITIONAL EXERCISES

**24.** Define or explain the following.

| | | |
|---|---|---|
| character string | string variables | substring |
| string | string expression | concatenation |
| length (of a string) | string array element name | concatenation operator |
| string constants | subscripted string variable | built-in string functions |
| string values | array element | user-defined string functions |

**25. Form letter revisited.**    Solve Exercise 22 in Chapter 3 on page 104 based on the following additional considerations.
  **a.** Use concatenation where appropriate.
  **b.** Before the loop that prints the form letter for each person, read the constant portions of the form letter into a one-dimensional string array, where each array element is a line in the letter. Use DATA statements to store the letter. Thus, the form letter is not contained in the lists of PRINT statements.
  **\*\*c.** Instead of using DATA statements, use an external file to store the name/address list and another external file to store the form letter.

**26. Case letter conversion.**    Develop a program that:
  **a.** Converts every letter in a text from uppercase to lowercase. The ASCII code for any lowercase letter is 32 greater than the corresponding uppercase letter. If the letter is already lowercase, don't change the letter.
  **b.** Leaves the first letter at the beginning of each sentence in uppercase. *Hint:* The program must identify the beginning of a sentence.
Use the following test text:[3]

> DEC SENT THIS MACHINE TO MARKET IN 1965. IT WAS A HIT. IT MADE DEC'S FIRST FORTUNE. THE PDP-8 . . . "ESTABLISHED THE CONCEPT OF MINICOMPUTERS, LEADING THE WAY TO A MULTIBILLION DOLLAR INDUSTRY."

**27. Word extraction.**    Write a program that extracts words from a text and prints each on a separate line. A word is defined as a string of characters followed by a space (this is a simplified definition). Include contractions such as *don't* in the definition of a word, which means that the apostrophe is treated as a letter. Also count and print the number of words. Use the following test text:[4]

> In 1979 Tracy Kidder went underground into the closely guarded research basement of Data General to observe a crack team of computer wizards about to embark on a crash program to design and build a new computer.

**28. Course queries.**    The course numbers at a university are coded as six-character strings, where the first three characters represent the department where the course is offered and the last three characters are digits that signify the academic level. For example, BIO405 is a valid course number. Write a program that answers administrative queries as described below. Use the following data file.

Course Number File
_____

BIO405
CSC201
CSC465
HIS101
HIS265
MGS105
MGS207
MGS500

  **a.** Sample run:

```
Department?  HIS
                  HIS101
                  HIS265
Department?  BIO

                  BIO405
Department?  ENG

                  * * * *  *    No courses in data base
Department?  END

End of run.
```

  **\*\*b.** Use a menu instead of the approach in part **a.**

```
Select one:
  1. List of all courses in a department
  2. List of all courses by academic level
  3. List of all graduate courses (500 and above)
  4. Stop processing
```

---

[3] Tracy Kidder, *The Soul of a New Machine*, Boston: Little, Brown and Company, 1981, p. 15.
[4] *Ibid.*, jacket cover.

Selection?  1
   (Same as part **a** above)
Selection?  2
   Level?  100

        H I S 1 0 1
        M G S 1 0 5

   Level?  300

        * * * * * *   No courses in
   Level?  0             data base

Selection?  3

        M G S 5 0 0
Selection?  4

End of run.

  \*\***c.**   Store the course number file as an external file.

The following texts are used as test data by Exercises 29 to 32.

*Column 1*

### Text 1

Jack and Jill went up the hill
  To fetch a pail of water;
Jack fell down and broke his crown,
  And Jill came tumbling after.

### Text 2

  Among other duties, a regional office of the Environmental Protection Agency (EPA) is charged with investigating complaints regarding industrial pollution, when "warranted." A complaint is investigated by sending a panel of three experts, collectively called the "proboscis patrol," to the site of the alleged offender. By consensus, the proboscis patrol then renders one of three opinions: low level, medium level, or high level of pollution. (We might note that the human nose has yet to find an electronic "equal" in detecting offending odors.) Following an opinion, the regional director of the EPA then has the option of issuing or not issuing a citation to the offender. Alternatively, the EPA may choose not to investigate the complaint and then make a decision regarding issuance of a citation.

*Note:* In the programs for Exercises 29–32, try accessing Text 1 and Text 2 from an external data file (see Module E).

**29.**  **Character frequency text analysis I.**   Write a program that processes *any number* of separate texts and prints the following for *each* text.
  **a.**  Number of characters
  **b.**  Number of letters and proportion of characters that are letters

  **c.**  Number of vowels and proportion of letters that are vowels
  \*\***d.**  Number of lowercase letters and proportion of letters that are lowercase
Process each text one line at a time (maximum line length is 80 characters) and ignore trailing blanks in a line. Process the two given texts in your run. It would be a good idea to output your results in the form of a bar chart, as in Example 7.1.

**30.**  **Character frequency text analysis II.**   Write a program that processes *any number* of separate texts and prints the number and proportion of *each* letter in the alphabet for each text. Make no distinction between lowercase and uppercase letters for purposes of the count. Process each text one line at a time, where the maximum line length is 80 characters. Process the two given texts in your run. It would be a good idea to output your results in the form of a bar chart, as in Example 7.1.

**31.**  **Word frequency text analysis.**   Write a program that processes *any number* of separate texts and prints the following for each text.
  **a.**  Number of words
  **b.**  Number and proportion of words specified by the user (use *the* or *The* and *and* or *And* as test input)
  **c.**  Number and proportion of words that end in a substring specified by the user (use *ing* as test input)
  **d.**  Number and proportion of words that begin with a letter (or more generally any substring) specified by the user (use the letters *a* or *A* and *e* or *E* as test input)
Process each text one line at a time, with the maximum line length of 80 characters. Process the two given texts in your run.

**32.**  **Keyboard text analysis.**   A typing textbook contains numerous paragraphs for students to type. These exercises vary in difficulty according to the following criteria.

  **1.**  *Number of strokes* in the exercise. A stroke is any keyboard act, such as typing a letter, typing a space, and returning the carriage to the next line (except for the last line in the exercise), and so on.
  **2.**  *Number of words* in the exercise. Words can include a single letter. For example, the phrase "I love computers" has three words.
  **3.**  *Average word length* in the exercise. This is defined as the number of strokes divided by the number of words.

  The usual approach to developing these exercises is for someone to count strokes, words, and word length for each proposed exercise, to ensure that exercises with various levels of difficulty are selected. This is a tedious task. This is where you come in. You are to computerize this task.

Write a program that processes *any number* of separate exercises and outputs each line of the exercise followed by a count of the number of strokes and words for that line. For example, the first two lines of Exercise 1 (Text 1) might be printed as follows:

|  | Strokes | Words |
|---|---|---|
| Jack and Jill went up the hill | 31 | 7 |
| To fetch a pail of water; | 28 | 6 |

At the end of each exercise print summary values for the three criteria discussed. Process each exercise one line at a time, with the maximum line length of 70. Use the two given texts as test data.

33. **Cryptography.** Keyword coding is a variation on the increment coding described earlier. Consider a scheme whereby letters in a keyword are used to establish variable increments as illustrated below.

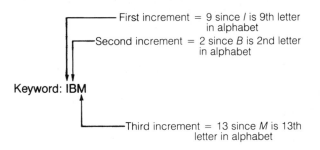

| Actual Message | Increment Used | Encoded Message |
|---|---|---|
| H | 9 | Q |
| E | 2 | G |
| L | 13 | Y |
| P | 9 | Y |
| I | 2 | K |
| S | 13 | F |
| O | 9 | X |
| N | 2 | P |
| T | 13 | G |
| H | 9 | Q |
| E | 2 | G |
| W | 13 | J |
| A | 9 | J |
| Y | 2 | A |

Increments are repeated in sequence as often as necessary.

a. Write an encoding program that inputs a keyword of up to ten characters and an actual message and outputs the actual message together with an encoded message. In your test runs, use the above message and the keywords IBM and DIGITAL.

b. Write a decoding program that inputs an encoded message and keyword and outputs the encoded message together with the decoded message.

34. **Text editor revisit.**   Complete our text editor program as follows.
   a. Finish the delete module. Note that the parse module also requires modification.
   b. Finish the insert module. Note that the parse module also requires modification.
   **c. Use external files to input the original text and to store the revised text. Use a new command *end* to end editing and store the revised text.

To debug your program, use the original three text lines in our example and then insert the following four new lines after the third line:

Jack fell down and broke his crown,
and jill came tumbling after.
and jill came tumbling after.
Up got jack, and home did trot.

Finally, delete the repeated line.

# Matrix Operations

A **matrix** is a rectangular array of numbers. For example, the matrices

$$\mathbf{A} = \begin{pmatrix} 10 & 15 \\ 20 & 25 \\ 30 & 35 \end{pmatrix}_{3 \times 2} \qquad \mathbf{B} = \begin{pmatrix} 1 & 2 & 3 & 4 \\ 5 & 6 & 7 & 8 \end{pmatrix}_{2 \times 4}$$

$$\mathbf{C} = \begin{pmatrix} 100 \\ 200 \\ 300 \\ 400 \\ 500 \end{pmatrix}_{5 \times 1} \qquad \mathbf{D} = (6 \quad 5 \quad 4 \quad 3 \quad 2 \quad 1)_{1 \times 6}$$

identify **A** as a $3 \times 2$ matrix (3 rows and 2 columns of elements, or 6 elements), **B** as a $2 \times 4$ matrix, **C** as a $5 \times 1$ matrix, and **D** as a $1 \times 6$ matrix. Alternatively, **C** may be called a **column vector** and **D** a **row vector**.

As you can see, a matrix is equivalent to our use of one- and two-dimensional *arrays*, where as usual the first subscript refers to the number of rows and the second subscript refers to the number of columns.[1]

Many systems include the option of using **MAT statements**, a set of BASIC instructions that greatly facilitates reading, inputing, printing, and manipulating one- and two-dimensional arrays.

---

*This module can be covered following Chapter 9.
[1] Systems that include row 0 or column 0 in one- and two-dimensional arrays ignore this row or column when applying the operations in this chapter.

## G.1 MAT READ, INPUT, AND PRINT STATEMENTS

Matrices are named in the same manner as the arrays discussed in Chapters 8 and 9, and they must be dimensioned by using a DIM statement. For example, the four matrices illustrated earlier could be dimensioned as follows:

100 DIM A(3,2), B(2,4), C(5,1), D(1,6)

Note that C(5,1) and D(1,6) essentially define the one-dimensional arrays C(5) and D(6).[2]

Read, input, and print operations of arrays are much less tedious with the use of the following MAT statements:

**MAT I/O Statements**

> **MAT READ** *list of array names*
> **MAT INPUT** *list of array names*
> **MAT PRINT** *list of array names*
>
> MAT READ A
> MAT INPUT B(N,M)
> MAT PRINT B;C,D

Keep in mind the following points when using these statements.

1.  The MAT READ statement assigns values from DATA statements to array elements.
2.  The data are read in on a *row-by-row basis*; that is, row 1 is stored before row 2, row 2 is stored before row 3, and so on.
3.  If several array names are listed in one MAT READ, PRINT, or INPUT statement, the first array is processed completely before the second array is processed.
4.  One-dimensional arrays may be included in the list of arrays.
5.  The MAT INPUT statement assigns values entered from the keyboard to array elements. This statement prompts with the standard input prompt for the system. Typically we cannot include a string or conversational prompt with the MAT INPUT statement.
6.  The MAT PRINT statement prints the contents of one- or two-dimensional arrays at the terminal or monitor. The values are printed in *row order*.
7.  The trailing separator (comma or semicolon) in the MAT PRINT statement determines the appearance of the output.
    a.  The semicolon causes array element values to be packed on a line. Each row is started on a new line.
    b.  The comma causes each array element value to be printed in a separate zone. Each row is started on a new line.
    c.  If neither a trailing semicolon or comma follows the array name, then each array element value in a 1-D array is printed on a new line.

**WARNING**  Our programs and runs in this module have been implemented on the VAX-11 system. Although the basic syntax of MAT I/O statements is reasonably uniform across systems, there can be variations. In general, it would be a

---

[2]Whether we dimension **C** and **D** as row vectors, column vectors, or 1-D arrays makes a difference in the algebraic operations of Section G.3.

good idea to try our examples and exercises on your system. Note any differences and consult with your instructor or systems manual.

We could have used the MAT I/O statements in any of the examples of Chapters 8 and 9. The next example illustrates their use.

## EXAMPLE G.1   FOR/NEXT and MAT READ/PRINT Equivalence

Study the following two equivalent versions for reading and printing the matrices

$$\mathbf{A} = \begin{pmatrix} 10 & 15 \\ 20 & 25 \\ 30 & 35 \end{pmatrix} \quad \text{and} \quad \mathbf{C} = \begin{pmatrix} 100 \\ 200 \\ 300 \\ 400 \\ 500 \end{pmatrix}$$

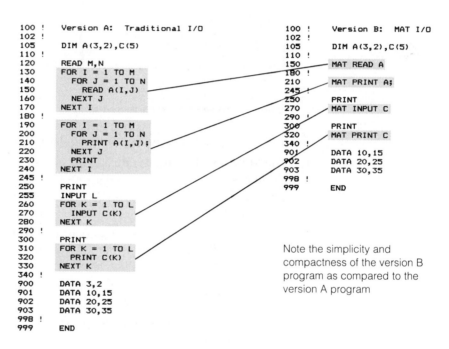

```
100 !    Version A:  Traditional I/O        100 !    Version B:  MAT I/O
102 !                                       102 !
105      DIM A(3,2),C(5)                     105      DIM A(3,2),C(5)
110 !                                        110 !
120      READ M,N                            150      MAT READ A
130      FOR I = 1 TO M                      180 !
140        FOR J = 1 TO N                    210      MAT PRINT A;
150          READ A(I,J)                     245 !
160        NEXT J                            250      PRINT
170      NEXT I                             270      MAT INPUT C
180 !                                        290 !
190      FOR I = 1 TO M                      300      PRINT
200        FOR J = 1 TO N                    320      MAT PRINT C
210          PRINT A(I,J);                   340 !
220        NEXT J                            901      DATA 10,15
230        PRINT                             902      DATA 20,25
240      NEXT I                             903      DATA 30,35
245 !                                        998 !
250      PRINT                               999      END
255      INPUT L
260      FOR K = 1 TO L
270        INPUT C(K)
280      NEXT K
290 !
300      PRINT
310      FOR K = 1 TO L
320        PRINT C(K)
330      NEXT K
340 !
900      DATA 3,2
901      DATA 10,15
902      DATA 20,25
903      DATA 30,35
998 !
999      END
```

Note the simplicity and compactness of the version B program as compared to the version A program

```
RUNN

   10   15        Note row-by-row output of A in       RUNN
   20   25        packed form. See line 210 in ———→       10   15
   30   35        program.                                20   25
                                                          30   35
?  5
                  Note convenience of inputting ————→  ? 100,200,300,400,500
?  100            more than one value on a line.
                  See line 270 in program.              100
?  200                                                  200
                                                        300
?  300            One value per line is printed ———→    400
                  since there's no trailing comma       500
?  400            or semicolon in line 320 of
                  program.
?  500

   100
   200
   300
   400
   500
```

You should make note of the following:

1.  The DIM statement in line 105 of version B defines **C** as a one-dimensional array. We also could have defined **C** as a row vector using C(1,5) or as a column vector using C(5,1). It makes no difference with respect to MAT I/O statements.[3]

2.  The MAT READ statement in line 150 of version B replaces lines 130 through 170 in version A. Notice that *the MAT READ processes the matrix row by row* (first row is read, then the second row, then the third row). The DATA statement in line 901, therefore, is consistent with row-by-row read in of the data.

3.  The MAT PRINT statement in line 210 of version B replaces lines 190 through 240 in version A. Note that a trailing semicolon in the MAT PRINT gives packed output. Also note that output is *row by row.*

4.  The MAT INPUT statement in line 270 of version B replaces lines 260 through 280 in version A. Note that values in response to a MAT INPUT statement can be entered on one line using the comma as a separator. However, the INPUT statement in line 270 of version A requires that data values be entered on separate lines.

5.  The MAT PRINT statement in line 320 of version B replaces lines 310 through 330 in version A. Note that C is printed as a column of numbers, since there is no trailing separator following the array name.

6.  More than one array name can be used in the print list on most systems. For example, if in version B we eliminate line 210 and rewrite line 320 as

    320 MAT PRINT A;C

    then we would get the same output as before. Note that the semicolon packs the output of A. If we were to use

    320 MAT PRINT A,C,

    then this would be equivalent to

    320 MAT PRINT A,
    325 MAT PRINT C,

    and result in the following output.

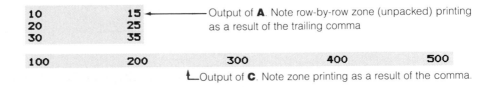

Output of **A**. Note row-by-row zone (unpacked) printing as a result of the trailing comma

Output of **C**. Note zone printing as a result of the comma.

---

## Follow-Up Exercises

1.  Make the following *successive* changes in version B of Example G.1. In each part first indicate the expected output on paper and then run the program on your system.

---

[3]But it willll make a difference in the matrix operations in Section G.3.

**a.** Change line 320 to

320 MAT PRINT C;

**b.** Eliminate line 210 and change line 320 to

320 MAT PRINT A,C

**c.** Change line 320 to

320 MAT PRINT A;C

**d.** Eliminate line 270, change line 150 to

150 MAT READ A,C

and add an additional data line.

**e.** Change line 120 to

120 MAT READ C,A

**f.** Eliminate line 270 and change line 150 to

150 MAT INPUT A,C

**2.** First indicate the output from this program and then run it on your system.

```
10 DIM R(1,4),S(4,1),T(4)
20 MAT READ R
30 RESTORE
40 MAT READ S
50 RESTORE
60 MAT READ T
70 MAT PRINT R;S;T;
90 DATA 10,20,30,40
99 END
```

Is T processed by the MAT statements on your system?

As demonstrated in Chapters 8 and 9, many applications programs conveniently "overdimension" an array to accommodate data having different numbers of rows and columns from run to run. *Subscripts can be specified after an array in a MAT INPUT or READ statement to indicate the last array element that is to be processed.* If the subscripts differ from the array size in the DIM statement, the array is said to be **redimensioned**.

**E X A M P L E   G . 2**   Redimensioning the Matrix during Execution

Our purpose is to define the matrix

$$\mathbf{X} = \begin{pmatrix} 10 & 1 & -2 \\ 20 & 2 & -1 \\ 30 & 3 & 1 \\ 40 & 4 & 2 \end{pmatrix}$$

then calculate the average of each column and store these in

$$\mathbf{A} = (25 \quad 2.5 \quad 0)$$

and finally to print **X** and **A**; however, we want our program to process matrices up to 100 rows and 10 columns, depending on the data. The program below demonstrates the redimensioning of the 100 × 10 array.

```
100 !    Redimensioning Arrays
110 !
120      DIM X(100,10),A(10)                    X gets redimensioned to M rows and N
130 !                                           columns
140      READ M,N
150      MAT READ X(M,N)
160      MAT READ A(N)
170 !
180      FOR J = 1 TO N
190        FOR I = 1 TO M
200          LET A(J) = A(J) + X(I,J)           The I-loop finds the sum of the Jth column in X
210        NEXT I                               and stores it in the Jth element in A
220      NEXT J
230 !
240      FOR J = 1 TO N
250          LET A(J) = A(J) / M                This calculates the average of the Jth column
260      NEXT J                                 in X and stores it in the Jth element in A
270 !
280      MAT PRINT X,A,                         Note how both arrays get printed by one statement
290 !
900      DATA 4,3                               M = 4 rows and N = 3 columns
901      DATA 10,1,-2
902      DATA 20,2,-1
903      DATA 30,3,1
904      DATA 40,4,2
905      DATA 0,0,0                             Elements in A get initialized to zero in line 160
998 !
999      END
```

RUNN

| 10 | 1   | -2 |
|----|-----|----|
| 20 | 2   | -1 |
| 30 | 3   | 1  |
| 40 | 4   | 2  |
| 25 | 2.5 | 0  |

Note that the execution of

150 MAT READ X(M,N)

effectively redimensions matrix X to 4 rows (value in M) by 3 columns (value in N). Thus, 12 items of data are read in from the DATA statements in lines 901 to 904. Also note that when X is printed in line 280, it is treated as a 4 × 3 matrix rather than a 100 × 10 matrix. In general, this program can process matrices up to 100 rows and 10 columns simply by changing the DATA statements. Finally, note that line 160 simultaneously initializes and redimensions A.

## Follow-Up Exercises

3.  Make the following changes in Example G.2.
    a.  Eliminate lines 900 through 905 and arrange the DATA statements to process the following array:

    $$\mathbf{X} = \begin{pmatrix} 10 & 1 \\ 20 & 2 \\ 30 & 3 \end{pmatrix}$$

    Run this version on your system.
    b.  Eliminate all DATA statements, enter M and N through an INPUT statement, enter X and A through a MAT INPUT statement, pack the output of X and A, and process the data given in part **a**.

4.  **Table Lookup Revisit**
    a.  Modify the program in Section 8.6 on page 293 according to the following: treat the premium schedule as a 6 × 2 matrix called PREMTABLE and read it into memory using the MAT READ statement.
    **b.  Run this program on your system.

*5.  **String Arrays Revisit**
    *a.  Use a MAT READ statement for the one-dimensional string array DAY$ in Example 8.7 on page 288. Include an echo print immediately following the read in of DAY$.
    **b.  Run this program on your system.

## G.2 MATRIX FUNCTIONS

Table G.1 describes and illustrates six common functions using MAT statements. The first two functions (ZER and CON) are primarily used to redimension and initialize matrices. We show these uses in the programs of Section G.4. The last three functions (IDN, TRN, and INV) are extensively used in **matrix (linear) algebra**, a field of study that manipulates matrices for solving systems of linear equations (see the program in Section G.4) and for describing certain real-world phenomena through mathematical modeling (see the brand switching program in Section G.4).

**NOTE**   Don't forget to describe any differences between the matrix functions on your system and those in Table G.1. Note these differences (if any) in the blank column. We also leave space at the bottom of the table for you to add any other available matrix functions of interest.

**Table G.1** Matrix Functions

| Function | Differences on your system (if any) | Purpose | Example |
|---|---|---|---|
| **MAT** *array name* = **ZER**<br><br>or<br><br>**MAT** *array name* = **ZER**(*rows, columns*) | | Stores a zero (0) in each element of the array. The alternative version redimensions the array during execution and stores a zero in each element of the redimensioned array. Useful for initializing a matrix that is to store sums (see Exercise 6). Can be used with one- and two-dimensional arrays. | ```
100  DIM X(3,4),Y(50,5)
110  MAT X = ZER
120  MAT Y = ZER(2,2)
130  MAT PRINT X;Y;
140  END
RUNN
```<br>Redimensions and initializes<br>Initializes **X** to zero<br><br>0 0 0 0<br>0 0 0 0 } **X**<br>0 0 0 0<br><br>0 0<br>0 0 } **Y** |
| **MAT** *array name* = **CON**<br><br>or<br><br>**MAT** *array name* = **CON**(*rows, columns*) | | Stores a one (1) in each element of the array. The array can be redimensioned, with a 1 stored in each element of the redimensioned array. Useful for initializing a matrix whose elements represent counters or switches (on–off states) and for certain operations in matrix algebra (see Exercise 9b). Can be used with one- and two-dimensional arrays. | ```
100  DIM K(100,50)
110  READ R,C
120    DATA 3,2
130  MAT K = CON(R,C)
140  MAT PRINT K;
150  END
RUNN
```<br>Redimensions and initializes **K**<br><br>1 1<br>1 1 } **K**<br>1 1 |
| **MAT** *array name$* = **NUL$**<br><br>or<br><br>**MAT** *array name$* = **NUL$**(*rows, columns*) | | Each element in the string array is set to the empty or null string. The array can also be redimensioned. Useful for initializing string arrays. Can be used with one- and two-dimensional arrays. | ```
100  DIM N$(3,2)
110  MAT N$ = NUL$
120  MAT PRINT N$;
130  END
RUNN
```<br>Initializes **N$** to null string<br><br>☺ } **N$** |
| **MAT** *array name* = **IDN**<br><br>or<br><br>**MAT** *array name* = **IDN**(*rows, columns*) | | The matrix is set to the **identity matrix**: Each element along the main diagonal stores a one (1), and all other elements store a zero (0). The matrix can be redimensioned with this function. Useful in matrix algebra. See Table G.2, Exercise 8, and linear equations example in Section G.4. Can be used *only* with two-dimensional arrays. | ```
100  DIM A(3,3)
110  MAT A = IDN
120  MAT PRINT A;
130  END
RUNN
```<br>Creates identity matrix<br><br>1 0 0<br>0 1 0 } Identity matrix **A**<br>0 0 1 |

**Table G.1** *(continued)*

| Function | Differences on your system (if any) | Purpose | Example |
|---|---|---|---|
| **MAT** *array name1* = **TRN** (*array name2*) | | The first matrix is the **transpose** of the second matrix; that is, the rows in the first matrix are set to the columns in the second matrix. Dimensions of the two matrices must be compatible (number of rows in the first equals number of columns in the second, and number of columns in the first equals number of rows in the second). Useful in matrix algebra. See Exercise 22. Can be used *only* with two-dimensional arrays. | ``` 100 DIM A(4,2),B(2,4) 110 MAT READ B 120    DATA 1,2,3,4 130    DATA 5,6,7,8 140 MAT A = TRN(B) 150 MAT PRINT A;B; 160 END  RUNN ``` Taxes transpose of **B** Note transposition of row and column declarations `1 5` `2 6` `3 7` `4 8` **A**, the transpose of **B** `1 2 3 4` `5 6 7 8` **B** |
| **MAT** *array name1* = **INV** (*array name 2*) | | The first matrix is the **inverse** of the second matrix (when the inverse exists). Both matrices must be square (number of rows equals number of columns) and the same size. Useful in matrix algebra. Similar to the inverse in scalar algebra whereby the scalar inverse $1/x$ times $x$ gives 1. See Table G.2 and the linear equations example in Section G.4. Can be used *only* with two-dimensional arrays. | ``` 100 DIM C(2,2),D(2,2) 110 MAT READ C 120    DATA 2,1,5,3 130 MAT D = INV(C) 140 MAT PRINT C;D; 150 END  RUNN ``` Takes inverse of **C** Note that these are square and of the same size `3 -1` **C** `-5 2` **D**, the inverse of **C** |

(Other matrix functions available on your system)

## Follow-Up Exercise

6.  Use an appropriate MAT function to simplify the initialization of A in Example G.2.

## G.3 ALGEBRAIC OPERATIONS

The five MAT statements in Table G.2 are used to perform certain algebraic operations in matrix algebra. Study this table before going to the examples in Section G.4.

**Table G.2**  Algebraic Operations Using MAT Statements

| Operation | Purpose | Example |
|---|---|---|
| $\mathbf{MAT} \, \begin{matrix} array \\ name\,1 \end{matrix} = \begin{matrix} array \\ name\,2 \end{matrix}$ | **Assignment.** Set each element in the first array equal to the corresponding element in the second array. Both arrays must have the same dimensions. Can be used with both one- and two-dimensional arrays. | Note same dimensions<br>100  DIM A(2,4),B(2,4)<br>110  MAT READ A<br>120    DATA 10,15,20,25<br>125    DATA 50,55,60,65<br>130  MAT B = A ← B is set to A<br>140  MAT PRINT A;B;<br>150  END<br><br>RUNN<br><br>10  15  20  25<br>50  55  60  65 ] A<br><br>10  15  20  25<br>50  55  60  65 ] B, the same as A |
| $\mathbf{MAT} \, \begin{matrix} array \\ name\,1 \end{matrix} = \begin{matrix} array \\ name\,2 \end{matrix} + \begin{matrix} array \\ name\,3 \end{matrix}$<br><br>$\mathbf{MAT} \, \begin{matrix} array \\ name\,1 \end{matrix} = \begin{matrix} array \\ name\,2 \end{matrix} - \begin{matrix} array \\ name\,3 \end{matrix}$ | **Addition/subtraction.** Set each element in the first array equal to the sum/difference of corresponding elements in the second and third arrays. All arrays must have the same dimensions. The same array may appear on both sides of the equal sign. Can be used with both one- and two-dimensional arrays. | Note same dimensions<br>100  DIM A(2,3),B(2,3),C(2,3)<br>130  MAT A = CON<br>140  MAT B = CON<br>150  MAT C = A + B ← C is the sum of A and B<br>160  MAT PRINT A;B;C;<br>170  MAT B = B - C ← B is B less C<br>180  MAT PRINT B;<br>190  END<br><br>RUNN<br><br>1  1  1<br>1  1  1 ] A<br><br>1  1  1<br>1  1  1 ] B<br><br>2  2  2<br>2  2  2 ] C = A + B<br><br>-1 -1 -1<br>-1 -1 -1 ] B = B - C |

**Table G.2**     *(continued)*

| Operation | Purpose | Example |
|---|---|---|
| $\text{MAT} \begin{array}{l} array \\ name\,1 \end{array} = \left( \begin{array}{c} arithmetic \\ expression \end{array} \right) * \begin{array}{l} array \\ name\,2 \end{array}$ | **Scalar multiplication.** Set each element in the first array equal to the value of the arithmetic expression times the corresponding element in the second array. Arrays must have the same dimensions. The same array may appear on both sides of the equal sign. The parentheses must be used. Can be used with both one- and two-dimensional arrays. | ```
100   DIM X(2,4),Y(2,4)
110   MAT X = CON
120   MAT Y = (5) * X
130   MAT PRINT X;Y;
140   END
RUNN
```  Note same dimensions;  **Y** is 5 times **X**  $\begin{bmatrix} 1 & 1 & 1 & 1 \\ 1 & 1 & 1 & 1 \end{bmatrix}$ **X**  $\begin{bmatrix} 5 & 5 & 5 & 5 \\ 5 & 5 & 5 & 5 \end{bmatrix}$ **Y** = 5**X** |
| $\text{MAT} \begin{array}{l} array \\ name\,1 \end{array} = \begin{array}{l} array \\ name\,2 \end{array} * \begin{array}{l} array \\ name\,3 \end{array}$ | **Matrix multiplication.** The array name1 is set to the matrix product of the second and third matrices. The second and third matrices must be compatible (the number of columns in the second matrix must equal the number of rows in the third matrix). The same matrix may not appear on both sides of the equal sign. Can be used *only* with two-dimensional arrays. See Exercise 13. | ```
100   DIM A(3,3),B(3,3),C(3,3)
110   MAT READ A
120     DATA 2,2,3,0,1,1,1,1,1
130   MAT B = INV(A)
140   MAT C = A * B
150   MAT PRINT A;B;C;
160   END
RUNN
```  Compatible dimensions (need not be square);  **C** is the matrix product of **A** and **B**  $\begin{bmatrix} 2 & 2 & 3 \\ 0 & 1 & 1 \\ 1 & 1 & 1 \end{bmatrix}$ **A**  $\begin{bmatrix} 0 & -1 & 1 \\ -1 & 1 & 2 \\ 1 & 0 & -2 \end{bmatrix}$ **B**, the inverse of **A**  $\begin{bmatrix} 1 & 0 & 0 \\ 0 & 1 & 0 \\ 0 & 0 & 1 \end{bmatrix}$ **C**, the product of a matrix (**A**) and its inverse (**B**) yields the identity matrix |

## Follow-Up Exercises

**7.**  Indicate printed output when the following program is executed:

```
010 DIM A(50,50),B(50,50),C(50,50)
020 READ M
030 MAT READ A(M,M)
040 MAT B = IDN(M,M)
050 MAT C = ZER(M,M)
060 MAT C = A − B
070 MAT A = (4*M − 1)*A
080 MAT B = TRN(C)
090 MAT PRINT A;C;B;
100 DATA 3
110 DATA 1,2,3,4,5,6,7,8,9
120 END
```

What would you say is the purpose of line 50?

8. In matrix algebra, the identity matrix plays a role that is analogous to the number 1 in scalar arithmetic. Thus, if we have a matrix **A** that's multiplied by a compatible identity matrix **I**, the result is the matrix **A**. In other words,

**IA = A**   or   **AI = A**

Modify the last example in Table G.2 as follows:

```
152 DIM D(3,3)
154 MAT D = A*C
156 MAT PRINT D;
```

What should be printed for D? Run this program on your system to confirm the expected results. Change line 154 to

```
154 MAT D = C * A
```

Same result?

## G.4 SELECTED APPLICATIONS

This section illustrates three applications programs that use MAT statements and functions.

### Financial Report Revisited

The financial report program in Section 9.6 on page 331 can be shortened considerably by using MAT statements, as the following revision demonstrates.

```
1000 REM * * * * * * * * * * * * * * * * * * * * * * * * * * * * * * * *
1020 REM *                                                             *
1040 REM *                    FINANCIAL REPORT                         *
1060 REM *                                                             *
1440 REM * * * * * * * * * * * * * * * * * * * * * * * * * * * * * * * *
1460 !
2000 ! ================== Control Module ================================
2020 !
2040     DIM SALES(10,10),COSTS(10,10),PROFITS(10,10)
2060 !
2080     GOSUB 3000              !Call subroutine initialization
2100     GOSUB 4000              !Call subroutine array entry
2120     GOSUB 5000              !Call subroutine profit calculation
2140     GOSUB 6000              !Call subroutine totals
2160     GOSUB 7000              !Call subroutine reports
2180 !
2200     STOP
2220 !
3000 ! ================== Subroutine Initialization ====================
3020 !
3040     LET ROW.LIMIT    = 9
3060     LET COLUMN.LIMIT = 9
3080 !
3100     READ REGIONS,MODELS
3120 !
3140     IF REGIONS > ROW.LIMIT OR MODELS > COLUMN.LIMIT THEN
            PRINT "Upper array boundary exceeded.  Check line 9000."
            PRINT "Limits:  Regions =";ROW.LIMIT; "Models =";COLUMN.LIMIT
            STOP
3160 !
3180     RETURN
3200 !
```

```
4000  ! ================== Subroutine Array Entry =====================
4020  !
4080      MAT READ SALES(REGIONS+1,MODELS+1) ←——— Replaces lines 4040–4120
4140  !
4200      MAT READ COSTS(REGIONS+1,MODELS+1) ←——— Replaces lines 4160–4240
4260  !
4280      RETURN
4300  !
5000  ! ================== Subroutine Profit Calculation ================
5020  !
5080      MAT PROFITS = SALES - COSTS ←——————— Replaces lines 5040–5120
5140  !
5160      RETURN
5180  !
6000  ! ================== Subroutine Totals ==========================
6020  !                          No need to initialize last columns to zero
6040      FOR I = 1 TO REGIONS⌐┘              ! Calculate totals for each
6120        FOR J = 1 TO MODELS
6140          LET SALES(I,MODELS+1)   = SALES(I,MODELS+1)   + SALES(I,J)
6160          LET COSTS(I,MODELS+1)   = COSTS(I,MODELS+1)   + COSTS(I,J)
6180          LET PROFITS(I,MODELS+1) = PROFITS(I,MODELS+1) + PROFITS(I,J)
6200        NEXT J
6220      NEXT I              No need to initialize last rows to zero
6240  !
6260      FOR J = 1 TO MODELS⌐┘              ! Calculate totals for each
6340        FOR I = 1 TO REGIONS
6360          LET SALES(REGIONS+1,J)   = SALES(REGIONS+1,J)   + SALES(I,J)
6380          LET COSTS(REGIONS+1,J)   = COSTS(REGIONS+1,J)   + COSTS(I,J)
6400          LET PROFITS(REGIONS+1,J) = PROFITS(REGIONS+1,J) + PROFITS(I,J)
6420        NEXT I
6440      NEXT J
6460  !
6480      RETURN
6500  !
7000  ! ================== Subroutine Reports =========================
7020  !
7040      PRINT "SALES"
7080      FOR J = 1 TO MODELS
7100        PRINT J,
7120      NEXT J
7140      PRINT "Region totals"
7160  !
7180      PRINT "------------------------------------------------------"
7200  !
7280      MAT PRINT SALES(REGIONS,MODELS+1), ←——— Replaces lines 7220–7340
7360  !
7380      PRINT "------------------------------------------------------"
7400  !
7420      PRINT "Model totals"
7440      FOR J = 1 TO MODELS
7460        PRINT SALES(REGIONS+1,J),
7480      NEXT J
7500  !
7520      PRINT
7540      PRINT
7560  !
7580      PRINT "COSTS"
7620      FOR J = 1 TO MODELS
7640        PRINT J,
7660      NEXT J
7680      PRINT "Region totals"
7700  !
7720      PRINT "------------------------------------------------------"
7740  !
7820      MAT PRINT COSTS(REGIONS,MODELS+1), ←——— Replaces lines 7760–7880
7900  !
7920      PRINT "------------------------------------------------------"
7940  !
7960      PRINT "Model totals"
7980      FOR J = 1 TO MODELS
8000        PRINT COSTS(REGIONS+1,J),
8020      NEXT J
8040  !
8060      PRINT
```

```
8080        PRINT
8100  !
8120        PRINT "PROFITS"
8160        FOR J = 1 TO MODELS
8180          PRINT J,
8200        NEXT J
8220        PRINT "Region totals"
8240  !
8260        PRINT "-----------------------------------------------------"
8280  !
8360        MAT PRINT PROFITS(REGIONS,MODELS+1),  ←—Replaces lines 8300 – 8420
8440  !
8460        PRINT "-----------------------------------------------------"
8480  !
8500        PRINT "Model totals"
8520        FOR J = 1 TO MODELS
8540          PRINT PROFITS(REGIONS+1,J),
8560        NEXT J
8580  !
8600        PRINT
8620        PRINT
8640  !
8660        RETURN
8997  !
8998  ! ==================== Data Section ============================
8999                                              ! Regions,Models
9000        DATA 3,2
9005                                              ! Sales array
9011        DATA 100,150,0
9012        DATA 60,40,0
9013        DATA 30,70,0   ←——— These initialize the last row and column
9014        DATA 0,0,0
9500                                              ! Costs array
9501        DATA 50,100,0  ←——┘
9502        DATA 40,10,0
9503        DATA 25,75,0
9504        DATA 0,0,0
9996  !
9997  ! ============================================================
9998  !
9999        END
```

```
RUNN

SALES
1                 2                 Region totals
-----------------------------------------------------
 100              150               250
 60               40                100
 30               70                100
-----------------------------------------------------
Model totals
 190              260

COSTS
1                 2                 Region totals
-----------------------------------------------------
 50               100               150
 40               10                50
 25               75                100
-----------------------------------------------------
Model totals
 115              185

PROFITS
1                 2                 Region totals
-----------------------------------------------------
 50               50                100
 20               30                50
 5                -5                0
-----------------------------------------------------
Model totals
 75               75
```

Try keeping the book open to both the original program on page 331 and the revised program above (put your fingers to work), and let's note the following points.

1. The two MAT READ statements in lines 4080 and 4200 replace ten lines of code in the original version. Note that these MAT READ statements redimension the matrices to augment each matrix by one row and one column; these eventually will store column and row sums, respectively. This means that we can initialize the last row and last column to zero using the existing DATA statements, as shaded in lines 9011–9504.

2. The calculation of the profit matrix PROFITS is illustrated in the five statements found in lines 5040–5120 of the original program. The single MAT statement in line 5080 replaces these original five lines.

3. We don't need the initialization lines 6060–6100 and 6280–6320 in the original program, since the last rows and columns of SALES, COSTS, and PROFITS already have been initialized to zero in lines 4080, 4200, and 5080.

4. The code that outputs SALES, COSTS, and PROFITS is simplified by the MAT PRINT statements in lines 7280, 7820, and 8360. By using MAT PRINT statements, however, we were not able to number the rows as in the original version. MAT PRINT statements simplify output coding, but at the expense of output design.

---

### Follow-Up Exercise

9.  a.  Where could we place the statement

    MAT PROFITS = SALES − COSTS

    to eliminate the need for lines 6180 and 6400?
  **b.  Can you show how matrix multiplication can be used to calculate total sales, costs, and profits by region? By model? *Hint:* If we premultiply an $M \times N$ matrix by a $1 \times M$ vector having 1s for each element, then we end up with a $1 \times N$ vector whose elements are the column sums of the $M \times N$ matrix. Similar logic can be used to calculate and store row sums.

---

## Brand Switching Problem*

The following problem illustrates a common application of matrix multiplication.

**Analysis.**   Brand switching behavior in the marketplace is a process that has been studied intensively by marketing analysts. The data given in Table G.3 illustrate a popular analytic approach for describing this behavior. These data summarize consumer brand purchase behavior for three brands from one week to the next. For example, the first row states that 90% of the consumers who purchased brand 1 in a given week repurchased brand 1 the next

---

*This example requires knowledge of matrix algebra.

**Table G.3**  Proportion of Consumers Switching from Brand $i$ in One Week to Brand $j$ in the Next Week

| Brand $i$ \ Brand $j$ | 1 | 2 | 3 |
|---|---|---|---|
| 1 | 0.90 | 0.07 | 0.03 |
| 2 | 0.02 | 0.82 | 0.16 |
| 3 | 0.20 | 0.12 | 0.68 |

week, 7% switched from brand 1 to brand 2, and 3% switched from brand 1 to brand 3. These proportions are termed transition probabilities, because they express the likelihoods that consumers switch (make a transition) from one brand to another.

The transition probabilities suggest certain changes over time in the overall purchasing behavior. For example, brand 1 customers appear to be the most loyal, since this brand has the highest probability of retaining its own customers from one week to the next (0.90 is higher than 0.82 for brand 2 and 0.68 for brand 3). Brand 3 has the least loyal customers, since only 68% of the consumers repurchase this brand from one week to the next. The third row, first column entry of 0.20 in the table further suggests that brand 3 is losing 20% of its customers to brand 1 from one week to the next.

Based on certain assumptions[4] the behavior of this process can be described for a specified number of weeks into the future. For example, if we define the matrix of transition probabilities by

$$\mathbf{P} = \begin{pmatrix} 0.90 & 0.07 & 0.03 \\ 0.02 & 0.82 & 0.16 \\ 0.20 & 0.12 & 0.68 \end{pmatrix}$$

then the matrix product

$$\mathbf{P}^2 = \mathbf{P} \cdot \mathbf{P} = \begin{pmatrix} 0.8174 & 0.1240 & 0.0586 \\ 0.0664 & 0.6930 & 0.2406 \\ 0.3184 & 0.1940 & 0.4876 \end{pmatrix}$$

defines transition probabilities 2 weeks into the future.[5] For example, 0.8174 means that 81.74% of the customers who purchase brand 1 this week repurchase brand 1 in 2 weeks. Similarly, purchase behavior 3 weeks into the future can be predicted by the product

$$\mathbf{P}^3 = \mathbf{P}^2 \cdot \mathbf{P}$$

Moreover, if we define the row vector

$$\mathbf{U} = (0.25 \quad 0.46 \quad 0.29)$$

as current market shares (brand 1 currently has 25% of the customers, brand 2 has 46%, and brand 3 has 29%), then the product

$$\mathbf{U}^2 = \mathbf{U} \cdot \mathbf{P}^2 = (0.32723 \quad 0.40604 \quad 0.26673)$$

---

[4]See, for example, F. Budnick, R. Mojena, and T. Vollmann, *Principles of Operations Research for Management.* Homewood, Ill.: Irwin, 1977, Chapter 15.

[5]You need not be concerned at this time how we calculated this product. The program on page 496 and Exercise 13 illustrate the mechanics of calculating matrix products. Just focus on the meaning of this product for now.

predicts market shares 2 weeks hence. Thus, it would appear that brand 1 is gaining at the expense of both brand 2 and brand 3, since over a 2-week period the expected market share of brand 1 will increase by about 8 percentage points (from 0.25 to 0.32723).

Let's develop a brand switching program with the following data requirements:

*Output*
Transition probabilities $k$ weeks into the future
Market shares $k$ weeks into the future

*Input*
Number of weeks into the future ($k$)

*Read*
Matrix of transition probabilities

**Design.**    The pseudocode for this program follows:

```
Read in size of matrix
Read in transition probability matrix
Redimension and initialize identity matrix
Redimension computational matrices
Input number of weeks
For each week
    Calculate transition probabilities for next week
    Copy transition probabilities to a "running product" matrix
Next week
Print future transition probabilities
Read in market shares for each brand
Multiply market shares by future transition probabilities
Print future market shares
Stop
```

**Code and Test.**    The following program and runs were implemented on a VAX-11 computer.

```
100  !    Brand Switching Program
110  !
120       DIM P(6,6),U(1,6),A(6,6),B(6,6),C(1,6)
130  !
140       READ M
150       MAT READ P(M,M) ◄————————P is redimensioned
155  !
160       MAT A = IDN(M,M) ◄————————A is initialized to identity matrix and redimensioned
170       MAT B = ZER(M,M)
180       MAT C = ZER(1,M) ◄————— B and C are redimensioned
190  !
200       INPUT "Enter number of weeks into future"; K
210       FOR L = 1 TO K
220          MAT B = A * P ◄————Calculates future transition probabilities
230          MAT A = B            A is a running product
240       NEXT L
250  !
260       PRINT
270       PRINT
280       PRINT "Transition probabilities"; K; "weeks into future'
290       MAT PRINT B;
292       PRINT
295  !
300       MAT READ U(1,M) ◄————————U is redimensioned
310       MAT C = U * B ◄——————— Calculates future market shares
315  !
```

```
320      PRINT "Market shares"; K; "weeks into future"
330      MAT PRINT C;
340 !
900      DATA 3
901      DATA .9,.07,.03,.02,.82,.16,.2,.12,.68
902      DATA .25,.46,.29
998 !
999      END


RUNN


Enter number of weeks into future? 2


Transition probabilities 2 weeks into future
 .8174   .124   .0586
 .0664   .693   .2406
 .3184   .194   .4876

Market shares 2 weeks into future
 .32723   .40604   .26673


RUNN


Enter number of weeks into future? 4


Transition probabilities 4 weeks into future
 .695035  .198658  .106307
 .176898  .535159  .287943
 .428394  .268518  .303088

Market shares 4 weeks into future
 .379366  .373708  .246926


RUNN


Enter number of weeks into future? 52


Transition probabilities 52 weeks into future
 .474077  .320985  .204936
 .474068  .320991  .204941
 .474074  .320987  .204938

Market shares 52 weeks into future
 .474072  .320988  .204939
```

**Discussion.**  Note the following points.

1.  The output from the first run (2 weeks into future) confirms the $P^2$ and $U^2$ results given earlier.

2.  All matrices are redimensioned in the program to the size stored in M. Proper dimensioning for compatibility is especially important in lines 220, 230, and 310. For example, in line 310 we must ensure that the number of columns in **U** equals the number of rows in **B**. Lines 170 and 300 properly redimension **B** and **U**.

3.  Matrices **A** and **B** in the program are used for computational purposes. Matrix **A** is initialized to the identity matrix in line 160; so the first time line 220 is executed, the result is **B** = **P** (see Exercise *8* for this result). Thereafter, the replacement in line 230 and the matrix product in line 220 ensure that **P** is successively multiplied by itself. Thus, using matrix notation, the successive calculations in line 220 give the following for **B**:

$$\mathbf{B} = \mathbf{I} \cdot \mathbf{P} = \mathbf{P} \qquad \text{when } L = 1 \ (\mathbf{I} \text{ is the identity matrix})$$
$$\mathbf{B} = \mathbf{P} \cdot \mathbf{P} = \mathbf{P}^2 \qquad \text{when } L = 2$$
$$\mathbf{B} = \mathbf{P}^2 \cdot \mathbf{P} = \mathbf{P}^3 \qquad \text{when } L = 3$$

$$\vdots$$

$$\mathbf{B} = \mathbf{P}^{K-1} \cdot \mathbf{P} = \mathbf{P}^K \qquad \text{when } L = K$$

In other words, when the FOR/NEXT loop is completed, **B** is equivalent to $\mathbf{P}^K$, which is the transition probability matrix $K$ weeks into the future.

4. The vector C in line 310 is equivalent to $\mathbf{U}^K$ in the matrix product

$$\mathbf{U}^K = \mathbf{U} \cdot \mathbf{P}^K$$

For example, when $K = 2$, C is equivalent to $\mathbf{U}^2$.

---

## Follow-Up Exercises

10. With respect to the output:
    a. Compare expected market shares 2, 4, and 52 weeks into the future, and comment on what the future holds for changes in market share conditions. Are brand 2 and brand 3 in trouble? Explain.
    b. Look at the matrix of transition probabilities 52 weeks into the future. Notice anything interesting? Explain what this means by relating it to the expected market shares at that time.

*11. a. Modify the program so that transition probabilities and market shares are printed for 1, 2, 3, . . . , and $K$ weeks into the future.
    b. Run this program on your system.

*12. Modify the program as follows:
    a. Define **R** as a revenue vector. Its elements equal expected total market revenue times corresponding market shares. Current total market revenue is $75 million. This market revenue, however, is expected to increase at the rate of half a million dollars per week.
    b. Define **S** as a cost vector. Its elements represent the total costs of each brand. It costs $20 million for brand 1, $18 million for brand 2, and $17 million for brand 3.
    c. Define **T** as a profit vector. Its elements represent revenue less cost for each brand.
    d. Print **R**, **S**, and **T** following the market share output.
    e. Run this revised program on your system.

**13. **Matrix multiplication.** If you're curious about the mechanics of matrix multiplication, then read on. If **A** has dimensions $m_1 \times n_1$ and **B** has dimensions $m_2 \times n_2$, then the matrix product **A·B** is defined if and only if $n_1 = m_2$. The result of this multiplication is a matrix **C** with dimensions $m_1 \times n_2$. Element $c_{ij}$ in **C** is calculated by multiplying the elements in *row i* of **A** by the corresponding elements in *column j* of **B**. For example, if

$$\mathbf{A} = \begin{pmatrix} 1 & 4 \\ 5 & -3 \end{pmatrix} \qquad \text{and} \qquad \mathbf{B} = \begin{pmatrix} 1 \\ 4 \end{pmatrix}$$

then

$$\mathbf{C} = \mathbf{A} \cdot \mathbf{B}$$
$$= \begin{pmatrix} 1 & 4 \\ 5 & -3 \end{pmatrix} \cdot \begin{pmatrix} 1 \\ 4 \end{pmatrix}$$
$$= \begin{pmatrix} 1 \times 1 + 4 \times 4 \\ 5 \times 1 - 3 \times 4 \end{pmatrix} = \begin{pmatrix} 17 \\ -7 \end{pmatrix}$$

Notice that the (2,1) element in **C**, or $-7$, is calculated by the product of row 2 in **A**, $(5 \quad -3)$, and column 1 in **B**, $\begin{pmatrix} 1 \\ 4 \end{pmatrix}$. Thus,

$$c_{21} = (5 \quad -3) \cdot \begin{pmatrix} 1 \\ 4 \end{pmatrix} = (5) \cdot (1) + (-3) \cdot (4) = -7$$

Also notice that attaching dimensions to

$$\mathbf{A}_{2 \times 2} \cdot \mathbf{B}_{2 \times 1}$$

clearly shows that the inner dimensions are equal, thereby defining the validity of the matrix product. Moreover, the result **C** will have dimensions equivalent to the outer dimensions; that is, **C** will be a $2 \times 1$ matrix.

**a.** Calculate the product **B·A**, where **A** and **B** are defined above.

**b.** Confirm the last result in Table G.2; that is, show that

$$\mathbf{C} = \mathbf{A \cdot B}$$

gives the identity matrix, where **A** and **B** are defined in Table G.2.

**c.** Confirm that a matrix multiplied by the identity matrix gives the matrix itself; that is, show that if

$$\mathbf{A} = \begin{pmatrix} 2 & 2 & 3 \\ 0 & 1 & 1 \\ 1 & 1 & 1 \end{pmatrix} \quad \text{and} \quad \mathbf{I} = \begin{pmatrix} 1 & 0 & 0 \\ 0 & 1 & 0 \\ 0 & 0 & 1 \end{pmatrix}$$

then

$$\mathbf{A \cdot I} = \mathbf{A} \quad \text{or} \quad \mathbf{I \cdot A} = \mathbf{A}$$

Is this result consistent with Exercise 8?

**d.** Confirm the result we got for $\mathbf{P}^2$ in the brand switching example.

**e.** Confirm the result we got for $\mathbf{U}^2$ in the brand switching example.

**f.** Show by example that **A·B** does not equal **B·A**, where **A** and **B** are square.

## Solving Systems of Simultaneous Linear Equations*

The following problem shows a common procedure in applied mathematics.

**Analysis.** The need to solve systems of simultaneous linear equations is very common in applications in mathematics, hard sciences, social sciences, and management. In precomputer days large systems involving hundreds of equations were quite costly to solve by "hand." Today, however, computer codes are readily available for efficiently solving simultaneous equations. The MAT statements in BASIC are especially convenient for carrying out this task.

Suppose we have the system of equations

$$\begin{aligned} x_1 + x_2 + x_3 &= 3 \\ 5x_1 - x_2 + 2x_3 &= 3 \\ 2x_1 - 3x_2 + x_3 &= -4 \end{aligned}$$

*This example requires knowledge of matrix algebra.

and we wish to solve for the values of $x_1$, $x_2$, and $x_3$ that satisfy this system. In other words, we wish to determine values of $x_1$, $x_2$, and $x_3$ that make each expression on the left-hand side equal to the corresponding right-hand-side constant. Using matrix algebra we would proceed as follows.

Represent the coefficients on the left side by the matrix

$$\mathbf{A} = \begin{pmatrix} 1 & 1 & 1 \\ 5 & -1 & 2 \\ 2 & -3 & 1 \end{pmatrix}$$

define the column vector for the unknown variables by

$$\mathbf{x} = \begin{pmatrix} x_1 \\ x_2 \\ x_3 \end{pmatrix}$$

and represent the right-hand constants by the column vector

$$\mathbf{b} = \begin{pmatrix} 3 \\ 3 \\ -4 \end{pmatrix}$$

The given system of equations can now be described by the matrix equation

$$\mathbf{A} \cdot \mathbf{x} = \mathbf{b}$$

To solve for $\mathbf{x}$, we premultiply both sides of this equation by the inverse of $\mathbf{A}$, which we label $\mathbf{A}^{-1}$. Thus,

$$\mathbf{A}^{-1} \cdot \mathbf{A} \cdot \mathbf{x} = \mathbf{A}^{-1} \cdot \mathbf{b}$$

Since $\mathbf{A}^{-1} \cdot \mathbf{A}$ yields the identity matrix (see Table G.2 on page 495 and Exercise 13b on page 505), we have

$$\mathbf{I} \cdot \mathbf{x} = \mathbf{A}^{-1} \cdot \mathbf{b}$$

But we know that $\mathbf{I} \cdot \mathbf{x}$ simply gives $\mathbf{x}$ (see Exercises 8 and 13c on pages 497 and 505); so we end up with

$$\mathbf{x} = \mathbf{A}^{-1} \cdot \mathbf{b}$$

Thus, we can solve a system of linear simultaneous equations by premultiplying the vector of right-hand constants by the inverse of the matrix of left-hand coefficients.

Let's develop a program with the following data requirements.

*Output*
The solution vector $\mathbf{x}$

*Read*
Number of equations
Matrix of coefficients $\mathbf{A}$
Vector of right-hand-side constants $\mathbf{b}$

**Design.**     The pseudocode for this program follows:

Read in number of equations
Read in matrix of coefficients **A**
Read in vector of right-hand constants **b**
Redimension **x** and inverse matrices
Calculate inverse of coefficient matrix
Multiply inverse matrix by vector of constants
Print solution
Stop

**Code and Test.**     The following program and run were implemented on a VAX-11 computer.

```
100  !     Solving Systems of Simultaneous Linear Equations
110  !
120        DIM A(50,50),X(50,1),B(50,1),C(50,50)
130  !
140        READ M
150        MAT READ A(M,M),B(M,1)  ←──────── A and b are redimensioned
160  !
170        MAT X = CON(M,1)  ←──────────── x and C are redimensioned
180        MAT C = CON(M,M)
185  !
190        MAT C = INV(A)  ←────────────── C is the inverse of A, or A⁻¹
200        MAT X = C * B  ←────────────── This is the solution of x = A⁻¹b
210  !
220        PRINT "X values:"
230        MAT PRINT X
240  !
900        DATA 3
901        DATA 1,1,1
902        DATA 5,-1,2
903        DATA 2,-3,1
904        DATA 3,3,-4
998  !
999        END


RUNN


X values:
  1
  2
  0
```

**Discussion.**     Note the following points.

1.  The matrices **A**, **b**, **x**, and **C** (or $A^{-1}$) are redimensioned in lines 150, 170, and 180. The CON function accomplishes this in lines 170–180 for matrices that are not read in. We could have used just as well the ZER or IDN function

2.  The inverse matrix $A^{-1}$ must be stored as a unique matrix. In line 190, the matrix **C** serves this purpose. Line 200 thus uses **C** to arrive at the solution.

---

### Follow-Up Exercises

**14.** Confirm that the solution for **x** satisfies the system of equations on page 505.

**\*15.** Implement the simultaneous equation program on your system.

**\*16.** Modify the program as follows:
  **a.** Print the elements in **x** as a row rather than a column. *Hint:* You need to use a function from Table G.1.
  **b.** Redesign the program to process *N* sets of *M* simultaneous equations each.
  **c.** Run and debug your program by processing the additional set of simultaneous equations below.

$$3x_1 + 2x_2 = 16$$
$$x_1 + 5x_2 = 27$$

Confirm the solution by plugging it into these two equations.

---

## G.5 POINTERS

### Design and Style

The use of MAT READ, INPUT, and PRINT statements presents us with a trade-off: fewer lines of codes versus flexibility. Recall that the MAT command can read, input, and print row-wise. What if the data are provided in column-wise format, or output is desired in a column-wise arrangement? In these cases the FOR/NEXT approach is necessary. In addition, when using the MAT PRINT statement, we can't mix other values with the output of the array. Did you notice that the model (row) number does not appear in the output on page 499. Compare this to the output on page 334.

### Common Errors

Certain errors in the use of MAT statements occur commonly. We shall now summarize them:

1. **Forgetting dimensions.**    If we forget to dimension an array using the DIM statement, then the first use of the array in a MAT statement may provoke a syntax error. In some cases this may not be a problem since many systems implicitly dimension arrays to 10 rows and 10 columns when the DIM statement is omitted. As before, we strongly recommend the use of DIM statements regardless of the system.

2. **Redimensioning.**    We can redimension a matrix during execution using the READ, INPUT, and PRINT statements and the functions ZER, CON, NUL$, and IDN. An attempt to redimension using any other statement may give a syntax error. An execution error occurs when we attempt to redimension a matrix beyond the size defined in the DIM statement. For example,

```
10 DIM A(20,10)
20 READ M,N
30 MAT READ A(M,N)
    .
    .
    .
90 DATA 50,5
```

would not be allowed since line 30 attempts to redimension A as a matrix of 50 rows, which exceeds the 20 rows specified in line 10.

3. **Nonconformity.**    The functions TRN and INV and all operations require compatibility or conformity in matrix dimensions, as follows:

| | |
|---|---|
| 10 MAT B = TRN(A) | The number of rows in B must equal the number of columns in A; the number of columns in B must equal the number of rows in A. |
| 20 MAT B = INV(A) | A and B must be square (the number of rows equals the number of columns) and of the same dimensions. |
| 30 MAT B = A | A and B must have identical dimensions. |
| 40 MAT C = A ± B | A, B, and C must have identical dimensions. |
| 50 MAT B = (75)*A | A and B must have identical dimensions. |
| 60 MAT C = A*B | The number of columns in A must equal the number of rows in B; the number of rows in C must equal the number of rows in A; the number of columns in C must equal the number of columns in B. |

Any violation of these conformity rules results in an execution error. Thus make sure your DIM statements conform. If you redimension during execution, make sure these conform.

4. **Other violations.**    In certain functions and operations, the same matrix may not appear on both sides of the equal sign. For example, the following are not allowed:

```
70 MAT A = TRN(A)
80 MAT A = INV(A)
90 MAT A = A*B
```

Also, multiple operations are not allowed. For example,

```
100 MAT D = A + B − C
110 MAT D = A*B*C
```

provoke syntax errors. Line 100 could be rewritten as

```
100 MAT D = A + B
105 MAT D = D − C
```

and line 110 as

```
110 MAT E = A*B
115 MAT D = E*C
```

## ADDITIONAL EXERCISES

**17.** Define or explain the following terms:

matrix   ZER function   inverse
column vector  CON function  matrix assignment
row vector   IDN function   matrix addition
MAT statements NUL$ function  matrix subtraction
MAT READ statement TRN function scalar multiplication
MAT INPUT statement INV function matrix multiplication
MAT PRINT statement identity matrix
redimensioned array transpose
matrix algebra

**18. Revisits.** Modify one of the following problems as indicated.

 **a.** Go back to one of our examples in Chapters 8 and 9 (except for the financial report example!) and use MAT statements and functions where appropriate.

 **b.** Go back to one of our exercises at the end of Chapters 8 and 9 and use MAT statements and functions where appropriate.

**\*\*19. Faculty flow model.** The current distribution of faculty at State University is given in Table G.4. The transition probability data in Table G.5 illustrate the typical "flow" behavior of faculty from one year to the next. The administration wishes to utilize these data in a planning and budget model that generates future faculty needs and budgets. Your program should:

 **a.** Determine the number of faculty in each rank for each of the next 5 years. Assume a policy of attrition, whereby no new faculty are hired during this period.

**b.** Assume the administration wants to maintain the current number of faculty positions of 300. Determine the number of faculty that need to be hired for each of the next 5 years. Include the calculation of number of faculty in each rank. Assume that all new faculty hirings are at the rank of Assistant Professor.

**c.** The average faculty salary for each rank is listed in Table G.6. Develop salary budgets for each of the next 5 years, first under the hiring policy in part **a** and then under the hiring policy in part **b**. Build in a 6% inflation rate into average faculty salaries.

**Table G.6** Average Faculty Salaries by Rank

| Rank | Salary($) |
|---|---|
| Full Professor | 38,000 |
| Associate Professor | 30,000 |
| Assistant Professor | 25,000 |
| Instructor | 15,000 |

**Table G.4** Distribution of Faculty by Rank

| Rank | Number of Faculty |
|---|---|
| Full Professor | 50 |
| Associate Professor | 100 |
| Assistant Professor | 100 |
| Instructor | 50 |

**\*\*20. Multiple linear regression analysis.** The data in Table G.7 show residential sales of 50 single-family residences. Real estate analysts use data of this type to study the relationship between the sale price of a house and characteristics of the house such as size, number of bedrooms, number of bathrooms, total rooms, age, whether there is an attached garage (0 = no; 1 = yes), and whether there is a view (0 = no; 1 = yes).

**Table G.5** Year-to-Year Changes by Rank

| Status at Start of Year \ Status at End of Year | Full | Associate | Assistant | Instructor | Leave or Retire |
|---|---|---|---|---|---|
| Full | 0.80 | 0.00 | 0.00 | 0.00 | 0.20 |
| Associate | 0.10 | 0.80 | 0.00 | 0.00 | 0.10 |
| Assistant | 0.00 | 0.20 | 0.65 | 0.00 | 0.15 |
| Instructor | 0.00 | 0.00 | 0.25 | 0.50 | 0.25 |

**Table G.7**  Real Estate Data

| Residence $i$ | Sales Price $y(\times \$1000)$ | Square Feet $x_1$ ($\times$ 100) | Bedrooms $x_2$ | Bathrooms $x_3$ | Total Rooms $x_4$ | Age $x_5$ | Attached Garage $x_6$ | View $x_7$ |
|---|---|---|---|---|---|---|---|---|
| 1  | 51.0  | 8.0  | 2 | 1 | 5  | 5  | 0 | 0 |
| 2  | 52.1  | 9.5  | 2 | 1 | 5  | 8  | 0 | 0 |
| 3  | 55.5  | 9.1  | 3 | 1 | 6  | 2  | 0 | 0 |
| 4  | 76.5  | 9.5  | 3 | 1 | 6  | 6  | 0 | 0 |
| 5  | 79.0  | 12.0 | 3 | 2 | 7  | 5  | 0 | 0 |
| 6  | 81.5  | 10.0 | 3 | 1 | 6  | 11 | 0 | 0 |
| 7  | 86.0  | 11.8 | 3 | 2 | 7  | 8  | 0 | 0 |
| 8  | 88.5  | 10.0 | 2 | 1 | 7  | 15 | 1 | 0 |
| 9  | 90.0  | 13.8 | 3 | 2 | 7  | 10 | 0 | 0 |
| 10 | 90.4  | 12.5 | 3 | 2 | 7  | 11 | 0 | 0 |
| 11 | 92.0  | 15.0 | 3 | 2 | 7  | 12 | 0 | 0 |
| 12 | 92.8  | 12.0 | 3 | 2 | 7  | 8  | 0 | 0 |
| 13 | 94.2  | 16.0 | 3 | 2 | 7  | 9  | 1 | 1 |
| 14 | 96.3  | 16.5 | 3 | 2 | 7  | 15 | 0 | 0 |
| 15 | 97.2  | 16.0 | 3 | 2 | 7  | 11 | 1 | 0 |
| 16 | 100.0 | 16.8 | 2 | 2 | 7  | 12 | 0 | 0 |
| 17 | 101.5 | 15.0 | 3 | 1 | 7  | 8  | 1 | 0 |
| 18 | 101.9 | 17.8 | 3 | 2 | 8  | 13 | 1 | 0 |
| 19 | 104.0 | 17.9 | 3 | 2 | 7  | 18 | 1 | 0 |
| 20 | 105.6 | 19.0 | 2 | 2 | 7  | 22 | 0 | 0 |
| 21 | 107.0 | 17.6 | 3 | 1 | 6  | 17 | 0 | 0 |
| 22 | 110.5 | 18.5 | 3 | 2 | 8  | 11 | 1 | 0 |
| 23 | 110.9 | 18.0 | 3 | 2 | 7  | 5  | 0 | 0 |
| 24 | 112.0 | 17.0 | 2 | 3 | 8  | 2  | 1 | 0 |
| 25 | 114.0 | 18.7 | 3 | 1 | 6  | 6  | 0 | 0 |
| 26 | 114.5 | 20.0 | 3 | 2 | 7  | 16 | 0 | 0 |
| 27 | 115.1 | 20.0 | 3 | 2 | 7  | 12 | 0 | 0 |
| 28 | 116.0 | 21.0 | 3 | 2 | 7  | 10 | 1 | 0 |
| 29 | 118.9 | 20.5 | 2 | 2 | 7  | 11 | 1 | 0 |
| 30 | 120.1 | 19.9 | 3 | 1 | 7  | 13 | 1 | 1 |
| 31 | 124.9 | 21.5 | 2 | 2 | 7  | 8  | 0 | 0 |
| 32 | 125.5 | 20.5 | 3 | 1 | 7  | 9  | 1 | 0 |
| 33 | 130.0 | 22.0 | 3 | 2 | 7  | 10 | 0 | 0 |
| 34 | 134.9 | 22.0 | 3 | 2 | 7  | 6  | 1 | 1 |
| 35 | 135.1 | 21.8 | 2 | 1 | 6  | 15 | 1 | 0 |
| 36 | 139.0 | 22.5 | 3 | 2 | 7  | 11 | 1 | 0 |
| 37 | 140.0 | 24.0 | 3 | 2 | 7  | 17 | 0 | 0 |
| 38 | 143.5 | 23.5 | 3 | 2 | 8  | 12 | 0 | 0 |
| 39 | 145.0 | 25.0 | 3 | 2 | 7  | 11 | 1 | 0 |
| 40 | 150.5 | 25.6 | 3 | 2 | 7  | 15 | 1 | 0 |
| 41 | 160.0 | 25.0 | 4 | 2 | 8  | 12 | 1 | 0 |
| 42 | 169.0 | 25.0 | 2 | 2 | 8  | 8  | 0 | 1 |
| 43 | 176.5 | 26.8 | 3 | 2 | 7  | 6  | 1 | 0 |
| 44 | 185.5 | 22.1 | 3 | 2 | 8  | 18 | 1 | 0 |
| 45 | 187.5 | 27.5 | 3 | 2 | 8  | 12 | 1 | 0 |
| 46 | 190.3 | 25.0 | 4 | 2 | 8  | 10 | 1 | 0 |
| 47 | 192.6 | 24.0 | 3 | 2 | 8  | 13 | 1 | 1 |
| 48 | 195.0 | 31.0 | 4 | 3 | 9  | 25 | 1 | 0 |
| 49 | 215.0 | 21.0 | 4 | 2 | 9  | 18 | 1 | 0 |
| 50 | 275.0 | 40.0 | 5 | 3 | 12 | 22 | 1 | 0 |

A statistical methodology called *multiple linear regression analysis* directly assesses the relationship between $y$ (sale price) and the set of variables, $x_1, x_2, \ldots, x_7$ (as defined in the table) by fitting the linear function (model)

$$y = b_0 + b_1 x_1 + b_2 x_2 + \ldots + b_7 x_7$$

to the given data. The symbols $b_0, b_1, \ldots b_7$, called *regression coefficients*, are calculated by a procedure called the *least-squares technique*. For example, suppose the model reads as follows:

$$y = -67 + 5.1x_1 + 8.2x_2 - 19.3x_3 + 14.5x_1 - 0.10x_5 + 6.3x_6 - 6.4x_7$$

The regression coefficient of 5.1, for example, means that an increase of 1 unit in the variable $x_1$ (an additional 100 square feet) increases $y$ by 5.1 units (the average price of a house increases by $5100), all other variables being held constant; an increase of 1 unit in $x_2$ (one additional bedroom) increases the average price of a house by $8200. Can you interpret the other $b$-values?

A model of this type can be used not only to study the relationships between variables (for example, what is the effect on price of an extra bedroom?) but also to predict the values of similar homes. For example, realtors are interested in predicting the potential sales price of a given home, and tax assessors are interested in assessing the value of homes to establish "fair" taxes.

**a.** Write a program that uses the data in Table G.7 to fit a linear model (that is, find the values of $b_0, b_1, \ldots, b_7$) by the least-squares method. If we define the matrices

$$\mathbf{y} = \begin{pmatrix} 51.0 \\ 52.1 \\ \cdot \\ \cdot \\ \cdot \\ 275.0 \end{pmatrix}_{50 \times 1}$$

and

$$\mathbf{x} = \begin{pmatrix} 1 & 8.0 & 2 & 1 & 5 & 5 & 0 & 0 \\ 1 & 9.5 & 2 & 1 & 5 & 8 & 0 & 0 \\ \cdot \\ \cdot \\ \cdot \\ 1 & 40.0 & 5 & 3 & 12 & 22 & 1 & 0 \end{pmatrix}_{50 \times 8}$$

and

$$\mathbf{b} = \begin{pmatrix} b_0 \\ b_1 \\ \cdot \\ \cdot \\ \cdot \\ b_7 \end{pmatrix}_{8 \times 1}$$

then the least-squares method calculates regression coefficients by the formula

$$\mathbf{b} = (\mathbf{X}' \cdot \mathbf{X})^{-1} \cdot \mathbf{X}' \cdot \mathbf{y}$$

where $\mathbf{X}'$ is the transpose of $\mathbf{X}$ and $(\mathbf{X}' \cdot \mathbf{X})^{-1}$ is the inverse of the matrix product $\mathbf{X}' \cdot \mathbf{X}$. In your program represent the number of rows in the data by the variable $n$ (50 in the example) and the number of columns in $\mathbf{X}$ or rows in $\mathbf{b}$ by the variable $k$ (8 in the example).

**b.** The model derived in part **a** can be used to predict the sale prices of similar homes. For example, a home having 2000 square feet ($x_1 = 20$), three bedrooms ($x_2 = 3$), two bathrooms ($x_3 = 2$), eight total rooms ($x_4 = 8$), that was built 10 years ago ($x_5 = 10$), that has an attached garage ($x_6 = 1$), and that has no view ($x_7 = 0$) can be expected to sell for

$$\begin{aligned} y &= -67 + 5.1(20) + 8.2(3) - 19.3(2) \\ &\quad + 14.5(8) - 0.10(10) + 6.3(1) - 6.4(0) \\ &= 142.3 \end{aligned}$$

or $142,300.

If we let $\mathbf{p}$ represent a $k \times 1$ vector of predictor values given by

$$\mathbf{p} = \begin{pmatrix} 1 \\ x_1 \\ x_2 \\ \cdot \\ \cdot \\ \cdot \\ x_7 \end{pmatrix}_{k \times 1}$$

then the product $\mathbf{b}' \cdot \mathbf{p}$ calculates the predicted value of $y$.

Add an interactive feature to the program that requests predictor values and calculates the corresponding $y$ value. Loop as often as the user desires and process the following data:

| $x_1$ | $x_2$ | $x_3$ | $x_4$ | $x_5$ | $x_6$ | $x_7$ |
|-------|-------|-------|-------|-------|-------|-------|
| 17.0 | 2 | 3 | 8 | 2 | 1 | 0 |
| 25.6 | 3 | 2 | 7 | 15 | 1 | 0 |
| 20.0 | 3 | 2 | 8 | 10 | 1 | 0 |
| 40.0 | 4 | 2.5 | 10 | 4 | 1 | 1 |

# Answers to Selected Follow-up Exercises

## Chapter 2

1. **(a)** Incorrect. No commas permitted. **(b)** Correct. **(c)** Correct. **(d)** Normally the plus sign is not printed with a positive number. **(e)** Correct. **(f)** Incorrect. Minus sign is misplaced. **(g)** Correct. **(h)** Depends on system. The proposed ANSI standard does not permit a space within a numeric constant. Most systems, however, would ignore this space. We recommend not using a space within a numeric constant, as it hinders readability. **(i)** Incorrect. Asterisk doesn't belong. This describes multiplication of 5 and 7. **(j)** Incorrect. Exponent is too large. **(k)** Incorrect. Exponent should be an integer. **(l)** Incorrect. Quote after T is missing. **(m)** Correct, but not recommended. **(n)** Incorrect. $ is not allowed. **(o)** Incorrect. Number is too large in this format. Use 6.57890E10. **(p)** Incorrect. Number has too many digits to be represented as is. Use 154.613: otherwise the computer may truncate to 154.612. **(q)** Correct. **(r)** Correct.

2. **(a)** $-6.142E15$ **(b)** $-6142E12$ **(c)** $7E - 5$ **(d)** $7E - 5$

3. **(a)** 123000000000 **(b)** 123000000000 **(c)** 0.0456 **(d)** 0.0456

4. **(a)** Incorrect. First character must be a letter. **(b)** Numeric. **(c)** Incorrect. No space permitted. **(d)** Correct string on some systems. **(e)** Correct string on some systems. **(f)** Incorrect. Plus sign not permitted. **(g)** Correct numeric on most systems. **(h)** Incorrect. First character must be a letter. **(i)** String. **(j)** Numeric. **(k&l)** Incorrect. First character must be a letter.

5. **(a)** I love BASIC   I love BASIC
   **(b)** I love BASIC   I love BASIC

6. **(a)** 5000   5000   2500
   **(b)** 5000   5000   10000
   **(c)** 5000   5000   2.5E+07

7. A=7.4   B=9   C=5   D=81

8. K=3    S=15    X=5

9. C=85.77779

10. P=20   R=.002

11. **(a)** 116 **(b)** 28 **(c)** 28 **(d)** 8.5 **(e)** 4 **(f)** 4 **(g)** 10.5

12. **(a)** X^(I+1) **(b)** X^I + 1 **(c)** S^2/(P−1) **(d)** (X−A)^2/(P−1) **(e)** (Y−3^(X−1) + 2)^5 **(f)** (7−X)^(1/2) **(g)** SQR((X−A)^2/(P−1)) **(h)** INT (A/B) **(i)** LOG(X+3)

13. **(a)** Only one variable to left of equal symbol. Use 5 LET A = B + C. **(b)** Two arithmetic operation symbols cannot be together. **(c)** Variable must appear on

left side of equal symbol. Use 15 LET A = 5. **(d)** Allowed on some systems but not others. The following works on all systems:

20 LET X = 5.3
22 LET Y = 5.3

**(e)** Cannot raise a negative value to a non-integral power. **(f)** Correct. **(g)** Many systems allow omission of LET, but it's not stylistically recommended.

14. Unique to each system.

15. Unique to each system.

16. Unique to each system.

17. **(a)**  50                          −100
    **(b)**  50                              −100
    **(c)**  50                       −100
    **(d)**              5.7
    **(e)**              −100
    **(f)**              RED
    **(g)**      RED
    **(h)**              RED
    **(i)**  RED
    **(j)**  5                      6

18. **(a)**  PRINT "A = ";A
    **(b)**  PRINT "B = ";B
    **(c)**  PRINT "QUANTITY PRICE REVENUE"
    **(d)**  PRINT A,B,C
    **(e)**  PRINT "MY NAME IS"

25. The input prompt (?) would appear on a separate line if we were to omit the trailing semicolon.

26. **(a)**  Input college name, tuition, enrollment
    Calculate revenue
    Print revenue
    Stop

**(b)**

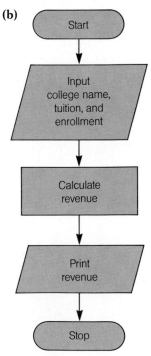

27. **(a)**  INPUT "Enter name, SS number and age (separated by commas)"; N$,S,A
    **(b)**  INPUT "Do you wish to print output (Y/N)"; R$

28. N$ will store Bogart, which gives the output Bogart. Place quotes around the input string "Bogart, H."

33. **(a)** Syntax error, extra comma. **(b)** No effect on the IBM PC. **(c)** Execution error in line 30—data type mismatch when numeric variable ZIP is matched with data

item "Miami,   ". Some systems, like the **IBM PC**, indicate a syntax error in line 60. **(d)** Kingston, RI 2881—make zip code a string variable to avoid missing leading zeros. **(e)** Execution error: Out of data in line 30.

**34.** **(a)** July 21 **(b)** July 21, 2001

**35.** **(a)** No change. **(b)** No change. **(c)** Out of data execution error. **(d)** Data type mismatch execution error. Some systems, like the **IBM PC**, indicate a syntax error in line 901.

**36.** A = 100   B = 150
Out of DATA in 180

**37.** All but c.

**38.** **(a)** Points to 10. **(b)** Points to 40. **(c)** Points to end of data, or just after the 50.

# Chapter 3

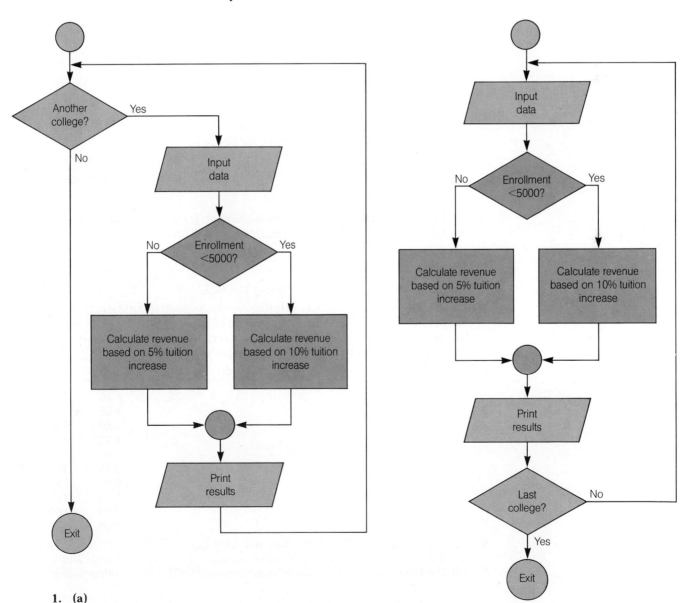

**1.** **(a)**

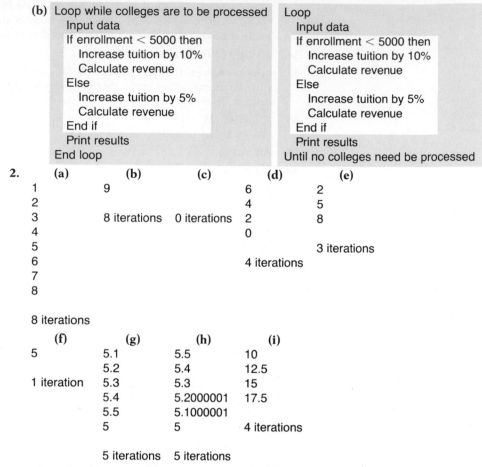

**(b)**

| Loop while colleges are to be processed | Loop |
|---|---|
| Input data | Input data |
| If enrollment < 5000 then | If enrollment < 5000 then |
| Increase tuition by 10% | Increase tuition by 10% |
| Calculate revenue | Calculate revenue |
| Else | Else |
| Increase tuition by 5% | Increase tuition by 5% |
| Calculate revenue | Calculate revenue |
| End if | End if |
| Print results | Print results |
| End loop | Until no colleges need be processed |

**2.**

| | (a) | (b) | (c) | (d) | (e) |
|---|---|---|---|---|---|
| 1 | | 9 | | 6 | 2 |
| 2 | | | | 4 | 5 |
| 3 | | 8 iterations | 0 iterations | 2 | 8 |
| 4 | | | | 0 | |
| 5 | | | | | 3 iterations |
| 6 | | | | 4 iterations | |
| 7 | | | | | |
| 8 | | | | | |

8 iterations

| (f) | (g) | (h) | (i) |
|---|---|---|---|
| 5 | 5.1 | 5.5 | 10 |
| | 5.2 | 5.4 | 12.5 |
| 1 iteration | 5.3 | 5.3 | 15 |
| | 5.4 | 5.2000001 | 17.5 |
| | 5.5 | 5.1000001 | |
| | 5 | 5 | 4 iterations |
| | 5 iterations | 5 iterations | |

**3.** **(a)** 0 increment. **(b)** Need a negative increment. **(c)** Control variable in FOR and NEXT don't match. **(d)** Control variable K is redefined within loop.

**4.** Change line 900 to

900 DATA 15

Add 12 additional data lines following line 903.

**5.** **(a)** Heading is repeated before printing results for each institution. **(b)** 41 dashes are printed beginning in position 1 instead of position 5. **(c)** No difference—Tab function on line 240 forces output to begin on a new line; otherwise the name of the first college would be printed to the right of the dashes.

**6.**

| PRINCIPAL | PERIODS | INTFIRST | INTLAST | INTSTEP | INTEREST | FUNDS |
|---|---|---|---|---|---|---|
| 1000 | 20 | 1 | 3 | .25 | 1.00 | 1220.190 |
| | | | | | 1.25 | 1282.039 |
| | | | | | 1.50 | 1346.854 |
| | | | | | 1.75 | 1414.780 |
| | | | | | 2.00 | 1485.946 |
| | | | | | 2.25 | 1560.510 |
| | | | | | 2.50 | 1638.616 |
| | | | | | 2.75 | 1720.430 |
| | | | | | 3.00 | 1806.111 |
| | | | | | 3.25 | |

**9.** **(a)** No change. **(b)** Yes. SUM does not include last college (SUM=3250000). **(c)** Not likely, but it's best to initialize summers for reasons of style and safety. **(d)** The label Total and a running sum are printed after each college's line.

**12. (a)**

| | |
|---|---|
| 1 | 5 |
| 2 | 10 |
| 3 | 15 |
| 4 | 15 |

**13.**

| Just before line | M | N | STUDENT | SNAME$ | J | SCORE | SUM | AVG |
|---|---|---|---|---|---|---|---|---|
| 340 | 4 | 3 | 1 | Smith | 1 | 90 | 90 | 0 |
| 340 | 4 | 3 | 1 | Smith | 2 | 80 | 170 | 0 |
| 340 | 4 | 3 | 1 | Smith | 3 | 100 | 270 | 0 |
| 380 | 4 | 3 | 1 | Smith | 4 | 100 | 270 | 90 |
| 340 | 4 | 3 | 2 | Jones | 1 | 50 | 50 | 90 |
| 340 | 4 | 3 | 2 | Jones | 2 | 90 | 140 | 90 |
| 340 | 4 | 3 | 2 | Jones | 3 | 70 | 210 | 90 |
| 380 | 4 | 3 | 2 | Jones | 4 | 70 | 210 | 70 |
| 340 | 4 | 3 | 3 | Ellie | 1 | 85 | 85 | 70 |
| 340 | 4 | 3 | 3 | Ellie | 2 | 75 | 160 | 70 |
| 340 | 4 | 3 | 3 | Ellie | 3 | 65 | 225 | 70 |
| 380 | 4 | 3 | 3 | Ellie | 4 | 65 | 225 | 75 |
| 340 | 4 | 3 | 4 | Budzirk | 1 | 88 | 88 | 75 |
| 340 | 4 | 3 | 4 | Budzirk | 2 | 72 | 160 | 75 |
| 340 | 4 | 3 | 4 | Budzirk | 3 | 86 | 246 | 75 |
| 380 | 4 | 3 | 4 | Budzirk | 4 | 86 | 246 | 82 |

**14. (a)** The sums and averages for all students but the first are incorrectly calculated.

```
Name                 Average
---------------------------
Smith                90
Jones                160
Ellie                235
Budzirk              317
---------------------------
```

**(b)** The output is unchanged, but the extra (and meaningless) calculations of AVE are inefficient.

**16. (a)** 16 iterations **(b)** 12 iterations

| | | | | |
|---|---|---|---|---|
| 1 | 1 | | 1 | 1 |
| 1 | 2 | | 1 | 1.5 |
| 1 | 3 | | 1 | 2 |
| 1 | 4 | | 2 | 1 |
| 2 | 1 | | 2 | 1.5 |
| 2 | 2 | | 2 | 2 |
| 2 | 3 | | 3 | 1 |
| 2 | 4 | | 3 | 1.5 |
| 3 | 1 | | 3 | 2 |
| 3 | 2 | | 4 | 1 |
| 3 | 3 | | 4 | 1.5 |
| 3 | 4 | | 4 | 2 |
| 4 | 1 | | | |
| 4 | 2 | | | |
| 4 | 3 | | | |
| 4 | 4 | | | |

# Chapter 4

**1.**

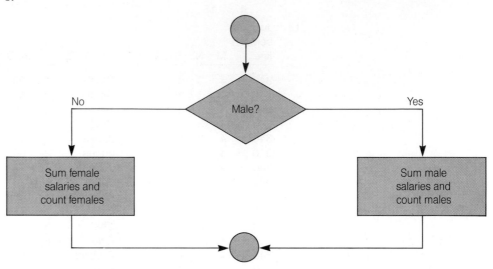

**2. (a)**

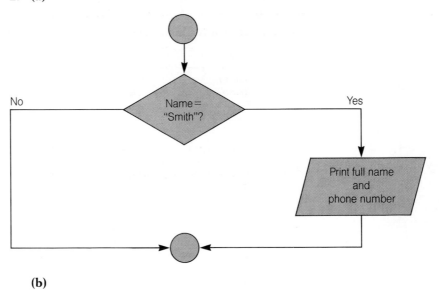

**(b)**

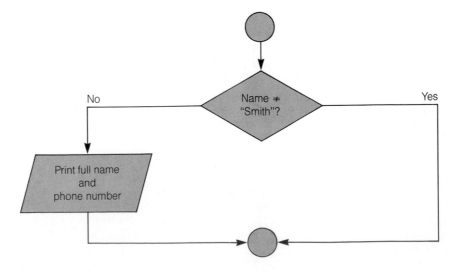

**(c)**

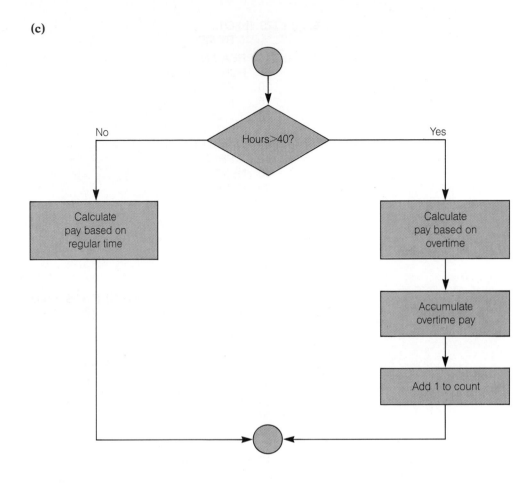

3. **(a)** T **(b)** T **(c)** T **(d)** T **(e)** F **(f)** F **(g)** T **(h)** Invalid **(i)** T **(j)** Invalid

4. **(a)** SALES > 10000　**(b)** LNAME$ = "Smith"　**(c)** LNAME$ <> "Smith"
   **(d)** B^2 > 4\*A\*C

5. 30　IF GPA >= 3.4 THEN 35
   32　　GOTO 45
   35　　LET K = K + 1
   40　　PRINT N$,GPA
   45 . . .

6. 25　IF AGE < 65 THEN 30
   27　　PRINT "Senior Citizen"; K
   30 NEXT K

7. On the IBM PC it would look like this:

170 IF SEX$ = "F" THEN LET FSAL = FSAL + SAL : LET FCOUNT = FCOUNT + 1
　　　　　　　　 ELSE LET MSAL = MSAL + SAL : LET MCOUNT = MCOUNT + 1

This shows one *program* line but two *visual* lines. To get from the first line to the second, the <Ctrl> and <Enter> keys are simultaneously pressed.

Compared to Example 4.5a, this approach is more readable and eliminates the error-prone explicit line number transfers given by THEN 180, ELSE 210, and GOTO 230.

Compared to Example 4.6, this approach is just as good; however the Example 4.6 approach does not limit the size of (number of statements in) else or then blocks, while the approach used in this exercise is restricted by the length of a program line. On the IBM PC this limit is 255 characters, or just over three visual lines.

8.  (a) 123  (b) O.K.
                  BY ME

9.  (a)    10   READ N
           15   FOR J = 1 TO N
           20      READ S
           25      IF E > 32400 THEN 40
           30         LET F = S * .067
           35      GO TO 45
           40         LET F = 0
           45      PRINT F
           50   NEXT J
           90   DATA . . .
                 .
                 .
                 .
           99   END

    (b)  As in part **a** except:

           25   LET F = 0
           30   IF E <= 32400 THEN LET F = S * .067
           (Delete lines 35 – 40)

    (c)  As in part **b** except:

           (Delete line 25)
           30   IF E > 32400 THEN LET F = 0 ELSE LET F = S * .067

    (d)  As in part **a** except:

           25   IF E > 32400 THEN
           30      LET F = 0
           35   ELSE
           40      LET F = S * .067
           42   END IF

    The approaches in parts **c** and **d** are preferable since they visually reproduce the
    if-then-else control structure, and unlike the approach in part **a** they avoid explicit
    line number transfers.

10. (a)    10   READ A,B,C,D,E,F
           20   IF A*C < B/D THEN 60
           30      LET X = A + B
           40      LET D = B − A
           50   GO TO 80
           60      LET C = D/E
           70      LET F = F − 1
           80   PRINT A,B,C,D,E,F
           90   DATA . . .
           99   END

    (b)  Not appropriate here. Would need to have the same form as part **a**.

    (c)    20   IF A*C < B/D THEN 30 ELSE 60
           30      LET C = D/E
           40      LET F = F − 1
           50   GO TO 80
           60      LET X = A + B
           70      LET D = B − A
           80   PRINT . . .

    Here it would be best to use the multistatement line approach of Exer-
    cise 7.

**(d)**
```
20   IF A*C < B/D THEN
30      LET C = D/E
40      LET F = F - 1
50   ELSE
60      LET X = A + B
70      LET D = B - A
75   END IF
80   PRINT . . .
```

The approach in part **d** is best since it avoids explicit line number transfers and visually reproduces the if-then-else control structure. Part **c** would also be fine if rewritten according to the approach in Exercise 7.

**11.** **(a)** IF SALES > 10000 THEN LET PAY = PAY + 150

**(b)** IF CREDITS >= 12 THEN LET TUITION = 1200 ELSE LET TUITION = CREDITS*100

**(c)** IF PART.NAME$ = "WRENCH" THEN PRINT QUANTITY

**(d)**
```
20   IF FIXED + VARIABLE < SALES THEN
30      LET PROFIT = SALES - (FIXED + VARIABLE)
40      PRINT "Profit ="; PROFIT
50   ELSE
60      LET LOSS = (FIXED + VARIABLE) - SALES
70      PRINT "Loss ="; LOSS
80   END IF
```

**(e)** IF M=N THEN LET I = I + 3 : LET J = J + 2 : LET K = K + 1

**12.**

| N | J | C$ | Q | MINQ | MINC$ |
|---|---|-----|-----|-------|-------|
| 5 | – | —— | —— | 10000 | —— |
|   | 1 | Test 1 | 700 | 700 | Test 1 |
|   | 2 | Test 2 | 500 | 500 | Test 2 |
|   | 3 | Test 3 | 900 | 500 | Test 2 |
|   | 4 | Test 4 | 200 | 200 | Test 4 |
|   | 5 | Test 5 | 600 | 200 | Test 4 |

**13.** **(a)**
```
225   LET MAXQ = 0
285      IF Q > MAXQ THEN MAXQ = Q : MAXC$ = C$
325   PRINT
326   PRINT "Maximum quantity ordered      :"; MAXQ
327   PRINT "Customer with maximum order:"; MAXC$
```

**14.  (a)**

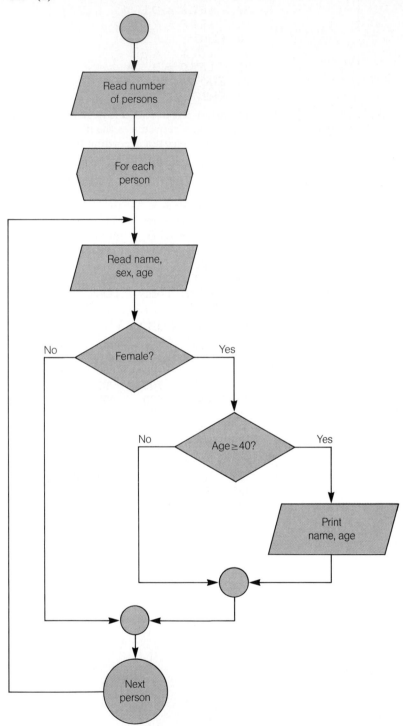

**(b)** First approach:

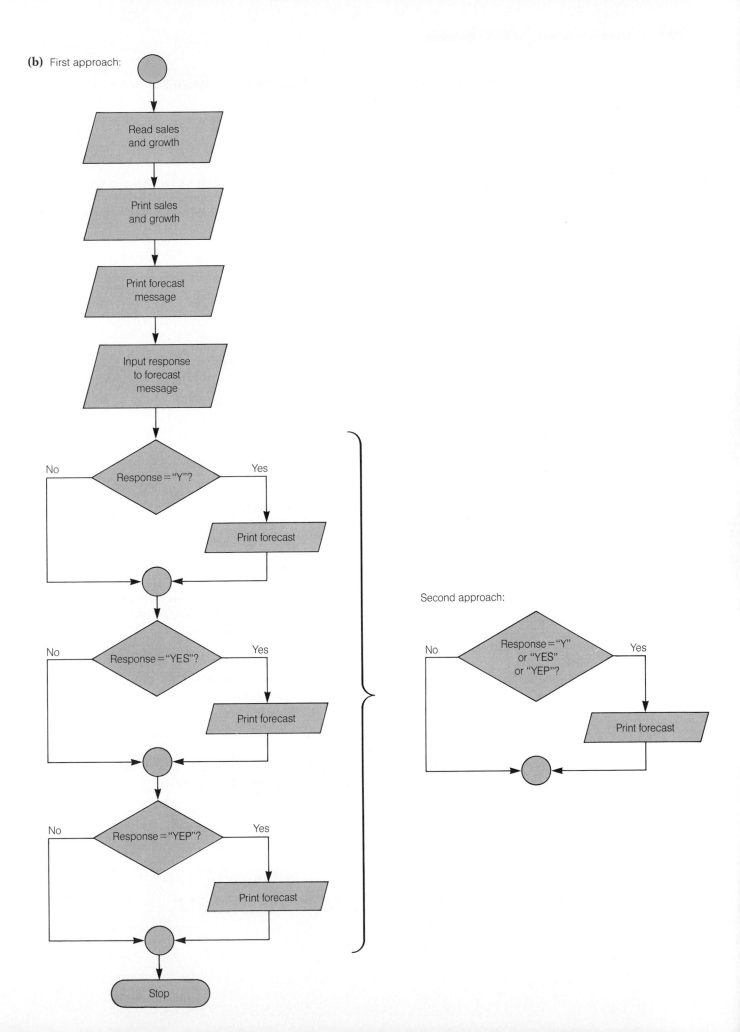

15. (a) Missing V in V < 200. (b) Missing MAJOR$ in MAJOR$ = "MATH". (c) Correct.

16. (a) No  (b) Yes  (c) No

17. (a)   IF GRADE > 0 AND GRADE < 100 THEN PRINT GRADE ELSE PRINT "Grade
             out of range"

    (b)   IF GENDER$ <> "F" OR GENDER$ <> "M" THEN PRINT "Error in gender
             data"

19. It's primarily a question of how much detail to include in any one step. For example, we could eliminate step 1 altogether; move the initial and concluding tasks from old step 3 to new step 1; and delete old step 4 by including its tasks in new step 2.

20. 2.1  For each order
    2.2    Read order data
    2.3    Compute charge
    2.3.1    Compute charge based on discount
                If quantity < 50 then
                   Charge = quantity * unit price
                End if
                If 50 <= quantity <= 99 then
                   Charge = .9 * quantity * unit price
                End if
                If quantity >= 100 then
                   Charge = .75 * quantity * unit price
                End if
    2.3.2    Compute charge based on surcharge
                If foreign country then
                   Charge = 1.25 * charge
                End if
    2.4    Accumulate totals
    2.4.1    Add quantity to cumulative quantity
    2.4.2    Add charge to cumulative charge
    2.5    Print order data
    2.6  Next order

    3.1  Print summary data

    This approach is precise in its numbering scheme, but gets rather tedious. It's simpler to refine a step by indenting from its preceding step without numbering, as done above following steps 2.3.1 and 2.3.2.

21. (a)  315    LET DISCOUNT1 = .05
         320    LET DISCOUNT2 = .10

    The use of variable names for parameters simplifies the task of updating data, since we don't have to dig into the program to find these values. In practice, this translates into lower maintenance costs.

22. (a)

| Step 2 | Step 3 |
| --- | --- |

    Read order data
    Edit order ⟍  ⎡ If not (foreign = "YES" or foreign = "NO") then
                  ⎢    Print "Incorrect yes/no entry"
                  ⎢    Quantity = 0
                  ⎣ End if

## Chapter 5

1. Unique to system.

2. Unique to system.

3.

| CCOST | PIRATE | Year | FCOST |
|-------|--------|------|-------|
| 90000 | .10 | | |
| | 10 | | 90000 |
| | | 1 | 99000 |
| | | 2 | 108900 |
| | | 3 | 119790 |
| | | 4 | 131769 |
| | | 5 | 144945.9 |
| | | 6 | 159440.5 |
| | | 7 | 175384.6 |
| | | 8 | 192923 |

4. **(a)** Infinite loop. FCOST is zero and is always less than
   MULTIPLE * CCOST.

   **(b)** Infinite loop. FCOST is always 99000 and always less than
   MULTIPLE * CCOST.

   **(c)** Output values for YEAR would be one higher than they should be. Move line 430 to line 455.

   **(d)** Place the constant expression

   (1 + PIRATE/100)

   in the initialization section as follows:

   405    LET FACTOR = (1 + PIRATE/100)

   Modify line 440 as follows:

   440    LET FCOST = FCOST * FACTOR

   **(e)** Chance of these two expressions being equal is very unlikely. Thus, an infinite loop would occur.

   **(f)** 10%; 20% (interactively forced to enter value between 1 and 100)

5. 420 WHILE FCOST < MULTIPLE*CCOST OR YEAR < 10

6. a.    262 READ N
   263    DATA . . .
   265 FOR J = 1 TO N
   281    DATA . . .
   . . .    . . .
   495 NEXT J

8. Unique to system.

9. Unique to system.

10. **(a)** Delete lines 270 – 300.
    260    . . .
    300 IF PIRATE < 1 OR PIRATE > 100 THEN 260

13. Unique to system.

14. **(a)** The sentinel − 99 gets printed following the 40. **(b)** The sentinel − 99 gets printed following the 40.

**15.**

| Line executed | Action | Result |
|---|---|---|
| 340–380 | Print report heading | See output |
| 400 | Read data | Test1,5000,300 stored |
| 410 | Test for eof | True |
| 420 | Cutoff test | False; PAY = 300 |
| 430 | Print results | Test1  5000  300  300 |
| 440 | Accumulate TOTBASE | 300 |
| 450 | Accumulate TOTPAY | 300 |
| 460 | Accumulate TOTSALES | 5000 |
| 470 | Read next record | Test2,4000,250 |
| 480 | Loop back | |
| . | | |
| . | (Get the idea?) | |
| . | | |
| 470 | Read next record | eof,0,0 |
| 480 | Loop back | |
| 410 | Test for eof | False |
| 500–510 | Print summary | 17000  875  975 |
| 999 | END executed | Execution ends |

**16.** **(a)** Same results.

**(b)** The last line in the table gets printed

.

.

.

Test3  8000  325  425

and then we get the error message

Out of data in 470

Thus, the totals never get printed.

**(c)** A fourth line gets printed in the table

end    0    0    0

and then we get the error message

Out of data in 470

**(d)** Replace "eof" with "end" in line 410.

**17.** Unique to system.

# Chapter 6

**1.** Unique to system.

**2.** IF S <= 50000                      THEN LET B = 0
   IF S >   5000 AND T <   600  THEN LET B = 100
   IF S >   5000 AND T >= 600  THEN LET B = 50

**4.** **(a)** The outer if-then-else structure determines the marital status of the person (married or not married). The inner if-then-else structure within the then block of the outer if-then-else structure (for married persons) is separated on an age cut-off over 55 and not over 55. The inner if-then-else structure within the else block of the outer if-then-else structure (for persons not married) is separated on an age cut-off 30 and above and under 30.

5. **(a)**
```
100 IF A > 10 THEN 130          or      IF A > 10 THEN
110    LET R$ = "F1"                       LET R$ = "T1"
120 GO TO 180                              IF B > 20 THEN LET R$ = "T2"
130    LET R$ = "T1"                                     ELSE LET R$ = "F2"
140    IF B > 20 THEN 170               ELSE
150       LET R$ = "F2"                    LET R$ = "F1"
160       GO TO 180                     END IF
170       LET R$ = "T2"
180 . . .
```

**(b)**
```
100 IF A > 10 THEN 160          or      IF A > 10 THEN
110    IF C > 30 THEN 140                  IF B > 20 THEN LET R$ = "T2"
120       LET R$ = "F3"                                  ELSE LET R$ = "F2"
130       GO TO 200                     ELSE
140       LET R$ = "T3"                    IF C > 30 THEN LET R$ = "T3"
150 GO TO 200                                         ELSE LET R$ = "F3"
160    IF B > 20 THEN 190               END IF
170       LET R$ = "F2"
180       GO TO 200
190       LET R$ = "T2"
200 . . .
```

**(d)**

|       | Part a | Part b |
|-------|--------|--------|
| i.    | F1     | F3     |
| ii.   | F2     | F2     |
| iii.  | T2     | T2     |

6. Unique to system.

7. Ok ◄———————— Logic error
   Ok
   Excellent
   Poor

8. **(a)** The approach taken is system-dependent. Here's the multiline if-then-else approach:
```
IF D = 0 THEN
   PRINT "Excellent"
ELSE
   IF D > 0 AND D < 1 THEN
     PRINT "Ok"
   ELSE
     IF D >= 1 AND D <= 100 THEN
       PRINT "Poor"
     ELSE
       PRINT "Error in defect %"
     END IF
   END IF
END IF
```
Yes. *Every else-if structure is a nested decision structure (in sheep's clothing).* The else-if structure is much easier to follow than the equivalent nested structure. Just compare the above code with the ANS or VAX versions in Table 6.2.

(b) No. Usually, nested decision structures express the logic more clearly when *two or more attributes* are being tested. In the coding below, sales and travel conditions are the two attributes being tested.

```
IF S > 5000 AND T < 600 THEN           or     IF S <= 5000 THEN
   LET B = 100                                   LET B = 0
ELSEIF S > 5000 AND T >= 600 THEN             ELSEIF T < 600 THEN
   LET B = 50                                    LET B = 100
ELSE                                          ELSE
   LET B = 0                                     LET B = 50
END IF                                        END IF
```

Some programmers would prefer the ANS/VAX approach in Table 6.1 to the above approaches.

9. (a) 7    8
   (b) 7    15
   (c) 10   25
   (d) 5    15

11. Unique to system.

12. (a)
```
IF C = 1 THEN PRINT "Single"
IF C = 2 THEN PRINT "Married"
IF C = 3 THEN PRINT "Divorced"
IF C = 4 THEN PRINT "Widowed"
IF C < 1 OR C > 4 THEN PRINT "Error in code"
```
   (b)
```
IF C = 1 THEN
   PRINT "Single"
ELSE
   IF C = 2 THEN
      PRINT "Married"
   ELSE
      IF C = 3 THEN
         PRINT "Divorced"
      ELSE
         IF C = 4 THEN
            PRINT "Widowed"
         ELSE
            PRINT "Error in code"
         END IF
      END IF
   END IF
END IF
```

   (c)
```
IF C = 1 THEN
   PRINT "Single"
ELSEIF C = 2 THEN
   PRINT "Married"
ELSEIF C = 3 THEN
   PRINT "Divorced"
ELSEIF C = 4 THEN
   PRINT "Widowed"
ELSE
   PRINT "Error in code"
END IF
```

Parts **a** and **c** are clean implementations. Part **b** is brutal, isn't it?

13. (a) The ON GOTO statement doesn't work with string values. Use an else-if structure.
   (b)
```
SELECT CASE C$
   CASE "S"
      PRINT "Single"
   CASE "M"
      PRINT "Married"
   CASE "D"
      PRINT "Divorced"
   CASE "W"
      PRINT "Widowed"
   CASE ELSE
      PRINT "Error in code"
END SELECT
```

17. Unique to system.

18. (a) Change line 250 to

    250 DATA 1400,1300,1100

20. (a) Replace LET FLAG = 0 in line 385 with STOP. The disadvantage is we can't continue processing other orders.

22. Unique to system.

23. (a) Exact root = 0.5; iterations = 1. (b) Estimated root = 0.500977; maximum error = 0.976563E-03; iterations = 9. (c) Estimated root = 0.499023; maximum error = 0.976563E-03; iterations = 9.

24. 215 DEF FNF (X) = 2^X

    Root can't be found within interval −3 to 1.

# Chapter 7

1. | Line executed | Action |
   |---|---|
   | . | . |
   | . | . |
   | . | . |
   | 290 | Read in B for LABEL$ and 15 for LENGTH |
   | 300 | Call subroutine |
   | 420 | Print label B |
   | 430 | Set FOR/NEXT parameters |
   | 440 | ⎤ |
   | 450 | |
   | 440 | Print 15 = signs |
   | 450 | |
   | . | |
   | . | |
   | . | ⎦ |
   | 460 | Print length 15 |
   | 470 | Return |
   | 310 | Next bar |

2. Yes and no. The only problem would be large frequencies that wrap the bars around the screen or paper. For example, 300 Cs in a large class would give a bar that wraps around to a fourth line in an 80-column display. The program could be modified to scale down all frequencies whenever any one frequency exceeds the maximum screen display.

   (a)  905 DATA "Age Distribution of Employees"
        910 DATA 6
        911 DATA "Under 20",5
        912 DATA "20 − 29",30
        913 DATA "30 − 39",50
        914 DATA "40 − 49",70
        915 DATA "50 − 59",40
        916 DATA "Over 59",10

3. The message "Break in 330" is printed. *Alternative 1:* Use GOTO 999 at line 330 instead of STOP. Our preference is to avoid GOTOs. *Alternative 2:* Use END instead of STOP at line 330. This is fine if the system allows it, since no break message is printed. Try it on your system.

4. Unique to system.

5.

| N | K | X | F | J | FACN | FACNK | FACK |
|---|---|---|---|---|------|-------|------|
| 10 | 4 | 10 | 2 | 2 | 0 | 0 | 0 |
| 10 | 4 | 10 | 6 | 3 | 0 | 0 | 0 |
| 10 | 4 | 10 | 24 | 4 | 0 | 0 | 0 |
| 10 | 4 | 10 | 120 | 5 | 0 | 0 | 0 |
| 10 | 4 | 10 | 720 | 6 | 0 | 0 | 0 |
| 10 | 4 | 10 | 5040 | 7 | 0 | 0 | 0 |
| 10 | 4 | 10 | 40320 | 8 | 0 | 0 | 0 |
| 10 | 4 | 10 | 362880 | 9 | 0 | 0 | 0 |
| 10 | 4 | 10 | 362880 | 10 | 0 | 0 | 0 |
| 10 | 4 | 6 | 2 | 2 | 3628800 | 0 | 0 |
| 10 | 4 | 6 | 6 | 3 | 3628800 | 0 | 0 |
| 10 | 4 | 6 | 24 | 4 | 3628800 | 0 | 0 |
| 10 | 4 | 6 | 120 | 5 | 3628800 | 0 | 0 |
| 10 | 4 | 6 | 720 | 6 | 3628800 | 0 | 0 |
| 10 | 4 | 4 | 2 | 2 | 3628800 | 720 | 0 |
| 10 | 4 | 4 | 6 | 3 | 3628800 | 720 | 0 |
| 10 | 4 | 4 | 24 | 4 | 3628800 | 720 | 0 |
| 5 | 0 | 5 | 2 | 2 | 3628800 | 7 | 24 |
| 5 | 0 | 5 | 6 | 3 | 3628800 | 720 | 24 |
| 5 | 0 | 5 | 24 | 4 | 3628800 | 720 | 24 |
| 5 | 0 | 5 | 120 | 5 | 3628800 | 720 | 24 |
| 5 | 0 | 5 | 2 | 2 | 120 | 720 | 24 |
| 5 | 0 | 5 | 6 | 3 | 120 | 720 | 24 |
| 5 | 0 | 5 | 24 | 4 | 120 | 720 | 24 |
| 5 | 0 | 5 | 120 | 5 | 120 | 720 | 24 |

6.

| N | K | C |
|---|---|---|
| 5 | 2 | 10 |
| 10 | 4 | 210 |
| 5 | 0 | 1 |
| 5 | 5 | 1 |
| 4 | 10 | 6.61375e-06 | ◄─── Note error whenever K exceeds N (see Exercise 7a). |
| 100 | 30 | overflow | ◄─── The factorials of 100 and 70 cause overflow. |

7. (a)
```
436   WHILE N < K
437     PRINT "***K must not exceed N***"
438     INPUT "N — — — — —>";N
439     INPUT "K — — — — —>";K
440   WEND
```

(b)
```
345   WHILE NOT (M$ = "C" OR M$ = "c" OR M$ = "S" OR M$ = "s")
          .
          .    ]— Repeat lines 320 – 340
          .
350   WEND
355   RETURN
```

**10.**

| Line Executed | Action/Result |
|---|---|
| 2070 | Customer module called |
| 4070 | Print prompt |
| 4080 | Enter car group E |
| 4090 | False |
| 4200 | Print prompt |
| 4210 | Enter estimated miles |
| 4220 | Print prompt |
| 4230 | Enter rental days |
| 4240 | Car group module called |
| 7060 | Reset pointer |
| 7070 | Read data |
| 7080 | False |
| 7110 | Return to customer module |
| 4250 | Return to process module |
| 2080–2110 | Print report headings |
| 2130 | Call daily module |
| 5050 | Compute daily cost |
| 5060 | Print daily cost |
| 5070 | Return to process module |
| 2140 | Call weekly module |
| 6060 | Compute number of weeks |
| 6070 | Compute weekly cost |
| 6080 | Print weekly cost |
| 6090 | Return to process module |
| 2160 | Print dashes |
| 2190 | Return to control module |
| 1580 | Call menu module |

For choice L, 800 miles, and 12 days:

Daily cost   = $868
Weekly cost = $886

For choice L, 300 miles, and 5 days:

Daily cost   = $350
Weekly cost = $432

**17.** **(a)** M$   is pseudo-global to control, menu, and combinations.

C   is pseudo-local to combinations.

N   is pseudo-local to combinations.

K   is pseudo-local to combinations.

F   is local to factorial.

J   is local to factorial.

FACTORIAL   is global.

X   is global.

**(b)** No. J is truly local to function factorial. Replacing J by N within this function would make N local also. This N would have a different storage location from the N in subroutine combinations, so no problem arises; however, from the standpoint of readability, we don't recommend two different uses for the same variable name. **(c)** Yes. X is global, so changing its value affects corresponding values in other modules. For example, consider the case where N = 5 and K = 2. When FACTORIAL(N) is evaluated in line 465, X temporarily shares the value in N. Thus, function factorial uses 5 for X and proceeds to evaluate the factorial as F = 120. When LET X = F is executed, the value in X is changed to 120. Since X and N are one and the same storage location for this particular function reference, it follows that N has been changed to 120. The problem now arises at the next function reference when FACTORIAL(N − K) is evaluated. Since N now stores an incorrect value, the factorial of (N − K) will be wrong. **(d)** Yes. The function returns a value of zero for FACTORIAL, giving a "division by zero" execution error in line 465.

**18.** 530  IF X <= 1 THEN
　　　　　LET FACTORIAL = F
　　　　　EXIT FUNCTION
　　　　END IF

**24.** LET F = 1
IF X <= 1 THEN EXIT SUB

**28. (a)** Prog. 1 executed
　　　　Prog. 3 executed

**(b)** RUN
Prog. 1 executed
Prog. 2 executed
Prog. 2 executed
Prog. 3 executed

```
LIST
10 '   Main program 3
15       PRINT "Prog. 2 executed"
20       LET P$ = "B:THREE"
95       PRINT "Prog. 3 executed"
99       END
```

# Chapter 8

**1.** Look up these definitions again if you're unclear about the distinctions.

**2. (a)** Invalid **(b)** Valid **(c)** Invalid **(d)** Valid

**3. (a)** Variable number of locations reserved for X in line 20; the DIM statement must precede the READ statement. **(b)** A has not been dimensioned; the subscript in line 50 (M − 2*N) has a value of −11, which is not permitted; the subscript 0 in line 30 may not be permitted on some systems. **(c)** The subscripts in D and E will exceed the upper limits specified in the DIM statement when J = 11 in line 30 and when J = 10 in line 60. E(3) = 36.

**5. (a)** Change lines 130 and 900 to

130 DIM DEPOSITS(100)
900 DATA 100

In version B we would need 97 more READs, 97 more LETs, and 97 more PRINTs. The expression in line 170 would contain 100 variables. Brutal, huh?

**6.** 110 READ N
120 FOR J = 1 TO N
130    INPUT B(J)
140 NEXT J

**8. (a)** Yes. The original approach is preferable because it is easier to locate and modify departmental data. This is because each data line corresponds to a specific department. For example, the 3rd department's data is found in line 903.

**(b)**

| Line | Action/Result |
|------|---------------|
| 210 | 3 stored in DEPT |
| 230 | False |
| 250 | PROFIT = SALES(3) − COSTS(3) |
|     | = 175 − 140 |
|     | = 35 |
| 270−290 | Report printed |
| 210 | 5 stored in DEPT |
| 230 | True; error message is printed and processing stops. |

9. (a) DAY$(1) = MONDAY,     DAY$(2) = TUESDAY,     DAY$(3) = WEDNESDAY,
DAY$(4) = THURSDAY
DAY$(5) = FRIDAY, DAY$(6) = SATURDAY, DAY$(7) = SUNDAY

(b) FRIDAY
\*\*\* 10 out of range
\*\*\* 0 out of range

10. T(K) = 0 doesn't initialize 200 positions: T(K) must be within a loop. If K is undefined for the system, then an execution error results: otherwise, T(0) is initialized to 0. T = 0 initializes a simple numeric variable to 0.

```
20 FOR K = 1 TO 200
30    LET T(K) = 0
40 NEXT K
```

11. 20
15
10
5

12. (a) BAL(1) = 150.30   BAL(2) = 850.75

13. N = 1    M = 3    X = 2    Y = 8    VALUE(3) = 3    VALUE(4) = 1

17.
```
RUN
Name       :? Rip Van Winkle
Age        :? 99
Uninsurable-- over 65


Another quotation (y/n)? y


Name       :? Rip Van Winkle
Age        :? 55
Premium is:$ 327


Another quotation (y/n)? y


Name       :? Rip Van Winkle
Age        :? 63
Premium is:$ 357


Another quotation (y/n)? y


Name       :? Rip Van Winkle
Age        :? 20
Premium is:$ 277


Another quotation (y/n)? n

See you tomorrow at 8 sharp!
```

18. Change line 270 and move line 290 to 265:

```
265  READ ROWS
270  DIM AGELIMIT(ROWS),PREMIUM(ROWS)
```

19. Change line 900, move line 906 to 907 and add new line 906:

```
900  DATA 7
906  DATA 75,500
```

The use of ROWS has two advantages, both relating to less program maintenance whenever the number of rows in the table changes: we need not change the upper limit in the FOR statement (line 300); we don't tie the uninsurable message to a constant such as "Uninsurable—over 65," as this constant can change in the data section.

**20.** This logic works as long as age is 65 or under. For an age above 65 a premium of zero, or PREMIUM(6), is output instead of an error message. This error problem can be corrected by an if-then-else structure at line 470 that checks for a J-value of 6. In fact, this approach to the table look-up problem is the traditional approach. We don't recommend it because it's unstructured (the loop has two exit points at lines 450 and 460), and the GOTO statement increases the likelihood of error.

**24.**

| J | TEMP | ID(1) | ID(2) | ID(3) | ID(4) | SWITCH |
|---|---|---|---|---|---|---|
| 2 | 3076 | 3076 | 8321 | 2501 | 7771 | 1 |
| 3 | 2501 | 3076 | 2501 | 8321 | 7771 | 1 |
| 4 | 7771 | 3076 | 2501 | 7771 | 8321 | 1 |
| 2 | 2501 | 2501 | 3076 | 7771 | 8321 | 1 |
| 3 | 2501 | 2501 | 3076 | 7771 | 8321 | 1 |
| 4 | 2501 | 2501 | 3076 | 7771 | 8321 | 1 |
| 2 | 2501 | 2501 | 3076 | 7771 | 8321 | 0 |
| 3 | 2501 | 2501 | 3076 | 7771 | 8321 | 0 |
| 4 | 2501 | 2501 | 3076 | 7771 | 8321 | 0 |

**(a)** Two passes; three passes.

**25.** Line 320 would test true, the error message would be printed, and processing would stop.

```
250 DIM ID(3000)
280 LET ARRAY.LIMIT = 3000
900 DATA 3000
  .
  .  ]— Additional data lines
  .
```

**32.**

```
Enter plot symbol such as * or +? *

Enter polynomial coefficient 0 ? 1
Enter polynomial coefficient 1 ? 4
Enter polynomial coefficient 2 ? 0

Enter first X-value? 1
Enter last  X-value? 5
Enter step  X-value? 1
```

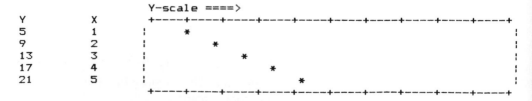

```
                                    GRAPH OF Y-FUNCTION

                        Y-scale ====>
    Y       X       +----+----+----+----+----+----+----+----+----+----+
    5       1       ¦      *                                          ¦
    9       2       ¦        *                                        ¦
   13       3       ¦          *                                      ¦
   17       4       ¦            *                                    ¦
   21       5       ¦              *                                  ¦
                    +----+----+----+----+----+----+----+----+----+----+

Another plot (y/n)? n
```

**33.** Line 640 would test true, the error message would be printed, and processing would stop.

**34.** Line 900 would test false, and the plot symbol would not be printed.

**35.** The plot symbol would be printed in column 12 after wrapping around the screen.

```
900  IF Y(J) > = 0  AND  Y(J) < = MAX.SCALE THEN . . .
                                        ELSE . . .
```

## Chapter 9

**1.** 1000  800  500  1200  500  2000  2000  500  1500  300  700  1500

**2.**
```
1000    500   1500
 800   2000    300
 500   2000    700
1200    500   1500
```

**3.** As in the original version. The arrangement of data in the original version is preferable because it's visually consistent with the data table or array.

**4.** DEPOSITS

| 1000 | 1200 | 2000 | 300 |
|------|------|------|------|
| 800 | 500 | 500 | 700 |
| 500 | 2000 | 1500 | 1500 |

The array now gets filled in column by column. Enter data as follows:

```
901 DATA 1000, 500,1500  ◄——— Column 1
902 DATA  800,2000, 300  ◄——— Column 2
903 DATA  500,2000, 700  ◄——— Column 3
904 DATA 1200, 500,1500  ◄——— Column 4
```

**9.** Add TOTAL(4) to the DIM statement in line 130 and insert between lines 270 and 280:

```
271  FOR COL = 1 TO QUARTERS
272    LET TOTAL(COL) = 0
273    FOR ROW = 1 TO BANKS
274      LET TOTAL(COL) = TOTAL(COL) + DEPOSITS(ROW,COL)
275    NEXT ROW
276  NEXT COL
```

After line 340 insert:

```
341  FOR COL = 1 TO QUARTERS
342    PRINT TOTAL(COL);
343  NEXT COL
```

**13.**
```
FOR  I = 1 TO 100
  FOR J = 1 TO 50
    LET WEIGHT(I,J) = 100
  NEXT J
NEXT I
```

**14.**
```
FOR I = 1 TO 4
  FOR J = 1 TO 4
    IF I = J THEN LET X(I,J) = 1 ELSE LET X(I,J) = 0
  NEXT J
NEXT I
```

15. (a)
```
100 INPUT "Enter number of rows ......"; ROWS
110 INPUT "Enter number of columns ..."; COL
120 PRINT
130 PRINT "Now enter each row in array A:"
140 FOR I = 1 TO ROWS
150   FOR J = 1 TO COLS
160     PRINT "Row"; I; ", Column"; J;
170     INPUT A(I,J)
180   NEXT J
190 NEXT I
200 PRINT
210 PRINT "Now enter each row in array B:"
220 FOR I = 1 TO ROWS
230   FOR J = 1 TO COLS
240     PRINT "Row"; I; ", Column"; J;
250     INPUT B(I,J)
260   NEXT J
270 NEXT I
```

(b)
```
100 INPUT "Enter number of rows ......"; ROWS
110 INPUT "Enter number of columns ..."; COL
120 PRINT "Now enter corresponding elements in arrays A and B:"
130 FOR I = 1 TO ROWS
140   FOR J = 1 TO COLS
150     PRINT "Row"; I; ", Column"; J;
160     INPUT A(I,J),B(I,J)
170   NEXT J
180 NEXT I
```

19. You're on your own with this one.

20. The upper boundaries are 10 for both rows and columns. The 10th row and 10th column store column and row totals, respectively. Therefore, we don't want data in these array elements.

21.

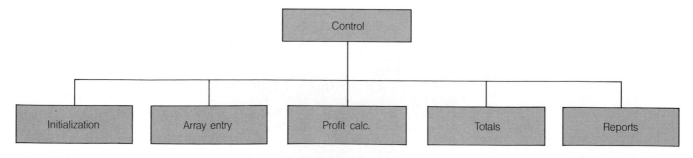

22. Line 3140 would test true, the message

```
Upper array boundary exceeded. Check Line 9000.
Limits:  Regions = 9 Models = 9
Break in 3140.
```

would be printed, and processing would stop.

26. So any taxable incomes above $55,300 would give a false result at line 715. Thus, loop exit would be achieved and the proper tax would be computed.

27. 330 LET MAX.CONTRIBUTIONS = 50
310 LET EXEMPTION            = 1500

By using variables for these and other parameters we can simplify this type of program maintenance; otherwise, we would have to search the program for the occurrence of these parameters. For example, the maximum contribution parameter is used three times in line 540; the exemption parameter is used in lines 565 and 575.

28. Yes, the comma indicates the end of string data, yet additional string data are entered. A "Redo from start" error message would be printed on the IBM PC. To correct this problem we could
(a) use quotes, which is undesirable for this application;
(b) use two string variables in the input list;
(c) use the LINE INPUT statement

LINE INPUT CITY.STATE.ZIP$

## Module C

1. **a.** 6.70925E-04   **(f)** 3
   **(b)** 16.0944          3
   **(c)** 80               3
   **(d)** 3.3             −3
        2            **(g)** −1
   **(e)** 3                1
        3                0
        3
       −4

2. **(a)** Replace INT(A) in line 190 with INT(A + 0.5). **(b)** Replace INT(A) in line 190 with INT(A*100 + 0.5)/100.

8. **(a)** 3    28.5279    127
   **(b)** 10 PRINT 1^3+1+3−2*SQR(2*1−1),3^3+3−3−2*SQR(2*3−1),5^3−5
                              +3−2*SQR(2*5−1)

   20 END

   The version in part **a** has 14 characters less code than the version in part **b** (excluding blanks), and is more aesthetically appealing.

9. 6    4    8

10. **(a)** DEF FNA(N) = 1/N^2 + 1/SQR(N)

11. **(a)** Usually correct. Some systems may not allow a missing formal parameter list. **(b)** Function name in calling statement FNB does not match function name FNE in the DEF statement. **(c)** Function called in line 10 before it's defined in line 20. **(d)** Formal parameter cannot be subscripted on most systems. (Subscripted variables are discussed in Chapters 8 and 9.) **(e)** FN5 is an illegal function name on systems that require FN as the first part of the name. **(f)** Okay, although it's simpler to assign the string value to the variable TITLE$ using a LET statement. String functions are best used when the string expression is more elaborate (as illustrated in Module F).

**12.** Yes, they both return the same results: 5.75 and −7.

**15.** **(a)** 135 IF ITEM$ = "D" THEN LET PRICE = 6

## Module D

**1.** **(a)** `4645.8`
  **(b)** `4,645.82`
  **(c)** `    3.20`
  **(d)** `   $3.20`
  **(e)** `$****$3.20`
  **(f)** `*****$3.20`
  **(g)** `0.46E+04`
  **(h)** `%4646`
  **(i)** `   3    4646`
  **(j)** `      3    4646`

**2.** **(a)** `PRINT USING "     ###"; B`
  **(b)** `PRINT USING "B=  ###"; B`
  **(c)** `PRINT USING "### ##.##"; B,C`

**3.**
```
 1  PRINT "12345678"
10 LET X = 3.283
20 PRINT USING "        #";X
30 PRINT USING "        #.";X
40 PRINT USING "     #.#";X
50 PRINT USING "    #.###";X
60 PRINT USING " #.#####";X
99 END

run
12345678
        3
        3
      3.3
    3.283
    3.28300
```

**4.**
```
10 LET FM1$ = "     \    \"
20 LET FM2$ = "     \ \"
30 LET FM3$ = "     \\"
40 LET A$ = "GOOFUS"
50 PRINT USING FM1$; A$
60 PRINT USING FM2$; A$
70 PRINT USING FM3$; A$
99 END

RUN
     GOOFUS
     GOOF
     GO
```

**5.**
```
            11111111112
   12345678901234567890
```
  **(a)** `-50   15.3`
  **(b)** `Number =  -50`
  **(c)** ` 15.320 INCHES`
  **(d)** ` scale in INCHES`
  **(e)** `%8196.177`
```
Type mismatch in 90
```

**6. (a)** LET FM1$ = " ####      ####     ##.##^^^^"
    PRINT USING FM1$; A,B,C

**(b)** LET FM2$ = "    MONTHLY PAYMENT = ###.##"
    PRINT USING FM2$; B

**(c)** LET FM3$ =      "    \                        \"
    LET FM4$ =      "    \                        \"
    PRINT USING FM3$; "** THERMAL REPORT **"
    PRINT USING FM4$; "********************"

**(d)** LET FM5$ =          "\                                        \"
    LET FM6$ =          "\              \  \          \  $#.##   $$###.##  "
    PRINT USING FM5$;"   EMPLOYEE    SOCIAL        PAY"
    PRINT USING FM5$;"   NAME        SEC. NO.    RATE  GROSS PAY"
    PRINT
    PRINT USING FM6$;N$,S$,R,P

**8. (a)** 170 LET FMT6$ = "                                \        \"
    325 PRINT USING FMT6$; "========="

**(b)** 150 LET FMT4$ ="\          \          ##.##  $$##.##   $$###.##"

**(c)** 150 LET FMT4$ ="\                \   ##.##   ##.##    ###.##"

## Module E

**1.** Unique to system.

**2. (a)** In line 10 of each program, replace "grades" with "mgs207." **(b)** Replace #1 with #3 in all OPEN, CLOSE, PRINT, and INPUT statements. Yes, the file names must be the same for both programs, but the file numbers need not be the same for different programs. Within the same program, however, there must be consistency in the file number. **(c)** In the first program, change the 5 to a 7 in line 90, and add 65 and 95 to the data list in line 95.

**3.** Possible record layout:

| Field | Type | Bytes |
|---|---|---|
| Student ID | String | 11 |
| Student name | String | 30 |
| Course number | String | 6 |
| Section | Numeric | 2 |
| Date enrolled | String | 8 |
| Grade | String | 1 |

The likely storage medium is hard magnetic disk.

A relative file is best for query programs, since the few records required can be accessed directly.

A sequential file is best when a high percentage of records in the file are processed, as in an end-of-term grade report.

**4.** The relative file is more efficiently updated than the sequential file. The new record is simply placed in an available (empty) record space. If the file were sequential, then the entire file would have to be processed to append a record. If the record had to be inserted alphabetically by name, then the sequential file approach requires the creation of a new file that places Clark's record between Bomberg's and Drury's. This would not be necessary if the file were a relative file with an accompanying index file. (See Exercise 23 for index files.)

5. **(a)**   5 <cr>

     90  75  85  95  70 <cr><eof mark>

  **(b)**   5<cr>

     90<cr>

     75<cr>

     85<cr>

     95<cr>

     70<cr><eof mark>

  **(c)**   No.

6. **(a)**   2 <cr>

     East 5000 <cr>

     West 4000 <cr><eof mark>

  **(b)**   2 <cr>

     East, 5000 <cr>

     West, 4000 <cr><eof mark>

  **(c)**   2 <cr>

     5000 East<cr>

     4000 West<cr><eof mark>

  **(d)**   2 <cr>

     "East",5000<cr>

     "West",4000<cr><eof mark>

7. **(a)**   The file has not been set up properly. A comma is needed after each string value.

  **(b)**   10 OPEN "SALES.DAT" FOR INPUT AS #1

     15 INPUT #1, N

     20 PRINT "Number of regions = "; N

     25 PRINT "------------------------"

     30 PRINT "Region         Sales   "

     35 PRINT "------------------------"

     40 FOR J = 1 TO N

     45    INPUT # 1, R$,S

     50    PRINT R$,S

     55 NEXT J

     99 END

  **(c)**   Change line 45 in part **b** to

     45   INPUT S,R$

  **(d)**   Same as part **b**.

**14.**

| Line | Result/Action |
|------|---------------|
| 245 | Enter 1 for DROP.ID |
| 255 | False |
| 260 | Record for Abatar with ID of 1 is input |
| 265 | False (Thus, this record doesn't get written to revised file.) |
| 285 | Enter 6 for DROP.ID |
| 290 | Return to beginning of loop. |
| 255 | True |
| 260 | Record for Bomberg with ID of 3 is input |
| 265 | True |
| 270 | Record for Bomberg is written to revised file |
| 275 | Record for Drury with ID of 6 is input |
| 280 | Return to beginning of loop |
| 265 | False (Drury's record doesn't get written to revised file.) |
| 285 | Enter 0 for DROP.ID |
| 290 | Return to beginning of loop |
| 255 | False |
| 310–315 | Eof condition |
| 335 | Files closed |
| . . . | |

**20.** We would have to delete the record with ID = 4 and add a new record with the proper ID number.

**22. (a)** The change in record length requires the following changes:

In line 360, replace 29 with 34.
In line 365, replace the first 4 with 9.

Using social security numbers represents a range from 1 to 999,999,999. Theoretically, we may need this many relative positions or records in the file. This means we would need an impossibly huge disk of about $3.4 \times 10^{10}$ bytes ($999,999,999 \times 34$), or about 34 billion bytes (gigabytes). Moreover, an incredible number of records would remain unused (the maximum social security numbers less the number of employees)

**25.**

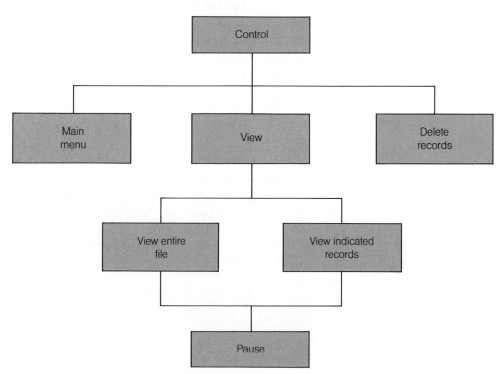

**26. (a)** Main menu (screen 2) is repeated until V,D or S is entered

**(b)** ID? 6

| | | | | |
|---|---|---|---|---|
| Drury | David D. | 6 | 18000 | m |

ID? 2

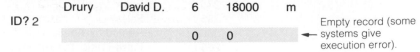

|  |  |
|---|---|
| 0 | 0 |

Empty record (some systems give execution error).

**(c)** Screen 9 would just show Drury's record, leaving 1 as the number of employees in the file.

## Module F

**1.** No. L, V, and E are not adjacent characters in LOVE.

**2.** Unique to system.

**3. (a)** SeeJanerun **(b)** See Jane run **(c)** Jane See **(d)** runrunrun

**4. (a)** 160 PRINT CITY\$ + "," + STATE\$ + " " + ZIP\$

This approach is simpler than the approach in our sample program, since we don't have to create the variable CTY.ST.ZP\$; however, in longer programs that might require the same concatenated string in several places, the use of CTY.ST.ZP\$ would be convenient.

**(b)** 110 READ FULL.NAME\$,ADDRESS\$,CTY.ST.ZP\$
120    DATA Rory Calhoun, 117 Macintosh Drive,"Cranston,RI 02878"

This approach would not be desirable if a program had to separate the city, state, and zip data items. It would be possible to break these out by methods that we illustrate later in this module, but at the price of programming complexity.

**5. (a)** 33

```
START = INT((LINE.LENGTH − HEAD.LENGTH)/2)
      = INT((      80      −      14      )/2)
      = INT( 33 )
      = 33
```

**(b)** 115 LET DASH\$ = "------- ------"
155 PRINT TAB(START); DASH\$

**6. (a)** Yep.

**(b)** Line 120 would test false, the "End of run" message would be printed, and processing would end.

**7. (a)** 160 LET MONTH\$ = LEFT\$(SALES.DATE\$,2)
165 PRINT "Month of sale:"; MONTH\$

**(b)**    120 LET YEAR\$ = "19" + RIGHT\$(SALES.DATE\$,2)
or
   125 LET YEAR\$ = "19" + YEAR\$
or
   130 PRINT "Year of sale: 19" + YEAR\$

**14.** Insert the following lines:

107 DEF FNYEAR\$(SALES.DATE\$) = RIGHT\$(SALES.DATE\$,2)
108 DEF FNDAY\$(SALES.DATE\$)  = MID\$(SALES.DATE\$,4,2)

Delete lines 120 and 140.

Replace YEAR\$ by FNYEAR\$(SALES.DATE\$) in line 130 and DAY\$ by FNDAY\$(SALES.DATE\$) in line 150.

This approach would have a coding efficiency advantage if different years and days had to be broken out at several different points in a long program. *Note:* We could use the function names YEAR\$ and DAY\$ instead of FNYEAR\$ and FNDAY\$ on some systems.

16. (a) `Enter increment key (1-26)? 10`

`Actual message ? HELP ISN'T ON THE WAY`
`Encoded message: ROVZ SCX1D YX DRO GKI`

└─The apostrophe has an ASCII value of 39.
Adding the increment 10 gives 49, which is
the ASCII value for the digit 1. (Check an
ASCII table.)

(b) 220 IF ASC(MID$(TEXT$,J,1)) > = ASC.LOW AND ASC(MID$(TEXT$,J,1)) < =
ASC.HIGH

THEN GOSUB 300
ELSE MID$(TEXT$,J,1) = BLANK$

17. (a) Change line 170 to

170 INPUT "Enter day of week (1−7)"; INCREMENT

`RUN`
`Enter day of week (1-7)? 2`

`Actual message ? HELP IS ON THE WAY`
`Encoded message:`

`RUN`
`Enter day of week (1-7)? 5`

`Actual message ? HELP IS ON THE WAY`
`Encoded message:`

20. (a) The program goes on to the next line without making the requested change, since lines 195–205 all test false.

21. (a) We have an illegal function call in line 630. FIRST.POS is zero and FIRST.POS − 1 is negative when used in the function LEFT$.

22. (a) We have an illegal function call in line 590. LEN.NEW is negative when used as an argument in the MID$ function.

23. (a) We could enter a change command that replaces an old string with the identical string. For example,

chg/Jack/Jack/

The skip command described in part **b** would be better, however.

## Module G

1. (a) The output for vector C is packed on one line:

100  200  300  400  500

(b) The output is similar to the original example, except each line in matrix **A** is printed in zones, instead of packed.

(c) The output is identical to the example.

(d) 902 DATA 100,200,300,400,500

The output of **A** and **C** is identical to the example.

(e) If we forget to interchange lines 901 and 902, we get the following output:

35    100
200   300
400   500

10
15
20
25
30

**(f)** ?10,15
?20,25
?30,35
?100
?200
?300
?400
?500

The output is identical to the example.

**2.** 10  20  30  40

10
20
30
40

10  20  30  40

**3. (a)** 900 DATA 3,2
901 DATA 10,1
902 DATA 20,2
903 DATA 30,3
904 DATA 0,0

**(b)** Eliminate lines 900 to 905. Change or add the following.

140 INPUT "Rows, Columns"; M,N
145 PRINT "Enter X row-by-row"
150 MAT INPUT X(M,N)
155 PRINT "Enter initial values in A on one line"
160 MAT INPUT A(N)
280 MAT PRINT X;A;

Input would appear as follows:

Rows, Columns? 3,2
Enter X row-by-row
?10,1
?20,2
?30,3
Enter initial values in A on one line
?0,0

Output would appear as follows:

10  1
20  2
30  3
20  2

**6.** Delete lines 160 and 905. Add line 135:

135 MAT A = ZER(N)

**7.** 11  22  33
44  55  66
77  88  99

0  2  3
4  4  6
7  8  8

0  4  7
2  4  8
3  6  8

Line 50 sets array C to same dimensions as A and B so that subtraction can take place in line 60.

8. Both runs should give the following output for D:

$$\left.\begin{array}{ccc} 2 & 2 & 3 \\ 0 & 1 & 1 \\ 1 & 1 & 1 \end{array}\right\} \text{—— Same as } \mathbf{A}$$

9. **(a)** Place at line 6450.

10. **(a)** The market share of brand 1 is gaining at the expense of brands 2 and 3. **(b)** Rows of the transition matrix are nearly identical to one another and to the market share vector. The market shares beyond period 52 will remain essentially the same, a condition called *steady state*.

14. $1(1) + 1(2) + 1(0) = 3$
    $5(1) - 1(2) + 2(0) = 3$
    $2(1) - 3(2) + 1(0) = -4$

# Index

| Reserved Words (Keywords) | Dialects[b] | Your System[c] | Pages |
|---|---|---|---|
| ABS | 1 2 3 4 | | 370 |
| AND | 2 3 4 | | 125 |
| AS | 3 4 | | 407, 429, 432 |
| ASC | 3 4 | | 466 |
| ATN | 1 2 3 4 | | 371 |
| BASE | 1 2 3 4 | | 278 |
| BEEP | 4 | | 244 |
| CALL | 2 3 4 | | 260 |
| CASE | 2 3 | | 194 |
| CHAIN | 2 3 4 | | 261, 262 |
| CHR$ | 2 3 4 | | 466 |
| CLOSE | 2 3 4 | | 414 |
| CLS | 4 | | 216 |
| CON | 2 3 | | 493 |
| COS | 1 2 3 4 | | 371 |
| CVS | 4 | | 431 |
| DATA | 1 2 3 4 | | 56 |
| DATE$ | 2 3 4 | | 371 |
| DEF | 1 2 3 4 | | 376, 381 |
| DIM | 1 2 3 4 | | 278, 316 |
| DO | 2 | | 148, 156, 162, 169 |
| ELSE | 2 3 4 | | 117, 119, 189, 194 |
| ELSEIF | 2 | | 188 |
| END | 1 2 3 4 | | 31, 119, 189, 194, 252, 255, 260, 381 |
| EOF | 4 | | 415 |
| ERR | 3 4 | | 415 |
| ERROR | 3 4 | | 415 |
| EXIT | 2 3 | | 169, 258, 261, 353 |
| EXP | 1 2 3 4 | | 370 |
| EXTERNAL | 2 3 | | 255, 257, 260 |
| FIELD | 3 4 | | 429 |
| FIX | 3 4 | | 370 |
| FOR | 1 2 3 4 | | 79, 407 |
| FUNCTION | 2 3 | | 252, 255, 257, 258, 381 |
| GET # | 2 3 4 | | 431 |
| GO | 1 2 3 4 | | 114, 148, 162, 188, 193 |
| GOSUB | 1 2 3 4 | | 229, 232 |
| GOTO | 1 2 3 4 | | 148, 162, 188, 193 |
| IDN | 2 3 | | 493 |
| IF | 1 2 3 4 | | 114, 115, 117, 119, 148, 156, 188, 189 |
| IMAGE | 2 | | 387 |
| INKEY$ | 4 | | 447 |
| INPUT | 1 2 3 4 | | 52, 487 |
| INPUT # | 3 4 | | 412 |
| INSTR | 3 4 | | 466 |
| INT | 1 2 3 4 | | 370 |
| INV | 2 3 | | 494 |
| IP | 2 | | 370 |
| LEFT$ | 3 4 | | 466 |
| LEN | 2 3 4 | | 429, 466 |
| LET | 1 2 3 4 | | 34, 462 |
| LINE | 2 3 4 | | 55, 412, 413 |
| LINPUT | 3 | | 55 |
| LIST | 2 3 4 | | 354 |
| LOAD | 4 | | 355 |
| LOC | 3 4 | | 437 |
| LOCATE | 4 | | 51 |
| LOF | 4 | | 447 |
| LOG | 1 2 3 4 | | 370 |
| LOOP | 2 | | 148, 156, 162, 169 |
| LPRINT | 4 | | 51 |
| LSET | 3 4 | | 430 |
| MAP | 3 | | 431, 432 |
| MAT | 2 3 | | 487, 493, 495 |
| MERGE | 4 | | 262 |
| MID$ | 3 4 | | 466 |
| MKS$ | 4 | | 430 |
| MOD | 2 3 4 | | 439 |
| NEW | 4 | | 354 |
| NEXT | 1 2 3 4 | | 79, 148, 156, 162 |
| NOT | 2 3 4 | | 128 |
| NUL$ | 3 | | 493 |
| OLD | 3 | | 353 |
| ON | 1 2 3 4 | | 193, 240, 415 |
| ON ERROR | 3 4 | | 415 |
| OPEN | 2 3 4 | | 407, 429, 432 |
| OPTION | 1 3 4 | | 278 |
| OR | 2 3 4 | | 126 |
| ORD | 2 | | 466 |
| ORGANIZATION | 2 3 | | 432 |
| PI | 2 3 | | 65 |
| POS | 2 3 4 | | 466 |
| PRINT | 1 2 3 4 | | 43, 387, 487 |
| PRINT # | 3 4 | | 409, 410 |
| PROMPT | 2 | | 53 |
| PUT | 2 3 4 | | 430 |
| RANDOMIZE | 1 2 3 4 | | 373 |
| READ | 1 2 3 4 | | 56, 487 |
| RECORDSIZE | 3 | | 432 |
| RELATIVE | 2 3 | | 432 |
| REM | 1 2 3 4 | | 31 |
| RESET | 2 3 | | 417 |
| RESTORE | 1 2 3 4 | | 59, 417 |
| RETURN | 1 2 3 4 | | 230 |
| RIGHT$ | 3 4 | | 466 |
| RND | 1 2 3 4 | | 370 |
| RSET | 3 4 | | 430 |
| RUN | 3 4 | | 351, 355 |
| SAVE | 4 | | 352, 355 |
| SELECT | 2 3 | | 194 |
| SGN | 1 2 3 4 | | 370 |
| SIN | 1 2 3 4 | | 371 |
| SQR | 1 2 3 4 | | 370 |
| STEP | 1 2 3 4 | | 79 |
| STOP | 1 2 3 4 | | 203 |
| STRING | 2 3 | | 431 |